BEAUTY MEMORY UNITY

Selected Volumes from the Classical America Series on Art and Architecture

For a complete list of titles in the Classical America Series, visit www.classicist.org

Edifices de Rome Moderne
Paul M. Letarouilly

Americans in Paris: Foundations of America's Architectural Gilded Age
Jean Paul Carlhian and Margot Ellis

The Secrets of Architectural Composition
Nathaniel C. Curtis (Author), J. S. Weiner (Introduction)

The New York Public Library: Its Architecture and Decoration (updated edition)
Henry Hope Reed and Francis Morrone

Comparative Architectural Details: A Selection from Pencil Points 1932-1937
Milton Wilfred Grenfell (Editor)

The Original Green: Unlocking the Mystery of True Sustainability
Stephen A. Mouzon (Author), Robert F. Kennedy Jr. (Foreword)

The Future of the Past: A Conservation Ethic for Architecture, Urbanism, and Historic Preservation
Steven W. Semes

The Study of Architectural Design
John F. Harbeson, John Blatteau, and Sandra L. Tatman

Get Your House Right, Architectural Elements to Use and Avoid
Marianne Cusato and Ben Pentreath with Richard Sammons and Léon Krier

Antiquities of Athens
James Stuart and Nicholas Revett (Authors), Frank Salmon (Introduction)

Building Details
Frank M. Snyder (Author), Peter Pennoyer and Anne Walker (Introduction)

The Theory of Mouldings
C. Howard Walker (Author), Richard Sammons (Foreword)

Classical Architecture for the Twenty-first Century: An Introduction to Design
Jean-François Gabriel

The United States Capitol: Its Architecture and Decoration
Henry Hope Reed

The Architecture of the Classical Interior
Steven W. Semes

Bricks and Brownstone: The New York Row House 1783-1929 (2nd Edition)
Charles Lockwood

The Elements of Classical Architecture
George Gromort (Author), Henry Hope Reed (Editor/Introduction)

Letarouilly on Renaissance Rome
John Barrington Bayley

The Library of Congress: Its Architecture and Decoration
Herbert Small (Author, Editor), Henry Hope Reed (Author)

Monograph of the Work of McKim, Mead, and White, 1879-1915, Student Edition
Allan Greenberg, Michael George

Greek and Roman Architecture in Classic Drawings
Hector d'Espouy

Man as Hero: The Human Figure in Western Art
Pierce Rice

The Classic Point of View
Kenyon Cox

The Decoration of Houses
Edith Wharton and Ogden Codman, Jr.

The Architecture of Humanism: A Study in the History of Taste
Geoffrey Scott

The American Vignola
William R. Ware

The Golden City
Henry Hope Reed Jr.

BEAUTY MEMORY UNITY

A THEORY OF PROPORTION
IN ARCHITECTURE AND DESIGN

STEVE BASS

LINDISFARNE BOOKS

In Association with the Institute of Classical Architecture & Art

2019

Lindisfarne Books
An imprint of Anthropsophic Press/SteinerBooks
402 Union Street, No. 58, Hudson, New York 12534
www.steinerbooks.org

ISBN: 978-1-58420-967-6 (paperback)
ISBN: 978-1-58420-968-3 (ebook)

Printed in the United States of America

Contents

II. Number Harmony Design

III. Proportion in Practice

Dedication

This book is dedicated to all the teachers who contributed to my understanding of Proportional matters; to Hermes Trismegistus, guide of souls and teacher of teachers; and to Aphrodite, goddess of physical love and beauty who provided constant inspiration.

Foreword

What can be *said* of the essence of architecture is definitely far, far less than can be *illustrated*. One carefully researched drawing is worth a thousand words because it can express facts and ideas that enter our awareness immediately. This is opposed to the necessary and procedural nature of lines of explanatory words.

This has had massively influential consequences for whole civilizations. One of the most powerful examples is the effect that the translation of the opening statement of the St. John's Gospel has had in the Christian world:

> "In the beginning was the word," which came from "En arche en O Logos" in the original Greek, ἐν ἀρχῇ ἦν ὁ λόγος, and has at least seventeen possible meanings according to the Liddle & Scott Greek/English dictionary. Of all these meanings of logos, one particularly stands out and that is "proportion."

It can be relatively easily pointed out that proportion was expressed well before any "words" were used — especially by the multi-various races and divisions of the human family.

Even the word "proportion" does not lend itself to comfortable verbal explanation — and too few questions have ever been asked as to *what* "word" was meant by St. John. Proportion is well expressed by graphic and mathematical means, as this book by Steve Bass so well demonstrates. We get the statement "Geometry is the art of the ever-true" from Socrates in Plato's *The Republic*, (Rep. VII 527.b.). This statement is very unusual for Socrates, as his most characteristic method of debate was normally questioning.

We may well ask ourselves what does the "ever-true" actually mean? When, how, and where else are we offered the ever-true?

This book is a very valuable contribution as to why and how great buildings are great.

It is not necessarily "style" — this word is a useful invention of scholars and historians who find words easier than actually experiencing buildings or, certainly, drawing them.

Steve Bass is a practitioner — a lifelong architect and builder. In this book he puts forward precious reasons as to why the important buildings have lasted. A great deal can be learned by studying this book carefully. I highly recommend it.

Keith Critchlow

Invocation

May we be guided by Truth
May we have Beauty revealed to us
& May it result in the Good

"All those possessing even a small share of good sense always call upon the Divinity at the outset of any undertaking, small or great; therefore we who are proposing to present a discourse concerning the universe must invoke the Gods and Goddesses, praying that all we say may be approved by them in the first place, and secondly by ourselves. Grant then that we have duly invoked the Deities; we must also invoke ourselves so that you may most easily learn and I may most clearly expound on the subjects before us."

"And if, Socrates, in our treatment of a great host of matters regarding the Gods and the generation of the Universe we prove unable to give accounts that are always in all respects self-consistent and perfectly exact, do not be surprised; rather we should be content if we can furnish accounts that are inferior to none in likelihood, remembering that both I who speak and you who judge are but human creatures, so that it becomes us to accept the likely account of these matters and forebear to search beyond it."

Timaeus 27 & 29

Introduction

It has been many years since this author started on the path that has brought him here. In the mid-1970s I began architectural practice and almost immediately found that I had no intelligible basis for making aesthetic judgments. Sometimes my work was acceptable but at other times not, and I couldn't tell why. I began to read various modern authors on design but they were romantic and opaque, offering nothing specific. One afternoon I walked by an entry doorway to a modest commercial building built in the 1910s or 20s. Struck by what seemed to be an elegant, noble arrangement of elements I began to draw it, but my linework quickly degenerated into "squiggles." I realized that I didn't know quite what I was looking at. I remembered having been told by a college teacher that if you wanted to understand a subject properly you should start at the beginning, with the oldest statement rather than starting with present-day commentaries as I had been trying to do.

Back in my studio I opened a copy of the Morgan *Vitruvius.* Turning to Book III, the canon of the Ionic mode, there seemed to be an intelligible method described. I quickly taped down a sheet of paper and followed his directions — 18 units wide, 9.5 units high. Column diameter of 1, spacing of 2.25 D, etc. In a few minutes I had drawn a credible Ionic portico. A short time later a person who had no formal design training walked by my board. She stopped, and I could just hear an inhalation. "That's beautiful," she said. My classical career began that day.

The next thing I needed was a teacher. Vitruvius had taken me 90% of the way, but there were still a raft of details that weren't clear from the text. It's said that in the spiritual world if you seek you'll find; if you ask, you'll be answered. I now had the temerity to ask, and I would soon be answered beyond my expectations. I became aware of an evening course called "Drawing the Five Orders," taught by architect Alvin Holm. It was given at the National Academy of Design in NYC, sponsored by Classical America, under the direction of Henry Hope Reed, and with the support of Arthur Ross. When Alvin presented the Corinthian capital while reciting the myth of the Maiden of Corinth, it became clear that, as is said, "love had something to do with it." A door connecting this mundane world to a metaphysical realm had opened. I had undergone a kind of initiation, a journey of consciousness from which one returns changed for the better. I had escaped from a minimalist-functionalist architectural fate.

Now I began to search for more. In his text, Vitruvius refers repeatedly to the philosophy of Pythagoras and Plato, saying that the numbering system he gives grows out of and is related to their work. I had taken a basic philosophy course in college but Plato got short shrift. The teacher had us read one page from *The Republic* before declaring that Plato was a fascist who hated art and would have had degenerate hippies like my friends and myself run out of town. Most of the rest of the term was spent on Aristotle. I did not expect the academies to be of help here.

Eventually I received a flyer for a talk on Gothic architecture by British artist, architect and teacher Keith Critchlow. Having read his early book *Order in Space,* I knew he understood the metaphysical connection. However the lecture was rather disappointing — Keith presented various tracery windows compared to various flower geometries — three-, four-, five-, sixfold, etc. At the end I asked if he gave other classes in the U.S., and he invited me to a weekend workshop at the Omega Institute in Rhinebeck, N.Y. There, with a more restricted audience, Keith began to unfold the Platonic mysteries. When he said, at the outset, that he didn't know any more than anyone else and that his task was to help us remember what we already knew, a resonance was struck with things I had learned in my earlier yoga study. I had found my guide to the Platonic realm.

This book began with the crossing of what I received from Alvin Holm and Keith Critchlow. Alvin taught the Vignolan numbering system, while Keith taught how the Platonists used those same numbers to describe metaphysical states. This completing of a circuit energized the work I was to do in the coming years.

From 1989 to 1991, I studied at the Royal College of Art, London, in the department of Visual Islamic and Traditional Arts chaired by Critchlow. Perhaps the most important experience during those years was my participation in the first Prince of Wales' Summer Course in Architecture. This was the architecture school you wished you had gone to. The classical approach was central, expounded by teachers like Critchlow, Demitri Porphyrios, Robert Adam, Leon Krier, Christopher Alexander, and others. During this remarkable program one of my fellow students was architect Richard Sammons. When we found that we lived a few blocks from each other in New York's Greenwich Village we resolved to meet on our return to the city. A few months later we did meet, and Richard introduced me to Don Rattner and Richard Cameron, cofounders of what is now called the Institute of Classical Architecture and Art. Sammons had taught a proportion course for the Institute and suggested that I take his place. I agreed, and so began teaching the course that constitutes the bulk of this book.

Special thanks needs to be given to the ICAA National Books Committee, formerly chaired by Steven Semes, for encouraging the proposal for this book; former ICAA president Paul Gunther for approving a generous grant to cover the costs of production; and current committee chair Matt Enquist and current ICAA president Peter Lyden for their continuing support. Thanks also to Lindisfarne Books, Christopher Bamford, Gene Gollogly and Mary Giddens for their work on my behalf.

Steve Bass
March 2019

I

THE SEARCH FOR THE BEAUTIFUL

Position of Proportion

Among those few living architects and designers who show any respect for or interest in the classical, most would argue that the study of the elements and the orders is a rational art. By this they mean that even the most complex or intricate elements can be specified by numerical and sometimes geometrical patterns expressed as "modules" and "parts." Such patterns, known as "canons of proportion," have come down to us in various architectural treatises, which designers use as references. This is a rational approach to achieving propriety in design; an Apollonian path, fully visible and based in text. The idea of using number and geometry as design tools is called "proportion."

If classical architecture is favored only by a minority of architects and designers, study of the theory and application of proportion in design is shunned even by many within that small group. Most deny that they use proportion at all, others see it as a stifling restriction, while a few even hint darkly about "madness"; that is, seeing things that aren't there.

The position taken here, however, is that although the subject of proportion transcends the strictly rational it can be understood, it is intelligible. Far from being a symptom of "madness" the use of proportion in design may turn out to be a way out of the genuine madness of alienation, fragmentation and depowerment into which our aesthetic sensibilities have been plunged in the last century-and-a-half. It might just provide a literal kind of psychotherapy, a modality of soul-healing for contemporary civilization.

In very direct ways proportion can be utilized by designers to guide them as they work, regardless of the function of the object, the medium of expression, the scale of the work or even the age in which they live. It allows the designer to endow the elements of their work with a consistent character—to give them a weightless elegance or titanic solidity. In its highest aspect the use of proportion allows designers to project qualities of vitality and animation into their work; a phenomenon that in an earlier time might have been called magical.

As criteria for the evaluation of architecture, Vitruvius gives the qualities of "firmitatis, utilitatis, venustatis," generally translated as "structure, function and beauty."[1] Structure and function are givens in architecture, at least of the traditional kind. But if architecture is the "Art of Building," as Alberti considered it, this aspect is actualized in the achievement of beauty.

The point for us today, if not always, in using the classical system is beauty. Structure and utilitarian function can be satisfied by any proper form of construction; architecture requires beauty. Nikolaus Pevsner begins his history of architecture with the statement *"A bicycle shed is a building, Lincoln Cathedral is a work of architecture."*[2] The difference being that the cathedral exhibits images going beyond construction itself, wherein the elements of construction are deliberately used to express ideas. This is the realm of Vitruvian "venustatis," of beauty. In this view, beauty is integral, not peripheral, to successful architecture.

Number and Beauty

If the goal of classical design is beauty and the guide to its achievement in the canons is number, then there must be a relation of number to beauty. To explore this relationship and establish a theory the reader is asked to accompany this author on a journey of sorts along a path where human sensibilities are balanced and focused so that unity is more important than division; a different stratum in the structure of consciousness where we can more clearly hear the "music of the spheres," the harmonies of number as they sing of the existence of a living, beautiful cosmos.

In what follows we will explore this path, which is perhaps more often associated with Orpheus, Dionysius, or Hermes than with Apollo; a path less traveled though no less worthy; not a dark path, just less-well lit. This path is not irrational but rather trans-rational, one that includes the rational and more. It might be called a mythopoetic or even ecstatic path. Such a journey is justified not on romantic or hedonistic grounds, but is necessary to explore the inner, hard-to-see aspects of number that are alien to the modern preconceptions we all unconsciously assume.

Experience of this path also leaves the door open to design as more than an academic exercise or workaday grind. Proportional study was considered by Plato a method of "clarifying the orbits of the soul," what we might call the elevation consciousness; or in more ancient terms, a preparation for discovery of the True Self, alluded to at the gate of Delphi.

Pythagoras and Qualitative Number

The foremost ancient explorers of number as a guide and analog to the shaping of the cosmos were the Pythagoreans. Pythagoras was a widely revered philosopher-mathematician, who is said to have coined the term "philosopher" meaning "lover of wisdom." He was born about 600 BC on the Greek island of Samos. In his teens he traveled in Ionia, studying with several teachers, including Thales of Miletus, who advised him to continue his studies in Egypt. Pythagoras is said to have studied in the Egyptian temple school system for twenty-two years, and then for another twelve years in Mesopotamia where he may also have picked up influences from Persia and India. Returning to Greece, Pythagoras, now middle-aged, set up a school on Samos. As his fame spread, his disciples formed schools in other cities in Greece, Southern Italy and Sicily. But as they gained prominence and political influence, opposition arose. Adherents of the school were eventually persecuted; many were killed and the survivors dispersed. During the next century Pythagorean teachings were passed down privately through families. In this period, aspects of the philosophy were recorded in writing for the first time; and it is the writing of one of these authors, Philolaus, that Plato is said to have used as the basis for his mathematical creation myth in the dialog of *Timaeus*.

Although Pythagoreanism was a comprehensive lifestyle including social, political, religious and even dietary aspects, number as quality, or state of being, was central to Pythagorean philosophy. For Pythagoreans there existed three kinds of number. The first, *quantitative* number, is the number of counted things; the kind of number we use when taking inventory or operating a cash register. The second, *mathematical* number, is a magnitude that we manipulate, as in addition or subtraction, without reference to actual objects. Finally, *qualitative* number refers to an essential differentiating aspect of each number, without reference to mathematical manipulation or to actual objects. It treats number as a symbol. It is in this sense that number may become an archetype of a particular state of being, and it is in this sense that number was used by Pythagoreans to model the coming into being of an orderly cosmos. Qualitative, or symbolic number may be a guide to understanding the principles that inform sensible matter because it has the ability to link the apparent separateness of objects to unity.

Psyche

The term *soul*, in the context of qualitative number, refers that aspect of ourselves which is our connection to Unity. Soul is the presence of ontological Unity on an individual level, an analog of the cosmos; its unity a refraction image of cosmic unity. Soul's function is to vitalize and govern matter. The principal Greek philosophical term for soul is *psyche,* meaning non-physical animating principle. Psyche is also the root of our word *psychological*, meaning related to mind. It is thus not without foundation to translate psyche as soul-mind or even as consciousness.

Psyche is structured by harmonic division. Such a pattern of division of Unity, which allows for its own re-integration, is known as a "logos." The sensible order of the cosmos arises in the realm of psyche by the result of the impression of logos upon matter. To make such an impression is the function of psyche. This is how we come to see an orderly world from the chaotic mix of raw sense input.

Timaeus, who represents the Pythagorean worldview, tells us that "*...this cosmos has come into existence as a living creature endowed with soul and reason* [life and intelligence] ...[3] and "... *when the structure of the* [world] *soul had been finished ... the Divinity proceeded to fashion the whole corporeal world within it; fitting the two together centre to centre; and the soul was woven right through from the centre to the outermost heaven....*"[4]

The cosmos and the soul are spherical as "*A suitable shape for a living being that was to contain within itself all living beings would be a figure that contains all possible figures within itself. Therefore the Divinity turned it into a rounded spherical shape....*"[5]

The two-dimensional representation of a sphere is a circle. The center of the circle is a point equidistant from all points on the circumference. Such a center point can be said to have location in space, but by definition, no measurable dimension. As such, the point constitutes an essential mystery at the center of materiality.

Timaeus says that the soul has a three part structure composed of "sameness, difference and intermediate being."[6] Sameness may be equated with the realm of cosmic mind expressed by the Greek word "nous," unchanging principle; idea without matter. Difference may be equated with the constantly changing, sensible, physical world called "hule," matter without idea. The median or balance between these two extremes is called intermediate being, which may be equated with the individual soul. A likely geometric model of psyche is shown in **figure 1.**

Critchlow writes, "*The Soul is the essential intermediary in the Platonic tradition ... it is to be thought of as having a threefold nature ... conceived diagrammatically as comprising three circles. Firstly, a higher circle represents the Heavenly domain of transcendental principles, home of the "eide" or formal ideas. Secondly, a lower circle (touching the upper one at its lowest point), which represents the earthly domain of the created order, the immanent enactment of the principles in*

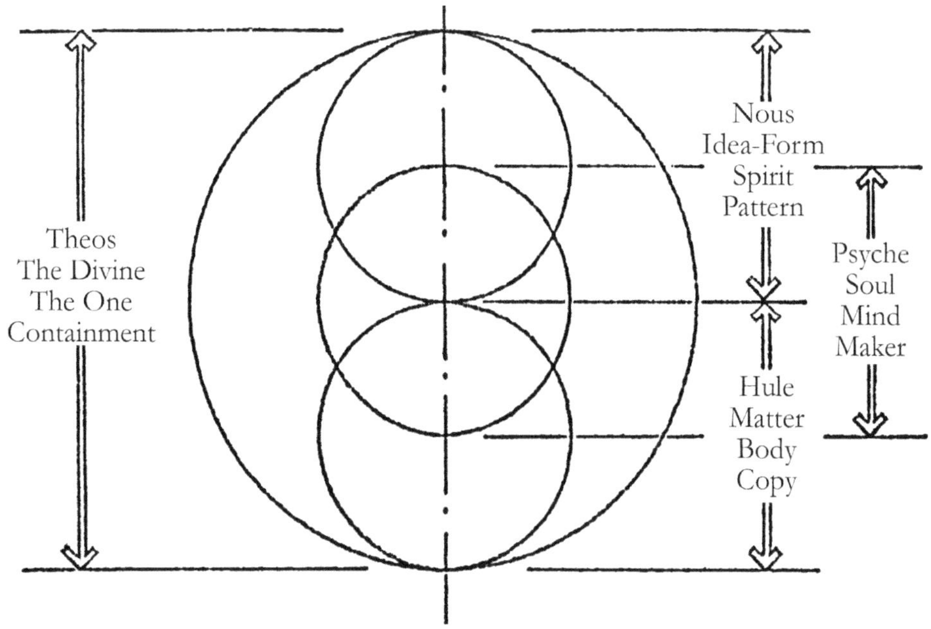

FIGURE 1
Geometric Representation of the Platonic Psyche

matter — our world of sensory experience. Thirdly, a joining circle representing the domain of the Soul. This latter circle is centered on the meeting point of the heavenly and earthly circles with its topmost point reaching to the center of the heavenly and its lowest point reaching to the center of the earthly circle. It thus symbolizes the threeness of Soul, as well as demonstrating its balancing role. The upper part of this Soul sphere can be taken as the most subtle in nature and as like its heavenly prototype as is conceivable. The lower part animates matter and totally permeates it, the center being a balance between the two."[7]

Analogous contemporary terms for the three circles might be spirit, mind and body, or in a more mythic reading the circles might be called pattern, copy and maker. In **figure 1** the three circles are shown within the larger circle of the world soul called here "the One," the principle of Unity, or Containment, the *chorha* in which the orderly cosmos takes place. Psyche looks up through the imagination and down through the senses. This joining of the above and below also represents an act of memory, giving psyche access to the nous, complete awareness of our ultimate nature.

Remembrance and the Journey of the Soul

In the Pythagorean tradition, the soul makes a journey towards its merger or wedding to materiality at birth, and another on the dissolution of its materiality at death. Timaeus[8] associates the individual souls with the stars, and in Plato's *Republic,*[9] the myth of Er describes the soul's journey from the divine realm beyond the fixed stars, where it partook of the nous, through the seven planetary spheres to earth. As the soul descends below the moon it becomes denser, more immersed in materiality until, upon reaching the earth, it has forgotten its original nature. In this view, the task of education actually is one of remembrance, or in Greek, *anamnesis*. Plato provides a demonstration of anamnesis in the *Meno* dialog, in which he uses a geometrical pattern to elicit a mathematical proof from an uneducated boy.[10]

Harmonic mathematical pattern appears, for Plato, to be a primary prompt for the soul to recall its original state of Unity. This remembrance of the true self, anamnesis, is an essential part of the process of the soul's re-ascension. The anamnesic model assumes that you already have the knowledge of the logos within you and the power to recall it because of the presence of unity presumed to exist in the individual soul.

Memory, ultimately the memory of Unity, is thus a key factor in the soul's re-ascension. This transcendent Unity differentiates into multiplicity where it can be apprehended by psyche, through memory of geometrical archetypes. Sense information is then compared by the mind to these archetypes of Unity, or "Ideas," to form our image of the physical world.

For Pythagoreans, one's actions might be judged against the goal of achieving and maintaining a dynamic balance or harmony of elements in the soul. Study of the harmonic patterns in body, mind, or spirit would lead to increased understanding of the harmony of elements in the individual's soul; this being possible because the soul of the world and the individual soul were constructed on the same harmonic pattern, the logos. The individual could thus be considered a microcosm.

Plotinus on Beauty

What is meant by beauty has certainly been a contentious topic for an extended period of time. Current popular opinion seems to be that beauty is subjective, with no possibility for firm or fixed criteria; it is "in the eye of the beholder." It is perceptual, therefore unreliable in scientific terms. In this view beauty is relative and judgments can only be made on the basis of personal experience or "taste." Beauty can have no "function" today except pleasure. But of course such analysis is confined to the sensible realm.

For a classical view of beauty we might look to the work of the third-century AD Neoplatonic philosopher Plotinus. He begins his discussion by noting that most would say beauty derives from being well proportioned. However, because proportion is a relation of more than one number, *"nothing single and simple, but only a composite thing will have beauty. It will be the whole which is beautiful and the parts will not have the property of beauty by themselves.... But if the whole is beautiful the parts must be beautiful too; a beautiful whole cannot be composed of ugly parts.... And when the same face sometimes appears beautiful and sometimes does not, though the same good proportion is there all the time, surely we must say that being beautiful is something else over and above good proportion, and good proportion is beautiful because of something else."* [11]

Plotinus points out that there is also beauty of virtue; but, he asks, *"what can be meant by good proportion in beautiful ways of life, laws, studies or branches of knowledge? How can speculations be well proportioned in relation to each other? If it is because they agree, there can be agreement between bad ideas.... virtue is a beauty of the soul, a truer beauty than those mentioned before; but how is virtue well proportioned?"*[12] Plotinus' questions here are rhetorical, as he does not consider virtue to be composite, and therefore it would not be beautiful in the theory of "beauty as proportion."

Plotinus says that the soul is drawn towards beauty and repelled from ugliness, *"Our explanation of this is that the soul ... is related to the higher kind of reality in the realm of being, and when it sees ... a trace of its kindred reality ... remembers itself.... But how are both the things in that* [higher] *world and the things in this beautiful? We maintain that the things in this world are beautiful by participating in form; for every shapeless thing ... is ugly as long as it has no share in formative power.... Form, then, approaches and composes that which is to come into being from many parts into a single ordered whole ... for since* [form] *is one itself, that which is shaped by it must also be one, as far as a thing can be which is composed of many parts. So beauty rests upon the material thing when it has been brought into unity, and* [beauty] *gives itself to parts and wholes alike... the beautiful body comes into being by sharing in a formative power which comes from the divine forms."* [13]

The forms of which Plotinus speaks are the same as those described by Plato in the *Timaeus* and other dialogues. These forms exist as "Ideas" in the intelligible realm, called nous in **figure 1**, and they give shape to material, hule, which otherwise would have none.

It may be said, *"Form is what raises chaos to cosmos."*[14] Cosmos, the Greek term for the sensible universe, is related to the English word cosmetic, meaning a surface covering or layer. In this sense the material universe is a surface covering on the form of the One; or we might say physical appearances "adorn" the One, or Unity. The One, which corresponds to the outer circle in **figure 1**, might also be thought of as Theos, meaning the Divinity, or as God. Nous, divine intelligence, or ideal form is a part of the One, which, when projected through psyche, gives rise to perceptible order in the otherwise chaotic or formless material ground, the hule.

Plotinus, in finishing this section, says that sensible beauties are, "... *images and shadows which, so to speak, sally out and come into matter, adorn it, and excite us when they appear."*[15]

Beauty and the Good

For Plotinus the value of beauty is that it turns the attention of the soul from the changing material realm to the unchanging realm of nous, or divine intellect. But perception of beauty is only possible to the degree that the soul is "pure," as purity is related to unity. *"This is the soul's ugliness, not being pure and unmixed, like gold, but full of earthiness; if anyone takes the earthy stuff away, the gold is left and is beautiful when it is singled out from other things and is alone by itself....*[16] *and every virtue is a purification, as is wisdom ...*[17] *the soul when it is purified becomes form and formative power, altogether bodiless and intellectual, entirely belonging to the divine, whence beauty springs."*[18]

In the realm of nous "... *beautifulness is reality ... so for God* [or in the realm of the divine intellect], *the qualities of goodness and beauty are the same ...* and *we must posit beauty, which is also the good; from this immediately comes intellect, which is beauty, and soul is given beauty by intellect. Everything else is beautiful by the shaping of soul ...."*[19]

In describing this state of beauty fused with intellect or truth, and with goodness, which can be viewed when the soul is pure, Plotinus writes, *"Anyone who has seen it knows what I mean when I say it is beautiful. It is desired as good and the desire for it is directed to good, and the attainment of it is for those who go up to the higher world and are converted and strip off what we put on in our descent (just as for those who go up to the celebrations of the sacred rites there are purifications, and stripping off of the clothes they wore before, and going up naked) until, passing in the ascent all that is alien to God, one sees with one's self alone... that alone, simple, single and pure, from which all depends, to which all look and are and live and think;*

for it is cause of life and mind and being. If anyone sees it, what passion they will feel ... what a shock of delight! ... [the person] *who has seen it glories in its beauty, is full of wonder and delight, enduring a shock which causes no hurt....*[20] *Here the greatest, the ultimate contest is set before our souls; all our toil and trouble is for this, not to be left without a share in the best of visions."*[21]

Plotinus offers this guidance for our journey, *"Shut your eyes, and ... wake to another way of seeing, which everyone has but few use....*[22] *Go back into yourself and look; if you do not yet see yourself beautiful, then, just as someone making a statue which has to be beautiful cuts away here, polishes there, makes one part smooth and clears another till the statue has a beautiful face, so you too must cut away excess, straighten the crooked, clear the dark and make it bright, and never stop "working on your statue" till the divine glory of virtue shines out on you, till you see self-mastery enthroned on its holy seat."*[23]

For Plotinus, study and work in the outer, material world is just the prelude to the "real" work, the ascent of the soul, which must take place within one's self; using only that which is really yours, your memory. In another part of his writings[24] Plotinus will continue the explication of beauty on the intellectual level and again leave us on the doorstep of the divine.

Diotima's Lecture on Beauty

In the Platonic system love is the attractive power, exerted by unity through beauty, that holds the elements of the cosmos in their proper harmonic relationships. The intermediary between love and beauty is desire, Eros, the child of Venus. An account of the relation of beauty, love and desire is given in Diotima's speech in Plato's *Symposium,* which outlines a process of self-elevation.

Diotima defines love as the *"desire for perpetual possession of the good."*[25] She goes on to relate that in the human realm love is centered on reproduction as a manifestation of the eternal in time. It is a form of participation in Oneness.

Diotima then describes a four-stage process of self-elevation through meditation on the beautiful.[26] The first stage is contemplation of a beautiful physical being. *"Those who would pursue the right way to this goal must begin, when they are young, by applying themselves to the contemplation of physical beauty ... they will first fall in love with one particular beautiful person...."*

The second stage is to understand that beauty is a quality, not a physical thing and is not restricted to a single object. We might call this beauty as symbol. *"Later they will observe that physical beauty in any person is closely akin to physical beauty in any other, and that ... it is great folly not to acknowledge that the beauty exhibited in all bodies is one and the same; when they have reached this conclusion they will become a lover of all physical beauty, and will relax the intensity of their passion for one particular person ...."*

The third stage is to recognize beauty of virtue and intelligence, which must be completely nonphysical; or, as Diotima calls it, "beauty of soul." *"The next stage is for them to reckon beauty of soul more valuable than beauty of body; the result will be that, when they encounter a virtuous soul in a body which has little of the bloom of beauty, they will be content to love and cherish it ... in this way they will be compelled to contemplate beauty as it exists in activities and institutions, and to recognize that here too all beauty is akin ... . From morals they must be directed to the sciences and contemplate their beauty also, so that, having their eyes fixed upon beauty in the widest sense, they may no longer be the slave of... an individual example of beauty... but, by gazing upon the vast ocean of beauty to which their attention is now turned, may bring forth ... beautiful and magnificent sentiments and ideas, until at last... they catch sight of one unique science whose project is the beauty of which I am about to speak."*

In the final stage one recognizes a beauty not drawing its power from anything else, Beauty itself. *"This beauty is first of all eternal; it neither comes into being nor passes away ... next, it is not beautiful in part and ugly in part ... varying according to its beholders; nor again will this beauty appear like ... anything else corporal, or like the beauty of a thought or a science, or like beauty which has its seat in something other than itself...; they will see it as absolute, existing alone with itself, unique, eternal, and all other beautiful things as partaking of it, yet in such a manner that, while they come into being and pass away, it neither undergoes any increase or diminution nor suffers any change."*

Diotima concludes, *"This is the right way of approaching or being initiated into the mysteries of love, to begin with examples of beauty in this world, and using them as steps to ascend continually with that absolute beauty as one's aim, from one instance of physical beauty to two and from two to all, then from physical beauty to moral beauty, and from moral beauty to the beauty of knowledge, until from knowledge of various kinds one arrives at the supreme knowledge whose sole object is that absolute beauty, and knows at last what absolute beauty is. This is where a person's life should be spent, in the contemplation of absolute beauty."*

This process is an inner esoteric road of personal transformation. No one can force anyone else on such a journey, but people can be persuaded of its value, or at least turned toward it. The classical designer's task is to create objects that turn us toward beauty. We may begin our approach to beauty by looking at its manifestation in the outer world through the four traditional sciences of number, keeping in mind the goals which Diotima has set before us.

The Liberal Arts

Intellectual study as a means to clarify the orbits of the Soul came to be taught in seven aspects or subjects in the schools of the Pythagoreans and as imparted in Plato's dialogs of the *Republic*, *Timaeus*, *Laws* and others. There are three "verbal" subjects: grammar, rhetoric and dialectic; and four "mathematical" subjects: arithmetic, geometry, music and astronomy. As the study of these subjects was meant to help harmonize the soul and assist its return journey to unity, they became known as the liberal arts. Liberal, used here in its original sense, implying that these studies help to liberate the soul from entrapment in matter. This system became the basis of the curriculum at the Platonic Academy in Athens, founded in the fourth century BC. This is the system which the early Christian fathers studied, and it was refined in the Middle Ages in the Islamic and Christian worlds, for example, at the School of Chartres. It was the same system that was reinterpreted in the Italian Renaissance.

The classical Greek works of Plato and others of his time are the earliest written formulations of this study of number and harmony. But reason and history point to these archetypes as existing outside of any particular time or place. They seem to have been developed over the entire span of known human existence, and may well be seen as evidence of our emerging humanness.

The four mathematical subjects of Plato are known as the Quadrivium. In each of the subjects it is the harmonic, qualitative aspects that we are to study and we are not to overly focus on the mechanical details. Arithmetic is number in concept. Geometry is number in space. Music or harmony is number in time. Astronomy or cosmology is number in time and space. Each subject constitutes an ontogeny, a story of coming into being, of its own. This allows us to recount a combined numerical and geometrical story of how things come to be.

A Pythagorean-based Creation Myth

A Brief Theology of Arithmetic and Geometry

Oneness — the Monad

All manifestation must have a starting point, **figure 2a.** This point contains a fundamental mystery—it has location without dimension. The point contains the All in potential as it is the necessary initial manifestation of anything. But the point cannot be perceived with the senses as it is unextended in dimension It is represented in geometry by the dot.

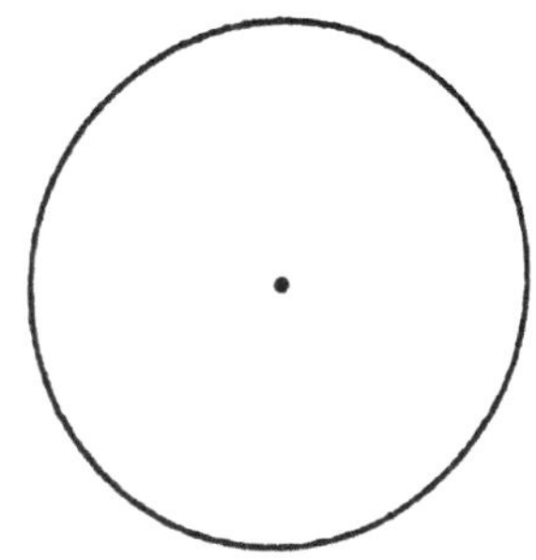

Figure 2a

The first shape is the circle. It is a kind of inflation of the point that allows the potential of the point to be actualized. It embodies the mystery of the point as its shape is entirely guided by the point and its circumference is a line whose curvature is uniform, undifferentiated. Perhaps more important is that the relation between the circumference and the area it encloses, though perfectly visible, is not fully expressible in rational units. This implies that the cosmos is not fully rationalizable and must always contain an element of mystery.

This first stage of our ontogeny, our story of coming into being, may be thought of as that of transcendent unity. Unity as an applied unit of measure consistent with its character of Sameness is called the *monad*. In architecture such a key unit of measure is called the *module*. An early image of the primal undifferentiated state of unity is the uroboros, a snake with its tail in its mouth, symbolizing continuous self-generation.

Further illustrating the nature of these ontological levels are descriptions of them that appear in religious, philosophical and mythological literature. In the first book of Genesis we read: "*In the beginning God created the heaven and the earth. And the earth was without form and void; and darkness was upon the face of the deep. And the spirit of God moved upon the face of the waters.*"[27]

Timaeus tells us that "*to discover the maker and father of the universe is a task indeed, and when discovered, to reveal him to all through the ministry of discourse is a thing impossible.*" The experience of transcendent Unity is not communicable through words. Then he adds, "*Let us declare then on what account the composing artificer constituted generation and the universe. The artificer was good.... Hence ... he was willing to produce all things as much as possible similar to himself.... Do we rightly conclude that there is but one universe; or is it more right to assert that there are many and infinite? But indeed there can be but one if it is fabricated according to its exemplar. For that which comprehends all intelligible living creatures can never be second to any other.*"[28] Unity is thus an ontological necessity.

Twoness — the Dyad

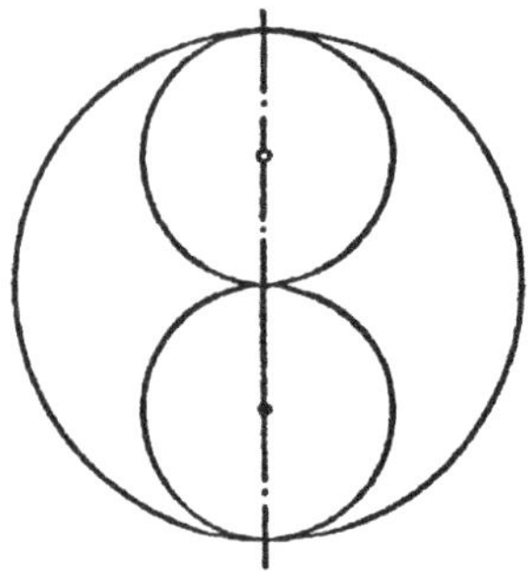

Figure 2b

If Unity contains the All, everything manifest and unmanifest, then it must also contain its own opposite, separation from unity, **figure 2b**. For such a separation to occur there must be a direction prior to any movement. This first form of extension is known variously as the ray of creation, lightning flash, world tree or axis mundi. Geometrically it is the line. Its movement is not an external separation but is division of Unity from within.

In Genesis we read: *"And God said, Let there be light: and there was light. And God saw the light, that it was good: And God divided the light from the darkness. And God called the light Day, and the darkness Night. And the evening and the morning were the first day."*[29]

Timaeus tells us: *"We must ... distinguish between that which always is and never becomes from that which is always becoming but never is. The One is apprehensible by intelligence with the aid of reasoning, being eternally the same, the other is the object of opinion and irrational sensation, coming to be and ceasing to be, but never fully real."*[30] "That which always is and never becomes" is called the real. "That which is always becoming and never fully is," is called the actual. These are also called the same and the different.

In an Orphic creation story *"... black winged Night, a goddess of whom even Zeus stands in awe, was courted by the wind and laid a silver egg in the womb of darkness; and Eros, whom some call Phanes* [light], *was hatched from this egg and set the world in motion."*[31]

For something to be perceivable with the senses a difference must exist. The beginning of difference in the dyad is symbolized by the separation of light from darkness, the separation of opposites. This is the ontological level of division within unity; also of moral choice, the good vs. the not good.

For Pythagoreans the dyad symbolized polar opposites such as: limit-unlimited; odd-even; one-many; right-left; rest-motion; same-different. Order is connected to the idea of limit, for recognizable order must fall within some limit. Disorder and the not-good are unlimited. In Taoism the polar opposite qualities of the dyad are known as yang and yin, the creative and receptive.

Threeness — the Triad

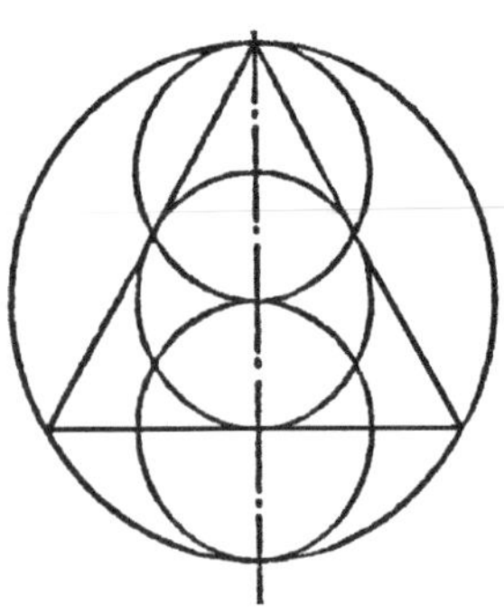

Figure 2c

Any two separate things must have a relationship. This requires the triad, **figure 2c**. For sensible perception or any act of communication to take place there must be at least a sender, a receiver and a medium of transmission. For any kind of structural stability a triangulation is required. The triangle resists deformation because none of its inner angles can change without a change in the length of the opposite side. The triad is the ontological level of structure. As the minimal stable cycle, the proceeding, maintaining and returning is triadic; it may also be considered the ontological level of the symbolic. The equilateral triangle is the first plane 2-dimensional figure. Geometrically we may represent the triad by placing a third circle "mediating" between the extremes of the same and the different. This circle governs the creation of the equilateral triangle.

In Genesis we read: *"And God said, Let there be a firmament in the midst of the waters, and let it divide the waters from the waters. And God made the firmament, and divided the waters which were under the firmament from the waters which were above the firmament: and it was so. And God called the firmament Heaven. And the evening and the morning were the second day."*[32]

Timaeus tells us: *"He composed* [the world soul] *in the following manner and out of the following constituents. From the indivisible, eternally unchanging Existence and the divisible, changing Existence of the physical world he mixed a third kind of Existence intermediate between them.... and taking these three components he mixed them into a single unity."*[33]

Fourness — the Tetrad

For anything to fully manifest it must have at least three dimensions, length, width and height, see **figure 2d**. These three intervals are marked off by a minimum of four points:

• length • width • height •
1 2 3 4

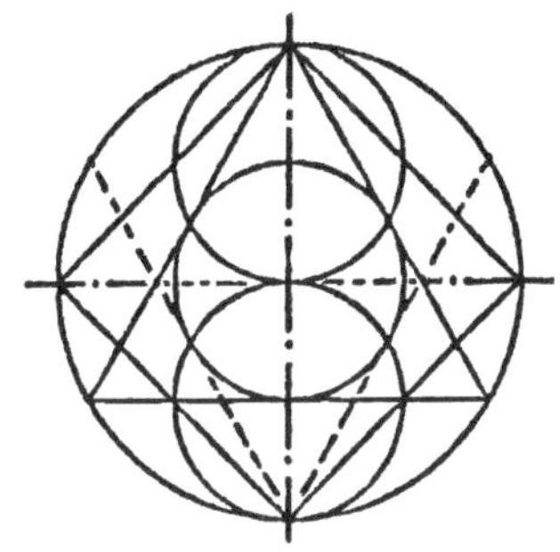

Figure 2d

The tetrad may be seen as the double dyad or as a crossing of opposites such as warp and weft, which cross to create a fabric; or male and female, whose paths must cross to allow physical birth. Geometrically this is represented by the square. We still use the expression, "the four corners of the world."

In Genesis we read: *"And God said, Let the waters under the Heaven be gathered together unto one place, and let the dry land appear: and it was so. And God called the dry land Earth: and the gathering together of the waters he called Sea."*[34]

Timaeus tells us: *"Anything that has come to be must be corporal, visible and tangible: but nothing can be visible without fire, nor tangible without solidity, and nothing can be solid without earth. So when the creator began to put together the body of the universe, he made it of fire and earth.*

But it is not possible to combine two things properly without a third to act as a bond to hold them together. And the best bond is one that effects the closest unity between itself and the terms it is combining; and this is best done by a continued geometrical proportion [a:b :: b:c].... *If then the body of the universe were required to be a plane surface with no depth, one middle term would have been enough to connect it to the other terms; but in fact it needs to be solid, and solids always need two connecting middle terms.*

So the creator placed water and air between earth and fire, and made them so far as possible proportional to one another ... and in this way he bound the world into a visible and tangible whole. By these means and these four constituents the body of the universe was created to be at unity owing to proportion; in consequence it acquired concord, so that having once come together in unity with itself it is indissoluble by any but its compounder."[35]

Taylor writes that since the tetrad *"causally contains all mundane natures, it may very properly be called the fountain of natural effects. Because likewise it opens and shuts the recesses of generation, it is denominated ... the key bearer of nature, as is also the mother of the gods, who is represented with a key."*[36] This also may be related to the symbol of St. Peter [from the Latin *petra*, rock], whose two keys of the kingdom are crossed at right angles.

. . . .

With this we have reached the sensible world. In the Platonic tradition, as the soul transits various levels on its journey to incarnation it becomes literally "turned around" or forgetful of its ideal nature and confuses itself with its material aspect. Remembrance or anamnesis thus becomes a primary life task. This process begins with a kind of turning around to begin a journey of return to Unity.

Fiveness — the Pentad

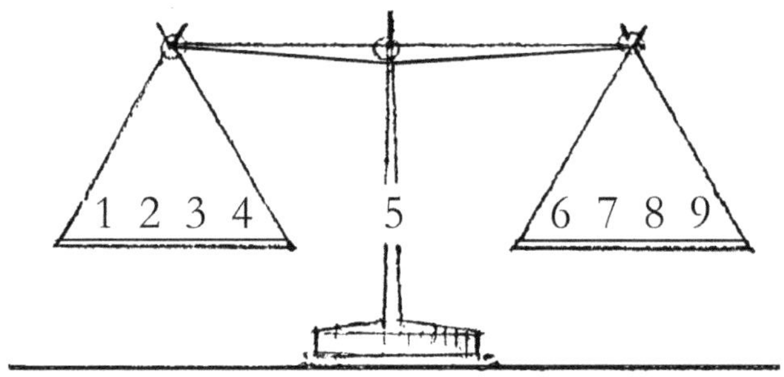

FIGURE 3
The Pentad as Balance or Turning Point

Pythagoreans considered the Pentad the "balance point" as it stands midway between the first four numbers of the decade and the last four. We may also see the Pentad as the turning point, **figure 3.**

In Genesis we read: *"And God said, let the earth bring forth grass, the herb yielding seed, and the fruit tree yielding fruit after its kind, whose seed is in itself, upon the earth. And the evening and the morning were the third day."*[37]

Concerning this image Lawlor writes, *"The rose family is one of those based on five, as are all the flowers of the edible fruit bearing plants. Thus five signals to man his proper foods.... The very exotic flowers ... the flowers of love such as the orchid, the azalea and the passion flower, are all governed by pentagonal symmetry."*[38]

Timaeus, after assigning each of the four elements to one of the Platonic solids, seems reticent to mention the one assigned to the Pentad saying only, *"There still remained a fifth construction, which the god used for embroidering the constellations on the whole of heaven."*[39] These are references to the 3-dimensional figure called the dodecahedron, which has twelve pentagonal faces.

The Pentad and Phi

The Pentad is most strongly associated with harmonic balance through its relation to the phi ratio [1 : .618...], which governs the growth of many living things. Known in ancient Greece as the "extreme and mean ratio," in the Renaissance as the Divine Proportion, it was later called the Golden Section. In more recent times it has been denominated by the Greek letter phi, Ø. Phi is defined mathematically as [√5-1]/2. It begins with the square root of five, √5, which equals 2.236.... Subtracting Unity we have 1.236... ; dividing by two gives .618....

The properties of phi answer to a special need in philosophical arithmetic and geometry. For Pythagoreans the Quadrivium was studied to accomplish the Delphic-Socratic motto, "Know Thyself." This may be paraphrased as "experience the One within yourself," or "experience that aspect of yourself that connects you to the One." Whatever points the way from the many to the One, is considered valuable. Just as the golden sun and the metal gold have been symbolically related to Oneness by Plotinus, the Golden Section embodies an approach to Oneness in terms of arithmetic and geometry.

In arithmetic a ratio is a comparison of any two numbers, a:b. A proportion is a relationship of equality between ratios and may be written, a:b :: c:d, for example, 2:4 :: 3:6. This is called a four term, discontinuous proportion. To get closer to unity we note that the relationship between some ratios can be expressed as a three term, continuous proportion, a:b :: b:c, for example 2:4 :: 4:8. This may also be written as a progression, a:b:c, or 2:4:8. This particular three-term proportion has the property that the product of the extremes equals the square of the mean, $b^2 = ac$ or $b = \sqrt{ac}$. Because of the arithmetic act of "squaring" it is known as a Geometric proportion.

Pursuing the path to Unity we may reduce the number of terms even further, to two, by setting c = a+b. We then have $b = \sqrt{(a^2+ab)}$. If we now set b = 1, we have $a+a^2=1$. That is, root plus square equals unity. The only magnitude that satisfies this condition is: a = 0.618..., or Ø. This creates a mathematical metaphor for the return to Unity, to Oneness, through division. Phi may be considered *"the ultimate reduction of proportional thought to the causal singularity."*[40]

Numerically substituting $(\sqrt{5}-1)/2$ for "a" in the equation $a+a^2=1$, we have $(2.236-1)/2 + [(2.236-1)/2]^2 = .6180... + .3819... = .9999...$. Phi, as a transcendental, does not actually reach 1 but makes a "near approach." This is because Ø is categorically not a number — it is a relationship.[41]

Pursuing Unity geometrically, we may ask, "Is there a rectilinear figure that can be continuously, proportionally divided, and produce unity, as symbolized by the square, through division?" Such a rectangle, shown in **figure 4a**, has its sides in the geometric progression a^2:a:1, such that $a^2+a=1$. A further iteration produces $a^2+a^3=a$.

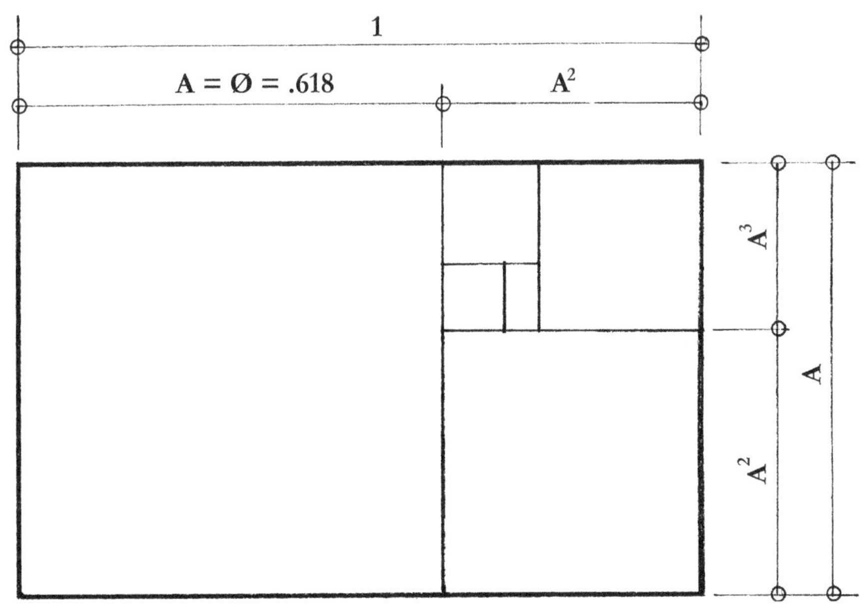

FIGURE 4A

Geometric Derivation of Phi

A further geometrical relationship of the Pentad and Ø is shown in **figure 4b**. Just as the diagonal of the square is related to the √2 and the altitude of the equilateral triangle is related to the √3, the diagonal of the pentagon is related to Ø. If the side of the pentagon is equal to 1, the diagonal is 1+Ø = 1.618.... The diagonals of the pentagon in figure 4b further divide the diagonals at its phi points, dividing Ø into $Ø^2 + Ø^3$. Either of these geometrical patterns produces a phi progression or scale.

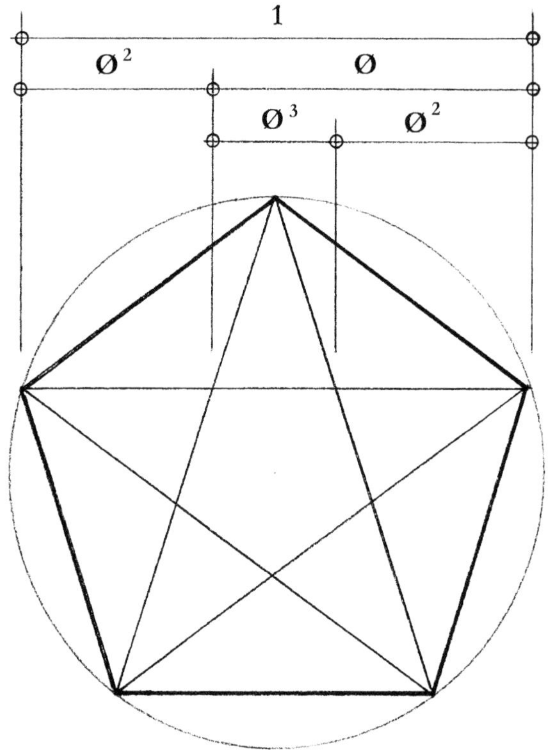

FIGURE 4B

Phi and the Pentagon

The Root Powers

Also ascribed to Pythagoras is the discovery that the numbers 3, 4, and 5, taken as intervals of length, are the smallest whole numbers that will form a right triangle. Thought of as formative powers rather than numbers this archetype forms the basis of a family of rectangles starting with the square. In this view the formative numerical powers are represented by "roots," √; a number that when multiplied by itself creates the number under the root symbol. The √2 is a number that multiplied by itself makes 2. Because $4 = 2^2$ and 2 = √4 a progression can be created, √2:2:2√2:4; thus the 4 in the 3-4-5 archetype is related to or can be represented by √2. The archetype can then be expressed as the root powers √2, √3, and √5.

The diagonal of the square whose side is 1 is equal to the √2, **figure 5.** A rectangle whose short side is 1 and whose long side is √2 is called a "root 2 rectangle." The diagonal of a root 2 rectangle is equal to the √3. A rectangle 1 by √3 is called a root 3 rectangle. Its diagonal is equal to the √4 = 2. A rectangle of 1 by 2 is a double square, its diagonal is equal to the √5. Ø may be derived by subtracting a square from a √5 rectangle and then dividing the remainder in half.

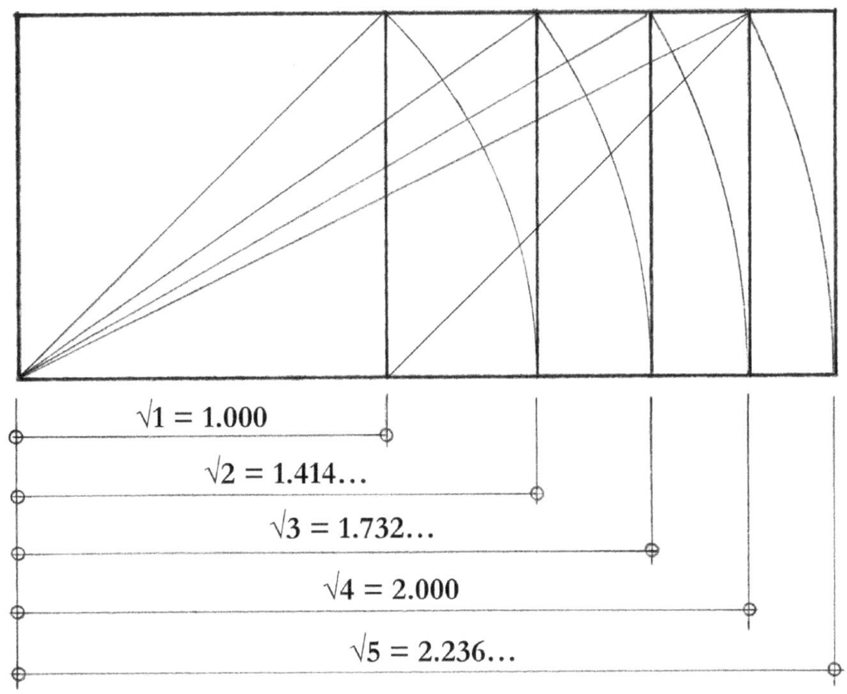

FIGURE 5

The Root Rectangles

The $\sqrt{2}$ symbolizes the Generative because it "... *contains the power which instantaneously transforms 1 into 2,*"[42] and it establishes the principle of Alternation; the $\sqrt{3}$ is said to be Formative as the equilateral triangle "*is the formative power giving rise to the polygonal 'world'*"[43]; and the $\sqrt{5}$ can be considered as Regenerative, because through its relation to phi, it may be said to "return to unity through division." "*The $\sqrt{5}$ is the proportion which opens the way for the family of relationships called the Golden Proportion. Ø generates a set of symbols which were used by the Platonic philosophers as a support for the ideal of divine or universal love. It is through the Golden Division that we can contemplate the fact that the Creator planted a regenerative seed which will lift the mortal realms of duality and confusion back toward the image of God.*"[44]

The root powers can thus represent the three stages of a cosmological cycle of proceeding, $\sqrt{2}$, maintaining, $\sqrt{3}$ and returning, $\sqrt{5}$. The Pentad is thus well suited to symbolize the turning or re-turning. The root powers and the golden section are treated further in Section II.

The Decade

The remaining numbers of the decade also have symbolic characteristics.

Sixness – the Hexad is symbolic of perfection and Pythagoreans considered six to be a "perfect" number. Perfect numbers in this sense are equal to the sum of their factors. For example, 6 is equally divisible into six parts of one unit each, or two parts of three units each, or three parts of two units each; 6/6=1, 6/2=3, 6/3=2, 1+2+3=6. Note that 6/4 and 6/5 do not yield whole numbers. In the case of 28 we have 28/28=1, 28/14=2, 28/7=4, 28/4=7, 28/2=14. 1+2+4+7+14=28.

In geometry the radius of a circle may be used to divide its circumference into six equal, or perfect parts.

Sevenness – The **heptad** is considered a "virgin" because it does not multiply within the decade; that is, seven as a prime number is created only by addition, not multiplication, and there is no whole number multiple of seven that is ten or less. Seven is associated with wisdom, especially with the virgin wisdom goddess Athena. Seven is also associated with the idea of ascension through the seven planetary spheres.

Eightness – The **octad** represents the eighth sphere of the fixed stars. It also symbolizes harmonia, as the octave is complete at eight notes.

Nineness – The **ennead** symbolizes completion, as nine is the last integer. It is the all inclusive, the boundary. It also is associated with the ocean, as in ancient times the ocean was presumed to completely surround the land.

Tenness – The **decade** represents the new monad. It is the realization of the potential of the monad. For our purposes here it may represent our return to a new higher unity. The decade's most important representation is called the tetraktys.

The Tetraktys

The decade is the sum of the first four numbers, 1+2+3+4=10. If each integer is represented as a dot and the ten are arranged in a triangular pattern, **figure 6a**, the image of the decade is known as the tetraktys. This kind of morphic or geometric arithmetic was common in ancient times. The number sigils we take for granted today were not used in Europe until the early Renaissance. Prior to that time arithmetic was taught with small round pebbles similar to marbles called "calculi," a term related to our word calculation. This morphic aspect was the source of the Pythagorean koan that ten is "complete at four."[45]

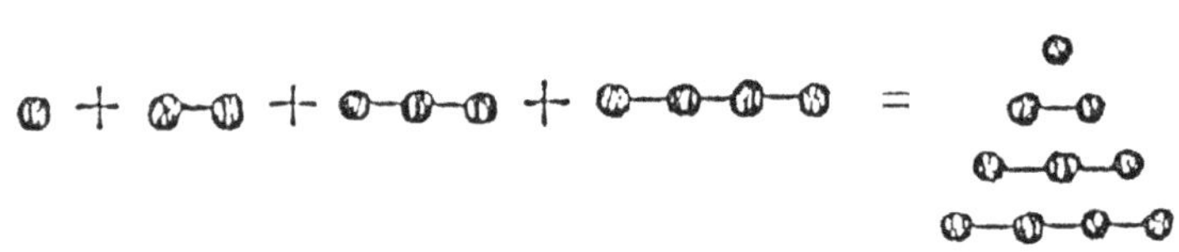

Figure 6a – *Building the Tetraktys*

Figure 6b – *The Tetraktys*

The four levels of the tetraktys may represent four stages of coming into being: unity, division, structure and manifestation; as well as the four subjects of the Quadrivium: Number, Geometry, Music and Astronomy. The tetraktys is a combination of number and geometry. Musically, the first four integers are the only numbers needed to obtain the ratios of the Pythagorean tetrachord; the fundamental 1:1; the octave 2:1; the fifth 3:2; and the fourth 4:3.

In the tetraktys "*... we have a most interesting Pythagorean idea to contend with — that ideal number is not necessarily subject to a sequential or causal progression from one through to ten, but is rather a unity with ten essential or potential qualities, simultaneously present in the Decade or Tetraktys.*"[46]

"In this way we can see a progression that embraces Plato's doctrine that "images" in the human mind reflect the universal source in the mind of the Divine Artificer. So we get one reflecting as a single dot or shadow on a surface for us to "imagine" or remember oneness from. If we should take the Pythagorean tradition literally, the first and comprehensive evidence of "ideal" or archetypal number is an array of dots in triangular form [**figure 6b**]. *This pattern might be called a refraction pattern of a single triangle.... This Decade or pattern can be taken both as a graphic (differentiated) form of ten dots in four rows and/or as one triangular form outlined in nine dots with a center point.* [It thus represents] *both a minimal oneness and a maximal tenness simultaneously."*[47]

Some correspondences to the tetraktys as an ontological model are indicated in the table below:

Tetraktys	Ontological Development	Dimensional Development	Spatial Dimension	Platonic Element	Quadrivium Subject
•	Unity	point	none/all	fire	number
• •	Division	line	one	air	geometry
• • •	Structure	plane	two	water	music
• • • •	Matter	solid	three	earth	astronomy

The Platonic Lambda

The Platonic Lambda is a geometric arrangement of the double and triple geometric progressions. Lambda, the Greek letter "L," is shaped like an inverted "V." The lambda is used as an ontological model by Plato in the *Timaeus*.[48] It starts at the first stage, with unity at the apex, and proceeds downward with the double series, the powers of 2, on one side and the triple series, the powers of 3, on the other. The second stage is the principle of odd and even, expressed in the first odd and even numbers, 2 and 3. In the third stage, that of the 2-dimensional plane, the odd and even principles are "squared," expressed in the numbers 4 and 9. In the fourth stage the still idealized 2-dimensional forms enter the solid, 3-dimensional, sensible world, expressed in the first two cubic numbers, 8 and 27.

The chart below shows the lambda and the four stages of coming into being. Also shown are some of the correspondences of four mentioned by Theon.[49]

Lambda	Number	Geometry	Element	3-d Figure	Social Scale
1	n^0 unity	point	fire	tetrahedron	species
2 3	n^1 odd-even	line	air	octahedron	community
4 9	n^2 square	plane	water	icosahedron	family
8 27	n^3 cube	solid	earth	cube	individual

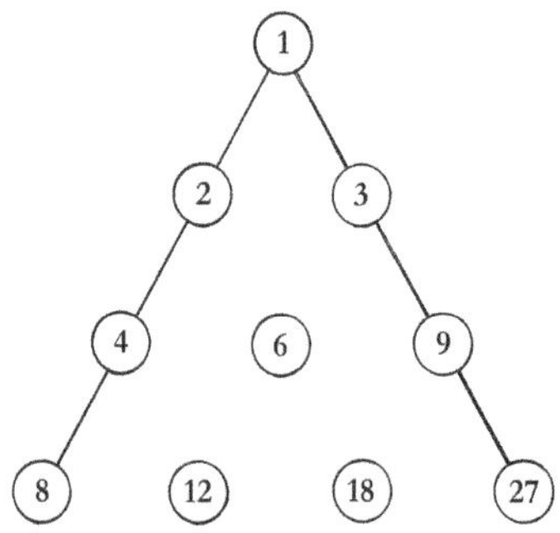

FIGURE 7a – *The Lambda and the Tetraktys*

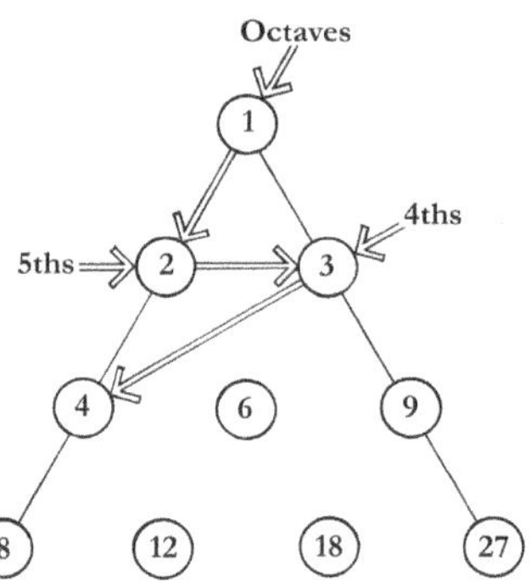

FIGURE 7b – *The Lambda and Music*

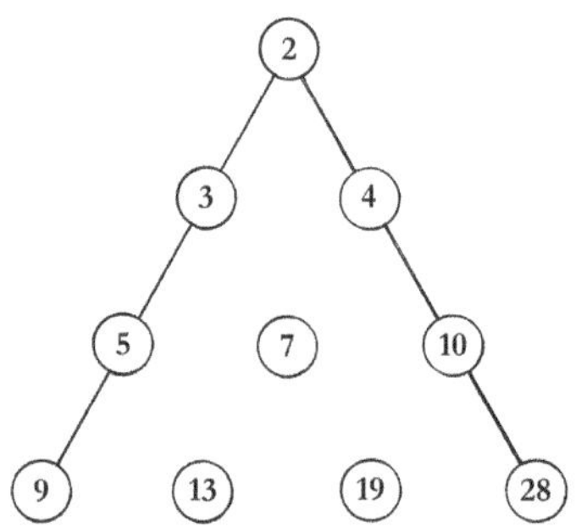

FIGURE 7c – *The Lambda and Astronomy*

The lambda may be considered a tetraktys with three positions missing, **figure** 7a. Filling in the open positions *"If we start from the monad ... and follow down the right hand slope the fourfold progression is 1x3=3, x3=9, x3=27. If we now shift down from 1 to the position of 2 and follow a similar angle down through the pattern, we pass through the center point, which becomes 2x3=6, and arrive at the point at the base, which becomes 6x3=18. If we do the same with the diagonal that moves down from 4, we have 4x3=12."* This produces a sequence: 1, 2, 3, 4, 6, 8, 9, 12, 18, 27.

"The point positions, one by one, represent the decade ... the allocated number progressions represent "states of being" of the refraction of one, we might say, and particularly of two and three respectively as they move from plane to cubic form and thereby provide a pattern that has within it the essential numerical harmonies [including those] *proposed by Plato for the generation of the 'world soul.'"*[50]

The musical ratios of the octave, 5th and 4th are present in the ten allocated numbers, **figure 7b.** By adding 1 to each number in the lambda decade, **figure** 7c, a new set of ten numbers is produced, each of which has astronomical significance.[51] The lambda-tetraktys may thus be linked to the four subjects of the Quadrivium; arithmetic, in the squaring and cubing; geometry, in the triangular structure; music, in the musical ratios; and astronomy, through a kind of "inflation" to a new monadic level.

2. Sun/Moon, day/night
3. Retrograde loops of Mercury per year
4. Four seasons
5. Retrograde loops of Venus in eight years
7. One-quarter of Moon cycle
9. Jupiter/Saturn triune conjunctions in 60 years
10. Tetraktys
13. Lunar months per year
19. Years in Metonic ecipse cycle
28. Days in full lunar cycle

NUMBER, GEOMETRY, MUSIC

Recalling the principle of the monad, the One can be taken as the beginning, as well as the all-encompassing, and may be represented by the circle, **figure 8a**; In terms of a ratio, Unity may be stated 1:1; musically, Unity might be called the fundamental. But, as we have seen, complete, fundamental unity is unmanifest, unperceivable. In order for something to be perceivable there must be a difference, a differentiation or separation, within unity. The start of this differentiation is for One to transform into Two. In music this relationship of 2:1 is called the octave, **figure 8b**, and is expressed through the length of strings or pipes. If a string of any given length, taken as an interval of 1, is vibrated, it produces a note called the fundamental. A string twice as long, or an interval of 2, will vibrate at a rate that produces a consonant sound one octave lower than the fundamental.

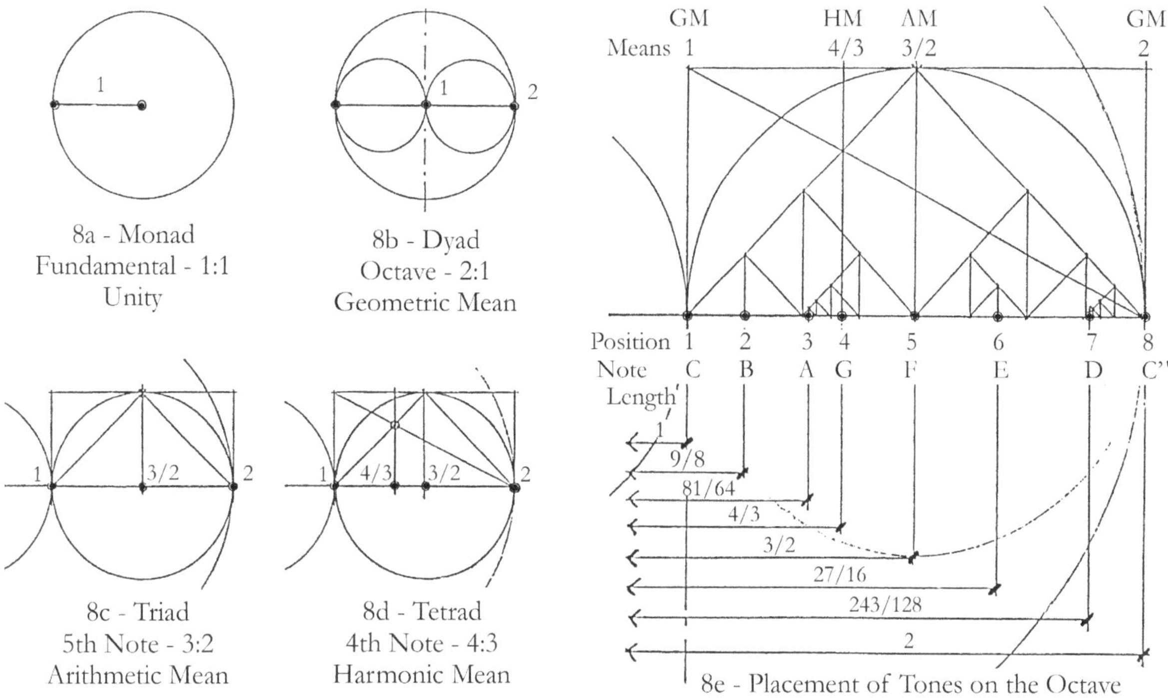

FIGURE 8
Geometric Construction of the Natural Octave

The extremes of Twoness are mediated by Threeness. In music the 3:2 ratio is known as a "fifth." That is, if the octaval distance is from 1 to 2, a string when plucked or struck at the 3/2 point will produce a consonant sound five notes lower than the fundamental; a geometric method of locating this point is shown in **figure 8c**. The next step in the manifestation of number is Fourness; which can be considered as both a doubling of two and a unit increase from three. The ratio 4/3 is known in music as a "fourth." That is, with an octaval distance of 2:1, a string when plucked or struck at the 4/3 point will produce a "consonant" sound four notes lower than the fundamental, **figure 8d**. The remaining four notes can be located geometrically by further subdivision, **figure 8e**.

The first four numbers can be seen to form four ratios; 1:1, 2:1, 3:2 and 4:3. These in turn define the octave and its two essential musical divisions. These first four numbers can also be taken to represent the four levels of the tetraktys; and the four stages of becoming; point, line, plane, solid. The parallel may be extended to see four "stages" of musical consonance, a fundamental, its octave, its fifth consonance, and its fourth consonance. This grouping of notes is known as the Pythagorean tetrachord.

Ratio, Proportion, Logos

A ratio is a comparative relationship between two numbers such as 2:1. A proportion is a relationship of equality between ratios.[52] for example 2:1::8:4. This is a four-term, discontinuous proportion, a:b::c:d. It is also possible to have a three-term, continuous proportion such as a:b :: b:c, which may be written a:b:c. In such a proportion the first and last term are called the "extremes" and the middle term is called the "mean." There are three types of continuous proportions used in ancient musical theory, which generate the significant ratios within the octave.

1. In the **Geometric proportion,** the product of the extremes equals the square of the mean, $b^2=ac$, $b=\sqrt{ac}$. For example, 2:4:8, where $4=\sqrt{[2 \times 8]}$. Or, it may be said that "the mean differs from each extreme by the same ratio"; in this example, the double ratio, $4=2 \times 2$ and $8=4 \times 2$.

2. In the **Arithmetic proportion,** the sum of the extremes is equal to twice the mean, $2b=a+c$ or $b=[a+c]/2$, for example, 2:3:4 where $3=[2+4]/2$. Or it can be said that "the mean differs from each extreme by the same number." In the above example 2, 3 and 4 differ from each other by 1. In this way the arithmetic mean may be said to give rise to the "natural" series, 1, 2, 3, 4.... In the mathematical sense the arithmetic mean may be considered primary[53]. In the context of music however, the geometric mean may be considered primary because it generates continuous octaval relationships; 2:4:8:16.

3. The **Harmonic proportion** can be said to combine the qualities of the other two means. The harmonic mean is equal to the product of the extremes divided by the arithmetic mean, $b=2ac/a+c$, for example, 2:3:6 where $2[2 \times 6]/[2+6]=24/8=3$. It can also be said to be "the mean which exceeds one extreme, and is exceeded by the other extreme, by the same fraction of each extreme." In our example, 3 is greater than 2 by 1/2 of 2 and 6 is greater than 3 by 1/2 of 6.

The three means are interrelated. They contain *"the general formula for all our basic mathematical operations. The arithmetic proportion contains the law for addition and its inverse, subtraction, and describes the natural series of cardinal numbers 1, 2, 3, 4, etc. The geometric proportion contains the law for multiplication and its inversion, division, and describes the relationship which gives any series of geometric progressions.... The most important and mysterious character of the harmonic proportion is that the inverse of every harmonic progression is an arithmetic progression. Thus 2, 3, 4, 5, is an ascending arithmetic progression while the inverse series, 1/2, 1/3, 1/4, 1/5, is a descending harmonic progression. In music it is the insertion of the harmonic and arithmetic means between the two extremes in double ratios — representing the octave double — which gives us the progression known as the "musical" proportion, that is, 1, 4/3, 3/2, 2."*[54]

Ratio and proportion were called "logos" in ancient Greece. This word had a range of meanings all having to do with comparative relationships determined through reasoning with or without the aid of speech. Theon writes, *"The relation of proportion or ratio is called this* [logos] *and it is in this sense that it is said that there is a relationship of one thing to another thing. It also has the meaning of the explanation of the elements of the Universe: the recognition of things which honor and are honored, and it is in this sense that we say: taking account of something, or not taking account of it (word of honor). The calculation of bankers is also called logos, as is the discourse of Demosthenes and Lysias in their written works (speech); the definition of things which explains their essence (reason).... The name logos is also given to the eulogy, to the tale and to the proverb."*

"According to Plato, the word logos is used with four different meanings: for mental thought without words; for discourse proceeding from the mind and expressed by the voice; for the explanation of the elements of the universe; and the ratio of proportion.... The ratio of proportion of two terms is a certain relationship that these terms have to each other, such as the double or triple."[55] One may thus define logos as "proportional relationship which gives meaning" or, to use a phrase attributed to Gregory Bateson, "the difference that makes a difference."[56] The passage from Theon also indicates a common ground, in ancient times, of proportional relationship, music, geometry, number, and "the explanation of the elements of the universe," to be found through rational discourse.

Astronomy

In ancient astronomy the key concept may be said to be the cycle of light and dark, particularly of the sun but also of other planets and fixed stars. The undifferentiated light of the sun is followed by a period of darkness. A simple yet fundamentally correct way to measure the changing nature of the light source, the sun, is by observing a shadow. One method of controlling the measurement of a shadow is by setting up a shadow stick vertically in flat ground. The stick may be thought of as a mediating third element in the sun-shadow or light-dark relationship. As the sun changes its position in the sky, the shadow changes its position inversely on the ground. As the sun represents the source of light, the shadow represents the absence of light and its movement is inverse to the source of light. As the sun moves to the right the shadow moves to the left, **figure 9a**.

Observation of the movement of shadows, whether natural or artificial, yields information in pattern form. An elemental piece of information obtained from the shadow stick is the east–west axis. This is found by describing a circle with the shadow stick as its center, marking the position of the shadow where it crosses the circumference of the circle just after sunrise, then again just before sunset, and connecting the two points on the circumference to give the east–west axis, **figure 9b**.

The north–south axis, which marks the high point of the sun's movement through the sky, can be found by constructing a perpendicular to the e–w axis, **figure 9c**. This is done by using the two points of shadow intersection as centers and the length of the e–w line as a radius, AB, generating the vesica piscis whose two "points" position the n–s axis.

Repeating the vesica construction along the east–west axis, **figure 9d,** creates square CDFG, which has approximately the same perimeter as circle AB. This squaring of the circle constitutes a new Unity, a kind of sacred marriage.

In its use of the circle, triangle and square this procedure recalls the Far Eastern great triad of heaven and earth mediated by the human being.[57] A fourfold imagery of the orientation process generates correspondences of the subjects of the Quadrivium with the tetraktys: the first four numbers, the first four geometric forms, the first four musical consonances, and four basic astronomical observations:

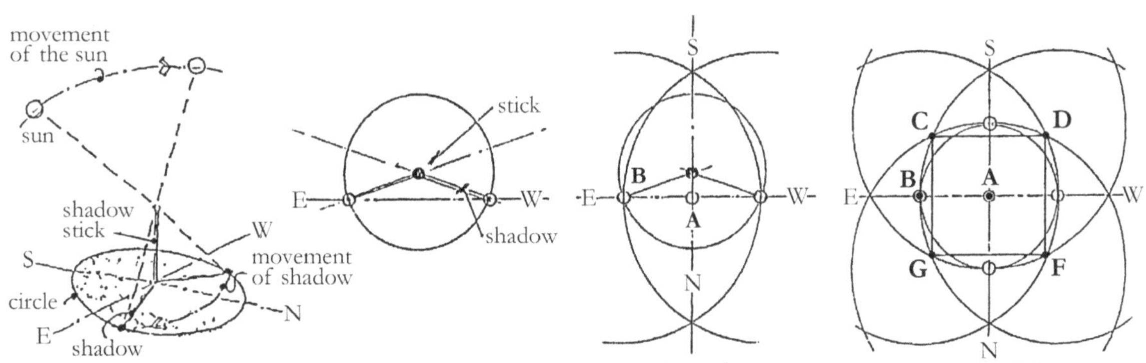

Figure 9a
Sun and shadow
Monad becoms Dyad

Figure 9b
East-West axis
The Triad

Figure 9c
North-South axis
The Tetrad

Figure 9d
Squaring the Circle
New Unity

FIGURE 9
Geometry of Orientation

Number		Geometry	Music	Astronomy	Ontological Term
1	•	point - circle	fundamental 1:1	the sun	unity - Theos
2	• •	line	octave 2:1	the shadow	division - Nous
3	• • •	plane - triangle	fifth 3:2	e - w axis	structure - Psyche
4	• • • •	volume - cube	fourth 4:3	n - s axis	matter - Hule

The theme of the division of the circle is important in the relation of time to astronomy. Segmenting the continuous circumference of the circle is analogous to order being brought out of chaos, or to establishing a moment in eternity. In modern terms we say we have become "oriented" when we know where we are. Orient means east, where the sun rises, so to be oriented implies being aligned with the sunrise and therefore with the patterns of movement of the cosmic bodies. The point of sunrise is the point of scission of the limitless circumference and it establishes the axis.

The vertical shadow marker itself represents the third directional axis. This third vertical element, or mean, can be taken to establish the structural relation between heaven and earth. Its linear aspect may be characterized as, *"the potency of creation or vertical ray: the axis of the lightning flash; the division of light from darkness; the ontological axis of being; related to the Greek letter Ø, phi as in phyla, to bring forth, and physis, nature, and phylon, race, sex."*[58]

A good natural shadow marker would be a freestanding tree, recalling the symbol of the tree of knowledge. In many traditions the wisdom teacher sits beneath a tree; the Buddha, for example, receives enlightenment beneath a tree. A good artificial marker would be a stick, which is a part of a tree. If the stick were marked or notched to record observations, it recalls the Biblical symbol of Jacob's ladder, perhaps an image descended from paleolithic counting sticks.

In ancient Greek times the shadow marker was called a "gnomon"; a word related to "gnosis" meaning experienced knowledge. In geometry the gnomon is associated with proportional transformation, and here we see it associated with transformation of light and dark through time. Its relation to the concept of "gnosis," inner knowledge, indicates that the experience of pattern, and the study of transformation, is a pathway to such knowledge.

Looking Up and Down

It is hoped that this exploration of philosophical number begins to accomplish our goal of understanding the relation of number to beauty. In brief we may say it is because number is the means by which ultimate unity is divided to become the sensible world; and because psyche, that aspect of ourselves that connects us to that unity is based in the same principles, it is constructed by analogy. The significance of this is that construction by analogy of the individual and the cosmos leaves open the possibility of self-dignification through participation with unity; and the communication of that elevated state to others by one's actions or work.

In Plato's *Republic,* Socrates puts it this way: *"the philosopher holding converse with the divine order, becomes orderly and divine, as far as human nature allows.... And if a necessity be laid upon him of fashioning, not only himself, but human nature generally, whether in states or individuals, into that which he beholds elsewhere, will he, think you, be an unskillful artificer of justice, temperance, and every civil virtue? … Will* [the world] *disbelieve us, when we tell them that no state can be happy which is not designed by artists who imitate the heavenly pattern?"*

To proceed with the design *"they will often turn their eyes upward and downward … they will first look at absolute justice, beauty and temperance, and again at the human copy; and will mingle and temper the various elements into the image of a man; and thus they will conceive according to that other image, which, when existing among men, Homer calls the form and likeness of the Divine."*[59]

II

NUMBER HARMONY DESIGN

Introduction

THE OPENING SECTION EXPLORED the concept of qualitative number, in which each number has a unique character in relation to unity. This concept was used to develop a theory of beauty as the memory of unity and then to tell a story of coming into being, an ontogeny, illustrated by the four sciences of qualitative number, arithmetic, geometry, music and astronomy. These subjects, known as the Quadrivium, which guided our ontogeny also form the background to the methods of application of proportion in design.

To approach the achievement of beauty in material works we might wish to use methods analogous to our ontogenic story; "proportional" methods in which qualitative number mediates between philosophy and aesthetics, between the ideal and the actual. The methods, images and examples in this section are presented in the spirit of illustrating such possibilities. Several methods and techniques are described for constructing "archetypal" building compositions that are in keeping with an analogic cosmos beginning in unity and proceeding to multiplicity. Examples begin with four, six and eight-column porticos, which often form the core or seed of more complex compositions, then expand and modify these.

Proportion in design is taken here to mean the use of symbolic number as a design tool. Proportional concepts are traditionally applied to the archetypes through three techniques: geometrical construction, arithmetical counting and use of small whole number ratios. They are called here the Geometric, Arithmetic and Harmonic Ratio methods in honor of the three well known mathematical "means" used by Plato in his construction of a musically related cosmos. They constitute only a fragment of the ancient science of mediation. Use of these terms in this section is not indicative of Platonic or musical usage, but rather is drawn from the actual operations utilized in each of the methods. The use of such methods in design essentially constitute the practice of Proportion.

What is here called the **Geometric Method** is one of pure construction. It begins with representatives of unity, particularly the circle and the regular polygons such as the equilateral triangle, square and pentagon. These are further subdivided through the use of their diagonals or other features. Hints of such geometrical methodology are found in Serlio's first book, *On Geometry*.[1]

Historically speaking arithmetic, geometry, music and astronomy have undoubtedly had a complex and inter-related path of development; but viewed from the position of the designer, it may be considered that the geometrical method is primary. Geometric constructions can be performed independently of arithmetic operations. Further, many geometrical constructions embody what mathematicians call "transcendental" ratios, such as π or Ø, which cannot be expressed as whole numbers. These are here referred to as *trans-rationals* because they transcend our ability to completely quantify them. Yet another aspect indicating its primacy is that geometric construction requires both mental and physical activity in a coordinated manner. This quality of being "psycho-physiological" gives geometry an "intuitive" aspect that would have appealed to people in early times when distinctions between mind and body were not as severe as they are today.

The **Arithmetic Method** is based on the addition of a unit or module. The module may be further subdivided into parts and minutes so that all elements may be described at any scale. This method is often manifest as a grid or graph on which points may be found by directional or linear counting. This is the method used by Vitruvius in his canon of the elements. Because the arithmetic method is more abstract than the geometrical method in the sense that calculation can be performed entirely in the mind, it may be considered subsidiary to geometry in architectural practice. It would have served the purpose of translating the trans-rational geometric constructions into buildable measurements without having either to teach the constructions or reproduce the geometry on a large scale.

The **Harmonic Ratio Method** consists of musical and geometrical relationships expressed as ratios of small whole numbers. The ancient musical octave utilized four notes known as the tetrachord. Expressed as ratios the tetrachord consists of: 1:1 – the fundamental, 2:1 – the octave, 3:2 – the fifth note, and 4:3 – the fourth note. These comprise what may be called "rational" ratios. Geometrical construction provides numerous "trans-rational" ratios. Although there are an indefinite number of trans-rationals, those used in traditional design are 1:√2 or 1:1.414…, approximated as 5:7; 1:√3, 1:1.732…, or 4:7, 1:√5, 1:2.236..., or 4:9, the Golden Section known as Ø, 1:.618, or 8:5; also two modifications of Ø, 1:1.236…, or 5:6; and 1:.809…, or 5:4.

An integral premise of this method is that a trans-rational ratio can be taken as an aesthetic equivalent to a small whole number ratio. This is necessary because at this point we come up against an ontogenic "fact of life": that in design an "idea" must somehow be applied to an "object." Since objects are material they are by definition not ideal. They are material reminders of ideals. In the arts and the pursuit of beauty this raises the question of how close an approximation is close enough. If your answer is zero, as it appears to be for some, then much of what appears in this book will be meaningless. Such readers are advised to stick to the "hard" sciences and forsake the arts. But for others who are willing to take this psychological plunge into the symbolic, the harmonic ratio method is very useful.

Although Vitruvius, Alberti and others offer sets of ratios recommended for various architectural elements, the use of small whole number ratios as a conscious method emerges in the work of Palladio. This may be related to the influence of Palladio's patron Daniele Barbaro, one of the leading musical theorists of his era. Through the influence of Palladianism the harmonic ratio method is the most widespread form of proportional application today. The method may be seen as a middle way between the pure construction of the geometrical method and the abstract calculation of the arithmetic method. While geometry keeps us close to unity it may be difficult to communicate or apply directly. Linear arithmetic is easy to communicate and apply but by immersing us in multiplicity it turns us away from unity. Use of harmonic ratios keeps us aware of unity while allowing us to translate that sense into rational measurements.

Since the goal of any such method is to create a sense of unity that allows the experience of beauty, as opposed to the achievement of a mathematically correct answer, the three techniques are not exclusive but essentially recapitulate one another. In operative projects any combination of them that achieves the desired result is acceptable. Thus in the examples that follow arithmetic canons are combined with geometrical constructions and harmonic ratios. One method may pick up where the other leaves off, at the designer's convenience.

Nor are these methods to be confused with design itself, but are a means to an end. They are formative but should not be preemptive of the design process. They are the guiding ground of the elements and orders of architectural language but should not be confused with the message. If a work looks too much like geometry the design is probably not finished. The designer also needs to keep in mind that the sense of unity is always an illusion. A building is made from thousands of individual components. It is the task of the designer to make these disparate parts, which lack any inherent coherence, appear to be one thing. It is to this end that methods of proportion contribute.

Proportion was not taught as an independent subject in the great European schools such as the French École des Beaux-Arts or the British Royal Academy. It was learned in the working studio, passed from one designer to another or from artisans to designers. This appears to have been the case as late as the nineteenth-century New York atelier of R. M. Hunt.[2] But the "modern" era has so thoroughly trashed the concept of proportion that in a certain way it needs to be reinvented. In the pre-modern era proportion was a series of methods, not an academic subject. It is hoped that this book it will be a step forward in the public profile of the proportional concept, making it accessible, taught, and utilized in the academy, the studio, the shop, and the field. To that end the constructions in this section are intended to be treated as workbook exercises. Perform them yourself. Draw them with instruments. Draw them freehand. Use them as a ground for experiencing psycho-physiological effects. In spiritual traditions such as Sufism and Yoga such practices are associated with the experience of Unity.

The images and designs presented in this section are didactic in nature, that is, done for explanatory purposes. Practical application always requires some alteration of the archetypes. Though the examples given here are intended to correspond fairly closely to the canons of number given by Vitruvius, Vignola and others the goal is not specifically to imitate or reconstruct past forms. No claim is made that these specific methods were actually used by the ancients or anyone else. The designer should use such methods and techniques, after careful study, as starting points for their own work; not as laws to be rigidly obeyed. The examples presented here are intended to develop an understanding of timeless principles and explore the possibility of their expression in the present moment. They are presented in the spirit of inspiring designers to seek solutions to contemporary issues in the timeless realms of Beauty, Love and Unity.

Figure 1. A Geometrical Creation Story

In the first section we recounted a story of creation, an ontogeny, to illustrate the concept of qualitative or symbolic number, **figure 1a.**

1. The Monad. Creation begins with the point of origin, embodying the quality of oneness, called the monad. It represents the state of transcendent unity which is the necessary starting point of our world of multiplicity. This point contains a fundamental mystery – it has location without dimension. Though the point contains everything in potential it cannot be perceived with the senses as it is unextended in dimension. It is represented in arithmetic by the number one and in geometry by the dot. The first shape is the circle. It is an inflation of the point that allows its potential to be actualized. This first stage of our story of coming into being may be thought of as that of transcendent unity. When taken as an applied unit of measure consistent with its character of sameness such a key unit is called the module.

2. The Dyad. If unity contains all, everything manifest and unmanifest, then it must also contain its own opposite, division or separation from unity. For such a separation to occur there must be a direction prior to any movement. This initial form of extension is known variously as the ray of creation, lightning flash, world tree or axis mundi. Geometrically this is the line. This movement is not an external separation but is division of unity from within. It is represented here by two equal circles centered on the axial ray. Twoness, called the dyad, is the ontological level of moral choice; the good versus the not good. For Pythagoreans, the dyad symbolized polar opposites such as: limit-unlimited; odd–even; one–many; rest–motion; same–different. Order is connected to the idea of limit, for recognizable order must fall within some limit. Disorder and chaos are unlimited.

3. The Triad. Any two separate things must have a relationship. This requires threeness or the triad. For sensible perception or any act of communication to take place, there must be at least a sender, a receiver and a medium of transmission. For any kind of physical structural stability, a spatial triangulation is required. As it contains the beginning, middle and end the triad is the ontological level of the symbolic, of the image and of the individual soul. We represent the triad in our diagram by placing a third circle between those of the same and the different. This circle governs the creation of the equilateral triangle, the first regular polygon.

4. The Tetrad. A fully manifest object must have at least three dimensions, length, width and height. These three intervals are marked off by a minimum of four points:

⋆ length ⋆ width ⋆ height ⋆

Fourness or the tetrad is the ontological level of manifestation. It may be visualized as a crossing of dyadic opposites, such as warp and weft which cross to create a fabric, or male and female polarities which must be crossed to allow physical birth. Geometrically, the tetrad may be represented by the square. It is in this sense that we still use the expression "the four corners of the world."

Our ontogeny takes us from the mysterious point of emergence to full manifestation in four stages. The building blocks of this creation myth are the qualitative aspects of number and geometry. In the fifth century BC, about a century and a half after the life of Pythagoras, this qualitative aspect of number was taken up by Plato, most notably in the dialog of *Timaeus*. In that work, Plato weaves a wonderfully complex and subtle creation myth using the four an-

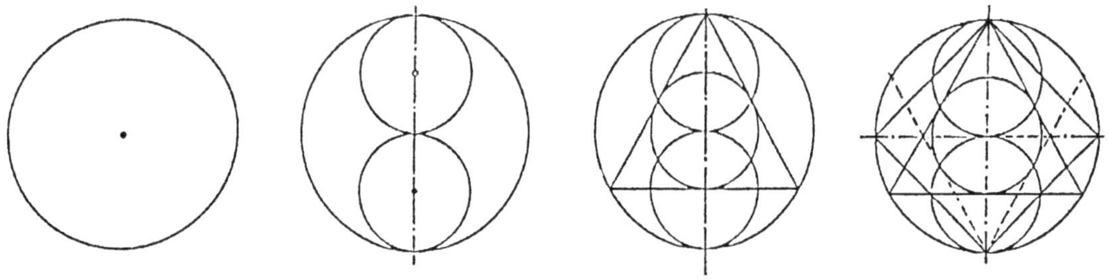

1 - Monad Unity Point	2 - Dyad Division Line	3 - Triad Structure Plane	4 - Tetrad Manifestation Solid

Figure 1a - The four stages of the Geometrical Creation Story

Symbol	Ontological Stage	Subject	Number	Geometry	Music	Astronomy	Platonic Element
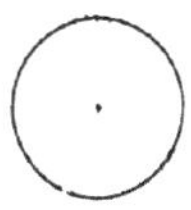	Unity	Number	1 Monad	Point	Fundamental 1 : 1	Light	Fire
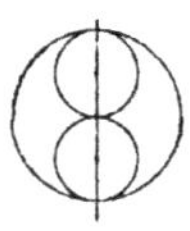	Division	Geometry	2 Dyad	Line	Octave 2 : 1	Dark	Air
	Structure	Music	3 Triad	Plane	Fifth Note 3 :2	Gnomon	Water
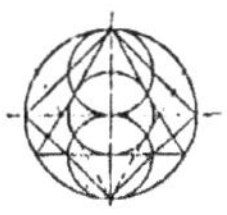	Matter	Astronomy	4 Tetrad	Solid	Fourth Note 4 : 3	Orientation	Earth

1b - Correspondences of the Four Mathematical Subjects of Plato

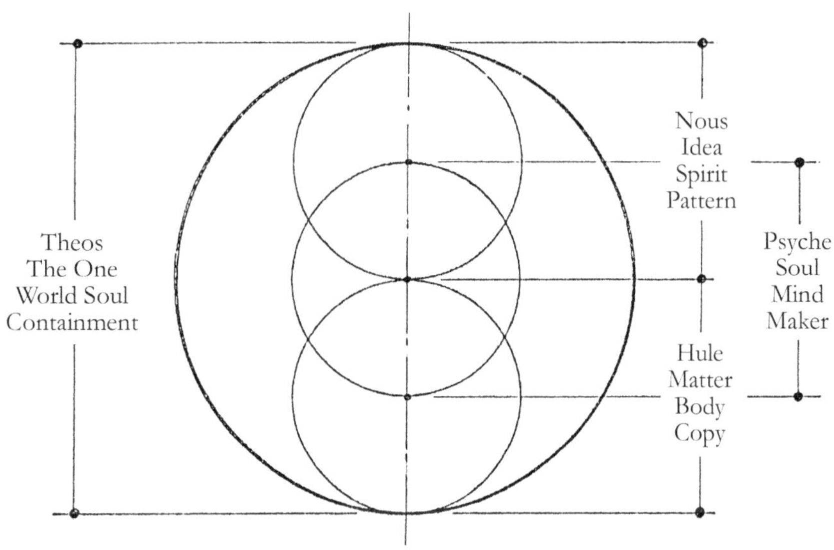

1c - Geometric Diagram of the Platonic Psyche

cient numerical sciences: Arithmetic – number in concept; Geometry – number in space; Music – number in time; and Astronomy – number in space and time.

These four sciences correspond to the ontological stages of our creation myth. In **figure 1b** each of the subjects is viewed in four stages, suggesting that they are each cosmologies of their own. The physical world of the Platonic elements also known as the sub-lunary world, corresponds to the cosmological stages as well. The elements — fire, air, water and earth — are listed in order of energy and density; fire being the most energetic and least dense.

In the *Timaeus* and the *Republic*, Plato employs the sciences of number to model what he calls the "world soul." A geometric image of this concept is shown in **figure 1c**. Though Plato uses the sphere to represent the world soul, for brevity's sake we represent it with the circle, in effect, a sphere in elevation. Soul or psyche may also be thought of as "mind." The diagram indicates that the individual soul is similar and concentric to the world soul; it is "analogous." The function of psyche is to project Nous, Idea, or Form, into matter, which has no inherent form.

Figure 2. The Musical Octave

One of the great discoveries attributed to Pythagoras is that relationships between consonant sounds may be expressed in terms of number. Ancient music used a natural or untempered octave and composition was based on four notes known as the tetrachord. When expressed as ratios of string length the tetrachord is; 1:1 – the fundamental, 2:1 – the octave, 3:2 – the fifth note, and 4:3 – the fourth note. Thus a string twice as long as the string that produces the fundamental produces a consonant or harmonic sound one octave lower.

These relationships are illustrated in Ptolemy's *Harmonics*, **figure 2a**, with the diagram called the "Helikon," after the mountain where the Muses lived. One must imagine an actual instrument with a square frame, four strings and a diagonal bridge. The length of the string to create the fourth note of the octave is given by the point of intersection of the square's diagonal and its semi-diagonal. The length of the string to create the fifth note is given by the intersection of the semi-diagonal and the centerline of the square. This geometrical formula which divides the sides of the square into two and three parts can also be used to create architectural elements.

In **figure 2b** the vertical diameter of the outer circle is seen as a string, The inner circle above gives the fundamental interval. The inner circle below is subdivided by the same pattern as the "Helikon." If we think of the outer circle as the world soul the diagram may be seen as a kind of cosmic monochord

A four column temple portico may be constructed on the same geometrical net as the musical octave, **figure 2c**. Both utilize the division of the square into thirds. The height and position of the inner column is given by the one-third point, which also gives the position of the 4th note. The depth of the entablature is one-forth of the column height and also equal to the interval of the whole tone, the distance between the 4th and 5th note. The lower diameter of the column is one-eighth its height, and one-twelfth of the width of the portico, thus relating the diameter to both the whole tone and the semitone. The height of the pediment is equal to the entablature and completes the square. This construction conforms to the canon of Vignola and comes within 5% of the canon of Vitruvius.

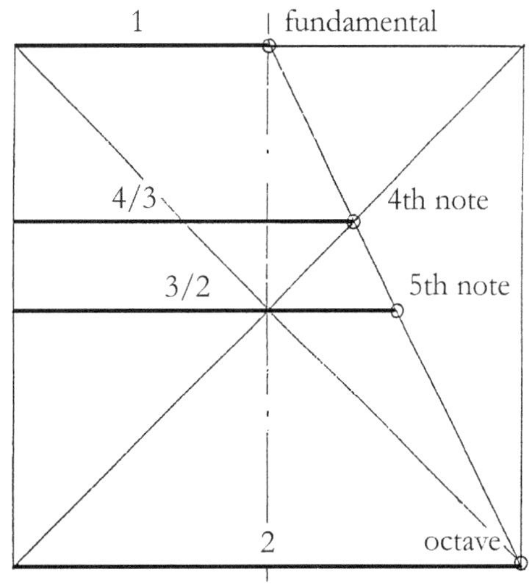

Figure 2a - Ptolemy's Helikon

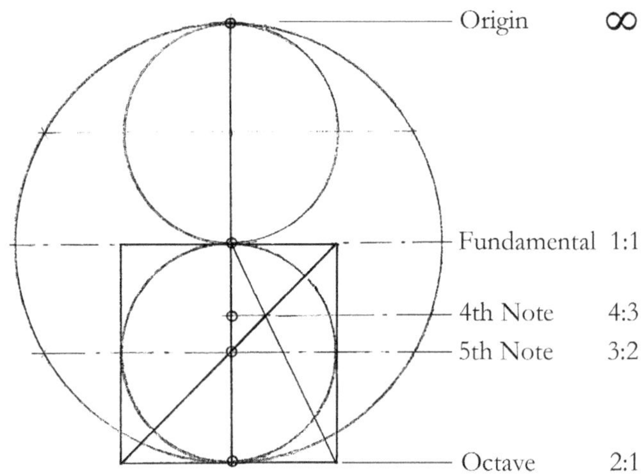

Figure 2b - Geometrical Construction of the Natural Octave

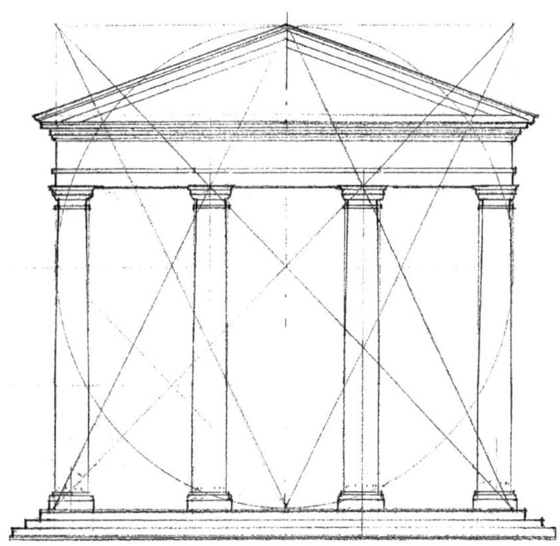

Figure 2c - A Tetrastyle Portico

FIGURE 2 – *The Musical Octave*

Figure 3. A Tetrastyle Portico Using Division of the Square

To look closer at the construction of the portico of **figure 2c** the design process may be divided into four stages which recapitulate the stages of our creation myth, **figure 3.**

1. Unity – Begin by restating the Pythagorean geometrical model—monad, dyad, triad, tetrad. From the inner tetrad construct an outer square, a material representation of unity, which will be the limit of the height and width of our design.

2. Division – The essential scission of unity. The square is divided by means of its diagonals and semi-diagonals. The intersection of these two sets of diagonals divides the sides of the square at the 1/3rd points. These points will mark the centers of the two inner columns and also their height.

3. Structure – The disposition and demarcation of the major parts of the design. By the canon of Vignola, if the height of the columns, including base and cap, is divided into four units, the height of the entablature is one additional unit. The lower diameter of the columns will be 1/8th of their height. In our design this is 1/12 of the side of the enclosing square. The sizes of other elements are derived from the lower diameter. Here we may see an integration of incommensurable geometry and the linear measures of the canon. The decimal equivalent of 1/3 is .333... ; that of half the side of the square is .500. The difference between them is 1/6 or .166... half of which is 0.083... , or 1/12. Thus geometrical manipulation alone could have been used to size and position the major elements.

4. Manifestation – Full articulation of the details and ornaments. The order selected for this design is Doric. Of the three Greek orders, Doric may be most associated with the Apollonian or rational function; the initial phase of the triadic cycle, the proceeding or coming forth. According to Vitruvius it may be selected to represent senior male divinities such as Zeus, heroes like Herakles, or certain female divinities such as Athena. The portico also references Apollo as overseer of the Muses in that it is based on the same geometry used to construct the intervals of the ancient musical tetrachord, shown in **figure 2**. In **figure 12** the Doric capital is constructed on the same geometrical pattern as that of the facade as a whole.

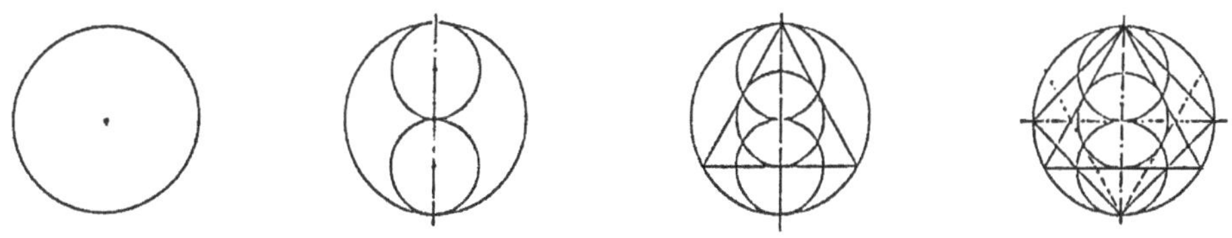

Monad Unity	Dyad Division	Triad Structure	Tetrad Manifestation

Four Stages of the Platonic Ontogeny

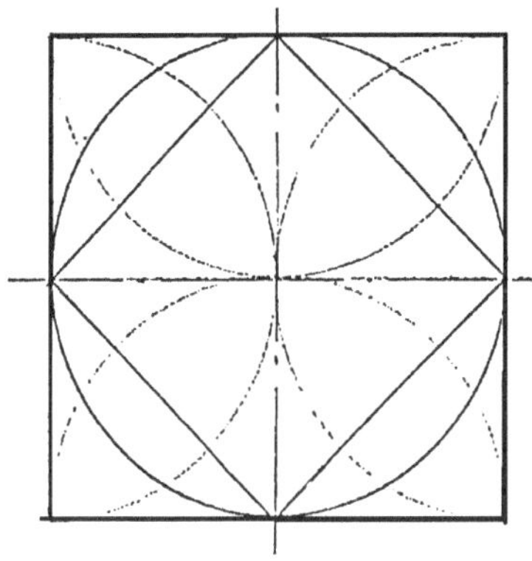

1-Unity and its Representative - the Square

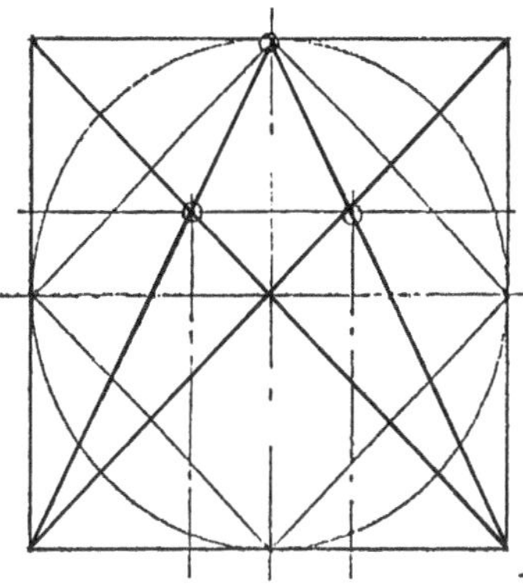

2 - Division of Unity - the Major Cuts

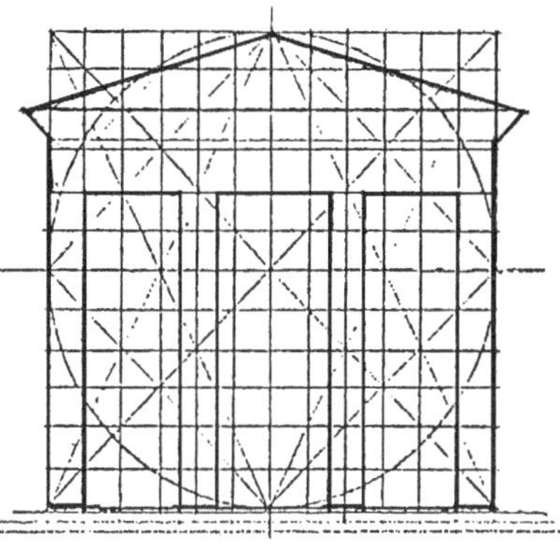

3 - Definition of the Major Elements

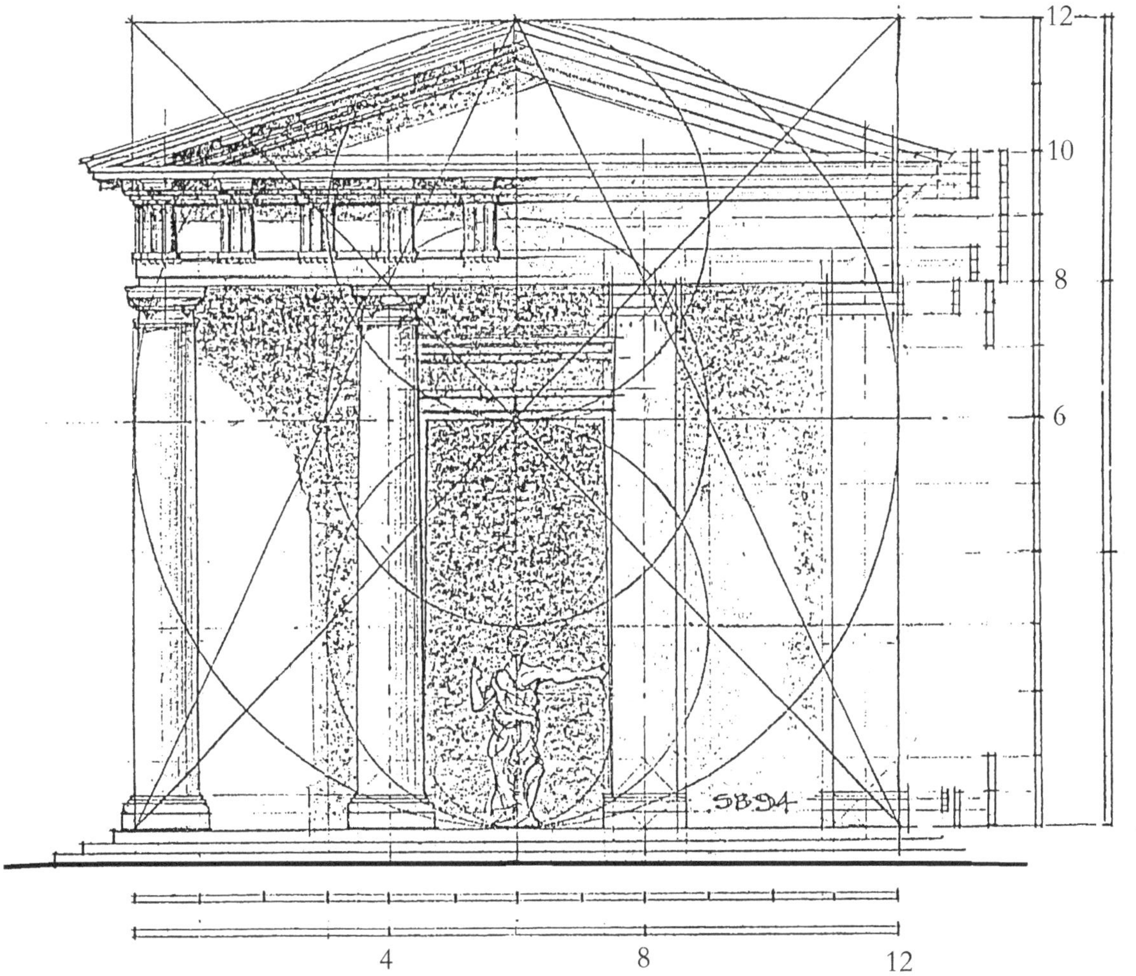

4 - Detailing and Ornamenting the Elements

Figure 4. An Ontogeny of the Root Powers

The ontogenic story, or creation myth told with arithmetic and geometrical images, in **figure 1** and in the first section of this book, is not unique nor is it an isolated instance. Indeed, there may be an indefinite number of such stories. The earlier story was used to model the emergence of the "rational ratios," a series comprised of small whole numbers that are related to the musical octave. Presented here is a variant of that story which gives rise to a series of "transcendental" or "trans-rational" ratios, that is, ratios that are not composed of whole numbers but of components that are not determinable in rational units. The most commonplace of such ratios is that of the circle's diameter to its circumference, known as pi, $\pi = 1:3.14\ldots$; the three dots after the figure indicates that the sequence of numbers does not have a knowable termination but continues indefinitely. Pi has been calculated, not just to millions of digits but to millions of pages of digits. All the computers in all the world, working for all the time there is will not pin it down.

These trans-rationals have a special character in that we can see directly the relation of the factors when they are drawn graphically, but we cannot fully express these relationships in rational mathematical units. We may take this stubborn "fact of life" as an indicator that the rational aspect of the human being, while important in the expression and communication of knowledge, is not the whole story. To put it another way, the existence of the trans-rationals suggests that there may never be a fully rational explanation of existence and the cosmos, or as the humorist puts it, to "life, the universe and everything." This may account for the persistence of the power of myth. Certainly, in the stimulation of remembrance the artist must, in some way, enter the realm of the trans-rational.

As earlier, the story begins on the level of the monad, with the mysterious point of emergence and its inflation into the circle, **figure 4a**. We project the initial ray of creation or lightening flash, **figure 4b**. In the earlier story, **figure 1**, this stage of Division, from the monad to the dyad, was represented by placing two circles within the circle of Theos, each half the diameter of the larger circle. Both these circles, symbolizing the Same and Different, Idea and Matter, are aspects of "Theos," and they divide within Theos, thus preserving a single unified cosmos. In the earlier story they continued their division until their circumferences were tangent at the center of the circle of Theos, forming a figure eight or meniscus.

In this story we must envision, **figure 4c,** that in response to the ray of creation the circle of the Same begins as the circle of Theos itself and withdraws upward, decreasing in diameter, while maintaining its tangency at point A; and simultaneously the circle of the Different, also beginning as the circle of Theos, withdraws downward, diminishing in diameter while maintaining its tangency at point B. In our earlier story the differentiation continued until the circles of the Same and Different were tangent at the center, point C. Here we stop the differentiation at a place where the center of one circle lies on the circumference of the other. The centers of these two circles may be found, **figure 4d,** by placing the circle of Theos in square DEFG then drawing the diagonals and semi-diagonals. Where these intersect, at H, J, K and L, the side of DEFG is divided into thirds, as in **figures 2** and **3**. Points M and N give the centers of the circles of the Same and the Different.

The football-shaped area of overlap of the circles of the Same and Different, **figure 4e,** represents the area of Psyche, Soul or Mind; the triadic level of our ontogenic story. This shape is

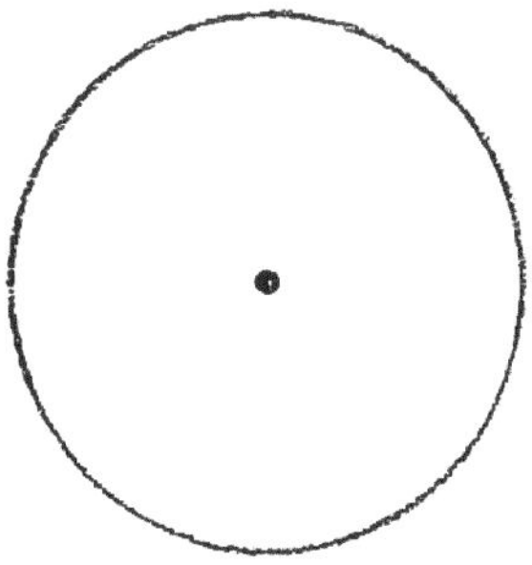

4a - Circle of Theos

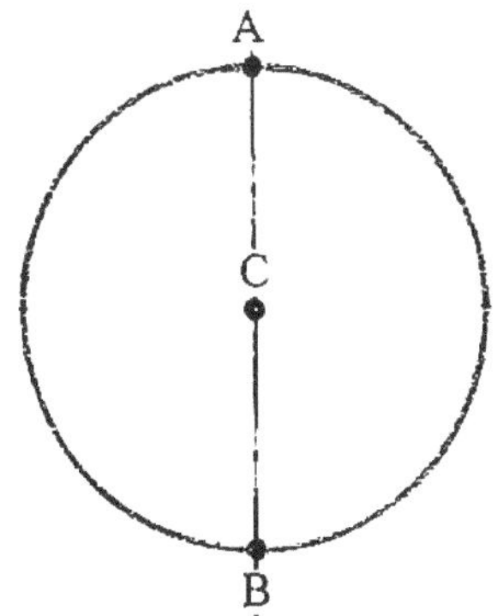

4b - Ray of Creation

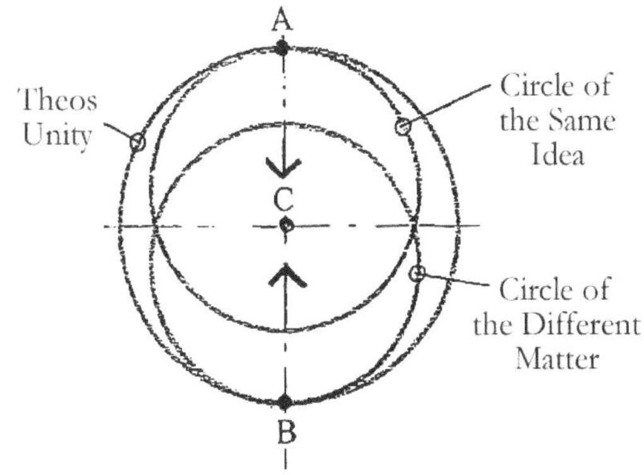

4c - Same & Different
Separate Within Theos

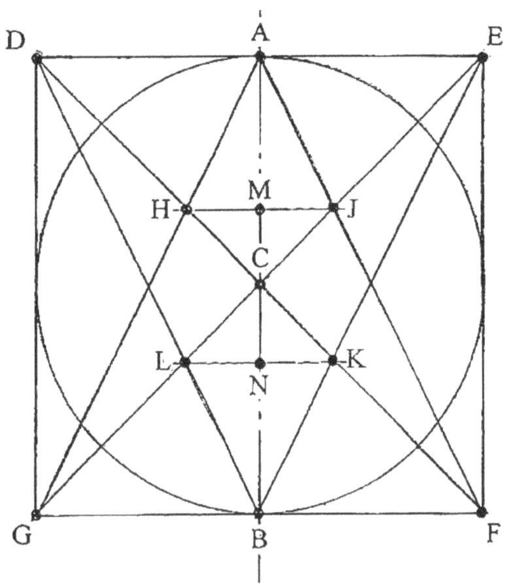

4d - Finding the Centers
of the Vesica Piscis

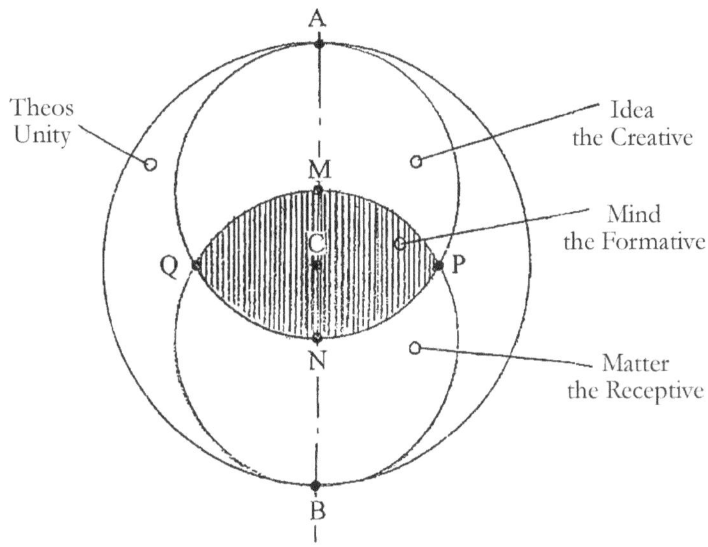

4e - The Vesica Piscis

called the Vesica Piscis or Vessel of the Fish. If we connect MN and PQ the lines will meet at C, the center of the circle of Theos, and will cross at a right angle, 90°, **figure 4f**. If we take this as symbolizing the tetradic or fourth ontological stage we will have recapitulated the steps in **figure 1**. Because intervals MN, MP and NP are all radii, shape MNP is an equilateral triangle. If the distance MN, from center to center is taken as 1, the distance from point to point, PQ is equal to the √ 3 = 1.732… .

The vesica piscis played a role in early Christianity. As a graphic sign it is said to have marked Christian meeting places during the time when the religion was illegal. In a deeper way it is related to Christianity symbolically as the birth of Jesus occurred at the start of the Piscean age, when the sun on the spring equinox began to rise in the constellation Pisces. For the previous two thousand years it had been moving through the constellation Aries; it is now about to enter the constellation Aquarius. The Christian era has thus taken place in the Piscean, or water age.

Water imagery surrounds Jesus; he is the "fisher of souls," his disciples are fishermen, he walks on water, and feeds the multitude with loaves and fishes. In John 21:11 the resurrected Christ bids fishermen to cast their net into the water and causes the miraculous catch of 153 fish. This may be a reference to the Pythagorean "measure of the fish" or 265/153, a whole number approximation of the $\sqrt{3}$.[3]

The vesica piscis may also symbolically represent the yoni or female birth organ. As the vesica piscis gives birth to the initial form, the equilateral triangle, it may also give birth to any regular polygon. The "trick" being how far to separate the two radii, MP and NP. Stated another way, the task is to find the center of the circle which will circumscribe the desired polygon. Construct a semicircle, **figure 4g**, centered at C with radius CM and find point R, the center of the square's circumscribing circle. Extend a line through MR until it intersects the circle at S. Repeat the process from N through R to point T. MNST is a square, and the diagonal $MS=NT=\sqrt{2}=1.414...$.

The triangle and square have been constructed on the right side of the vesica piscis. Constructing a mirror image square on the left side, **figure 4h**, gives rectangle UTSV. If $ST = 1$, $VS = 2$; and 2 is the $\sqrt{4}$. By the Pythagorean theorem, $a^2+b^2=c^2$, the diagonal of double square UTSV is equal to the $\sqrt{5}=2.236...$. This represents a movement beyond the story in **figure 1**. If the first four stages represent our descent from Unity into Materialization, the Pentad, fiveness, symbolizes the balance point, or the "turning point" of our return.

In the Pythagorean myth the individual soul begins its journey by projecting into the cosmos from the divine realm as a ray of light. As the psyche approaches the earth it passes through the shells of the seven planets, acquiring character. When it passes below the level of the moon it begins to take on material form. At last it reaches the earth where physical birth occurs. But according to Plato[4] the effect of the journey into incarnation is to cause the psyche to, in effect, become disoriented, forget its identification with divine unity and to identify with the body. Thus our earthly work is one of remembrance or in Platonic terms "anamnesis"; a necessary precursor for psyche's return journey to the divine. This turning from multiplicity to unity is symbolized in the ratio called phi, Ø, or the Golden Section.

In **figure 4j** the interval UC is "applied" along vertical axis AMC to find point W. $UC=\sqrt{5}/2=1.118...$, and $MC=1/2=.5$, thus the numerical value of $phi=.618...$. If we draw a line through W parallel to UM, and extend UV the two lines will meet at point Y creating a phi rectangle. Point Y falls on the circle of Theos, the divine. This is because $WC = 1.118...$ and $YW = 1$; $YC = 1.118...^2+1=\sqrt{2.249...} = 1.499...$ and $AC = 1.5$. Thus phi has geometrically reenacted the metaphor of Platonic remembrance and returned us to unity via a journey through multiplicity.

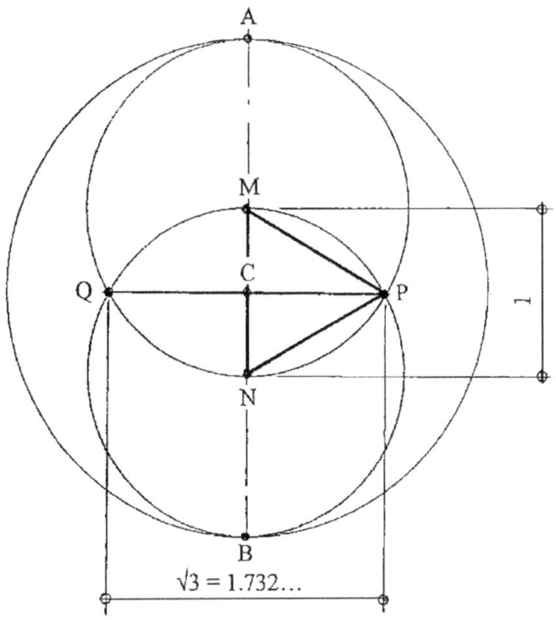

4f - The Equilateral Triangle
and the √3

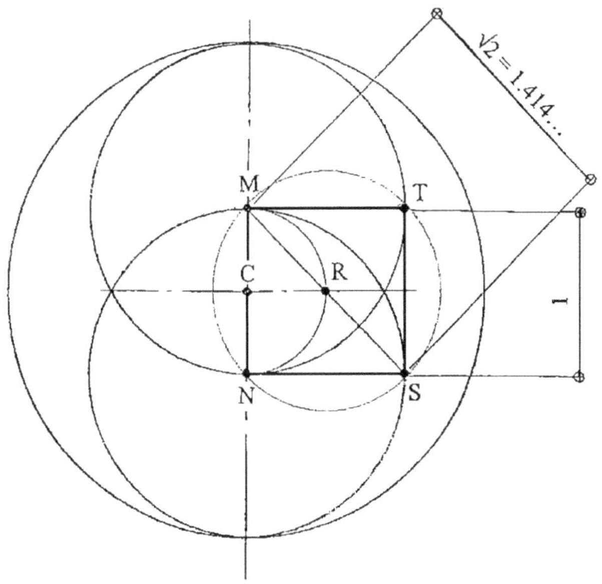

4g - The Square
and the √2

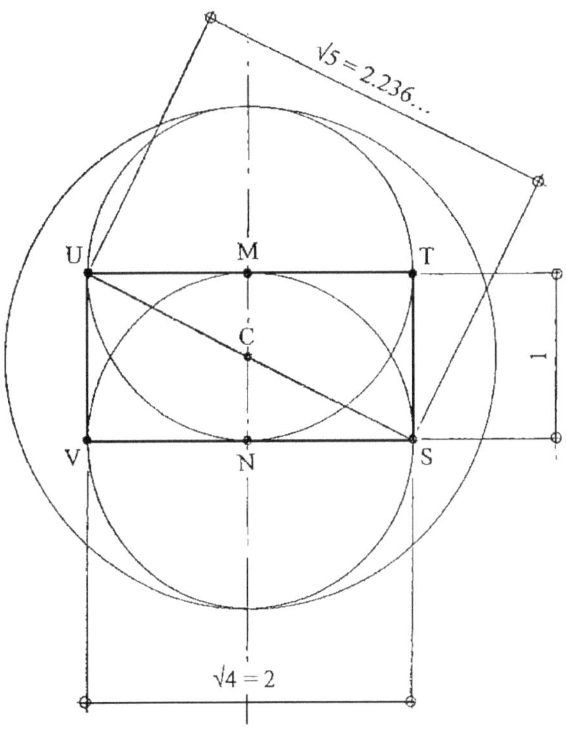

4h - The Double Square
and the √5

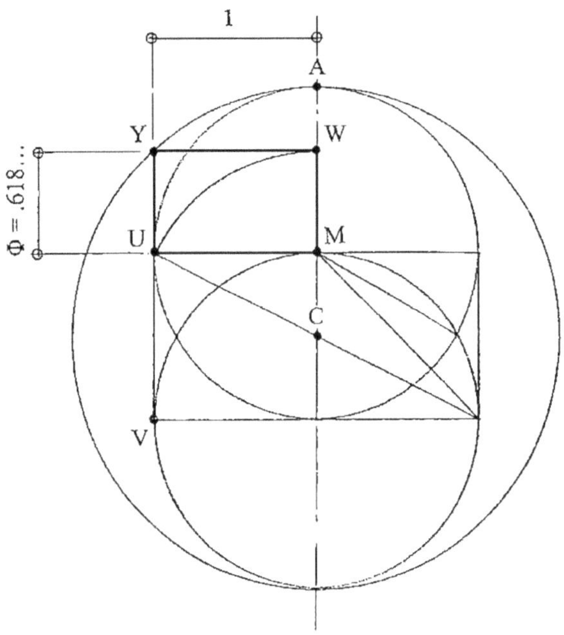

4j - Phi Returns to
Unity Through Multiplicity

Figure 5. Properties of the Root Rectangles

The root powers form a series of rectangles exhibiting a family-like resemblance, starting with the square, **figure 5a**. The diagonal of a square whose side =1 is √2=1.414.... Rotating the diagonal down to the horizontal, or as geometers might say, "applying" the diagonal upon the extended edge, produces a rectangle whose sides are in the ratio of 1:1.414..., called a "√2" rectangle.

In a remarkable aspect of the nature of number, the diagonal of a √2 rectangle =√3, 1.732.... Continuing the process, it is even more remarkable that the diagonal of a √3 rectangle is equal to √4=2, producing the double square. This constitutes a "crossover" point between the rational and the trans-rational ratios. Continuing another step, the diagonal of a double square =√5=2.236....

Although we could continue indefinitely, design tradition has not found it necessary to go beyond the √5 rectangle, most likely because this is a source of the Golden Section, as Ø=[√5-1]/2. A geometrical version of this algebraic procedure, **figure 5b**, starts with a √5 rectangle. Subtract a square, then divide the remaining interval by 2, leaving a Ø rectangle.

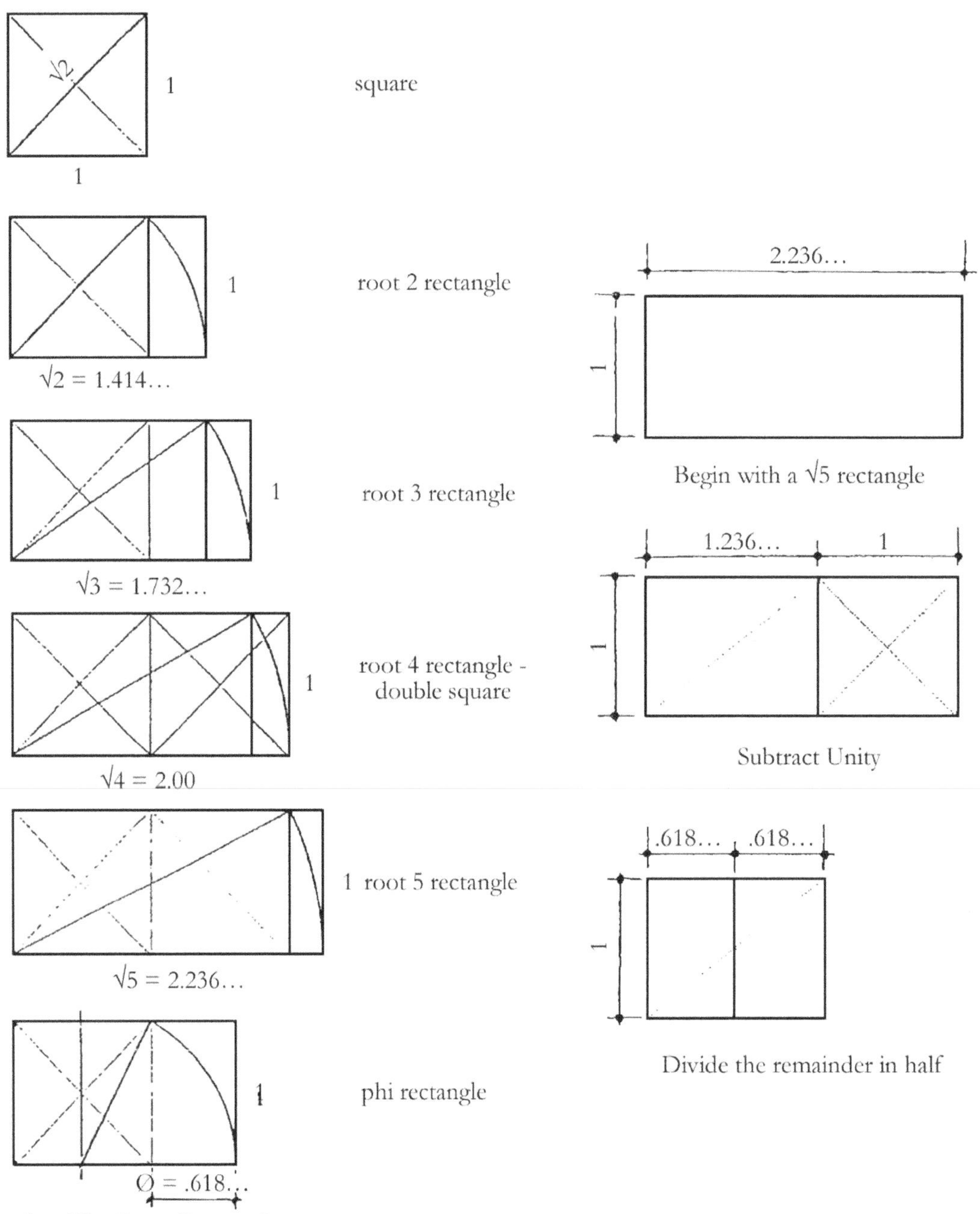

5a - The Root Rectangles - Individual Construction

5b - Geometrical Algebra of Phi

In a superimposed view of the root rectangle family, **figure 5c**, we see the "crossover points" between the rational and trans-rational ratios marked by the square and the double square. An extension of this, **figure 5d**, illustrates the area relationships of the family. The square, initial representative of unity, has an area of 1; a square whose side is equal to the √2 has an area of 2; and so on.

All rectangles have a "reciprocal"; **figure 5e**, that is, if the short side of a rectangle is 1 and the long side is 2, if we then set the long side equal to 1 the short side is now equal to 1/2; or if the sides are 1 and √2 the reciprocal is 1 by 1/√2, or 1:.707… The reciprocal of the √3 rectangle is 1:1/√3=1: .557…; of the √5=1:1/√5=.447… The reciprocal of a √2 rectangle divides its parent rectangle into two equal parts; the reciprocal of a √3 rectangle is 1/3rd of its parent; and so on. The reciprocal of a Ø rectangle is another Ø rectangle plus a square because 1 : .618… = 1.618… : 1. The square is its own reciprocal. The diagonal of a rectangle intersects the diagonal of its reciprocal at a right angle, called by Le Corbusier the "place of the right angle."

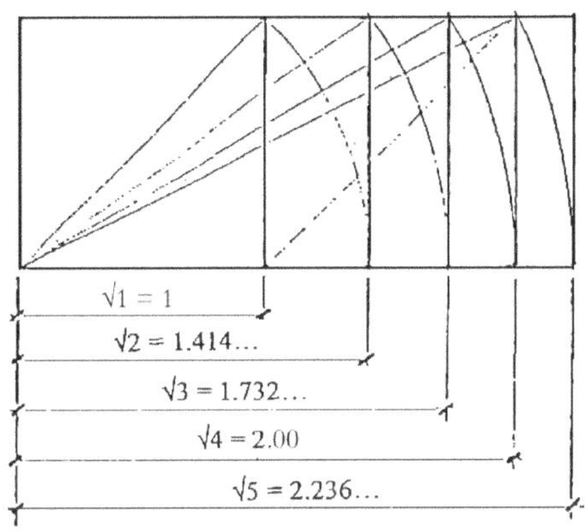

5c - The Root Rectangles Superimposed Construction

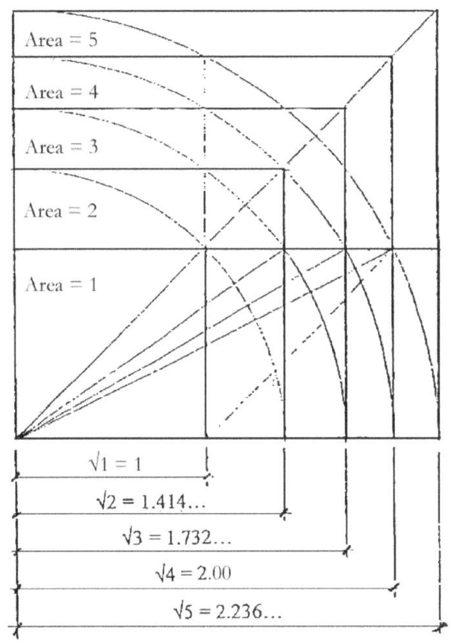

5d - Area Relations of the Root Rectangles

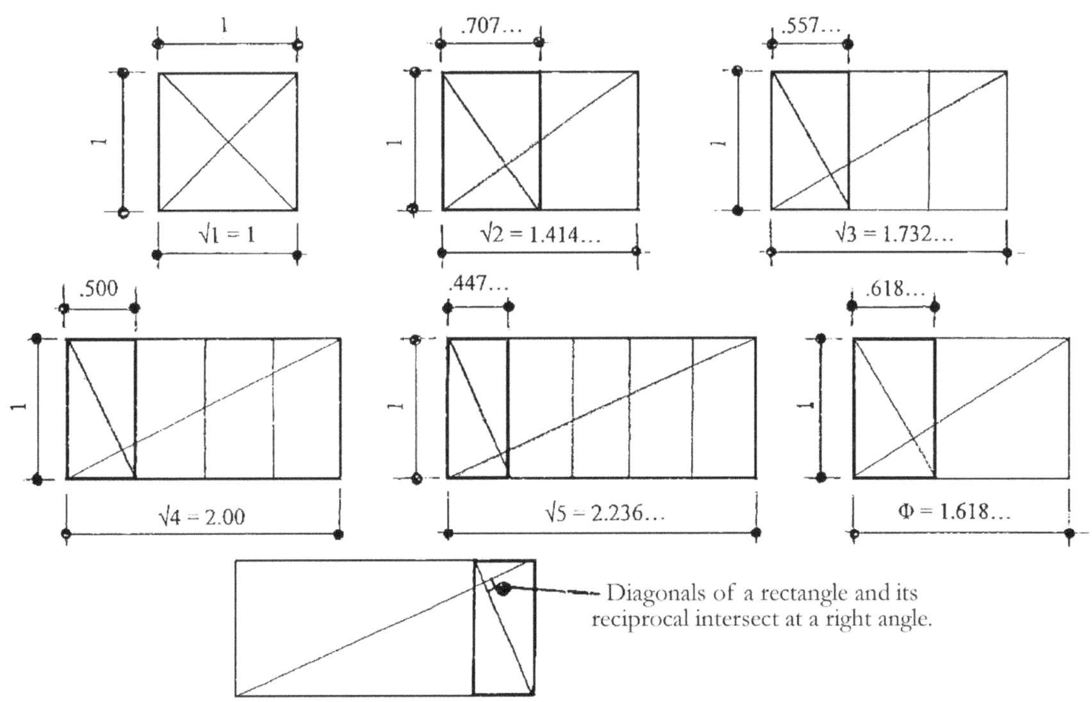

5e - Reciprocals of the Root Rectangles

Figure 6. The Golden Section

In classical times mathematical and geometrical descriptions of the universe were contained within the philosophy of the Pythagoreans. They considered the sensible cosmos to be "analogos" that is, "like the logos." Although the term "logos" has many meanings, for our purposes here it is taken to be "a numerical pattern used by the Divinity to divide Unity in such a way as to allow for its reunification." This reunification or remembrance of Unity, which Plato[5] called "anamnesis" is associated with the experience of Beauty. The captivating quality of Beauty, Plotinus tells us, is the outer aspect of the attractive power of Love.[6] The rush of Erotic emotion and captivation we feel in the experience of Beauty, according to this theory, results from the Soul's identification of Unity within apparently separate objects. This identification is a function of Soul and is a kind of remembrance.

In the *Republic*[7] Plato directs designers, whether of nations or buildings to *"turn their eyes upwards and downwards ... first look at absolute justice, beauty and temperance, and again at the human copy."* He adds that the designer should *"mingle and temper the various elements of life into the image of a man,"* that is, an image like ourselves, a copy of the divine pattern. This pattern is the logos expressed as number.

The most prominent numerical pattern associated with the idea of logos was known in ancient times as the "extreme and mean ratio," called the Divine Proportion in the Renaissance and the "Golden Section" [ratio, proportion or division] in more recent times. Today it is denominated by the Greek letter phi, Ø. In nature Ø governs the proportions of many living forms. In Pythagorean philosophy it is associated with the magical animation of matter. It is also the key to the Aristotelian theory of "mimesis,"[8] which may be broadly stated as "art imitates life" or more specifically visual art imitates organic life. However, mimesis should be in the service of anamnesis.

Symbolically Ø represents return to Unity through division. The portico of **figure 3**, in its twelvefold division, may be said to have used the symbolic numerical powers of 3 and 4, as 3x4=12. But 3+4+5 also =12. Among many discoveries ascribed to Pythagoras is that the numbers 3, 4, and 5, taken as intervals of length, are the smallest whole numbers that will form a right triangle whose sides satisfy the famous equation $a^2+b^2=c^2$. This "3-4-5 archetype" forms the basis of an ontogeny of its own, that of the triadic cycle. Four may be taken here to represent the twofold power, as $2^2=4$. It is associated with the proceeding aspect of the cycle in that the $\sqrt{2}$ that governs the doubling of the area of the square, symbolizing the essential division of unity, is the first step toward manifestation. The threefold power is associated with the maintaining aspect through the relation of the $\sqrt{3}$ to the altitude of the equilateral triangle, symbolic of both mediation and structure. The fivefold power represents the returning aspect through its relation to Ø, which is mathematically derived from the $\sqrt{5}$.

Defined mathematically, Ø=[$\sqrt{5}$-1]/2; beginning with the square root of five, $\sqrt{5}$, which equals 2.236..., subtracting unity we have 1.236...; and dividing by 2 gives .618.... Ø is the only expression that satisfies the equation $a+a^2=1$, that is, root plus square equals unity as .618...+.381...=.999... ≈ 1.0. Phi, as a transcendental, does not actually reach 1 but makes what might be called a "near approach." The Phi ratio, in creating a progression in Ø proportion, can have two values: 1:1.618... if the progression is increasing and 1: .618... if the intervals are decreasing. For the sake of consistency Ø will be taken as .618... unless otherwise noted.

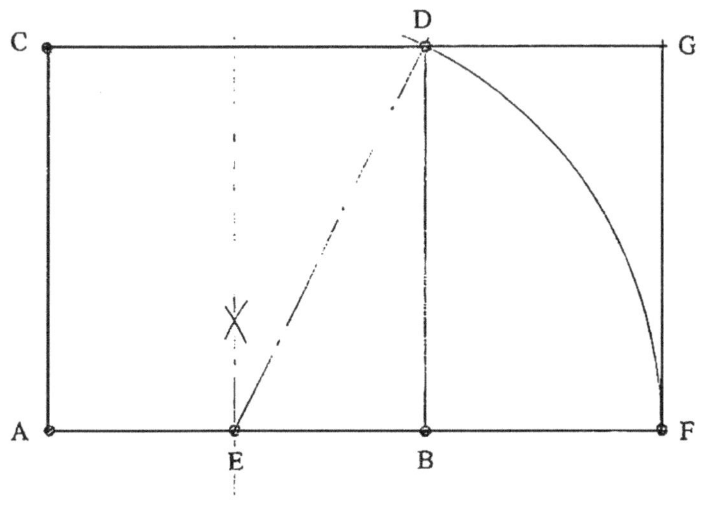

1. Given line AB
2. Construct square ABCD
3. Bisect AB to find E.
4. Draw arc with center at E and radius ED to find point F on the extension AB.
5. Construct a perpendicular on F and extend CD to find point G. AC : AF = 1 : 1.618…

6a - Construct a Rectangle with Sides in the Ratio of the Golden Section

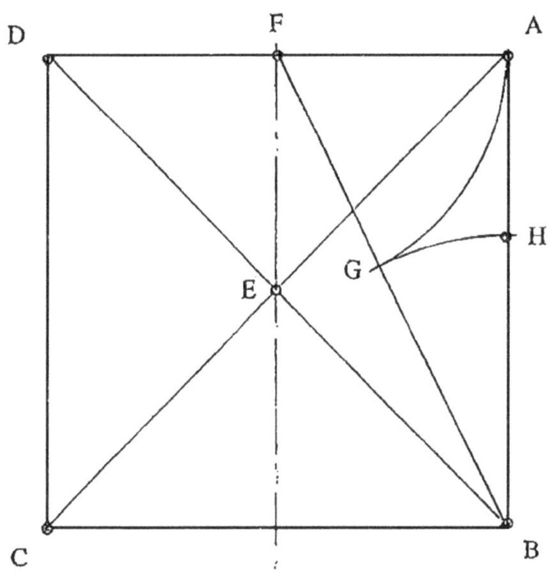

1. Given line AB. Construct square ABCD.
2. Draw diagonals AC and BD to find center E. Draw centerline EF
3. Draw semi-diagonal FB.
4. With center at F draw arc AG. With center at B draw arc GH.
5. AB = 1; BH = $\varnothing$ = .618…; AH = $\varnothing^2$ = .382… .

6b - Divide a Line by the Golden Section

Just as the golden sun and the metal gold are symbolically related to unity, the golden section embodies an approach to oneness through geometric construction. To construct increasing intervals, **figure 6a**, the side of a square is set equal to 1. The semi-diagonal ED of the square $=\sqrt{5}/2$. The semi-diagonal is then applied on the extension of AB to find point F. The extension BF is equal to $\sqrt{5}/2$ minus 1/2. $\sqrt{5}/2=1.118...-.5=.618...=\text{Ø}$. To obtain the next interval construct a square on side AF. AF + FG = 1.618...

To construct decreasing intervals the side of the square is divided at Ø, **figure 6b,** by constructing semi-diagonal FB. With center at F and radius FA, find point G. With center at B and radius BG, draw arc GH. If AB = 1, BH = Ø and HA = Ø^2.

The relationship of the Pentad and Ø is shown in **figure 6c**. Just as the diagonal of the square is related to the $\sqrt{2}$ and the altitude of the equilateral triangle is related to the $\sqrt{3}$; if the side of the pentagon, DK, is equal to 1, its diagonal, GK, is $1+\text{Ø}=1.618....$ **Figure 6d** shows the derivation of two Ø related ratios. Half of a 1:1.618... ratio gives a ratio of 1:.809..., a small whole number approximation of which is 5:4. Doubling a ratio of 1:.618... gives 1:1.236... or approximately 5:6.

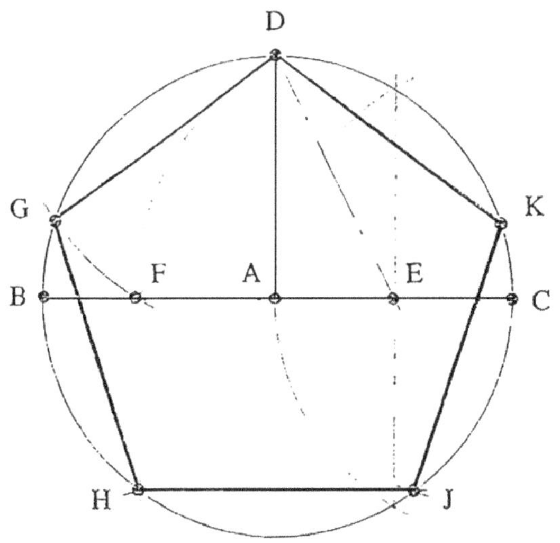

1. Given a circle with center A and diameter BAC.
2. Erect a perpendicular from A to find D.
3. Bisect AC to find E.
4. Draw arc with center at E and radius ED to find point F.
5. With center at D and radius DF draw arc FG.
6. Mark off interval DG on the circumference to find points H, J and K. DGHJK is a pentagon.

6c - Construct a pentagon within a circle.

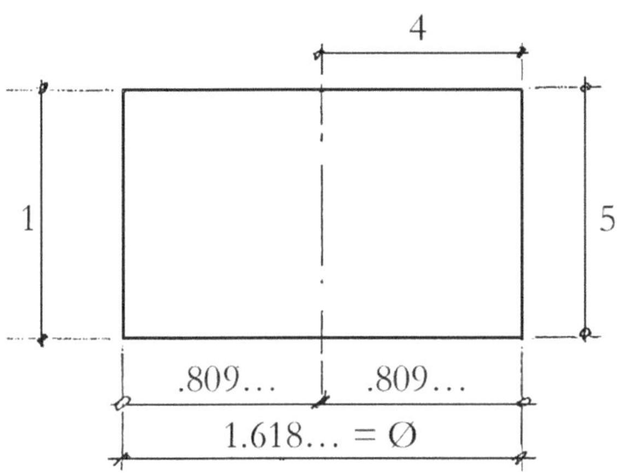

The 5:4 ratio is created by dividing a Golden Rectangle

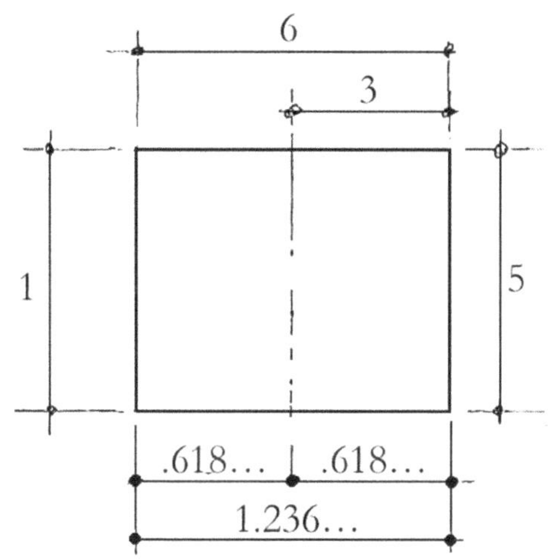

The 5:6 ratio is created by combining two Golden Rectangles

6d - Two ratios derived from the Golden Section

Figure 7. Squaring the Circle

Vitruvius[9] prefaces his method of designing temples by saying "*Without symmetry and proportion there can be no principles in the design of any temple; that is, if there is no precise relation between its members, as in the case of those of a well shaped human body.*" A little later he adds in illustration, "*if a man be placed on his back, with his hands and feet extended, and a pair of compasses centered at his navel, the fingers and toes of his two hands and feet will touch the circumference of a circle…* [and] *…if we measure the distance from the soles of the feet to the top of the head, and then apply that distance to the outstretched arms, the breadth will be found to be the same as the height,*" thus forming a square.

In the geometrical creation story, **figure 1**, the circle is a symbol of transcendent unity and the square is a symbol of unity in the material realm. In the Pythagorean–Platonic worldview our lives as intelligent human beings result from a kind of intimate or loving embrace between spirit, the circle, and matter, the square. This concept could be symbolized by creating a relationship of equality, a proportional relationship, between a square and a circle.

To construct a circle and square that have equal perimeters set the side of the square equal to 1. Its perimeter will equal 4. The diameter of a circle whose perimeter or circumference equals 4 is $4/\pi$ or 1.273..., making the radius .636... as compared to 1, the side of the square. The ratio of approximately .6/1 or 6/10 may be taken as a reference to Ø. Its geometric construction is shown in **figure 5.** Ø is not a number but rather a relationship, a ratio. In practical terms it is a multiplier used to relate other magnitudes to achieve an equality of ratio, that is to say, proportionality.

For example, 1:2::4:8 is a proportion in double ratio; that is, the ratios are equal, in each ratio the second term is double the first. There may also be a proportion in Ø ratio. Although any number can be used to create a proportional group of ratios, Ø occupies a special position which may be stated mathematically as $Ø + Ø^2 = 1$. This may symbolize the interweaving of matter and spirit; where Ø represents spirit, the unmanifest, and $Ø^2$ represents matter, the manifest. Together they equal 1, unity, which may also represent life and intelligence comprising the soul.

This relation to unity also implies that the individual and the cosmos are created on the same pattern, that they are constructed by analogy. Implied in Vitruvius' discussion, then, is the idea that the temple or perfect building is a living mediator between the individual and the cosmos. Proportion, in this context, can be seen as the soul of the building, uniting and vitalizing the idea of the building with its physical body. This Vitruvian comparison of the building and the body, called "anthropos," was visualized in the Renaissance by Leonardo da Vinci in his famous drawing known as the Vitruvian Man.

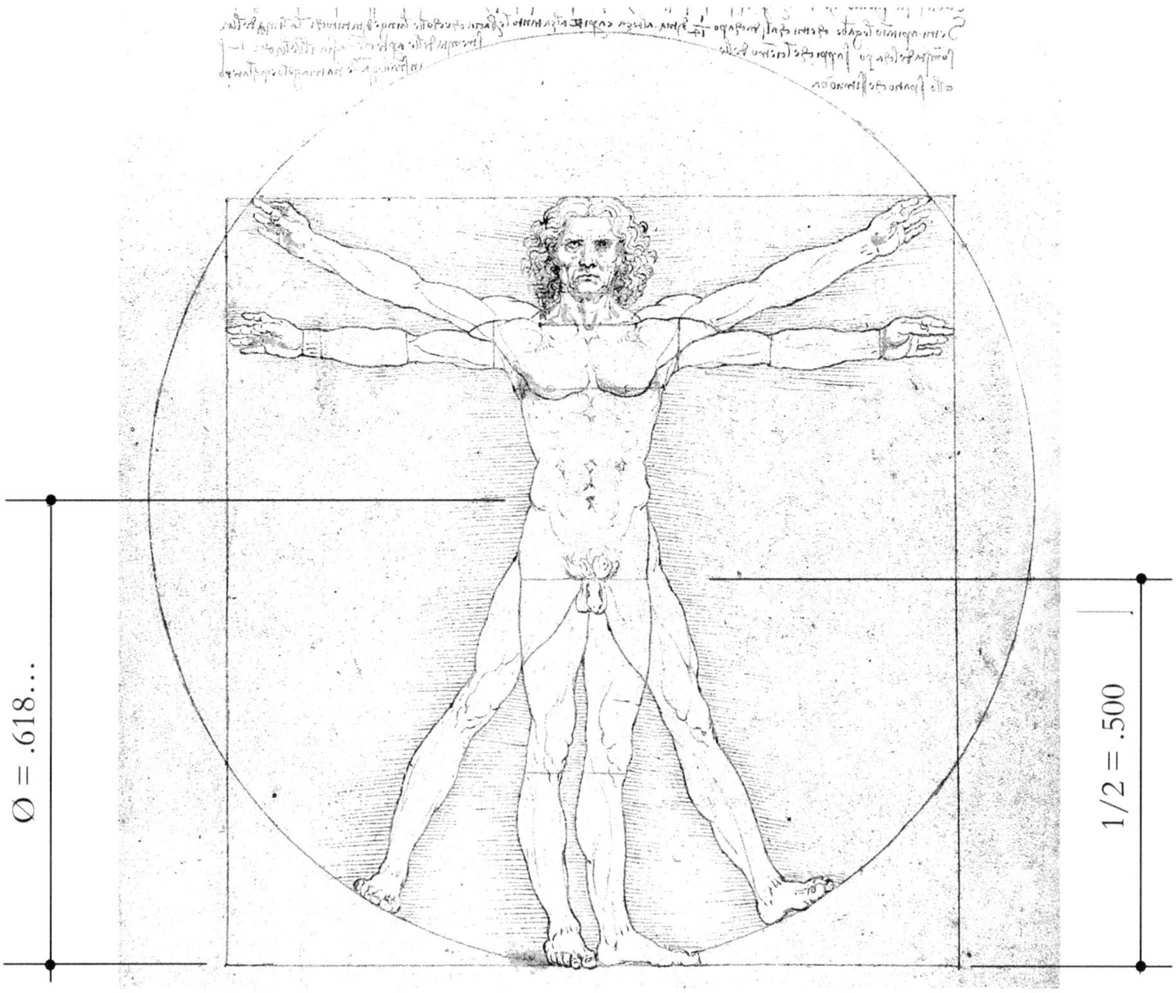

Permeter of square = side x 4 = 1 x 4 = 4
Circumference of circle = π x D = 3.14… x 1.236… = 3.88…
Ø squares the circle within 3%

Figure 8. A Tetrastyle Portico
Using Ø and the Squaring of the Circle

The method of division of the circle into five parts, the internal divisions of the pentagram and the squaring of the circle could provide appropriate geometrical keys for another tetrastyle design. As in **figure 3** the process can be seen to unfold in four stages:

1. Unity – As in the first example we repeat the steps of our ontogeny, arriving at the square.

2. Division – As a fundamental act of division we apply the Ø ratio to the height of the square and use this distance as the radius of a circle, which will mark the apex of the pediment.

3. Structure – To obtain the size and placement of the two inner columns divide the circumference of the circle into five parts as in **figure 6c**. Connecting these points, construct the pentagram. Intersecting points on its diagonals mark the column diameter and its position. The horizontal diagonal will mark the lower edge of the entablature. The top of the original square gives the top of the entablature. The square and circle are in the relationship of the "squaring of the circle" symbolizing a harmonic union of spirit and matter.

4. Materialization – Having placed and sized the major elements we now complete the elevation and move to detailing the elements. The Corinthian order is selected for this design because of its inner relationship to the pentagon and phi. This is hinted at in the myth of Callimachus as told by Vitruvius in which the artist is seen meditating at the grave of the "maiden of Corinth." His design for a capital is inspired by leaves, flowers and volutes that have grown up around a basket of the maiden's grave objects, which was weighted down with a square stone tile. The "maiden" may be taken as a reference to Venus–Aphrodite. Though outwardly the spirit of the maiden has taken the form of vegetation, the inner structure of the capital's composition may be based on the double pentagon, **figure 13,** suggesting that Ø has been the medium of this transformation.

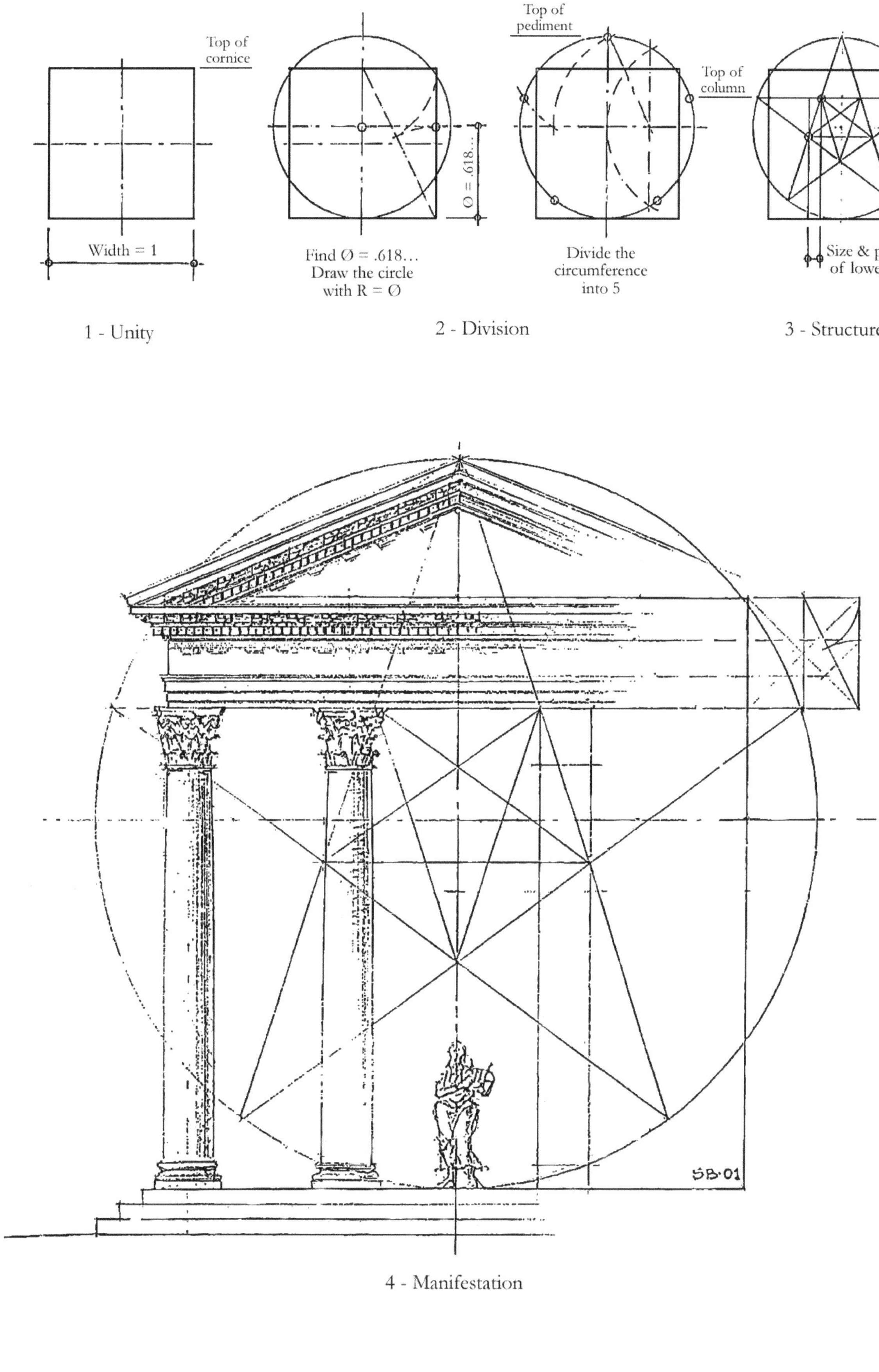

FIGURE 8

A Tetrastyle Portico Using Ø and the Squaring of the Circle

Figure 9. Creating a Ø Scale

Beginning with an interval defined as unity we may continue the procedure of **figure 6b** to construct a series of Ø-related intervals, or a Ø scale.

1. Given square ABCD with E as the midpoint of AB. Draw semi-diagonal EC. With center at E and radius EB draw arc BB'. With center at C and radius CB' draw arc B'F. CF is Ø, .618... of BC, and BF is Ø^2, .382... of BC.

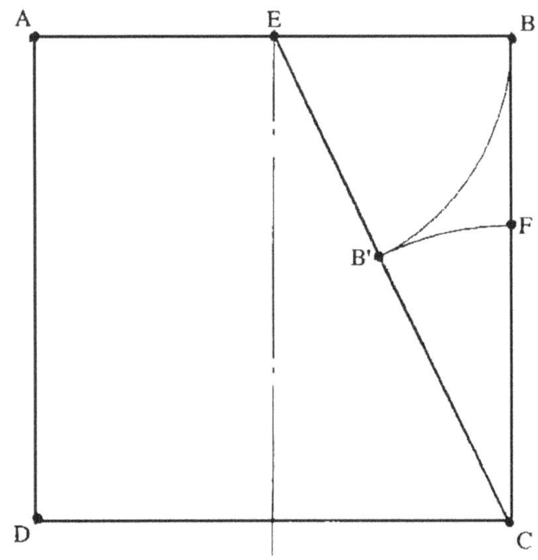

2. Draw line FG parallel to AB. Repeating the procedure in step 1, with center at G and radius GF draw arc FF'. With center at C and radius CF' draw arc F'H. HC = Ø^2 and FH = Ø^3.

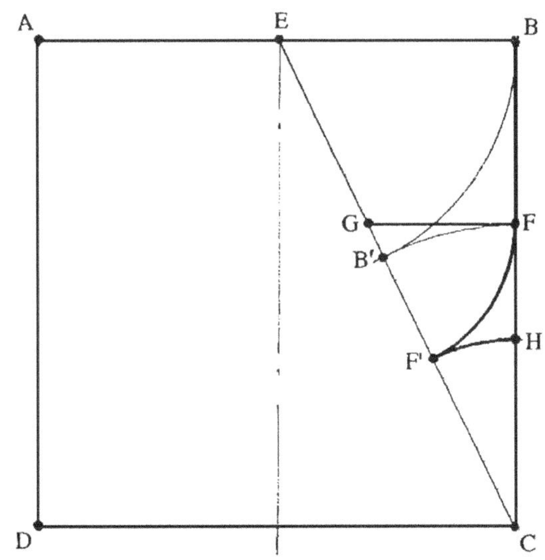

3. Repeat the procedure to obtain the next interval. Draw line HJ parallel to AB. With center at J and radius HJ draw arc HH'. With center at C and radius CH' draw arc H'K. CK = Ø^3, KH = Ø^4.

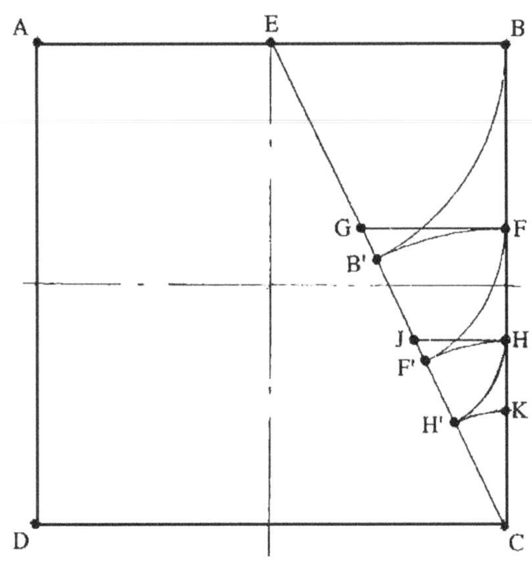

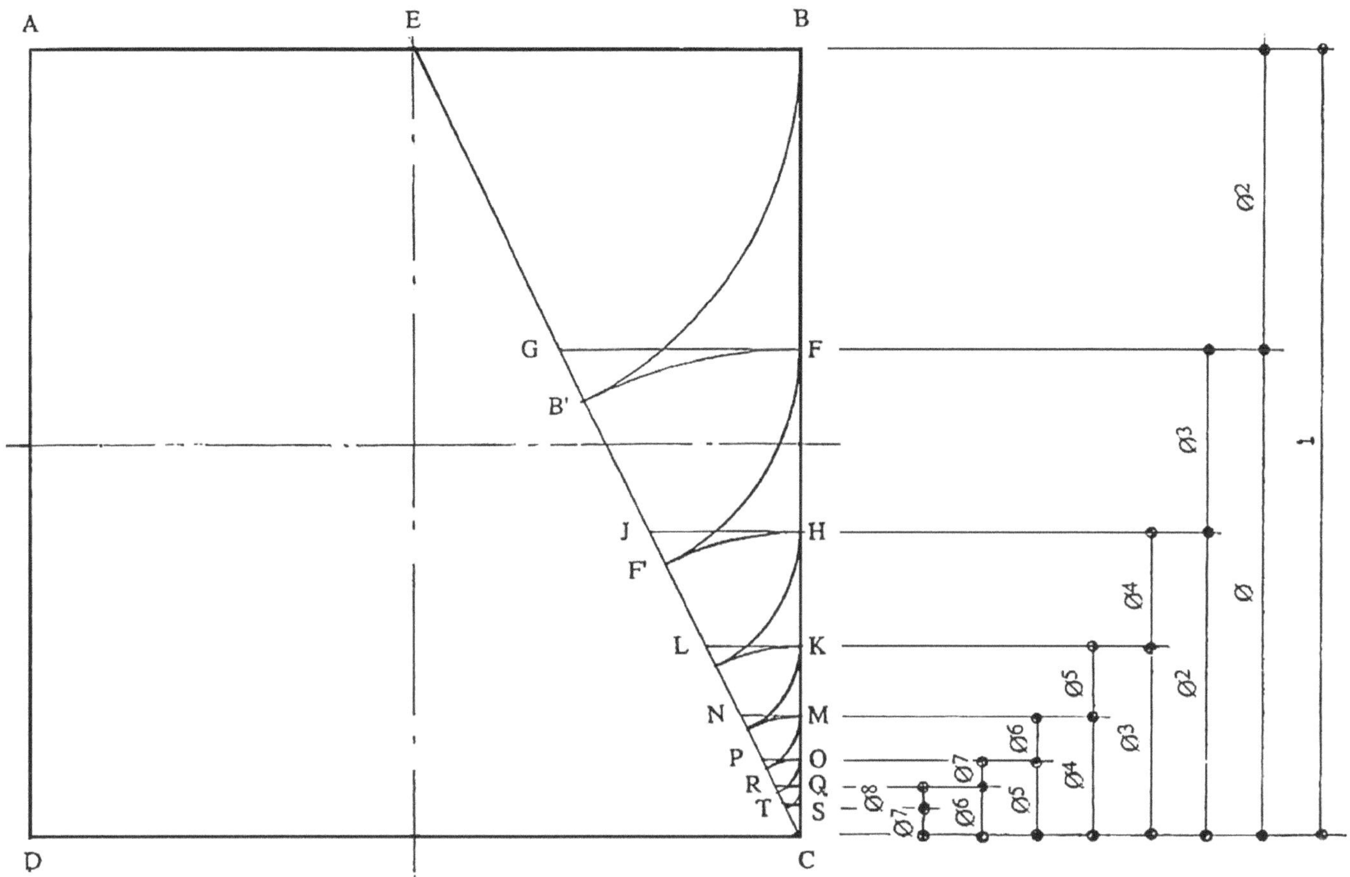

4. The scale may be carried on indefinitely, to the limit of practicality. Here we have gone to $Ø^8$.

Decimal Equivalents of the Ø Scale

Ø = .618…	$Ø^5$ = .090…
$Ø^2$ = .382…	$Ø^6$ = .056…
$Ø^3$ = .236…	$Ø^7$ = .034…
$Ø^4$ = .146…	$Ø^8$ = .021…

Figure 10. A Tetrastyle Portico
Using Ø and the √2

Set up a square as in the previous examples but here subdivide it with a Ø scale, as in **figure 9**. Setting the side of the square as 1, Ø=.618... and Ø^2 =.382.... Ø^2 divided in half, =.191..., is the depth of the entablature. Ø gives the position of the inner columns. The diameter of the columns is given by Ø^5=.090..., but may also be given by the difference between Ø and the √2, .707...-.618...=.089.... As the height of the columns in this design is .809..., Ø^5 gives a ratio of 1:9 and .089... gives 1:9.1. Vitruvius gives a ratio of 1:9.5 and Vignola gives 1:9 for the Ionic order. D of .090... is 1/11th of the width of the portico; D of .089 = 1/11.24; Vitruvius divides the width into 11.5 parts; the design in **figure 3** used division into 12 parts. The height of the pediment is set by an interval of Ø^2/2, giving an overall height of 1.191... or approximately a width to height ratio of 5:6, recalling the squaring of the circle, **figure 7.**

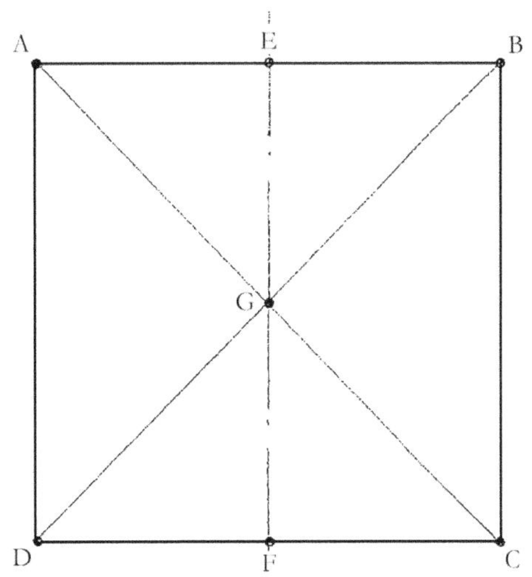

1. The portico is constructed within square ABCD, its centerline is EF with center at G.

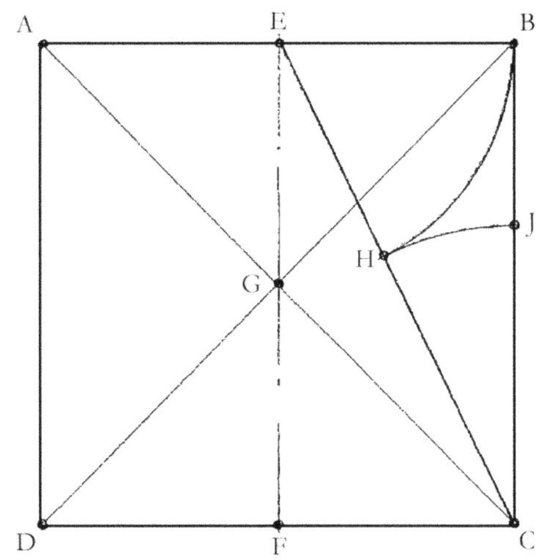

2. Draw the semi-diagonal EC. With center at E and radius EB draw arc BH. With center at C and radius CH draw arc HJ. If BC=1 then CJ=Ø=.618... and BJ=Ø^2=.382....

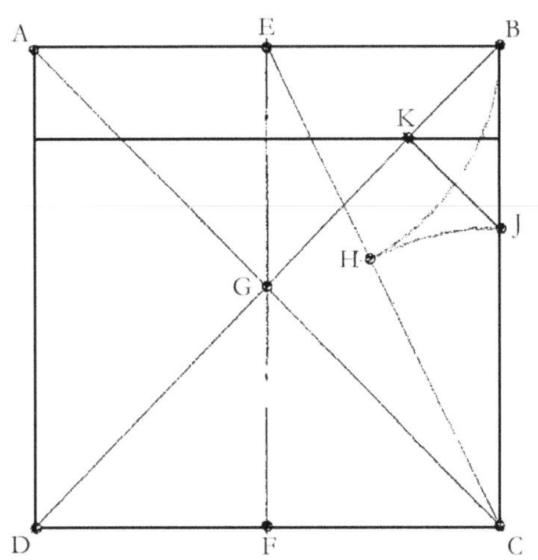

3. Divide BJ in half to find point K. BK=Ø^2/2 = .191... CK=.618...+.191...=.809... marking the top of the columns.

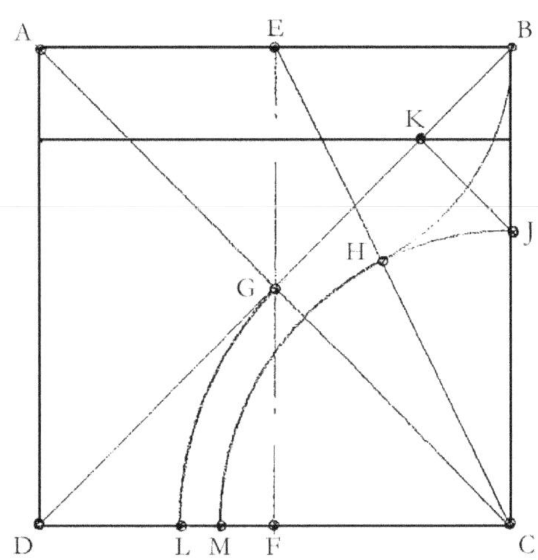

4. With center at C and radius CG draw arc GL. With center at C and radius CH draw arc HM. LM gives location and size of the column.

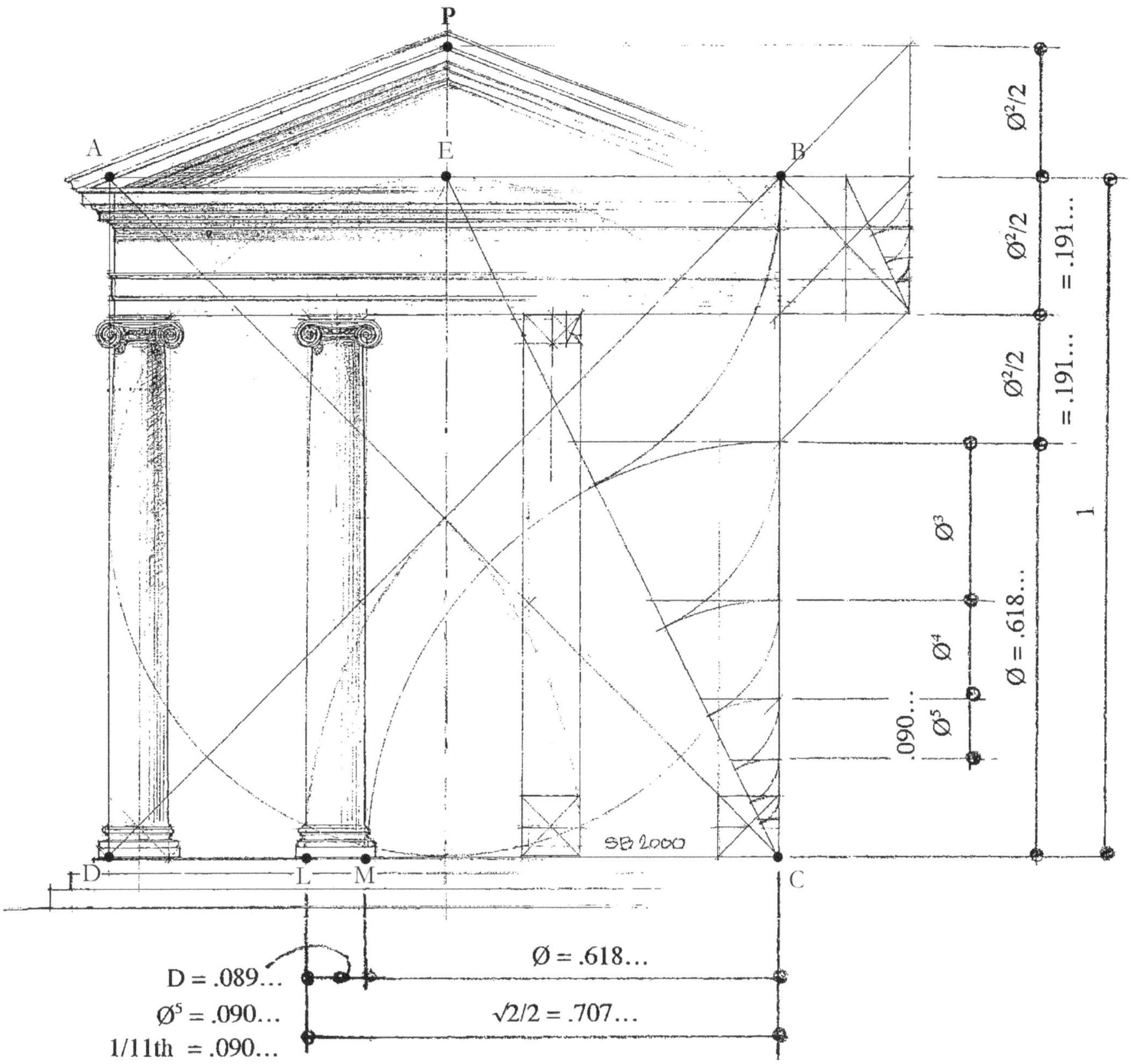

5. Completed portico.

Figure 11. A Tetrastyle Portico Using Harmonic Ratios

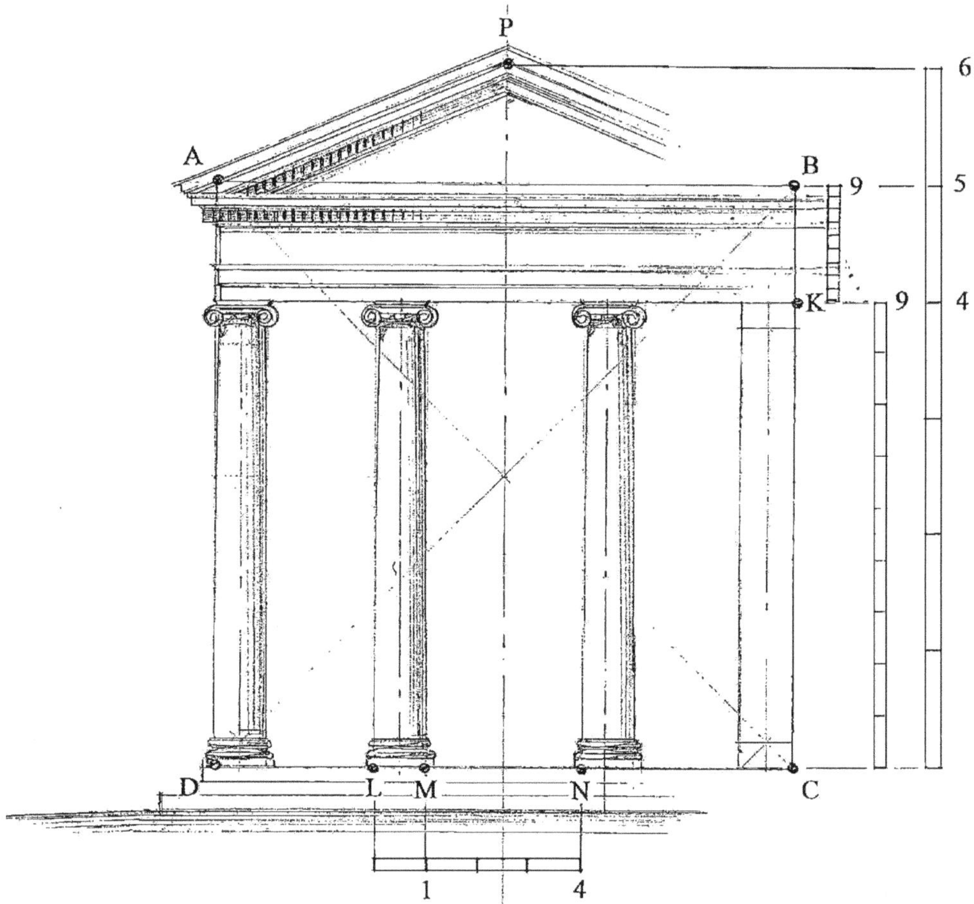

Constructing a four column portico using the harmonic ratio method begins with square ABCD. Divide its height BC into 5 parts. The topmost interval BK will be the entablature. This makes the shape under the entablature a 5:4 rectangle. The apex of the pediment will be one part higher, point P, fitting the elevation as a whole into a 6:5 rectangle. Both these ratios are phi related; 5:4 is half of a phi rectangle and 6:5 results from addition of two phi rectangles, **figure 6d.**

To size the columns divide the 4 lower parts, interval CK, into 9 units. The column diameter, LM, will be 1 unit; the central intercolumniation, MN, will be 3 units. Although the column height complies with Vignola's canon, the 4:9 relation may not seem harmonious but it is also phi related. The 4:9 ratio may be expressed as 1:2.25, a very close approximation to 1:√5, 1:2.236.... If the 9-unit scale were extended up to the top of the square it would measure 11.25 units, very close to the Vitruvian arithmetic division of the tetrastyle portico into 11.5 units.[10]

If the central intercolumniation is 3 units, and allowing 4 units for the diameters of the columns, that leaves 4.25 units for the two side intercolumniations, or 2.125 units each. Thus interval MC would equal 3+1+2.125+1=7.125 D; 7.125/11.25=.633..., very close to phi =.618..., which marked the location of point M in **figure 10**. The entablature in the canon of Vignola is divided into the same number of parts as the column, in this case 9. The architrave is 2.5 parts, the freeze is 3, and the cornice is 3.5. Ø divides 9 units at 5.5 and 3.5. While more such close approximations could be cited, the point is that the geometric, arithmetic and harmonic ratio methods may be used to produce canonical structures and elements.

Figure 12. A Tetrastyle Portico
Using the √3

Previous tetrastyle examples have utilized the musical ratios of the tetrachord, the √2, and Ø-related ratios to construct porticos. In this example the portico is guided in part by the equilateral triangle. It creates a higher column and lighter entablature, giving an elegant elongated character.

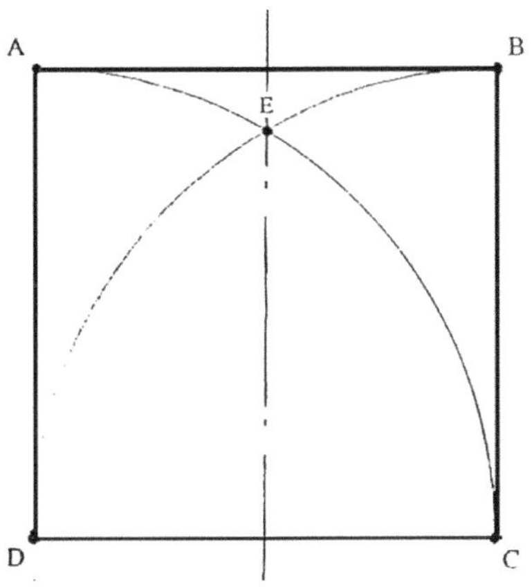

1. Begin with square ABCD. DC will be the width of the portico. With center at C and radius CD, draw arc DB; with center at D and the same radius draw arc CA Their point of intersection is E, the apex of an equilateral triangle.

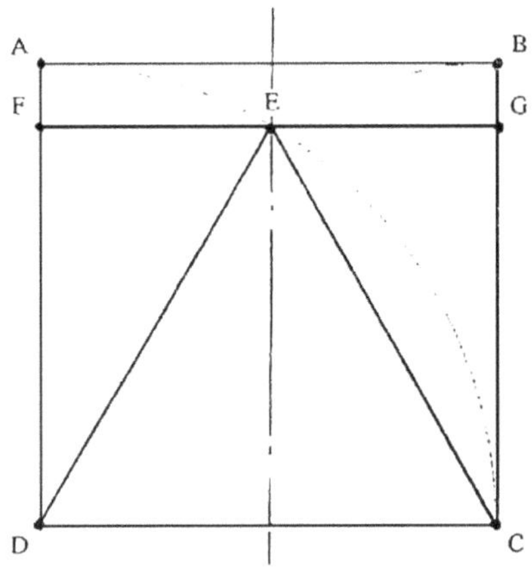

2. Draw line FG through E, parallel to AB. Line FEG sets the height of the columns.

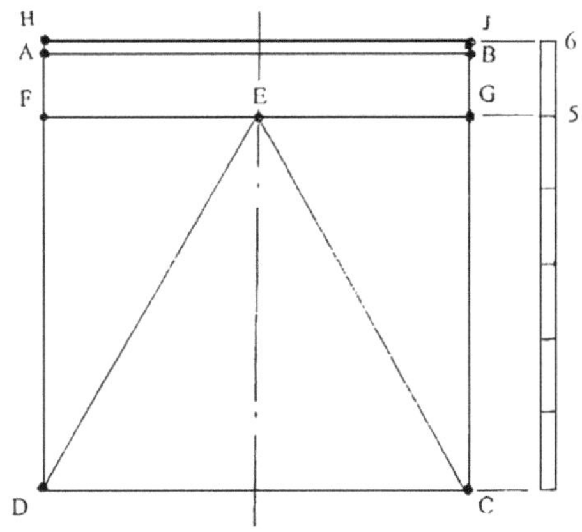

3. Divide the column height into 5 parts. Add an additional part to create interval GJ, giving the depth of the entablature. The top of the entablature is HJ, which is slightly higher than the top of the square AB.

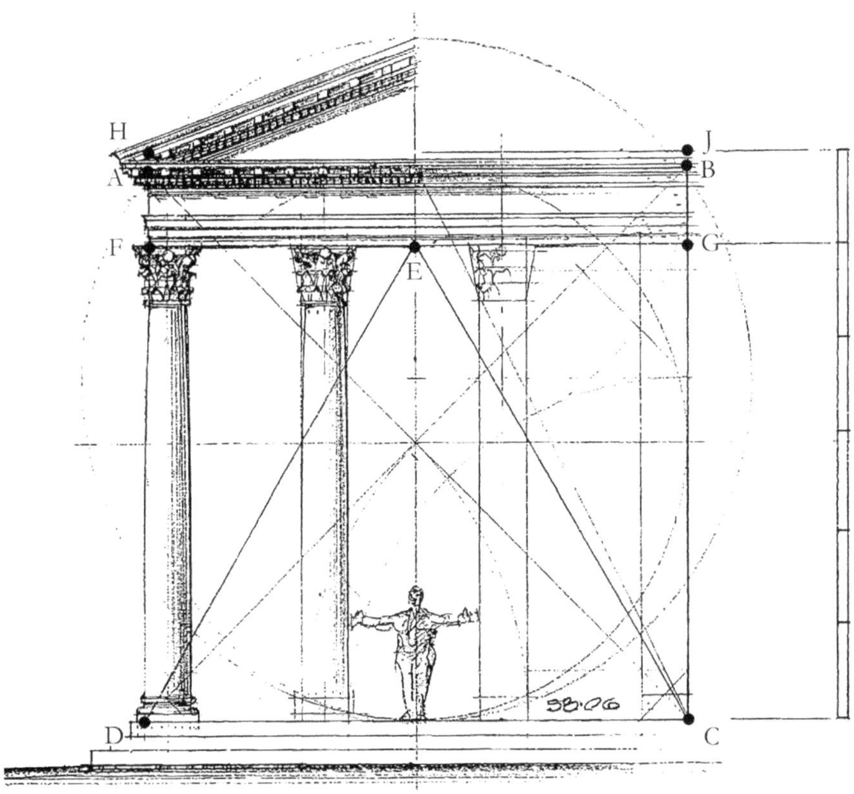

4. The column diameter and placement may be done according to the method of **figure 10.** If D is 1/11th of the width or .089… and the column height =√3/2, the altitude of an equilateral triangle or .866…, then H=9.75 D; or the height may be simply divided into 10 for a D of .086…. These ratios are within the canonical range for the Corinthian order as given by Vitruvius [D = 9.5 H] and Vignola [D = 10 H]. Vignola provides for an entablature to column ratio of 1:5 as well as 1:4. The pediment may be added according to any of several methods, see **figure 22 – Pediments.**

Figure 13. A Hexastyle Portico Using Ø and the Ø Scale

The hexastyle portico may be constructed using Ø as a key, following the four steps in our ontological myth, **figure 1**, Unity, Division, Structure and Manifestation.

Figure 13.1: Draw a circle whose diameter is the width of the portico and set it equal to 1. Enclose the circle, representing spirit or inner Unity, in a square, ABCD, representing matter, the manifest or outward Unity. The half-point of the square, line HF, will be the height of the columns. HFCD is a 2:1 or octaval rectangle.

Figure 13.2: Apply a key pattern of division, internally dividing the square by Ø using the method of **figure 6b.** Draw semi-diagonal EC. Apply radius EB on EC to find point B'; with center at C and radius CB' draw arc to find point J. Apply arc CJ to the base CD to find point K. CJ=Ø=.618... as CF=.500, JF=.118... or $Ø^3/2$.

Figure 13.3a: Place the elements of structure. JF, .118..., will be the depth of the entablature. Continue to develop the phi scale by the method of **figure 9** to find point L. CL= $Ø^2$=.382.... Applying this interval along CD gives point M. Points K and M are the centers of the inner pair of columns. The interval between them KM=JL=$Ø^3$=.236....

Figure 13.3b: Continue the phi scale to find points N, P, Q and R. The interval CR=$Ø^6$=.056.... This will be the lower diameter of the columns. Interval PQ is also equal to $Ø^6$, as $Ø^5$[CQ]+$Ø^6$[QP]=$Ø^4$[CP]; thus, construction of the scale need only be pursued to point Q.

The last element of structure is the pediment. Its apex is found by bisecting interval BJ to find point S. BJ=$Ø^2$=.382...; divided by 2=.191.... The overall height of the portico will be SG=.618...+.191....=.809....

Figure 13.4: To complete the portico, locate the outer columns at the perimeter of the square and the middle columns equally between the inner and outer. The capital and base heights are taken to be 1/2 of lower D. The entablature is subdivided by the same pattern of Ø division as the whole portico, see **figure 21**.

This construction falls within the canonical range established by Vitruvius and Vignola. Both of these systems will be taken up in later sections, but for the moment note that Vitruvius divides the width of the six-column portico into 18 units; 1/18th=.0555... and that our lower D=$Ø^6$=.0557.... This interval compared to the height of the columns, .500, gives a D/H ratio of 1/8.98... where Vignola gives 1/9 and Vitruvius gives 1/9.5. The Vitruvian entablature =1.93 D. Our entablature is .118÷.056...=2.11... D. Vignola gives 2.25 D when the entablature is 1/4 of the column height, but he also says the ratio may be 1/5, which gives a ratio of 1.8 D. The central intercolumniation given by Vitruvius is 3D. Ours is .236...-.056...=.180, or 3.21D. Thus, the major elements of our construction fall within the canonical range established by Vitruvius and Vignola.

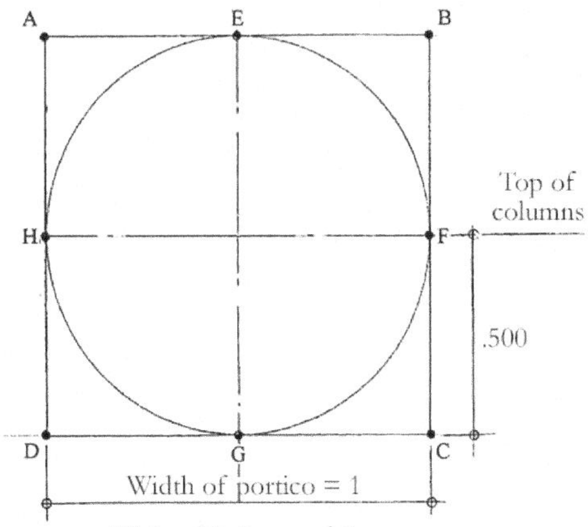

13.1 - Unity and Its
Representatives

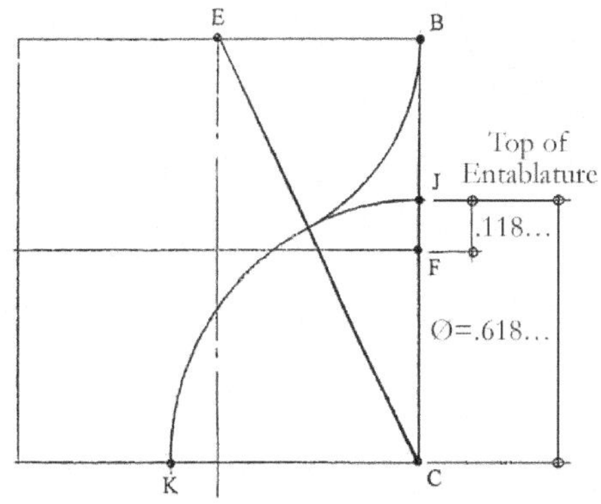

13.2 - Division, the Major Cuts
The Double Square and Ø

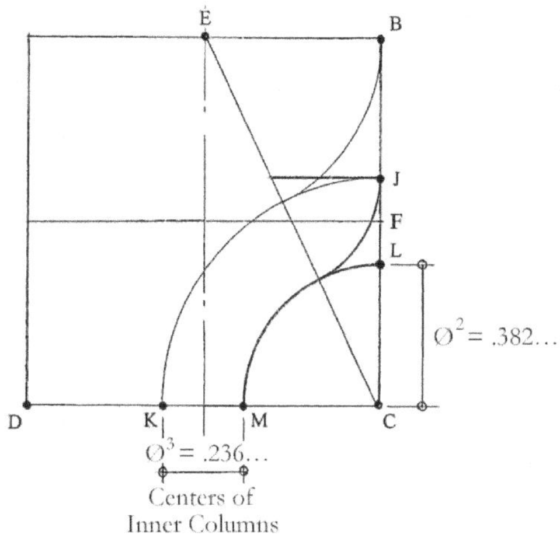

13.3a - Structure, Placement
of the Inner Columns

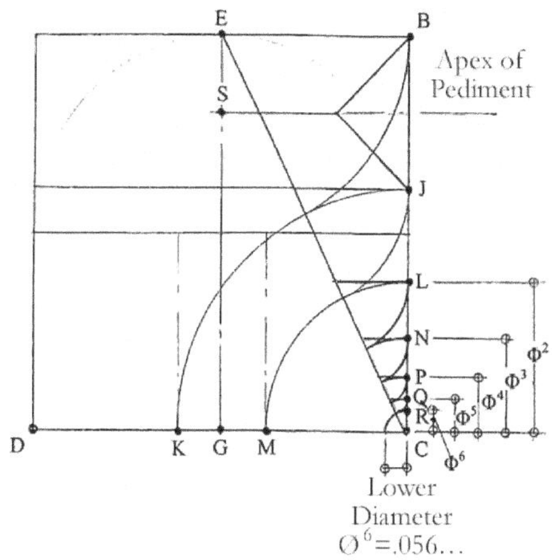

13.3b - Structure
Column Diameter

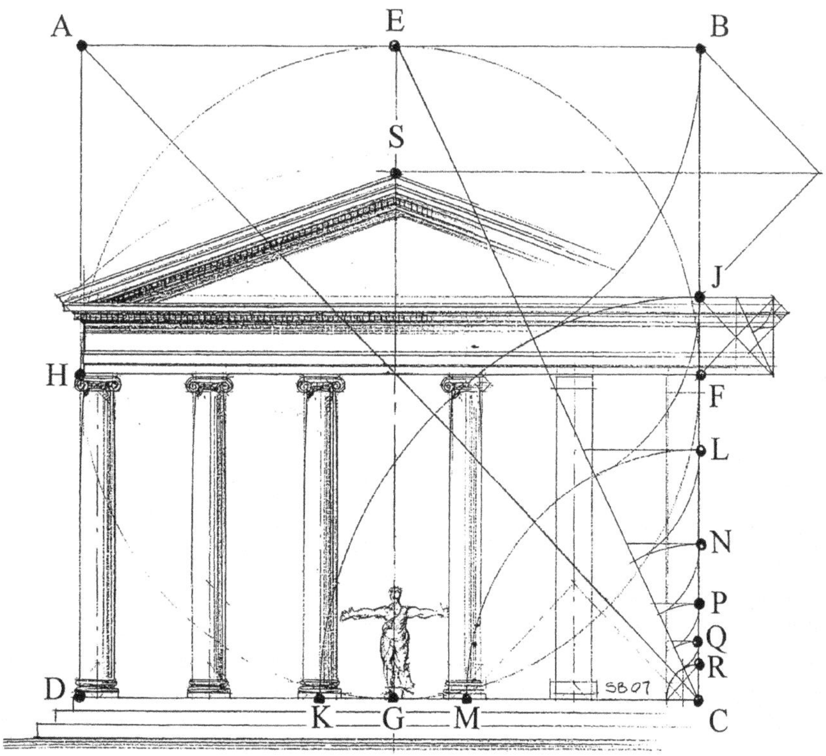

13.4 - Manifestation
Ornamenting the Elements

FIGURE 14 - A HEXASTYLE PORTICO
Using Harmonic Ratios

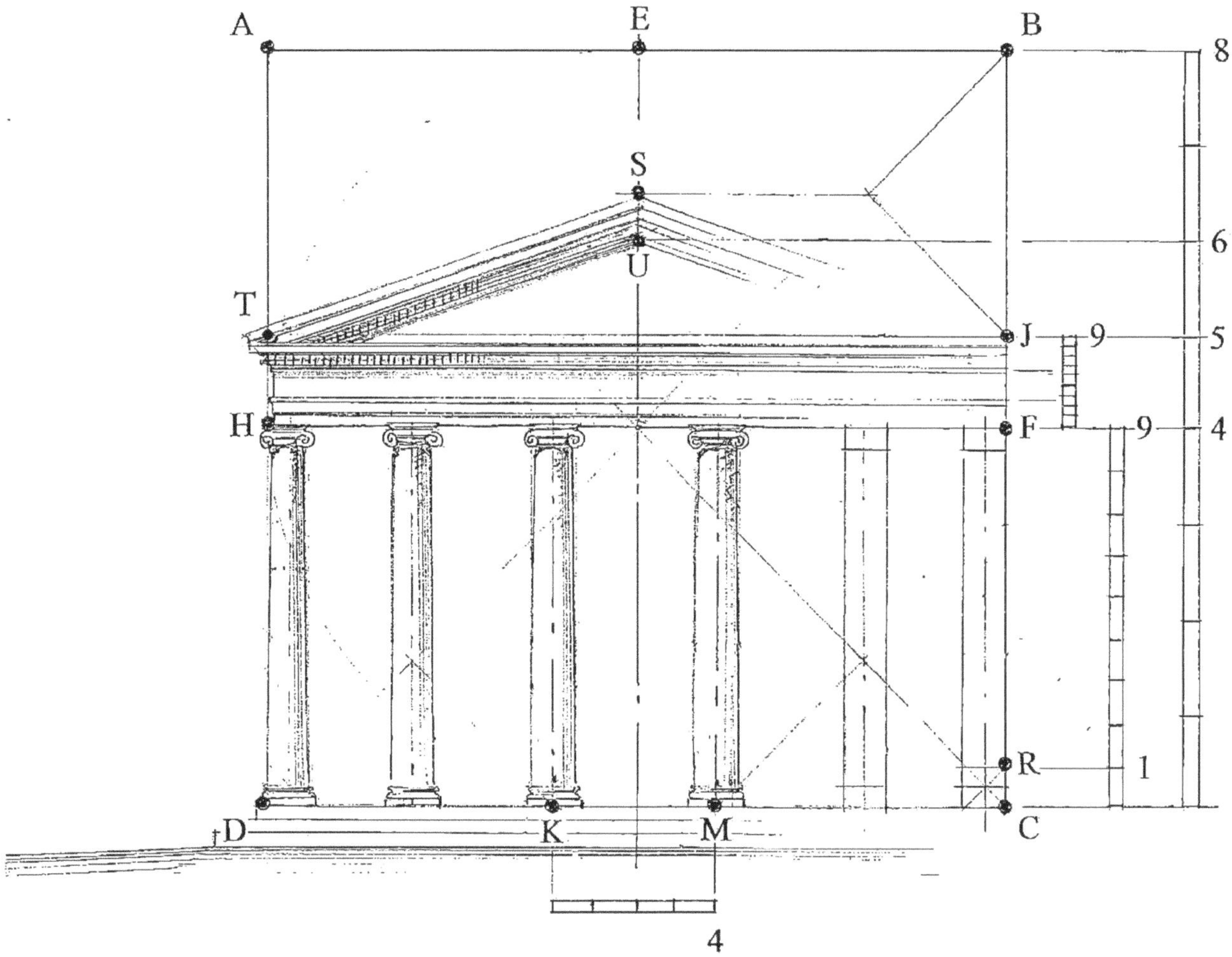

The six-column portico can be constructed with harmonic ratios as was done with the four-columned portico, **figure 11**. Begin with the square ABCD and the half-square HFCD. Point F will mark the height of the columns. Divide CF into 4 parts; adding a fifth part will give the depth of the entablature. Adding a sixth part will give the apex of the tympanum, U; or dividing the upper 3 units, interval BJ, in half will give the apex of the pediment, point S. As in **figure 11,** the column height, CF, is divided into 9 parts; each will be 1 diameter; the central intercolumniation will be 3 diameters. Since CF is half the side of square ABCD the width of the portico, CD may be divided into 18 column diameters, in exact agreement with Vitruvius' division.

The entablature is divided into 9, or if one wishes, into 18 parts, as in **figure 11**. In terms of ratios, the colonnade is 8:4 or 2:1, the double square and the ratio of the octave; the rectangle CDTJ is 5:8 or Ø. The top of the tympanum, point U is at the 6/8 or 3/4 point, the musical fourth and one of Palladio's recommended room ratios. Each side intercolumniation is 2.25 column diameters. Interval CK is 11/18 or Ø, as it was in **figure 13.**

Figure 15. An Octastyle Portico
Using a Ø Scale

Figure 15.1-2. To construct the octastyle portico, follow a similar procedure as in **figures 10 and 13**. Set up square ABCD as the representative of unity. AB, set equal to 1, will equal the width of the portico. The key pattern of division is once again the Ø scale, but we will have to be more flexible in its application. Ø intervals will be divided in half and taken out of sequence, translating them to where they are required.

Figure 15.3-4. In structuring the elements, the Ø interval, FC = .618..., will be the overall height of the portico to the top of the pediment. The $Ø^2$ interval, GC = .382..., will be the height of the columns. The depth of the entablature will be $Ø^5$, interval HJ = .090.... Apply this interval by placing it atop point G. The central intercolumniation will be the interval NP = GL = $Ø^3/2$ = .118....

The diameter of the columns will be PQ = HM, $Ø^5 \div 2$ = .045.... With a column height of $Ø^2$ = .382... the diameter-to-height ratio [D/H] = 8.5. Vignola gives 9.0 which would give a D of .042...; Vitruvius gives 9.5 or a D of .040. The pure geometry differs from the Vitruvian arithmetic canon by an interval of .005.... This is 1.3% of the column height, .382...; or 0.5% of the overall width of the portico.

The center intercolumniation, .118..., is 2.6 D. Vitruvius gives 3 D or .120. The entablature is .090 in depth. In the Vignolian canon it would be 1/4 of the column height, .382..., or .095...; in the Vitruvian canon it would be 1.95 D or .078 differing by .017, or 4.5% of the column height. This comes within 5% of Vitruvius' construction and considerably closer to Vignola's.

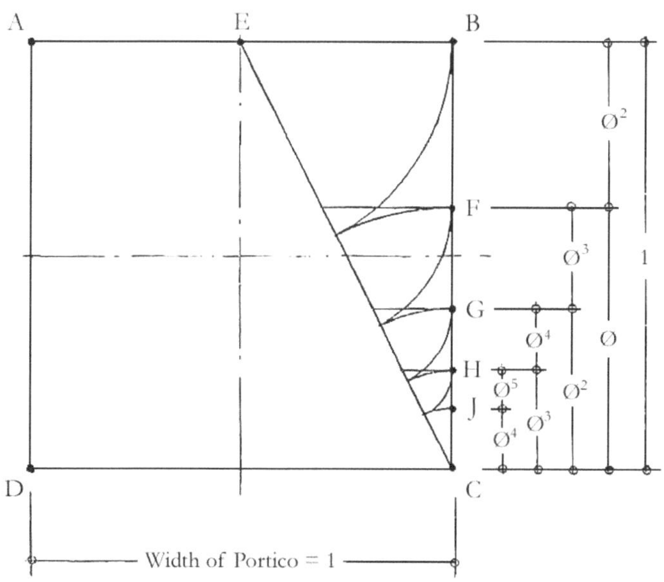

15.1-2 - Unity & Division

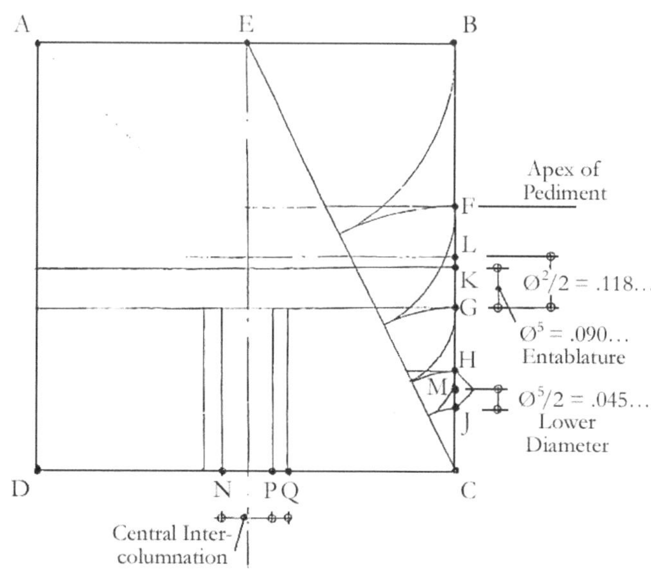

15.3 - Placement of Elements

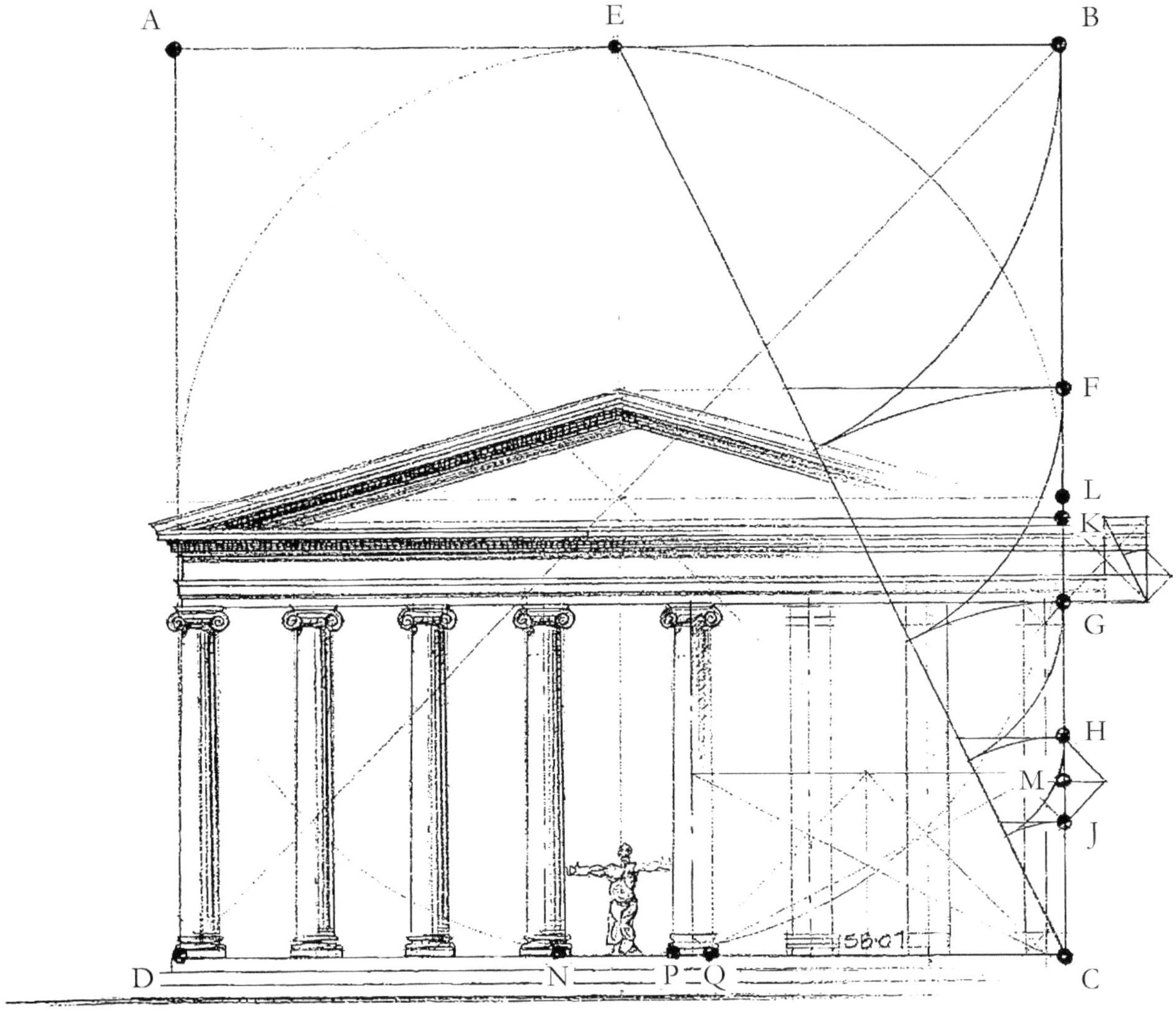

15.4 - Manifestation

FIGURE 16. AN OCTASTYLE PORTICO
Using Harmonic Ratios

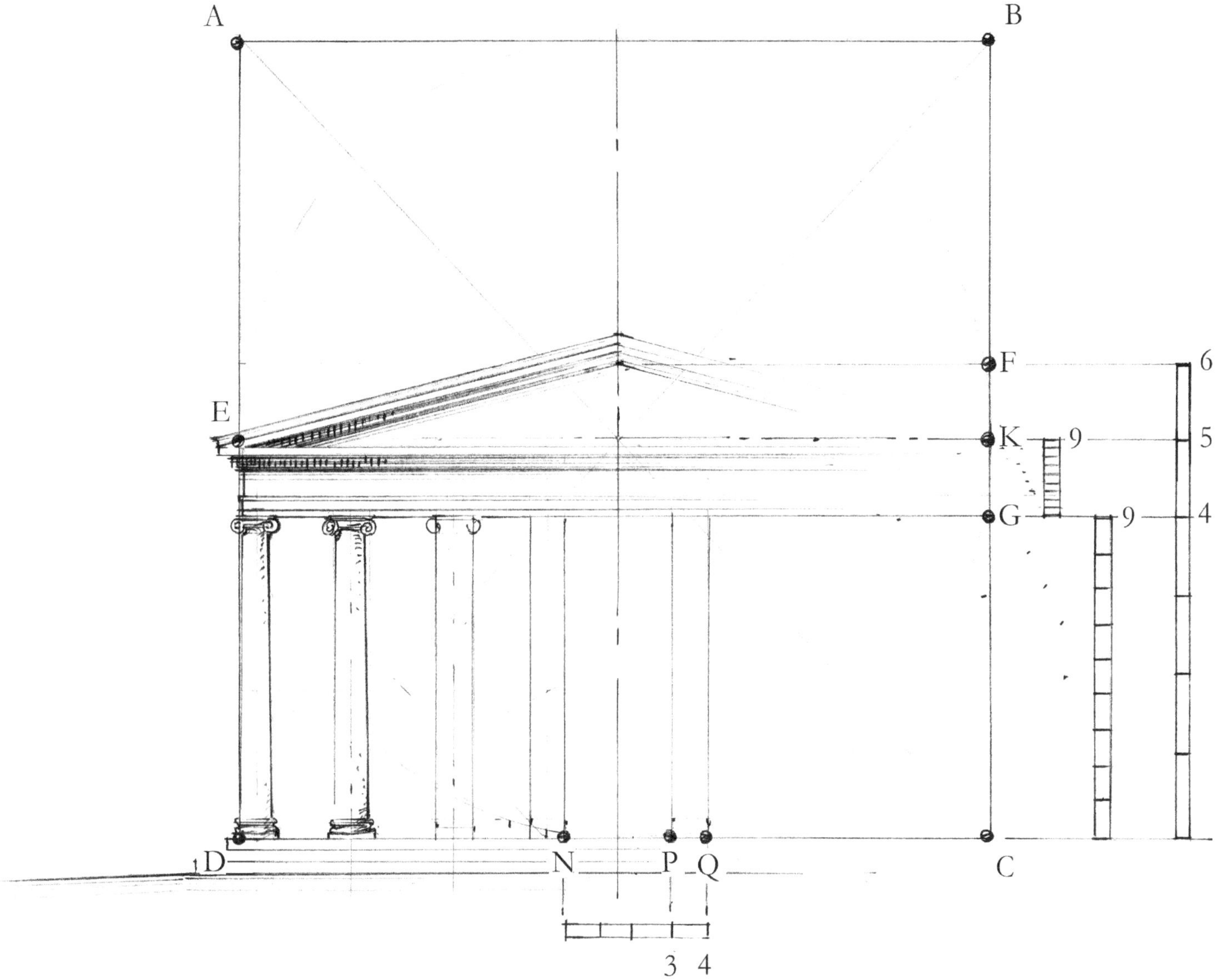

To construct an octastyle portico using small whole number ratios, begin with square ABCD. Divide it in half to create a 2:1 rectangle, EKCD. Divide the height CK into 5 parts; the columns will be 4 parts high, CG, and the topmost part will give the location and depth of the entablature, GK; a 6th part will place the apex of the tympanum, point F. Divide the 4 parts of the column height into 9 units, each of which will be 1 column diameter. The central intercolumniation will be 3 diameters, NP. Column D will be 1 part, PQ, and equal .044… of the overall width of the portico; dividing it into 22¾ D. Vitruvius gives 24½D. If we had divided the column height interval into 9½ parts, D would be .042…, coming even closer to the Vitruvian .040.

Figure 17a-b. The Classical Order and the Canon of 19

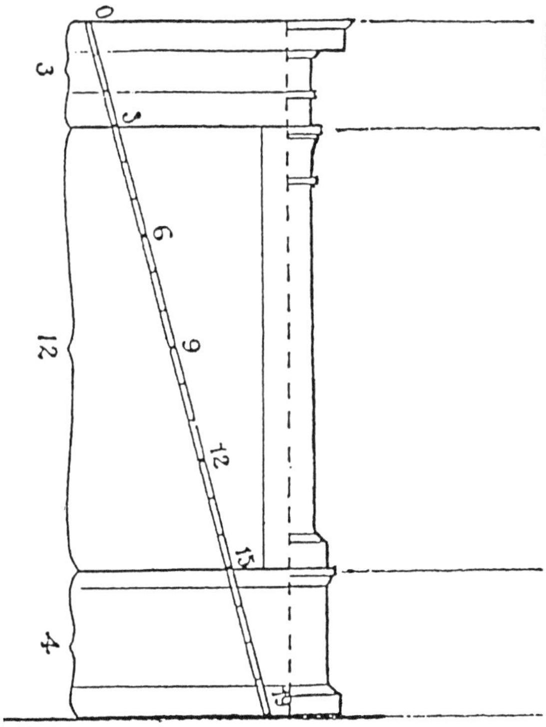

Classical order of 19 units
after Ware's *American Vignola*

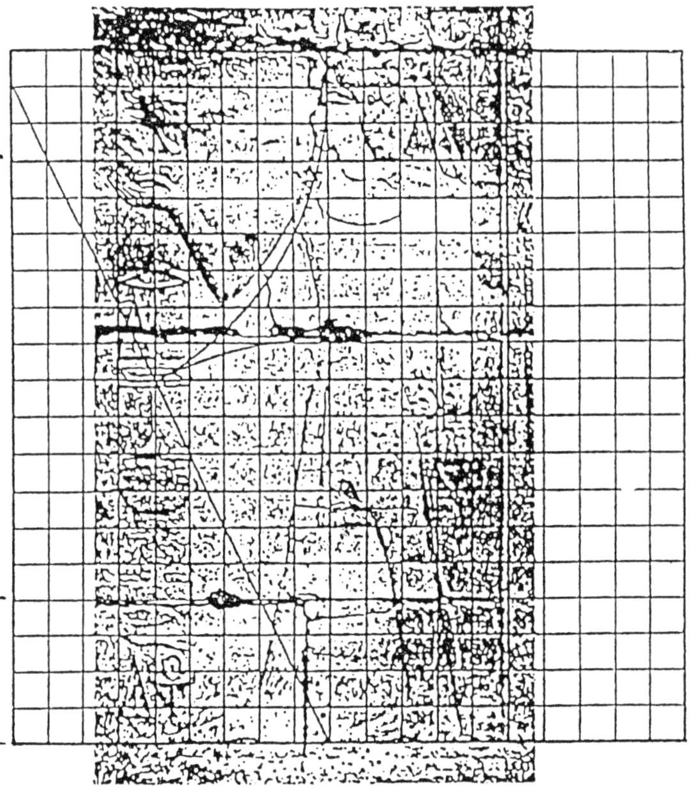

System of 19 units applied to a figure
in room 20 of the Temple of Luxor
after Schwaller's *Temple in Man*

17a - Examples of the Classical Order of 19 Units

The number 19 plays a notable role in the four mathematical subjects of Plato. In geometry the ratio of 18:19 is the relation of the altitude of the pentagon to its diagonal. In music 19/18ths is one measure of the interval of the semitone (Lawlor, 1982, p. 51, fig.5.4b). Arithmetically 4+3=7 and 4x3=12 and 7:12 is a whole number approximation of Ø. In astronomy the number 7 is associated with the movements of the moon and 12 with the sun. Although these two bodies meet once a month, at the new moon, they only meet at the same point in the zodiac once in every 18.6 years, that is in every 19th year; the arithmetic of this cycle being essential for the prediction of eclipses.

The ancient Egyptians had an aesthetic canon of 19 in which the height of the human body was divided into 19 units.[11] The number 19 may have been associated in the Egyptian Mysteries with the magical animation of matter. In **figure 17a**, a figure is divided into 19 parts, 4 parts give the bottom of the knees, 12 parts give the height of the upper legs and torso, the navel is at the Ø point at the 11th unit above the ground, and the remaining 3 parts give the head. This is also the formula for an archetypal classical architectural order, as given by Ware in the *American Vignola,*[12] in which the pedestal is 4 units, the column is 12 units and the entablature is 3 units. The eighteenth unit marks the point on the forehead known in the east as the brow "chakra." The Egyptian figure in the illustration wears a headband with a cobra projecting from his forehead at this point. The serpent takes the same cyma-recta shape and size as the topmost crown moulding on the classical entablature.

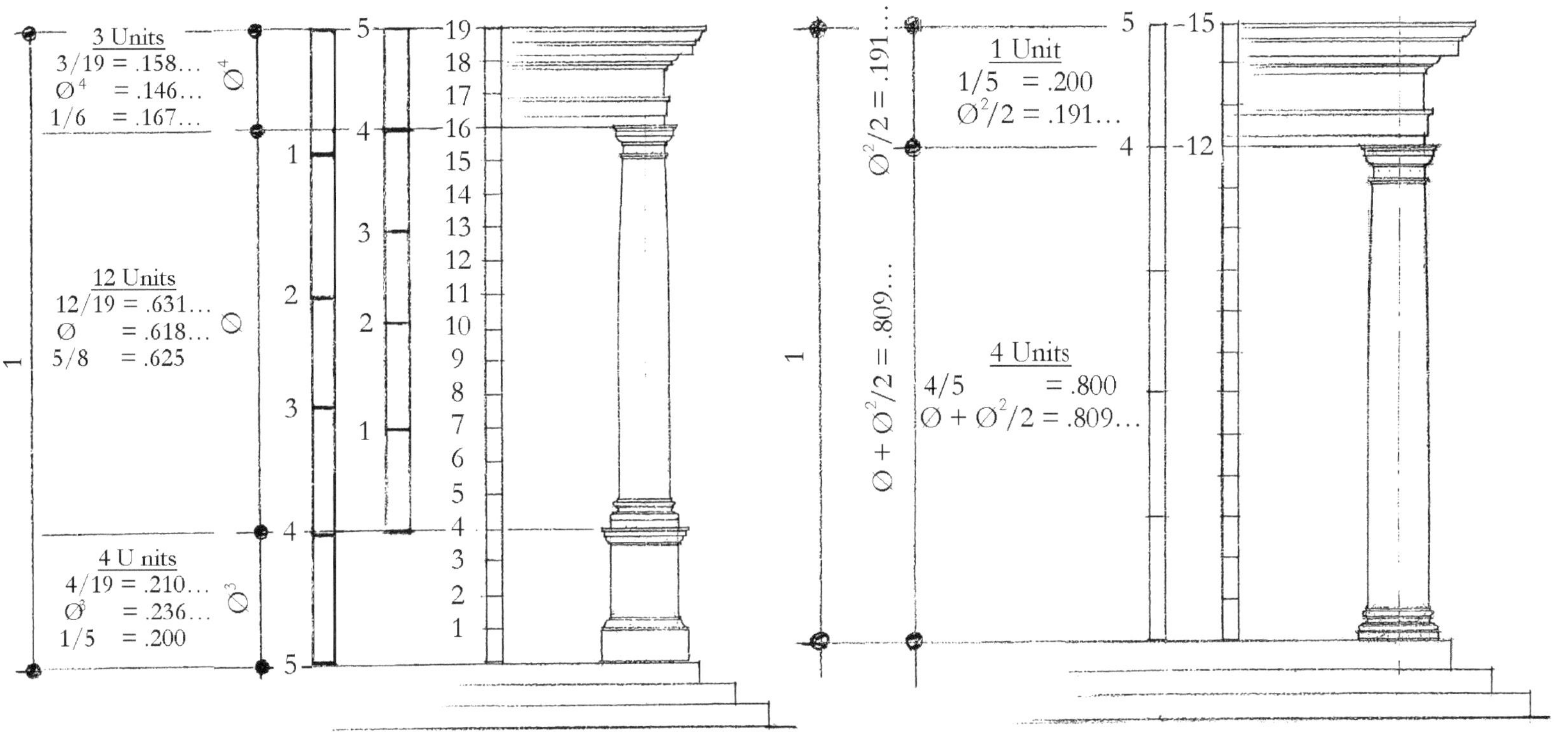

Order with Pedestal

Order without Pedestal

17b - Classical Order in Relation to the Canon of 19

Linking the classical order with the canon of 19, **figure 17b**, creates a similar anthropic analogy to that used by Vitruvius. And Ø, that mystery factor that's not there in Book III, but is there within the measures of the temple Vitruvius gives, emerges here to be a key factor. Set the overall height of the order as 1 and divide it into intervals of Ø and $Ø^2$. $Ø + Ø^2 = 1$, $Ø^3 + Ø^4 = Ø^2$, thus $Ø^3 + Ø^4 + Ø = 1$. $Ø^3$ gives the pedestal, Ø gives the column height and $Ø^4$ gives the entablature. These geometrical increments vary less than 5% from the arithmetic canon of 19 and even less from the small whole number ratios 1/6, 5/8 and 1/5. The process may be simplified further by dividing the overall height of the order into 5 parts. The lowest part will be the pedestal. Divide the remaining 4 parts into 5 smaller parts. The top part will be the entablature. The use of a proportional divider set to Ø will reduce this procedure to a few turns of the hand.

We may see here a kind of intersection of the three methods of application of proportion in architecture. The existence of such intersections indicates that the three methods are not distinct and unrelated, but may be seen by artists as three ways to say the same thing. The anthropic analogy and the musical analogy provide hints of what this "same thing" might be.

Figure 18. The Doric Capital

The Doric capital is based on division of the square into thirds, as performed in **figure 3.** The height of the capital is half D. The necking is 1/3 of this, the echinus 1/3, and the abacus 1/3. The width of the necking is 5/6ths of D; the abacus projects 1/6th of D on either side, total = 7/6ths of D.

The echinus is reduced by 1/3 for its torus and fillet. The abacus is also reduced by 1/3 for its cymatium. The torus and fillet at the top of the column shaft are 1/12th of D, which may also be found on the diagram. Each of these elements is, in its turn, subdivided by thirds to give the relation between the fillet and torus or cyma.

18a 1-4 – Constructing a Doric Capital

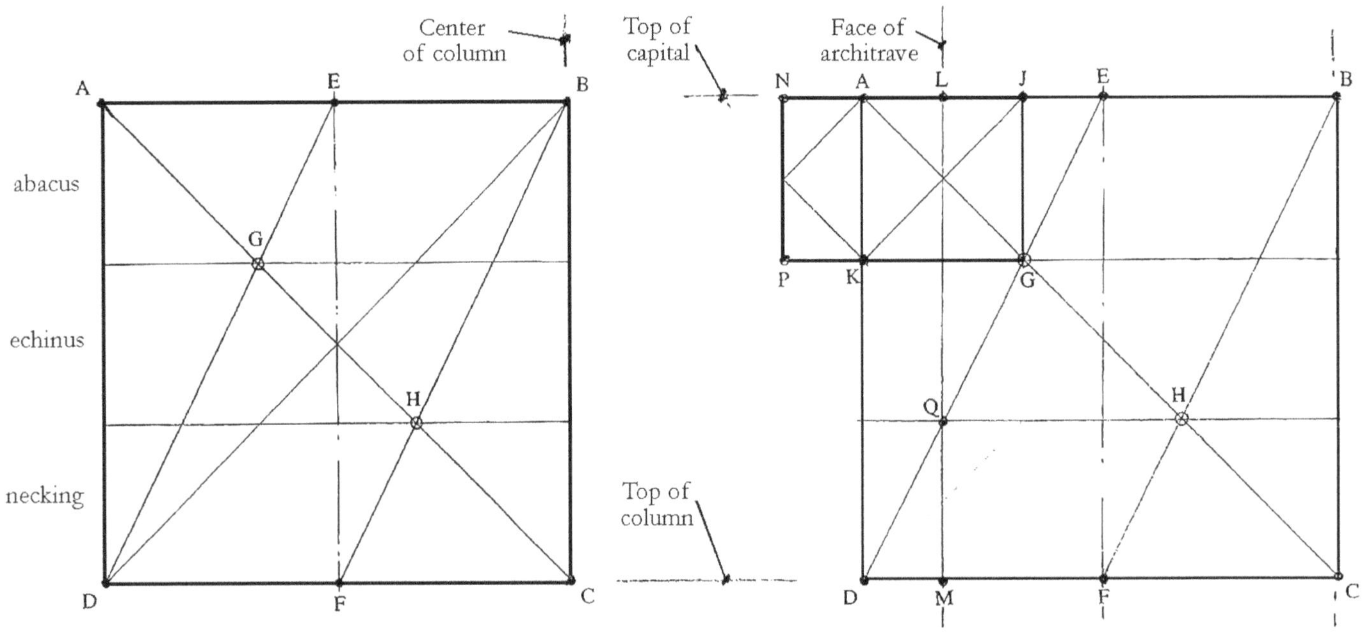

1. Set up square ABCD with centerline EF. AB = half of the lower column diameter. The height of the capital is AD = 1/2 of lower diameter. DC is the top of the column. The centerline of the column is BC. Draw diagonal AC and semi-diagonals DE and FB. Points G and H divide the square into thirds. The upper third is the abacus, the middle third the echinus, the lower third the necking.

2. Set up a square on AG and divide it by its diagonals to find point L. Draw line LQM. L marks the edge of the architrave and M marks the upper column diameter. AJ = 1/6 of D, AL = 1/12 D. Extend AB to point N, NA = AL, NP is the outer face of the abacus.

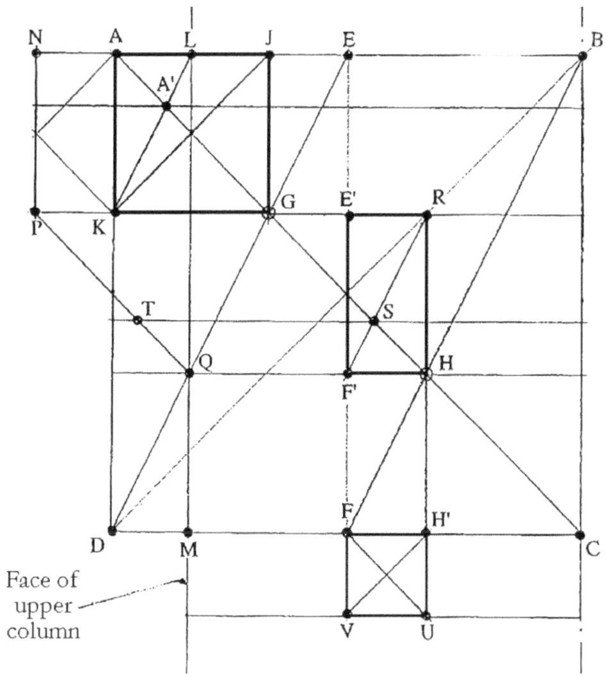

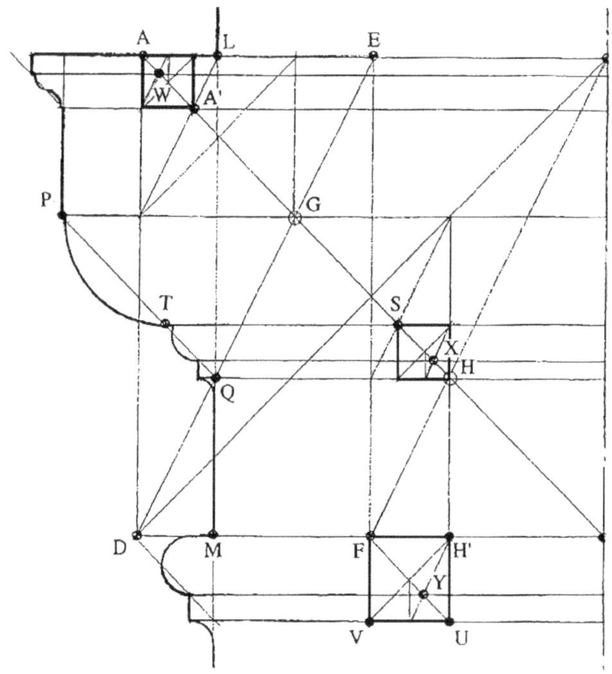

3. Draw semi-diagonal KL to find A'. This gives the cap of the abacus. Set up half-square E'RHF', draw semi-diagonal F'R to find S. This gives the echinus and its bed mould. The necking is undivided. The astragal at the top of the column is given by the interval FH' = 1/12 of lower D.

4. Find the 1/3 point between AA'. Point W gives the fillet of the cap of the abacus. Point X, the 1/3 point of SH gives the fillet of the bed mould of the echinus. Point Y gives the fillet of the column's astragal.

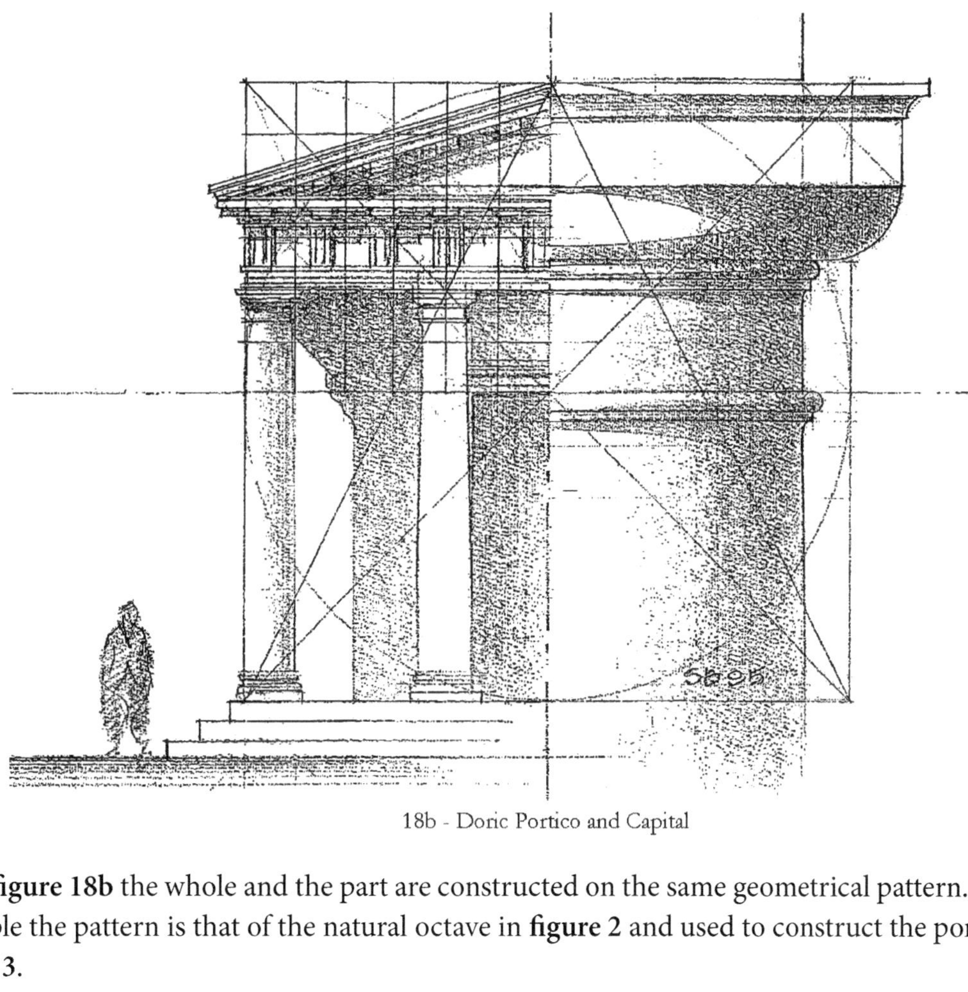

18b - Doric Portico and Capital

In **figure 18b** the whole and the part are constructed on the same geometrical pattern. In this example the pattern is that of the natural octave in **figure 2** and used to construct the portico in **figure 3**.

Figure 19. The Ionic Capital

An arithmetic method is given by Vitruvius based on the canon of 19, described in **figure 17**. 1/2 D is divided into 18 parts and 1 part is added.[13] The overall width of the abacus is to be 19/18ths of half D. The overall height of the capital including the abacus and the volutes = 1/2 its overall width, 19/18ths of half D. The vertical center of the eye is 3 parts in from the edge of the abacus. The horizontal center is located 7 parts up from the bottom of the capital. The eye is 2 parts in diameter. The abacus thickness is 3 parts. The echinus is 4 parts high, its astragal 2 parts. The fillet of the volute is 1 part wide.

A harmonic ratio method is given by Vignola. Half D is divided into 6 parts. The top 1/6th is struck off for the abacus. The remaining 5/6ths are divided into 8 parts. The eye is 1 of these parts in diameter and its bottom is placed at the 3/8ths point. Note the presence of the Fibonacci series - 1, 1, 2, 3, 5, 8, …. The vertical centers of the eyes are 1 D apart. Vignola's construction of the spiral volute centers within the eye is based on division of the square into thirds, as in **figure 2.**

A geometric construction emerges if we consider the height of the capital as 19 units with the eye centered at the 7/12th point. 7/12 is an arithmetic approximation of the phi ratio, = .583… ≈ .618…. In this geometrical layout, if the overall height of the capital is 1, the eye is centered at the Ø point, its diameter is $Ø^5$ = .090…. The depth of the abacus is $Ø^4$ = .146… ≈ 1/6th of D = .167…. The echinus is $Ø^3$ = .236…; its bottom edge on center with the eyes. The distance between the centers of the eyes may "slide" from a maximum of 1 D to a minimum of the eyes being tangent to 5/6ths of D. In this illustration the eyes are centered at 11/12ths D.

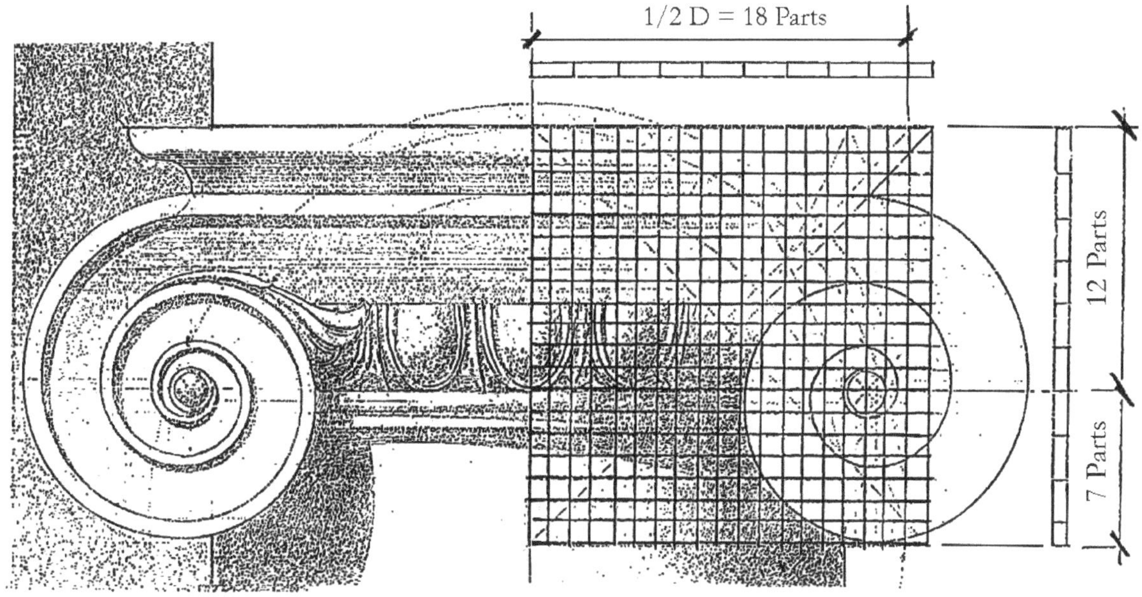

Vitruvius' Arithmetic Construction Using 19

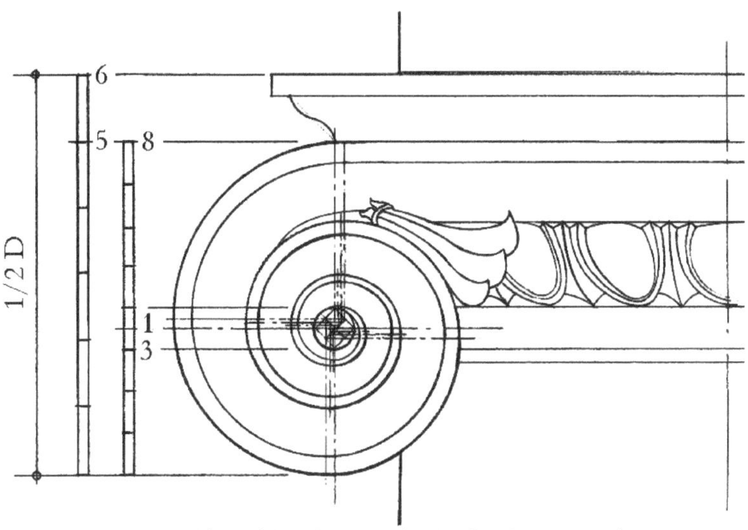

Vignola's Harmonic Ratio Construction

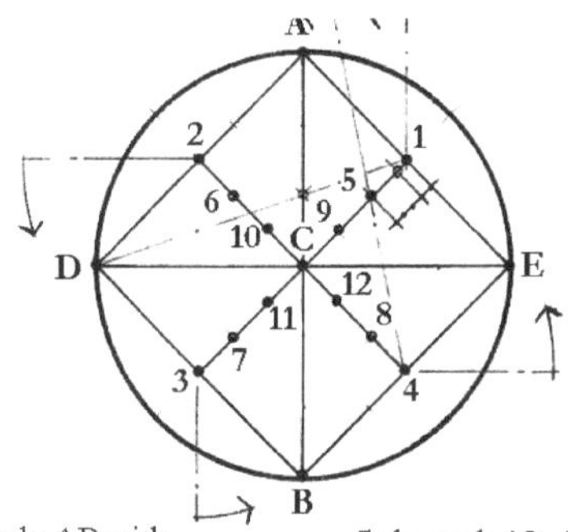

1. Given circle AB with center C
2. Draw diameter DE perpendicular to AB and draw squareABCD.
3. Bisect the sides of the square to find points 1-4. Divide lines 1C to 4C into 3 to find points 5 through 12. Points 1 to 12 are the centers of the volute segments.
4. To find centers for the fillet divide interval 1-5 into 4 parts. The first part is the center of the fillet.

Eye of the Volute - Vignola's Construction

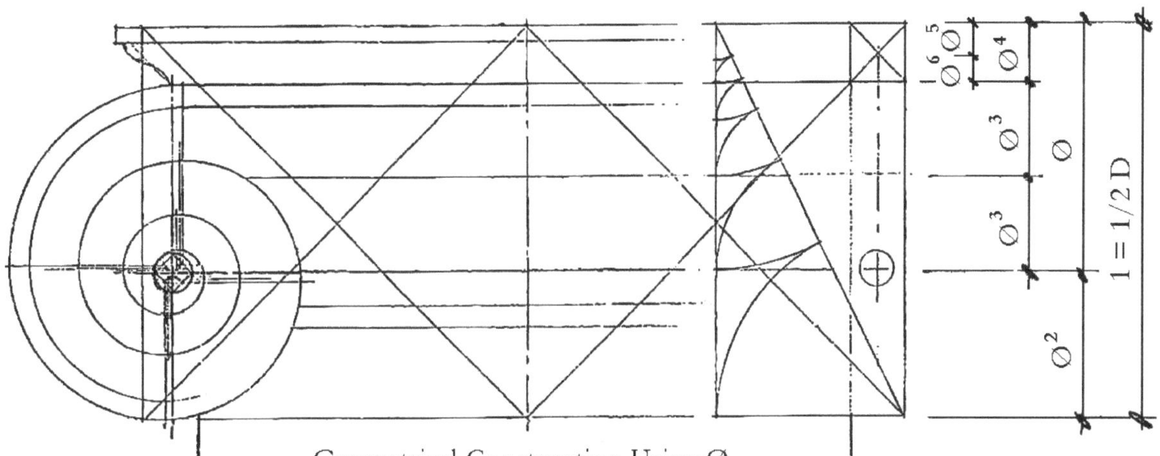

Geometrical Construction Using Ø

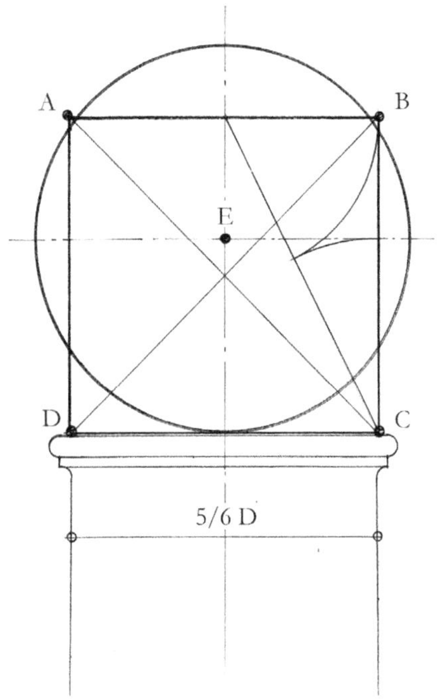

1 & 2 - Unity and Division

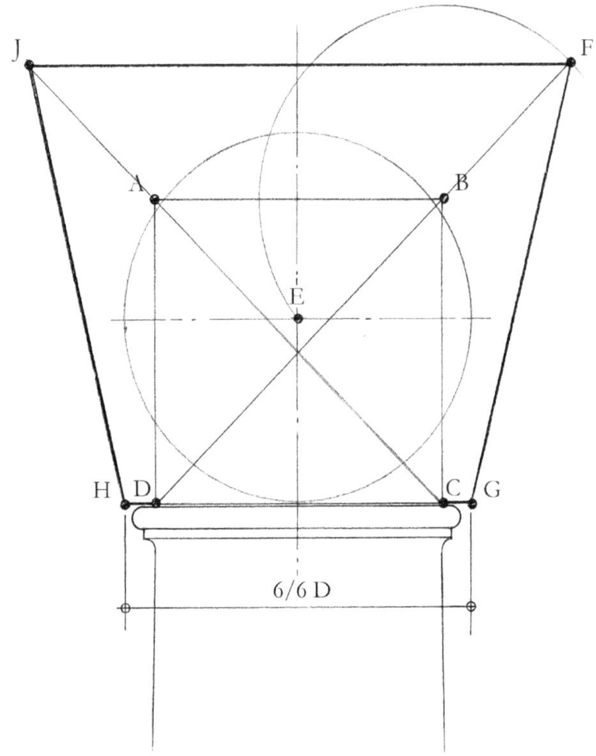

3.1 - Structure the Elements

Figure 20. The Corinthian Capital
Using the Squared Circle and the Pentad

1 & 2. Unity and Division. The representatives of unity are the square and the squared circle. The major cut is Ø. The side of the square, ABCD, is upper D, 5/6th of lower D; The diameter of the circle is lower D, its radius, centered at E, is Ø of the side of the square. The perimeters of the square and circle are approximately equal, as in **figure** 7. This implies that the entasis of the column, the relationship of lower to upper D, is Ø related.

3.1. Begin to structure the elements – with center at B and radius BE find F on the extension of diagonal DB. Extend DC to find G and H, GH = lower D. JFGH will guide the outer edges of the elements.

3.2. The circumference of the circle is divided into 5 and diagonals drawn to create the pentagram, KLMNP, as in **figure 6c**. The horizontal diagonal of the pentagram, LP, gives the top of the upper row of leaves. The top of the square, AB, gives the bottom of the volutes and the uppermost part of the circle, K, gives their height. The abacus is in the interval between K and JF.

3.3 Draw an inverted pentagram, QRSTU; its horizontal diagonal, SU, gives the top of the lower row of leaves.

4. Manifestation. The leaves, volutes, caliculi, bell, abacus and fleuron are placed and refined to the desired degree. Diagonals NK and KM frame out the central upper leaf and the two central lower leaves. V marks the return of the leaves. K marks the center of the fleuron. Lines JC and QR give the center of the volute and QR marks the bottom of the fleuron.

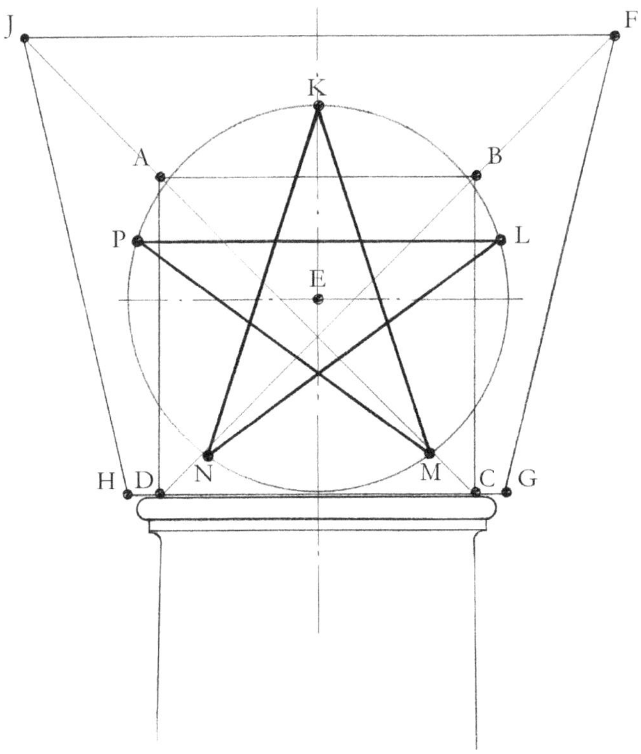

3.2 - Structure Continued

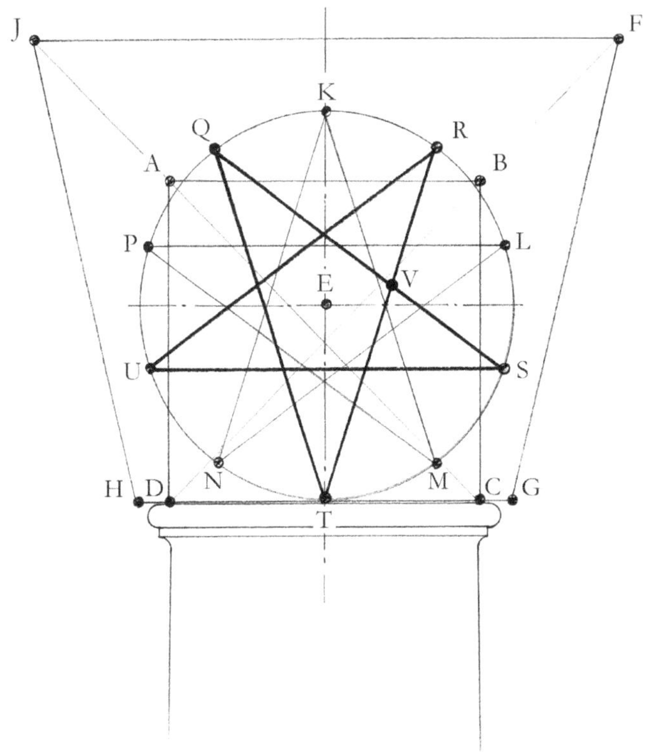

3.3 - Structure Continued

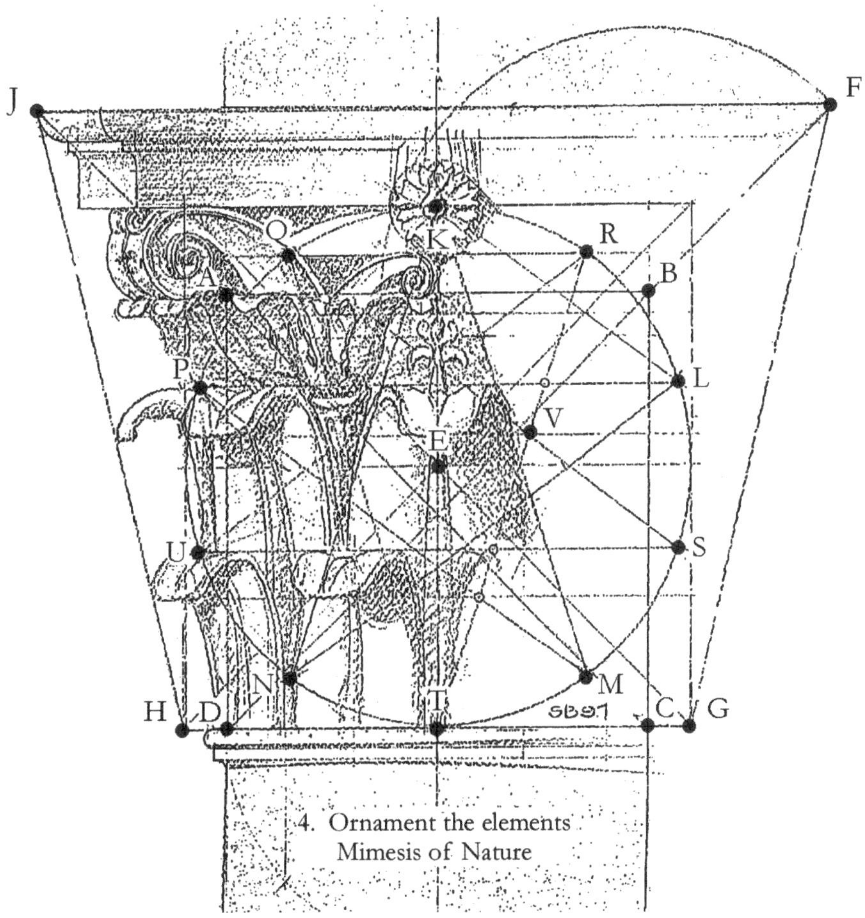

4. Ornament the elements
Mimesis of Nature

FIGURE 21. ENTABLATURES OF THE THREE PRINCIPAL ORDERS

In the canon of Vignola each of the orders has a key number; Doric – 8, Ionic – 9, and Corinthian – 10. These keys give the ratio of the column's lower diameter to its height. In each order the depth of the entablature is 1/4th of the column's height.

Each entablature is, in turn, divided into the key number. In the Doric order the cornice is 3 parts, the frieze is 3, and the architrave is 2 = 8. The Ionic entablature is divided into 18 parts, twice 9, cornice = 7, frieze = 6, and architrave = 5. The Corinthian entablature is: cornice = 4, frieze = 3, and architrave = 3, giving 10 parts total.

Geometrically, however, each is a Ø construction. The 2, 3, 5, 8, … pattern of the Doric is the Fibonacci series. The 3.5/5.5 or 7/11 split of the Ionic is a Ø approximate ≈ .611…; also note that 5/6 ≈ .833…, or about 1.618…/2. The Corinthian 6/10 split is a Ø approximate.[14]

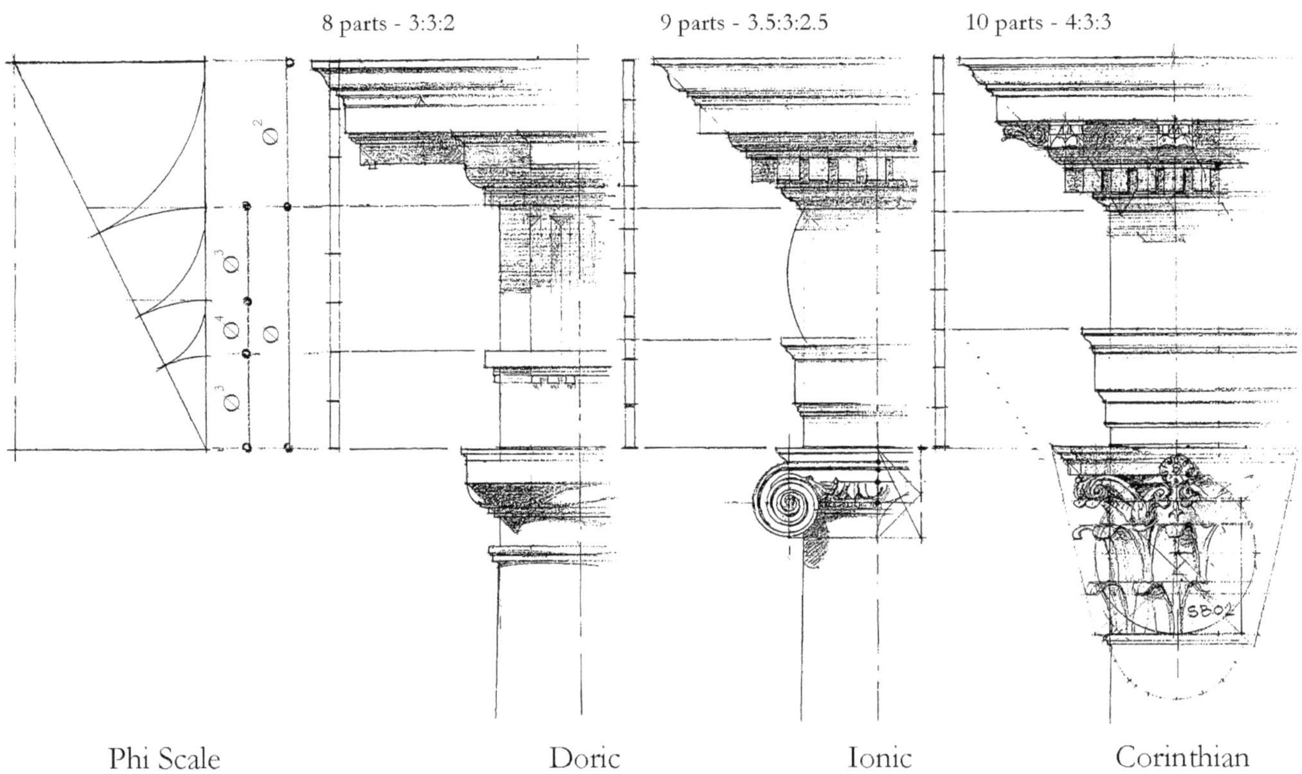

Figure 22. Pediments

The pediment is an important centering and culminating device in traditional composition. To begin its construction take the distance from its center to the outer edge of the cornice, interval AB, **figure 22a**. With center at A and radius AB draw arc BC. With center at C and radius CB draw arc BD, **figure 22b**. Point D is the apex of the top of the cyma. The crown moulding rides on top of the split fillet. CD:AB = $1:\sqrt{2}$. The rake angle formed is 22.5°. This is the construction of the octagon. AD = .414… . This is very close to $Ø^2$ or .382…. It can be rounded off at 2/5 of the half or 1/5th of the overall length of the entablature. 1/5 is an approximation of $Ø^2/2$ or .191…. This method is given by Serlio[15]

A variant of this is the construction attributed to L'Eveille, **figure 22c**. The top extremities of the split fillet are points A and B. With center at A and radius AB draw arc BC. ABC is an equilateral triangle. With center at C and radius CA draw arc AD. D will mark the bottom edge of the bed mould of the cornice and the apex of the tympanum. With center at E open the compass or divider to radius EF, which is equal to the depth of the cornice from the bottom of the bed mould to the top of the split fillet. Apply interval EF to point D to find point G. Line AG will be the top edge of the raking split fillet. As EF = GD the raking shapes under the split fillet are slightly thinner than the equivalent ones in the horizontal cornice.

Arithmetically we may follow Vitruvius who recommends 1/9th of the length of the split fillet for the height of the tympanum, **figure 22d**, but we note that 1/9 = .111… and that $Ø^3/2$ - .118…. This produces a relatively low rake angle of about 16°. Vitruvius allows for higher tympanums if sculpture is to be included.

Part of the compositional tradition concerning pediments is that the rake angle decreases as the entablature gets wider. Thus an individual window could have a high raking angle while an octastyle portico would have a comparatively low angle. A guide for this is that the area of the entablature and pediment should be about equal to the area of the columns carrying them.

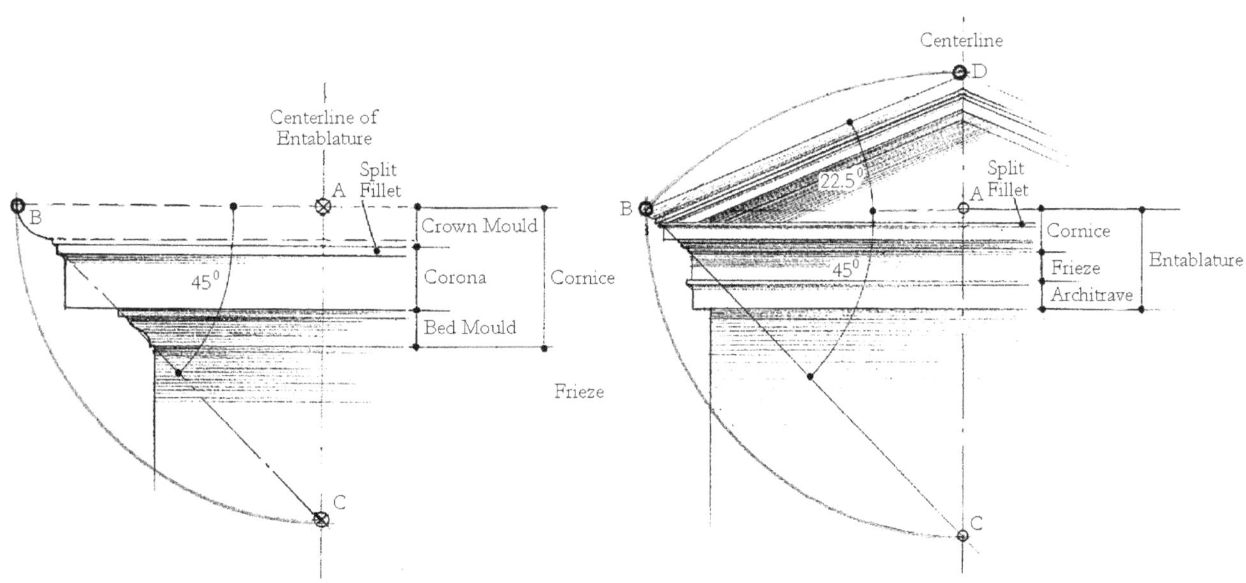

22a & b - Serlio's Geometric Method

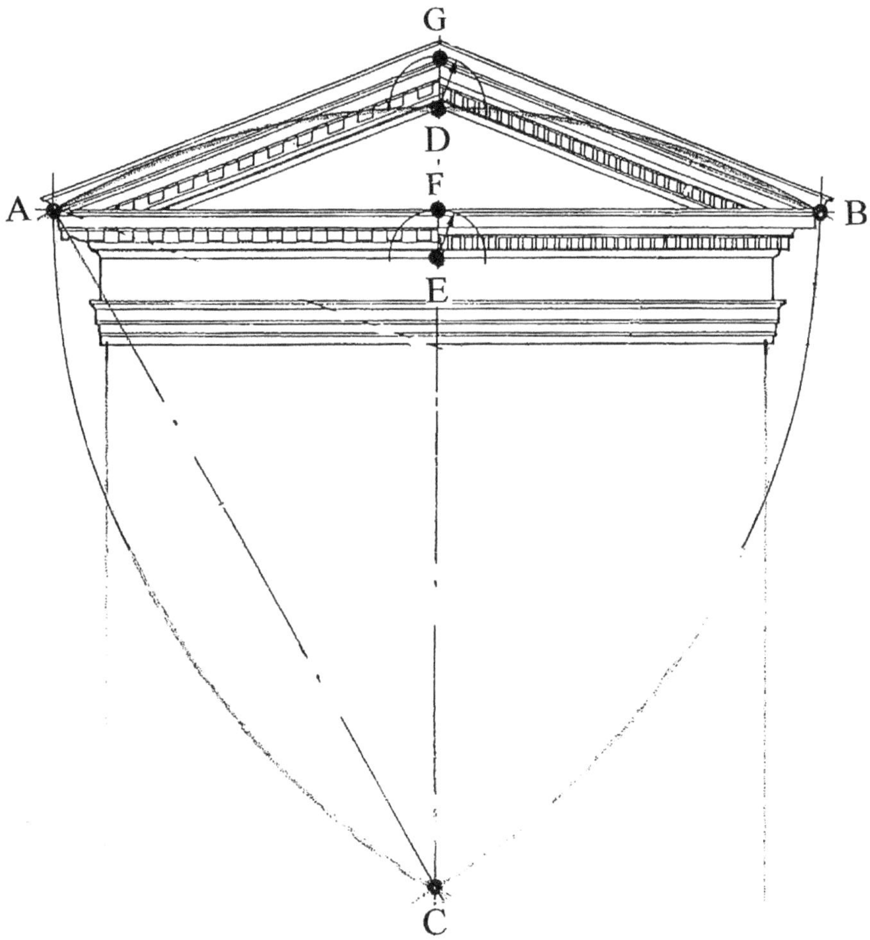

22c - L'Eveille's Method

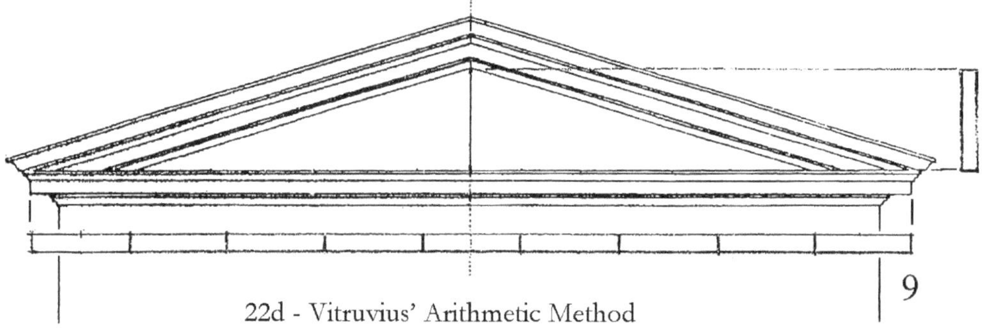

22d - Vitruvius' Arithmetic Method

For example, in **figure 22e**, the columns, as in the Doric genera, have a face area of 1 x 8 x 4 = 32. The entablature area is 2 x 10 = 20 and the area of the pediment is 5 x 2 = 10. If we add 1 unit for the angular projection of the cornice, that = 31. Since the area of the columns is slightly greater than the area of the entablature and pediment the massing seems stable; but if the diameter of the columns is decreased to .8, or a ratio of 1/10 as in the Corinthian genera, then their combined area is only 25.6, implying that we might wish to reduce the depth of the entablature as well as the rake angle of the pediment.

In **figure 22f** we use a Corinthian column ratio of 1/10. The same 10 x 12 grid is used. The top of the column is 8.5 units high and the columns are .85 units in diameter; the entablature and pediment are each 1.75 units high. This approximates the Vignolian canon in which the entablature may be 1/5th of the column height. The area of the columns is 8.5 x .85 x 4 = 28.9.

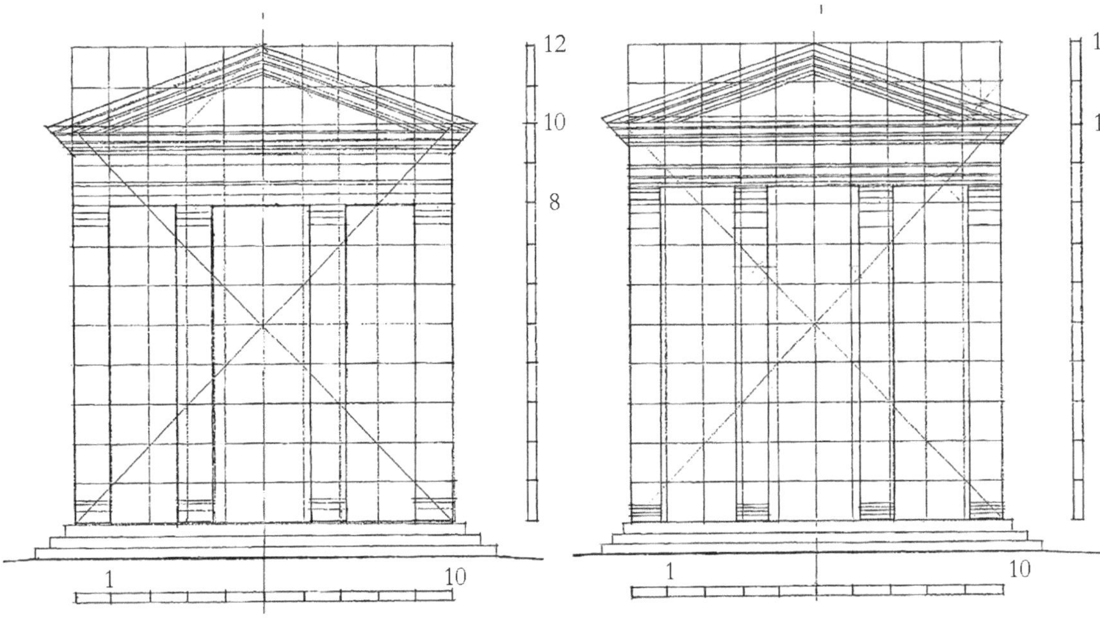

22e & 22f - Area Equivalence of Columns and Superstructure

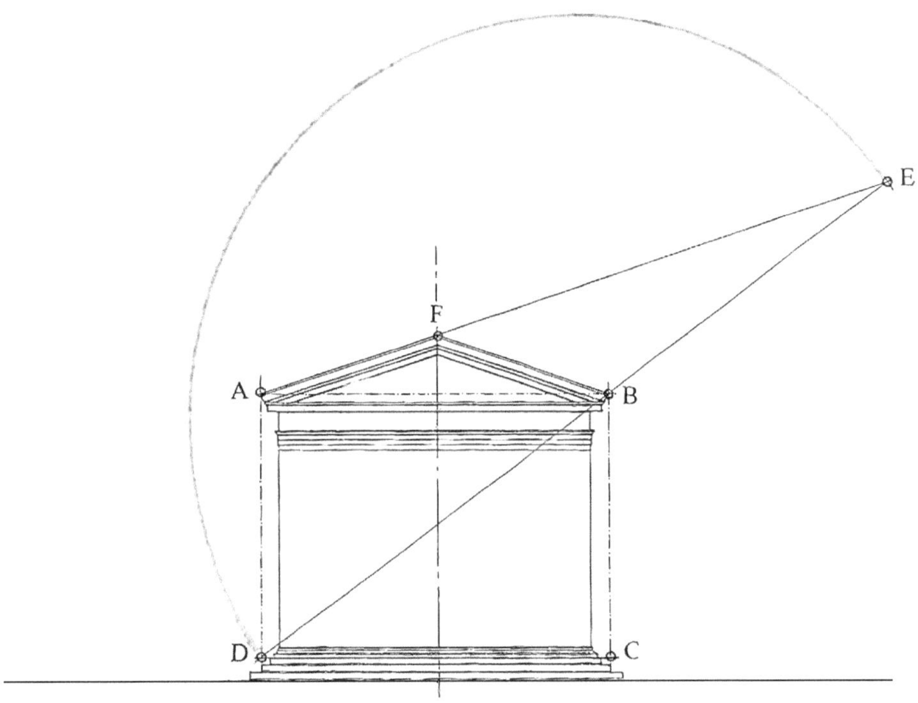

22g - A Geometrical 'Sliding Scale' for Pediments

The entablature is 1.75 x 10 = 17.5 and the area of the pediment is 1.75 x 5 = 8.75; adding 1 unit for the cornice projection = 27.25, thus achieving visual stability.

A geometrical method, a kind of sliding scale, for finding an appropriate rake angle for any needed width is offered in the 1936 Tiranti edition of Normand's *Parallel,*[16] shown here as **figure 22g.** Construct rectangle ABCD the length of which runs from the outermost points of the top of the entablature, points A and B, and the height of which runs from the top of the entablature to the floor of the portico or opening, points C and D. Draw diagonal DB. Extend DB beyond point B and with center at B and radius BD draw arc DE to intersect the projection of DB. The line AE gives the rake angle of the pediment AFB.

Figure 23. Superposition

Figure 23a stacks the genera from the most robust to the most delicate – Tuscan, Doric, Ionic, Corinthian, and Composite. Each column diminishes through entasis so that it is 5/6 of its lower diameter at the top of the shaft. A column placed above another should have its lower diameter equal to 5/6 of the diameter of the column below it. **Figure 23a** and the table below give the arithmetic. To make the results comprehensible lower D of the Tuscan column is a starting interval and is divided into 6 units that are then used as a consistent measure. The D for each genera is determined by multiplying the diameter of the column below by 5/6 to get its diameter in Tuscan D units.

Each of the genera has a particular D:H ratio, 7, 8, 9, 10 and 10 respectively in the canon of Vignola. The diminished diameter for each genera is then multiplied by its D:H ratio to get its height. Each height is divided by 4, as per Vignola, to find the depth of each entablature. The "floor to floor" heights can be equalized, if necessary, through the use of extended plinths or pedestals.

In elevation the columns are set directly above one another but in section the plinth of each column is aligned with the upper diameter of the column below, thus the centerline of each successive column is "setback" by 1/6th of its own diminished diameter. This setback interval is also given in Tuscan D units. Thus in **figure 23b** the setback of the Doric centerline is 1/6th of its diameter, which is 5 Tuscan D units, making the setback 5/6 of one of those units.

Though this seems like a complicated arithmetic method keep in mind that 5/6 is a whole number Ø-related ratio, being the equivalent of a half a Ø rectangle with sides 10/6. The setback of the centerlines is an important subtlety in that it gives the entire building a kind of entasis, a tapering inward that contributes to a sense of stability; it is mimetic of natural objects that diminish as they rise and alludes to the building as sacred mountain.

Genera	Tuscan D = 6 Units Diameter	Height	Entablature	Setback
Tuscan	1 = 6/6 = 6 Units	7D = 42	10&1/2	0
Doric	6/6 x 5/6 = 5/6 = 5 Units	8D = 40	10	5/6
Ionic	5/6 x 5/6 = 25/36 = 4&1/6	9D = 37	9&1/4	2/3
Corinthian	25/36 x 5/6 = 125/216 = 3&1/2	10D = 35	8&3/4	7/12
Composite	125/216 x 5/6 = 625/1296 = 2&8/9	10D = 29	7&1/2	1/2

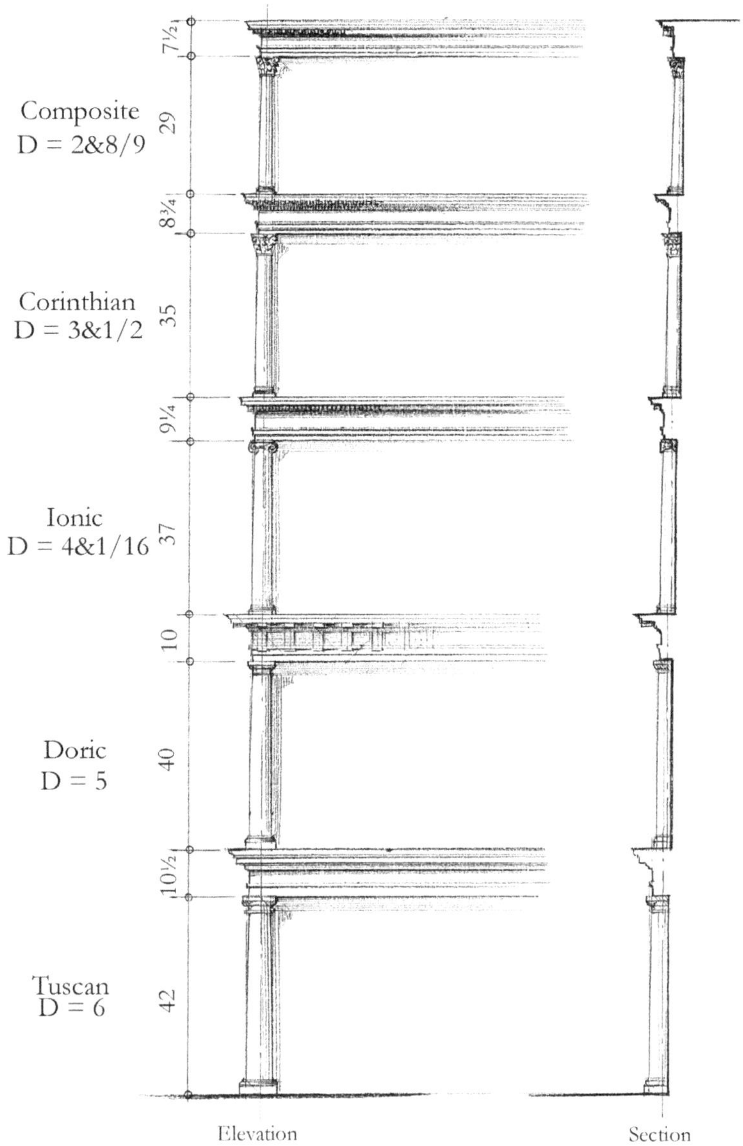

23a - Superposition in Elevation

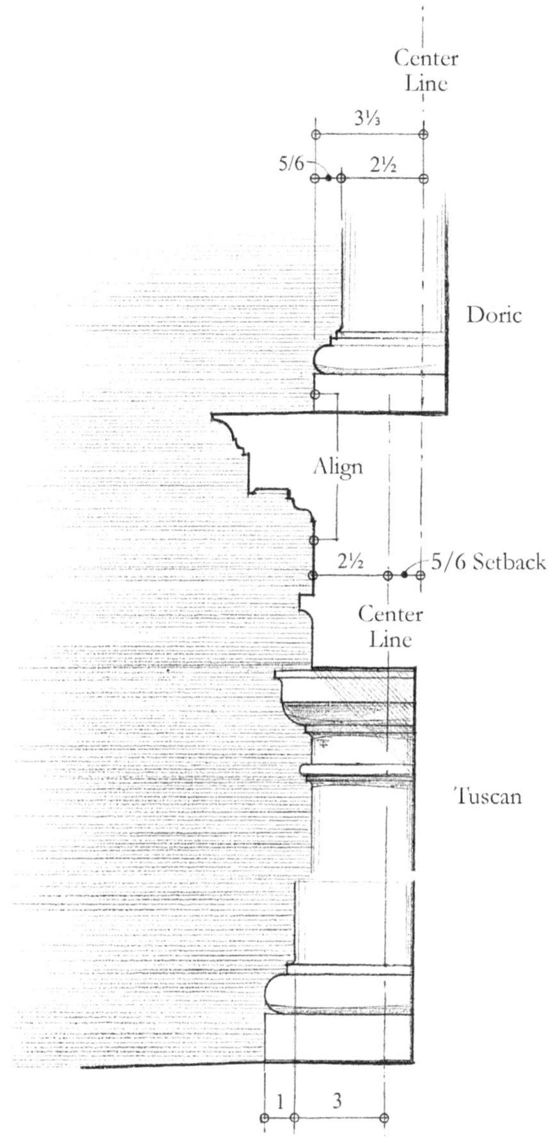

23b - Setback of Column Centerlines in Section 1 = 1/6th Tuscan D

Figure 24. Arcades

In **figure 24a** the orders or generas are combined with arches to form an arcade. The key to this marriage [according to Ware] is to add a plinth of .75 D to the column and entablature. In the Corinthian genera, for example the column is 10 D high and the entablature is 1/4 of that or 2.5 D. This adds up to 13.25 D. The arch is also 10 D high and for a nominal 2:1 ratio for the opening, it is 5 D wide. The pier is nominally 2 D wide but it can be varied somewhat to accommodate the requirements of column spacing; in the Corinthian the piers are 2.33 D wide and the column centers are 7.33 D apart to mesh with the .66 D spacing of the modillions.

The same kind of process is followed to superpose arcades as was used in **figure 23**. Though each column is 5/6ths of the column below, and the intercolumnation is slightly wider. The proportion of the arch openings may be varied anywhere from 4:9 to 1:1, or floor heights may be equalized by varying the heights of plinths or pedestals.

A geometric ratio such as phi or whole number ratio such as 1:2 could be utilized to proportion an arcade. In **figure 24b** phi is used to locate the column centers [13.25 x .618... = 8.188... or 8&3/16 D] and place the arch as another phi ratio, 6/10. To make up the extra 3/16 D each modillion interval would need to be about 1/64th of D wider than the canonical 2/3 D.

The arcade motif exhibits a good deal of proportional flexibility. In **figure 24c** two modifications are made to the arcade in **figure 24b** that noticeably alter its character. First, the depth of the entablature is reduced from 1/4 of the column height to 1/5th, making the vertical count 10 parts for the column, 2 for the entablature, and 3/4 for the plinth, totaling 12&3/4 D. Multiplying this by phi gives 7&7/8 or 7.875 D for the column centers. Second, the arch is adjusted to be 2:1; its height will be 10 and its width 5. This leaves 2.875, 1 for the column D + 1&23/32nds or about .75 D for each pier. The modillion spacing is reduced by 1/8 D over 12 intervals; or alternately the column spacing may be increased by that 1/8 of D to 8 D without sacrificing the proportional character of this version.

Figure 24d is an exercise in the placement of a single-story Corinthian arcade in a rectangle whose sides are in the ratio of 1:4. If we divide the height into 13.25 D parts, 2.5 for the entablature, 10 for the column, and .75 for the plinth, the overall length will be 13.25 x 4 = 53 D. The column centers will be 7.33 D; multiplying this by 6 gives 44 D, leaving 4.5 D on either end to act as an abutment. Alternately, using a thinner entablature **figure 24e** divides the height into 12.75 parts using 8 D as our column center. This divides the length into 51 D parts; 8 D x 6 intervals = 48, leaving 1.5 parts on either end, just enough to position a Corinthian capital.

In **figure 24f**, the number of arches is reduced to five. The piers get too wide and may be further articulated into the form of the "Serliana" or "Palladian" opening. This example returns to the height of 13.25, giving 5 intervals of 10 D leaving 1.5 D on either side, just enough to position a Corinthian capital.

In each of the examples the 2:1 ratio of the arched opening has been held, but it is not necessary to maintain this or any other individual variable. There are an indefinite number of settings or "tunings" possible using such methods. This process of stretching, squeezing, removing or adding mass may be seen as a kind of morphic transformation, a shifting of one element into another in an almost alchemical way; or it could be seen as a form of rhythmical movement. In these examples, proportional techniques become tools for the designer in the service of composition and the search for character; geometric, arithmetic and harmonic ratio methods used separately or together inform compositional choices.

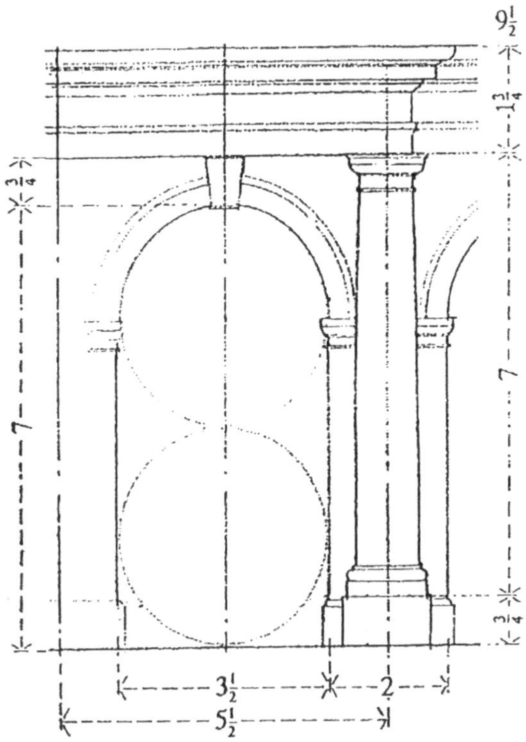

Tuscan Arcade

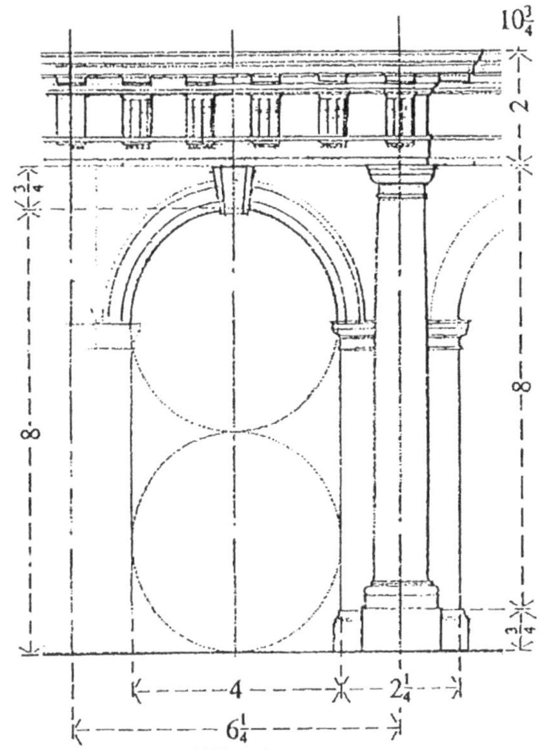

6 Triglyphs

Doric Arcade

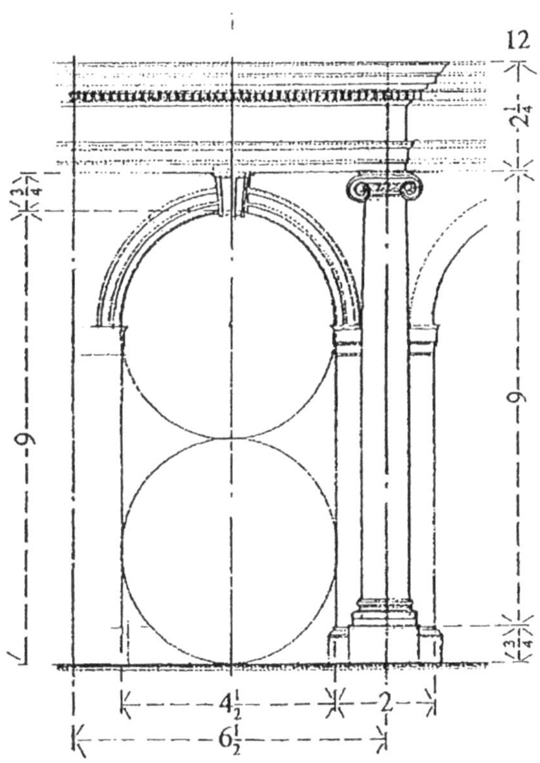

39 Dentils

Ionic Arcade

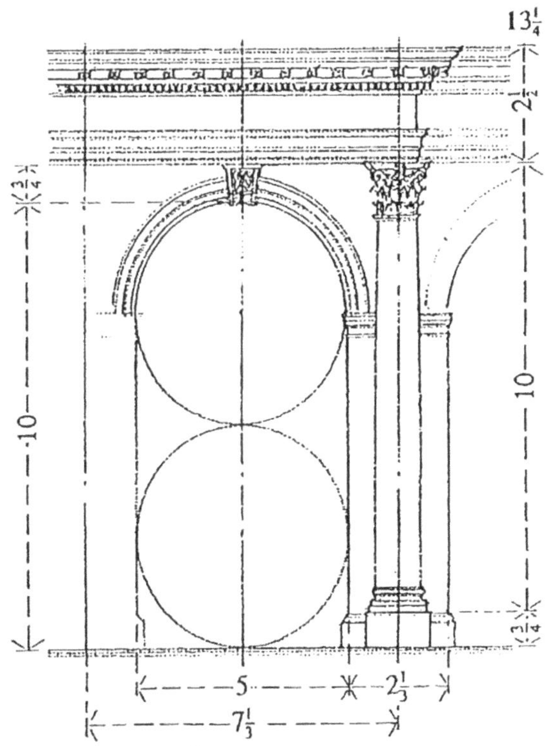

12 Modillions = 44 Dentils

Corinthian Arcade

24a - Arcades Based on Vignola

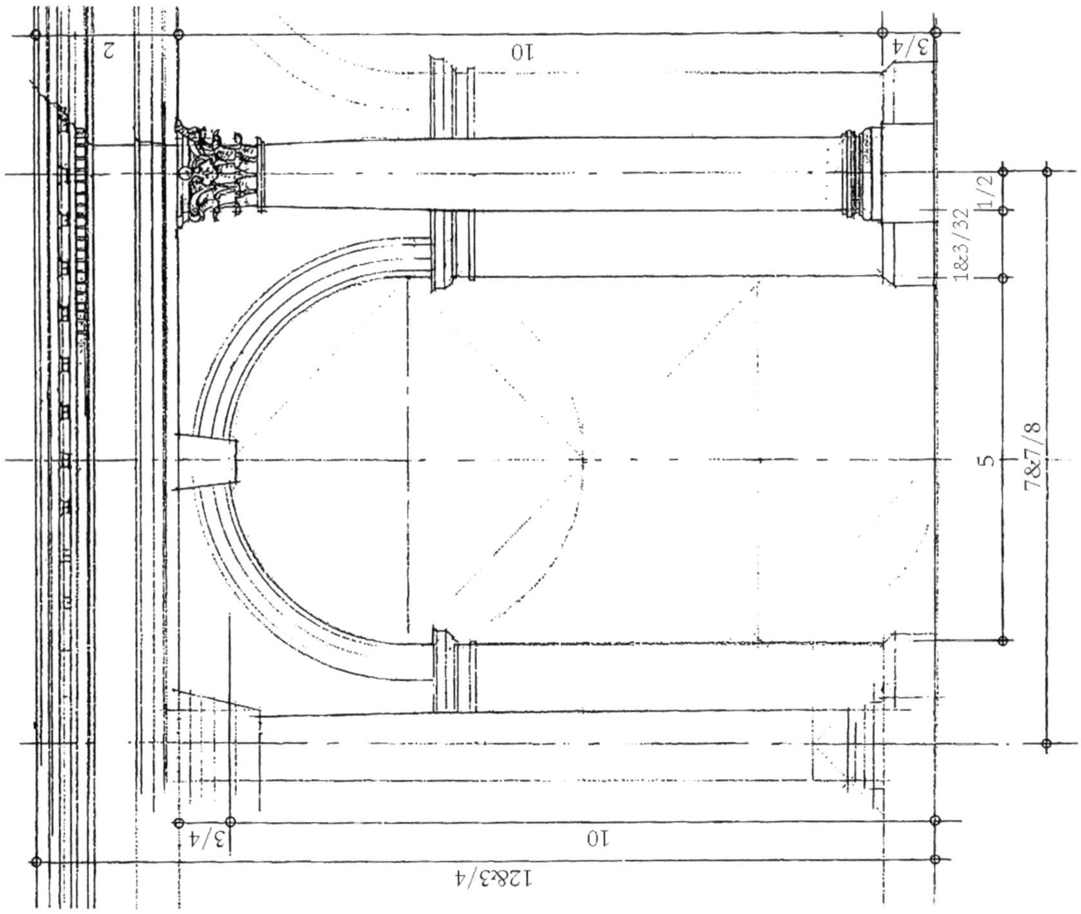

24c - Arcade Based on Phi and 2:1

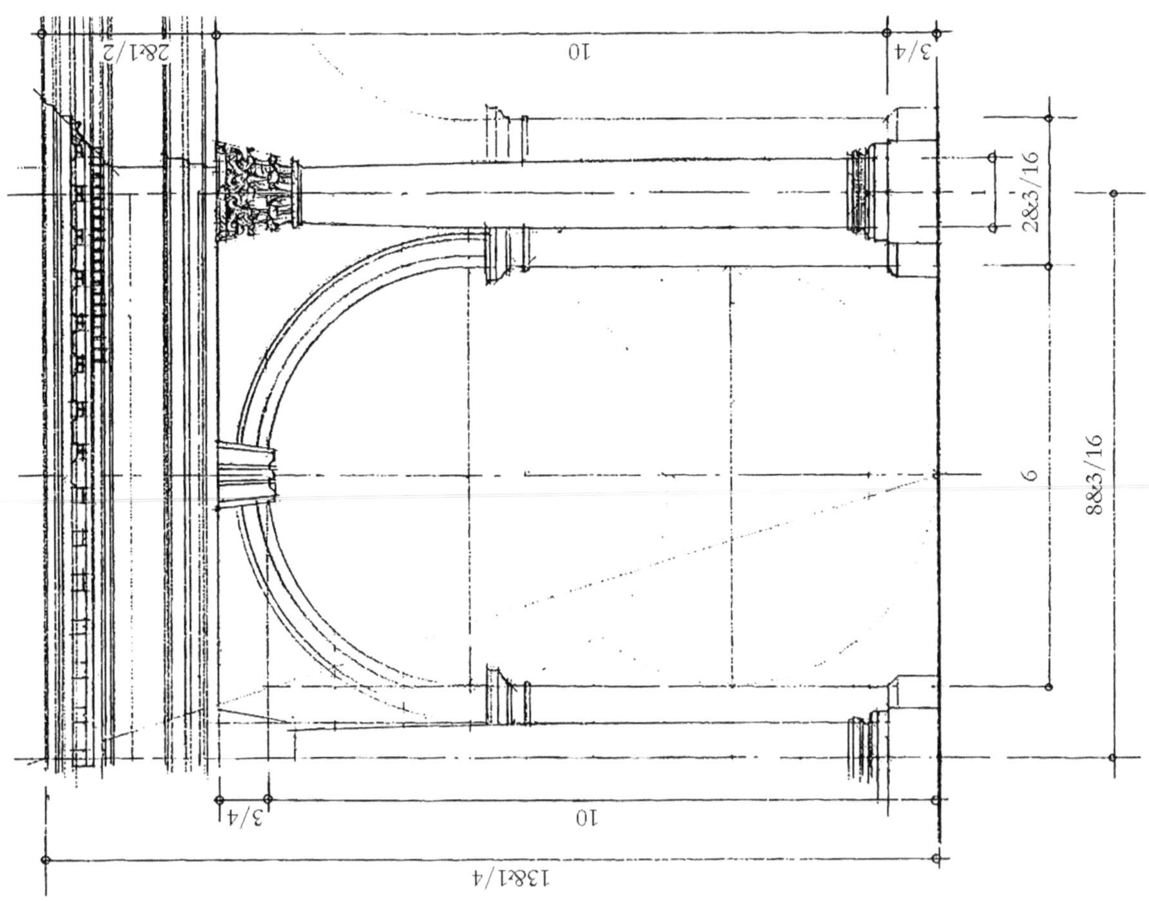

24b - Arcade Based on Phi

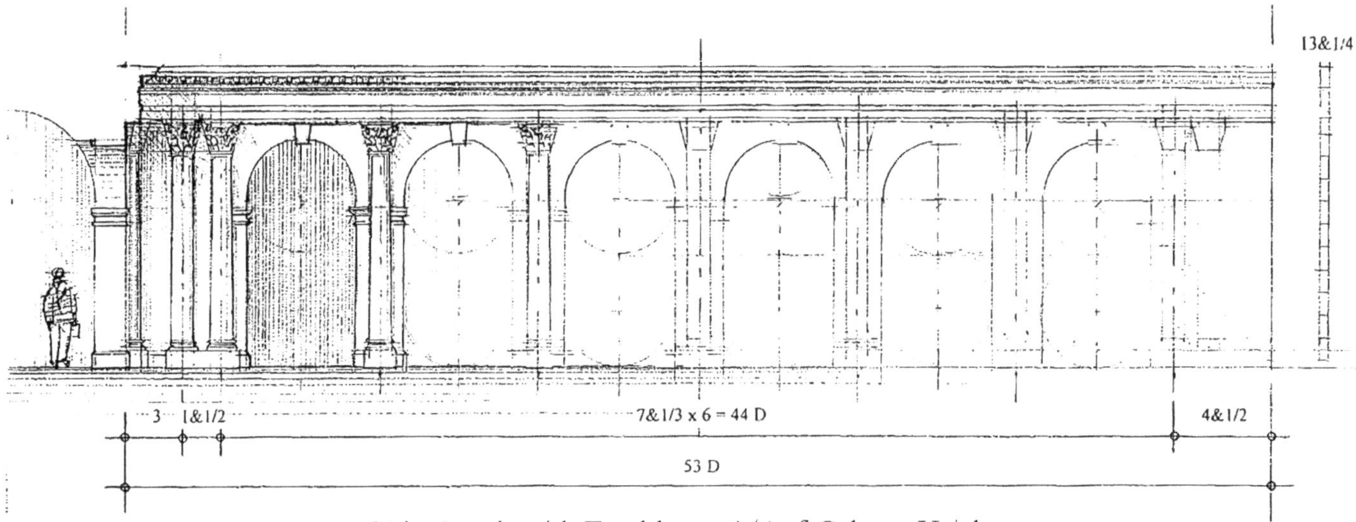

24d - Arcade with Entablature 1/4 of Column Height

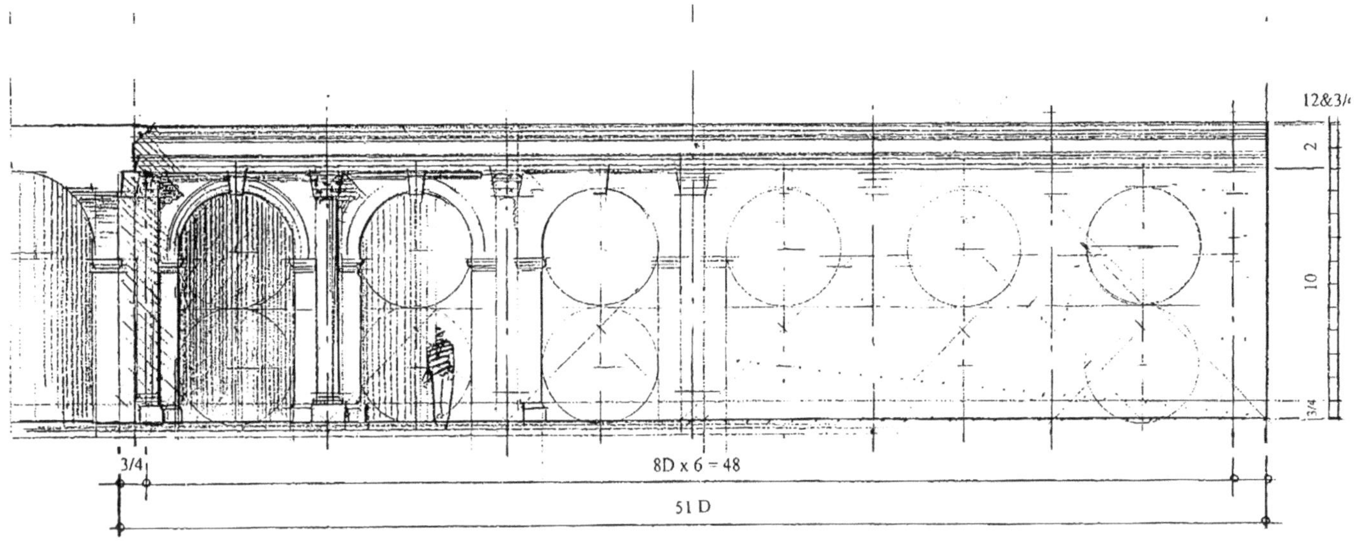

24e - Arcade with Entablature 1/5 of Column Height

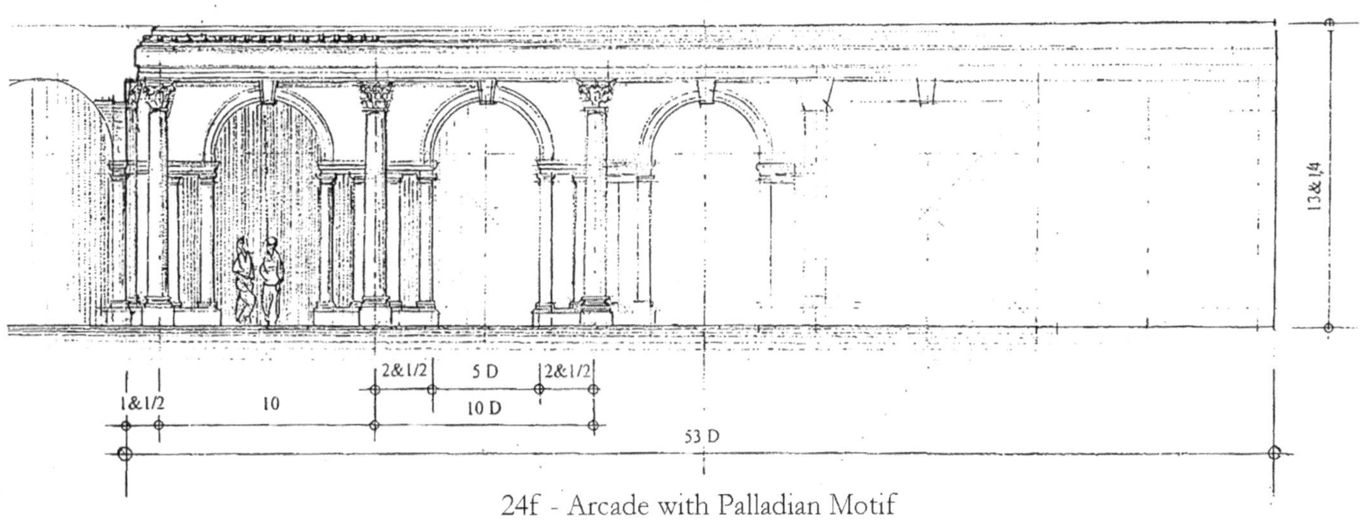

24f - Arcade with Palladian Motif

Figure 25. Palladio's Harmonic Ratios for Rooms

In the Renaissance the ancient geometric and arithmetic methods were synthesized to form a system of harmonic ratios. This may also be thought of as a "small whole member method," as the incommensurable geometrical ratios are rounded off to ratios of small whole numbers. One of the earlier appearances of this system are the group of seven shapes for the plans of rooms given by Palladio.[17] Through publication in his *Four Books,* this method had widespread influence and still affects the theory and practice of classical architecture today.

The seven shapes are: 1, the circle, 2, the square, 3, the ratio of 4:3, 4, the ratio of 1:√2, 5, the ratio of 3:2, 6, the ratio of 5:3, and 7, the double square. The circle is the first image in the geometrical creation myth, **figure 1**, representing idea or spirit and is the origin of all the regular polygons. The second shape, the square, is last in the myth and represents manifestation. It is a source for the remaining five shapes. The sides of the double square are in the same ratio as the interval of the octave; the 4:3 and 3:2 ratios are those of the fourth and fifth notes respectively. The ratio of 1:√2 is that of the diagonal of the square. Other than the circle this is the only pure geometrical. Its inclusion by Palladio may be taken as a reference to Vitruvius, where this ratio is also the only geometrical given. The 5:3 ratio is a whole number approximation of Ø. This ratio is specifically not mentioned by Vitruvius but is the subject of the opaque and perhaps intentionally confusing presentation in Book III, see **figure** 5. The selection of seven shapes may be taken as a reference to the seven visible planets of ancient cosmology, the seven intervals of the musical octave, and the seven liberal arts.

To create volumes, Palladio[18] uses the "three means" used in the creation of the musical octave in Plato's *Timaeus:* geometric, arithmetic and harmonic. The arithmetic mean, for example, is the "average" between the extremes, 25 being the average between 20 and 30. The two others are very close to that suggesting the arithmetic mean as a starting point for planning.

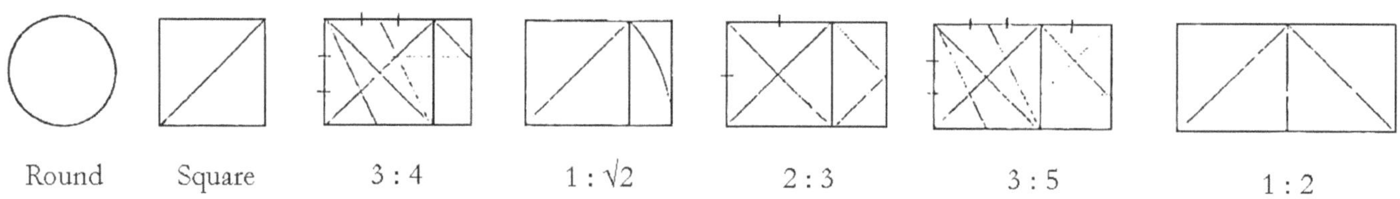

Palladio's Seven Room Proportions

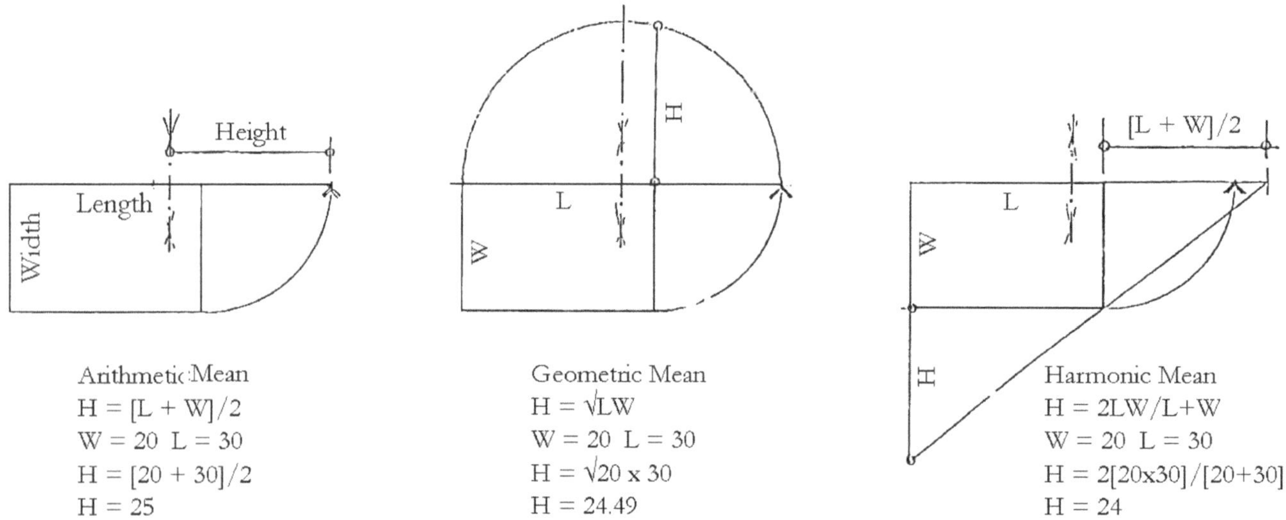

Palladio's Guide to Room Heights

Figure 26. Harmonic Volumes of Robert Morris

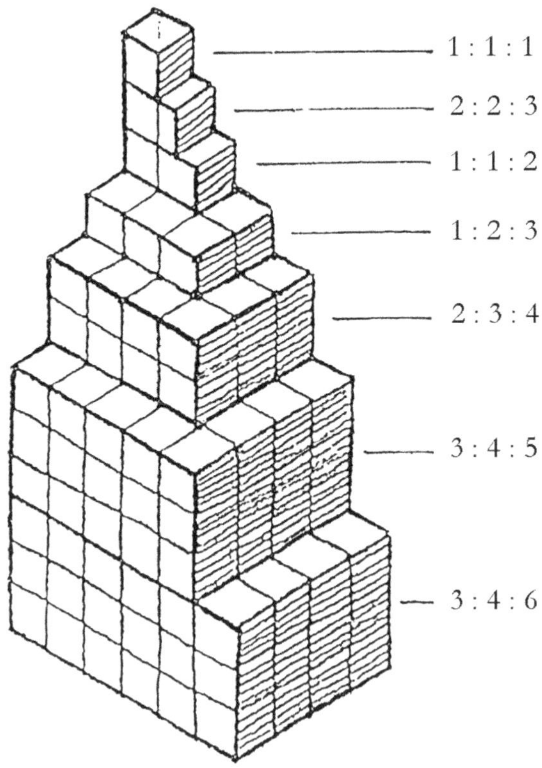

The Seven Room Proportions of Robert Morris

The Palladian system allows designers to create rooms of powerful nobility and intense erotic character. However, when transported to northern Europe the system has a climatic drawback. The heights of the rooms, based on the three musical means, essentially prohibit proper heating in winter. In his 1734 lectures at the Royal Academy, the British architect Robert Morris offers an alternative method of proportioning rooms using musically related ratios.

Two aspects of his modification to the Palladian system interest us here. 1) the essentially proportional character of his design theory and 2) the direct reference to the harmonic ratio method. Morris's method utilized three term proportions, what in mathematics might be called "progressions," or in music "chords," to proportion rooms. His "breakthrough" is that he uses the lowest number, not as the width of the room as Palladio had done, but as the height of the room, thus lowering the ceilings relative to the size of the room. While this makes the room easier to heat it also reduces the intensity of the proportional effect, as both of the rooms' vertical planes are horizontally orientated rectangles; though perhaps not an unwelcome outcome for Protestant England in the Enlightenment era.

Morris writes, "*As I consider the affinity between architecture and music, so I have produced those proportions from the same rules: In music are only seven distinct notes, in architecture likewise are only seven distinct proportions, which produce all the different buildings in the universe.*"

He then gives the following ratios:

		H W L	**Ratio L : W**	**Ratio H : L : W music term**
1	cube	1 : 1 : 1	fundamental	fundamental unison
2	cube & a half	1 : 1 : 1&1/2	fifth	fundamental & fifth
	or	2 : 2 : 3		
3	double cube	1 : 1 : 2	octave	fundamental & octave diapente
4		1 : 2 : 3	fifth	octave & fifth diapason
5		2 : 3 : 4	fourth	fifth & fourth sesqualter
6		3 : 4 : 5	tempered third	fourth & third
7		3 : 4 : 6	fifth	fourth & fifth

Morris concludes, "*These are the seven proportions of rooms, which are founded upon the same rules as the Unison* [fundamental], *the Diapente* [octave], *the Diapason* [fifth], *the Sesqualter* [fourth], *& etc., are in music, and may be varied to all kinds of magnitudes whatever...*"[19]

Figure 27. An Expansion of the Tetrastyle Using the Octave, √2, and Ø

The tetrastyle may become a core or seed for larger compositions through horizontal and vertical expansion. The first modulation to be considered is the octaval ratio 2:1. This exercise sizes and places a tetrastyle portico within a double square by utilizing the √2 cut. The portico is constructed within a square using the method of **figure 10**. This example indicates an overlap, or interlocking, a kind of occult relationship between the √2 and Ø. The √2/2 is approximately equal to 7/10 and Ø/2 is approximately equal to 3/10. It also illustrates the interlocking of geometrical, arithmetical and harmonic ratio methods.

1. Set up square CDEF with center at G. Through G draw line AB parallel to CD. ABCD may be considered a double square with AD and BC = 1 and AB and CD = 2. With center at C and radius CG, draw arc GH. This interval = √2 = 1.414…. Repeat the procedure to find point J.

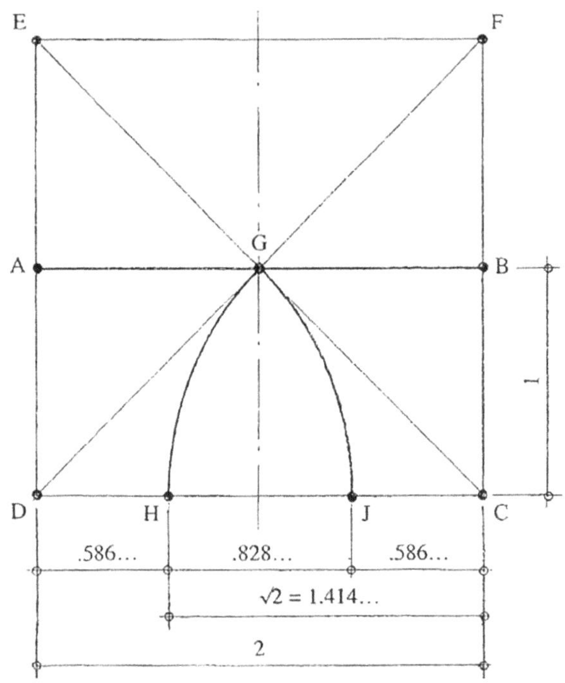

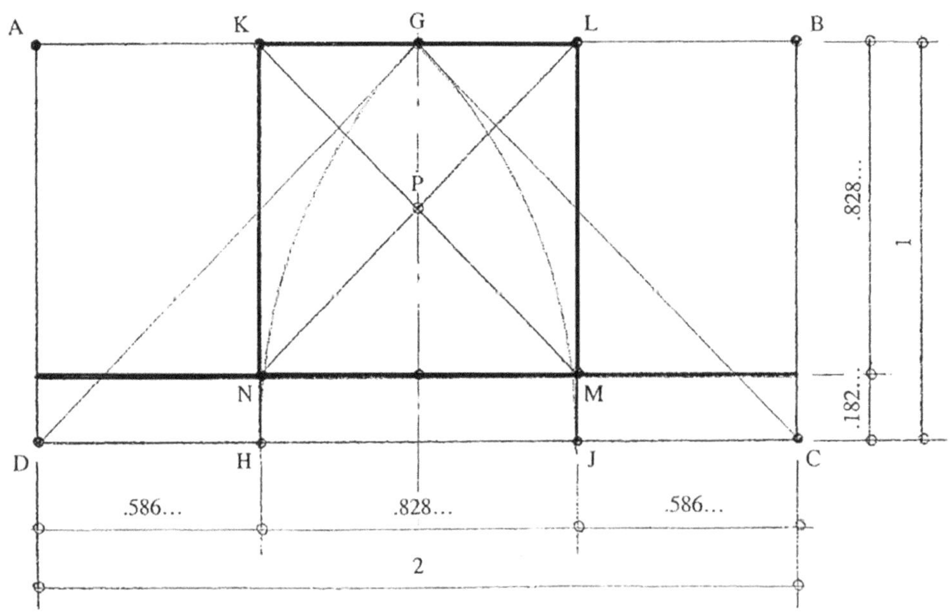

2. Draw lines HNK and JML. Draw square KLMN with center at P; extend MN to AD and BC. AB will be the top of the entablature, CD will be the ground, and MN the main floor level.

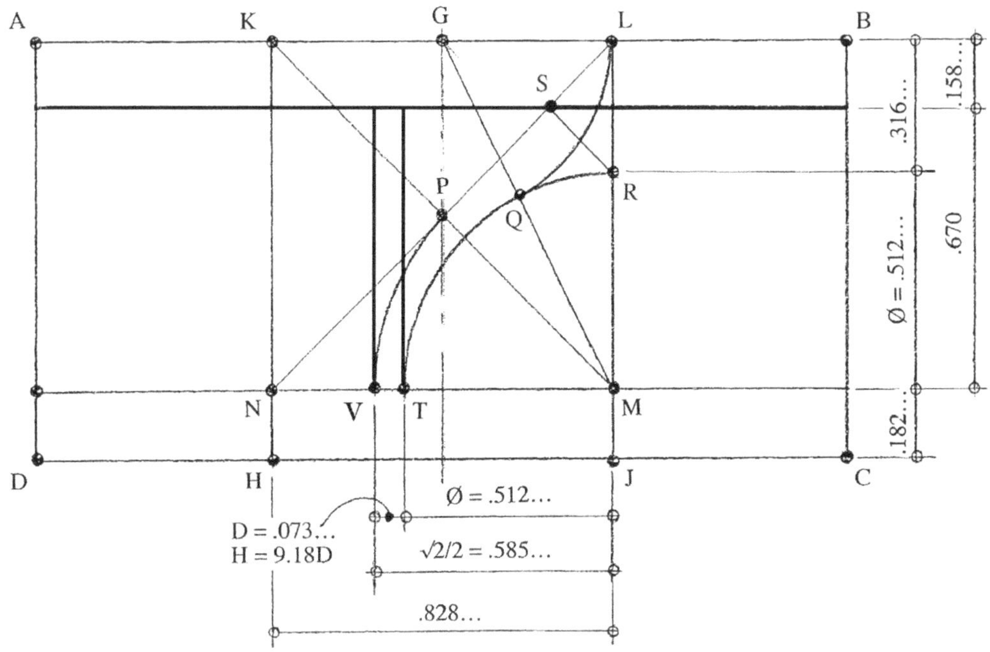

3. To size and place the elements of the portico we use the method of **figure 10.** Draw the semi-diagonal GM. With center at G draw arc LQ, with center at M draw arc QR. RM = Ø of LM. As LM = .828… of LJ then Ø = .512… of the overall height. Find point S midway on LR, marking the underside of the entablature. Extend arc QR to T and with center at M draw arc PV. MT = Ø of MN = .512… MV = √2/2 of MN = .585…. The interval VT= .073… is the column's lower diameter. As the height of the columns is .670, their height = 9.18 D.

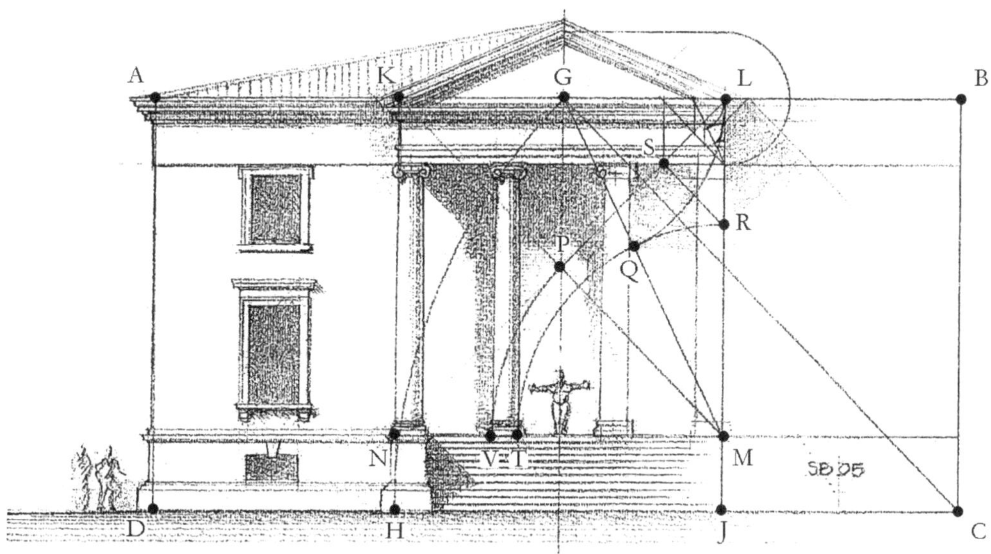

4. At the final stage the Ionic order is applied. The cornice is subdivided as in **figure 21**; $Ø^2$ of the entablature gives the cornice and $Ø^3$, or a slightly greater interval gives the architrave. The width of the window is 1/5 of the side bay. The first floor window is 2:1, the second floor is 6:5, and the basement is 1:2. Each window is ornamented in the character of the room it opens into. The exercise ends here as character depends on a specific program.

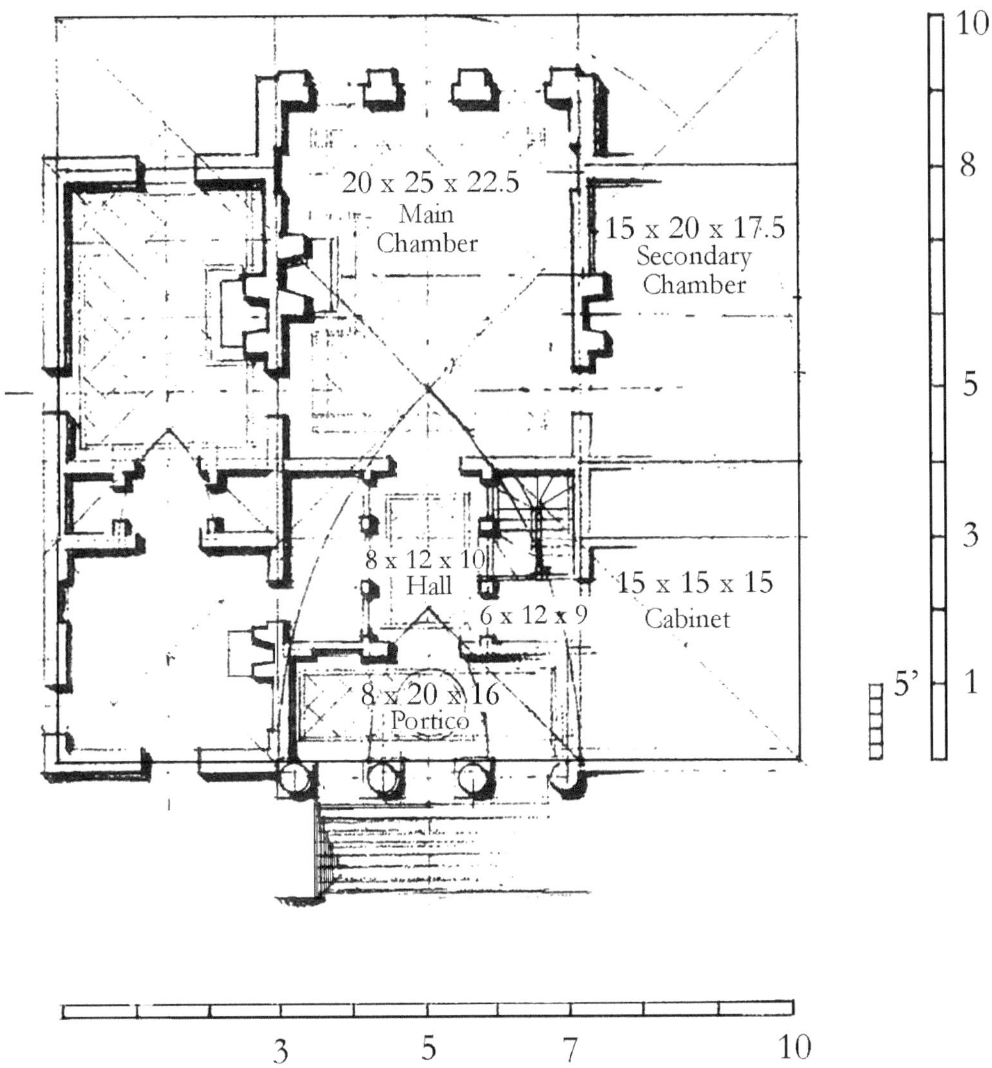

5. The plan of such a house is related to its elevation by the same patterns of division. The √2/2 cut that gives the portico width is carried through the plan providing a portico, interior hall and main chamber sequence. The right and left sides are divided into a secondary chamber, a utility area and a small chamber or cabinet. The utility area is in turn divided by the √2 pattern into a passage and two small spaces suitable for bathrooms, dressing space or closets.

Assuming a width of 50 feet, each of the 10 modules is 5 feet in length. The rooms are shaped by harmonic ratios: the main chamber is 20 x 25 feet. Its arithmetic ratio or average gives a 22.5-foot ceiling height. As the exterior cornice line is 20 feet, some part of the ceiling will penetrate above it. There are many designs that could accommodate this and its high point could be lowered a bit by using the harmonic ratio of the length and width instead of the Arithmetic. The secondary chambers are 15 x 20 x 17.5. The cabinet is 15 x 15 feet; its ceiling could be 15 feet high but if a second story is desired this could be lowered to 12 or even 10 feet while still maintaining some harmonic relations of the dimensions. Here we enter the larger realm of design, where proportion is the tool, not the decider.

6. Here we see a transition, or transformation of the three methods — geometric, arithmetic and harmonic — into and through one another. Interval DC = 2, DP = CP = BC = 1. DJ = √2 = 1.414…, leaving a remaining interval JC = .585… Ø of BC = CN = .618… Thus the overlap = .033 is less than 2% of the overall length CD. The location of the transition, interval NJ, contains the 2/5 + 3/5 point of CP.

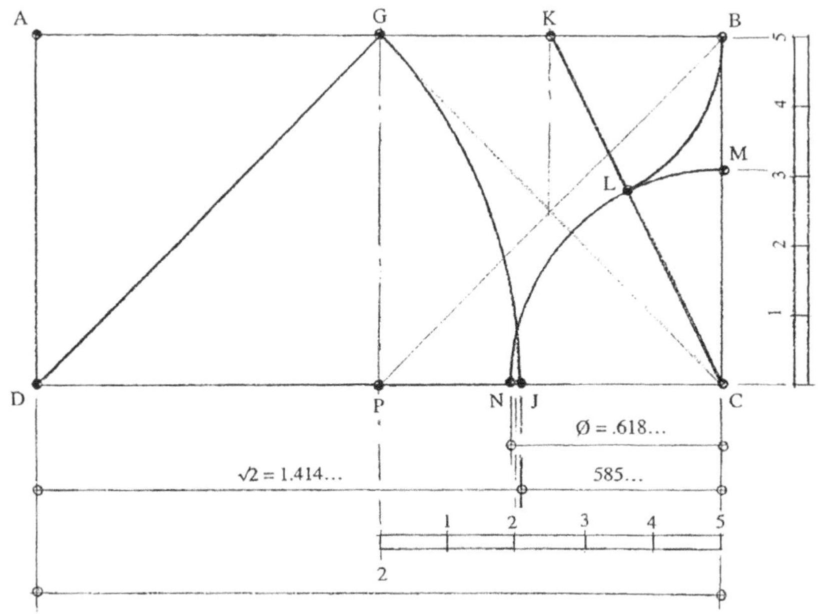

7. DC may now be divided into 10 units, BC into 5. Guided by the points of overlap, redesignated H and J, we see ABCD divided into a 3 – 4 – 3 pattern with a predominant 4:5 rectangle JHKL and two supporting 3:5 rectangles AKHD and BCJL.

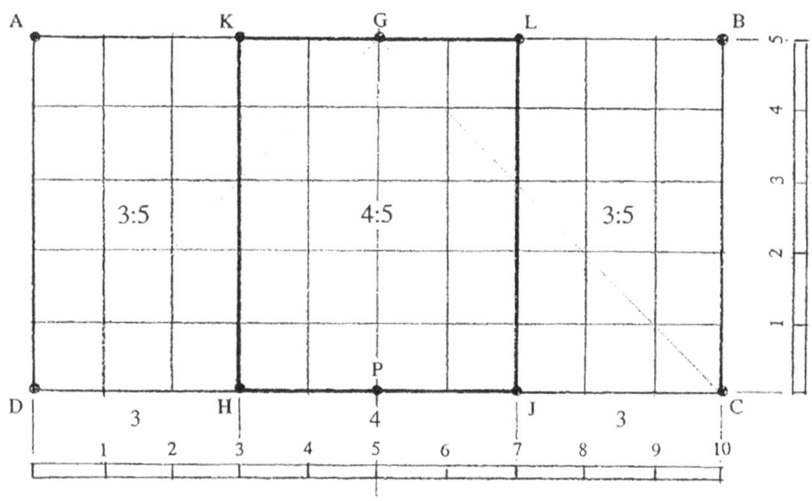

8. A tetrastyle centerpiece may now be placed within 4x4 square KLMN. It is raised on a base 1 unit x 4, a double octave. The side wings are 3x4 rectangles, each on a 1x3 base, an octave and a fifth. To define the elements of the portico arithmetically each unit is divided into 6 parts, totaling 24. Set the inner column centers at 8 and 16 units, which is a crossover point to the geometry of the octave in **figure 2**. If lower D is 2 units the column height = 9.5 D = 19 units and an entablature of 4.75 ≈ 5 units. For a more elegant character raise the columns 1 unit to 20 with 4 to the entablature.

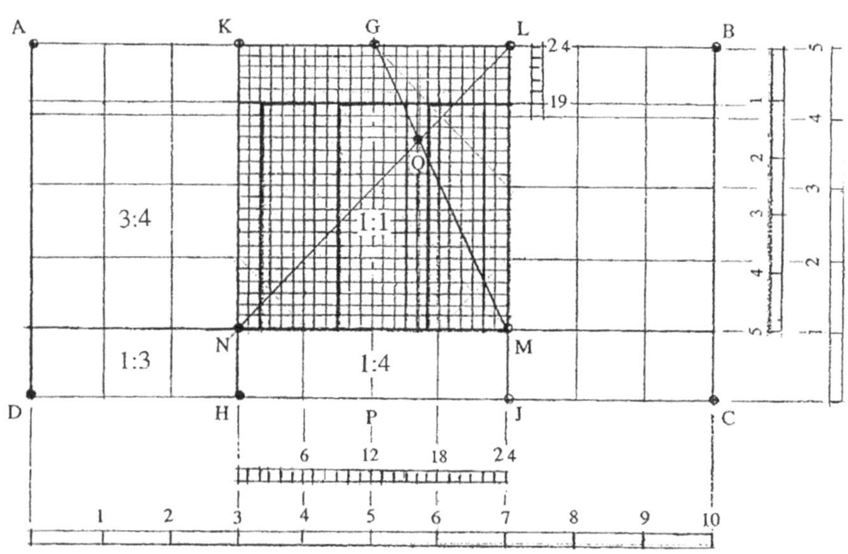

Figure 28. An Expansion of the Hexastyle Using Ø and the Double Square

This exercise places a double square within another double square. The hexastyle colonnade is quided by the double square and divided by Ø as in **figure 13**.

1. Begin with 2:1 rectangle ABCD. FC = 1. Find point J using the procedure of **figure 6b**, FJ = Ø = .618..., JC = Ø² = .382.... Find point K halfway between J and C.

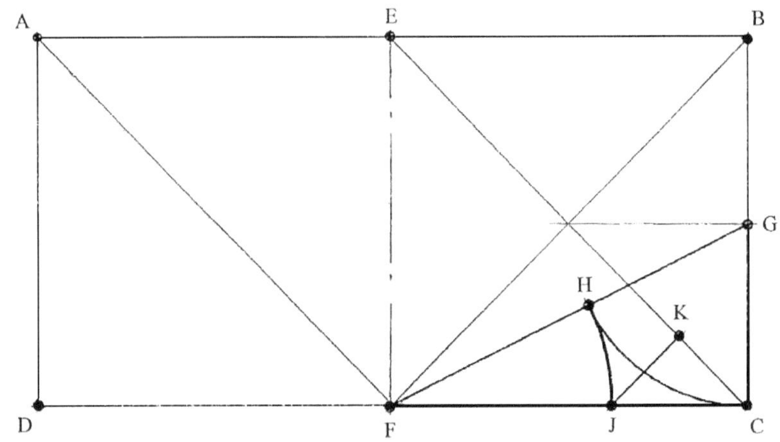

2. Draw LN through K. Where LN intersects FB draw line QM, where QM intersects AF draw line PQR. FN = [1+Ø]/2 = .809... and NC = Ø² = .191... We have placed Ø rectangle PLNR within octaval rectangle ABCD. Because AF and FB are semi-diagonals of ABCD, QMNR is another double square.

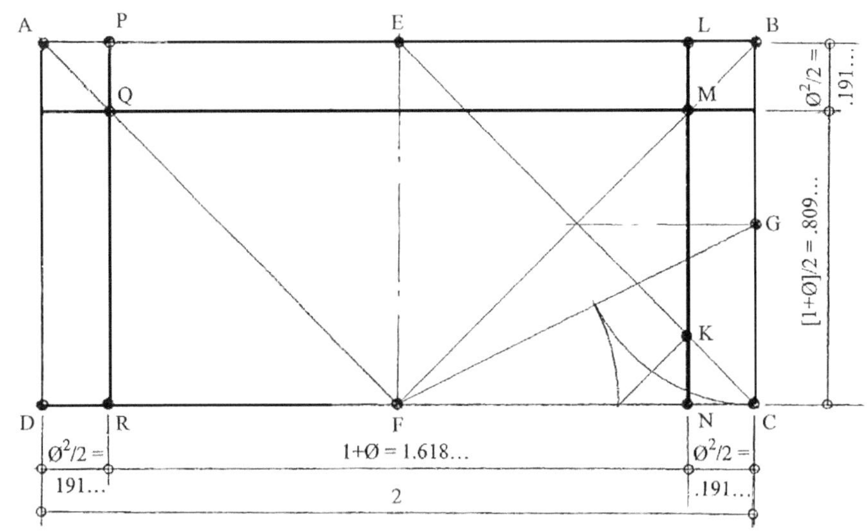

3. To size and place the columns apply the Ø scale procedure of **figure 9** to double square QMNR. MS = Ø, QS = Ø². Because of the arithmetic of Ø, QS = MT = Ø² and ST, which is centered on EF, = Ø³. S and T are the centers of the inner columns.

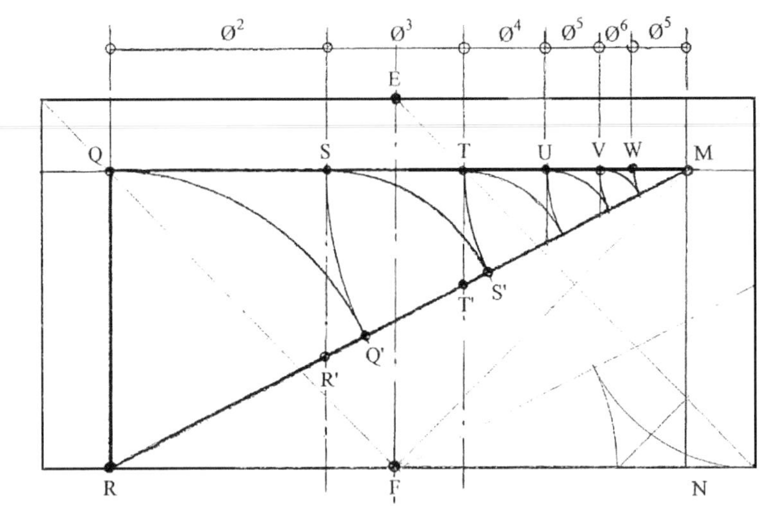

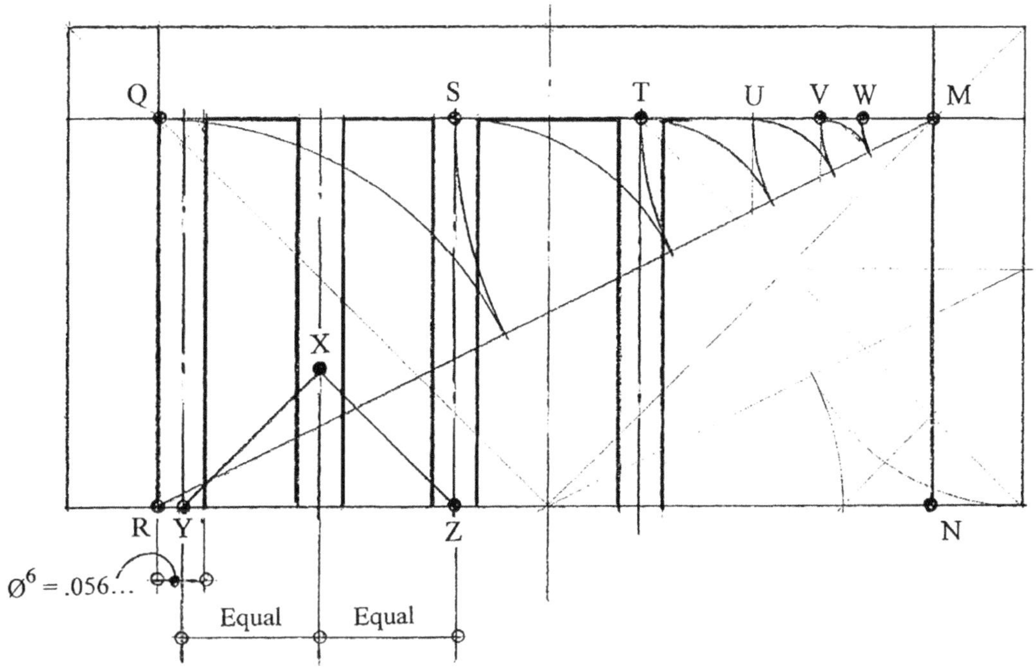

4. Taking QM as 1, lower D = VW = $Ø^6$ = .056..., QS = $Ø^2$ = .382..., interval YZ = . 382... - .028... = .354..., divided by 2 to find point X, center of the second column = .177.... The intercolumniation is .121... or a little less than the canonical 2.25. The central intercolumniation = .0236... - .056... = .180, which is 3.2 D, slightly greater than the canonical 3.

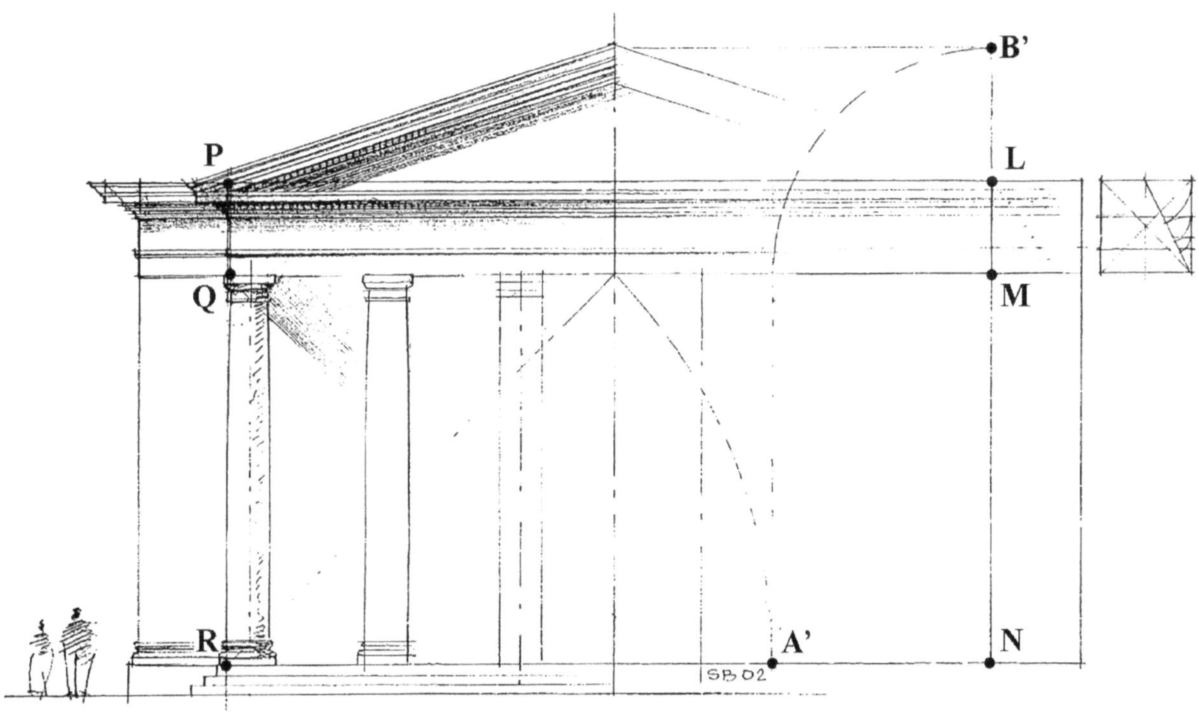

5. Articulate the entablature using a Ø scale and add a base of about 1/16th of the overall height. The height of the pediment may be found by taking the interval RN = 1.618... x √2 = 1.144... = RA'. Subtracting 1.618 - 1.144 = .474 = A'N. Apply this interval on the extension of NM to find B'. Subtracting .191, LM, = .283 from the top of the cornice to the top of the cyma, B'L.

Figure 29. The "Pillar" of Egypt

The ancient Egyptians expressed the idea of ratio in the image of the "pillar"[20]; that is to say, the ratio 2:1 may be seen as a right triangle whose base is 1 and altitude is 2. The pillar is discussed further in Section III. Here it is used as a method of dividing an interval into a variety of fractional parts. In this example the 2:1 pillar is set in the square although any ratio would produce similar results. The pillar was symbolized on the "royal apron" worn by the king, **figure 29a**, in the scene depicting the "stretching of the cord" for the foundation of a temple. On the left is the goddess Seshat, keeper of the cord and the "plan-net." The radiating lines on the pyramid-shaped apron are interrupted by a staircase formed by the interweaving of two cobras.

29a - The King and Seshat Stretching the Cord

1. Begin with square ABCD, center at E. Points F and G mark the centers of the sides of ABCD. Where AC and FG intersect find point H. Draw line HJ parallel to AB. Point J marks the 1/4 point of height AD. Draw semi-diagonal DF to find point K.

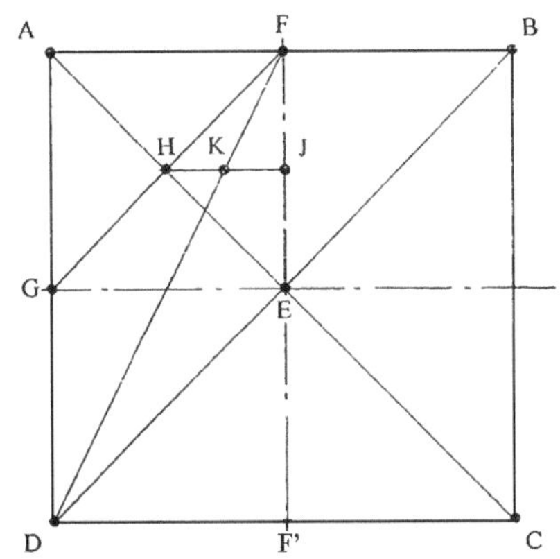

2. Draw line CJ to intersect DF at L and draw line LM parallel to AB. Draw line CK and mark point N on centerline FF', then draw line NP parallel to AB. Repeat this procedure three more times to find QR, ST and UV.

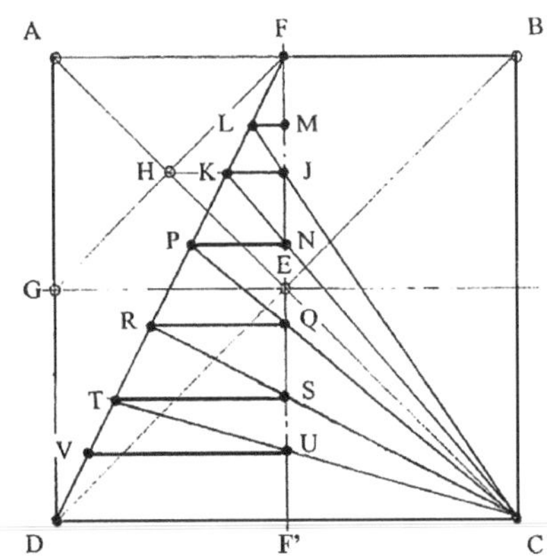

3. Draw semi-diagonal CF. Where it intersects diagonal DB mark point W and draw line WX parallel to AB. Mark point Y at the intersection of CF and the extension of centerline EG. Draw line DY and mark point Z on centerline FF'. Draw line ZA' parallel to AB. Repeat this two more times to find B'C' and D'E'.

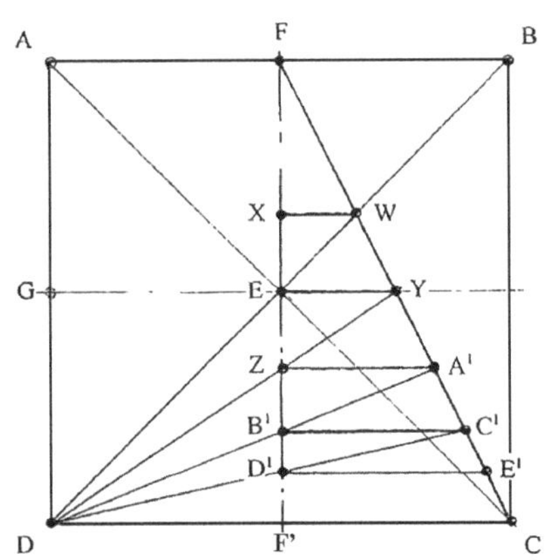

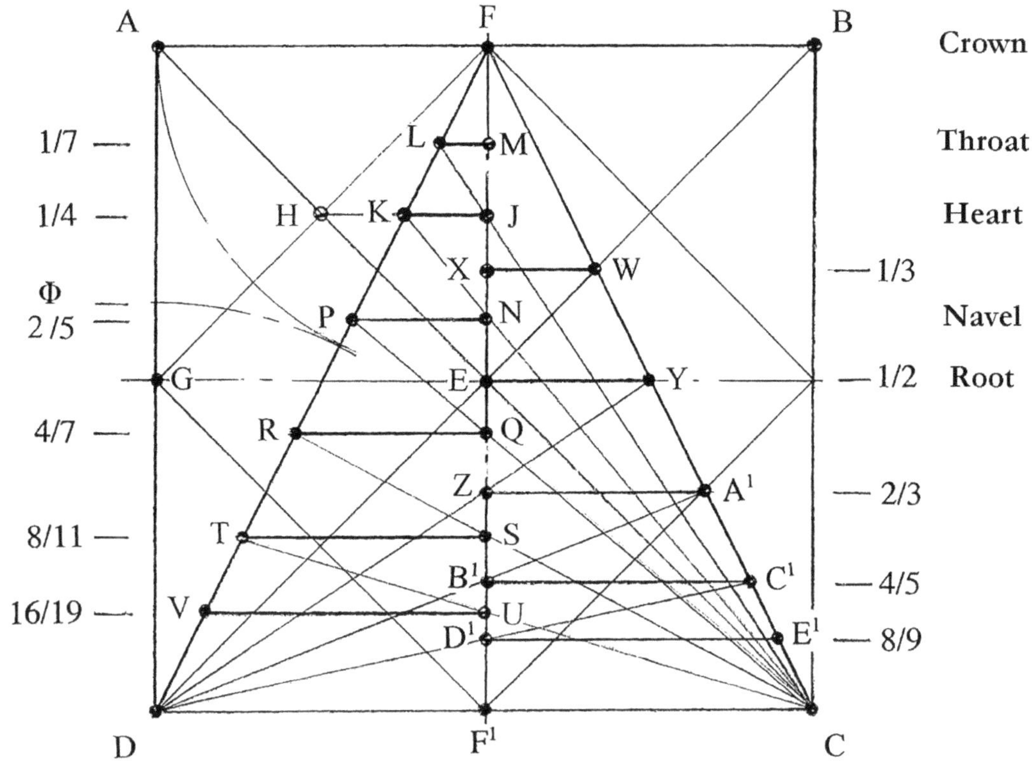

4. Combine the previous steps. On the left are listed the fractional parts beginning with the 1/4 point. On the right are the intervals that begin from the 1/3 point. On the left is indicated the geometric position of the Ø ratio.

The pillar is cited by Robert Lawlor[21] as a method of determining harmonic means. For example if the interval FF' is divided into 12, FE = 6, then FZ = 8, the harmonic mean between 6 and 12. This diagram is similar to the "Helikon" of **figure 2** on which the musical octave is derived. The square on its point is the symbol of materialization, the last stage in our myth of creation in **figure 1**.

On the left of the illustration we note that if a person's height is equal to BC, then F, M, J, N and E mark respectively the Crown, Throat, Heart, Navel and Root "chakras." Also note that 3/19ths is the depth of an entablature in an order with a pedestal and 1/5 is the depth of the pedestal, as in **figure 17**.

Figure 30. Vertical Expansion
A Portico with a Steeple Using the Pillar

This didactic example sets the vertical and horizontal divisions of a steeple using a variant of the pillar.

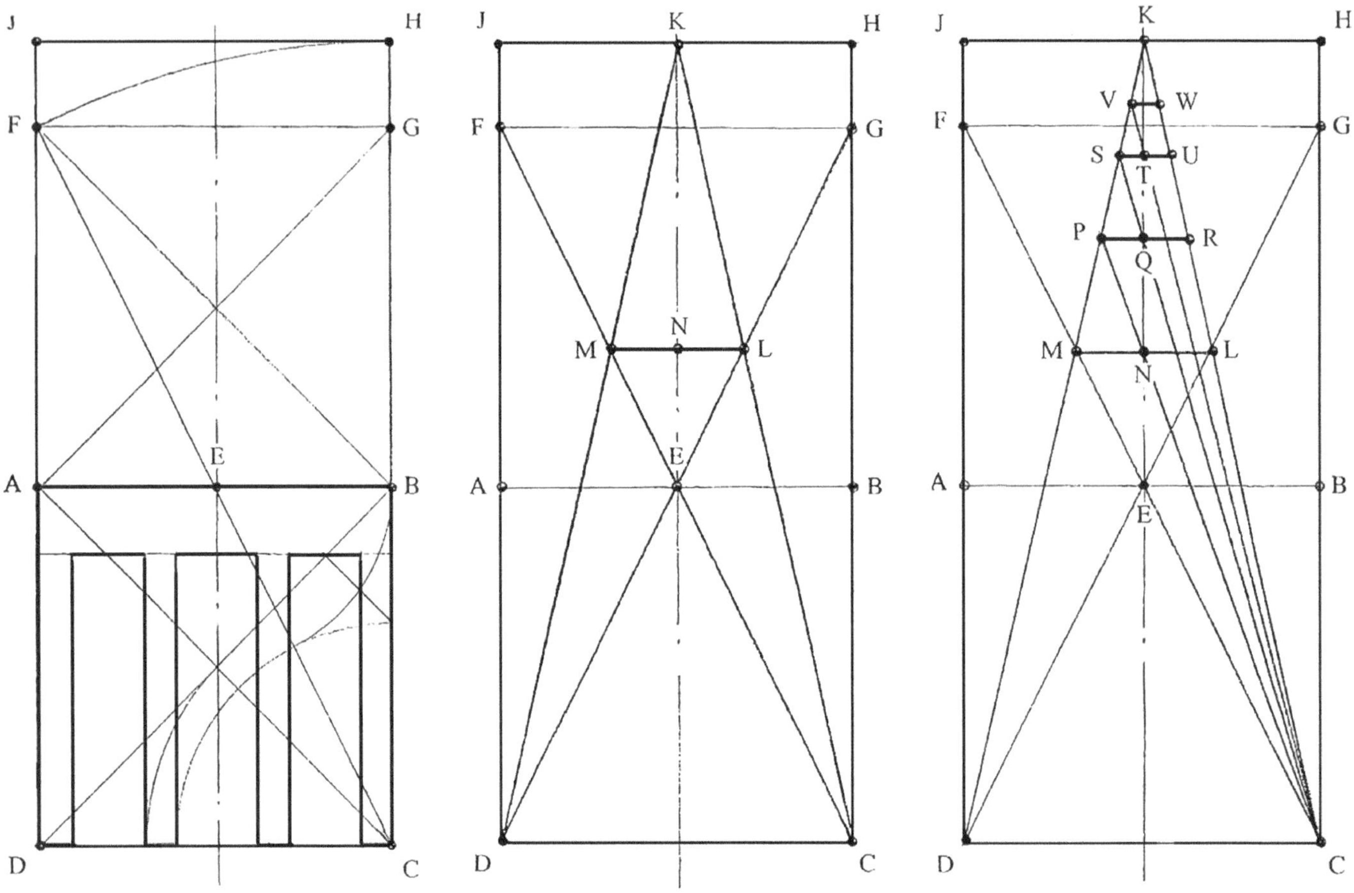

1 2 3

1. Given square ABCD with point E at the midpoint of AB. Create a portico within the square by the method of **figure 10.** To frame the steeple construct a √5 rectangle, selected for its elegant verticality. This will be our representative of unity. Extend semi-diagonal EC and side AD to meet at F. With center at C and radius CF draw arc FH. Rectangle JHCD is a √5 rectangle

2. Point K is the center of JH. Draw semi-diagonals KC and KD. Where they intersect at M draw line MNL parallel to AB. This relationship between the semi-diagonals of the square and those of the √5 rectangle will "set the tone," or pattern of division, for the steeple.

3. Draw line CN; and extend to meet KD at P. Draw PRQ parallel to AB. Continue this pattern to find points S and V. These points will mark the "steps" of the steeple.

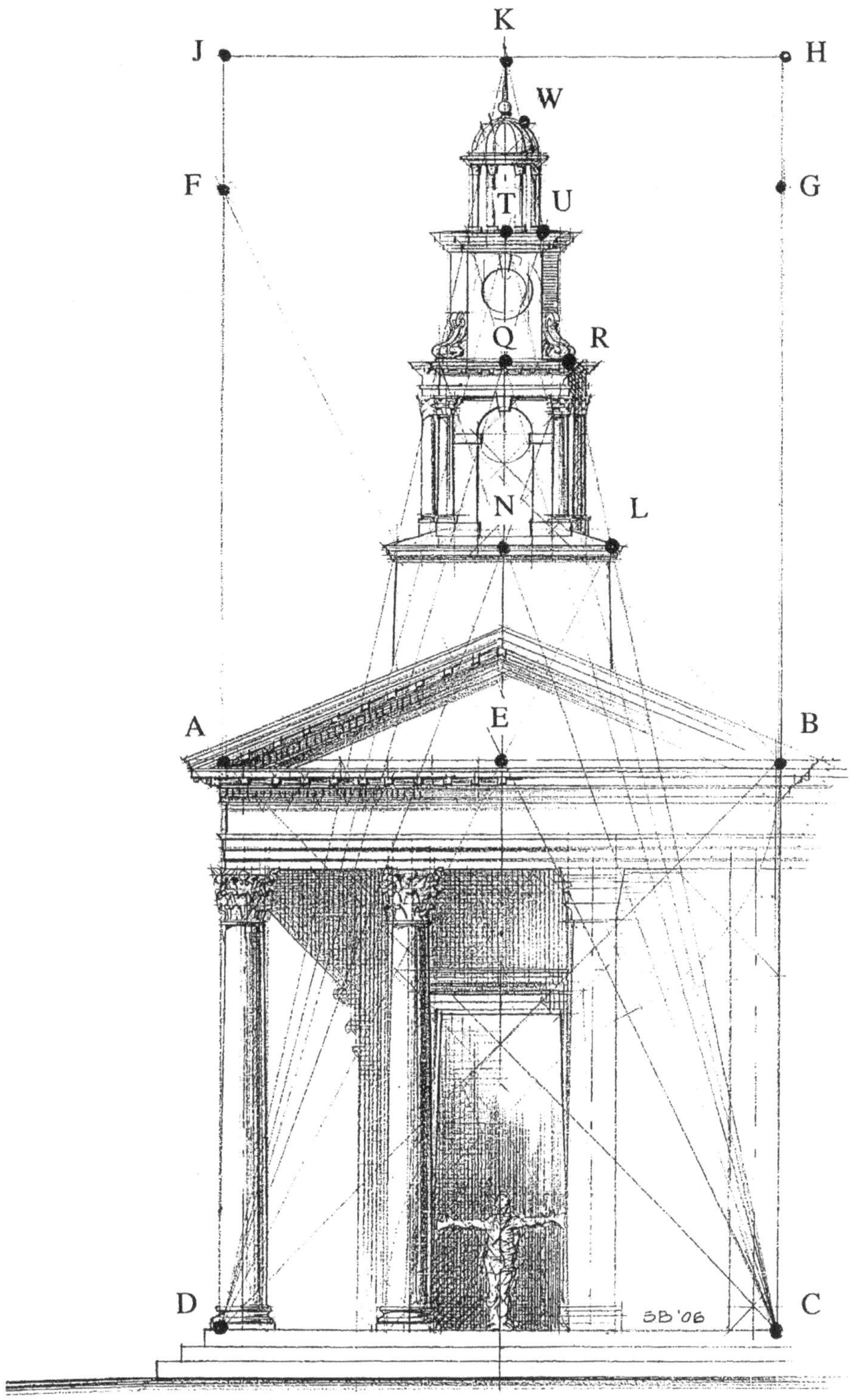

4. The completed elevation. The geometrical method used here is "impure" in the sense that we have not used the diagonals and semi-diagonals of the same rectangle but of two related ones. This grew from the wish to interrelate the semi-diagonals of the square, which give us the portico, and the "pillar," which is "extended" upward beyond the double square. Had we used the double square, or raised point E by using CJ instead of CF, the steeple would have been slimmer.

Figure 31. Geometric Rectangles of Hambidge

In his 1948 book *Elements of Dynamic Symmetry,* artist and analyst Jay Hambidge[22] based on his study of Greek art, particularly vases, proposes that a family of mathematically related rectangles was utilized by ancient designers. Hambidge begins by constructing a series of building blocks or "basic rectangles" also known as the root rectangle series starting with the square, **figure 5a.** Although the root rectangle series could continue indefinitely, Hambidge and the design tradition in general have not found it necessary to go beyond √5 most likely because it is a source of the Golden Section. For Hambidge, using a series based on rational, whole number ratios creates a static symmetry, whereas using a group of rectangles based on the trans-rational ratios, Ø in particular, creates a "dynamic symmetry."

Hambidge also emphasizes the use of the reciprocals of the root rectangles, **figure 5e**. To obtain a "reciprocal" invert the ratio of the sides; that is, if the short side of a rectangle is 1 and the long side is 2, if we set the long side equal to 1 the short side is now equal to 1/2; or if the sides are 1 and √2 the reciprocal is 1: 1/√2, or .707.... The reciprocal of the √3 rectangle is 1 : 1/√3 or .557...; of the √5 is 1 : 1/√5 or .447.... The reciprocal of a Ø rectangle is another Ø rectangle because 1 : .618... = 1.618... : 1. The square is its own reciprocal.

To fill out his family of related rectangles Hambidge focuses on the Ø and √5 rectangles suggesting what might be called "basic operations," essentially either doubling a rectangle and its reciprocal, or adding a square to them. The rectangles in **figure 31** include the angle made by the diagonal and the base of each rectangle. Setting an adjustable triangle to that particular angle, a set of "proportional" rectangles and reciprocals may be drawn.

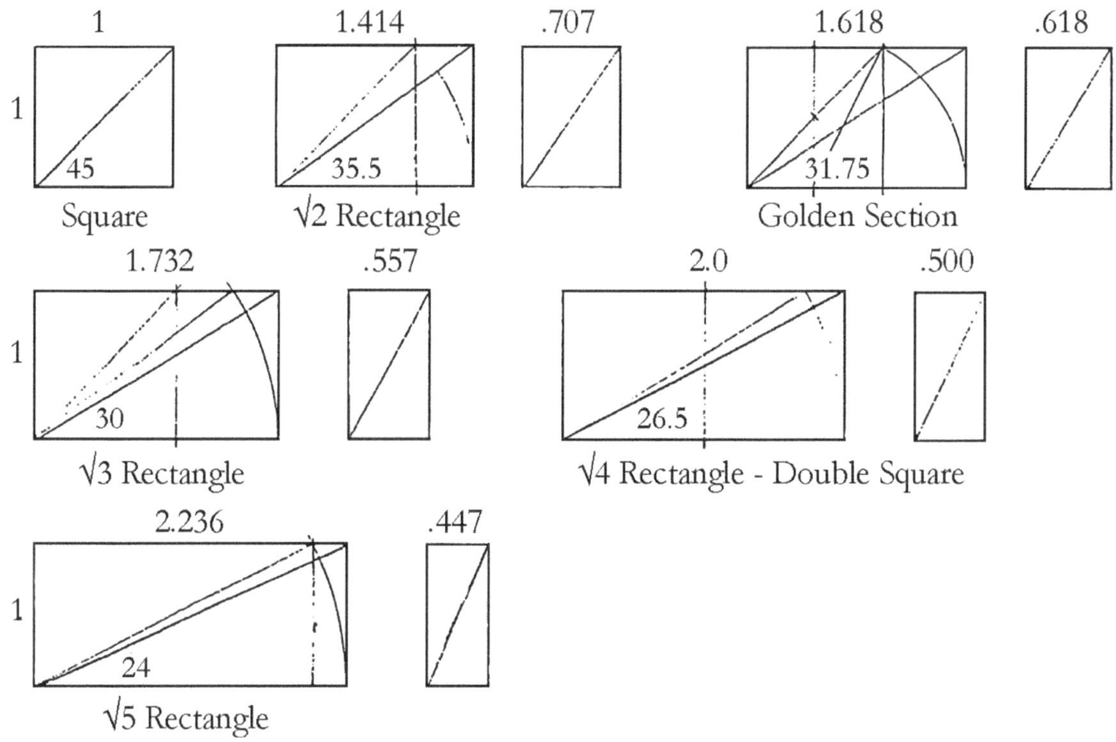

Basic Rectangles - the Root System and Phi

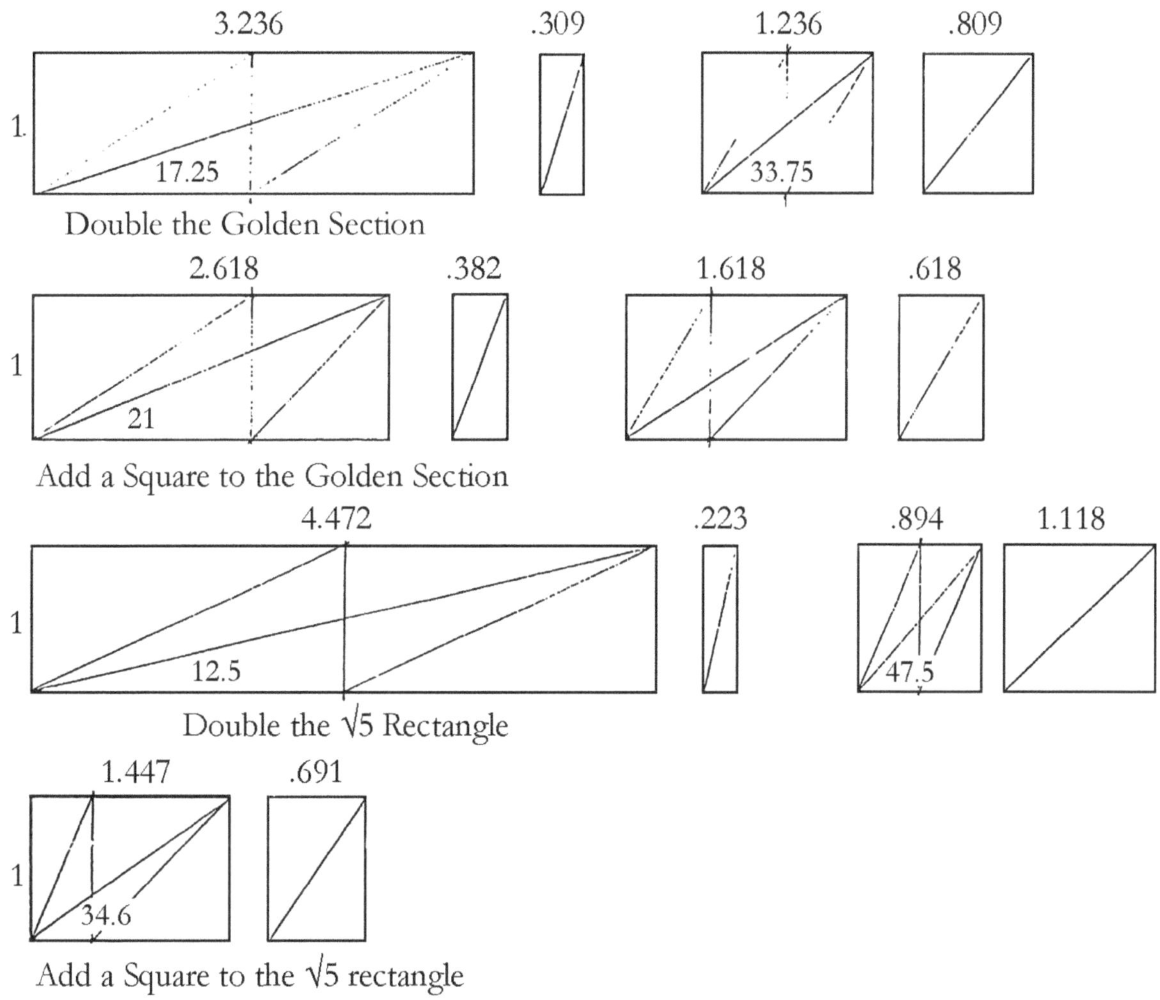

Basic Operations - Add a Square

Figure 32. Division of the Frame

In *The Painter's Secret Geometry,* author Charles Bouleau[23] proposes a number of traditional methods of division of the frame for pictorial composition. Like other methods in this section they are various ways of achieving the same thing — a sense of unity in the finished work. To this end they can be mixed, matched or modified to produce the desired result.

Geometrical Division. The most basic geometrical division of the frame is by its diagonals and semi-diagonals. This method which has been used throughout this section "naturally" divides any interval into parts that are multiples of 2 and 3, such as halves, thirds, quarters, sixths, eighths, ninths, twelfths, etc. In the method called "rabatment," the short side of the frame is "squared up," in effect the short side of the frame is subtracted from the long side. This is a simple yet powerful compositional technique as it divides the frame into unity, a square, and a remainder related to the frame through unity. Another geometrical method is to divide the sides of the frame into similar ratios such as Ø, shown here, or any ratio.

Arithmetic Division. The sides of the frame may be divided into the same number of parts, then the grid will be of rectangles "proportional," that is, in the same ratio as the frame itself. Alternately, one side of the frame may be divided into any number and a grid of squares constructed.

Musical Division. Though there may be many methods of applying the musical intervals to division of the frame, suggested here is a very basic approach of treating the long side of the frame as an octave interval and marking off the 4th and 5th note positions, in this case the 1/2 and 1/3 points of the interval; which may also be found geometrically.

Geometrical Division

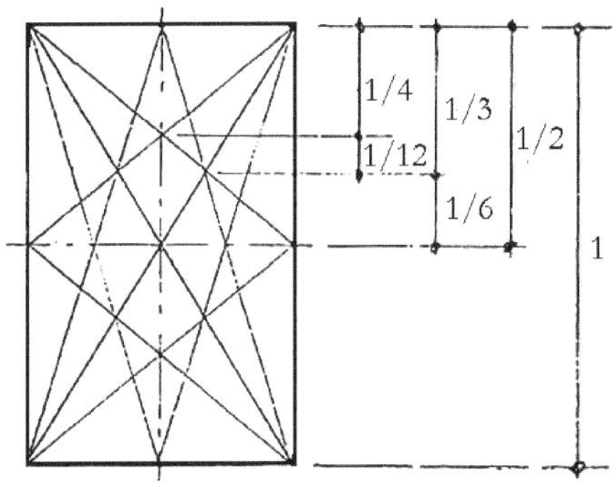

Divide by Diagonals
& Semi-diagonals

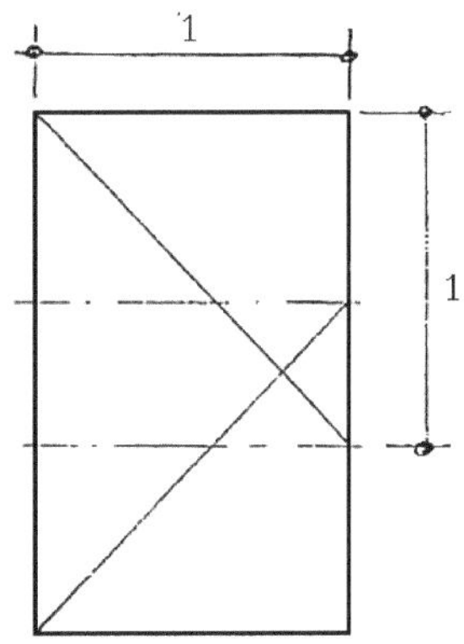

Rabatment -
Placing a Square

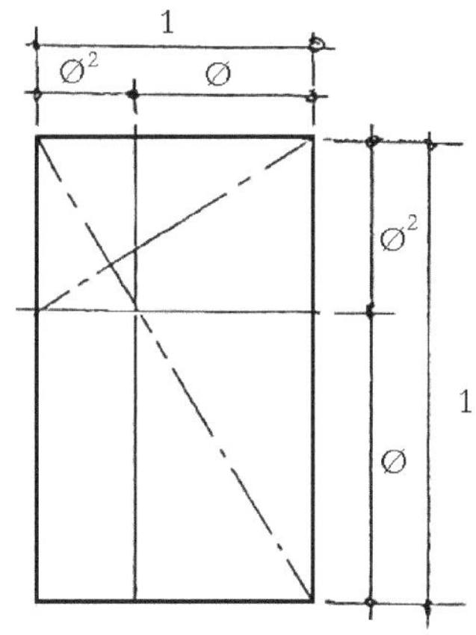

Divide the Sides
into the Same Ratio

Arithmetic Division

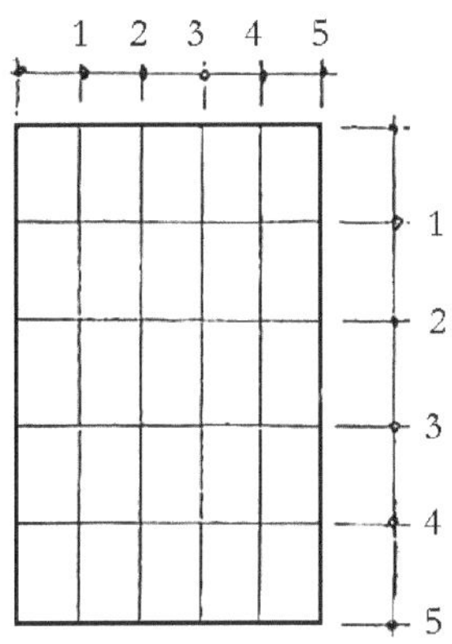

Divide the Sides
into the Same
Number of Parts

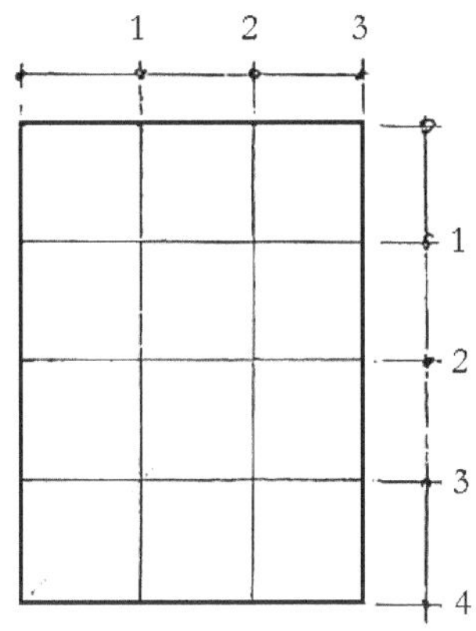

Divide into Square Modules
the Regular Grid

Musical Division

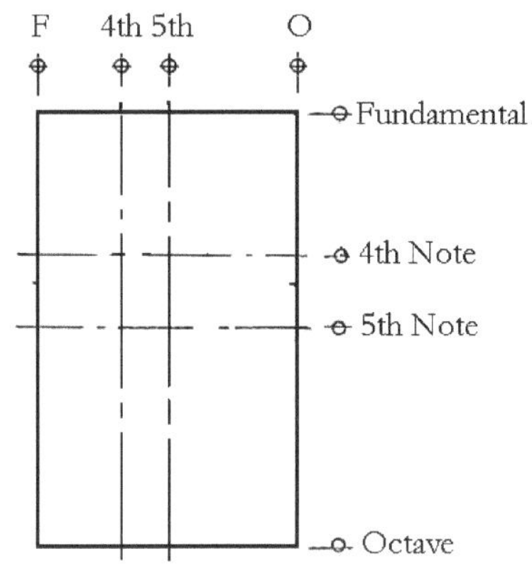

Divide at Nodal Points

III

PROPORTION IN PRACTICE

Introduction

History

PROPORTION IN CLASSICAL ART consists of the use of number and geometry as design tools. Described here is a theory of the nature of proportion in architecture rooted in the philosophical systems of the Pythagoreans, Plato, and certain later ancient philosophers such as Nicomachus, Iamblichus, Plotinus, and Proclus, known as Neoplatonists. These systems, in turn, utilize number in symbolic form to represent ontological states of being and relationship. In these systems the multiplicity of the physical world emerges or develops in stages from a state of transcendent unity. In such a system it is our spiritual challenge to realize the presence of that unity within ourselves, leading to an experience of re-ascension, a return to unity.

A key ally in the search for unity is beauty, said by Plotinus to be the joyous state of the psyche as it is reminded of its relation to transcendental unity. This reminding or anamnesis as Plato calls it, stimulates Eros, the desire to join or be one with the object of beauty. As unity is associated by Plato with beauty and the good, creating objects in a way that allows for the experience of the beautiful is acting for the good. Such relationships, however, can only be exerted or be meaningful in a cosmos that is constructed by analogy, whose parts respond through sympathetic resonance, and whose structure complies to the Hermetic maxim "as above, so below."

Methods of application of the proportional idea to the elements of classical architecture fall into three general categories: geometrical construction, arithmetical division, and harmonic ratios. The relation of these methods to ancient philosophical tradition establishes that the numerical and geometrical descriptions of the classical elements in the various canons are neither arbitrary, random nor superstitious, but rather may be used as keys to allowing the experience of the beautiful, the beginning of the journey of return.

The experience of beauty takes place within the individual. It is an experience of the psyche, the soul. Thus beauty is not in the object of perception or in its measures. In this context the canon becomes the starting point in the search for beauty and should not be confused with the beautiful itself, which is a state of the psyche that the canon is meant to help us induce. The canon is the starting point for design not its endpoint. Its visual forms need to be fully integrated by the designer so that invention or particularization can be achieved.

The theme of this section will be to follow the proportional idea through certain historical moments, looking at selected architectural examples. The goal is not to write a comprehensive history but to seek the presence and expression of the proportional idea, to make it available to designers in the present moment. To do this it is necessary to look, however briefly, at the extension and support of the proportional idea in philosophical and spiritual traditions.

Though the section is set up in roughly chronological sequence this is only a matter of convenience. The reader should not suppose that it is necessary to connect the visual or geometric concepts historically in order to establish their validity. In the view advocated here, proportional concepts spring from the human imagination. Their source is in a noetic, formal or ideal realm, a metaphysical state, the ultimate ground of knowledge in the Platonic system. All human beings have access to this realm all the time through the faculty of the imagination. The imagination is that aspect of psyche through which we contact the noetic entities and project them into consciousness.

Nothing stated here is meant to contribute to any kind of "historicism." By this is meant the reductionist notion that the manner of building in a certain time and place can be treated in a static, isolated way, like a stuffed creature in a display case, as something out there, lifeless, to be looked at but not touched. The classical tradition is treated here as a single living entity, a noetic entity, accessible through the imagination. The elements and archetypal compositions exist there in disembodied archetypal form. The designer's task is to enter this timeless realm and select the elements and relationships related to their particular issue in the moment. Of necessity, since physicality is by definition in constant change, the built solutions will always be unique.

Where historical documentation exists it may be cited in support of the proportional concept. But if proportional theory and esoteric philosophy are approaching a kind of truth, or correct description, then we should expect to find similar principles enunciated across geographic and temporal boundaries. For example, the pre-Columbian Maya and ancient Egyptians both used the pyramidal form for monumental buildings yet there is no established actual connection between them. Indeed, the two civilizations were not only divided by an ocean but by three millennia. In the terms used here the Maya and Egyptians were drawing from the same transcendental sources to solve a similar architectonic problem: the expression of hieratic order in stone.

Analysis and Synthesis

The presence of proportion will be sought in historical examples by a combination of analysis and synthesis. The search begins by applying various geometric constructions, arithmetic divisions and harmonic ratios to the plan, elevation and/or section of the building in question. The relevance of these factors to key aspects of the building's structure and elements can then be evaluated. For the sake of brevity not every possible variant of the methods will, or even could, be illustrated, just those with the most likely chance of having been employed or of being employed today.

From this analysis a possible method of synthesis is suggested. To establish that the method could have been utilized, it is made the basis of a reconstruction of the analyzed building. However, not all the constructive steps can be illustrated for every example. In some examples the analysis will be shown, others will be reconstructed in stages, and for some just the completed reconstruction will be presented.

There are many possible pathways to the designs analyzed. The ones shown here are the result of this author's journey through the material and are not meant to be exclusive or preemptive. They are not the only way to achieve the designs in question, but have been thought "most likely" by the author. The reader is urged to draw these reconstructions in the interest of determining their own view of the proportional landscape, remembering that design is an artistic process rather than a reductionist one.

In premodern times many, though not all, aspects of proportional methodology were held in private. Traditionally, artists and architects were not intellectuals. They learned what they knew by actual experience and regular practice in studios, shops or on building sites. In many cases the proportional techniques would have been couched in mythic terms, perhaps presented to the artisan in an initiatic context.

As professional design emerged in the post-medieval world, elements of proportional theory and method were widely published for the first time, but these were only its rationalized, outward aspects, presented in a mathematical context. Since the so-called Enlightenment, proportion's metaphysical underpinnings have been marginalized or denied outright by mainstream thought. Thus proportion, denied a "rational" foundation, never achieved the status of an independent academic subject in the pedagogy of the École des Beaux-Arts and other institutions. It was taught "on the board" so to speak, in the shop or studio, and not necessarily by noblemen, intellectuals or celebrated architects but often by artisans who had learned it in practice.[1]

In applying the methods of proportion to analysis and synthesis we are not looking for the "right answer" to a mathematical formula. What is sought is a "workmanlike" method, a pathway from unity to multiplicity that could credibly have been used by a designer, an artisan or a builder in their own day. A workmanlike method would be one that is as direct as possible, having the fewest number of steps or stages; with each step having a discernible motive and outcome. This applies the principle of Occam's razor; which cuts away the unnecessary parts of a theory or argument and asserts that the least complex answer or structure is the most probable. It is a logical method but not necessarily a reductionist one.

There might be an indefinite number of such proportional pathways to a given design. In the symbolic realm there are no absolute answers, only degrees of affinity or remembrance; therefore no proof of anything is claimed here. Nor is there a claim to have reproduced exactly any particular work of the past. Rather the attempt is to assist designers with the tasks at hand in the present moment. It is not claimed to know what went on in anyone's mind centuries ago, unless a specific written or graphic record was left behind. The present work may be considered an exercise in comparative symbolism; the reader must decide on the usefulness, in the present moment, of the methods described.

The best way to assess their value is to treat the constructions presented here as workbook exercises. Perform them yourself, draw them with instruments and freehand to experience the psycho-physiological effects. Such work creates an integration that opens the imagination to the presence of the noetic entities, including proportional entities.

Process

The process of applying proportion to design may be conceptually seen in four steps or stages, comprising an ontogeny of Unity, Division, Structure and Manifestation. 1) Establish a symbolic representative of unity, usually a regular polygon. 2) Divide unity in a way that establishes a key pattern, usually related to either arithmetic units, musical ratios, or geometrical construction, the latter most often using functions related to $\sqrt{2}$, $\sqrt{3}$, $\sqrt{5}$, and especially Ø. 3) Further divide by the same or an allied method to position and size the major elements of the design. 4) Fully materialize the design by defining the elements in detail and ornamenting them, if possible by again applying the key pattern or, if necessary, by making slight adjustments. These steps may be summed up as:

Step 1. Establish a relationship to unity.
Step 2. Divide unity by a key relationship or pattern.
Step 3. Define the size and location of the major elements of structure.
Step 4. Complete the materialization by detailing the elements and developing the ornaments.

This process will be used for both analysis and synthesis. Usually the key measure of unity will be taken as the width of the building. This will form the side of a square, equilateral triangle or pentagon. This polygon will then be subdivided, or sometimes expanded, by one or more of the arithmetic, geometric, or harmonic ratio methods. One must then make a judgment as to the precision of the relationship of the method chosen to the image being analyzed. Remember that more than one method may succeed in "explaining" the design.

A useful method to help avoid finding what one is looking for is to attempt to reconstruct the design on the drawing board through a re-enactment of the application of the geometrical idea that is hypothesized to be present. Such a procedure is intended to produce a concrete result: a geometrically accurate drawing that can be numerically, or at least consistently, compared to the original drawing or built work with the goal of either confirming the hypothesis or generating a new one. If dimensions of the building are available they can be mathematically analyzed to ascertain their relation to the proposed proportional method. This allows for a kind of reproducibility: someone else should be able to follow the same steps and come to the same result.

Toward an Ancient Science of Design

The reader must judge if the methods used here are anything more than the personal idiosyncrasies of this author or are acceptable as an introduction to a kind of "science." The author's personal or symbolic speculations need be taken as nothing more than that. The attempt here is to reclaim some part of what is taken to be an ancient "science" of design. This is not a modern, reductionist science; rather, a science more like that of Goethe, that is describable, measurable, and reproducible, but is not reductionist or even entirely materialistic. It is, in the ancient sense, a logically organized and developed form of study, but it is not limited by these aspects.

In such a context the question may fairly be raised, "how rational is rational?"; or "how close is close enough?" We must also respond to the "fat pencil" criticism of proportional methods; and to the issue of finding what we seek. In our analysis a difference of up to 5% is considered a likely match. With Ø for example, the ratio .618/1 (For the sake of brevity the three dots [...] for transcendentals will be omitted in this section of the book.) may be considered as equivalent to the ratio 6/10 as these differ by only .018 or 1.8%. The difference between √2/2, .707, and 7/10 is only .07% but the difference between .707 and 3/4, .750, is right at the margin, 4.9%; and it becomes a matter of context if one or the other of these marks more significant points on the object.

There are those who refuse to accept the notion that .618 could be taken as equivalent to 6/10. Such persons are asked to keep in mind that, literally, design is not rocket science and that in considering the symbolic we are in a realm where 2 + 2 does not always and inevitably make 4. For our purposes here design is closer to a kind of illusionism than it is to mathematics. The goal of design is to create what might be called the vitalistic illusion; that the object reminds us of something alive, that is to say, something unified.

This vitalistic illusion may be accomplished on an abstract or mass level by the use of geometrical shapes or harmonic ratios, and on the detail level by the achievement of what might be called "fictive structure,"[2] the appearance that the elements are actually carrying weight when they are not. It is appearance not mathematically correct answers that count. In this author's personal experience of both looking for such things and constructing them, if you come within 5% of a theoretical mark or point, that is close enough to support the illusion. 5% represents a kind of margin of perception and will be axiomatic in the following sections.

Furthermore, as the goal of design is to construct impressions or remembrances of unity the methods used need not be "pure"; they can be combined in a given work. Because the numerical structures of the three methods overlap, in effect they restate the same thing three different ways.

The examples and notes that follow are also offered to those professional colleagues who reject this kind of design method as being unduly restraining; who are subject to the superstitious fear that they will become "prisoners of geometry." To avoid this we need to put design in the context of the esoteric work of remembrance. The proportional system should be entered completely, integrated completely, thus mastered, after which it "works for you," so to speak. In this way it becomes a liberating, empowering force rather than a deprivation of freedom.

In the ancient sense there could be a science of design or even a magical science. Though some might find the idea of magic disturbing either for religious or psychological reasons, it needs to be remembered that for most of human existence magic, the creation of an appearance or of apparent action at a distance, was the basis of human governance and included the subjects of arithmetic and geometry. Though the magical tradition may at times be referenced, one certainly does not have to participate in any "theurgic" activities to utilize proportional ideas successfully.

In looking at history we will recap the role of Plato's demiurge, beginning in unity and making harmonically related divisions that ultimately give rise to the sensible cosmos. As human beings we are part of that cosmos and are constructed on the same pattern. We are constructed by analogy. We are "like the logos." If we in turn create objects in this same manner, they can become links in a chain of being. Such a human presence in architectural works or elements is known as anthropos. As we have linked our aesthetic theory to a cosmological story we will consider the presence of such stories current at the time of the architectural examples we are considering. Such stories are called myths and scriptures. They are "stories" that hold sway in the human imagination. They may be couched in religious, philosophical, or "scientific" terms, but stories of origin are always mysteries.

Egypt

Egyptian History

The recorded history of ancient Egypt as a united, self-governing entity is a remarkable spectacle spanning almost three thousand years. Within this vast panorama there were four major eras:

Pre-dynastic urban settlements in the Nile valley begin about seven thousand years before the unification of the nation and the institution of an imperial political system. The earliest calendar notations begin about 4200 BC.

The Old Kingdom, 3400–2200 BC, 800 years, dynasties I–VI, in which the unified national structure is created. After the fall of the Old Kingdom, about 2200 BC comes a less integrated feudal period known as the **Middle Kingdom**, dynasties VII–XII, 300 years. This is followed by a collapse associated with the somewhat mysterious invading group known as the Hyksos, 2500–1600 BC, dynasties XIII–XVII another 900 years.

The New Kingdom is initiated by the expulsion of the Hyksos, followed by a period of imperial expansion into the Middle East, 1600–1100 BC, 500 years, dynasties XVIII–XX. Another period of decline sets in from 1100–500 BC, 600 years, dynasties XXI–XXVIII, a kind of long twilight. After a run of 2,900 years, Egyptian political independence essentially ends with the Persian takeover in 525 BC.

Greco-Roman. The Persians retain influence to a greater or lesser degree for about 200 years, from 525 to 323 BC, when Alexander arrives. Egypt then remains firmly in the Greco-Roman orbit for another 900 years, serving as a critical breadbasket for Rome and later Byzantium, until the Muslim conquest about 600 AD.[1]

The outstanding architectural work of the Old kingdom may be the great pyramids of the IVth dynasty, but the key personality is Imhotep, architect of the IIIrd dynasty King Zoser. Imhotep initiated large-scale construction in stone and developed the pyramid as a monumental architectural form. The New Kingdom is the height of aesthetic refinement in Egypt, as well as its political and economic expansion. Of many wonderful buildings from this era the outstanding single work is the Temple of Hatshepsut, designed by her lover Senmut. In the later Greco-Roman period, the Temple of Horus at Edfu stands out as a complete example; it is said to be based on early patterns.

Egypt didn't simply die; rather, it was absorbed or digested by the Greco-Romans. In a kind of alchemical transformation, its vital energy, its magical ka, diffused through Western culture, like nutrient through living tissue, where it still flows today.

The Pillar

Badaway[2] sees two levels of design using harmonically related number. A kind of blocking out, the "constructional diagram," and internal divisions given by a "harmonic diagram." Both are composed of right triangles called "pillars," expressed as ratios of the base to the altitude. When placed back to back the right-triangle pillars form isosceles triangles that position rectangles. The concept of the pillar can hardly be unrelated to the symbol of the djed pillar, which appears in the myth of Osiris.[3]

The 1:2 pillar is the square, divided by its semi-diagonals,[4] **figure 1a**. The double square forms the 1:4 pillar used for overall proportions either internally in sanctuaries or externally as the enclosing wall. The 1:4 and 1:8 pillars are used as "virtual backbones" of the plan. Badaway uses the 1:8 pillar in combination with squares or 1:2 pillars to form a kind of stepped pyramid. He cites the 8:5 triangle, or 4:5 pillar, as being of great importance, saying that the harmonic sense of Egyptian architecture is based on this pillar, citing Viollet le Duc, who calls it the Egyptian triangle. Badaway also cites the Pythagorean 3:4:5 triangle, which Plutarch called the Osiris triangle; its primary use being as the template for the right angle.

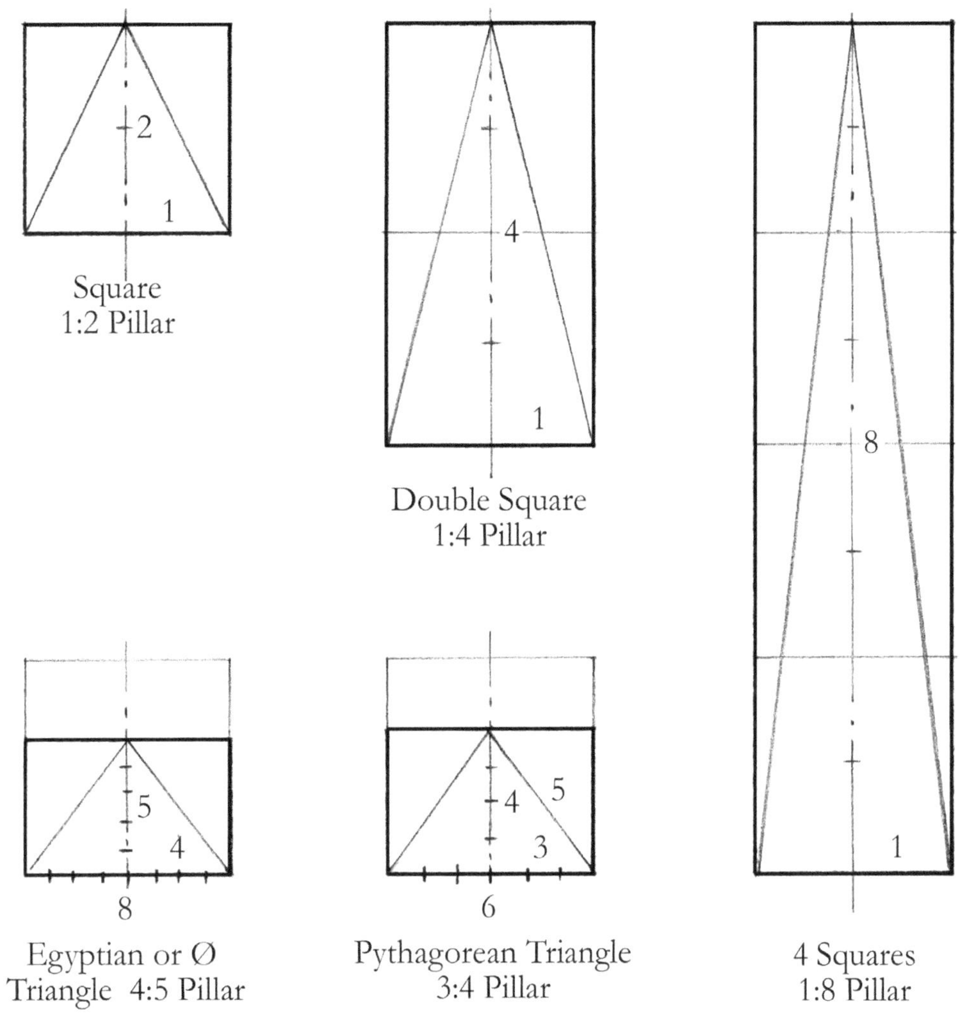

Figure 1a – *The Pillar*

Badaway describes Egyptian design methodology in five stages:[5]

1) The center line is marked, both on drawings and on foundations, though in many cases the bilateral aspect is not exact.

2) Putting squares and triangles together in a "constructional diagram," **figure 1b**: the square; two 8:5 triangles; a square and one 8:5 triangle, 8:13, 1:Ø; a double square; a more favored combination, a square flanked by two 8:5 triangles, 8:18, 1:√5; two squares and one 8:5 triangle, 8:21, 1:.381, 1:Ø²; two squares and two 8:5 triangles, 8:26, 1:3.25, 1:2/Ø; and a square flanked by two 8:5 triangles on either side, 8:28.[6] The number of such combinations of squares and phi triangles is indefinite.

3) The overall rectangular enclosure of the building is usually 1:2 or 1:4 for major interior and exterior limits. Badaway adds to these the 1:8 pillar used in combination with squares to set widths of various rooms and spaces. These pillars are likened to a "backbone" or spine, called a "prismatic" pillar.

4) Stages 2 and 3 set the overall parti and major internal divisions. Stage 4 sets the size and shape of individual rooms and interior wall patterns. These Badaway sees as guided mainly by 5:8 triangles placed on the spine to form the prismatic shapes.

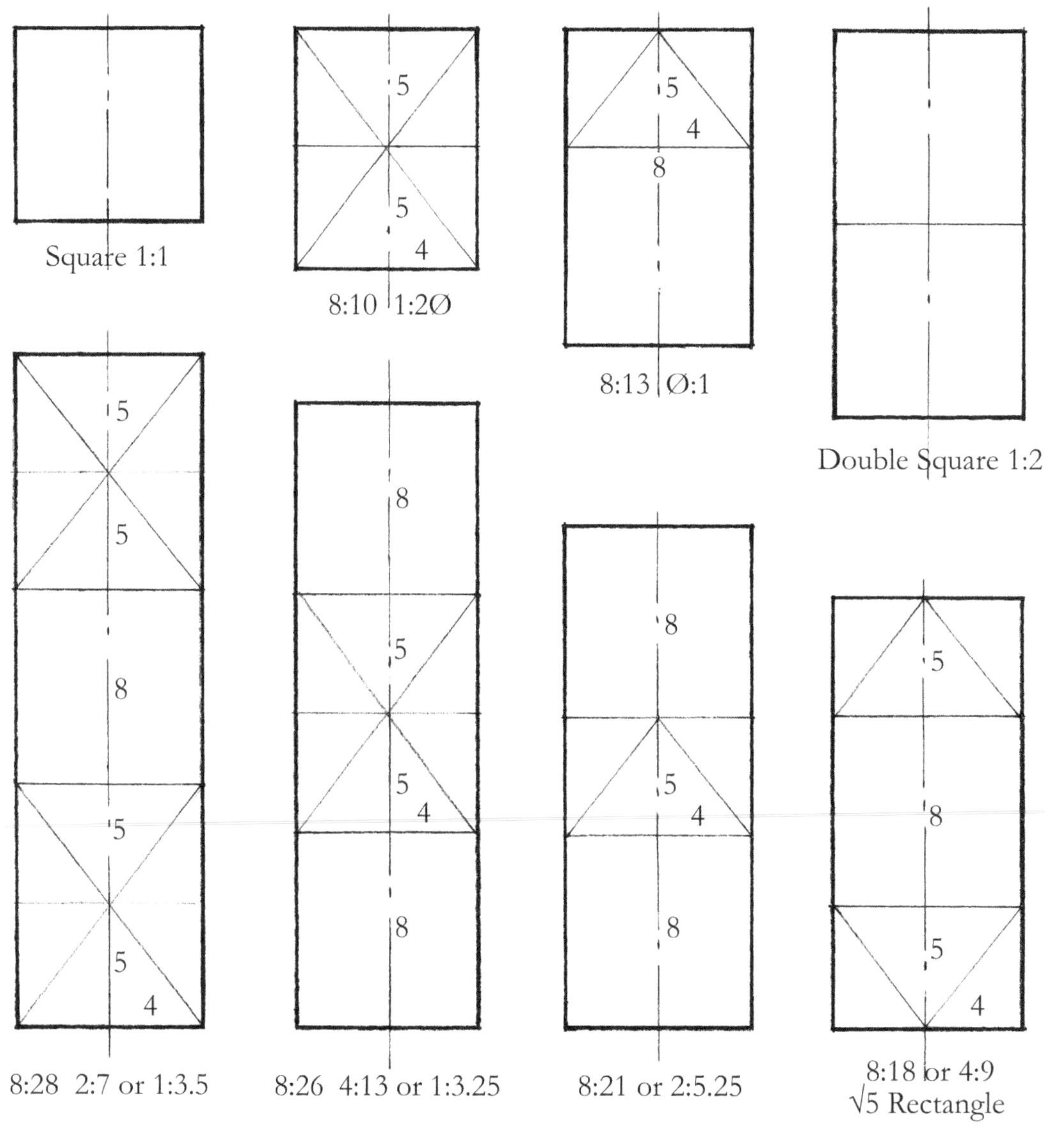

FIGURE 1b - *Constructional Diagrams*

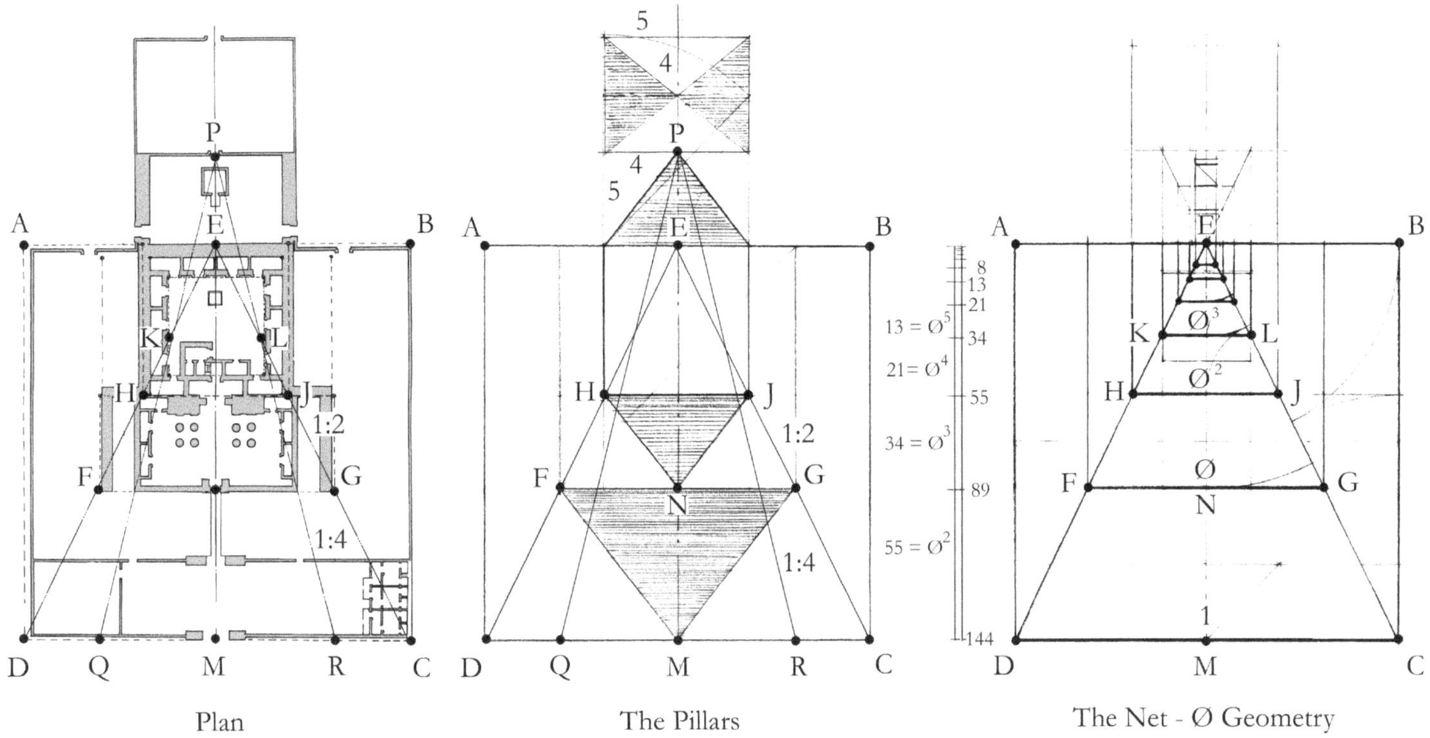

FIGURE 2
The Temple at Amarna

An example is the inner temple at Amarna,[7] **figure 2**. The main enclosure is square ABCD. This is subdivided by the semi-diagonals, DE and EC, a 2:1 pillar. A 5:4 pillar, triangle FGM with its apex at M intersects DE at F. FG is Ø of BC. The process is repeated with 5:4 pillar, triangle HJN, establishing interval HJ, which is $Ø^2$ of BC. These intervals give the location and size of the entry court and temple forecourt. Interval KL is $Ø^3$ and gives the width of the inner courtyard. We can continue to work with the 5:4 pillar to lay out the back courts. However, Badaway suggests the use of the 1:4 pillar, PQR, QR = FG.

5. Once the design is done according to such harmonic methods the plan is translated into a modular grid so that linear measurements can be given to artisans. The grid diagram is a rationalization of the pure geometry of the pillars. Badaway notes that internal divisions are often related by phi through the use of a Fibonacci series, in cubits. We might see the constructional diagram being made with the pillar and then the plan-net marking the steps on the spine-like pillar.

Unlike some modern commentators Badaway, consistent with the ancient manner, has no problem with 5:8 as a whole number approximation of phi.[8] Earlier a 5% guideline for such approximation has been suggested. In fact, phi, as a trans-rational can never be perfectly translated into actual measurements. Physical objects can only be reminders of such concepts as phi. Keep this in mind as we look more closely at Egyptian design methods.

The Canon of 19

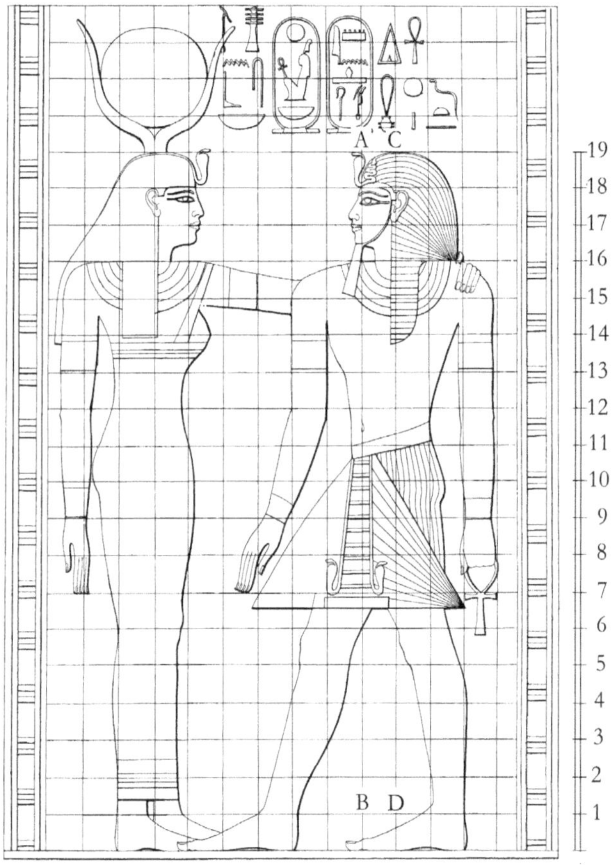

Figure 3
The Canon of 19

The Egyptians utilized a "canon of 19," in which the height of the human body is divided into 19 parts, from the ground to the top of the head, **figure 3.**[9] This division provides an approximation of phi that is adequate for use in practical crafts; small enough to give detail but not too small to apply in the field. The topmost unit represents the measurement of the cerebral cortex of the brain, where the "higher functions" are located. This is part of the physical ground of Mind and its Imaginative function; the mediating realm between the transient, material body below and the timeless, perennial, non-material realm of principles above. 18:19 is also the relationship of the altitude of the pentagon to its diagonal. To determine the position of the navel the lower 18 units were divided at the Ø point; about 6.875:11.125 units, or 7:11.

The grid was also used to compose the body horizontally. There is a vertical line of movement, AB, running through the eye down to the big toe of the back foot, the point from which we move forward, toward what the eye sees. One unit behind this is a line running just in front of the ear down to the ball of the back foot, CD, a point on which we balance.[10]

The 18th unit on the figure marks the "brow chakra," the third eye in the Indian tradition, the point of focus in meditation. In addition, the figure wears the Uraeus, the cobra crown representing the eye of Atum. The figure's head is 3 units high and the entablature of the classical order is also 3/19ths.[11] Thus its cornice would be approximately 1 unit and its topmost shape, the cyma recta, is the same profile as the rearing cobra.

The whole 19-unit interval may be divided at Ø to give 7/12, .583 only 2.5% from phi, Ø x 19 = 11.742.[12] 7 and 12 are symbolically associated with the periodicities of the moon and sun respectively. The Metonic cycle of sun-moon eclipses is a period of 19 years. In the Indian yoga system there are two principle energy channels, the ida and pingala, also associated with the sun and moon. The task of the yogi is to balance these energy flows and allow them to rise along the spine to the third eye where they are said to exit the body or "fly off," producing an elevation of consciousness. This flowing energy, which is often depicted in serpentine form is called prana in India, chi in China, and is very much like the Egyptian ka.

In discussing the relationship between Ø and the grid of 19, Fideler is not only undeterred by the translation of trans-rationals into whole number ratios but embraces the process as a key one, seeing the two kinds of number as complementary rather than contradictory.[13] "*Students of geometry draw a distinction between the principles of static and dynamic symmetry. The square grid is useful but static, the phi grid is dynamic and brings the piece to life. The square grid represents the body or raw material of the composition; the phi ratio is the animating principle which brings it to life. In the same way that the universe is a harmonic union of spirit and matter, so too did the Egyptians reflect this understanding in their temple art.*"

Seshat

In ancient Egypt, records of architectural plans as well as other key legal and financial records were stored in libraries located within temple or palace compounds.[14] While not denying that oral tradition played a major role in the transmitting of traditional practices, within an urban, literate culture that alone would not have been enough to guarantee continuity.

FIGURE 4a
Seshat and Her Symbol

Egyptian temples were built according to a "plan-net."[15] In the case of the late temple of Horus the net had been recorded in the Old kingdom, and associated with Imhotep. These nets were recorded both as drawings and written specifications. The temple libraries were under the purview of the goddess Seshat.[16] Seshat played two roles, librarian-archivist and keeper of the "cord and plan-net." Part of her ritual activity was to participate in the foundational "staking out" of the temple. It is said that she "stretches the line and spreads the plan-net," thus she is titled "Lady of the Builders." Because of her close association with writing she is considered Thoth's female consort, his girlfriend. Thoth, inventor of writing and governor of subtle knowledge, is later equated with the Greek Hermes.

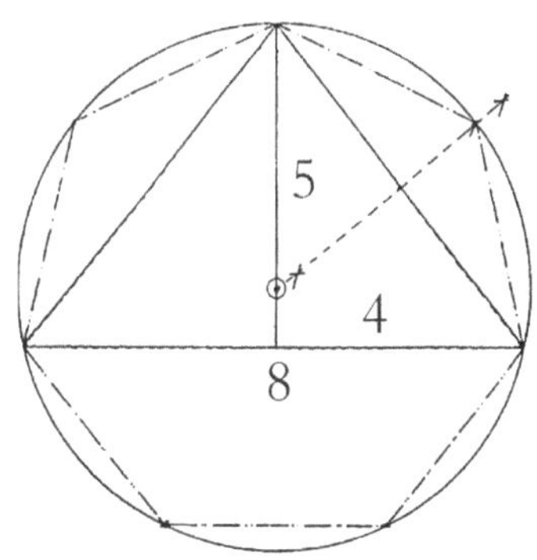

FIGURE 4b
Phi and the Heptad

Seshat's emblem or sign, **figure 4a**, is seven "leaves" or "lancets," atop a stem or cord, surmounted by a crescent shape described as a month sign, topped by a dual sign described as two "feathers" or "fingers." Badaway suggests that one interpretation for her name may be a pun on the number seven. He notes that the cubit was divided into 7x4 or 28 parts, which came from the measure of the human forearm. The seven leaves could thus represent 28 days and the two feathers atop the crescent would be the 2 remaining days in the Egyptian month.[17]

The relation of the seven "rayed" symbol to Seshat as "Lady of the Builders" and "keeper of the cord and plan-net" is illustrated in **figure 4b**. The isosceles triangle with base 8 and altitude 5, the 5:4 pillar, provides a template for the construction of the heptagon.[18] The numbers 7, 77, and 777 are associated with Athena and in later centuries with the Virgin Mary.

FIGURE 4c
Stretching the Cord

Figure 4c[19] illustrates the layout ceremony. The king faces Seshat, each holds a tall stake, the two connected by a cord. This image may represent the first stage in the staking-out ceremony, the stretching of the cord. This would establish the axis and overall enclosure outline. The second stage is the "spreading of the plan-net" containing the harmonic pattern of the building's internal divisions. A text at Edfu reads, "'*He excavated its foundation.... The cord was extended in it with Seshat the Great. Its plan-net has been loosened with Ptah. The angles have been fixed by the majesty of Khnum ... in excellent work of eternity. Its length and its width are according to the need. Its height and its depth are right.*'"[20] Ptah is associated with coming into form, Khnum with the molding of the body of the fetus during gestation.

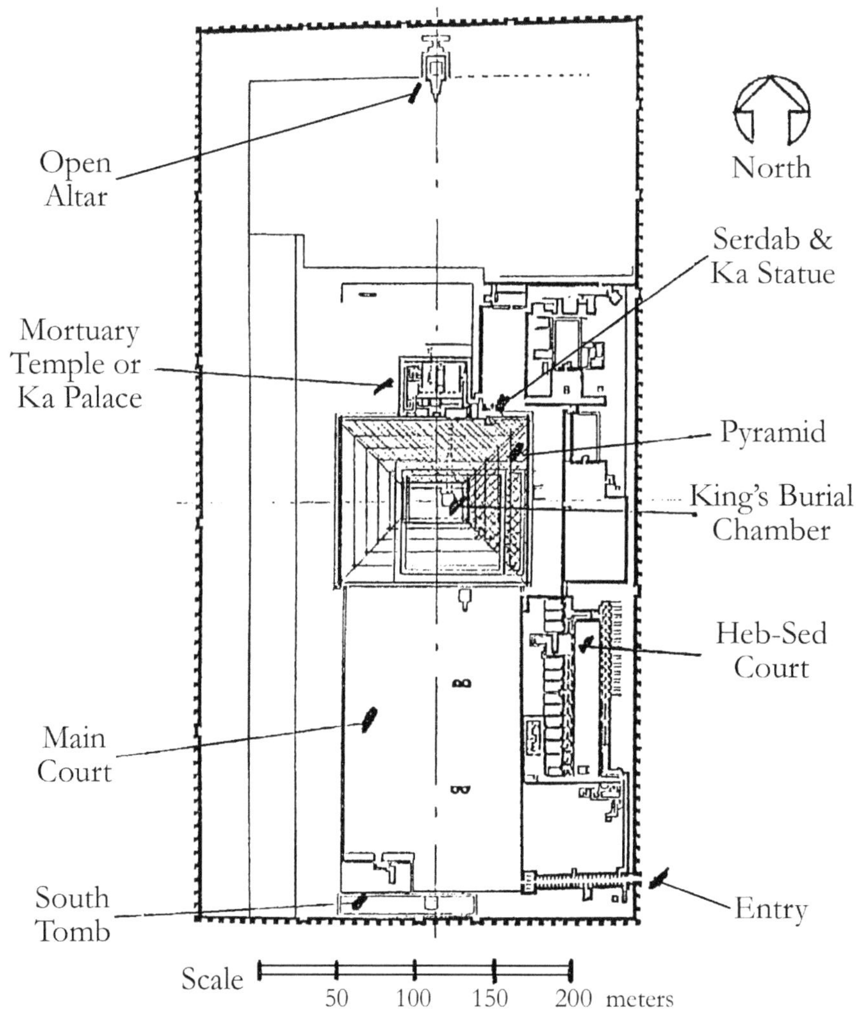

FIGURE 5
Zoser's Complex, Saqqara, Imhotep, c. 2700 BC

IMHOTEP

The earliest monumental architectural work done in dressed stone is the stepped pyramid at Saqqara, **figure 5**, a ritual complex built by the third dynasty King Zoser, c.2800 BC. The design is attributed to Imhotep, a remarkable individual, who held several of the highest offices in the Egyptian government. He was chief priest, prime minister, court doctor, astronomer and architect. Nothing is known of his early life, but the office of Master Builder, if not the priesthood itself, was hereditary,[21] indicating that he was likely a nobleman.[22] In playing all these roles he would have been what was later called a Renaissance Man.

Taken as a verb "htp" means "to satisfy"; as a noun it signifies satisfaction or peace.[23] "I" signifies "he who comes" and "m" means "in" or "in the guise of." Thus Imhotep may be translated as "one who comes in peace." If we expand the meaning of "htp" to include "the sacrificial offering that establishes peace, or harmony, with the god," then Imhotep could be translated as "one who comes to establish harmony." "Htp" is also the reverse of "Pth," or Ptah,[24] the divinity governing the coming into material form. The reverse is the returning to the ideal, the unified, for which harmony is the key. Thus we might translate Imhotep as "one who comes to realize harmony" or "realizer of harmony." In the sense that he is the inverse of Ptah we may say his work involves return to unity.

As prime minister Imhotep had access to the highest level of political power and planning. He was in charge of practical matters such as finances and resource management. The construction of monumental-scale buildings in stone is a tribute to the organizational level of the government and the craft skills of the artisans, already well developed on this first great monumental complex.

As high priest of Heliopolis he was head of the temple bureaucracy, but more importantly he was chief magician. This would put him squarely in the world of the secret books of Thoth and channeling of the ka. In the funerary ritual he would have pronounced the "words of power" that enabled the deceased to function in the realm of the afterlife. He would have officiated at the magical ceremony known as the "opening of the mouth," in which the mummy would have been enabled to speak.[25] In later eras Imhotep was portrayed as a conductor of the soul on its afterlife journey.

Imhotep was also a medical doctor, the healing arts of the day being strongly correlated with the magical system. It was as a god of medicine that he was deified, many centuries after his death, becoming a model for the Greek healer Asclepius. Imhotep wrote books on medicine and architecture. He was later called "patron of scribes."[26] As chief priest, in charge of scheduling rituals, he would have been familiar with the astronomical lore in the magical texts.

Imhotep's lasting contribution to architecture is the development of the pyramid form in stone. The technical and managerial expertise and the social and economic strength required speak to the power and **vision** of Egypt only shortly after its birth as a unified nation.

In certain ways Imhotep's career recapitulates the activity of the prehistoric shaman. He maintains the connection to the spirit realm, the shaman's journey, now contained within the astronomically guided ritual of the temple. He uses this power principally for healing, but also for governance. His activity as an architect both reinforces the state in practical ways and grows out of an understanding of manipulation of spiritual and psychic forces, in part at least, through visual-spatial symbols.

Zoser's Pyramid

The enclosure walls of the complex are a rectangle, 1,790 feet x 912 feet,[27] an approximately 2:1 ratio, oriented toward the cardinal points. The entry is at the southeast corner. It leads from a small vestibule to a long processional hall, with what might be called semi-columns or quasi-columns, that is, columns fused to wall ends, as will later be seen at Bassae. Its clerestory lighting set the tone for later hypostyle halls. This hall opens to the main court, where the king ran a symbolic race during the Heb Sed festival, a renewal of the king's rule celebrated every thirty years.

The stepped pyramid fronts on the main court. Its base is 396 feet x 352 feet.[28] The height of the six steps are, 38, 36, 34.5, 32, 31, and 29.5 feet, respectively, for a total of 201 feet.[29] The centerline of the main court and pyramid are slightly off axis to the east of the centerline of the enclosure wall. This may be due in part to a design that developed as it went along, or it may serve some subtle function not presently understood.

The pyramidal structure began as a mastaba, was enlarged several times, then built up, wedding-cake style, with smaller mastabas atop one another. The likeness to a Mesopotamian ziggurat cannot be accidental. Nor can the symbolism of stepped ascension be unrelated to a form of communication with and a movement back to a unified spirit realm. It was literally a stairway to heaven for the ka of the king to ascend and descend.

On the north side of the pyramid is the mortuary temple also called the ka palace. Just to its east, also along the north side of the pyramid is the Serdab, a small closet-like room containing the ka statue of the king. At the north end of the complex, on axis with the court, the pyramid, and the ka palace, is an open altar of undetermined function. Opposite it, on the south wall of the complex, is a mastaba-like structure called the south tomb, also of undetermined function.

On the east side of the main court is the Heb Sed court where the ceremony of renewal took place and where the djed pillar was erected, identifying the king with Osiris. This court was surrounded by "dummy" buildings said to represent government offices. Giedion sees an air of experimentation and enthusiasm in the work, concluding that it, *"radiates a joyous optimism."*[30]

FIGURE 6 -*The Ka Hieroglyph*

Giedion calls the complex "City of the Ka."[31] The ka is a kind of vital energy that permeates or "embraces" the physical body, a life force, subtle or quasi-physical, and flowing. Because of this embracing quality the ka is sometimes known as the "double."[32] Its hieroglyph is two outstretched arms, **figure 6**. This power has been transmitted from Atum to every individual living being, which could not have movement or consciousness without it. It connects the divine with the human, the earth with the sky. It has a positive protective power. Through association with sexual potency, the ka forms a link with ancestors and descendants. The hieroglyph is a *"compelling symbol of human affection."*[33]

The flowing character of the ka implies that like chi and prana it can be channeled and accumulated. The ka has no form of its own, it needs a material container; according to ancient belief, the denser the better. Thus brick would be better than wood or earth and stone better than brick. In the case of the king, Atum's representative on earth, standing at the apex of the social pyramid he is the point source connecting earth and heaven. As Atum provides the ka itself, the king is the ka of the nation. As long as the ka was regularly nourished with actual offerings the embrace of the ancestor's ka would continue indefinitely.[34]

Giedion writes, *"The beginning of stone architecture is inseparably bound up with the concept of the Ka, ... for only stone could provide an indestructible container for the Ka."*[35] In this view the complex is designed for the ka to flow through the rituals of renewal so that its beneficial power might continue to embrace the nation indefinitely. Imhotep, son of Ptah, would have been the ideal person to create this City of the Ka by virtue of his familiarity with the books of Thoth, both practical and theological.

Analysis of Zoser's Complex

A geometrical procedure to develop the plan of the complex begins with double square ABCD, **figure 7.1-5**. As a primary division find E, Ø of AB. If AB = 1, AD = 2, point E divides line AB so that AE = 1.191 and ED = 0.809, AE:AB = DC:DE, the two rectangles are similar geometrically. If we "rationalize" this division by setting AB = 5 and AD = 10, we get a 5:6 and a 5:4 rectangle. Though these ratios are not arithmetically identical both are half of a Ø rectangle. EF can also be found by placing two 8:5 triangles on CD.

As a second major pattern of division apply a 1:4 pillar, triangle DGC. The pyramid will front along line HJ. To find its length and width apply a 1:2 pillar, triangle HMJ and construct square KLJH. Apply a 4:5 pillar on HJ to find NP, Ø of KH, draw line QR marking the back edge of the pyramid. The plan of the pyramid is rectangle QRST, which is close to an .809 rectangle. The ka palace on the north side of the pyramid is also a 1:.809 rectangle whose width is $Ø^2$ of QR.

This dynamic geometrical aspect is matched or balanced by a fixed aspect in which the indefinite geometrical functions are "rationalized" to produce measurable quantities. The key being that 1/19 = .053 and $Ø^6$ = .056. If we apply a division into 19 units to the north-south axis

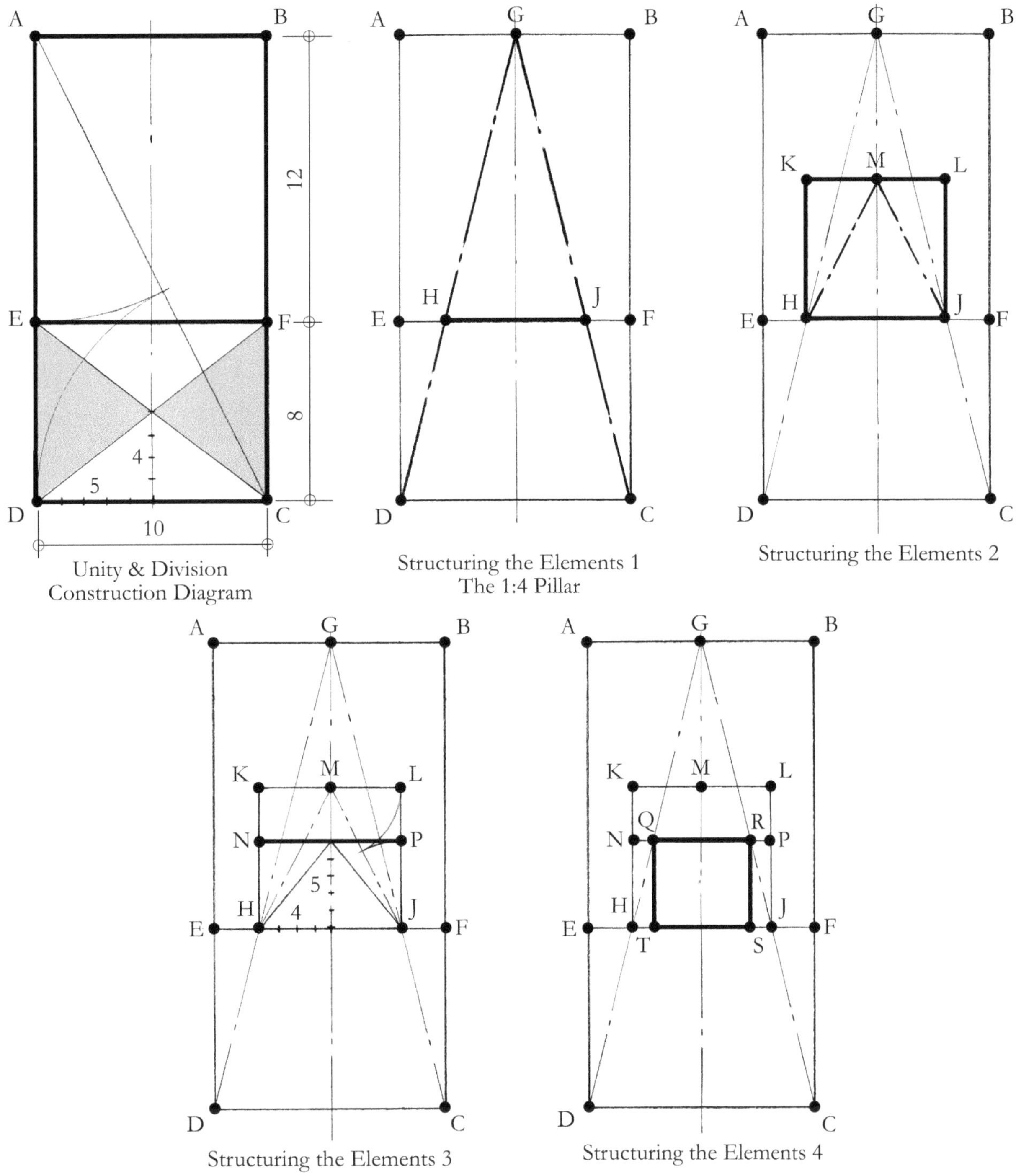

FIGURE 7.1-5

Zoser's Complex. Reconstruction

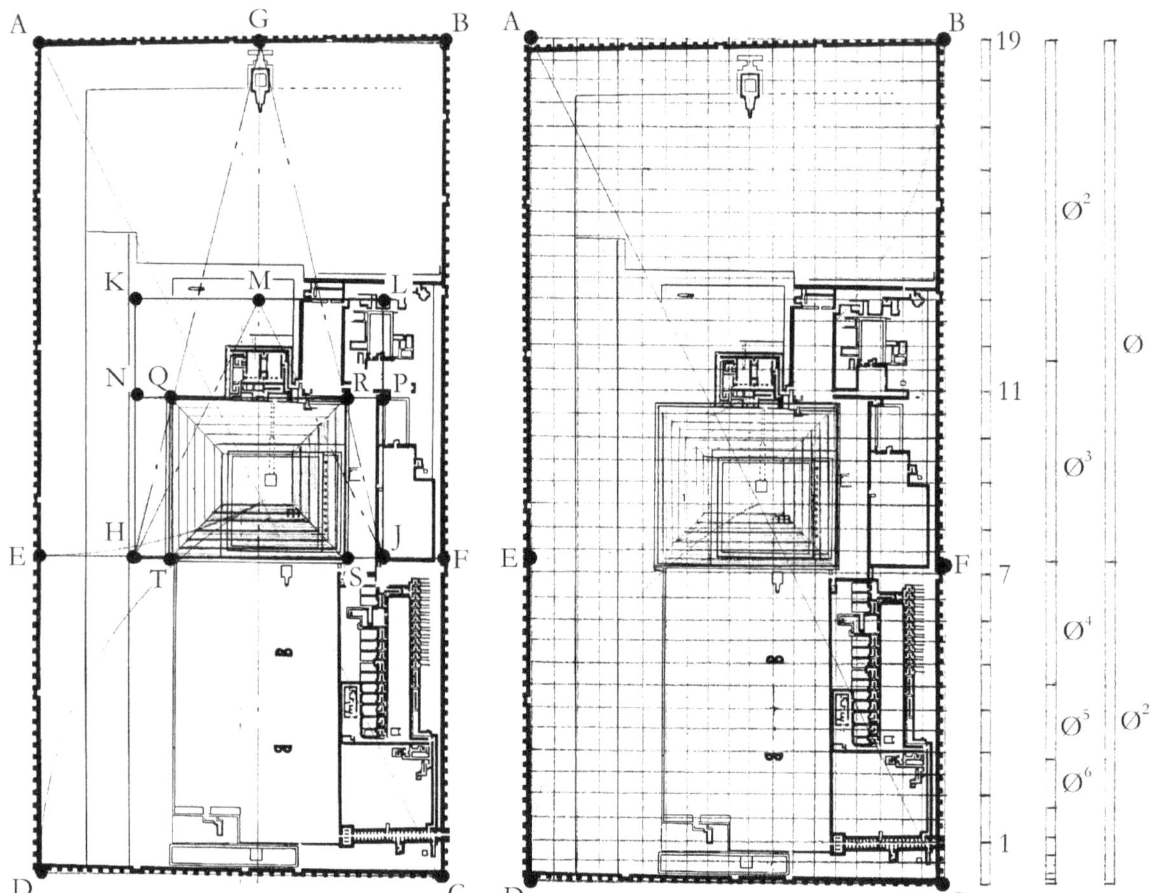

Manifestation
the Plan

Ø and the Canon of 19

FIGURE 7.6-7
Zoser's Complex. Plan Analysis

of Zoser's complex, **figure 7.7**, we find that the pyramid is located between units 7 and 11, a whole number approximation of phi. Assuming a human figure the same height as the complex, with the head lying to the north, **figure 7.8**, the entrance of the complex falls at the place of the foot, within unit 1. If we divide the width AB into 19, making AD equal to 38, the center axis of the pyramid and its major related structures fall on line 5. On this line, at unit 18, at the place of the brow chakra of the figure, is the small open altar or shrine. The king's burial chamber, at about the 9th unit, just below the center of the complex, is approximately at the location of the figure's genitals or root chakra, perhaps relating to the theme of regeneration. The main court where the king ran his symbolic race is at the position of the lower legs, while the entrance to the complex is at the position of the foot. **Figure 7.9** shows the major elements of the complex, the main court, pyramid, and ka palace, compared to a human figure. At this scale the "ka palace" is at the position of the head; the serdab and ka statue, is at the level of the throat; the king's burial chamber is about the position of the heart, the pyramid fronts at the navel, the main court remains at the position of the legs with the complex's entrance at the place of the feet.

The use of the numbers 19 and 38 might provide a key to the stepping of the pyramid. The first step is 38 feet high,[36] which is twice 19. If a fundamental interval was 19, its octave would be 38. If we calculate the value of each of the twelve semitones of such a "chromatic" octave, as shown in the chart below, we find that the measures of the six steps in the pyramid correspond rather closely.

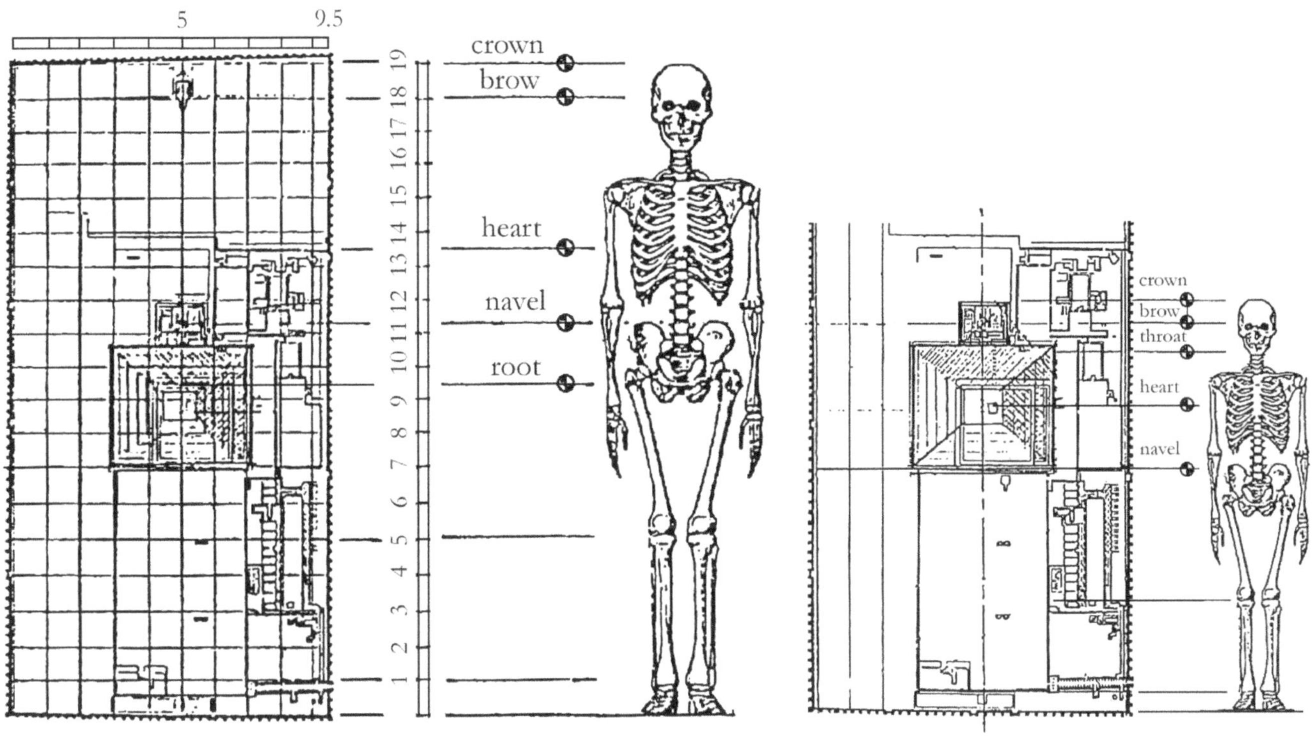

FIGURE 7.8-9 *Zoser's Complex and the Human Figure*

Means	GM					HM		AM					GM
Sounds	DO		RE		ME	FA		SOL		LA		TI	DO
Whole tones	1		2		3	4		5		6		7	8
Semitones	1	2	3	4	5	6	7	8	9	10	11	12	13
Interval length	19	20.2	21.4	22.6	23.7	25.3	26.9	28.5	30.0	31.5	33.6	35.6	38
Pyramid steps								29.5	31.0	32.0	34.5	36.0	38

There are several causes for ambiguity here; that the Egyptians did not use the English feet as their unit of measure; that the work we are discussing is forty-seven hundred years old and not especially well preserved; and that there are no extant records by its designers to indicate their intentions. Therefore, the above analysis must remain speculative. But enough has been shown to indicate that a proportional system of thought was at work. A system that included an integration of arithmetic in the use of the number 19; of geometry in the Ø ratio; of music in terms of the 1:2 ratio of the octave and the intervals of the semitone; and of astronomy in the cardinal orientation of the complex as well as the 19-year lunar–solar eclipse cycle. Comparison to the human figure reveals a deep anthropomorphism. Regardless of the actual method used, perennial patterns of harmony informed the deepest conceptual levels of Imhotep's career and work.

The Great Pyramids

The fourth dynasty was the era of pyramid building that we all associate with ancient Egypt. During the two centuries that followed Imhotep, the stepped mastaba developed into the "true" pyramid with sheer faces, culminating with the Great Pyramids at Giza. A huge amount of ink has been spilled concerning them. Nothing more could be added here to such an enormous output. Two points though might profitably be treated: the first, symbolic; the second, geometrical.

Symbolically the pyramid as an ontological element represents the emergence of light as a cosmic ordering force. The form of the pyramid is associated with the radiating point source. We may see in this form all four of our ontological stages—the point source, the dyadic vertical axis, the triadic radiation and the tetradic base—meeting the earth. The physical manifestation of this light is the sun. The sun in the cosmos occupies the same position as the king in the human realm.

The eye is the organ of light. It gives us access to space, volume and measure. Horus, divine child of Isis and Osiris, must fight his father's enemy Set. Though he is ultimately victorious, during the course of the battle Set rips out his left eye, tears it into pieces and hurls them into the chaos beyond the edge of the orderly universe. The pieces are found by Thoth, reassembled and returned to Horus. This eye that was divided and reunified is called the Wadjet. As the moon exhibits phases, the Wadjet is decomposable into fractions. The violent image of the myth has a numerical counterpart. The parts of the eye symbolize fractions representing the geometric progression 1/2, 1/4, 1/8, 1/16, 1/32 and 1/64, **figure 8**. These are the fractions of the "hekat," a standard unit of measure.[37] The summation of this series comes to 63/64. It will never come to 1, but will get closer and closer, making a near approach, called "asymptotic" in mathematics.

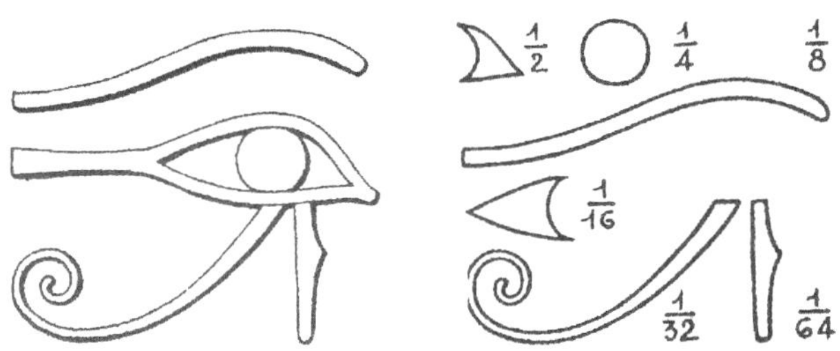

Figure 8 – *The Wadjet Eye*

But there is also another symbolic level here. The site at Giza contains three pyramids. Each of these is a different size, though each is oriented precisely to the cardinal points. They do not, however, fall in a straight line with regard to each other. It has been suggested that the three pyramids represent the stars in the belt of Orion. They align well and their relative sizes correspond the relative brightness of the three stars that make up the belt.

Geometrically, **figure 9**, the measures of the pyramid of Cheops are: base edge 440 cubits and the altitude 280 cubits. A section of the pyramid through its axis parallel to its side creates a right triangle with a base of 220 and a height of 280. This gives a ratio of .785; but Doczi suggests that this is an approximation of .750, or 3/4, making the height 293, a 4.3% discrepancy.[38] This implies the conceptual use of the 3:4:5 triangle. Moreover, the hypotenuse of this triangle would be 356 and 220/356 = .618, Ø. The practical significance is that this triangle would give the slope of the face of the pyramid.

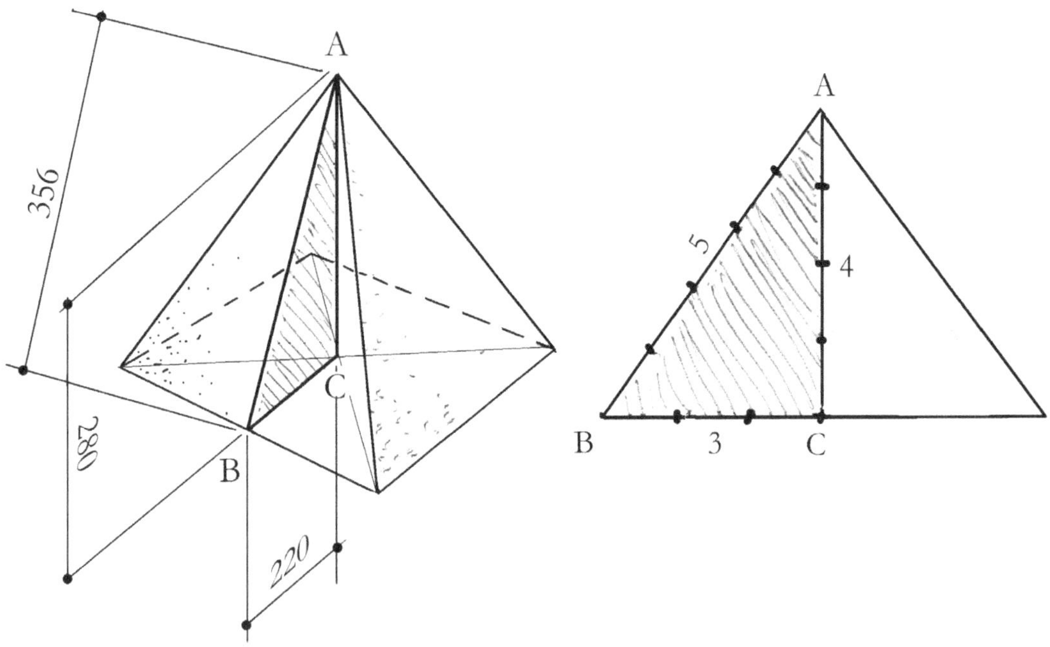

FIGURE 9
The Great Pyramid

HATSHEPSUT

Hatshepsut occupies an almost unique position in Egypt's history as a woman accepted as the national political leader. In fact, the eighteenth dynasty to which she belongs is a remarkable one, including its founder Ahmose I who reunited the country and expelled the Hyksos in 1580 BC; Hatshepsut herself whose peaceful, tasteful reign included the largest trade expedition in Egypt's history; and Thutmose III, Egypt's most successful military conqueror, whose writ ran from Ethiopia to the Euphrates. The climax of the dynasty comes with the religious reformer Ikhnaton, credited with being the first monotheist. In anticlimax the dynasty ends with the young Tutankhamen, whose magnificent funerary objects have mesmerized many in our time.

Hatshepsut's nominal husband, her half-brother later known as Thutmose III, is said to be a child during her twenty-year administration, about 1490–1470 BC. Thutmose III and Hatshepsut are at first acknowledged as co-rulers but his faction lost out and he was pushed away from the centers of power with Hatshepsut reigning independently. While out of sight he nurses his grievances and ultimately when reaching maturity makes a political comeback. Whether he had a direct hand in Hatshepsut's death is not known, but his hatred of her appears to have been extreme. After taking power he not only had her name chiseled off her monuments and inscriptions but, in an unusual move, also had the tombs of all of her major administrators similarly defaced, to the point that modern archeologists have had great difficulty reconstructing the events of the period.[39]

During most of her governing tenure the head of the queen's personal household and presumably her lover is Senmut. Though neither head of government nor official architect, this remarkable individual is the designer of her temple at Deir el Bahari.

Hatshepsut's Temple

The temple designed by Senmut is sited in a concave cliff formation with a pyramid-shaped mountain just behind it, as one faces west. The building approximately aligns with the Great Temple at Karnak, across the river to the east, where Semnut erected a pair of obelisks for Hatshepsut, which could be seen from the temple.[40] The spatial sequence from east to west had four levels, two terraces, and an enclosed courtyard as well as the rock-cut tomb itself. The two terraces were planted with myrrh trees obtained from the great trade expedition Hatshepsut had sent to the land of Punt, modern Ethiopia. Hatshepsut saw this as re-creating the "myrrh terraces of Punt" sacred to Amon and the original home of the gods.[41] Egypt had traded for myrrh, an important ingredient in temple incense, for a long time but had not cultivated the trees themselves.

The first and largest terrace is on the ground and defined by a wall. An avenue lined by sphinxes leads to a long elegant ramp up to the second terrace. On either side of the ramp is a colonnade of eleven square cut piers. At the second level is another ramp up to the temple level, also with square-cut colonnades on either side. Beyond these colonnades were specialized chapels, a Hathor chapel on the south and an Anubis chapel on the north. The north colonnade turns the corner and continues about halfway along the terrace. This northwest colonnade directly engages the live rock of the mountain providing entry to several small rock-cut chapels. It is done in what might be called a "proto-Doric" manner.[42] The third level had another pair of colonnades on either side of a ceremonial entry. This colonnade was backed by a wall. Beyond the wall was an open peristyle courtyard. On the south was a mortuary temple and on the north was another open court with a large altar, sometimes called a sun altar. Proceeding further to the west one enters the rock-cut tombs for Hatshepsut and her father Thutmose I.

The terraced myrrh gardens have the quality of an ideal landscape. In this context the building complex may be seen as a four-level "ontogeny" or story of coming into being, like the Tetraktys. In this analogy, the first terrace is the materialized realm, it is literally on the ground, the earth, enclosed in a four-sided wall symbolizing orientation. The second terrace is the realm of sustaining, the ideal garden, the level of vital flow, or water. Here is located the temple of Hathor. The third terrace is the level of intellect, discrimination, or differentiation, containing the shrines of the sun god Amon. The fourth level is the rock-cut tomb itself, representing oneness, the point of origin or reabsorption. Though there is no actual pyramid, the terraces and levels of the building complex themselves form a conceptual pyramidal structure. The physical journey within the building may be seen as recapitulating the spiritual journey of the soul in its return to unity.

Tetraktys	Building Level	Character	Ontological Level
•	Tomb	Transcendent	Unity
• •	Court	Mind	Division
• • •	Garden	Energy	Structure
• • • •	Terrace	Body	Matter

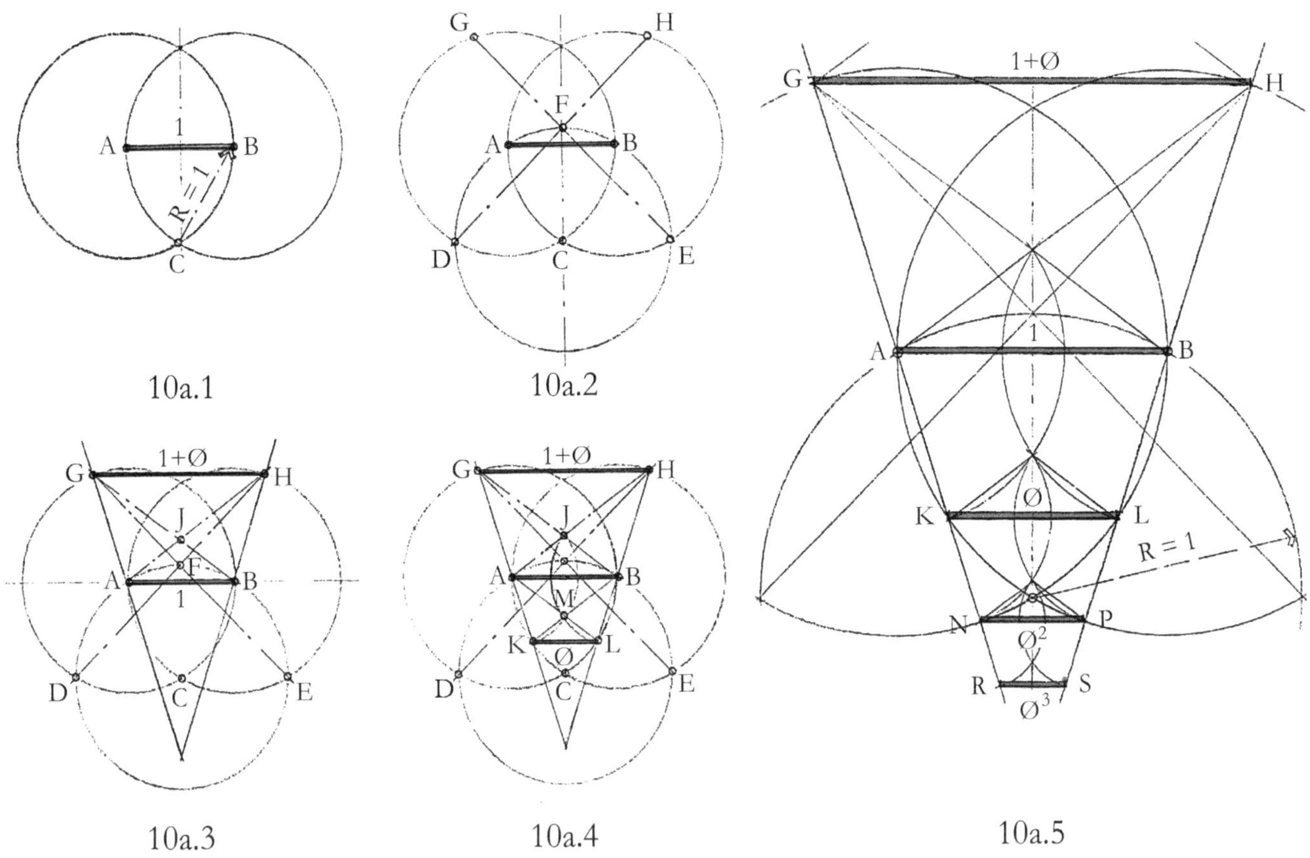

FIGURE 10a.1-5
Pentagonal Phi Scale

GEOMETRY OF HATSHEPSUT'S TEMPLE

Setting the width of the third terrace at 1, the width of the inner courtyard is Ø and the overall width of the second terrace, including the side chapels is 1+Ø. We may apply a version of the pillar that gives us phi scales in both axial directions. The construction of this "phi-scale pillar" was published for the first time by artist Albrecht Dürer but was almost certainly not invented by him and probably long predates the Renaissance.

Begin with interval AB set equal to 1, **figure 10a.1**. Use this as a radius to draw a vesica piscis. Using one of the "points" of the vesica, C, as center draw a third circle of radius AB. Where the circle centered on C intersects the circles centered on A and B, are points D and E, **figure 10a.2**; where the circle on point C intersects the centerline of the vesica find point F. Extend diagonal EF to G and DF to H. Draw line GH, **figure 10a.3**, its length is 1+Ø. Connect B to G and A to H to find point J. With center at A and radius AJ, draw arc JK, **figure 10a.4.** Point K lies on the circumference of circle B and on the extension of AG. Find point L in a similar manner. As AB = 1, KL = Ø. Figure AJBLK is a pentagon. These pentagonal constructions may be extended indefinitely in either direction, larger or smaller, **figure 10a.5**.

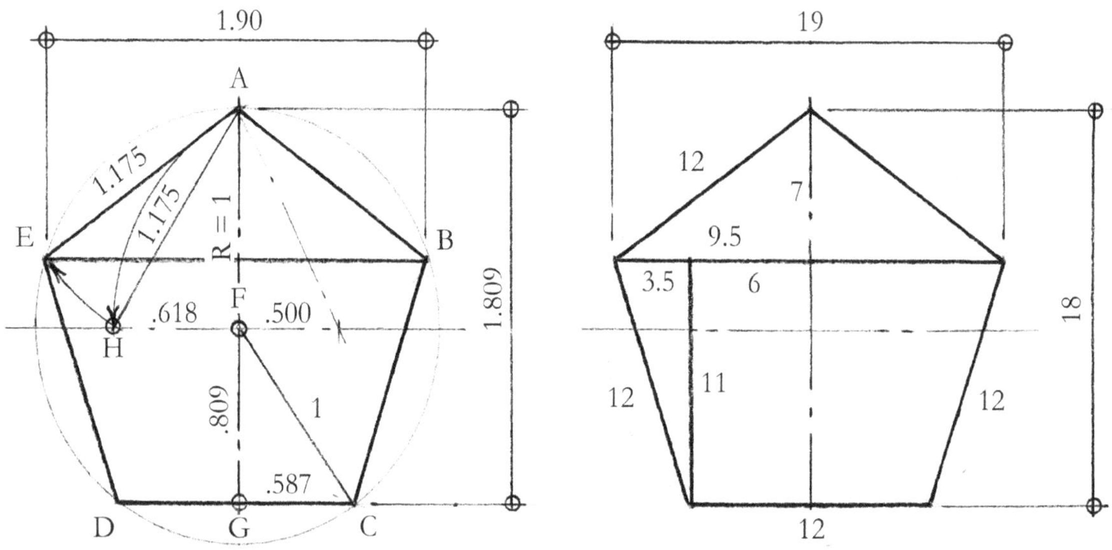

FIGURE 10b-c
The Pentagonal Pillar

What kind of pillar would this be? **Figure 10b** shows certain fundamental relations in the construction of the pentagon.[43] With the radius of the pentagon's enclosing circle as 1, the side of the pentagon is 1.175, its altitude is 1.809, and its diagonal is 1.90. In **figure 10c** these numbers are multiplied by 10 and rounded off to the nearest whole integer. The slope of the pentagon's side is set by a triangle with base 3.5 and altitude 11. Although all the ratios along the centerline and perpendicular to it are Ø related, the actual measure of the phi interval will differ in the two directions in the ratio of 11/12. Badaway would call this a 3.5:11 pillar but note that expressed as whole numbers the height to the half-base would be 22:7. This ratio may be recognized as an approximation of π, the transcendental function giving the ratio of a circle's diameter to its circumference. This figure may thus be described as a Ø pillar or as a π pillar. It reveals an "occult" or hidden relation between Ø and π. In the series of nested pentagons with their internal diagonals, **figure 10a**, we see the marriage of the pillar and the plan-net. Every interval is phi related including diagonals like AJH, where JH/AJ = Ø and KM/AJ = Ø and CM/MJ = Ø, and so on. Such a pattern could well have been woven in string or rope.

Applying this to the plan of Hatshepsut's complex, **figure 11a,** begins with setting the width of the third terrace, AB = 1. The width of the inner courtyard is Ø and its depth is $Ø^2$, making it a Ø rectangle. The two groups of rooms on either side of the courtyard are $Ø^2/2$ in width and $Ø^2$ in depth making them 2:1 rectangles. The width of the Hathor chapel on the south side of the second terrace is Ø/2. On the north side the width of the Anubis chapel and the colonnade with its rock cut chambers is also Ø/2. Hatshepsut's tomb chamber seems to be about $Ø^3$ in depth and $Ø^4$ at its widest and so is framed out within a Ø rectangle. The depth of the first and second terraces may be found by a reversal of the pillar. Inscribe pentagon AGTHB in a circle and divide each of the segments of the circumference in half. Draw pentagon UVWXY. The second terrace will end at WX. The west, south and east sides of the terrace have now been framed out. The north side may have been determined more pragmatically, as it is up against the rock face, but the width of the Anubis chapel is $Ø^2/2$. The ratio of AB to BX is about 3:4. Extend VW and YX to intersect on the complex's centerline at point Z, giving the entrance to the complex and the depth of the first terrace.

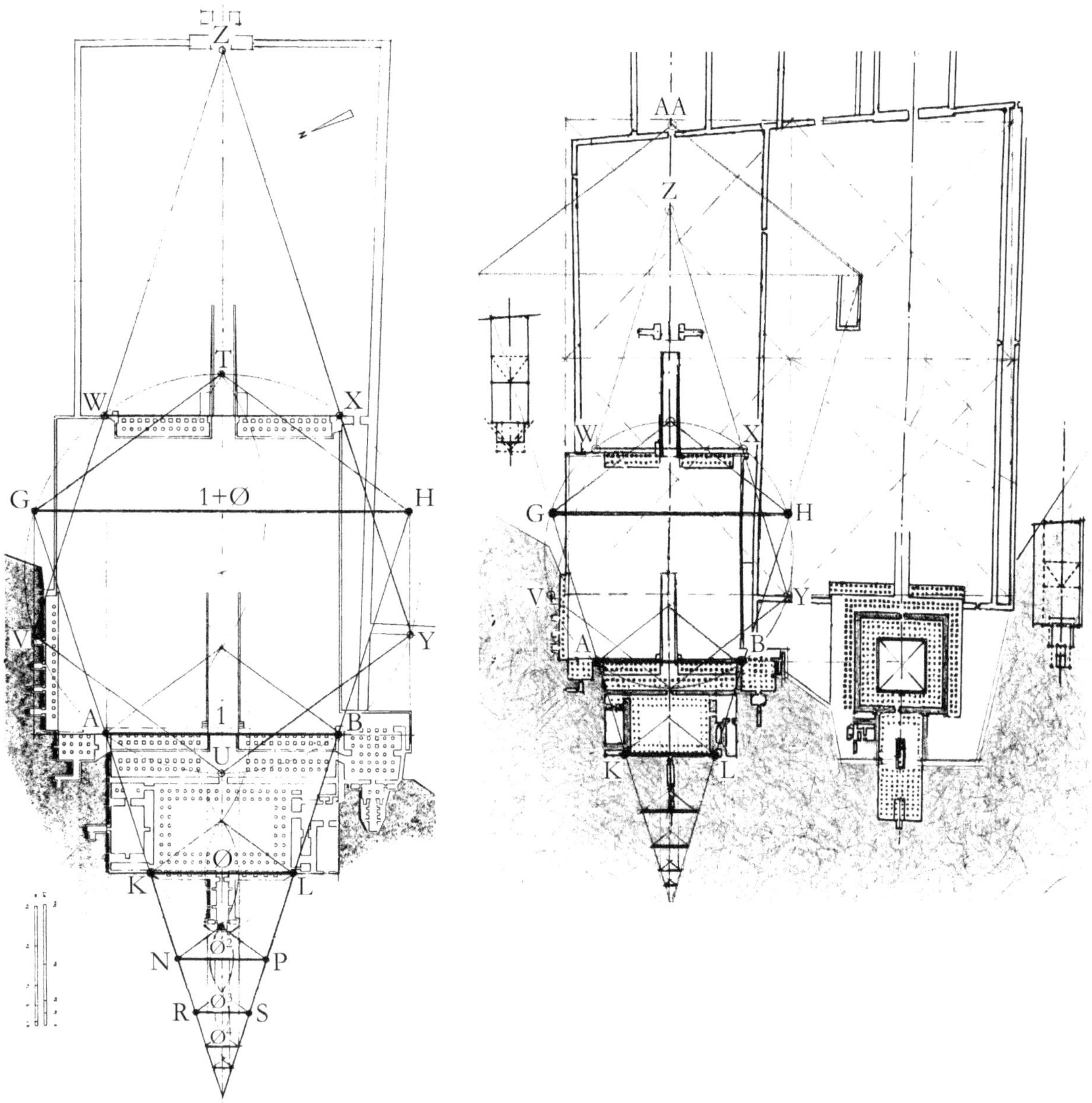

FIGURE 11a-b

Temples of Hatshepsut and Mentuhotep

Looking at the relation of Hatshepsut's complex to the adjoining complex of Mentuhotep, **figure 11b**,[44] indicates certain points of alignment. Line AB aligns with the center of Mentuhotep's pyramid and line KL marks the start of the rock-cut portion of Mentuhotep's tomb chamber. In this plan line VY lies on the side of a large square whose side equals 377 cubits, and the extension of VY marks the front of Mentuhotep's second terrace. The opposite side of the square marks the entry points of both lower courts. Point AA, on the centerline of Hatshepsut's complex, is the apex of a pentagon constructed on GH. The half-side of the square, which Badaway says is 188.5 cubits, is equal to the altitude of pentagon AGTHB. In **figure 11b**, based on a combination of the plans of De Cenival and Giedion,[45] the entry to Hatshepsut's complex is at point Z but here it is at AA. In addition, the width of Mentuhotep's terrace is Ø of this half-square interval. The centerlines of both complexes fall on the quarter points of the large square.

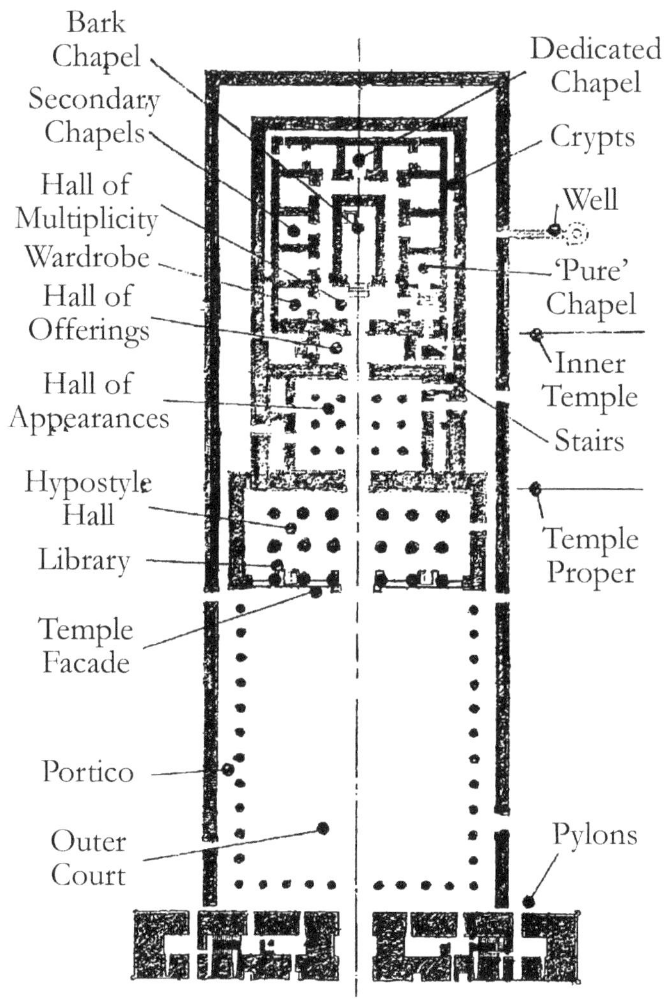

FIGURE 12a
Temple of Horus, Edfu, Plan

Geometrical analysis suggests that the phi ratio could have been a guiding principle of the design. Although such principles involving the pentagon would have been traditional in Egypt, one cannot help but feel that Senmut was not unaware of the five-part movement of the planet Venus, and the relation of that body to physical love and beauty; perhaps he had only to see his lover to be reminded. The temple remains to this day an ongoing monument to the power of love and beauty.

TEMPLE OF HORUS AT EDFU

The present temple, **figure 12a**, was begun during the reign of Ptolemy III, 221–203 BC. Its construction took "only" 180 years, from 237 BC to 57 BC.[46] The inner temple was built in about twenty years and decorated over the next eighty. The two outer "hypostyle" halls were completed by about 122 BC. The pylons, the fore-court and the enclosing walls were done by 100 BC and decorated until 5 BC.[47]

This however was the second temple on the site. Just when this older temple was built is not known but it is associated with Imhotep. It was designed "*according to a plan dropped down from heaven to earth near Memphis. The master craftsman was Imhotep, son of Ptah, the great god of Memphis; father and son united their powers and produced the first temple at Edfu.*"[48]

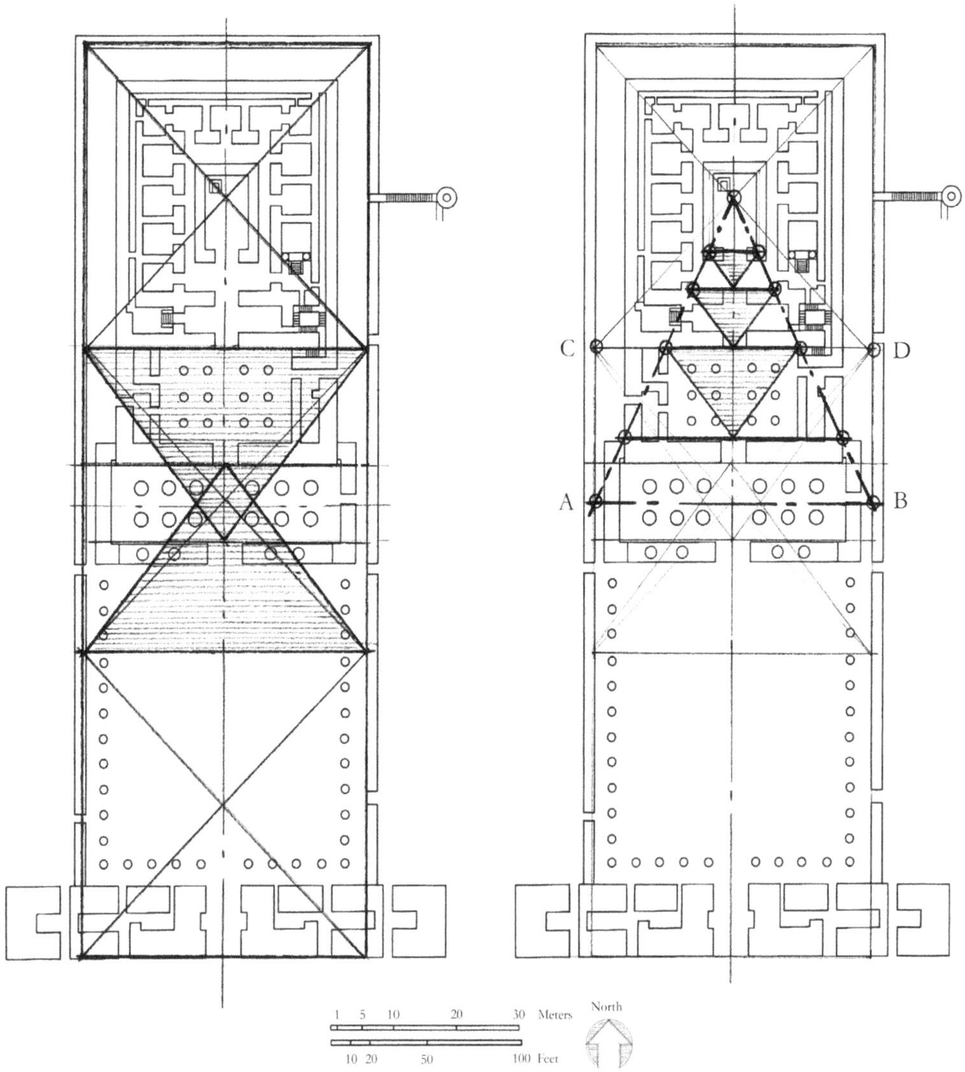

FIGURE 12b

Temple of Horus. Pillar and Plan. Net Reconstruction

Once again Imhotep is seen as a son of Ptah, associated with acting out heaven's plan on earth, embodying the Word of Thoth in matter, in this case, in the form of the temple. Unfortunately the first temple of Edfu, built in the earliest era of Egyptian history, was deconstructed to create the existing temple in the last period of Egypt's history. It was deconstructed rather than demolished, as material from earlier temples was, throughout Egyptian history, ritually reused in other temples.[49] The Egyptians claimed to have built the new Temple at Edfu in the same manner as the old but as we do not have either the building or the plans it is not possible to know in what way to take this statement.

Temple of Horus Reconstruction

A construction diagram may be formed from three squares. In the central square two 8:5 triangles are applied to place the Hypostyle Hall, **figure 12b**. From the center of the middle square, AB, a 2:1 pillar is set up, its apex at the center of the Bark Chapel. From line CD an 8:5 triangle is placed. Where it intersects the 2:1 pillar sets the Hall of Appearances, two further 8:5 triangles size the inner rooms.

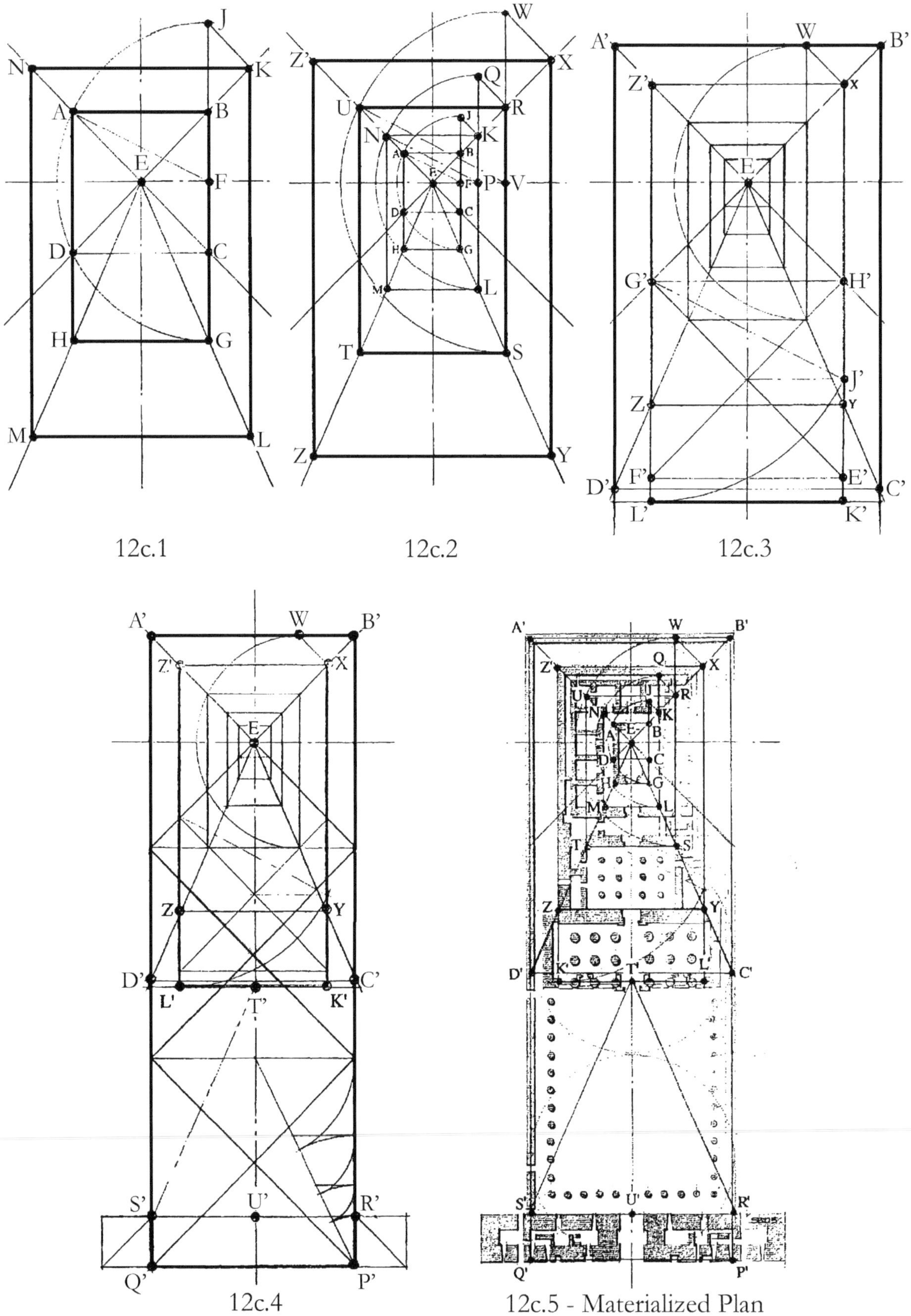

FIGURE 12C

Temple of Horus. Geometric Reconstruction

A less conventional but entirely geometric reconstruction working from the inside out begins with square ABCD, center at E, **figure 12c.1**. Draw centerlines and diagonals; project them out to a convenient distance. Extend line BC. With center at F, the midpoint of BC, and radius FA = FD, draw semi-circle JADG. Draw rectangle ABGH. Setting AB = 1, CG = BJ = .618, Ø. JG = 1 + .618 + .618 = 2.236, √5. Draw lines EG and EH; extend them to a convenient distance. Draw a line through J perpendicular to diagonal EB to find point K. Alternately divide JB by any method and draw KN parallel to AB. Draw rectangle KLMN.

12c.2. With center at P and radius PN draw semi-circle LNQ, Q is on the extension of KL. Divide KQ in half to find point R. Draw rectangle RSTU. Extend RS. With center at V and radius UV draw semi-circle SUW. Divide WR in half to find point X. Draw rectangle XYZZ'.

12c.3. Draw rectangle A'B'C'D' through point W. Find point G' on the extension of ED and H' on the extension of EC. Find point J', J'H' = 1/2 H'E'. With center at G' and radius G'J' find point L' on the extension of Z'Z. Draw line K'L' which marks the temple facade. ZY and ST mark the Hall of Appearances. ML defines the Hall of Multiplicity. ABGH locates and sizes the Bark Chapel.

12c.4. To determine the courtyard extend lines A'D' and B'C' to construct rectangle A'B'Q'P' with sides in the ratio of 1:3. The depth of the pylon R'P' is equal to $Ø^3$ of Q'P' and it extends an equal distance on either side. But we also note that diagonal S'T' is "congruent," as it were, to diagonal ED'. That is, triangle ED'T' = S'T'U'.

In these constructions we have examples of the work of people who did not see the world as we do; who did not see number mathematically but symbolically. Yet a method seems to be emerging. Triangular "pillars" and rectangles form an enclosing outline. The altitude or "spine" of the pillar is then divided by a harmonic method to place elements within the enclosure, like rungs on a ladder. An important topic here is the relationship between geometry and the grid. They are not antagonists but rather two means of attaining the harmonic idea. While it cannot be claimed in any of the examples shown that this was exactly the procedure used by ancient designers, it is hoped that these methods are close enough to assist contemporary designers. In that sense it is hoped that they would have been found worthy by Seshat to be placed in the plan room of the cosmic temple.

Greece

The Doric Order

Three "Orders" of architecture are indigenous to Greece: the Doric, Ionic and Corinthian. This section focuses on the Doric, as the story of the Ionic and Corinthian orders will be told in relation to Vitruvius. In presenting Greek architecture the modern term "orders" is somewhat misleading and restrictive in our attempt to comprehend these aesthetic phenomenon. Professor Gordon-Smith simply calls them "architectures."[1] They could be called "genera," with each particular application being a "species." The term "mode." as in the Greek modes of music is proposed here and used interchangeably with order, genera and architecture.

The one thing that can surely be said of the Doric mode of the sixth and fifth centuries, 600-400 BC, is that it is anything but a "pure" construction. It only looks that way. Nor is the design method "simple" either. In this era there was no architectural canon as we know it today. For the entire time from the seventh century BC through to Vitruvius in the first century BC, the Doric order was a "work in progress." The main sources of inspiration for the Greeks were in the eastern Mediterranean, particularly Egypt, as early as the eighth century BC. The rapid development of Greek monumental architecture in the late seventh century is directly related to the expansion of Ionian influence in Egypt through the Greek business colony at Naukratis, on the Egyptian coast.[2]

During this period the Greeks would have seen and learned from the Egyptians the nature of large dressed stone works; and these became a model for later Greek work. Coulton concludes, "*there is a considerable similarity in proportion and general effect between an early Doric colonnade and some Egyptian ones.*" In both instances the columns are five to six diameters high, and the entablatures they carry consist of three parts, a flush architrave above which is another vertical face and ending in a strong projected crown. Coulton is probably referring to Hatshepsut's temple at Deir el Bahari with its proto-Doric colonnade, **figure 1**, whose columns are cut with twelve straight faces.

Many commentators, especially those of a rationalist bent, maintain what might be called the "structuralist" concept of the origin of the Doric mode.[3] In this explanation the column, entablature and pediment elements were adopted from wood construction. The tapering of the column, like that of a tree trunk, the fluting or arising representing either the bark of the tree or the "bundling" of thinner trunks or reeds; the capital deriving from the tie-wraps holding the elements together. The key feature of the Doric, the triglyph and its relation to the metope, is said to be derived from a cap on the endgrain of the exposed crossbeams resting on the architrave. The mutules of the cornice are said to be exposed rafter ends and the guttae are the pegs that attach elements in traditional wood construction.

Although the structuralist story is not impossible it likely could only have played a small part in the development of the Doric.[4] If the triglyphs were literally structuralist, their pattern would be different on the sides and front. This would also be true of the mutules: why would they be run on the front? There are far too many guttae for them to represent pegs. Though there clearly is a structural logic here, it could only be the beginning of the story. Hersey suggests a dramatic symbolic interpretation;[5] that the triglyph is an abstraction of the thigh bones,

FIGURE 1
Proto-Doric Colonnade, North Side of Hatshepsut's Temple, Dier el Bahari, Senmut, c.1480 BC

or femurs, of sacrificial animals. The cap and regula are bindings and the guttae are drops of marrow dripping off the bound bones. More recently the theory of the triglyph as an abstraction of the sacrificial tripod has been advanced. This also has some archeological support, as a triple-mark border pattern appears as a decorative motif on various ritual objects as early as new kingdom Egypt.[6]

These early Doric works are not pure or simple and were likely designed using some sort of composite method. The didactic reconstructions here attempt to suggest possible methods in which a transition may be made from an incommensurable geometry to a rational arithmetic. No attempt is made here to put thoughts into the minds of dead builders; rather the attempt is made to help living designers apply ancient concepts of harmony, expressed through geometry and arithmetic, in their work of the moment.

Treasury of the Athenians, Delphi

The initial or minimum architectural archetype of the classical language may be said to be the tetrastyle or four-column facade. There is no complete facade type that has fewer parts, but the four-column unit forms the seed or centerpiece of many larger compositions, similar to the tetrachord in Greek music. The tetrastyle's close relation to the square, a representative of unity in the sensible realm, also indicates its "primacy."[7]

The four-column facade, whether "in antis" or "prostyle"[8] was used by the Greeks of the sixth and fifth centuries BC for small buildings known as "treasuries" located near the sites of large temples. They were essentially storage lockers for ritual objects often made of precious metals and rare minerals. Groups of such treasuries appear at Delphi for example, where they line the serpentine sacred way to the Temple of Apollo.

A well known Doric example is the "in antis" Treasury of the Athenians at Delphi, c.490 BC.[9] According to Coulton it illustrates a kind of minimum case in which the actual distance between the inner columns becomes critical.[10] The practical issue is that in the Doric mode the triglyphs are centered over the columns but when the building is small enough, the central intercolumniation, through which people and large objects must pass, becomes too small. In the Treasury of the Athenians the width of about 21'-3" would have given a central column spacing of 6'-4" and a clear space of 4'-1". The columns were slimmed down to H = 6 D from 5.5 D, but this was not enough. The inner column centers were moved out to the third points of the width of the building, a center to center interval of 7'-1" giving a 4'-10" clear opening in the center.

Archeological evidence indicates that the columns were moved after the stylobate was laid. The stylobate is composed of seven stones, four long, under the point loads and three short, between the columns. The two inner long blocks are centered below the triglyphs, not the columns, while the joints in the architrave align with the columns, not the triglyphs. Coulton concludes that the designers were, *"stretching existing modes to their limit"* to increase the central opening.[11]

Arithmetic Analysis

The elevation, based in the square, may have been planned on a grid of 16, 32, or perhaps 48, with the location of the columns moved to the 1/3rd points and their diameters trimmed to H/6. The keys to the horizontal placement of the triglyphs and metopes are that: a) the triglyph is in the ratio of 2:3; b) the metope is square, or 3:3; and c) the width of the triglyph is 1/2 D. For the purposes of our analysis the triglyph is made 2 modules wide, D = 4M. If a triglyph is to be placed over each of the four columns, and in the center of each of the three bays, this gives 7 triglyphs and 6 metopes, or 14 + 18 = 32 M, **figure 2.** This makes each triglyph 1/16th of the overall width and D 1/8th of the overall. However, the columns have been slimmed down to H/D = 6, D = 3.4 M. The width of the building is equal to its height up to the apex of the tympanum; and the height of the columns is 20.5 M, while Ø = 19.78 M. The frieze and the entablature are, by inspection, 3.5 M each, and the corona is 1.0, making the top of the cornice 28.5 M. The Greek frieze included the cap of the triglyph, which the Renaissance versions do not.

Geometric Reconstruction

As 16 is the sum of the two Pythagorean perfect numbers 10 and 6, and 4:6:10:16 or 8:12:20:32 are Fibbonacci progressions, a Ø construction is suggested, **figure 3. 3a,** Divide square ABCD by the diagonals AC and BD, and semi-diagonals CE and DE to find the 1/3rd points F and G. **3b,** Apply radius EB to EC to find point B'. With center at C draw arc B'H. HC = Ø, BH = $Ø^2$. Continue the arc to find point J. If CJ = Ø and DJ is $Ø^2$ then J also divides DC into intervals of 6 and 10. **3c,** the entablature is found by performing a Ø division of the $Ø^2$ interval. Construct 1:2 rectangle LBHM. The $Ø^3$ interval NH will give the depth of the entablature, 32 x $Ø^3$ = 7.6M.

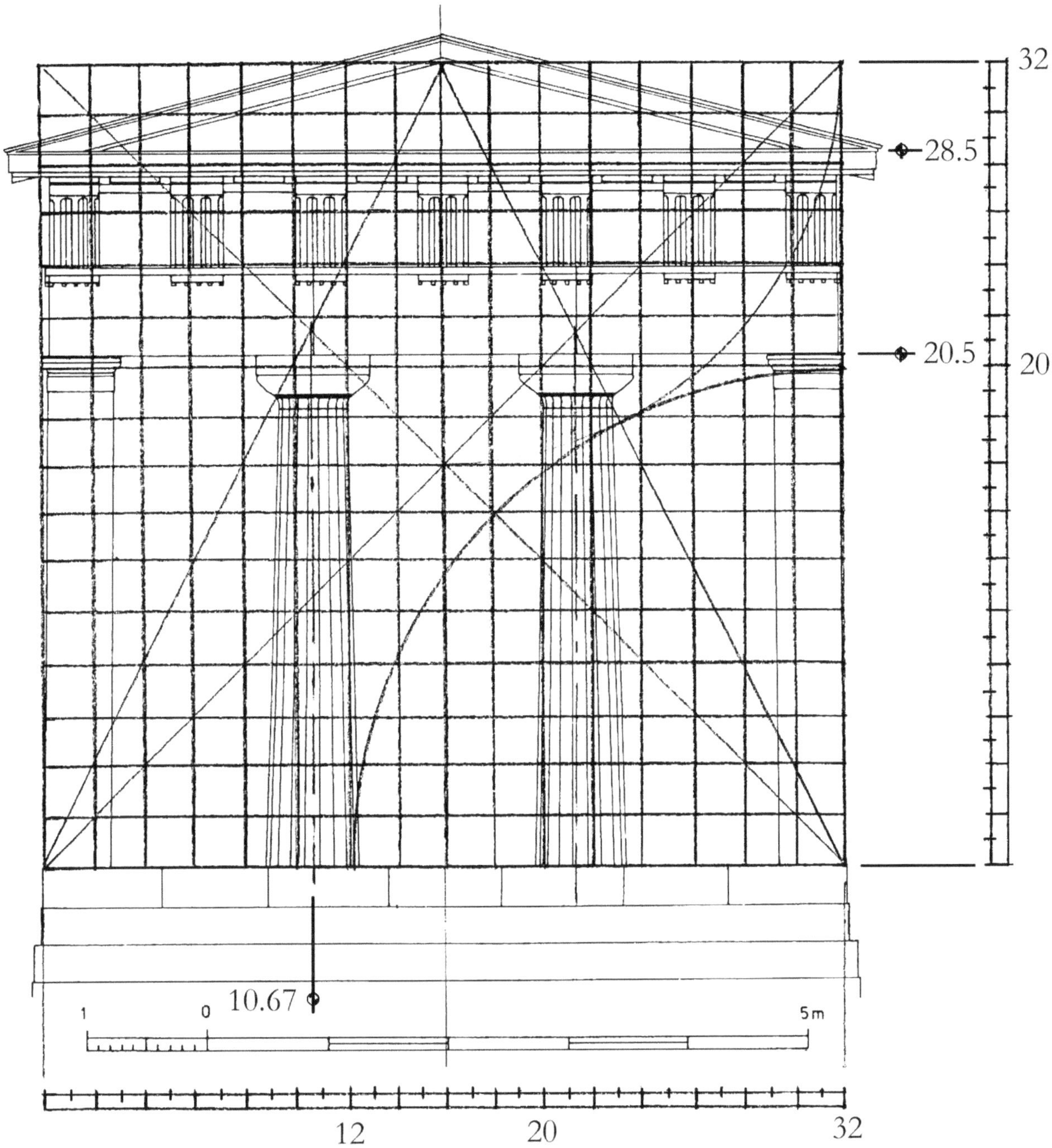

FIGURE 2

Treasury of the Athenians at Delphi. Arithmetic Analysis Using a Grid of 32

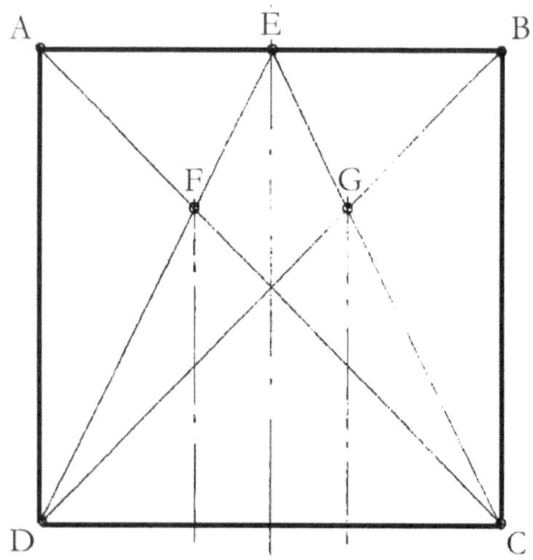

3a - Unity and Division 1

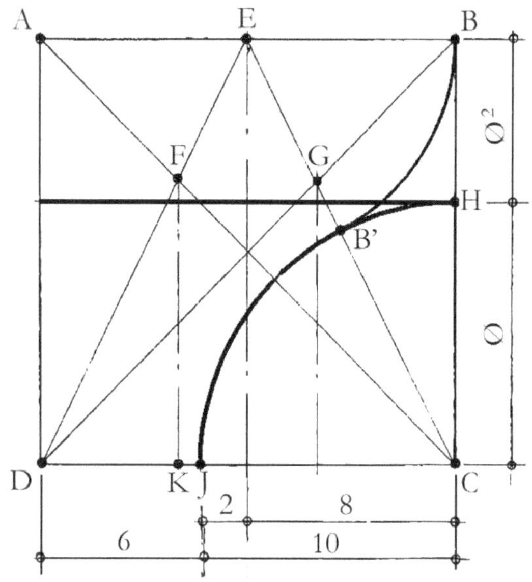

3b - Unity and Division 2

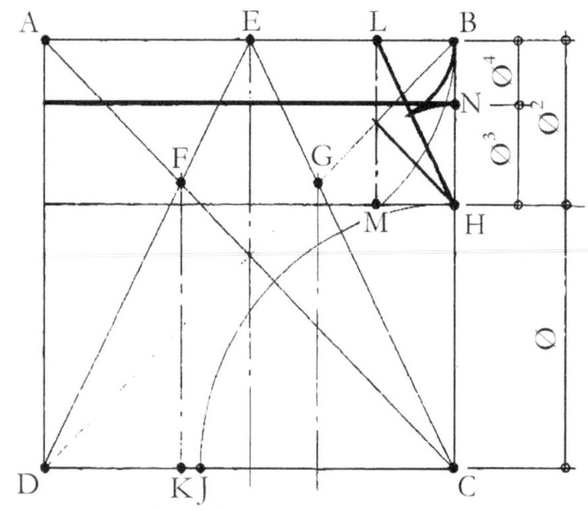

3c - Structure 1

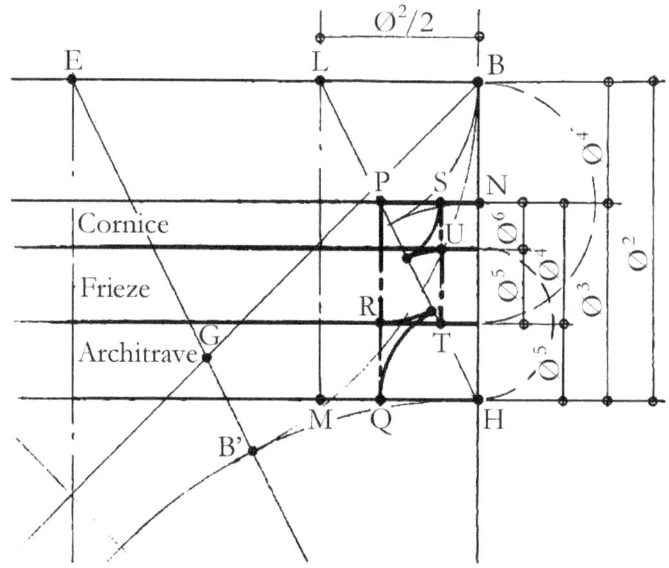

3d - Structure 2

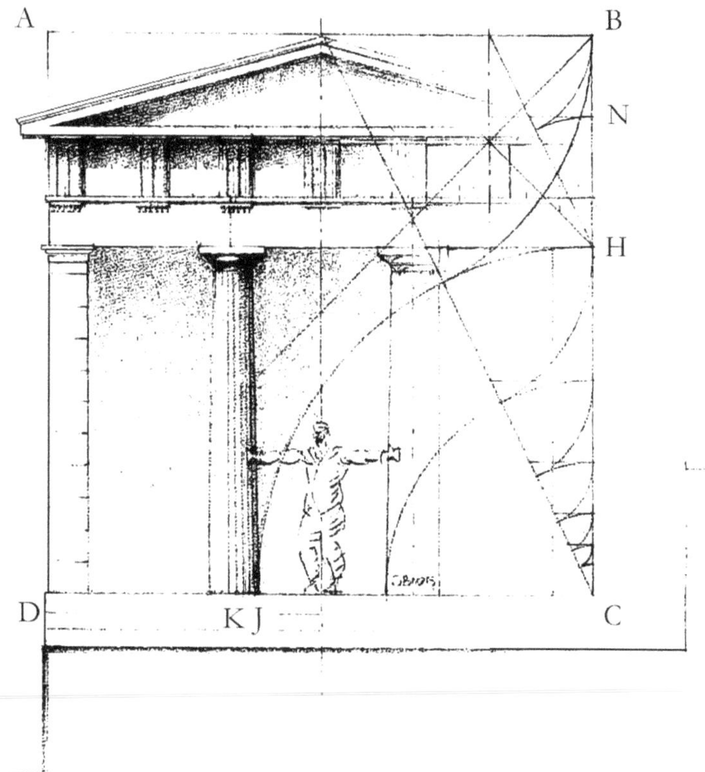

3e - Materialization

FIGURE 3

Treasury of the Athenians at Delphi. Geometric Reconstruction

3d, repeating the procedure, the $Ø^3$ interval is further divided into $Ø^4$ and $Ø^5$. $Ø^5$ gives the freeze and architrave while $Ø^6$ gives the cornice. **3e,** In the didactic reconstruction, setting the width equal to 1, the column height is Ø = .618. D may be set equal to twice the interval KJ, .667 - .618 = .049, D = .098. This gives a rather slender H/D ratio of 6.3. However we could have used $Ø^6$ = .056, giving D of .112 and H/D of 5.53; and that 2/18ths or 1/9th = .111, giving an H/D of 5.56. As to the freeze, the geometrical is $Ø^5$ = .090 and 3/32nds = .093, a difference that can be made up within the cap of the triglyph.

Comparing the geometric reconstruction with the arithmetic analysis, we note that the column height is 32 x Ø = 19.75 M + the entablature, 7.6 M makes 27.35 as opposed to 28.5, lowering the entablature and the pediment. The discrepancy is: 1.15/28.5 = 4.03%, suggesting that pure geometry, though close, may not be the complete explanation.

Composite Reconstruction

A closer result can be achieved using a composite method, **figure 4**. Begin with square ABCD. Find the 1/3 points F and G. Draw equilateral triangle DHC. Point H is at a height of 32 x $\sqrt{3}/2$ = 27.75 M. From H we count 7 M down for the frieze and architrave making the top of the columns 20.75. The frieze is 3 M with a .5M cap. Above H add 1 M for the corona, making the height 28.75M.

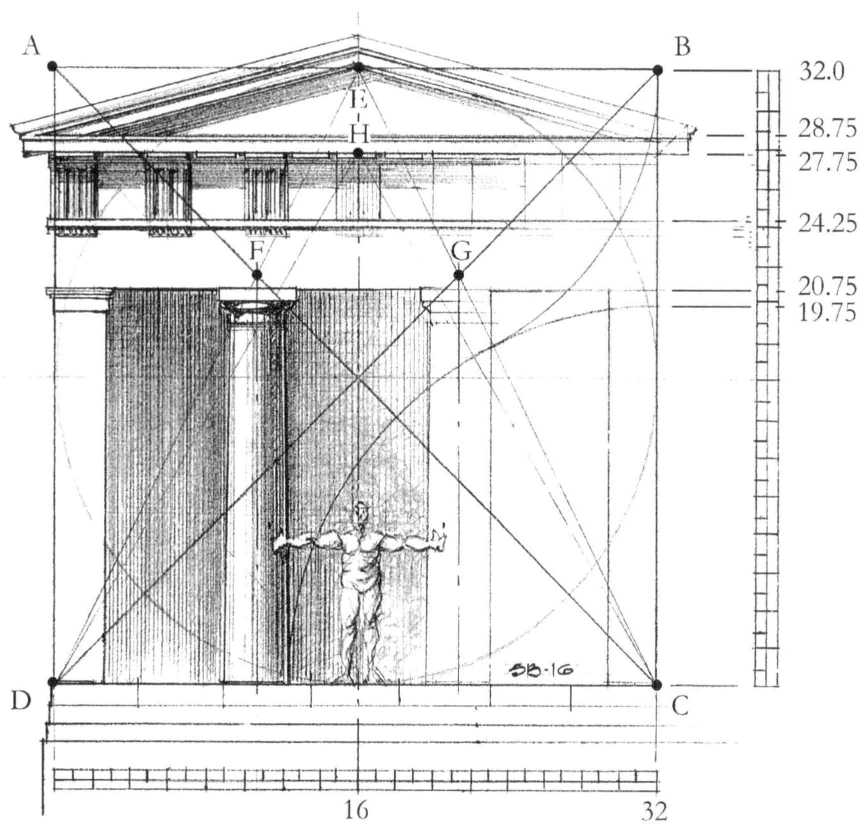

Figure 4

Treasury of the Athenians at Delphi. Composite Reconstruction

The Hephaisteion

An example of a six-column or hexastyle facade is the well-preserved Temple at Athens known as the Hephaisteion,[12] constructed c.450 BC. It sits on a rise at the south end of the agora, facing the sacred way that led to the Acropolis. Hephaestus, the Roman Vulcan, was the divinity whose province included fire, specifically the intensified and controlled fire of the furnace, leading to his patronage of the crafts, with a focus on metalwork and mechanics. Just the kind of guy you'd want to have around if you needed to move "megalithic" stone blocks and work them with metal tools.

The Myth of Hephaestus

Hephaestus is the son of Zeus and Hera, though some say he was Hera's parthenogenic child, that is, born of the goddess alone, without a father.[13] Others say that his father is Talos, a nephew of Daedalus, the mythic ancestor of artisans. Talos' mother was Daedalus' sister Perdix, which means partridge, whose mythic identity is merged here with Hera's.[14] Graves links Hera with the pre-Hellenic Great Goddess of the ancient Near East farming world. He notes that partridges were sacred to the old goddess, and that the spring equinox was celebrated with erotic rituals in which a hobbling, partridge-like dance was performed in her honor.

Hephaestus was so weak and sickly at birth that the embarrassed Hera dropped him off the side of Mount Olympus. He survived uninjured because he fell into the sea where he was rescued by the goddesses Thetis and Eurynome. They raised him in an underwater cave near Lemnos where he quickly set up a small shop and began to make various practical and ornamental metal objects. Nine years after his traumatic birth event Hera spots Thetis wearing an unusual pin. Stimulated by envy she forces Thetis to admit that it was made by Hephaestus. Hera immediately brings him back up to Olympus, sets him up in a big shop, and arranges for him to marry the hottest match on the block, Aphrodite, the goddess of physical beauty and lovemaking.[15]

Some time later, Hephaestus protested to Zeus over his harsh treatment of Hera.[16] Zeus had strung her up by the wrists after she had interfered in a plan of Herakles, one of the huge number of Zeus' illegitimate sons. For his interference, Zeus threw Hephaestus off Olympus again. This time he hit land, on the island of Lemnos, breaking both his legs. Zeus gets over his anger quickly and Hephaestus returns to Olympus, but from then on could only walk with metal braces. Lemnos is a volcanic island and a jet of asphaltic gas had burned steadily on Mount Moschylus for centuries during ancient times.

Hephaestus is described by Graves as *"ugly and ill-tempered,"*[17] but, though lame, has great upper body strength. He translates the name Hephaestus as "he who shines by day," a reference to the fire of the sun; and comments that he and Athena shared temples at Athens. As Hephaestos was solar, *"Athena was the moon-goddess, 'she who shines by night', patroness of smith-craft and of all mechanical arts."*[18]

Graves notes that the "hobbling" of the artisan divinity is a widespread tradition. The limitation on movement is similar to the Egyptian divinity Ptah, who governed coming into form. While Graves suggests that *"in primitive times smiths may have been purposely lamed to prevent them from running off and joining enemy tribes,"* he quickly adds that *"a hobbling partridge-dance was also performed in erotic orgies connected with the mysteries of smith-craft"* noting here his marriage to the erotic goddess Aphrodite. He further reminds us that *"every Bronze Age tool, weapon, or utensil had magical properties, and that the smith was something of a sorcerer."*[19]

The tenor of Hephaestus marriage to Aphrodite is related in the story of her relationship to Aries.[20] Being the governor of physical love Aphrodite "gets around" as they say, "making it" with a huge array of gods, demi-gods and heroes. But it is her persistent affair with Aries, whom Graves describes as *"the straight limbed, impetuous, drunken and quarrelsome God of War,"* and the actual father of her three children, Phobus, Deimus and Harmonia, that finally drives Hephaestus "around the bend."

As Graves tells it, Hephaestus was a happy fool until one morning Helios, the sun, as he rose saw the lovers in bed together when they overslept and told him; fire and the sun presumably being good friends. Enraged, Hephaestus creates a net of very fine bronze wires that he attaches to the posts of their bed. He then tells Aphrodite he will be away from Olympus for a few days. Aphrodite quickly arranges a date with Aries. Once they were in bed together Hephestus dropped the net on them. As the lovers awake at dawn and struggle to untangle themselves Hephaestus calls the other Olympians for a session of embarrassment and mockery. *"Up ran the gods, to watch Aphrodite's embarrassment.... Apollo, nudging Hermes, asked: "You would not mind being in Aries position, would you, net and all?" Hermes swore by his own head that he would not ... both gods laughed uproariously."* Zeus was disgusted and refused to interfere in such a vulgar domestic dispute. The lovers are eventually released from the net and Aphrodite baths in the sea to renew her virginity.

A significant symbolic aspect of this story is that that all the characters are planets. Aphrodite and Aries are Venus and Mars. Their synodic periods allow them to "conjunct" regularly, at approximately thirteen-month intervals, thus their ongoing affair in myth. Hermes is Mercury. Apollo is the sun or we might say, the concept of light, whereas Hephaestus is the fire of the sun, and Helios is the mover of the sun as a body, he drives the solar chariot. Thus there is a witty astronomical double entendre in the image of Apollo [the Sun] nudging Hermes [Mercury, which is never far from the sun], asking if he would like to be in the "position" of Aries [Mars] conjuncting with Aphrodite [Venus]. Zeus is Jupiter, whose period of movement is much longer than any of the other bodies in the story, thus he refuses to be moved.

Beyond astronomy the story is about the relationship of the artisan to beauty. The maker of objects or images is bound to seek beauty, but while married to beauty cannot possess it. This is because beauty is not a thing, or in things; it is a state of the observer, an inner experience. It cannot be owned or controlled. It cannot be given away or imposed upon, and the maker of things can only aspire to allow for the possibility of the experience which, for the observer, will be unique or virginal every time.

Arithmetic Analysis of the Hephaisteion

The Doric hexastyle portico is divided into 26 Modules, 11 triglyphs, and 10 metopes or 15 triglyph widths, M = 1/2 D, or into 52 units of 1/4 D. D = 1/13th of the overall width. Projecting a grid of 26 over the elevation,[21] **figure 5**, the columns are 11.25 units high, H/D = 5.625. The top of the corona is at 15, making the entablature = 3.75 units, plus .5 units for the cyma = 4.25 units. The apex of the pediment is at 18.5, plus the cyma, .5 = 19 units, recalling the Egyptian canon of 19 with all its symbolic implications.

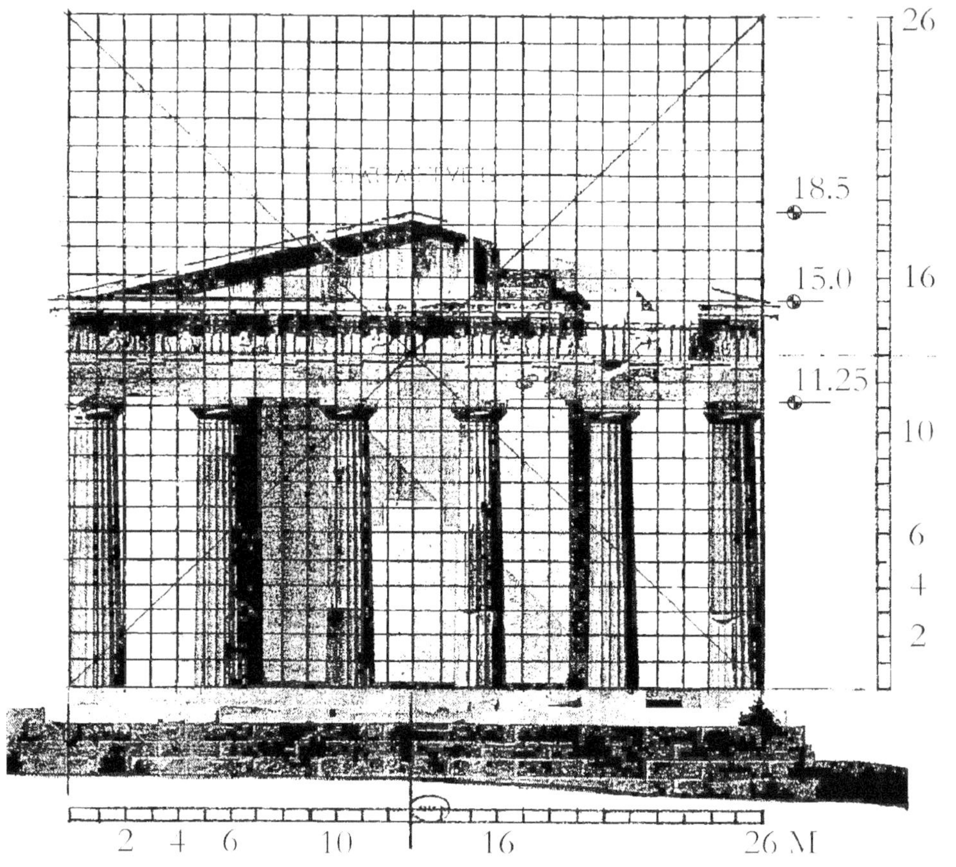

FIGURE 5

Hephaisteion, Athens, c.450 BC. Arithmetic Analysis

RECONSTRUCTION WITH √5

Figure 6a. A geometrical reconstruction utilizing Ø and √5 begins with square ABCD, vertical centerline EF, semi-diagonal EC, and horizontal centerline GH. With center at C and radius CF draw arc FH and find point J. Draw line JK parallel to CD. KC = 1/√5 = .447, 26 x 1/√5 = 11.62M, the height of the columns.

Figure 6b. With center at E and radius EB draw arc GB to find point L. With center at C and radius CL draw arc LM. CM = Ø = .618, 26 x Ø = 16.07 M, dividing BC into intervals of 10 and 16, giving the top of the cyma.

Figure 6c. With center at C and radius CG draw arc GN. NC = √2/2 = .707, 26 x √2/2 = 18.38M, the apex of the tympanum, plus 1M for the corona and cyma = 19.38 M.

Figure 6d. In the reconstruction D = 2/26 = .077 and $Ø^4/2$ = .073; the width of the triglyph, the key unit, =1/26 = .038 and $Ø^7$ = .034. The column height is 11.62 as opposed to 11.25. The entablature is .618 - .447 = .171 = 4.45 units, as opposed to 4.25. 18/26 = .692 and √2/2 = .707, although the tympanum's height of 3 units, 3/26 = .115 and $Ø^3/2$ = .118. The column height 11.25/26 = .432 and 1/√5 = .447. The geometrical version is about .37 M higher, or about 3.3% of 11.25. The entablature is .171 x 26 = 4.45 M, as opposed to 4.25. The overall height is 19.38 M, retaining the 14^0 degree rake angle, as opposed to 19.

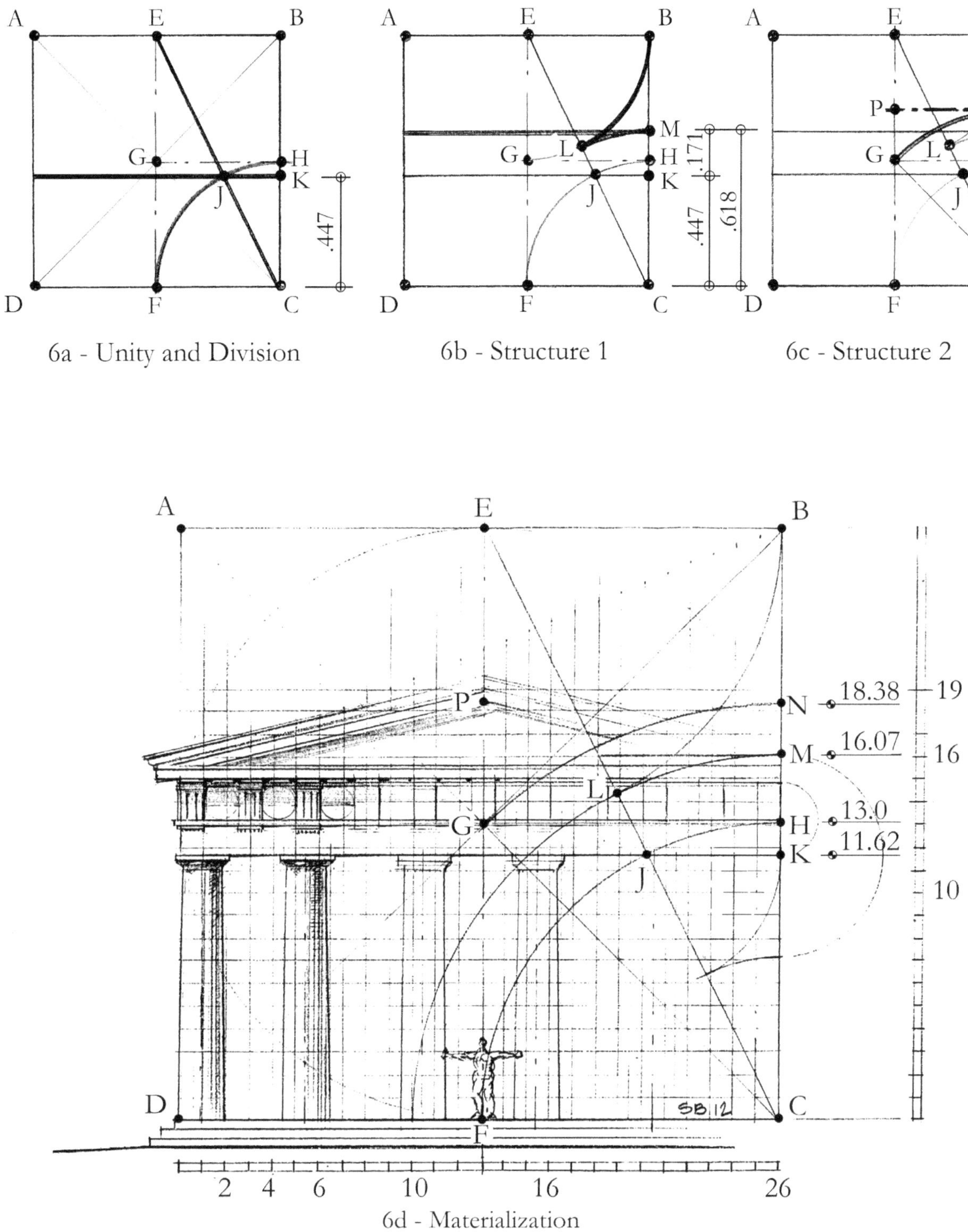

FIGURE 6a-d

Hephaisteion. Geometric Reconstruction

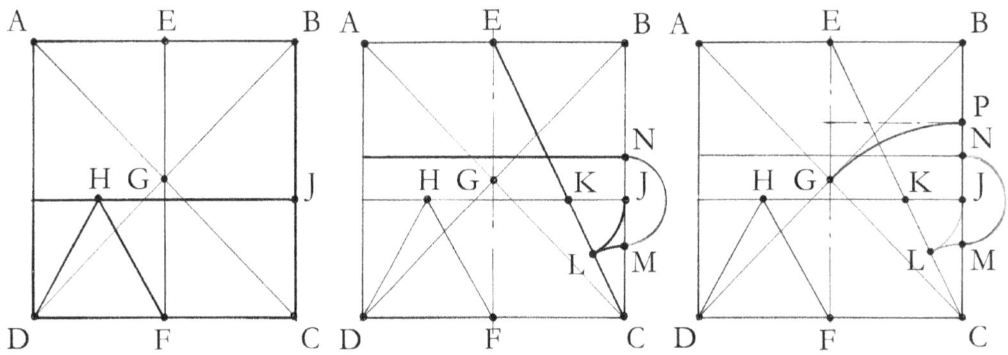

7a - Unity & Division   7b - Structure 1   7c - Structure 2

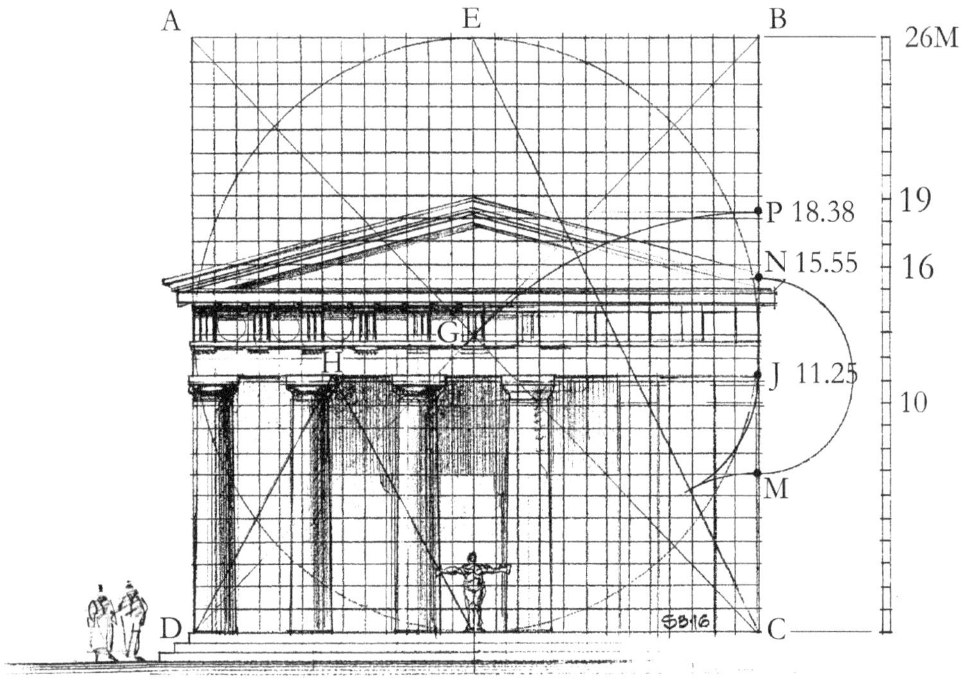

7d - Materialization

FIGURE 7a-d

Hephaisteion. Geometric Reconstruction Using √3

Reconstruction Using √3

Though André's elevation indicated by inspection that the columns are 11.25 M high, orthodox sources give 11 M.[22] 11/26 = .423 while $\sqrt{3}/4$ = .433, suggesting a reconstruction using a modulation of $\sqrt{3}$, **figure 7**.

7.a. Begin with square ABCD, vertical center line EF, center G. Draw equilateral triangle DHF and line HJ parallel to BC, marking the height of the colonnade, $\sqrt{3}/4$ = .433. 26 x .433 = 11.25 M

7.b. Draw semi-diagonal EC and find point K on JH. With center at K and radius KJ draw arc JL. With center at C and radius CL draw arc LM. With center at J and radius JM draw arc MN. Interval JN will be the depth of the entablature. It is $Ø^2$ of JC = .433 x .382 = .165 x 26 = 4.3 M.

7.c. With center at C and radius CG draw arc GP. CP = $\sqrt{2}/2$ = .707 x 26 = 18.38 M, the apex of the split-fillet, +.5 for the cyma = 18.88 M.

7.d. 11 to 11.25 is a difference of 2.7% in the height of the columns. The entablature is 4.3 M opposed to 4.25. The apex of the pediment is essentially at the orthodox location, 19 M.

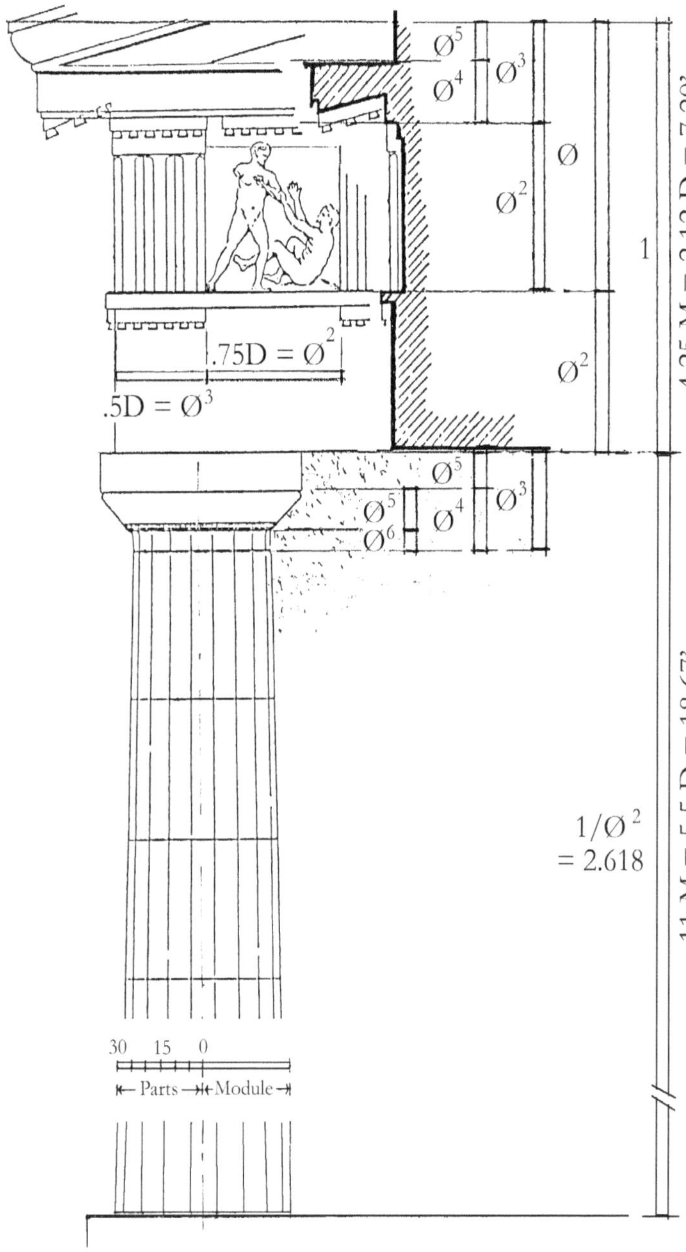

FIGURE 8
Hephaisteion Entablature

HEPHAISTEION ENTABLATURE

The column height is taken as 11 M and the entablature as 4.25 M, **figure 8.**[23] If the overall height of the order is taken as 1, the entablature is, 4.25/15.25 = .278 and the column is 11/15.25 = .721, very close to both $\sqrt{2}/2$ = .707, and to 1/3, or .25/.75. If the height of the column is taken as 1, the entablature is 4.25/11 = .386 close to $Ø^2$, .382. If the entablature is taken as 1 the column height is $1/Ø^2$ = 2.618. Thus the order could be constructed by starting with the overall height and striking off the $\sqrt{2}$ cut for the height of the columns; or starting with the height of the column take $Ø^2$ and apply it above the column.

If the depth of the entablature = 1, the architrave and frieze are $Ø^2$ and the cornice is $Ø^3$, while the cyma is $Ø^5$ and the corona, including the mutule band, is $Ø^4$.[24]

If the capital is .5 D deep it is $Ø^3$ of the entablature, the abacus and echinus are both $Ø^5$ and the necking is $Ø^6$. As the entablature is $Ø^2$ of the column height, the capital is $Ø^5$ of the column.

Hephaisteion's Plan

The width of the building is divided into 52 Parts, each P = .5 M and .25 D. A complete modulation of triglyphs and metopes for the length of the building is 25 triglyphs + 24 metopes giving a length of 122 P, **figure 9**. This gives an L/W ratio of 122/52 = 2.346 as opposed to the geometrical √5 x 52 = 116.27/52 = 2.236, a difference of 5.73P over 122, or 4.7%. The plan may thus be seen as a √5 rectangle "stretched" to the nearest Doric modulation.

The width of the inner temple, GH, is approximately equal to 1/2 of the overall width, EF. The back of the cella, KL, is centered on EF. The Adyton is set by half-square KLHG. The Naos is within double square GHMN the Pronaos, NMPQ can be set by taking Ø of MN.

A resonance of Egypt appears in that EF could have been located by 1:4 pillar STC and GH determined at UV, as half of EF. MNR is an 8:5 triangle, or 4:5 pillar and DRC is two 4:5 pillars, a 10:4 triangle, if DC = 1, RS = $Ø^2$.

In fairness the discrepancies here must be noted. The height of the colonnade is given as 11M by BF and Normand, while André's rendering indicates 11.25. Our √5 reconstruction has given a height of 11.62, while the √3 reconstruction gives 11.25, matching the arithmetic analysis. 11.25/11.62 is a difference of 3.3% of the column height, but only 1.9% of the overall height of 19. The entablature is 4.45 in figure 6 and 4.3 in figure 7, while the references give 4.25. These differing constructions establish a range or spectrum in which the designer should try to stay to keep the feeling of the old work.

But rather than focusing on such discrepancies what may be observed here is the transition from a geometrical to an arithmetic system growing organically from the design and construction process itself. The geometrical method, especially when using trans-rationals, represents the flowing, animating spirit; while the arithmetic method represents body, the crystallized earthly container, vehicle of the spirit.[25] Though these may be dyadic opposite qualities they are not separate, since a living being must have both; their combination gives rise to psyche, mind, or soul.

Allowing the design to undergo a similar process, that is, implanting spirit into matter, may be said to "ensoul" the temple. On one level, we may say that the designer has given the illusion of animation, but on another level, the numerical powers involved are the forces of creation themselves, and the life is "real." Since both ourselves as individuals and the cosmos are "analogic," a temple created with such methods becomes an "anthropic mesocosm," linking the individual to the universe.

Though the √5 construction is elegant and workmanlike it is further away from the original than the √3 construction. However, it appears that under all the gridded arithmetic we see the presence of the trans-rational formative powers, √2, √3 and √5; but especially Ø, as the sequence 2, 4, 6, 10, 16, 26, ... is a multiple of the Fibonacci series. We have to wonder what those old Greeks were studying at the Egyptian temple schools. Our absolute inability to pin the temple down perhaps gives us a glimpse of the marriage of Hephaestus and Aphrodite, of the search for beauty, which remains elusive, frustrating, even faithless, but for the fulfillment of which the artisan and builder are bound to strive.

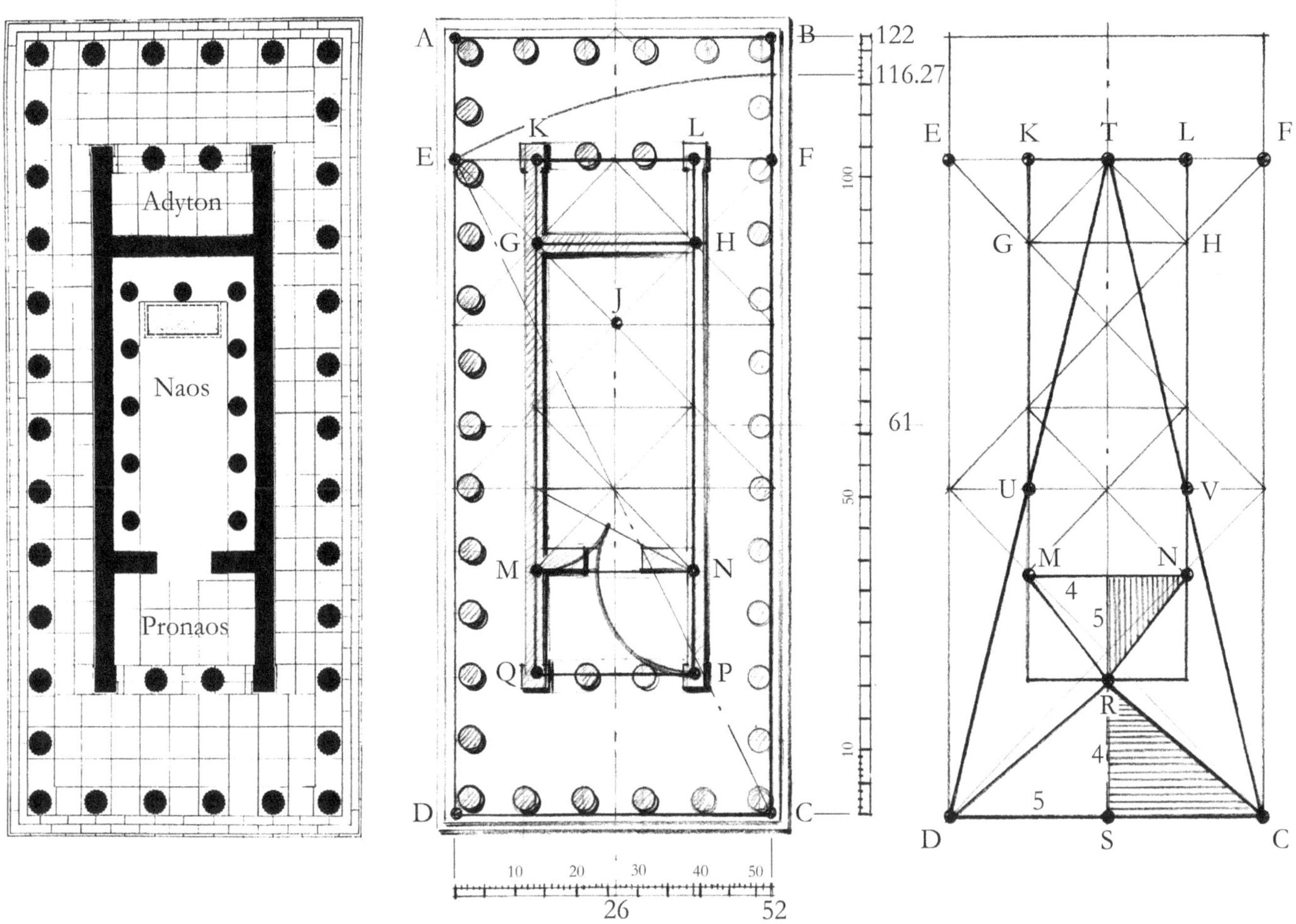

FIGURE 9
Hephaisteion Plan

THE PARTHENON

Although there can hardly be an architectural work more central to the self image of the West than the Parthenon it will not be dwelt on here. So much has been said, written and drawn about it that, like the Great Pyramid, nothing new can be presented here and no "secrets" will be revealed. The goal is not to determine some absolute methodological certainty or to find out "what they knew and when they knew it;" questions that are beyond the scope of this study. The goal here is to suggest, on the basis of reasonable analysis of available data, methods by which designers today can produce new work that contains a living spirit of precedential work. As the rational and trans-rational ratios are the representatives, or are metaphoric of the very powers of creation themselves, study and practice of their use are a path to implanting such vitality. This goal must be kept in mind when approaching a work like the Parthenon to avoid becoming hopelessly mired in minutia.

The facade, **figure 10a,**[26] is octastyle, monotriglyphic, having 15 triglyphs and 14 metopes. If the building were done according to later orthodoxy with M = 1/2D = 1 triglyph, and a metope =

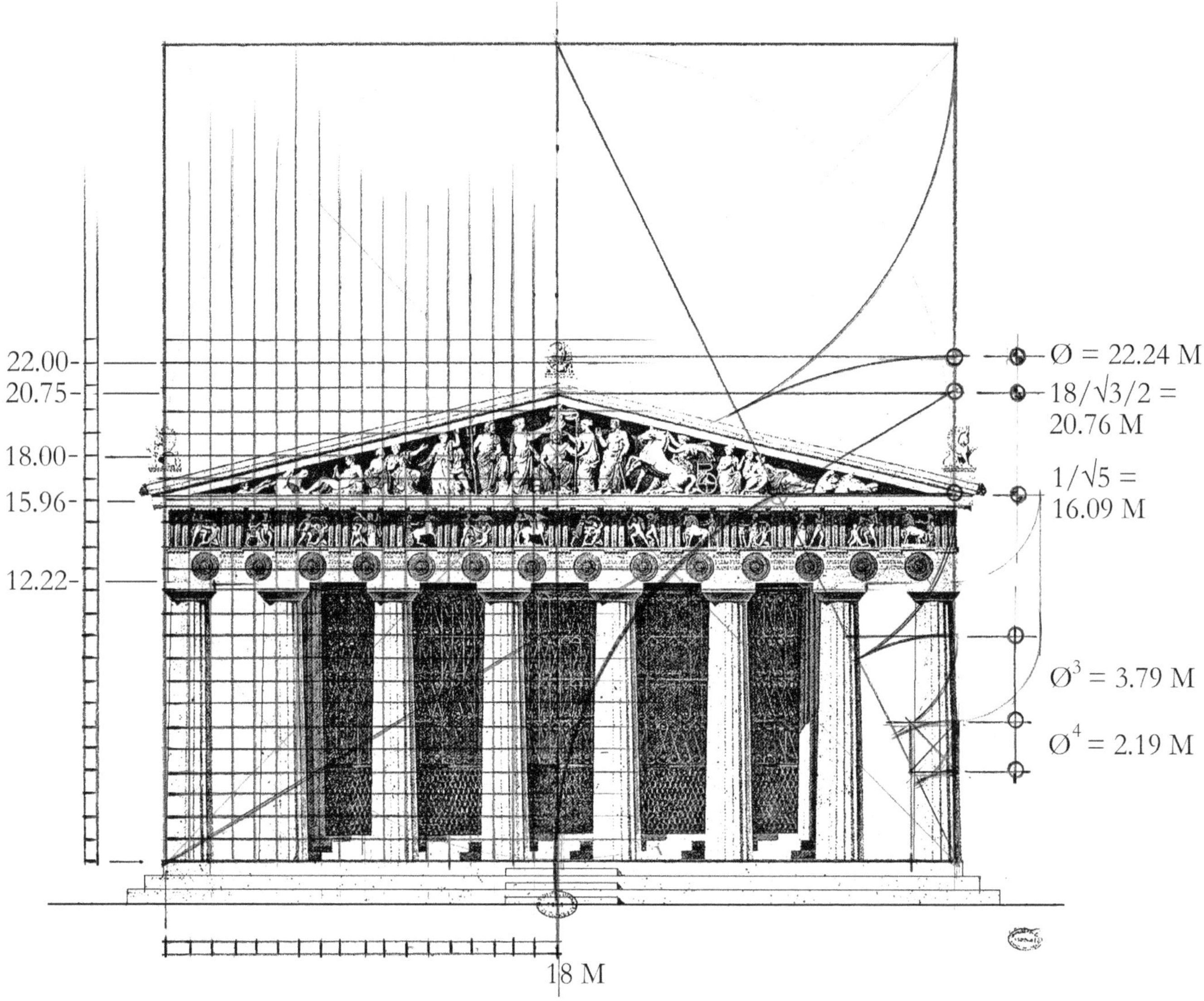

FIGURE 10a

The Parthenon, Athens, Ictinus, c.450 BC

1.5 M, then its facade width would have 15 M for triglyphs + 21 M for metopes = 36 M. The width of the building is 101.24', D = 6.17', M = 3.08'.[27] However, 101.24'/36M = 2.815' making D = 5.63'. If we maintain M at 3.08' then the overall width = 36 x 3.08'=110.88'. In the actual building the column module, CM, was maintained at 30 Parts while the freeze module, FM, was narrowed to 27 P. For analysis here the FM is used, making CM 33.33 P. Given the column height of 11 CM, 33.33 x 11 = 366.6 P which divided by 30 P/CM = 12.22 of the smaller FMs. The entablature, to the top of the corona is 101 P,[28] divided by 27 FM = 3.74 FM. 12.22+3.74=15.96 FM.

In the geometrical analysis the top of the corona is 1/√5 = .447 x 36 = 16.09. From this the entablature is "hung."[29] Taking 16.09, the height of the order as 1, $Ø^3$ = 16.09 x .236 = 3.79, 16.09 - 3.79 = 12.30, giving the top of the columns. The apex of the split fillet, by inspection is at 20.75 FM while the height of a half-equilateral triangle is 18/.867 = 20.76. Lastly the center of the anthemion is at Ø = 22.24 FM. The column diameter is 33.33 P, or 2.11 FM while $Ø^4$ of 16.09 = 2.19.

In plan, **figure 10b.1**, the building is 101.33' x 228.17', a ratio of 1/.443, very close to 1/√5 = .447. The "pure" geometrical shape would be 101.33 x √5 = 226.57'; an extension of 1.6', or 0.7% of the side length, to reach the next complete Doric modulation beyond the geometrical, rectangle AEFD.

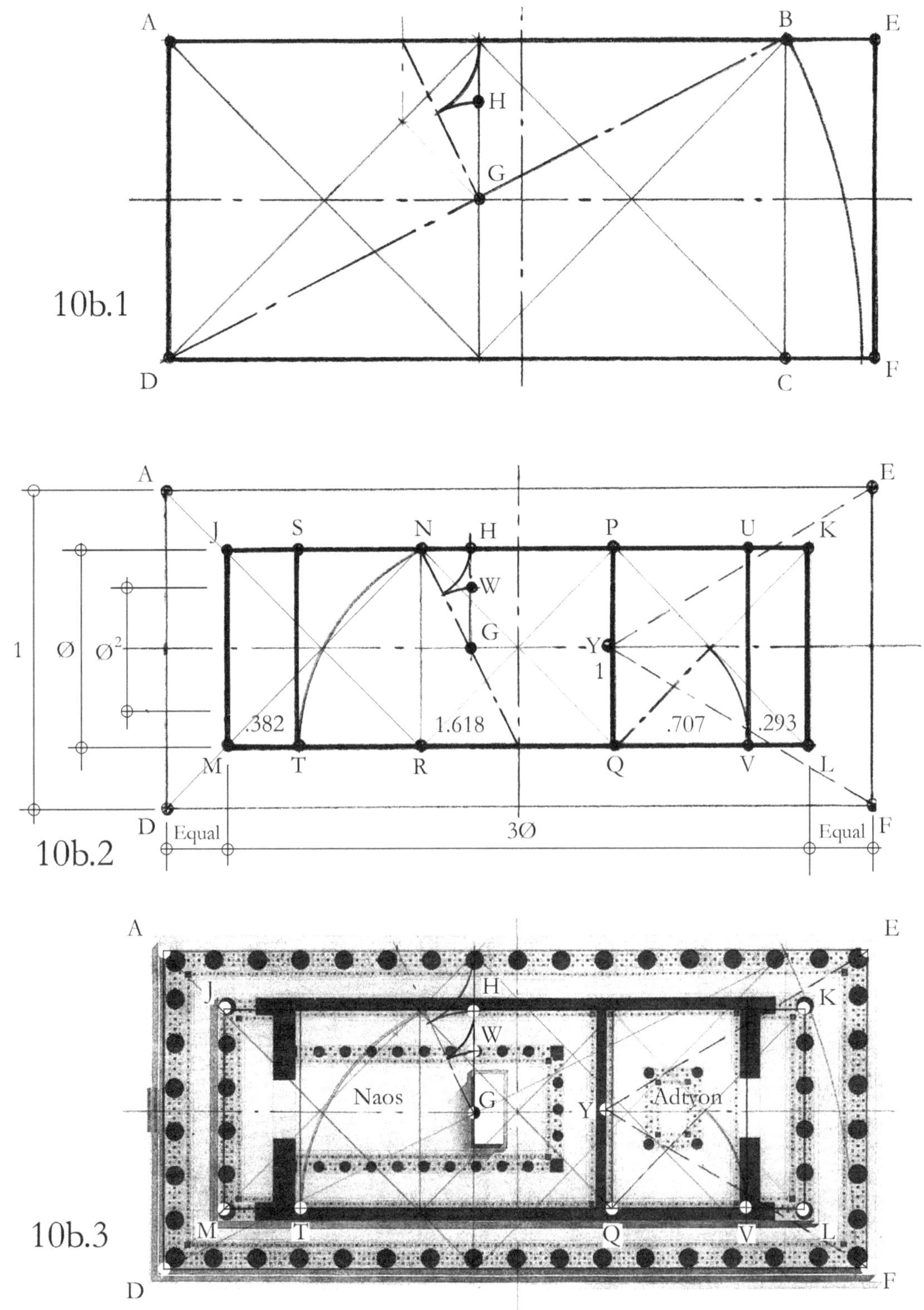

FIGURE 10b
The Parthenon Plan

The inner temple is 63.0' wide internally, while, 101.25' x Ø = 62.57', marked by point H in **10b.1-2**. By inspection, the length of the inner temple is ≈ 1:3, rectangle JKLM, centered on AEFD, **10b.2**. Central square NPQR is extended by Ø to position the naos. The adyton is framed by √2/2 of PQ, QV. The aisle of the naos, **10b.3**, is Ø of GH, point W; or Ø^2 of AB.[30] Line GH also

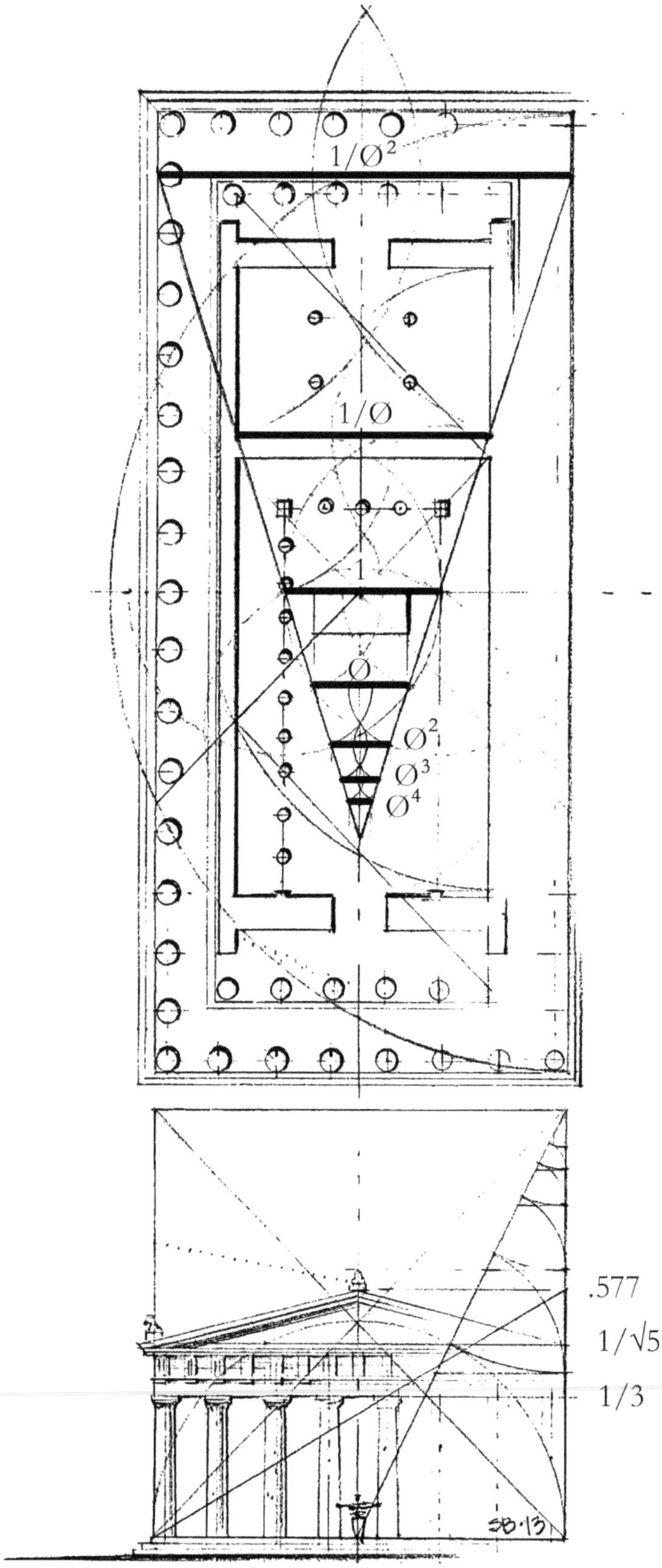

FIGURE 10c

The Parthenon. Reconstruction Using the Ø Pillar

positions the statue base whose width is $Ø^3$ x $Ø^5$. PQ, the joint of the naos and adyton could also have been positioned by the apex of equilateral triangle EYF, reminiscent of the Egyptian pillar.

An archetypal octastyle, a near approach to the Parthenon, could be made using a "pentagonal pillar" with a Ø scale, **figure 10c,**[31] to give all the major width increments, starting with a unit increment of 1 at the center of the plan. From these seeds a series of rectangles can be constructed. Taking the $1/Ø^2$ interval as the width construct a square of the $1/Ø^2$ interval centered on the building center. Then construct a √5 rectangle centered on this square giving the overall length and width of the building. With the interval of 1/Ø, the width of the naos, construct a 1:3 rectangle, centered on the √5 rectangle, giving the perimeter of the inner temple. This rectangle is divided at the 1/Ø line. The naos is a Ø rectangle, 1/Ø x $1/Ø^2$, its inside length equaling the building's width. The adyton is a √2 rectangle. To these are added the thicknesses of the "pylons" to give the pronaos and opisthodomos. Within the naos construct a square with side = 1, centered on the building center, three of whose sides give the naos' colonnade. The interval of Ø gives the width of the statue base. This is backed up to the building center and is $Ø^3$ deep. The $Ø^2$ interval gives the entry width.

To obtain the elevation redefine overall width, $1/Ø^2$, as 1 and square it up.[32] Strike off the lower 1/3 for the height of the colonnade, and a √5 rectangle for the top of the corona. The apex of the pediment is at 36/[√3/2] = .577. The triglyphs and columns are placed by division into 36, D = 2/36 = .056, while $Ø^6$ = .056.

On the Greek artistic process Plotinus writes, *"Phidias made the statue of Zeus upon no model among things of sense but by apprehending what Zeus would look like if he chose to become manifest to sight."*[33] Thus the temple may be said to be the formative powers of the cosmos made visible. Hambidge comments that the Greeks were not "artistic idealists," in the modern sense, *"The artistic idealists of today substitute themselves for nature. The classic Greek eliminated himself as much as possible and endeavored to let nature, at its best, tell the story.... Instead of brooding about himself he tried to understand the deeper meaning of natural phenomena and to become an unprejudiced interpreter."*[34] An important key to such a method is downplaying the ego, which allows oneself to become connected to the "deeper meaning," the sense of Unity carried by the proportional relationships.

These fifth-century BC Doric works are not pure or simple, they only appear to be so. They were likely created through some composite method of geometry adjusted by arithmetic. In these didactic reconstructions it is attempted to show possible methods in which a transition may be made from an incommensurable geometry to a rational arithmetic. No attempt is made here to put thoughts into the minds of long dead builders; rather the attempt is made to help living designers apply ancient concepts of harmony expressed through geometry and arithmetic, in their work of the moment.

No firm conclusions can be reached by the analysis or reconstructions here. The base illustrations used are secondary reproductions of drawings from a variety of sources. Any degree of certainty in such analysis must be based on actual measurements preferably taken in person, but at least from authoritative sources. We may say, however, that for the ancient Greeks the Doric mode was always a work in progress, perhaps utilizing an Egyptian background; and though there is a sense of proportion at work here, there is also a kind of "open-ended" spirit, a sense of optimistic self-development that has characterized the West ever since.

Mystery Religions

The major religious form of the Greco-Roman world was the Mystery religions. These were a series of homegrown Western and imported Eastern mythic systems. Some were of very ancient origin, some were newly synthesized, in a process known as syncretism.

In prehistory the predominant spiritual form was shamanic. The shaman makes a journey of consciousness that may include contact with "helpers" in plant, animal, or human form, sometimes one's own ancestors. Useful or even critical information relevant to physical survival is obtained from them, or in modern psychological terms, brought into consciousness. In the community of the shaman this helper or sacred ancestor, actual or imaginal, becomes an object of veneration.

As the community grows it becomes more elaborate and differentiated. The means of holding it together must now become more abstract. Thus the city-state is governed by law, rather than custom. Religion becomes governed by myth, spoken and later written by specialists, rather than the direct word of the shaman in the moment.

The shamanic system is thus "encapsulated" by temple religion. The ancestor-helper of the shaman becomes the sacred ancestor of the polis. This person is either identified with the deity itself or is said to be the descendant of a deity while the animate cosmos of the shaman is personified in various nature deities, perhaps related to the shaman's animal and plant "helpers." In this early period, writing is virtually a monopoly of the temples. New and more abstract knowledge, particularly about astronomy, is confined there. Also keep in mind that the social "mode of participation" in the early city-state is sanguinal, that is, one's social place is determined by maternal birth. Thus participation in the temple system becomes hereditary. The system is also localized in a particular place, with particular names and attached to particular landforms.

This relatively stable and well balanced world, however, is subject to conquest by warfare. The loser's spiritual system would either be destroyed or, if the city was large and economically significant, incorporated in the victor's system. Destruction of the city is not just a political or economic loss. It is also a loss of ties to the land, to one's ancestors, and therefore to one's divinities, indeed, to one's own spiritual center. People in such a situation became the dispossessed, the poor, and the slaves in the imperial capital. They are no longer participants in the traditional religious system.

On the positive side, the empire unites people of widely different backgrounds. This is both its political challenge and its creative possibility. A new "myth of governance" or national story must be created. Since the right to govern is still based on sanguinal descent, the governor's deity becomes the state deity, but these deities are only available directly to the governing family or clan. To govern such an enlarged state requires a long-distance administration. Literacy, and the higher knowledge associated with it begins to move beyond the temple.

This process, which had been under way for some time, was given a large boost by the conquests of Alexander the Great, c.330 BC. The incorporation of Anatolia, Mesopotamia, Egypt, Persia and even parts of India into the Greek world opened the doors to the era of syncretism. The job was finished by the workmanlike Romans, circa 50 BC, who united the entire circum-Mediterranean world. Mystery religions included those of Orpheus, Dionysus, Sibyl, Isis, Serapis, Mithra, Hermes, Demeter, Hercules and others. There were also official state Mysteries such as Sol Invictus and Jupiter Dolichenus.

In the late antique world the Mystery religions declined because: 1) daily life for increasing numbers of people became spiritually unclear and/or uncentered, largely because of physical dislocation; 2) state religion was political and not an answer to one's individual needs; 3) knowledge of the physical world, particularly about astronomy, became more refined and moved into the public realm beyond the temple, fostering rational speculation and challenging myth.

Angus gives these general characteristics of the Mysteries[35]: 1) they included a sacerdotal drama and ritual, constituting an initiation; 2) used mythic and iconic symbols; 3) involved the idea of "gnosis," direct knowledge of the deity through an actual experience of union, not based on faith; 4) included an "eschatology," a story of what happens after death; 5) were both a cosmology and a personal pathway, making an analogy between the individual and the cosmos, called anthropos; 6) participation resulted in redemption and salvation for the individual.

Angus cites three stages of a Mystery religion:

I. Preparation and probation, called in Greek "katharsis." This included: 1) investigation or confession, an opening up of one's life to inspection in some form; 2) purification, possibly including baptism or blood sacrifices; 3) ascetic practices including fasting, abstinence, or self-mortification; 4) pilgrimages; 5) vows of secrecy and their penalties; 6) elaborate rites including new names, costumes, makeup, lights, use of intoxicants, dancing, and use of ritual tools.

II. Initiation, called in Greek "muesis." This consists of a story of death and rebirth, reenacted as a ritualized participatory Mystery drama. The initiate, called a "mystes," is ritually murdered in such a way that they may not know whether they are alive or dead; presented to the divinity, given instruction, vowed to secrecy and returned to the world. During this drama the initiate undergoes an "apotheosis" or transformation in which "sympatheia," a communion, spiritual marriage, or joint identification with the deity is achieved.

III. Blessedness and Salvation, called in Greek "epopteia." Establishing sympatheia and beholding an epiphany of the deity is considered the same as the attainment of salvation and immortality, a release from fate.

The religious system of the Mysteries forms the cultural, spiritual and philosophical background to the aesthetics of the classical orders of architecture. The architectonic elements of the classical orders were developed for buildings in the service of, and with participation in the Mystery system. They would have formed the visual-spatial enclosure for the ritual drama of the individual's identification with the divinity.

Rome I – Vitruvius

Vitruvius on Number

Vitruvius opens his presentation on the design of temples with a lesson on number. *"The design of temples depends on symmetry, the principles of which must be carefully observed by the architect. They are due to proportion, in Greek "analogia." Proportion is a correspondence among the measures of the members of an entire work, and of the whole to a certain part selected as standard. From this result the principles of symmetry. Without symmetry and proportion there can be no principles in the design of any temple; that is, if there is no precise relation between its members, as in the case of those of a well shaped human body."*[1]

Vitruvius has previously told us[2] that "order" is a system of related linear measures of elements. When considered as ratios these create a specific pattern of "proportion" which establishes "symmetry." Symmetry is, in turn, the basis of eurhythmy, "good movement" or proper harmony in the finished work. Achievement of eurhythmy leads to a sense of unity in the work and contributes to the observer's "anamnesic" experience of beauty. Eurhythmy could also be seen as the establishment of a kind of initiatic "sympathia," particularly if a phi symmetry is used.

By immediately associating proportion and symmetry with the human body Vitruvius seems to be suggesting that achievement of proportion–symmetry–eurhythmy–beauty could also impart a vital, living quality to architecture. Beauty, or in Latin, "venustatis," is the province of the goddess Venus, the Greek Aphrodite. It is this goddess who, in the myth of Pygmalion, animates the perfectly wrought statue.

Vitruvius gives specific examples of symmetry from the human body: chin to hairline = 1/10th of overall body height; wrist to tip of middle finger also = 1/10th of height; head from chin to crown = 1/8th of height; pit of neck to hairline = 1/6th of height. The face from chin to hairline is divided into thirds, 1/3 from chin to bottom of the nose, 1/3 from nose to top of eyes, and 1/3 from eyebrows to hairline. The length of the foot is 1/6th of the overall height; from the center of the chest to the elbow and from the elbow to the fingertips are both 1/4th of the body's height.[3]

Next is the description of what has come to be called the Vitruvian Man, subject of the well-known sketch by Leonardo da Vinci,[4] **figure 1**. Vitruvius tells us here, in effect, that the body has two centers, one at the navel with the arms and legs in the shape of the letter "X" and another center at the perineum with the body in the shape of the letter "T." The circle and square created by these centers both have perimeters that are equal to each other within 3%. Thus the human body may be said to "square the circle." In Vitruvius' illustration the human being symbolically combines the heavenly circle and the earthly square thus geometrically recapitulating the Pythagorean-Orphic cosmogony of the "hieros gamos" or sacred marriage of matter and spirit from which life arises.

By equating the concepts of proportion and "ana-logia'[5] Vitruvius may be seen to be pointing to the "logos." Logos, as the concept appears in Plato's *Timaeus*, may be said to mean "the proportional relationship which gives order and meaning to the cosmos."[6] In that dialog logos is the numerical tool used by the Divinity to divide unity in such a way as to allow for its harmonic reintegration.

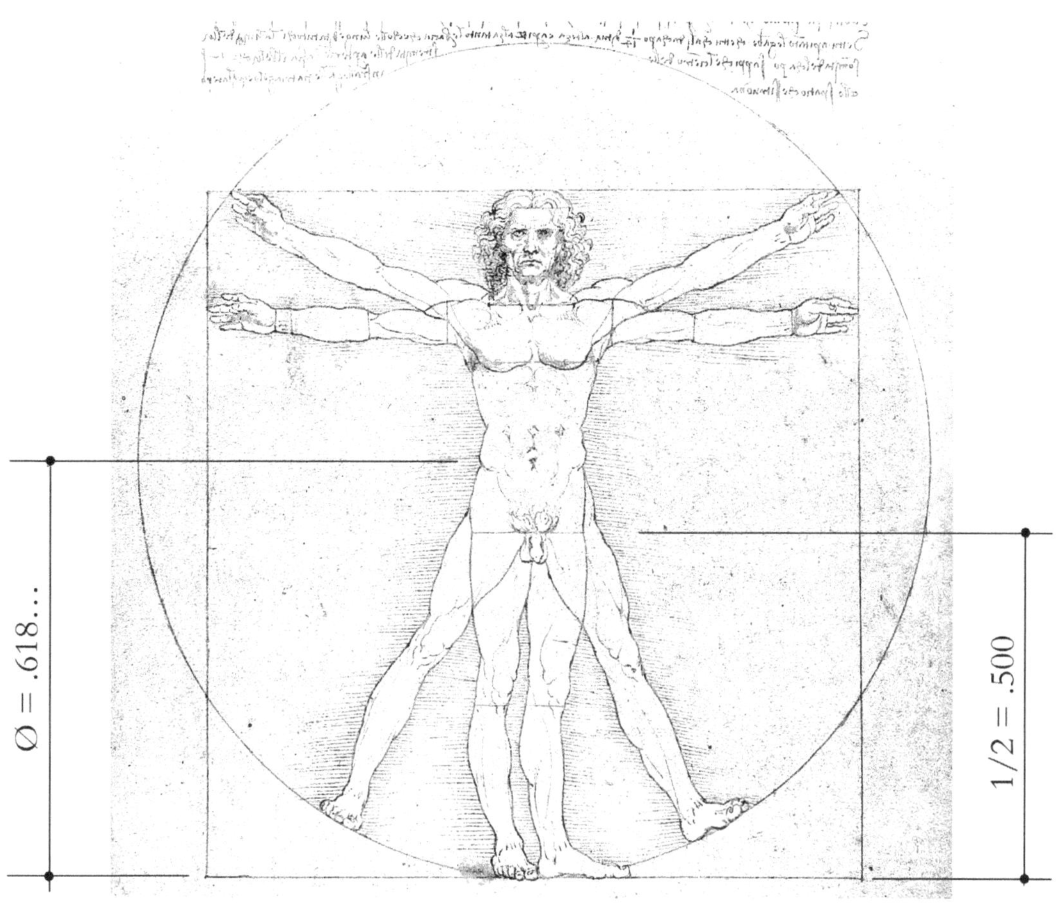

Permeter of square = side x 4 = 1 x 4 = 4
Circumference of circle = π x D = 3.14... x 1.236... = 3.88...
Ø squares the circle within 3%

FIGURE 1
Da Vinci's Vitruvian Man Squares the Circle

By illustrating analogia with the example of the human body Vitruvius seems to be making reference to the concept of anthropos, the ideal or cosmic man, who is constructed by analogy to the cosmos. In the Mystery traditions the individual human soul is said to be constructed by the same analogy. When this cosmic man lies down on the earth, as he does in Vitruvius' illustration, his measures give the paradigm for the plan of the temple.[7]

The work of many of the Mystery religions of Vitruvius' day was a series of initiations in which the candidate ultimately experienced an identification with the divinity called the "sympatheia." It is suggested by the nature of Vitruvius' presentation that this process could have been facilitated by the measures of the temple itself. In Pythagorean terms we might say the vital quality, life itself, was imparted by the Divinity to the cosmos through the logos, a pattern of proportion, a symmetry, which extends through the individual human soul to the body itself; thus allowing for the possibility of the individual's re-identification with unity. In this context it may be suggested that this living quality, or certainly at least some aspects of it, may also be imparted to the temple if it too is constructed by analogy. The temple may then become a

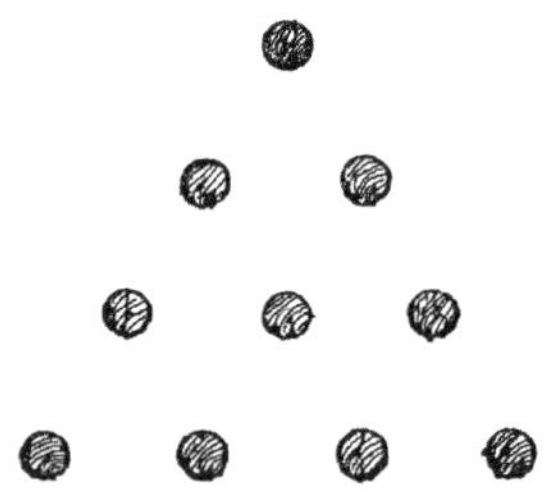

FIGURE 2 – *The Tetraktys*

conducive background for initiatic, or other such ceremonies. Such a technique of construction by analogy, which today would be called psychological, would in Vitruvius' day have been classed as magical. Its methods and content might have been considered part of restricted religious doctrine, known only to those initiated beyond a certain level.

To implement proportion and symmetry the ancients, as Vitruvius calls them, used the medium of "perfect numbers."[8] He singles out the numbers ten and six. The perfection of ten, according to Granger, is a reference to the Pythagorean tetraktys, **figure 2**, in which ten is considered morphically as the sum of one, two, three and four.[9] Six is mathematically perfect because it is the sum of its whole number factors; its aliquot parts, or fractions with numerators of 1. 1/6 of 6 is 1. 1/3 of 6 is 2. 1/2 of 6 is 3. No other whole numbers can be multiplied to make 6. Six is perfect because 1 x 2 x 3=6 and 1+2+3 =6. Now we have 1+2 +3 = 6 and 1+2+3+4=10. These are both perfect numbers in Pythagorean lore and they are two steps on the Pythagorean tetraktys. The numbers 1, 2, 3, and 4 also construct the Pythagorean musical tetrachord, **figure 3**; fundamental = 1/1, octave = 2/1, fifth note = 3/2, and fourth note = 4/3. The octave is a double interval thus a pattern of octaves would be 1, 2, 4, 8, 16 . . . , what might be called a geometric proportion in double symmetry.

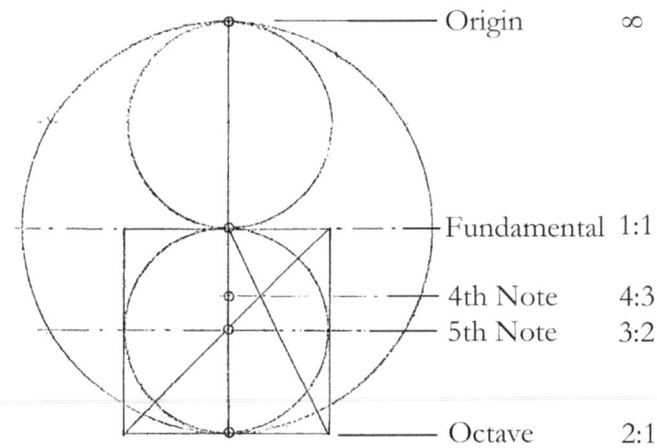

FIGURE 3 – *The Pythagorean Octave*

Vitruvius cites examples of the use of six and ten in measurement and monetary systems.[10] The palm = 4 fingers; the foot = 4 palms = 16 fingers = 1/6th of overall height; the cubit = 6 palms = 24 fingers = 1/4 of overall height. Thus a person's overall height = 4 cubits, 6 feet, 24 palms, or 96 fingers. In correspondence to these measures, Greek currency, the drachma, was set to = 6 obols = 24 dichalca. In Roman currency, the denarius was formerly = 10 bronze coins, but was later revised to = 16 asses.

In all Vitruvius has made use of the numbers 1, 2, 3, 4, 6, 8, 10, 16, 24, and 96. 1, 2, 3, and 4 comprise the tetrachord; 1, 2, 4, 8 are an octaval geometric progression, the left leg of the Platonic Lambda; 6 and 10 are "perfect"; 16 is the sum of 6 + 10, and = 4^2 or 2^4; 24 = 1 x 2 x 3 x 4, 6 x 4 or 8 x 3; 96 = 16 x 6 or 24 x 4.

Hermogenes

In presenting his canon Vitruvius introduces the personage of Hermogenes. The pseudodipteral temple of Diana at Magnesia is attributed to him.[11] He is said to have devised the pseudodipteral arrangement itself.[12] We hear of a hexastyle temple to Father Bacchus [the Greek Dionysius] he designed at Teos in Ionia.[13] Later we find that Hermogenes frowned on the use of the Doric order for temples and after beginning the temple to Bacchus, changed from the Doric order to the Ionic.[14] Finally we are told that Hermogenes published books on the temple of Diana at Magnesia and on the monopteral temple to Bacchus at Teos.[15]

More importantly, the entire numerical design system Vitruvius is about to present is credited to Hermogenes. "*These rules for symmetry were established by Hermogenes*[16] [who] *produced results which exhibit much acute ingenuity, and he left sources from which those who came after him could derive instructive principles.*"[17] Although Vitruvius mentions many other sources in the course of the Ten Books he rarely gives anyone else such broad credit.

It is presumed that Hermogenes was an actual person who lived circa 250–150 BC in Ionia. The name Hermogenes means "born of Hermes." This may indicate only that his father was named Hermes, but in the age of Vitruvius, the god Hermes was a well-known figure in the eastern Mediterranean. He was the subject of a syncretic Mystery religion developed in Greek Egypt from the time of the Alexandrine conquest, 332 BC, in which the Greek Hermes was merged with the Egyptian Thoth. This religion had a philosophical side related to the works of Plato, which has come down to us as the *Corpus Hermeticum*, and a practical side including astrology, alchemy and magic, which exists in various "technical Hermetica," much of which has never been published in English.

Hermes, called "thrice-greatest" and "guide of souls," was the divinity governing transformation and subtle intellectual knowledge. He is especially associated with the subjects of the Platonic Quadrivium: number, geometry, music and astronomy. Hermes is mythologically the inventor of the stringed musical instrument called the lyre, which he traded to Apollo. Orpheus, the great mythic musician was later given the lyre by Apollo. The divinities whom Orpheus honored with his lyre were Apollo and Dionysus, the Roman Father Bacchus. The music Orpheus made would have been constructed on the Pythagorean tetrachord whose number pattern, whose symmetry, is given by the numbers 1, 2, 3, and 4. Orphism may be considered a religious side of Pythagoreanism.[18]

A kind of mythic circle is completed in these images. As Hermes is the source of Orpheus' musical harmony, which is based on number, so the system "born from Hermes" will provide the numerical pattern for the visual-spatial harmony of the temple. Thus Vitruvius becomes a kind of architectural Orpheus. Now it may be only coincidence that the rules for symmetry in the temple are credited to a person named after Hermes. But it may just as likely be a "tip off" that the system is a very old one. A system, perhaps, having its roots in ancient Egypt, its branches in the Greco-Roman Mysteries and one of its many flowerings in the art of architecture.

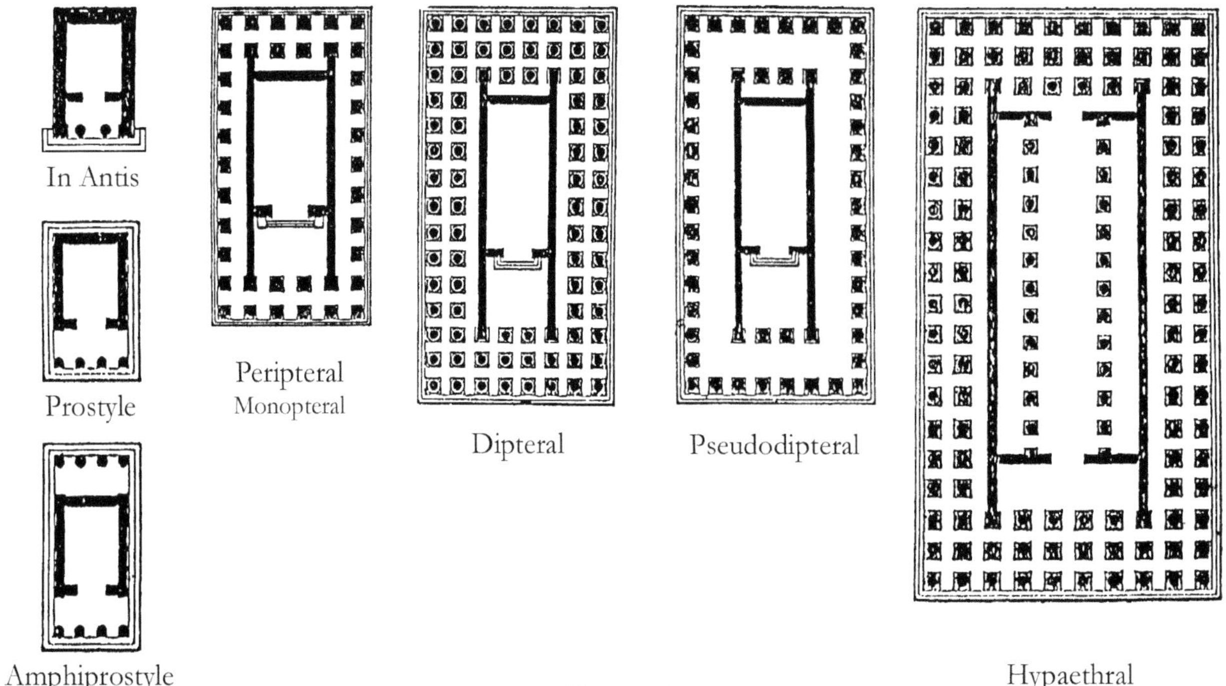

FIGURE 4
Arrangements of the Temple

Arrangements of the Temple

Vitruvius specifies seven arrangements of temples, **figure 4.**[19] The first three are variations of the tetrastyle, four-column facade: the **temple in Antis,** with two side walls and two free-standing columns; the **prostyle**, with a freestanding portico on the facade; and the **amphiprostyle**, with free-standing porticos on front and back. The **peripteral** arrangement is for the hexastyle, six column portico. The **dipteral** and **pseudodipteral** are for octastyle, eight column porticos. The pseudodipteral has the middle row of columns removed to create a wide peristyle. The **hypaethral** is decastyle, ten columned. Its central room, the cella, is partly unroofed. In the number of columns of these arrangements Vitruvius has again made use of the numbers 4, 6, 8, and 10. These numbers are factors of the usual Pythagorean suspects 3, 4, and 5; or they may be seen as representatives of the three formative root powers, √2, √3, and √5.

Footprint of the Temple

Regarding the plan of the temple, **figure 5,** Vitruvius writes that there should be twice as many intercolumniations along the sides as on the front, making the plan an octaval 2:1 ratio.[20] The interior structure is also an octaval rectangle 4:8 divided at its Ø point, 3:5.[21] The cella is 4:5 which is an arithmetic approximation of [1+Ø]/2. The pronaos is a 4:3 rectangle, the ratio of the musical fourth note.

Vitruvius provides the interesting injunction that *"The steps must be arranged so that there are an odd number of them; for thus the right foot, with which one mounts the first step, will also be the first to reach the level of the temple itself."*[22] Risers are to be from 9 to 10 inches and treads between 18 and 24 inches. In the reconstructions the first odd number, 3, is used for the number of risers.

Patterns of Column Spacing

Vitruvius further classifies temples by intercolumnation, **figure 6,** distinguishing five classes:[23]

1. Pycnostyle, with the columns close together; the intercolumniation, I = 1.5 D.

2. Systyle, with the intercolumniations a little wider, I = 2 D.

Vitruvius notes these two spacing patterns have practical disadvantages. Processions cannot pass through the colonnade except in single file; the periptory is too narrow for comfortable walking; and the statue in the cella is hard to see.

3. Diastyle, more open still; I = 3 D.

4. Araeostyle, I = >3D, where the columns are, *"farther apart than they ought to be...."*

Vitruvius adds that architraves in araeostyle colonnades need to be made of wood as stone would be overstressed and crack. This modulation produces buildings that are *"clumsy-roofed, low, and broad"* He associates araeostyle with the Tuscan mode.

5. Eustyle, intervals apportioned just right. I = 2.25 D; middle I = 3 D. It is the *"most approved class, developed with a view to convenience, beauty and strength ... the effect of the design will be beautiful, there will be no obstruction at the entrance, and the walk round the cella will be dignified."*

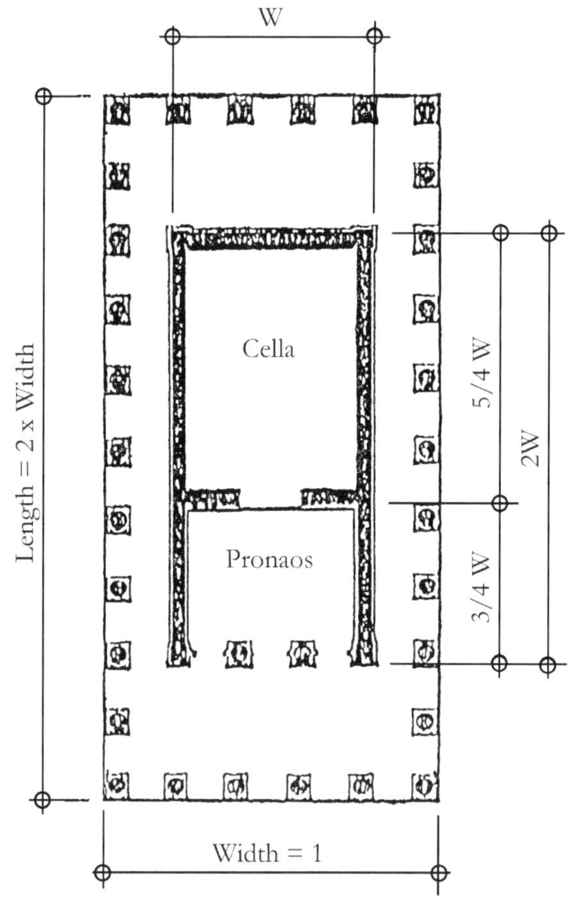

Figure 5
Footprint of the Temple

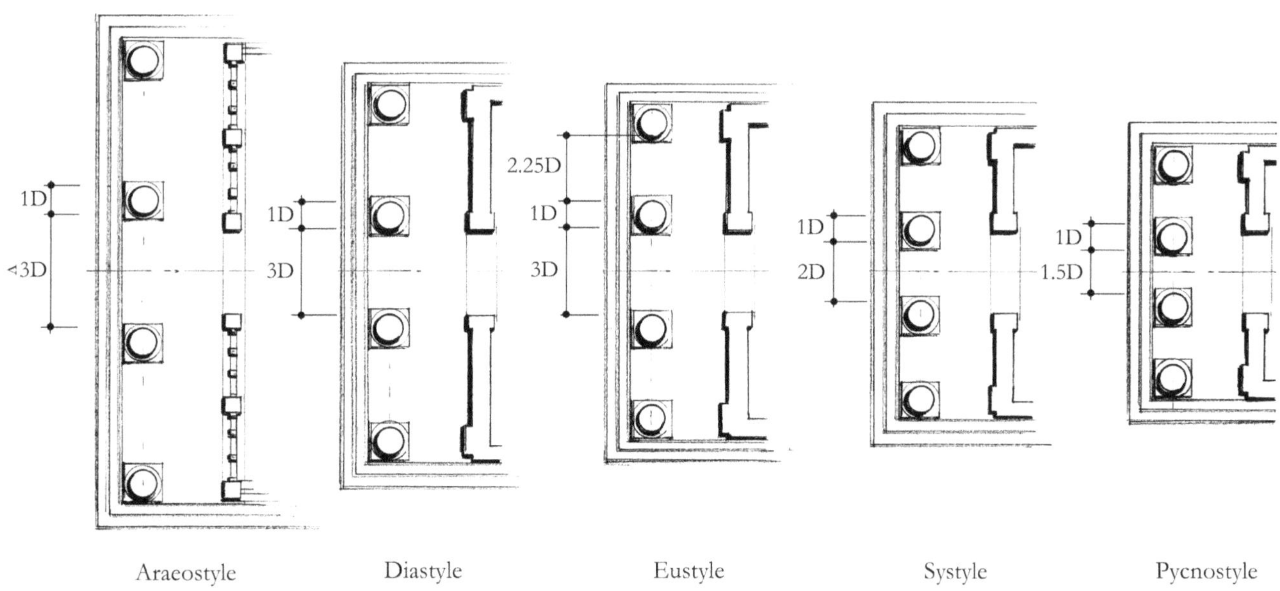

Figure 6 *Vitruvius' – Patterns of Column Spacing*

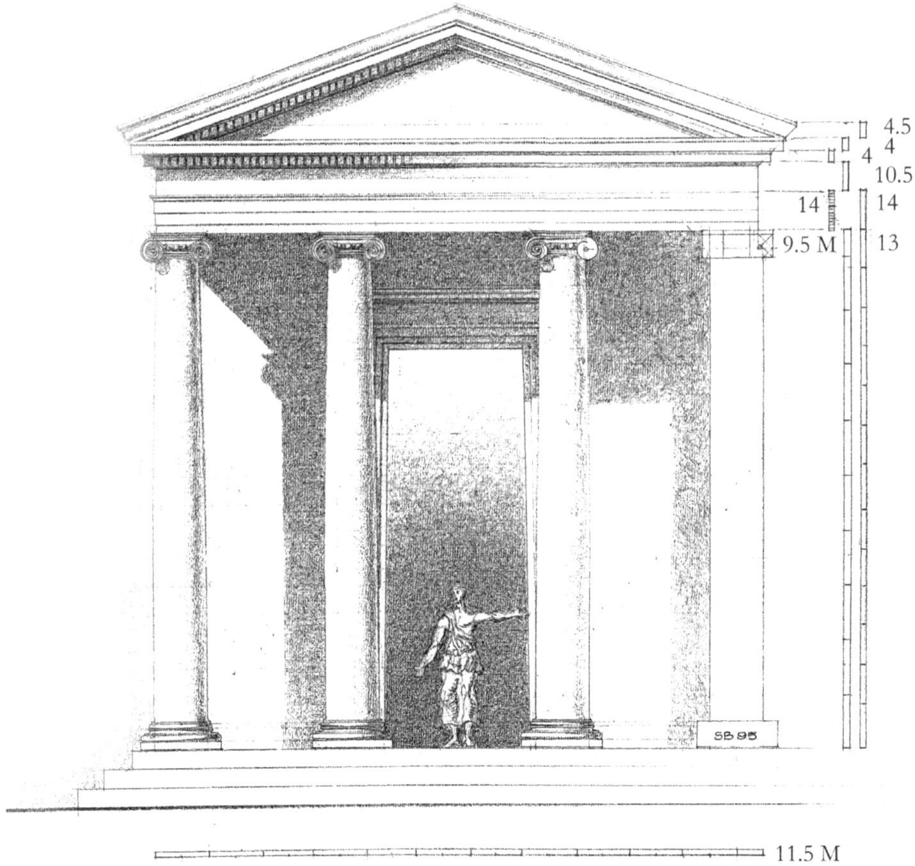

FIGURE 7a – *Tetrastyle Portico*

ESSENTIAL DIVISIONS OF THE TEMPLE FACADE

In **figures 7a-c** Vitruvius' directions are followed diligently, as one would those of a military officer, to reconstruct a tetrastyle, hexastyle and octastyle temple facade in the Ionic mode using eustyle spacing. For purposes of consistency in the reconstructions it is assumed that M, the module, and D, the lower column diameter = 2 feet in each elevation. Thus column height H will remain the same in each Ionic reconstruction.

Vitruvius divides the width of the temple, not including any projection of the base or cornice, into 11.5 parts for a four-columned tetrastyle facade; 18 parts for a six-columned hexastyle facade; and 24.5 parts for an eight-columned octastyle facade.

One of these parts is taken as the module. The thickness of the column, D, will be equal to one module, M. The side intercolumniations = 2.25 D. The middle intercolumniation = 3 D.

Column height H, including base and cap are:[24] Aerostyle, H = 8 D. Diastyle, 8.5 D. Systyle, H = 9.5 D. Eustyle, H = 9.5 D. Pycnostyle, H = 10 D. As the columns get closer together they get thinner.

FIGURE 7b – *Hexastyle Portico*

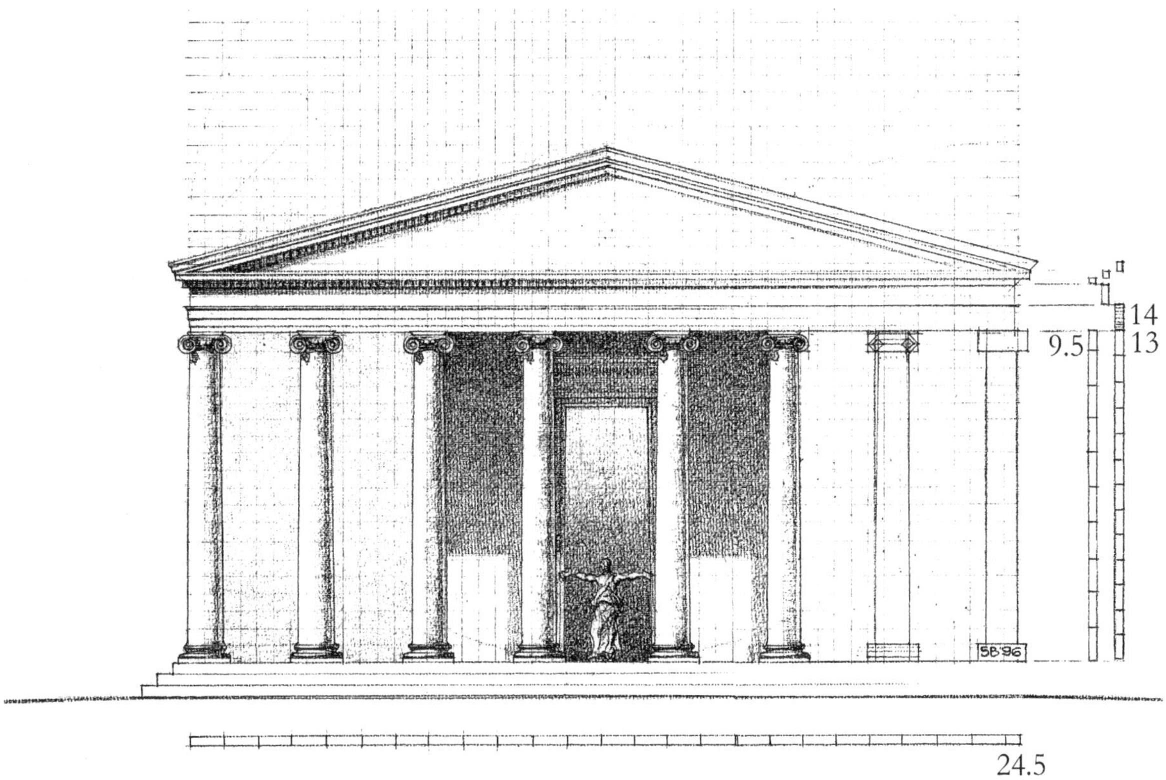

FIGURE 7c – *Octastyle Portico*

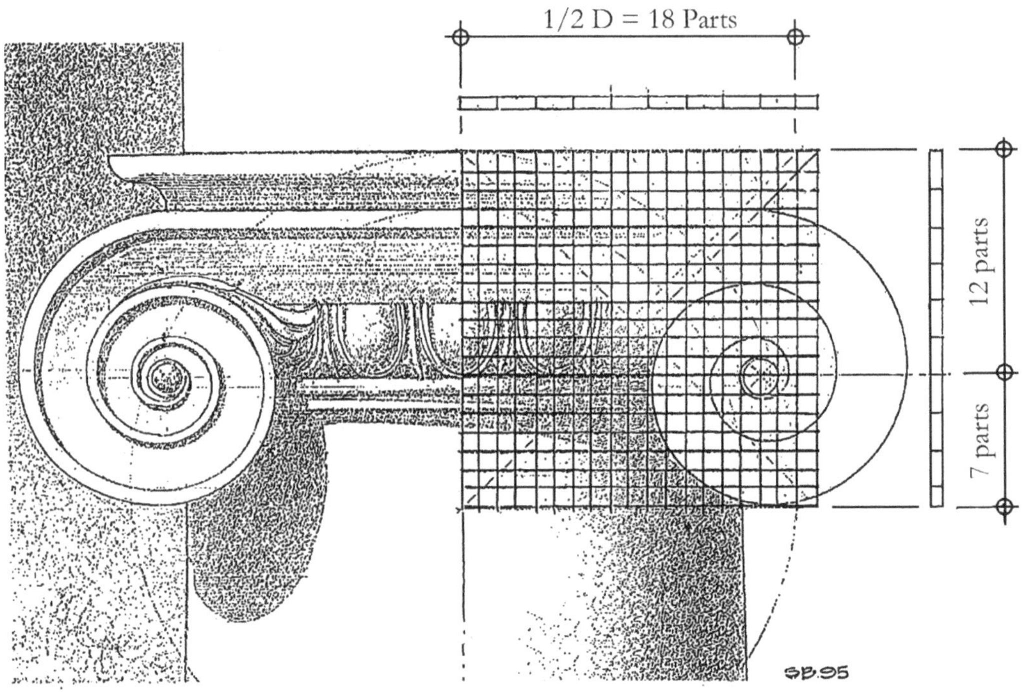

FIGURE 8
Ionic Capital of Vitruvius

The Ionic Capital

To construct the Ionic capital, **figure 8,** divide 1/2D into 18 parts, add 1 to get 19 parts, then square this up.[25] The overall width of the abacus will be 19/18ths of lower D. This may be restated as 38/36 D. The overall height of the capital including the abacus and the volutes = 1/2 its overall width, 9.5/18ths or 19/36 D. The abacus thickness is 3 parts or 3/36 D.

The vertical center of the eye is located 3 parts in from the edge of the abacus. Its horizontal center is located 7 parts up from the bottom of the capital. The eye is 2 parts in diameter. Vitruvius' method of constructing the volute is lost. Here the conventional 12-centered method is used.[26] The echinus is 4 parts high; the astragal below it is 1 part. The channel of the volute is 4 parts and the fillet 1 part wide.

The eye of the volute is centered 12/19 from the top and 7/19 from the bottom. $7/12 = .583 \approx$ Ø, .618. The ratio of the overall height of the capital to the distance between the centers of the eyes is $32/19 = 1.684 \approx 1/Ø$, 1.618 and the ratio of overall length, including the volutes, to height is $50/19 = 2.631 \approx 1{:}1/Ø^2$, 1:2.618.[27]

Note the prominence of the number 19 and its close relation to 18. 19/18 is one measure of the interval of the musical semitone.[28] 19/18 is the ratio of the diagonal of the pentagon to its altitude. In astronomy the Metonic cycle of 18.6 years governs solar eclipses. Arithmetically, 19 x 19 = 361; the number of degrees in a circle + 1, the symbolic center; and the number of days in a symbolic year, perhaps linking this icon to astronomical observations.[29]

The Entablature

The entablature, **figure 9,** consists of the architrave, frieze and cornice. Vitruvius gives a sliding scale governing the architrave.[30] If columns are 12' to 15' high the architrave A = 1/19 H, or

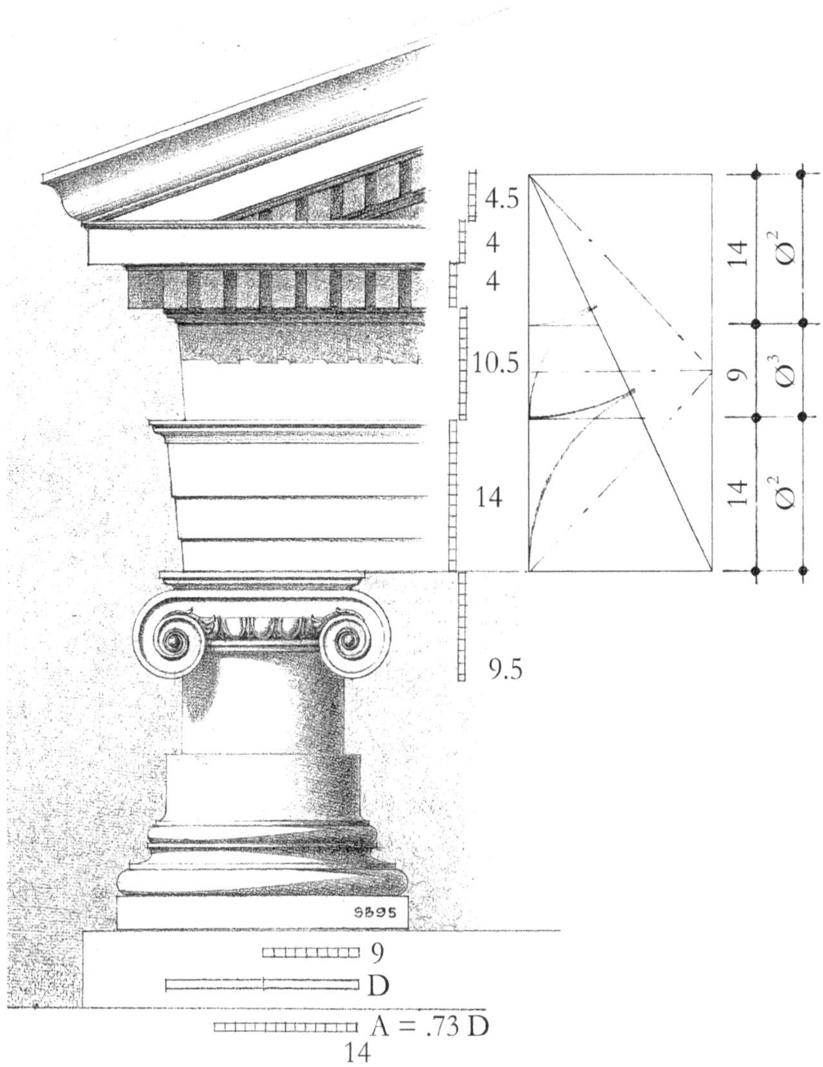

FIGURE 9
Ionic Entablature of Vitruvius

1/2 D. If H is 15' to 20', A = 1/13th H, .73 D. If H is 20' to 25' A = 2/25 H, about .76 or 3/4 D. If H = 25' to 30' A = 1/12 H, about .79 or 4/5 D. Thus the height of the entablature, which is based on the architrave, gets larger the higher it is from eye level. Since the eustyle column height H is 9.5 D and we have assumed D = 2', then H = 19'. The architrave in our reconstructions will thus be 1/13th H.

The architrave is divided into 14 parts.[31] It is formed into bands of 3, 4, and 5 parts with a cymatium of 2 parts. The use of the number sequence 3, 4, 5 may be seen as a reference to the Pythagorean 3–4–5 triangle and, by extension, to the root powers $\sqrt{2}$, $\sqrt{3}$, $\sqrt{5}$.

The frieze is either, 3/4 or 5/4 of the architrave = either 10.5 architrave parts = .55 D or 17.5 parts = .91 D, the larger frieze providing for sculpture. In the reconstruction the smaller frieze is used. The frieze has a cymatium equal to 1/7 of its height, or 1.5 architrave parts.[32]

The cornice[33] is made up of the dentil band and the corona, each 4 architrave parts and the sima, 4.5 architrave parts. The cornice projects out at 45°, its projection equaling its height. The height of the tympanum is determined by taking 1/9th of the distance from the outsides of the corona. This is measured from the top of the corona to the apex of the tympanum. The raking dentil band, corona and cymatium are run on top of the tympanum.

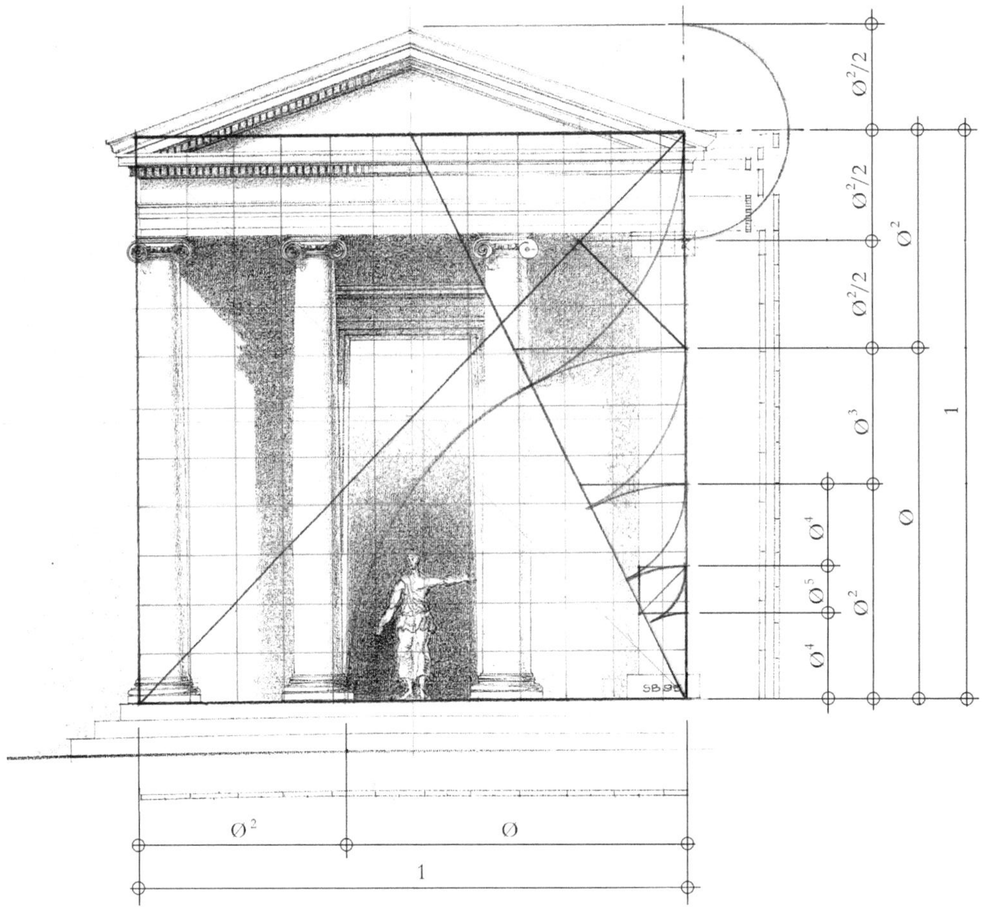

FIGURE 10a – *Tetrastyle Portico Geometry*

Geometric Relations of the Temple Facades

We now have three well-dressed Ionic porticos. Analyzing the reconstructions using the square and Ø the geometrical character of the system of Hermogenes is revealed. It may be seen as an arithmetical method of approximating geometrical constructions.

In the tetrastyle facade, **figure 10a**, the ratio of width to height of the order is 1:1. Column height = 9.5 D. The architrave, A = .73 D. The architrave is further divided into 14 parts. The frieze is 10.5 parts, the cornice is 12.5 for a total entablature of 37 parts. 37/14 = 2.67 A units x .73 = 1.95 D. The height to the cornice is 9.5 + 1.95 = 11.45. The width of the facade is 11.5.

Column D is 1/11.5 = .087 and Ø^5 = .090. The ratio of the height of the columns H to the width W = 9.5/11.5 = .825 and Ø + [Ø^2/2] = .809. The face of the inner column falls near the Ø point, 11.5 x .618 = 7.1, and Vitruvius gives 7.25.

The altitude of the tympanum is 12.5/9=1.4 D.[34] The apex of the pediment is 11.4 + 1.4 + .65 = 13.45 D,[35] 13.45/11.5 = 1.17, 1 + Ø^2/2 = 1.191, close to 2Ø = 1.236.

For the hexastyle, **figure 10b,** setting W=1 the height to the underside of the capitals is 1/2. Column height = 9.5/18 = .527, Ø^2 + Ø^4 = .528. Top of cornice is 11.45/18 = .636 ≈ Ø. D = 1/18 = .055, Ø^6 = .056. The center of the inner column is at 11.0 M, 18 x Ø = 11.12. The apex of the tympanum is 19/9 = 2.1 M + 11.4 = 13.5 M, while Ø^3/2, .736, = 13.25 M. The overall height to the apex of the pediment is 13.5 + .65 = 14.15 D, 14.15/18 = .786, close to Ø + [Ø^2/2] = .809.

For the octastyle, **figure 10c**, the overall height, as per previous examples, is 11.4 + 2.8 [altitude of tympanum] + .65 = 14.85 D, 24.5 x Ø = 15.14. D = 1/24.5 = .041, Ø^7 = .034, or Ø^5/2 = .045. The height of the columns = 9.5/24.5=.387, Ø^2 = .382. The outer edge of the inner column is at 14.75, 24.5 x Ø = 15.14. The top of the entablature is 11.45/24.5 = .467, $1/\sqrt{5}$ = .447.

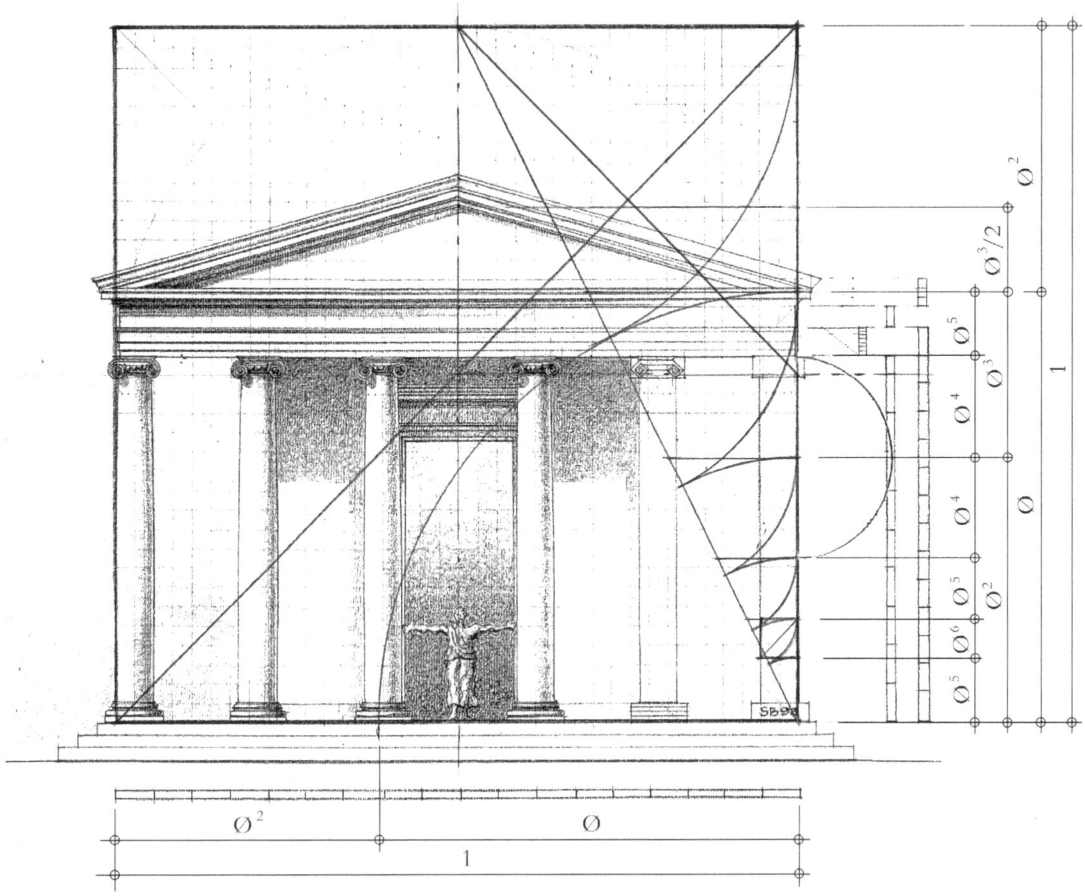

FIGURE 10b
Hexastyle Portico Geometry

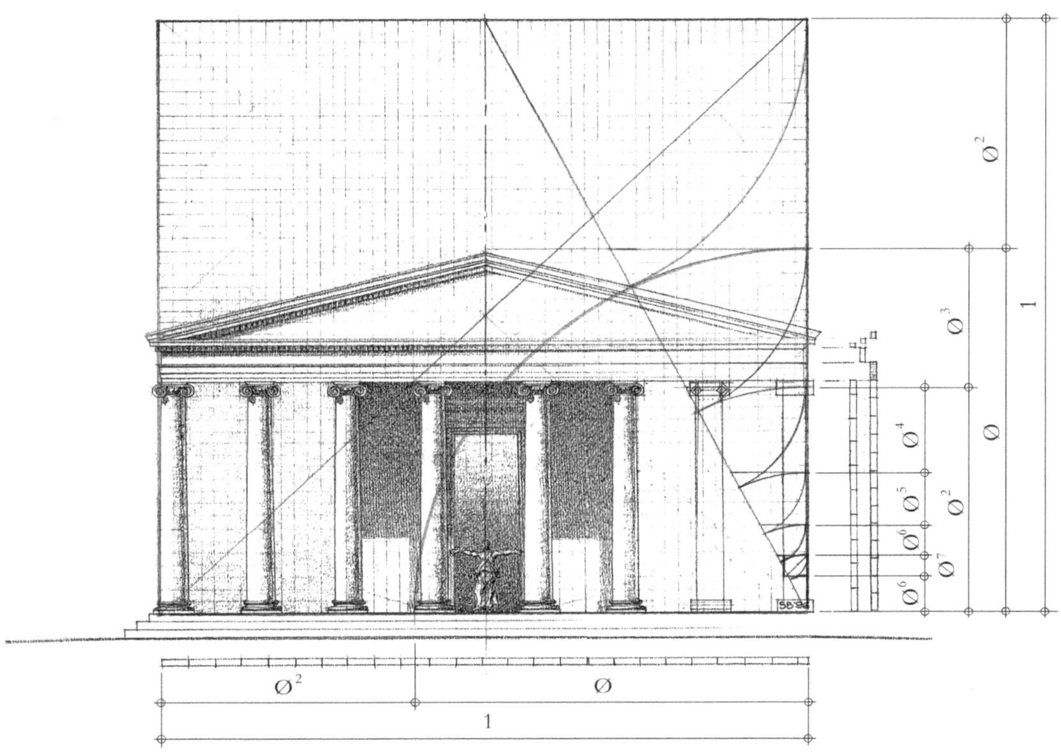

FIGURE 10c
Octastyle Portico Geometry

Vitruvius on the Doric

Vitruvius declares that he would rather not present the Doric canon because of its *"faults and incongruities"* but, since he said he would at the outset of the Ten Books, he will here, *"so that if anybody cares,"* as the Morgan translation puts it, the proportions will be given to keep the designer out of trouble.[36] Vitruvius' "problem" is that in the traditional Greek system the end triglyphs do not center over the end columns. If you want to keep the column centers equal and still keep the triglyph at the corner the metope will be stretched; or if the metopes are kept square the end bays will be shorter than the interior bays, as they are in actual Greek work. So something will have to be offbeat, so to speak, causing *"embarrassment and inconvenience to the work."* Amazingly, Vitruvius says *"the ancients appear to have avoided the Doric order in their temples."* He cannot mean the Greeks and may referring to the Tuscans.

Here is where the canonical Doric begins: the triglyphs are 1/2 D x 3/4 D and are aligned strictly with the centers of the columns. The width of the triglyph is taken as the module, M = 1/2 D [as opposed to the Ionic, where M = D]. The metopes are 3/4 x 3/4 D or 1.5 M square, and there will be a fragment of a metope at each corner, 1/3 M, accounting for entasis. The Doric is no longer a work in progress. There will be no more flexibly off-center triglyphs as on the Treasury of the Athenians at Delphi, the unruly Greeks have been brought under Roman control. If you want a larger opening in the center you must add one triglyph to the center span. This "chunky" modulation of 10/4 D or 5 M column centers can only be varied to 15/4 D at the center.[37] Intercolumniation in the Ionic mode, for example, is governed by the dentil, an interval of 1/6 D, a lot more flexible. This may also be part of Vitruvius' "problem" with the Doric.

Because of the triglyph placement, the count is different from both the Greek Doric and from Vitruvius' Ionic. The tetrastyle is divided into 19.5 Modules, M = 1/2 D, **figure 11a**. The columns are 7 diameters high = 14 M. The top of the columns is at 14/19.5 = .718, $\sqrt{2}/2$ = .707. The center of the inner columns is at 13.5 M, 13.5/19.5 = .692, $\sqrt{2}.2$ = .707. The architrave is 1 M and the frieze is 1.5 M. The cornice consisting of a corona and a cyma is 1 M,[38] total = 3.5 M or 1/4 H. The height of the tympanum is 1/9th of the length of the corona, as in the Ionic. For this length add 1.67 M[39], giving 21.17/9 = 2.35 M + 17 M = 19.35 M.

In addition to arithmetic and geometry a harmonic ratio method for reconstructing the monotriglyphic tetrastyle is shown in **figure 11b**. Divide the side of the square into 10. The lower 9 parts are divided into 5 parts. 4 of these 5 are the height of the columns and 1 part is the entablature. 4/5 x .9 = .72; 28/39 = .718, and 39 x .707 = 27.3. D = .72/7 = .103. M = .72/14 = .052; 1/19.5 = .051. As $Ø^6$ = .056, there could be a Ø method for this construction.[40]

The monotriglyphic hexastyle is divided into 29.5 M, **figure 11c**. All the height relationships are the same as the tetrastyle: top of order = 17.5 M, 17.5/29.5=.593, ≈ Ø; altitude of tympanum, 31.2/9 = 3.5 M; apex of the tympanum = 17.5 + 3.5 = 21, 29.5x.707=20.8 M. The inner column is centered at 18.5 M, Ø = 18.25 M.

Vitruvius also gives directions for intercolumniations of two triglyph intervals. Greek sacred buildings were always monotriglyphic, but multi-triglyphic intervals were used on commercial and civic buildings.

The bi-triglyphic tetrastyle, **figure 11d**, is divided into 27 M. The column height of 14 M is a bit higher than a half-square, 14/27 = .518. The top of the corona and base of the tympanum is at 17/27 = .629, ≈ Ø = .618, 16.7 M. The apex of the tympanum is 28.3/9 = 3.1 + 17 = 20.1/ 27 = .744, 3/4=.75. The center of the inner column is at 18.5 M, 27 x .707 = 19.1, 2/3 x 27 = 18 M.

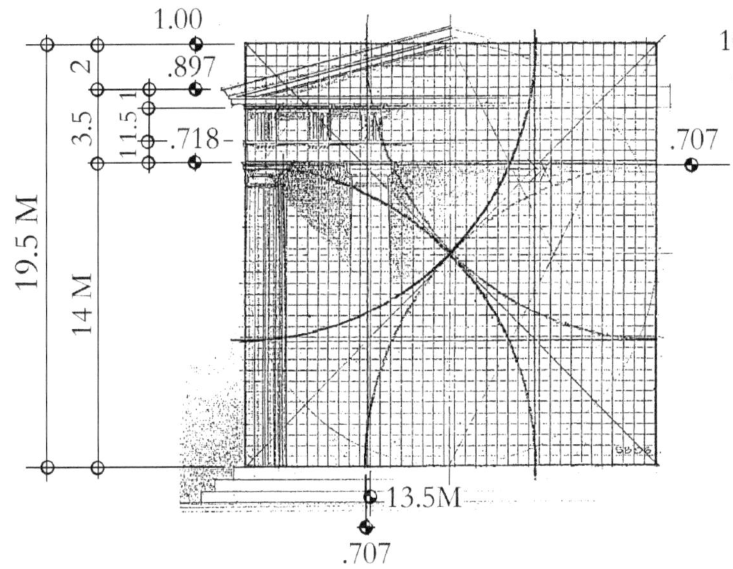

FIGURE 11a

Vitruvian Doric Tetrastyle. Width Divided into 19.5 M

FIGURE 11b

Harmonic Ratio Method for Doric Tetrastyle

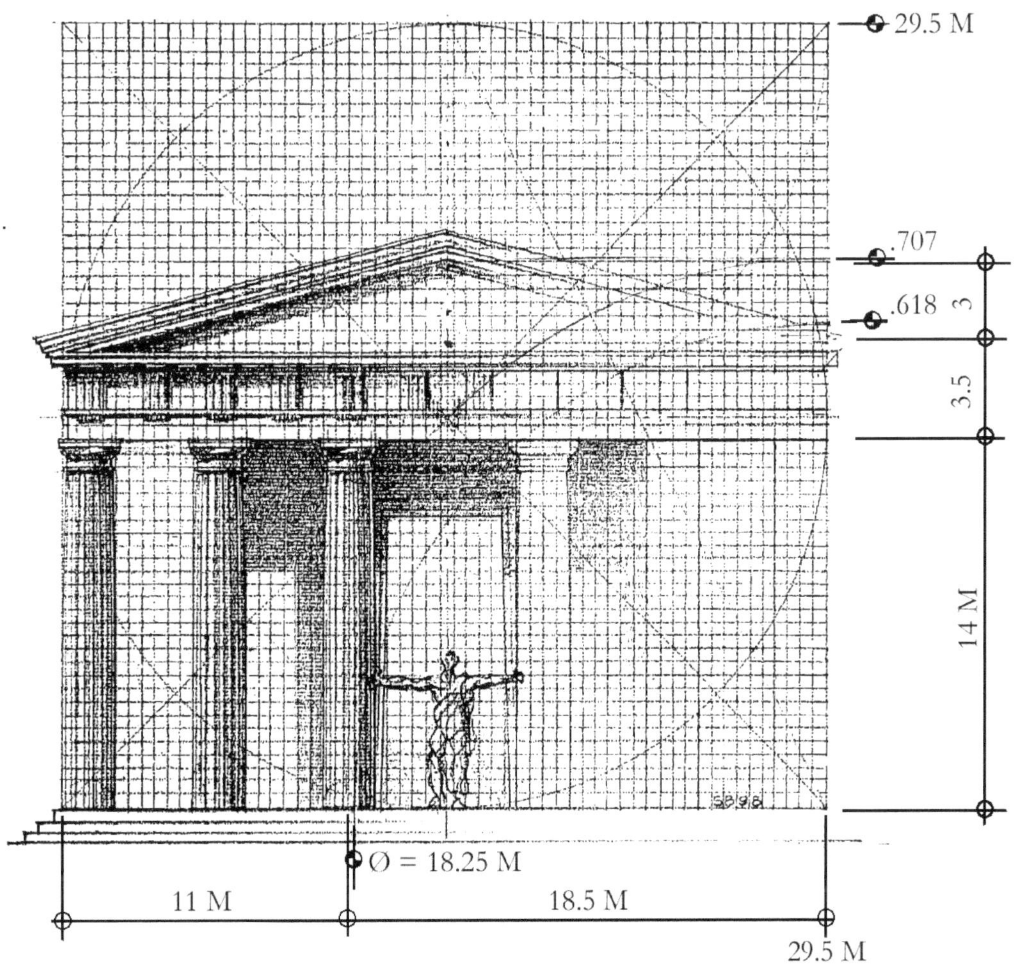

FIGURE 11c

Doric Hexastyle, Monotriglyphic. Width Divided into 29.5 M

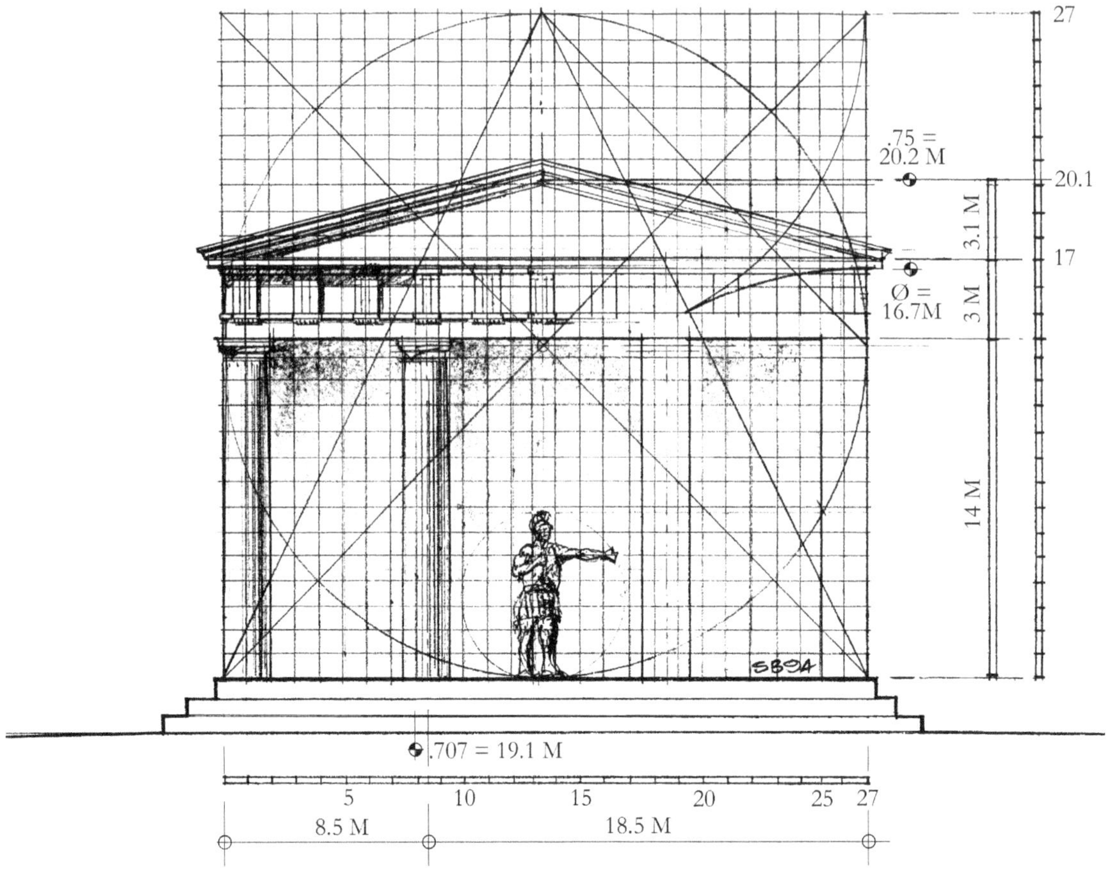

FIGURE 11d – *Doric Tetrastyle, Bi-triglyphic. Width Divided into 27 M*

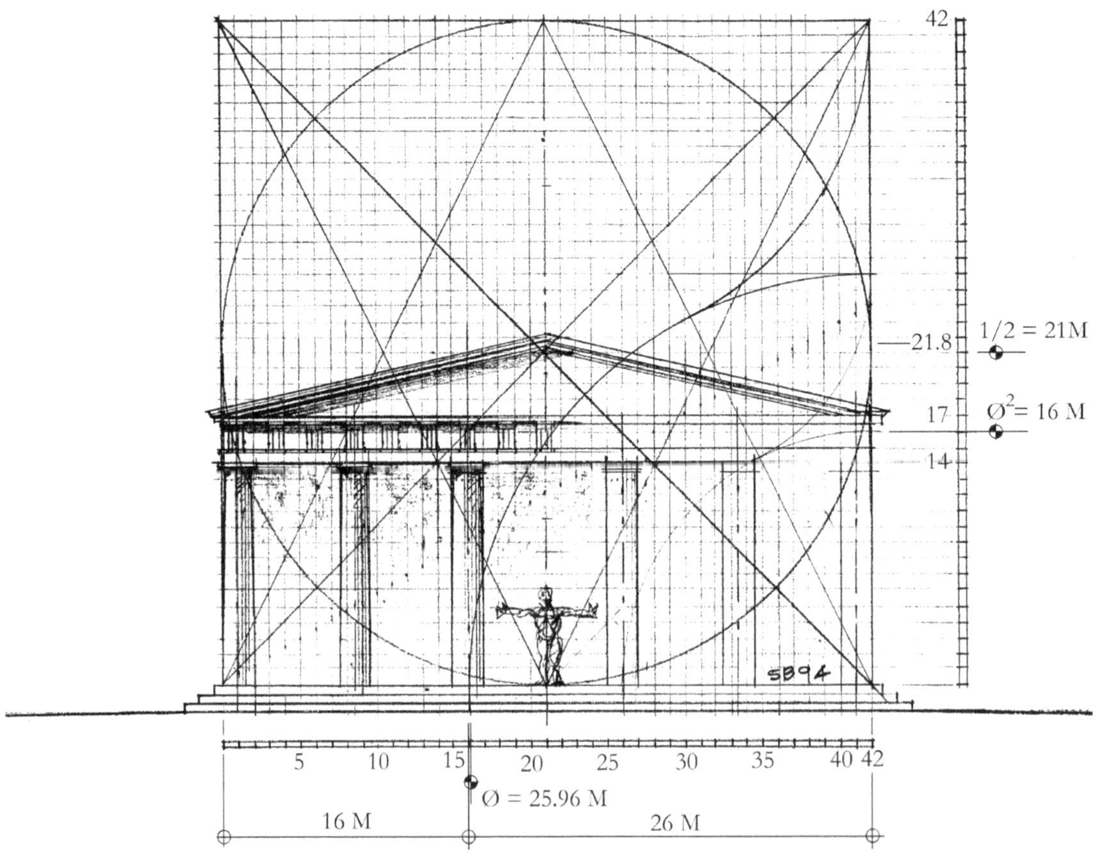

FIGURE 11e – *Doric Hexastyle, Bi-triglyphic. Width Divided into 42 M*

The bi-triglyphic hexastyle, **figure 11e,** is divided into 42 M: column height of 14 M creates a 1:3 ratio; center of the inner column is 26 M and 42 x Ø = 25.96; top of the corona is 17/42 = .404, $Ø^2$ = .382 x 42 M = 16 M, the underside of the corona; apex of tympanum is 43.3/9 = 4.8 M + 17 = 21.8, the half-square is 21 M.

Vitruvius, Ø, and the Mysteries

In the context of the reconstructions it may justly be asked if Vitruvius follows his own number theory. If we take Vitruvian symmetria to imply a harmonic pattern of division, there can be no greater carrier of symmetria than Ø. Mathematically Ø may be defined as Ø + $Ø^2$ = 1; that is, "root plus square equals unity." Symbolically Ø is the division that re-creates unity as the Ø rectangle may be divided into a square and another Ø rectangle. If we take "root" to represent unseen informing principle or limit and "square" to represent sensible matter or the unlimited, their combination as the monad is a symbolic restatement of the Pythagorean–Orphic cosmology. Organic life including the human body is governed in its growth by Ø, thus it is no accident that Vitruvius uses the human body as the illustration of proportion and symmetry. In this sense Vitruvius does follow his own theory. By apparently composing with the square and Ø Vitruvius is working with the ultimate conveyors of symmetry.

In his discussion of number Vitruvius never mentions Ø, yet his number specifications, which at first seem arbitrary and opaque, recapitulate geometrical constructions using Ø. Why wouldn't he just tell us to use Ø? One answer is that he didn't know about it and was just parroting a system that he read in some other book. A little more charitable answer is that he knew about Ø but chose not to include it because building construction was done arithmetically, with linear dimensions. While this may be so, Vitruvius doesn't hesitate advising us to use the diagonal of the square.[41]

But if Vitruvius was a participant in some form of Mystery religion it might be that he was under an obligation not to discuss Ø publicly. This would account for its total absence, even in theory. This odd condition also occurs when Timaeus[42] mentions by name four of the five Platonic solids but only alludes to the fifth; the dodecahedron, made of twelve pentagonal faces. Socrates also avoids mention of it in the *Phaedo*,[43] referring to it, in translation, as a "soccer ball." Even Euclid is surprisingly vague, separating parts of the dodecahedron's construction as far as possible in his narrative and not clearly cross-referencing them.[44]

The Ø ratio was part of the Egyptian Mysteries. Associated with the principle of animation, Ø is said to be the basis of their magical art of bringing statues of the gods to life. Fideler writes: *"According to the ancient Egyptian Hermetic writing entitled the* Asclepius *or* Perfect Discourse, *one of the magical arts of antiquity involved the animation of statues. Through this art, the statue became the home of a living spirit – so that what is of heavenly nature, being drawn down into the images by means of heavenly use and practices, may be enabled to endure with joy the nature of mankind, and sojourn with it for long periods of time.... And to this invention they added a supernatural force whereby the images might have power... and combined it with the material substance; that is to say, being unable to make souls, they invoked the souls of spirits and implanted them in the statues by means of holy and sacred rites.*

"The notion of statues being so carefully wrought that they come to life is an archetypal, universal notion, appearing in the Greek myth of Pygmalion.... In ancient Egypt, not only were the statues designed to become the receptacles of living spirits, but the temple itself was conceived of as the very

incarnation of the god.... In antiquity, the practice of animating temples and statues was conceived of as both an art and a science. In its scientific aspect, the art of animating statues drew upon the ancient canon of proportion."[45]

Fideler discusses the relation of Ø to the canon of 19: "*No one can deny the existence of the canon, for in some instances the gridwork is still visible on surviving temple walls.... The 19 square Egyptian canon was taken over by the early Greek artists and sculptors.... The 19 square grid is not a true canon of proportion, but a canonical rule of thumb. True proportion involves the use of ratio, and one of the most dynamic ratios is the Golden Section, reflected in the process of unfolding life. Students of geometry draw a distinction between the principles of static and dynamic symmetry. The square grid is useful but static, the phi grid is dynamic and brings the piece to life.... The square grid represents the body or raw material of the composition; the phi ratio is the animating principle which brings it to life. In the same way that the universe is a harmonic union of spirit and matter, so too did the Egyptians reflect this understanding in their temple art.*"[46] Pythagoras, the source of Plato's numerical logos in the *Timaeus*, studied in Egypt and the pentagram was a symbol of the Pythagorean school.

On this topic Critchlow notes, "*The fact is that the pentagonal Dodecahedron has been quite deliberately obscured by avoidance [in Plato's* Timaeus*], and that when the fifth solid which makes up 'the whole' is mentioned, the mention is significantly brief, occupying only one sentence. And yet this figure, the pentagonal Dodecahedron, the fifth solid, is immeasurably more important than the others, because it is not only 'the whole' but also the Heavens of the animal belt or the zodiacal constellations, and so constitutes the limits of our sense perception (aesthesis) ... the indications seem clear that there was a great deal 'unsaid' in the* Timaeus *'myth' — which echoes Aristotle's allusion to Plato's 'Agrapha Dogmata' in his* Physics *(V, 209b) where he says that Plato's account of the Receptacle in the* Timaeus *differs 'from what he says in his so-called unwritten teaching.' There is no way one may know much more about this. Plato's contemporaries seem to have observed the injunction that these teachings remain unwritten.*"[47]

Vitruvius has presented the human body as the exemplar of symmetry and proportion. He has also made the analogy between the temple and the human body. Although Ø is the prime giver of symmetry in the human body and many other animals and plants as well, Vitruvius gives us only opaque whole number ratios. There is almost a skillfulness with which he avoids saying that the navel is at the Ø point of the human height. Instead he diverts our attention, while still not spelling it out for us, to the squaring of the circle, in which the navel is one of the center points.

All this suggests that Ø may have been a symbolic part of the rituals of initiation in some of the Mysteries. If Ø was part of initiatic symbolism it could not have been publicly discussed and a measurement system based on Ø would not have been given to builders who may not have been part of the tradition. For construction purposes or for publication an arithmetic approximation would have been used. We might recall that as late as the sixteenth century, legend has it, Albrecht Dürer was expelled from his guild of engravers in Lübeck for publishing a particular construction of the pentagon. The $\sqrt{2}$ system, by contrast, appears to have been publicly known. It is the only geometrical mentioned by Vitruvius and was the basis of much day-to-day Roman architecture.

Since geometric-arithmetic translations can never be exact, it may be asked how close is close enough?[48] Certainly a tolerance of 5% should be adequate. A stricter tolerance might not even be practical in most constructions. Thus $Ø + Ø^2/2$, .809 could be approximated from .759 to .859. Expressed as whole numbers .75 = 3/4, .8 = 4/5, .833 = 5/6.

Origins of the Orders: Vitruvius' Account

Vitruvius gives the following account of the origins of the three principal architectural orders[49]—a fusion of myth and history involving the eponymous ancestors, Dorus, Ion and Corinthus.

The Doric, he tells us, *"was the first to arise, and in early times."* Dorus was the son of Hellen, king of Achaea, a general term for Greece, including the Peloponnesus, who gave his name to the whole of Greek culture. Dorus is the grandson of Deucalion, the last upright man, who is chosen to survive the flood. Dorus' eldest brother, Aeolus, succeeds his father as king in Thessaly. His middle brother, Xuthus, becomes king in Athens, marries Crusea, daughter of Erechtheus, and has two sons, Ion and Achaeus. Dorus becomes king in the Peloponnesus. *"Thus the four most famous Hellenic nations, namely the Ionians, Aeolians, Achaeans, and Dorians, are all descended from Hellen."*[50] However, both Dorus and Ion are said to actually be sons of Apollo. Dorus built temples at Argolis and other Peloponnesian cities in what might be called the Doric manner, *"although the rules of symmetry were not yet in existence."*

Vitruvius continues, *"the Athenians, in obedience to oracles of Delphic Apollo, and with the general agreement of all Hellas, dispatched thirteen colonies at one time to Asia Minor …, giving command to Ion."* This area of western Asia Minor was called Ionia. Americans might be interested to note the "thirteen colonies" motif in this ancient myth of national foundation.

After their takeover *"they set off precincts for the immortal gods and began to build fanes: first of all, a temple to Panionion Apollo such as they had seen in Achaea, calling it Doric because they had first seen that kind of temple built in the states of the Dorians."*

"Wishing to set up columns in that temple, but not having rules for their symmetry, and being in search of some way by which they could render them fit to bear loads and also of a satisfactory beauty of appearance, they measured the imprint of a man's foot and compared this with his height. On finding that the foot was one sixth of the height, they applied the same principle to the column, and reared the shaft, including the capital, to a height six times its thickness at its base. Thus the Doric column, as used in buildings, began to exhibit the proportions, strength and beauty of a man."

Vitruvius is again invoking the concept of anthropos. Just as there is an equivalence of the individual and the divinity at the moment of epiphany in the Mysteries, so here is there an analog created between the individual and the temple. If the divinity represents the macrocosm and the individual represents the microcosm then the temple may be said to represent the mesocosm, the middle ground, like the polis or civitas where the forces of the natural world are modulated and distributed to the individual through the "justly tuned" mechanisms of the state. As middle ground the temple may be said to represent the realm of mind or psyche and considered to be the soul of the community, or the symbolic center where the individual soul meets the world soul.

"Just so afterwards, when they desired to construct a temple to Diana in a new style of beauty, they translated these footprints into terms characteristic of the slenderness of women, and thus made a column the thickness of which was only one eighth of its height, so that it might have a taller look. At the foot they substituted the base in place of a shoe; in the capital they placed the volutes, hanging down at the right and left like curly ringlets, and ornamented its front with cymatia and with festoons of fruit arranged in place of hair, while they brought the flutes down the whole shaft, falling like folds in the robes worn by matrons. Thus in the invention of the two different kinds of columns, they borrowed manly beauty, naked and unadorned, for the one, and for the other the delicacy, adornment, and proportions characteristic of women.

"It is true that posterity, having made progress in refinement and delicacy of feeling, and finding pleasure in more slender proportions, has established seven diameters of the thickness as the height of the Doric column, and nine as that of the Ionic."

Both Dorus and Ion claim Apollo, the sun, as their sacred ancestor. We may say that the Doric order symbolizes the sun in its radiant aspect, as the source of fire, the coming forth of the ray, the proceeding mode. The Ionic order may thus be seen to symbolize the sun in its spiral, serpentine movement; or perhaps the movement of the moon [Diana] in its monthly journey around the zodiac. More deeply, since Vitruvius' geometrical pattern of the Ionic capital is the square of nineteen, the double-spiral motif may also symbolize the integration of the solar and lunar energies, thus providing an apt symbol for the maintaining mode. Ionic-like double-spiral capitals were used in Asia Minor and Persia and may also recall the Egyptian Hathor-head capital.

Thus the male-oriented Doric order symbolic of yang force, the fire element, is associated with Apollo and ascribed to Dorus; the female-oriented Ionic order symbolic of yin force, the earth element, is ascribed to Ion. We may see these as the proceeding and maintaining phases of the cycle, now Vitruvius introduces the third or returning phase. The Corinthian *"is an imitation of the slenderness of a maiden; for the outlines and limbs of maidens, being more slender on account of their tender years, admit of prettier effects in the way of adornment."*

The story of its "discovery" is as follows: *"A freeborn maiden of Corinth, just of marriageable age, was attacked by an illness and passed away. After her burial, her nurse, collecting a few little things which used to give the girl pleasure while she was alive, put them in a basket, carried it to the tomb, and laid it on top thereof, covering it with a roof tile so that the things might last longer in the open air. This basket happened to be placed just above the root of an acanthus. The acanthus root, pressed down though it was by weight, when springtime came round put forth leaves and stalks in the middle, and the stalks, growing up along the sides of the basket, pressed out at the corners by the tile through the compulsion of its weight, were forced to bend into volutes at the outer edges."*

The artist Callimachus, who was known *"for the refinement and delicacy of his artistic work, passed by this tomb and observed the basket with the tender young leaves growing round it. Delighted with the novel style and form, he built some columns after that pattern for the Corinthians, determined their symmetrical proportions, and established from that time forth the rules of the Corinthian order."*

The myth is illustrated in the famous eighteenth-century image, **figure 12**. The theme of the story is that of death and rebirth. The "maiden of Corinth" may be taken as a reference to Persephone, daughter of Demeter, in the Eleusinian Mysteries. Persephone is kidnapped by Hades, the Roman Pluto, and becomes queen of the Underworld. While Demeter the grain goddess disconsolately searches for her daughter nothing grows and the human food supply is cut off, preventing sacrifice to the gods. After much petitioning, Zeus cuts a deal in which Persephone will spend half the year below ground with Pluto and the other half with Demeter, above ground; thus giving rise to the seasons. The story also echoes the relation of Dante and Beatrice. Dante is "platonically" in love with Beatrice, he never touches or even speaks to her. She quickly passes away, but returns when Dante is at a low ebb to guide him to higher realms.

In Vitruvius' version Callimachus, we may say, is worshiping or meditating on the goddess as "death and rebirth" by observing the forms of nature. The acanthus itself is the maiden reborn through nature, and the "mimesis" of nature through art serves as an elevating inspiration.

As many natural forms, particularly plant forms, are governed by phi, we are reminded of that other maidenly goddess, Aphrodite, who governs beauty in natural form and whose star draws out the pentagram in the sky by virtue of its retrograde loops. The pentagram may be used as the geometrical net for the Corinthian capital.[51]

FIGURE 12
Origin of the Corinthian Order

Corinth is located at a narrow north-south isthmus connecting the Peloponnese with mainland Greece. At an early time the Corinthians dug an east-west canal to connect the Gulf of Corinth with the Aegean Sea. Thus much of the commerce in the major Greek regions had to pass through Corinth. The city became very wealthy and was known for its artistic refinement.

Graves recounts the story of another Corinthian maiden.[52] Corinthus is the city's eponymous ancestor. His grandson is called Sinis, though also said to be a descendent of Poseidon. Sinis got the nickname Pityocamptes, pine bender, *"because he was strong enough to bend down the tops of pine trees until they touched the earth, and would often ask innocent passers-by to help him with this task, but then suddenly release his hold. As the tree sprang upright again, they were hurled high into the air, and killed by the fall. Or he would bend down the tops of two neighboring trees until they met, and tie one of his victim's arms to each, so that he was torn asunder when the trees were released."*[53]

The civilizing hero Theseus encounters Sinis but does not fall for the trick. He overpowers Sinis, and *"served him as he had served others."*[54] Sinis' daughter Perigune *"ran to hide herself in a thicket of rushes and wild asparagus."* Theseus follows her and, *"found her invoking the plants, promising never to burn or destroy them if they hid her safely."* Theseus, rather charmed, promises not to harm her and the two become lovers.

Graves comments, *"Since the North Wind, which bent the pines, was held to fertilize women, animals and plants, 'Pityocamptes' is described as the father of Perigune, a corn goddess. Her attachment to wild asparagus and rushes suggests that the sacred baskets carried in the Thesmophoria Festival were woven from these."*[55] The scenes of tree murder are said by Graves to represent the sacrifice of the sacred king in early Pelasgian times which the Hellene Theseus would have put an end to. Graves notes, *"'Thes' has the same meaning in Thesmophoria as in Theseus: namely 'tokens deposited' — in the baskets woven of wild asparagus and rush which Perigune sanctified."*[56] The tokens were erotic in nature, indicated by the mutual seduction. The references to the basket are reminiscent of the "bell" of the Corinthian capital, on which the leaves and volutes rest. Even the nature-maiden hidden within plant forms appears in the story. The principle theme is sacrifice, which may be taken to represent the dramatic enactment of the returning mode.

A Vitruvian Context

All these stories, however, must be mythical, as a proto-Doric colonnade appears on Hatshepsut's temple c.1500 BC; the bell and leaves of the Corinthian capital appear in the complex of Zoser c.2600 BC; and the double spiral of the Ionic order is carved on the stones of the shaft-and-passage mounds in the Boyne Valley of Ireland c.3500 BC. Though no firm conclusions on the historical origins of the three genera can be reached from the above discussion, we do get a view of them as a form of encoded knowledge whose medium is number and geometry. In this view, where each of the three modes of the cycle is represented, we may say that the orders are "myths in stone," whose actualizations are guided by number and geometry.

The linear arithmetic Vitruvius gives us for the design of temples recapitulate geometrical constructions based principally on Ø, but also including √2 and the musical ratios. For practical and possibly religious reasons the arithmetic method was preferable for publication.

Assuming Ø to have been part of initiatic Mysteries shows our professional ancestor Vitruvius in a new light. We see him not as the overreaching bounder he is sometimes portrayed as, but as a link, knowing or unknowing, in a great chain of human wisdom; a chain that stretches over the historical horizon. We see him not just as the gruff hard-hat artillery officer he likely was but also as facilitator of the sympathetic magic of the initiations. And without presuming that he was personally a mystic, we may see here a more profound Vitruvius; indeed we may even see a Mystery Vitruvius.

The value of such a view is that it expands our professional inheritance and fully justifies the study of the classical elements in a philosophical and spiritual context. More importantly still, it allows for the possibility of our own personal elevation in the present moment through a conscious connection of our own work to the most ancient traditions of self-knowledge.

Rome II

The Pantheon

The Pantheon is certainly one of the great icons of Western architecture. The project was part of Hadrian's re-development of Rome's Campus Martius district, a part of his empire-wide building program substituting infrastructure development for territorial expansion. Construction took about 8 years, from 118–126 AD. It replaced an older structure built by Augustus' right-hand man, Marcus Agrippa c.25 BC. This initial building burned and was replaced under Domitian but burned again in Trajan's time. Domitian's building and perhaps even Agrippa's may have included a rotunda.[1] As Augustus steadfastly refused to be deified in his lifetime, Agrippa's building may have served to place Augustus, if not as a god himself, at least in the company of the gods. Hadrian's Pantheon may also have been a kind of audience hall where the emperor would hold court from the central niche, flanked by statues possibly of Caesar and Venus, patroness of the Julian gens.[2]

There is little doubt that Hadrian played a central role in the design of the Pantheon.[3] Though he was certainly not the supervising engineer, the technology of masonry in compression is pushed to its limits here by a vision so courageous that it is unlikely to have come from a consultant. Its combination of rectilinear and circular volumes, not seen at this scale before, strikes one as primal and deeply resonant. At the same time, and in common with the ancient world itself, the Pantheon embodies various mysterious aspects.

The most obvious mystery of the Pantheon is written on its frieze. Hadrian put someone else's name on the building; his own does not appear anywhere in the structure. Only recent archeology has determined that it was built entirely under Hadrian. The Pantheon was in a neighborhood loaded with Augustan-era buildings, thus in political terms Hadrian is attempting to identify with Augustus, in a form of imperial propaganda worthy of the pharaohs.[4]

The omission of his name from inscriptions on his public works was something of a habit of Hadrian's[5] and he is known to have published books under pseudonyms. He may have done this so the works could get a reasonable reception, free of the lavish praise of fawning courtiers or savage jibes of those excluded from the club. But we need to keep in mind that Hadrian also engaged in personal spiritual development through the Mysteries. He is one of only two or three Roman emperors to have completed the full initiation process of the Eleusinian Mysteries.[6] Thus it could be that he is displaying a personal reticence, a kind of humility born of an understanding of spiritual development in which the ego must of necessity be limited; in any event it could indicate a degree of self-reflection born of spiritual experience. The interior also has aspects that modern commentators have found problematic, particularly the discontinuity of vertical elements in the three interior layers, the base, attic and dome. However, the dome "hovers" like the sky because of this discontinuity of structure.[7] The floor is laid out in a square grid, much the way the Romans would survey a town; whereas the dome is laid out in rows of tapering coffers, recalling the mapping of the sky. The interior is lit by a single source: the oculus, eye of the divine, or of Horus.

There are sixteen columns on the entry portico and sixteen axial points on the rotunda plan. 16 is 10 + 6, the combination of the two Pythagorean perfect numbers, as a ratio it is Ø, 6/10. 16 is also 4^2. The attic layer of the interior has 16 openings. The 16 solid surfaces between them each have 4 pilasters for a total of 64 divisions or 4^3. The dome has 28 rows of coffers, 4 x 7, uniting the fourfold annual solar pattern and the 28-day lunar cycle.

A Reconstruction of the Pantheon

Let's say we wished to construct a building dedicated to the One and to be a model of the cosmos; not of the physical cosmos but of its formative powers, its psyche. We might begin by repeating a cosmological construction.[8] The point of emergence, **figure 1a,** is point A. The scope of the work is set by radius A-B1. Point A is "inflated" to create circle BC. After developing the dyad and the triad we arrive at the tetrad, square B1-B4. Rotating this 1/8th of the circle creates square C1-C4. Their points of intersection are at D1-D8 and these points which create an octagon give the inner diameter of our *chorha*, the space in which order will be manifest, the bubble within the *nun*, the sphere of the cosmic psyche, the form of Plato's world soul. Though it's represented here for brevity's sake as a circle we should remember that the building and Plato's world soul are spherical.

But starting here in the physical realm we will need to pass through a transitional zone. In keeping with the character of the physical it will be rectilinear. To size and place this element, the portico, **figure 1b**, draw a pentagon whose diagonal is B2-B4.

To accomplish this, draw a vesica piscis; with center at B4 and radius B2-B4, draw arc E1-E2 and extend it to G1 and F1. Repeat this with center at B2 and extend to G2-F2. With center at E2 and radius E2-B2 draw arc F2-B2-B4-F1. Draw a line from F1, at 45° to the axis of our construction E1-E2, through F3, continue to find point G2; repeat opposite hand to find point G1. Draw lines from G1 through B4; and from G2 through B2; extend both lines to find point H at the centerline. Triangle B2-B4-H is a Ø triangle.

If B2-B4 is set equal to 1, B2-H is 1/Ø, 1.618. To complete the pentagon, with center at G2 and radius G2-B2, draw arc to find point G3. With center at B2 and radius B2-G3 draw arc G3-J2, repeat opposite to find J1. Where the arcs cross the centerline find point J3. G3-B2-J2-J1-B4 is a pentagon.

If B2-B4 is 1 then each side of the pentagon is Ø. The process can be repeated to find intervals K, L, etc., whose lengths will form a Ø series. Line J1-J2 will give the width of the portico. Points G3 and J3 fall almost exactly on circle D, thus either the pentagon or the octagon could give the thickness of the enclosing wall.

The front of the portico can be set in several ways, **figure 1c**; 1, draw double square N1-N4 whose "back" is on line C1-C2 and whose short side is equal to J1-J2; or 2, draw equilateral triangle C1-C2-P; double the altitude of this triangle to get line N3-N4; or 3, where N1-N4 crosses line C4-C3 find points Q1-Q2 and construct equilateral triangle Q1-Q2-E2. Since E2 is given by the vesica piscis, B2-B4-E2 is also an equilateral triangle. Thus all the key relationships in the plan could be found using a pentagon and square with equal diagonals combined with an equilateral triangle whose side also equals that diagonal, **figure 1d.**

These primary, form-giving relationships appear even more clearly on the elevation, **figure 2,** and are reconstructed in **figure 3**. The width of the portico is the key interval, taken as 1. $Ø^2$ gives the top of the lower cornice, the 1/2 point gives the height of the order, Ø gives the height of the second cornice, $\sqrt{2}/2$ gives the apex of the tympanum of the portico, and $\sqrt{3}/2$ gives the start of the upper cornice. The height of the square gives the beginning of the "steps" that ballast the thrust of the dome, and the sides of the pentagon seem to govern their angle of ascent. The radius of the inner sphere is Ø of the side of the portico square, thus it is in the relationship of the squaring of the circle, of the "hieros gamos" or sacred marriage of spirit and matter, illustrated by the "Vitruvian Man." Another image would be that of a "sagrada familia" of, for example,

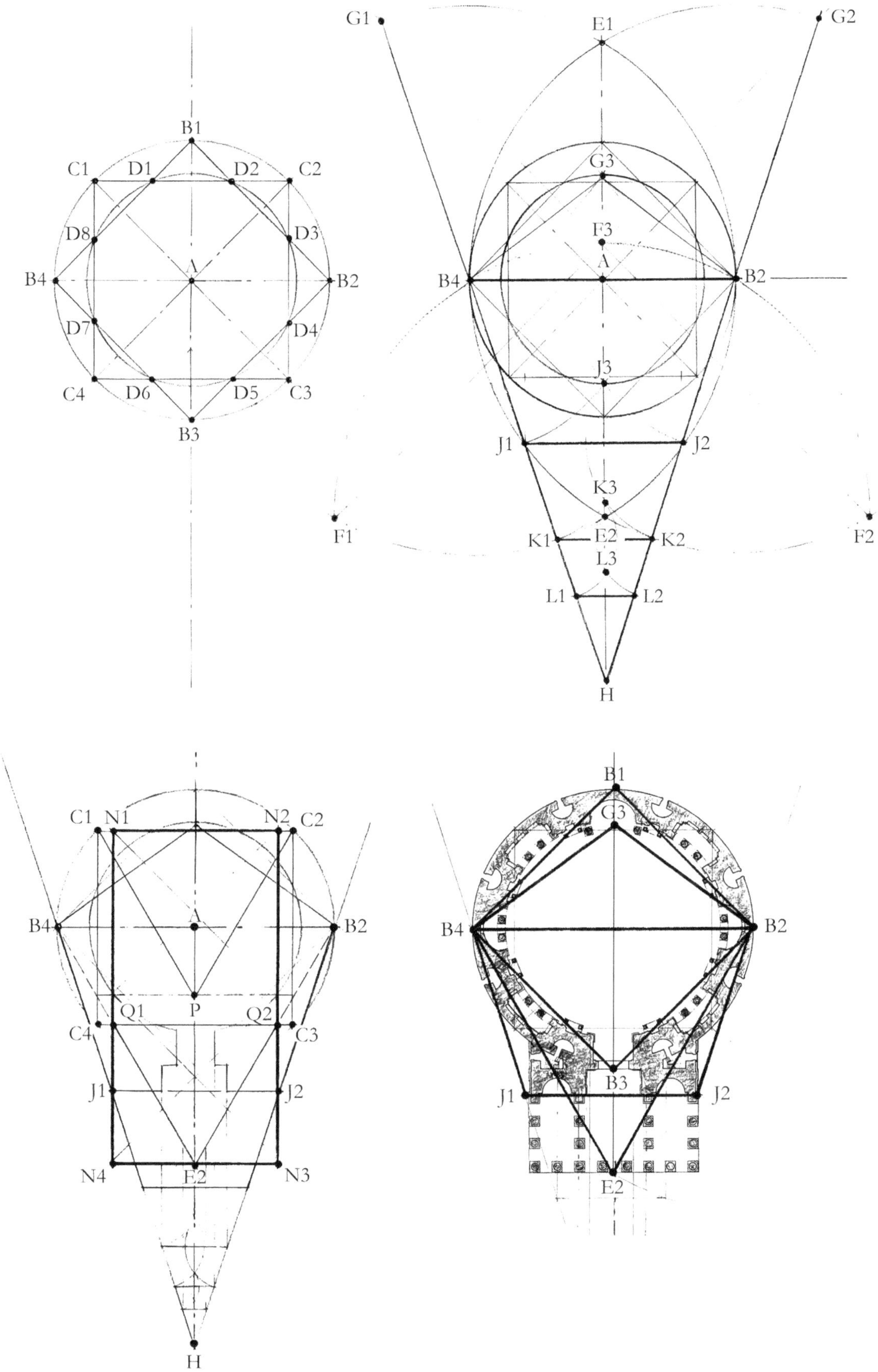

FIGURE 1a-d

Pantheon, Rome, 126 AD. Plan Reconstruction

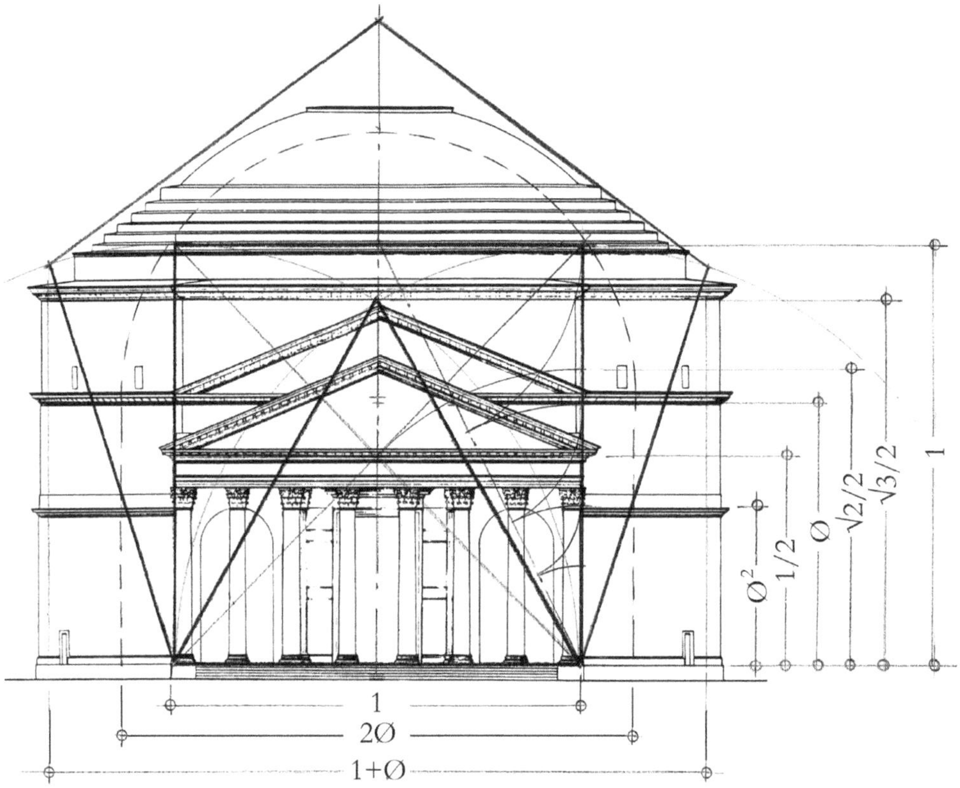

FIGURE 2

Pantheon. Elevation Analysis

the three most popular Egyptian divinities: Isis, the triangle; Osiris, the square; and Horus, the pentagon. Or we could see them as the powers of triad, tetrad, pentad , √2, √3, √5 or expressed in whole numbers as the Pythagorean triangle, 3, 4, 5. As each of these three figures is a face of a Platonic solid, there is most likely a creation myth involving the solids here though for brevity's sake discussion is restricted to two dimensional figures.

In actual dimension the rotunda's inner diameter is given[9] as 142'-6". The wall of the drum varies but is taken at 20'-0" giving 182'-6" for the outer diameter. The portico is 110'-10" wide; from the beginning of the portico to the face of the inner circle is 85'-7", giving a depth of 228'-1". Thus the relation between the width of the rotunda and the width of the portico, J1-J2 to B2-B4, is 182.5'/110.85 = 1/.607, a difference of about 1.7% of Ø. The relation of AD, the inner radius, to the front of the portico, J1-J2, is 71.25'/110.85 = .642, a difference of 4.0% from Ø. The relation of the sides of the double square N1-4 is 228.08'/110.85 = 1/2.06, a difference of 3%, but line N1-N2 is slightly forward of circle D; N1-N21 is about 6' less than 228.08', making the ratio 1/2.01.

In elevation the column diameter is 4'-11.5". The height of the columns is 46'-5" and the entablature is 10'-11.5" giving a total height of 57'-4.5". H/D = 46.4/4.96 = 9.355/1; very close to the Vitruvian 9.5/1. The ratio of the entablature to the overall height of the order, 10.96/57.375 = .191, Ø^2/2 . The ratio of the width of the portico to its height = 110.83/57.375 = 1/1.932, only 3.5% short of a double square.

An understanding of Platonic esoteric doctrines seems to underlie the Pantheon's conception. In the *Timaeus,* the world soul is said to be a sphere, whereas the manifest physical world is made from the Platonic solids, which in turn are built up of triangles derived from the three primary polygons. The clear appearance of these three archetypal polygons, triangle, square, and pentagon, in the building's plan and elevation – polygons that may also be taken to represent heaven-human-

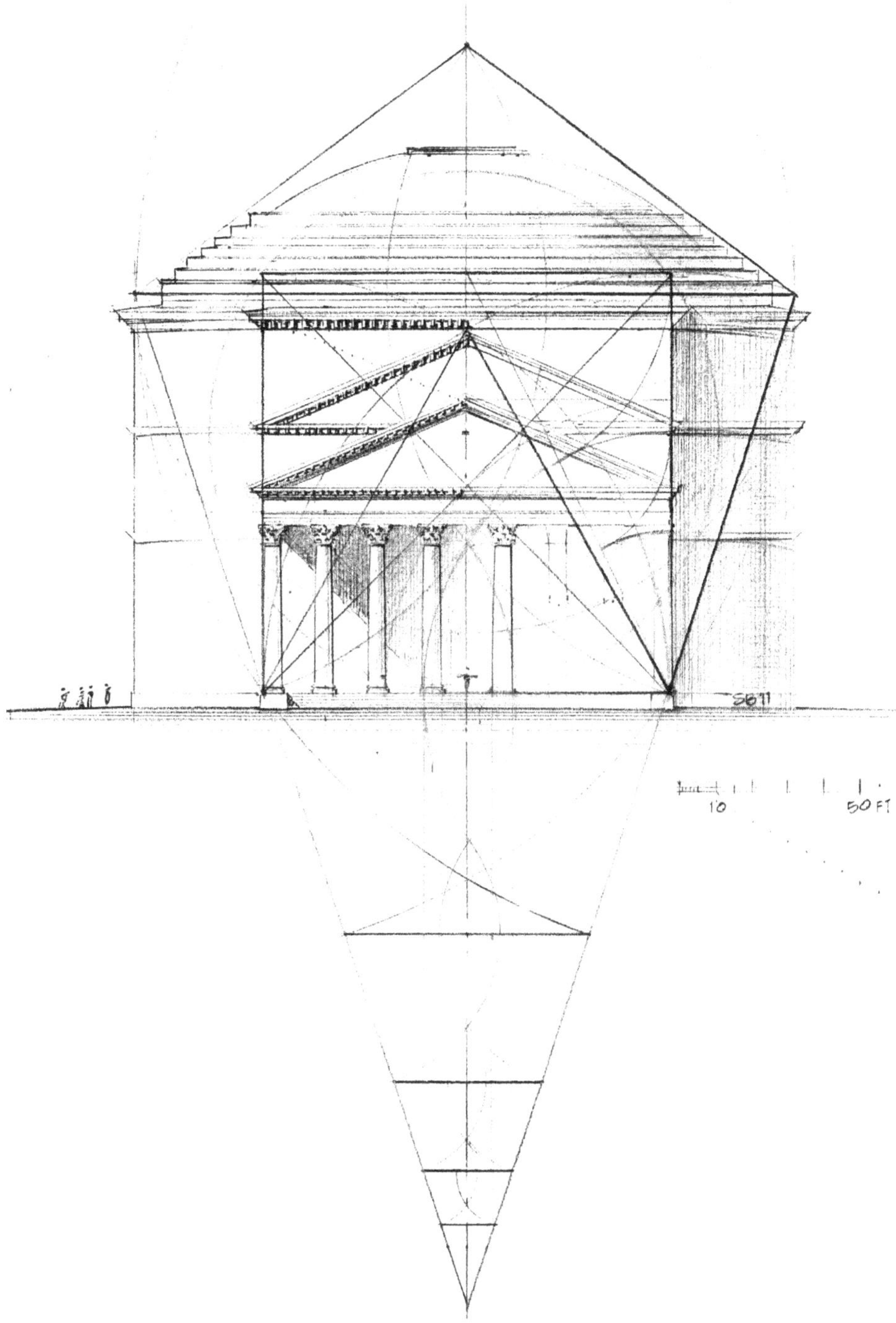

FIGURE 3

Pantheon. Elevation Reconstruction

earth or spirit-mind-body – reinforce the notion that the Pantheon is a cosmological construct. The multiple pathways possible to arrive at this design indicate that the story here is not definitive, indeed, there may not be one. Compound systems may be at work. The fecundity of geometric and arithmetic relations that appear in the Pantheon indicate the sophistication of the design. There may be no definitive proportional story for this building; like the cosmos itself, its mysteries will endure.

The Portico Question

Yet another abiding mystery of the Pantheon is the presence of a second raking cornice on the intermediate block that, along with a number of other "anomalies" on the exterior, seems to indicate that the portico was altered during the course of construction: the entablature of the portico does not align with either of the two string courses on the rotunda and steps out a few inches on each side where it meets the block; the central pilasters at the back of the portico are not properly modulated with respect to the pilasters of the block; foundations do not reflect the offsets of the two previous items; and the brickwork of the intermediate block is integral to the rotunda up to the portico height but not integral above, indicating that the upper portion was built a little later. Several other "anomalies," such as intercolumniation and tympanum height, are judgment calls rather than measurable misalignments.[10]

One explanation for the anomalies is that 50-foot column shafts, which would align the portico cornice to the rotunda's second string course, became unavailable, forcing the substitution of 40-foot shafts.[11] There may have been problems of sheer structural weight involved, or issues of quarrying and transport. In particular, it is suggested that one or more ships carrying some of the 50-foot shafts from Egypt sank, thereby depriving the Roman builders of these special order, long lead-time items.[12] But how many could have been lost? It's hard to imagine a single ship carrying more than two such enormous monoliths. Only eight of each type of stone were needed. This story assumes that forty footers of the required stone were in stock, and able to be reassigned from another project. But as few buildings of the period use 40-footers they may well have been special orders too.

A higher portico would have more fully hidden both the rotunda and the intermediate block, but was that necessary or desired?[13] And why is the intermediate block there at all? The "service stair" explanation is inadequate.[14] Perhaps the block and raking cornice are a reference to an earlier building or to another building. Perhaps the portico was intended to appear to back up against a flat wall like the temple of Mars in the forum of Augustus. Visually, the block reduces our awareness of the rotunda; symbolically, it is the opposite of the rotunda. Regardless of why the portico was set where it was, why was the higher pediment expressed at all? The explanation that the raking cornice visually ties the ends of the interrupted string course, while not incorrect, is not compelling.[15] Why was it necessary to run the rotunda's string courses on the block at all? Couldn't the surface have been treated as an attic, or in some other decorative manner?

In terms of construction sequence, wouldn't the entablature of the portico have been placed before the upper part of the block and its cornice had been built?[16] If the portico was lowered before the intermediate block was built, why was a pediment built on the front of the block at all? If these elements were built after the portico then they must have been intentional.

The sinking ship story requires that Hadrian insist on monolithic shafts.[17] Why? Was it just "bravado"?[18] Unusual materials, brought from a great distance, used in huge quantities or worked in novel ways, can strike awe, even terror, in the hearts of viewers. The stone types used are clearly a reference to Roman domination of Egypt, but as monoliths they would also symbolize a cultural continuity with Egypt. A possible reason to insist on monoliths may be the magical or esoteric phenomenon of resonance in a monolith, as opposed to a composite form, though there is no objective evidence that Hadrian knew of or practiced such a science. The objection to composite shafts, that carving the fluting was too time-consuming,[19] presumes that fluting was "de rigueur" for composite shafts.[20] Since shafts came to the site rough cut and were finished in situ, all columns, whether monoliths or drums, whether intended to be fluted or smooth, would have to be finished in place making the difference in working time between fluted and unfluted relatively minor.

The shipwreck scenario also depends on some sort of time pressure or constraint. It may be that the date of 127, when Hadrian assumed the title "father of the country," was critical, *"Waiting*

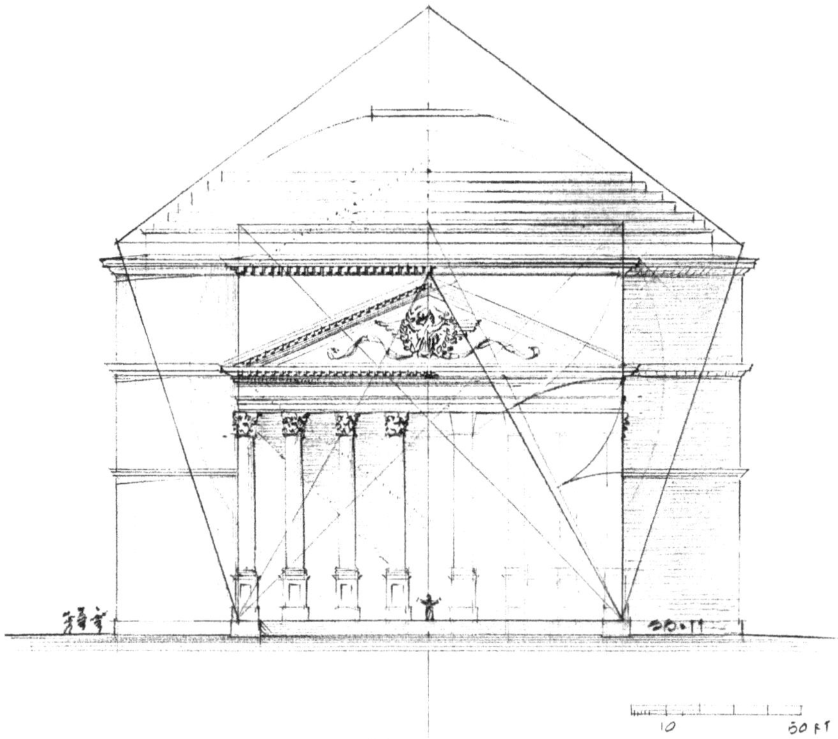

FIGURE 4
Pantheon. Reconstructed with Pedestals

appeared feeble,"[21] but Hadrian was in Rome until late 128. Regardless of dates, government officials often open public projects long before actual completion. Depending on the degree of completion some face-saving accommodation could have been made. On the other hand, would another two years in an eight-year construction process have been fatal to the political aims of the project?

To keep the "intended" portico height, assuming 40-footers could be quickly obtained, was there any other design solution? The shorter shafts could have been placed on pedestals, **fig. 4.** This retains the higher cornice, aligning with the rotunda's string course, eliminating the double pediment. It could also be that the designers decided the 50-foot portico was too high and that it needed to be lowered. Perhaps the intended effect was not primarily exterior but transitory; passing through a lower portico would intensify the effect of entering the spherical hall.

Ultimately, the shipwreck story is all speculation[22] and does not explain the existence of the second pediment. Furthermore, this kind of explanation, while perhaps not factually wrong, points our attention downward, keeping us, in effect, from "looking up." The aim of such stories is to trash the ancients, to always point out that "their feet smelled and their noses ran," as the joke goes; to show that they were "mortal flesh."[23] This attitude is expressed in the suggestion that Hadrian kept Agrippa's name on the frieze to avoid taking the blame for the butchered design.[24]

We could, by contrast, just accept the existence of the anomalous pediment.[25] Could it be that modern commentators have a limited or reduced understanding of ancient concepts? This certainly bedeviled them on the Pantheon's interior. Contradiction or alternation, the combination of opposites, which Hadrian seemed to relish and a key to the Platonic creation, was in fact banished from post-Renaissance design analysis. It may well be that the Romans, new to such an archetype, didn't see the non-alignments, and double pediment as errors. Perhaps the double pediment is a reference, the source of which is no longer available for us to read. Or perhaps our view of the ancient world is like a mirror revealing even more about ourselves than about the subject of observation.

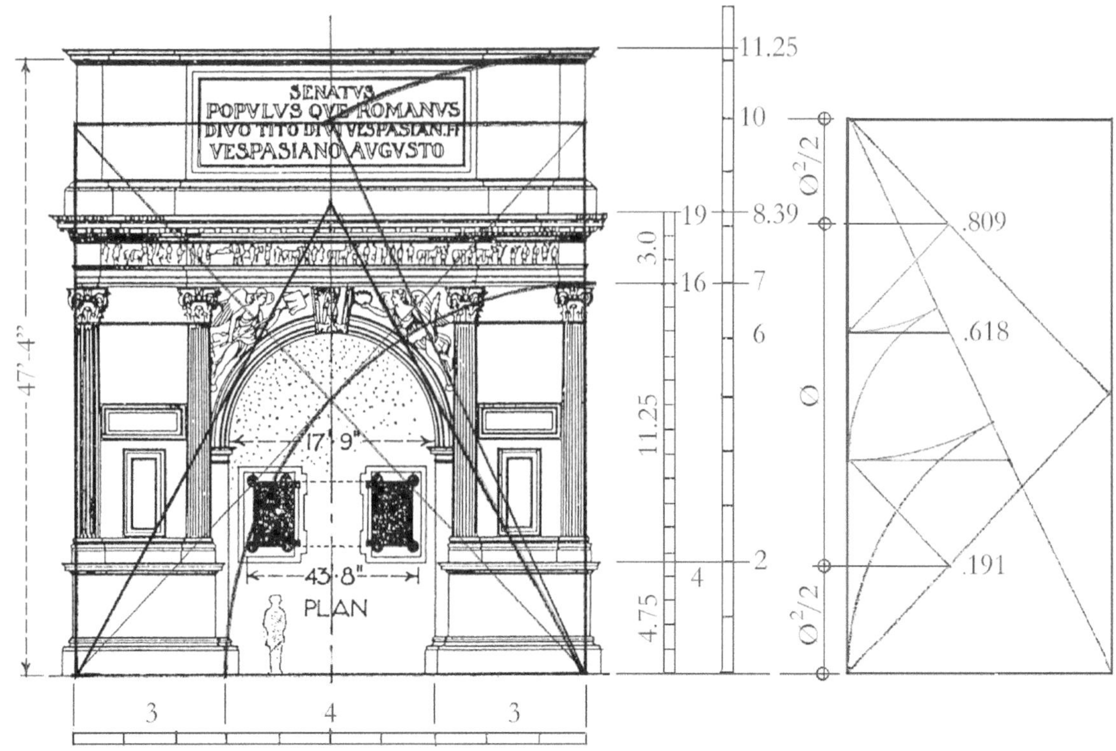

FIGURE 5a

Arch of Titus, Rome, 82 AD. Analysis

MONUMENTAL ARCHES

The Romans were the first to utilize the circular arch as a monumental form. Arches had been used in ancient Egypt, but only for utilitarian purposes, in lightless shrines, or in tombs. These vaults or domes were usually corbeled rather than segmented or were done in mud brick.[26] The Greeks used vaulting in some substructures, but in Greece, as in Egypt, the arch played no role above ground or in public buildings. The Romans elevated what had been a structural utility, best kept out of sight, to a symbol of public virtue.

In republican times[27] the monumental arch was "triumphal," the victorious general and the seized booty including prisoners were paraded before the populace, passing under a specially erected arch as they entered the city or forum. The arch form quickly became honorific in general. It was very common at urban gateways, crossroads and entrances of major buildings. Arches sometimes stood independently and were sometimes built into larger wall areas.[28] Though there are numerous variants most Roman monumental arches fall into two broad classes: the single bay with abutments and the three bay, in which the abutments are wide enough to be opened up with arches of their own, sometimes in two directions. Most monumental arches have an order with pedestal, column and entablature, above which is an attic. The central part of the attic had dedicatory inscriptions. Atop the attic were statues above the outer columns and a statue group, sometimes a quadriga, in the center. The space between the columns on the abutments contained reliefs telling the story of the arch, or niches for statuary. Sometimes the attics had similar ornamental treatment.

ARCH OF TITUS, ROME

This archetypal example of a single-bay arch was built in 82 AD in recognition of the sacking of Jerusalem at the conclusion of the first Jewish revolt by Domitian's son and successor, Titus.

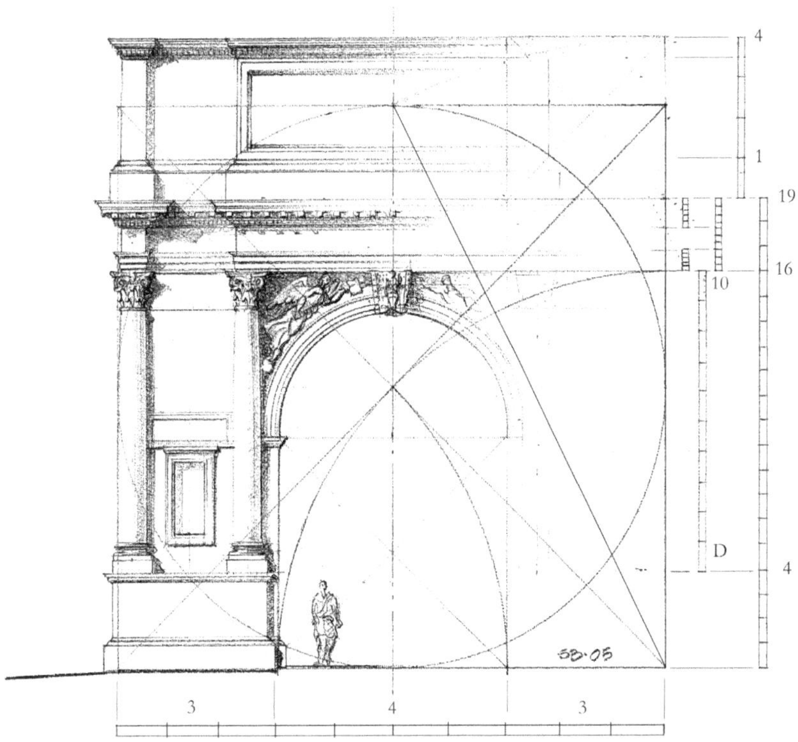

FIGURE 5b
Arch of Titus Reconstruction

Ornamental panels below the arch show the Romans carrying off loot from the Temple, including the seven-candled menorah. The arch is sited along the Via Sacra leading to the forum, adjoining the temple of Venus and Rome.

Setting the width of the structure as 1, **figure 5a,** the elevation is put in a square. The √2/2 cut provides the major horizontal division into the 3-4-3 pattern, while vertically marking the underside of the entablature. Applying an arithmetical scale of 19 to the order, the pedestal is 4.75 units high, the column 11.25 and the entablature 3. The height of the square may be divided into 10, with the pedestal 2 units, the columns 5 and the entablature 1.25. By inspection the attic is 3/10ths high, making it equal to the width of the pier, giving a total height of 11.25. The H/W ratio is 11.25/10, 1.125/1, 9/8, the interval of the whole tone.

The width is 43.66' and the height is 47.33' to the underside of the attic cornice.[29] Adding 1.5 feet to include that element the H/W ratio is 48.75/43.66 = 1.117, very close to √5/2 = 1.118. The height of the order is found by taking the interval of each unit: .707/16 units = .044 of the side of the square per unit; making the height of the order .707 + .132 = .839, close to [1+Ø]/2 = .809, also close to √3/2 = .867. The pedestal height is .044 x 4.75 = .209 approximately $Ø^2/2$, .191. The column height is .044 x 11.25 = .495, very close to half of the overall width, giving a column height to arch opening ratio of .495/.4 = 1.24/1, 5/4. Column center to center is, by inspection, .525; giving a ratio of .495/.525 = .943/1, not quite a square. The height of the apex of the arch to its opening is 1.5/1, putting it at 6/10, or Ø.

The reconstruction, **figure 5b**, begins with the square, the √2/2 cut to give the width of the arch and the top of the columns. The order is applied vertically by dividing the √2/2 interval into 16, giving the pedestal a conventional 4 [as opposed to 4.75 in the analysis], the column 12, and adding the last 3 for the entablature to equal 19. Alternately, the √3/2 point could be divided into 19, making the height of the order 10 x .867 = 8.67 units as opposed to 8.39, a

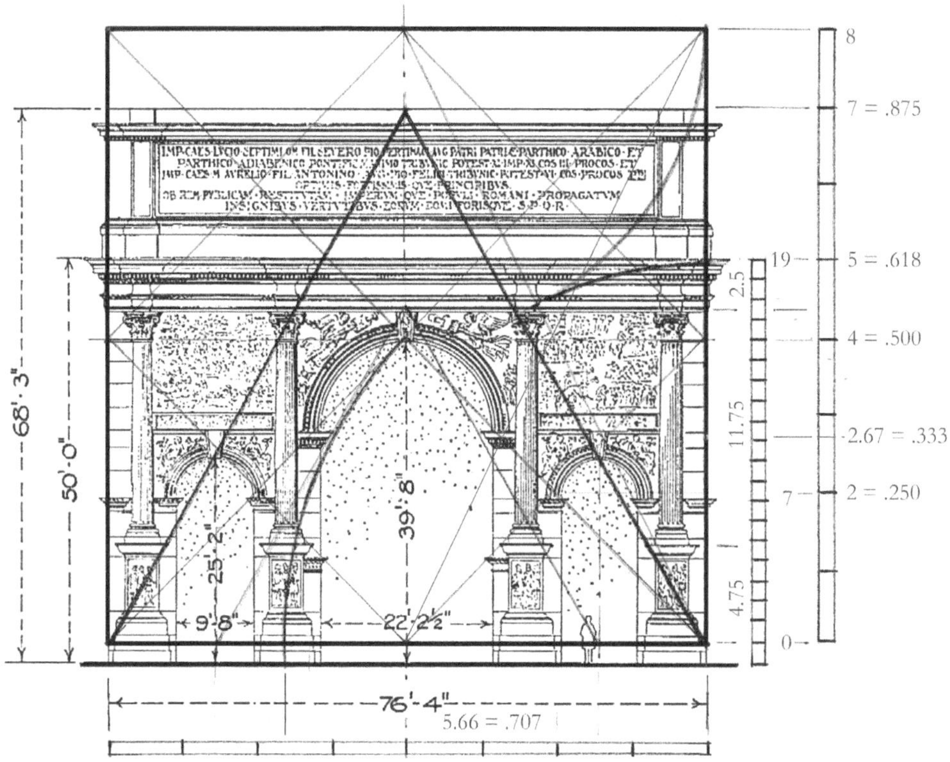

FIGURE 6a

Arch of Septimus Severus, Rome, 203 AD. Analysis

difference of 3.4%. The attic height is found by applying the √5/2, or squaring up 3/10ths, the width of the pier. The lower part of the central arch is a 4 x 4 square, putting the crown of the arch at 6/10 or Ø of the enclosing square.

The Arch of Septimus Severus

This archetypal three-bay arch was built in Rome in 203 AD to celebrate the victory of Severus and his sons, Caracalla and Geta, in fighting the Parthians in what is present-day Iraqi Kurdistan. The monument is prominently sited in the Roman Forum astride the Via Sacra, next to the Senate, at the opposite end of the movement path from the Arch of Titus.

Applying a scale of 19 to the order, **figure 6a**, gives a pedestal of 4.75, a column of 11.75 and an entablature of 2.5[30]; .75 units have been shaved off the column and entablature and given to the pedestal. To further elevate the pedestal in this design 1 unit is added below the canonical 19. The given height of the order, 50.0' divided by 20 gives 2.5' per unit making the pedestal 11.875', the column 29.375' and the entablature 6.25'. The height of the order and the attic is 68.25'-2.5'[for the sub-base] = 65.75/76.3 = .860 very close to the altitude of the equilateral triangle, √3/2 = .867. The top of the cornice is 50.0'-2.5' = 47.5' and Ø x 76.33' = 47.17'.

In the three-bay type the width or diameter of the central arch is about equal to the height of the column of the order. This ratio is stretched and squeezed in individual cases. Dividing the column height by 10 gives D = 2.94' or 2'-11". If a pier were 3 D wide it would be 8.82' or 8' -10"; whereas the given measures[31] indicate 8.71' ÷ 3 = 2.90' or D = 2'-10". The clear space between the central columns is, 22.2' + 5.8' [2 D] = 28.0', as opposed to the column height of 29.33', about 4.5% vertically off square.

The √2/2 point seems to position the inner columns: 2 piers, 8.71 x 2 = 17.42 + small opening, 9.67 + center opening, 22.2 + 1/2 a pier, 4.35 = 53.64' while the geometrical is 76.33' x .707 =

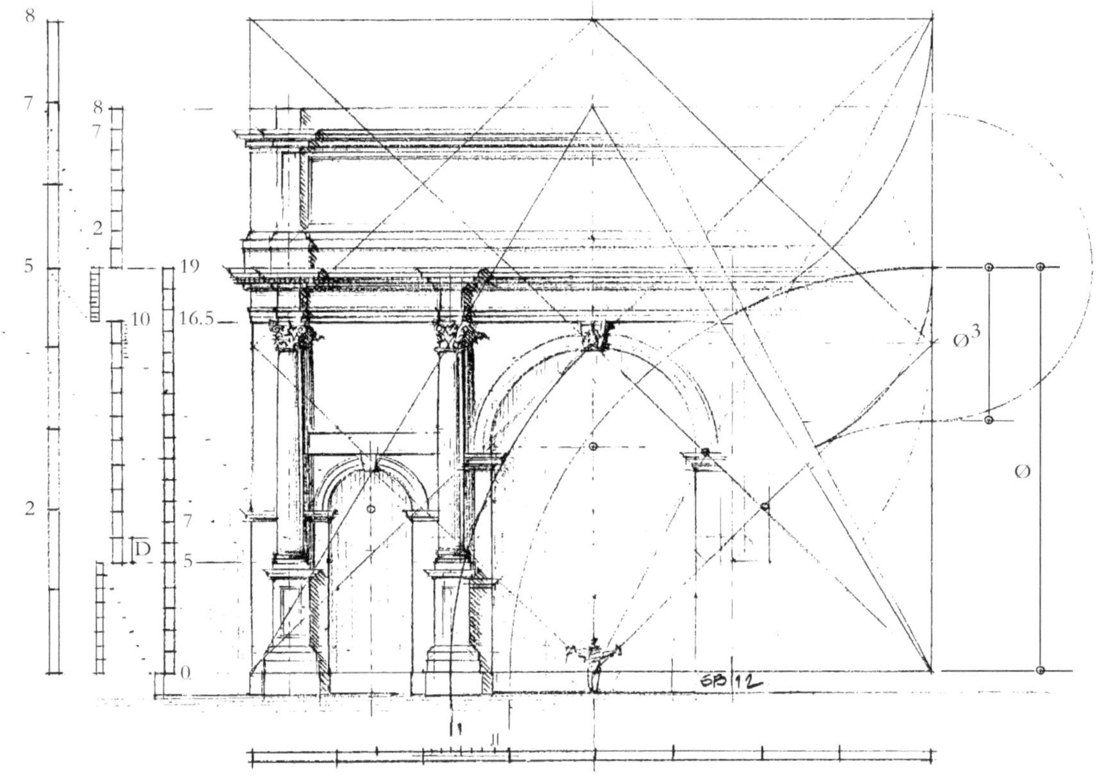

FIGURE 6b

Arch of Septimus Severus. Reconstruction

53.96'. The edge of the central arch is at 49.29', close to the given height of the order, 50.0.' The spring point of the central arch is, by inspection, 1/3rd of the overall width, 76.33' ÷ 3 = 25.44'. The apex of the central arch, by inspection, is at the half-point of the square, as are the tops of the column shafts: top of shaft = 8.83 D x 2.94' = 25.97' + pedestal 11.9 = 37.9', BF gives 37.2' a difference of about 6", while 76.33/2 = 38.16', 3" off.

The side arches spring from about the quarter point of the square, 2/8ths, .250, or 7/19ths, implying that it is at $Ø^3$ of the square, .236 x 8 = 1.89, about 5% off. The distance from the bottom of the square to the top of the columns is 41.25', while the altitude of an equilateral triangle with its base equaling the interval from the centers of the side arches is 49.2' x .867 = 42.65', and close to 2 x 22.2 = 44.4', twice the width of the central arch.

Reconstruction, **figure 6b**, begins with the square. Strike off Ø for the body of the arch and $Ø^3$ for the attic. Divide the Ø interval into 19 units and set the count at 5 for the pedestal, 11.5 for the column and 2.5 for the entablature. Divide the 11.5 interval of the column into 10 to get D. The piers are 3 D in width, with the inner pier centered on the √2/2 point.

The center of the enclosing square is the crown of the central arch. The central arch springs from the 1/3 point while the small arches spring from the 1/4 point. Add an additional 1/19th unit below the bottom of the square for the sub-plinth. Pure division by 8 would also give a reconstruction, as Ø = .618 and 5/8 = .625; a difference of .007 or only 1.2%. Thus division by 8 provides an "intersection" between the geometrical and arithmetic systems. By dividing each unit into 8 parts gives a width of 64 parts. Such a "pure" scheme could be modulated by moving the center of the interior column 1/64th toward the center.[32] As in the Pantheon, these archetypal constructions arise from the interplay of the formative powers, √2, √3, √5.

The Medieval Era

Hebrew Tradition – Solomon's Temple

Solomon's Temple at Jerusalem consisted of a sequence of three spaces, a porch, a sanctuary and an inner temple known as the "Holy of Holies" where the Arc of the Covenant was kept.[1] The temple, **figure 1**, was 20 cubits in width, the depth of the porch 10 cubits, the length of the sanctuary 40 cubits and its height 30 cubits. The Holy of Holies was 20 x 20 x 20 cubits. This gives the following ratios: the Holy of Holies is a cube with sides in the ratio of 1:1:1; the Sanctuary is 2:1 in plan, in elevation the short side is in the ratio of 3:2 and the long side is in the ratio of 4:3. These four ratios were the bedrock of the ancient musical system.

The Kabbalistic Tree of Life may be constructed within the 1:2 ratio on the floor of the sanctuary with Keter at the entry to the Holy of Holies and Malkhut at the entry from the porch. The Tree consists of ten Sephorat, depicted as dots arranged in a sixfold pattern, **figure 2.** The Tree may well be of prehistoric origin but the image only came to light in the early Middle Ages. This opens the possibility that in a venue such as ancient Alexandria, the ten dots of the tetraktys may have been rearranged into the Tree, as suggested in **figure 3.**

The left and right sides of the Tree are known as Jachin and Boaz, the pillars of justice and mercy. These are materialized in the temple as two freestanding columns placed in front of the porch. These columns are said to have had capitals that used the image of the lily, a flower which follows a sixfold symmetry as does the Tree. The pillars are reminiscent of the pairs of obelisks placed in front of the pylons of Egyptian temples.

If the Holy of Holies is included in the plan, an "extended" Tree may be placed in that 1:3 overall ratio.[2] The extended tree creates seven points of intersection that may be likened to the seven henads of the late Neoplatonist Proclus. In **figure 4**, the plan of Chartres Cathedral and one of its key ornaments are compared to an extended tree and to the cosmology of Proclus.[3]

The arrangement of Solomon's Temple utilizes arithmetic, geometry, music and, in its siting and orientation, astronomy. The integration of these "sacred sciences" established the individual's perception of cosmic order,[4] allowing the temple to become a link of above to below.

But beyond the physical temple a larger project may be glimpsed. The temple is said to have been located on the northern end of the platform at a site called the Dome of the Spirits,[5] built over an outcrop called the Rock of Foundation. This location forms an alignment or Ley line running east-west,[6] **figure 5.** It begins in the east on the summit of the Mount of Olives, moves west over the temple platform's "Golden Gate," through which Jesus entered the city on Palm Sunday, a gate that has since been sealed. The line runs between Jachin and Boaz, through the sanctuary, over the Tree imagined on the floor moving from Malkhut "back" to Keter at the foot of the Holy of Holies, and into that space, passing between the almost-touching wings of the cherubim placed over the Ark of the Covenant. On a certain day close to the vernal equinox, the sun would rise over the mount of Olives. Its rays would penetrate the Holy of Holies and be reflected off its gilded surfaces. The ray passing between the wings of the metal cherubim may have created an energetic discharge. This energy was directed into the earth through the rock of foundation and radiated fertilizing energy. Myths and legends surrounding the temple suggest that a thundering sound like rushing waters was audible from below.

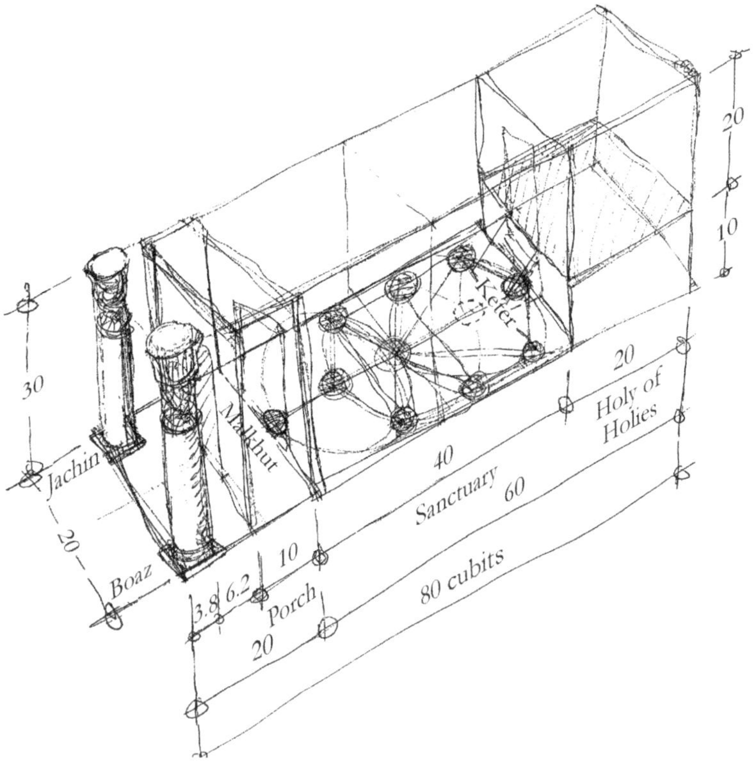

FIGURE 1
Dimensions of Solomon's Temple

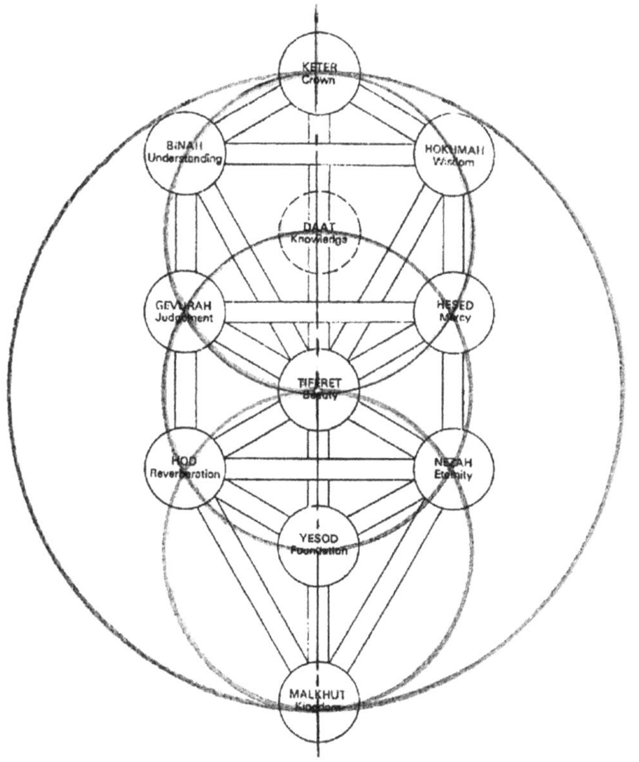

FIGURE 2
The Tree of the Kabbalah

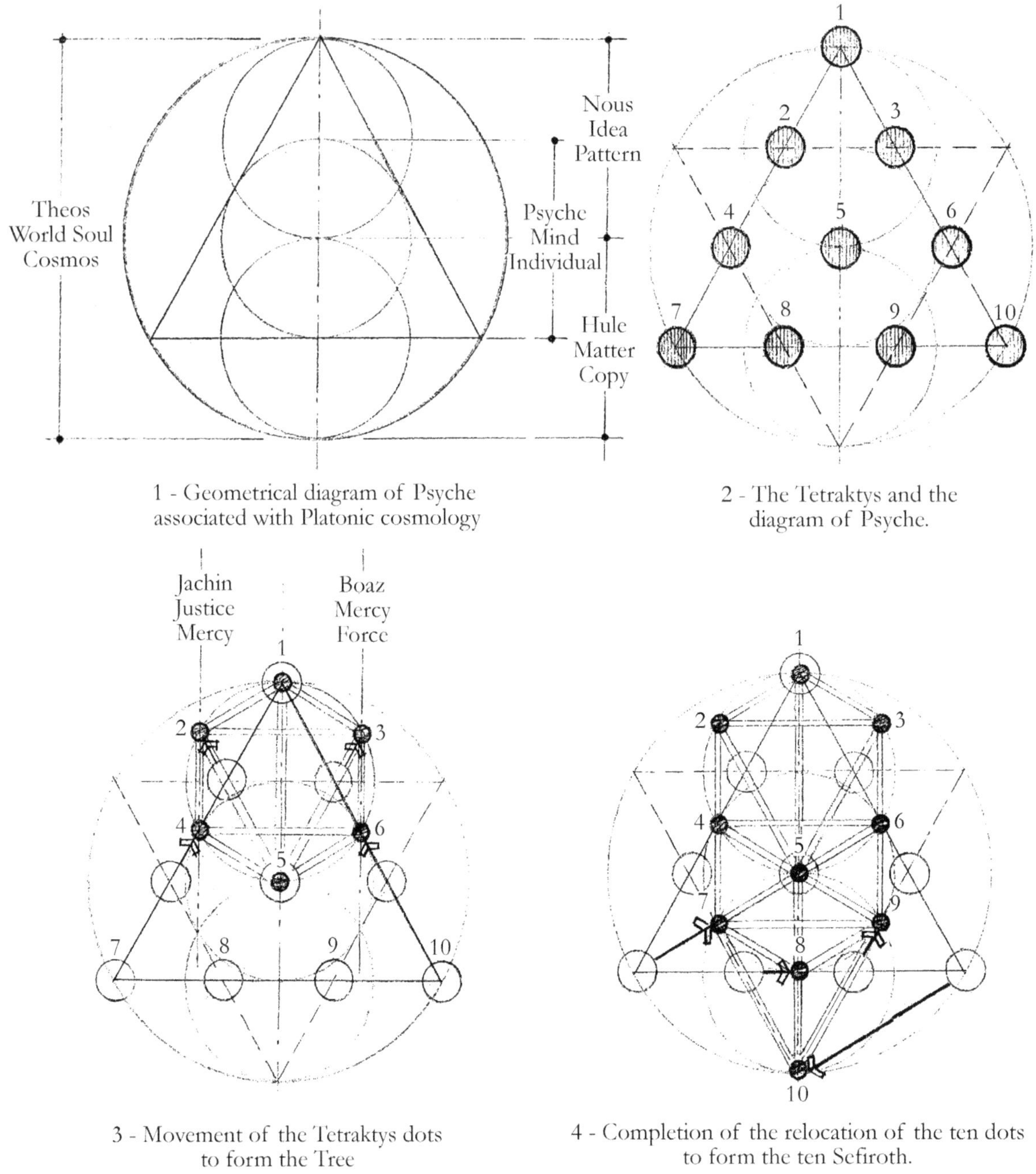

1 - Geometrical diagram of Psyche associated with Platonic cosmology

2 - The Tetraktys and the diagram of Psyche.

3 - Movement of the Tetraktys dots to form the Tree

4 - Completion of the relocation of the ten dots to form the ten Sefiroth.

FIGURE 3
The Tetraktys and the Tree

This interaction constitutes an alchemical union of opposites, a sacred marriage of celestial light yang power and terrestrial dark yin power taking place in the Holy of Holies.[7] This arrangement may be seen as a refinement of the "chamber and passage" monuments of the Old and New Worlds.

The temple however is not the end of the ley line. If continued farther west, the line crosses the Roman Cardo Maximus at a right angle. At its northern terminus the cardo joins two other streets in a radial pattern at the apex of which Hadrian placed a commemorative column. Continuing west the ley crosses Golgotha, site of the crucifixion. The terminus of the cardo and the radiating streets comprise one vertex of a pentagon whose base runs through the back of the temple, **figure 5**, with Golgotha lying near its apex.

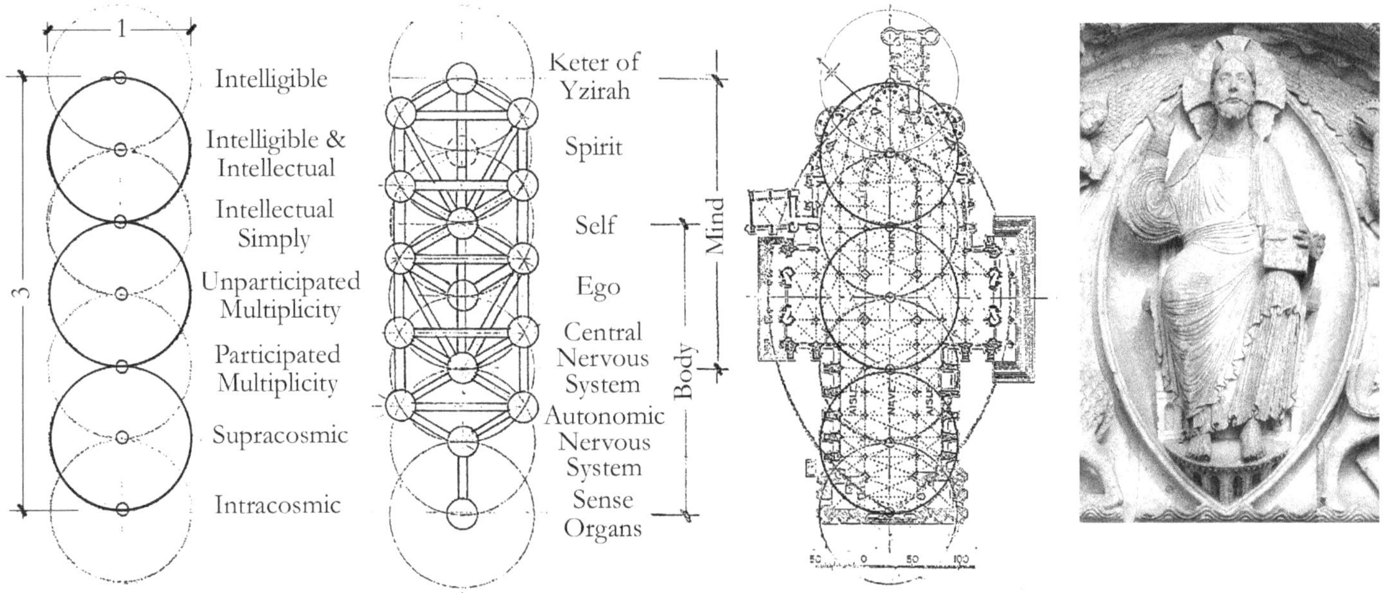

Procession of the Hennads after Proclus, 'On Parmenides'

Extended Tree of Body & Mind after Halevi, 'Kabbalistic Universe'

Plan of Chartres Cathedral

Christ in the Vesica West Portal, Chartres

FIGURE 4

Proclus, the Extended Tree and Chartres. Indicating Continuity of Ancient and Medieval Philosophy, Religion and Architecture

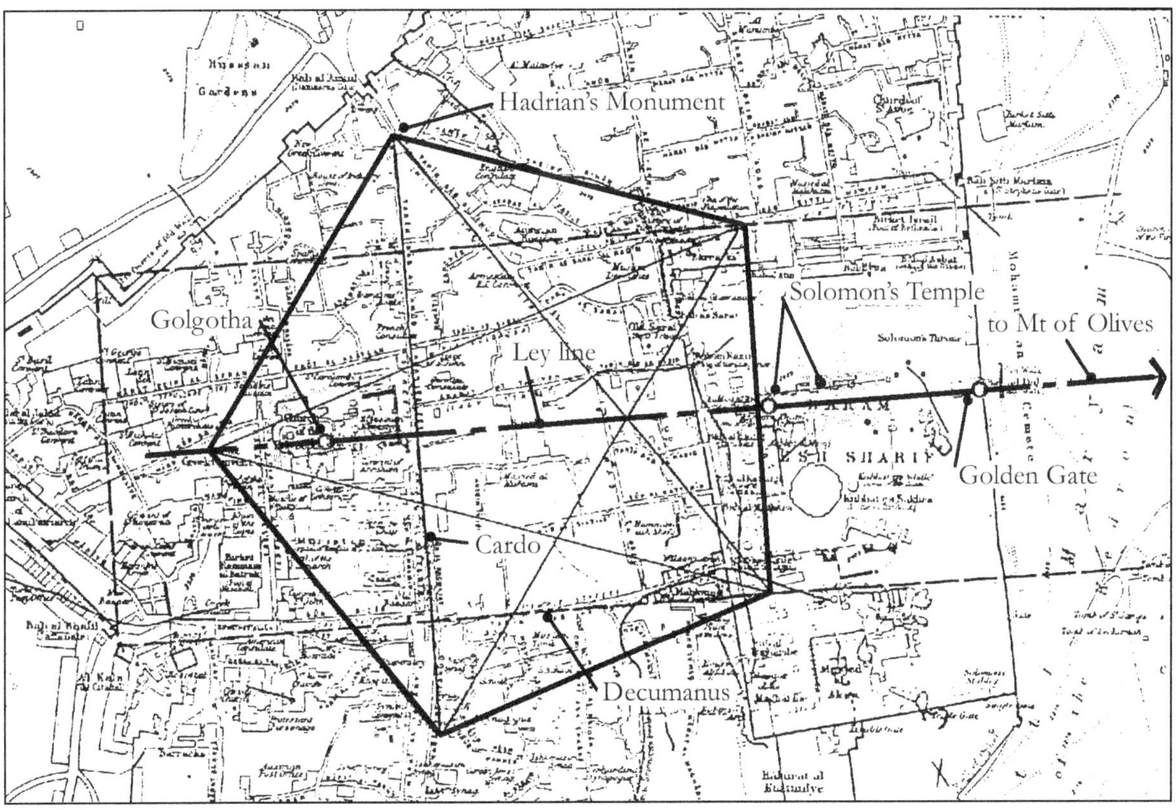

FIGURE 5

Geometry of Jerusalem

Romanesque Architecture – St. Front, Périgueux

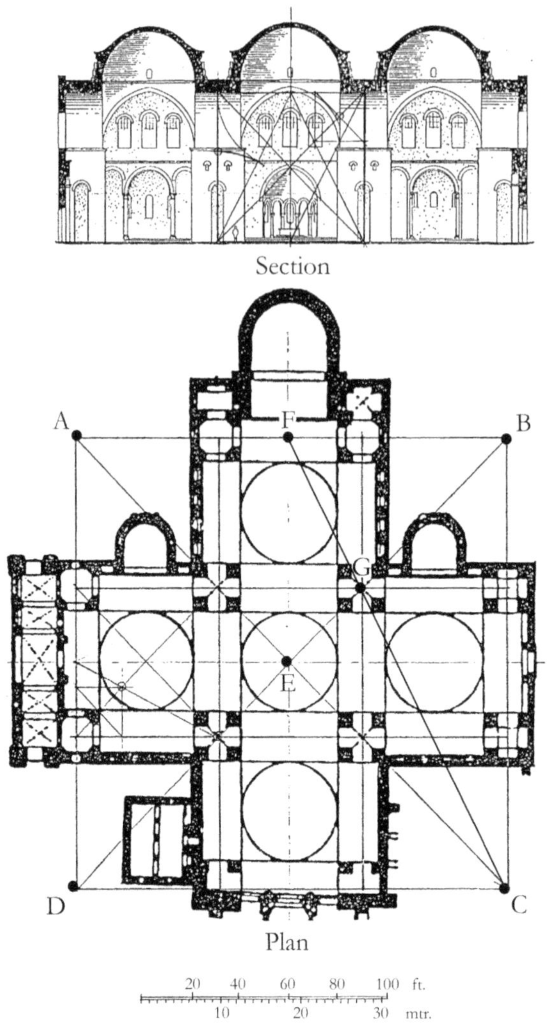

Figure 6a – *St. Front, Périgueux, 1120*

Romanesque architecture is based on the √2 pattern. This determines the size of the mass needed to resist the thrust of the spherical domes. Illustrated here is the Cathedral of St. Front, Périgueux, in central France, 1120, **figure 6a**. The plan is a cross arrangement of five cubes each of which has a dome and 1/4 of a retaining pier. It is put in square ABCD and divided into 1/3rds.

6b.1. Reconstruction begins with square ABCD, whose sides will be the center lines of the dome "modules." Divide the square by its diagonals AC and BD, and semi-diagonal FC. The intersection of these lines at point G divides the sides of the square into thirds and creates nine squares within ABCD.

6b.2. Create an octagon within the central square. With center at G and radius EG draw arc LEH. Repeat this at each corner of the square to create octagon H-Q. Setting the side of the inner square = 1, EG = √2/2 = .707. This creates a 3-4-3 pattern of division of the side of the square.

6b.3. Extending this octagonal construction to the squares adjoining the central square begins to construct a semi-regular, 2-dimensional grid of octagons and squares, such as RSKJ.[8]

6b.4. From the midpoints of the sides of square RSKJ, draw square TUVW. Interval TU gives the width of the main piers and, by subtraction, the diameter of the carrying arches. As point T is

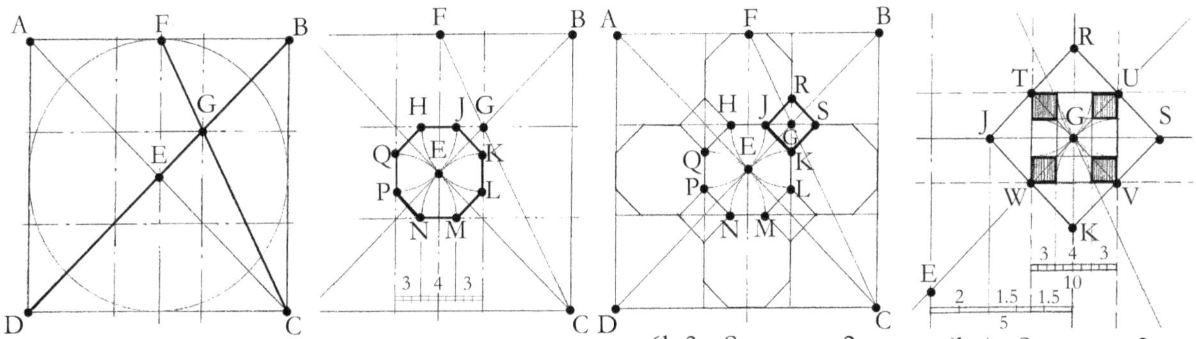

6b.1 - Unity and Division 6b.2 - Structure 1 6b.3 - Structure 2 6b.4 - Structure 3

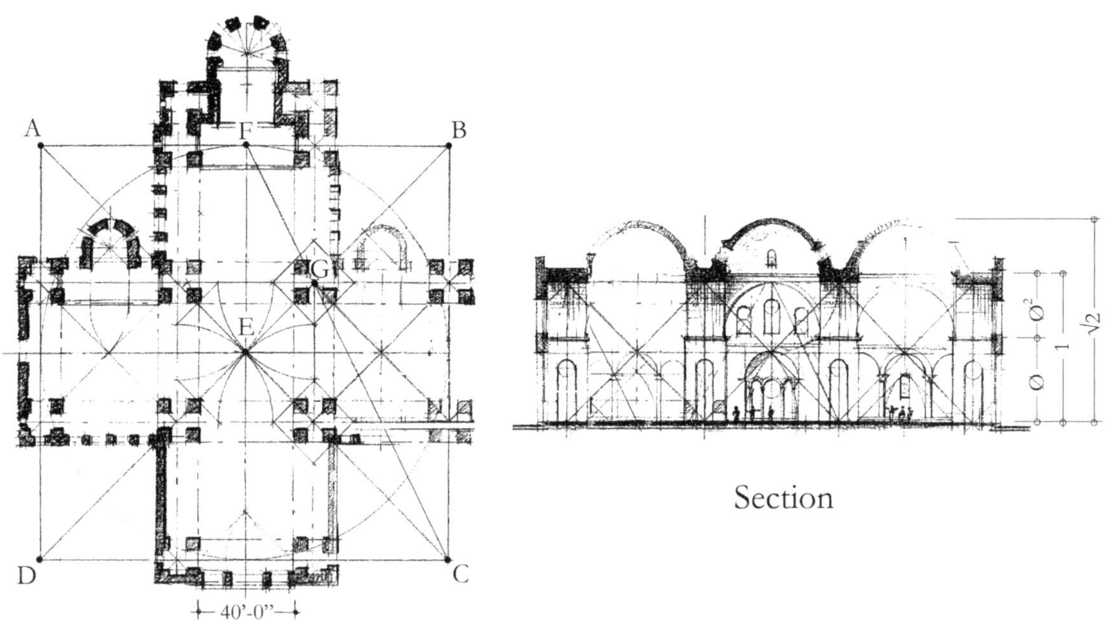

Plan

Section

6b.5 - Materialization

FIGURE 6b – *St. Front Reconstruction*

the midpoint of JG a structural pattern is created of a dome 7 units in diameter with a 3-unit support pier. The massive masonry piers are "lightened" by openings also shaped by the √2 pattern.

6b.5. Repeating this for each of the five squares in a cruciform pattern gives the plan of the church. In section the lower floor arches rise to the half-point of the central square. The upper tier of arches appears to spring from the Ø point of the interior interval and rises to the top of the central square. The semi-spherical domes spring from there, bringing their crowns to the √2 point.

Cosmatesque Ornament

Emerging from the Middle Ages, composed of fragments of the ancient Roman world, sometimes literally, and of influences from Sicily, Byzantium and Alexandria, the ornamental style called Cosmatesque is one of the more important geometrically guided design approaches in world aesthetic history. Like all good examples of such work its parts are perfectly obvious and it appears to use a few simple rules, yet the overall effect is captivating, promising deeper mysteries below the surface. The artisans who practiced it were called the Cosmati. Though they all claimed descent from a common ancestor, Cosma, they were actually a group of six or more families operating in and around Rome c.1000-1300 AD.[9] The name "Cosma" of course is derived from "cosmos," referring to the beautiful, orderly appearance of the material world, the surface covering of the divine. As in the case of Hermogenes, the name may be a "coincidence" or a "tip off" that there is more here than meets the eye.

The Cosmati shops were structured on the apprenticeship tradition, restricted almost exclusively to family members. The several families lived during the same period, in the same neighborhoods in Rome and were involved in the same geometrically based business. They would almost certainly have intermarried; but more pointedly, did they have a common guild that practiced initiation? Without doubt though, they shared a geometrical methodology.

The designs have two scales. A large scale circular enclosing pattern and smaller scale infill patterns. The enclosing pattern was a three-part stripe with two outer layers of marble and an inner layer of tile infill. The circular centerpieces were usually single pieces of spoliated marble, cut from columns like slices of a sausage. Additional tile rings could make up any difference in the center circular stones and the enclosing stripe. The tile infill was done in a variety of 2-D patterns based on 3, 4, 6, 8 and 12 fold regular and semi-regular patterns.[10]

The geometry of the guilloche pattern,[11] **figure 7a**, begins with square ABCD, center at E. Construct squares FGHJ and KLMN. With AB = 1 the radius of the inner circle EP = .25. The enclosing stripe is PG = EP. For the stripe of one circle to be tangent to the next circle their centers must be at 3/4 of AB. The stripe is divided by the √2/2 or 3-4-3 pattern giving a predominant tile center bounded by two thinner stone edge strips. To lay out a section on a floor or wall the length of the pattern needs to be divided into intervals of 3/4 of AB. Areas between the pattern and the frame available is made up of additional strips of marble or tile.

A typical quincunx, **figure 7b.1**, from the twelfth-century church of Santi Quattro Coronati, Rome,[12] begins with square ABCD. Divide by the √2 system to get squares FGHJ, KLMN, and PQRS. The center stone circle is radius EV. The outer circles are interval LT in diameter, center at U. In this example interval VL is divided into 6, though not exactly equally. If AB = 1, EF = .5 and EP = PF = .25. EB = .707, √2/2. EL = LB = .354, √2/4. Interval PW, the width of the enclosing stripe, is EW .354 - EP .25 = .104, or about 1/10th of AB. The diameter of the outer roundel, LT = ET, .5 - EL .354 = .146, or about 1/7th of AB. However the spoliated center stone was smaller than its allotted circle EP, necessitating the addition of three rings. In this example the inner roundel is EV, radius = .177, √2/8, about 1/6th of AB.

A similar pattern is reconstructed in **7b.2**. Interval LK is the diameter of the outer roundel. With center at M inscribe a circle tangent to AB with radius MN. If AB = 1, AE = .707, EL = .5, EK = .354, LK = .146, its radius MK = .073. From K vertically to the centerline of circle M = .073 x .707 = .0516. From M to AB = .25 - .0516 = .198, which also = MN. The enclosing stripe KN = MN .198 - MK .073 = .125 or 1/8th AB. NE, the center roundel radius, = .354 - .125 = .229, about 1/4 of AB.

In practice the centers of the four outer circles would have been slid along the diagonals of the informing square or rectangle until they accommodated either the designer's wishes or the spoliated material available, probably some combination of both. In **7b.3** the center of the outer circle is slid inboard a bit. EL = .25. EK = .354. LK, the width of the stripe = .104, slimmer than at **7b.2**. KM = LK, making LM, the radius of the outer circle = .208, larger than at **7b.2**. The vertical interval from K to AB is: K to M = .104 x .707 = .073, + ML .208 = .281. As this is 3% greater than .25 the inner circle may be reduced by this degree. Moving in the other direction, **7b.4**, sliding the outer circle outboard enlarges the center and makes the outer circles smaller. Here the radius of the center circle KE is .354, ME is .5, KM = .147 and the stripe = MK/2 = .074 = ML.

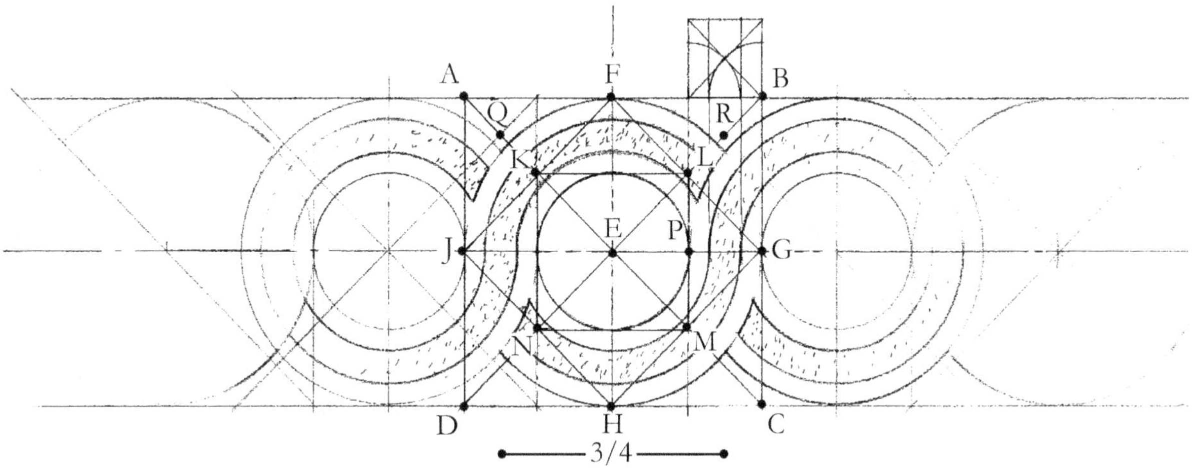

7a - The Guilloich

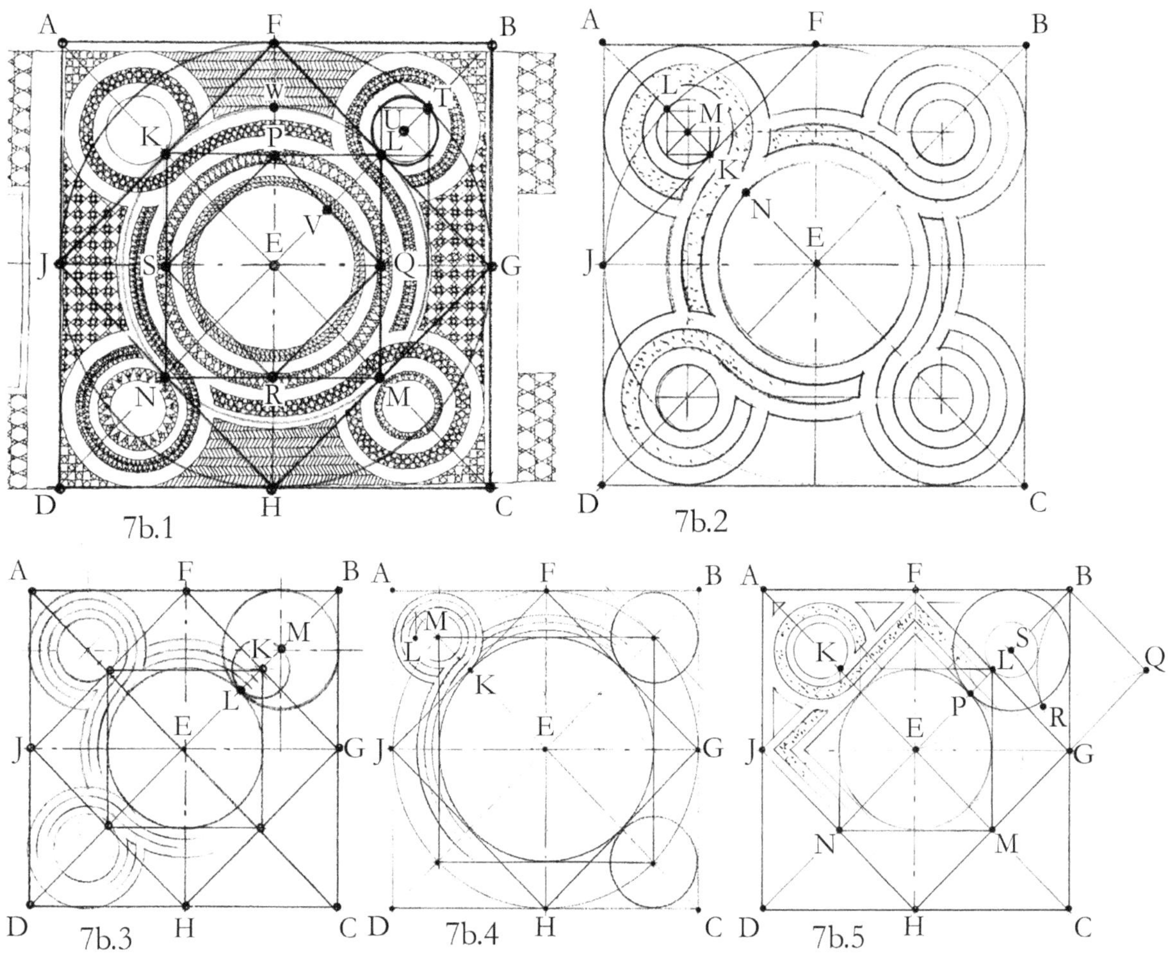

7b - The Quincunx

FIGURES 7a–b
Cosmatesque Ornament

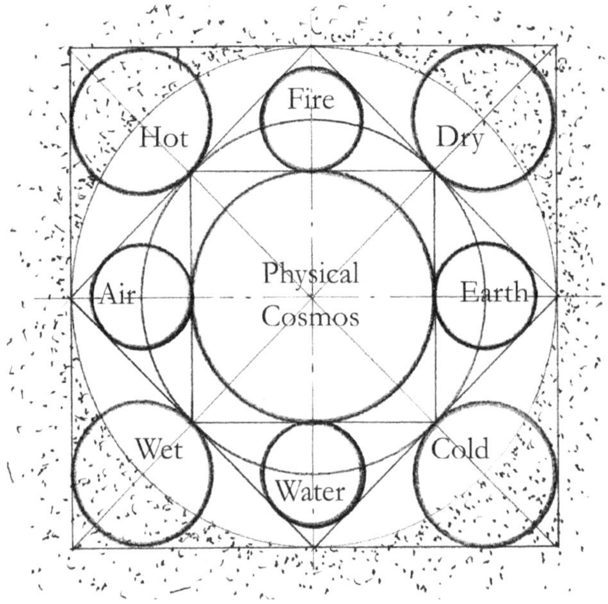

FIGURE 7C
The Quincunx Cosmos

Another modulation of this pattern is the diamond quincunx, **7b.5**, in which the center is not a roundel but a square with tile infill. Interestingly, here 1/4 of the side of the square is EP. The stripe PL is again .104. The center of the outer circle is at point S which is EB = .707 x Ø [.618] = .437 = ES. EL = .25 + .104 = .354. SL the radius of the outer roundel is .437 - .354 = .083. The distance from L to AB = the stripe, .104, + radius SL, .083 = .187, + LS x √2/2 = .059, total = .246 ≈ .25.

These geometrical patterns would only have been starting points or just one of several factors guiding the designers. The Middle Ages did not have our standards of accuracy in layout; looking for geometrical purity will be futile. Though the √2 system is clearly featured in the Cosmati patterns, there is a link between the √2 and Ø[13] and in **figure 7b.5** it reappears again, like Macavity the Mystery Cat, peeking out from the shadows.

Whatever meaning it had for its creators the quincunx is a remembrance of the center and fourfold differentiation completely appropriate for a Christian environment. The first stage of the design is the last stage of our ontogeny, the emergence of materiality. On one level the quincunx is related to the √2 planning of Romanesque buildings[14] but on another level the fourfold pattern lends itself to the cosmological interpretation of the four qualitative states informing matter: hot, wet, cold and dry, **figure 7c.** These qualities combine to form the four physical elements, earth is cold and dry, water is cold and wet, air is hot and wet, fire is hot and dry.

Islamic Architecture – The Dome of the Rock

One of the most sacred sites in the Islamic world is the Haram al-Sharif, the terrace within the ancient Temple precinct of Jerusalem. The major building on this site today is known as the Dome of the Rock, **figure 8.** The building is an enclosure of a rock outcropping identified with the site where tradition says Abraham brought Isaac for sacrifice; where some say Solomon's Temple stood; and the spot where the prophet Muhammad ascended to heaven after his "night journey" from Mecca.[15] The present building dates from c.690 AD, making it one of the oldest extant Muslim

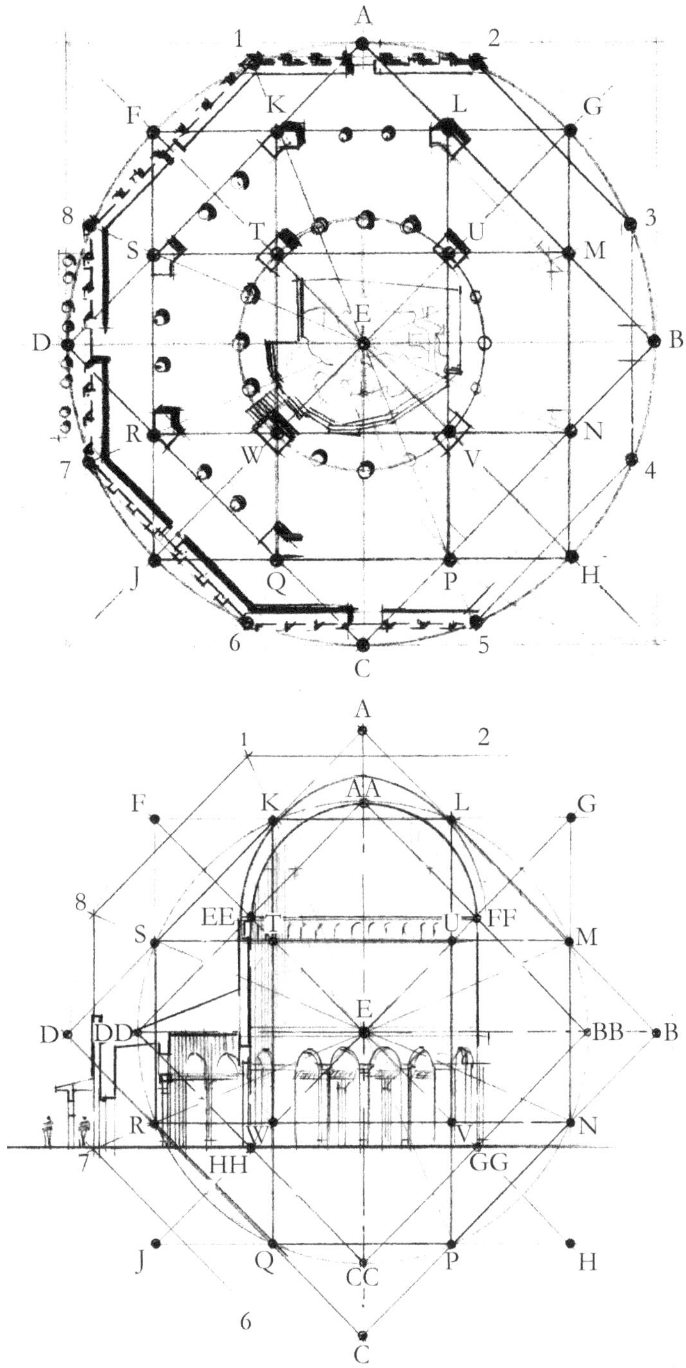

FIGURE 8 – *The Dome of the Rock*

sacred buildings. The "Platonic purity" of its octagonal, √2-derived shape, and its centralized plan, link it to contemporary Byzantine and Romanesque architecture. The transition from Byzantine to Islamic art was assisted by a *"Platonic element ... a certain aspect of contemplative wisdom"* inherent in both traditions.[16]

The exterior tile ornament was added in the fifteenth century. The building has a wooden dome, thus avoiding issues of thrust and the necessity for large buttressing. The four entries are oriented to the cardinal points, making the building a symbolic center. The relation of the exterior octagon and the circular dome is a marriage of the earthly crystal to the celestial sphere. In later Muslim architecture the octagon is used as an intermediary between a cubical base below and a circular dome above.

The inner ring supporting the dome has 4 piers and 12 columns arranged in a circle, creating a still center while inviting circumambulation. The outer ring is octagonal with 8 piers and 16 columns creating a linear transitional zone while maintaining a unified sense. The two supporting rings are related through the octagon and the √2 division of its diagonals. The 8 piers of the octagon, K-S and the 4 piers of the circle, T-W, are positioned on this pattern.

The ratio of the piers is 4:8 = 1:2; the ratio of the columns is 12:16 = 3:4; the ratio of all the supports is 16:24 = 2:3; comprising three of the four primary musical ratios. 16 + 24 = 40, and according to a saying of the Prophet there are 40 saints who at any one time constitute the world's spiritual pillars.[17] Thus the number of supports, regardless of size or material, creates a harmonic sense, reinforced by geometrical placement.

The plan may be reconstructed starting with circle and square ABCD, center at E. This is the last stage of our geometric ontology.[18] Rotate ABCD by 45°, or divide AD in half and project a line from center E to the circumference of circle AD, to find square FGHJ. Where the two squares intersect are points K-S. That these are the √2/2 points is confirmed by drawing an arc with center at F and radius FE, to find points L and R; repeat at G, H, and J. These diagonals intersect to form square TUVW marking the four piers of the inner circle. The outer eight piers are at K, L, etc. The outer enclosing octagonal wall is positioned with its vertexes on circle ABCD. Divide interval FA by projecting line EK to the circumference of circle ABCD to find point 1; repeat to find 2-8. In section, the same geometrical pattern is used. Square FGHJ is divided with square AA, BB, CC, DD, and that into square EE, FF, GG, HH, which gives the key interior heights and the inner diameter of the dome.

The √2 related plan *"is a Byzantine legacy which has a Pythagorean and Platonic antecedent in antiquity.... The result is that the various groups of pillars mark out square or rectangular areas whose proportions are all governed by the* [√2 which] *cannot be expressed in whole numbers, but is profoundly "organic."* The building's plan *"expresses the synthesis of the circle and the square, movement and repose, time and space."* This Pythagorean qualitative geometry *"has a speculative, even contemplative aspect; it is the art of combining the multiple and diverse with unity. If proof were necessary for the continuation of an element of ancient gnosis in Islamic art, it is here that it is to be found."*[19]

Pointed Arches

A major structural and visual aspect of Islamic architecture is the "pointed" arch. Any arched structure produces an outward pushing force called thrust. This force is directed downward at a typical angle of about 60° to the horizontal. In traditional stone structures, which can only work in compression, never in tension, thrust is counteracted by buttressing; the placing of mass on either side of the arch. About the year 1000 AD pointed arches begin to appear in Islamic architecture. This results in the thrust's line of action being directed more vertically, reducing the need for buttressing mass, **figure 9a**.

A circular arch is a single centered arch whose radius, R, equals 1/2 of the span, S, **figure 9b.1**.[20] To point the arch the ratio of R/S is set greater than 1/2. Once the radius is moved off the center point of the spring line the arch has two centers. Their positions are determined by dividing S into some number of parts. At the point where R = S, **9b.2**, the arch is congruent with the vesica piscis. As the radius gets longer the apex of the arch rises. In **9b3-5**, the centers A and B are positioned so that R = 3/5S, 2/3S and 3/4S. The radius may be increased further so that, for example, R = 6/5S, **9b.6**, further reducing the horizontal thrust.

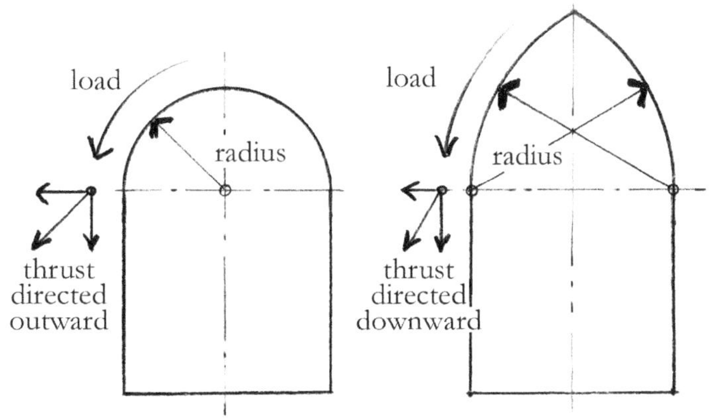

FIGURE 9a – *Pointed Arches. Directing Thrust Downward*

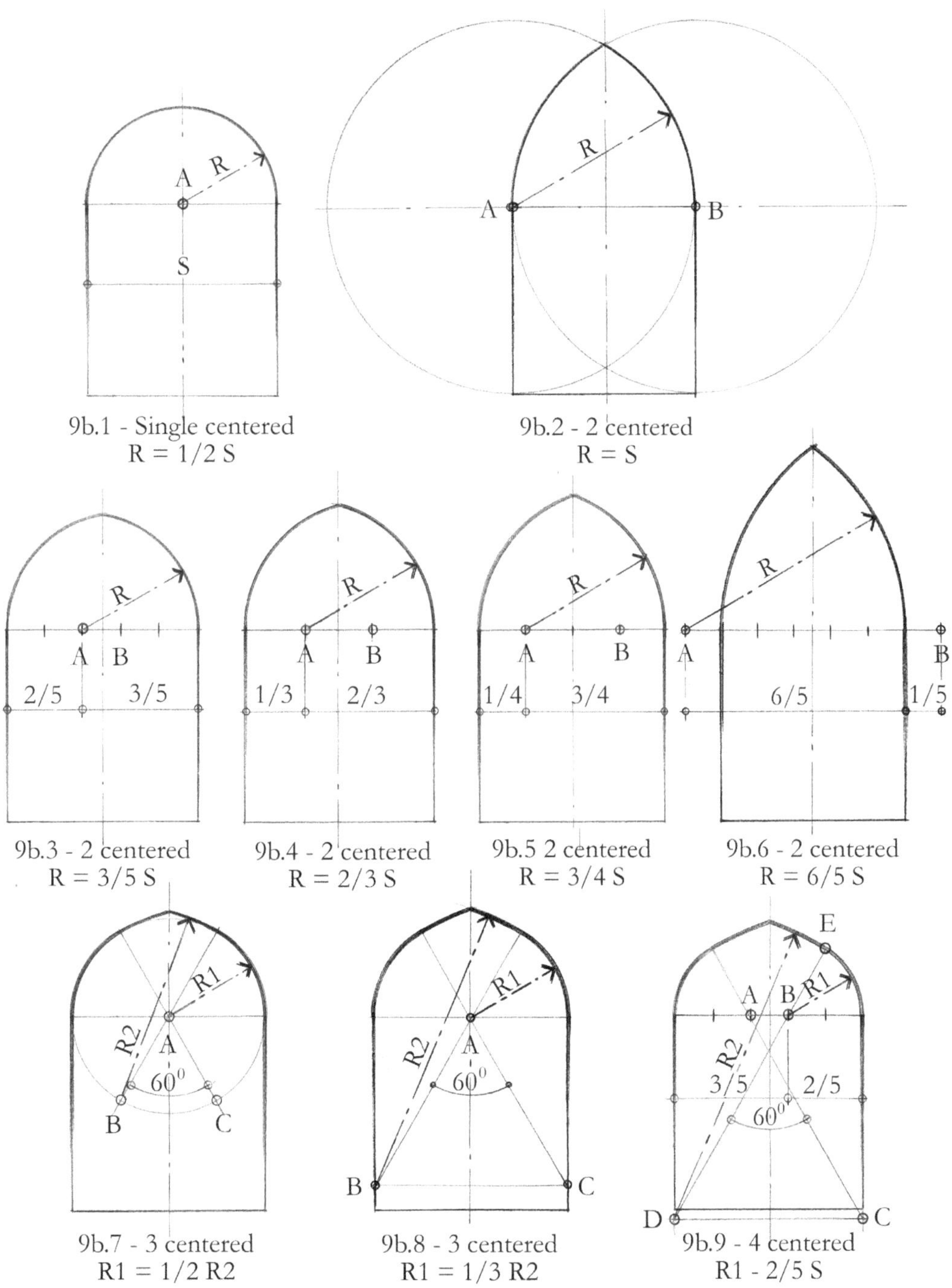

FIGURE 9b.1-9 –*Various Modulations of Pointed Arches*

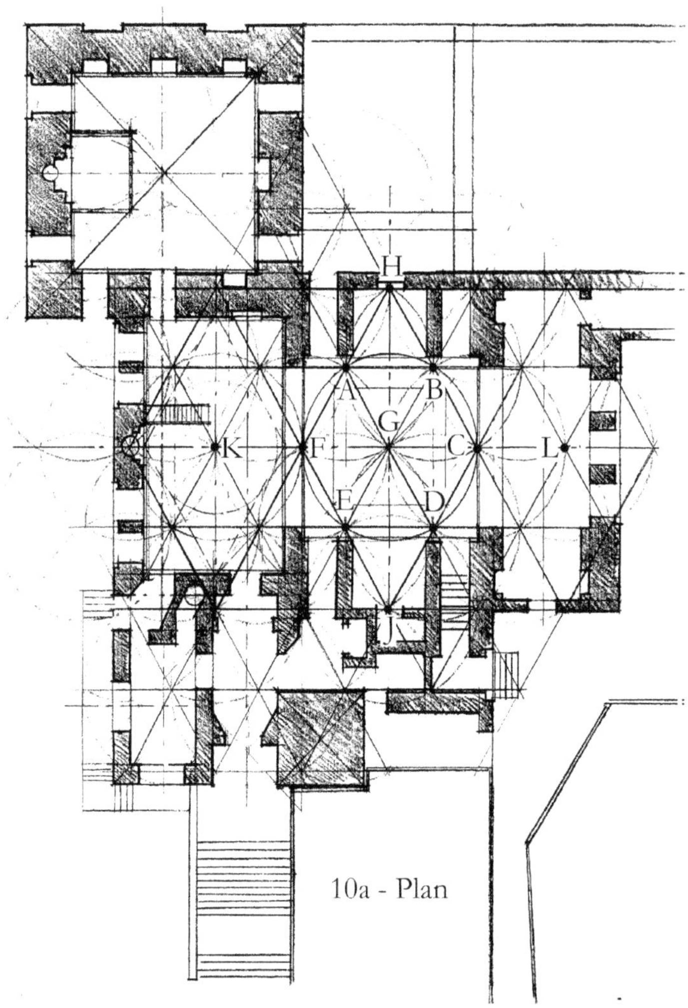

10a - Plan

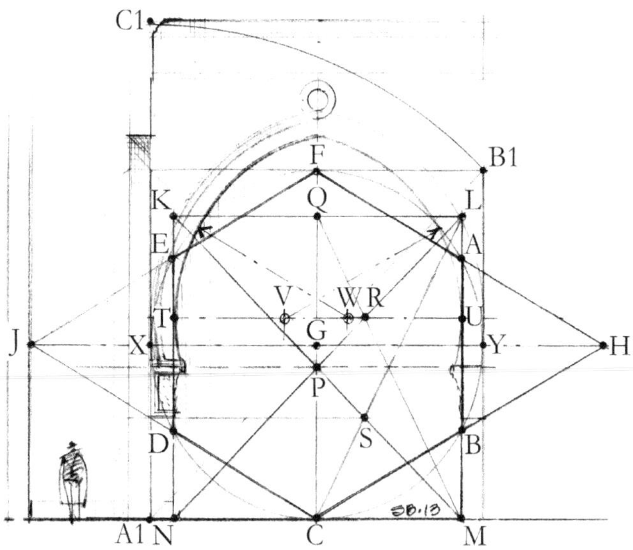

10b - Section along Plan Points H-J

FIGURE 10a–b

Qaitbay Complex, Cairo. Reconstruction

The relatively "pure" geometry of the two centered arches can be tempered by introducing a third or fourth center. In the three centered version there are two radii, R1 and R2. In **9b.7** the vertices of equilateral triangle ABC provide the centers, with B and C on the circumference of a circle whose radius is R1, making R1 = 1/2R2. A slightly lower apex can be obtained by lengthening R2, **9b.8**, so that CB = S and R1 = 1/3R2. An apex angle of 45° rather than 60° can also be used with either of these methods.

If the apex of the controlling triangle is lowered below the spring line four centers, A, B, C, D are created. In **9b.9,** R1 is set at 2/5S, as in **9b.3**. With the apex angle of 60°, DC = S, as in previous figures. If R2 were extended indefinitely then its arch segment would be a straight line tangent to E and perpendicular to DE, creating a "keel" arch. Adding the "horseshoe" arch, where the arcs are carried below the spring line, generates an almost indefinite number of combinations and characters.

Tomb of Qaitbay

A more fully developed example of Islamic architecture is the tomb, mosque and madrasa complex of Mamluk Sultan al-Ashraf Qaitbay, **figure 10a**, Cairo, 1474. The reconstruction uses a triangular-hexagonal network. Circle A-F with center at G marks the square madrasa. The circle is divided into six. Interval AE gives the width of the main arch, and interval AB the width of the alcoves and side arches. ABDE is a √3 rectangle. The triangular network is expanded along axes HJ and KL. The overall width of the interior of the madrasa is HJ. The interior mosque area is also a √3 rectangle centered at K.

The large arch, **figure 10b**, may be constructed starting with circle A-F, center at G. The diameter of this circle gives the overall width of the room, XY. Draw hexagon A-F. Edges AB and DE give the opening of the arch, the same interval as AE in the plan. Set up square KLMN with center at P, side equal to interval AE, and base at C, the floor. Divide LM into thirds using the intersection of the diagonals and semi-diagonals, points R and S. Draw horizontal line TU, the spring point of the arch. The centers of curvature of the arch, V and W, are found by dividing TU into fifths, VW = 1/5 of TU; or divide TU at its Ø points making VW = .236 rather than .20. The radii are TW and VU. The overall width of the room XY and vertical centerline FC are the centerlines of a square circumscribing circle A-F whose diagonal is A1B1. With center at A1 and radius B1 find point C1, the height of the ceiling. Setting height KN as 1, PC, the top of the impost, = .500. The bottom of the impost, at point S = .333. NT, the spring point of the arch = .67; if the radius is WT the crown of the arch is slightly below .667 + .600 = 1.267, very close to 2Ø = 1.236.

Islamic Pattern Ornament

In our geometrical ontogeny[21] the circle, **figure 11a.1**, symbol of monadic unity, with center at A, divided within itself to create two reflections of itself. These circles manifested by movement away from each other yet still within the primary circle along a single axis, BC. Their movement continued until their circumferences were tangent at A with radius AB, **11a.2**.

The indefinite quality of the dyad allows the two circles to rotate freely with respect to each other. To achieve stable form, a third circle is necessary, **11a.3**. This diagram is associated with psyche which also has a triadic structure of "same," "different" and "intermediate" being.[22]

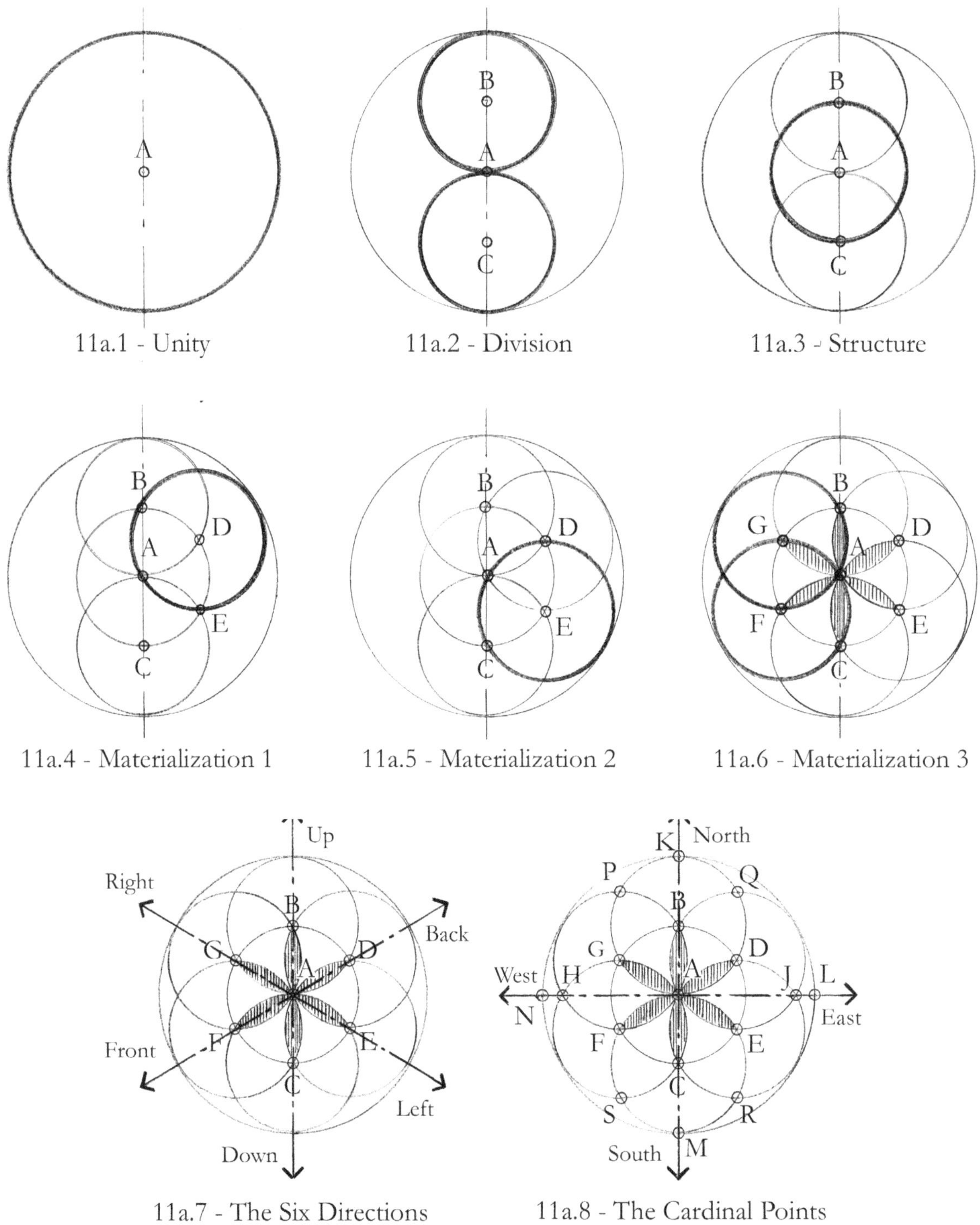

FIGURE 11a

Origin of the 3-, 4- and 6-fold Grids

To achieve material manifestation a fourth stage of differentiation is necessary. In the earlier story the square was used to symbolize this. Here a circle is added, centered at point D, with radius AB, **11a.4**. The process of differentiation is continued by placing circles of the same radius at points E, F and G, **11a.5-6**. This produces the hexagonal flower pattern B, D, E, C, F, G. In this geometrical creation myth the external six "perfectly" surrounds the central monadic one; suggestive of the six days of creation and the seventh day of rest; the journey of the soul through the seven planetary spheres; or the seven intervals of the musical octave.

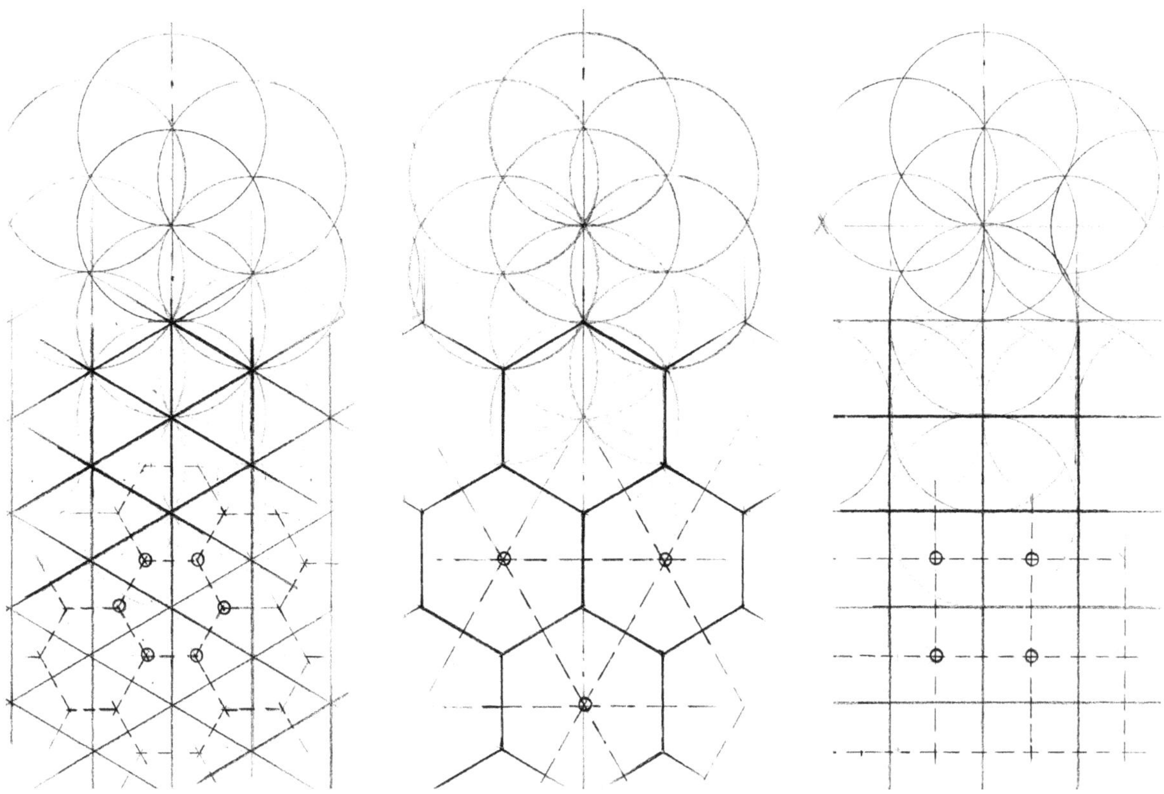

11b.1 - Regular Grid #1
The Triangle

11b.2 - Regular Grid #2
The Hexagon

11b.3 - Regular Grid #3
The Square

Figure 11b

The Regular Grids and Their Duals

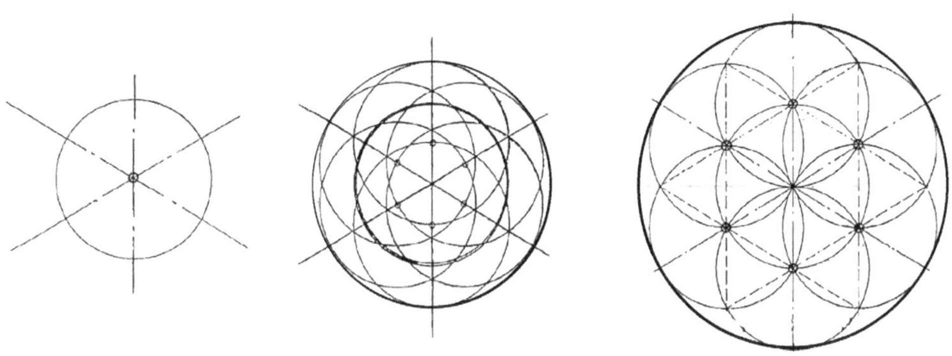

Figure 11c

Simultaneous Development of the Flower

From this pattern emerge three axes, **11a.7**, BC, DF and EG, indicating the six "directions" – up-down, forward-back, and right-left. These six axes position six faces of a cube, symbol of the earth element.[23] The three axes intersect at 60° angles, so that ABD is an equilateral triangle, giving the key shape to regular grid #1. Points B-G form a hexagon giving rise to regular grid #2.

The only other regular polygon that completely fills two-dimensional space is the square. It can also be derived from the arrangement of seven circles, **11a.8**. The grid is produced along axes BC and HJ by adding circles of radius AB, with centers at K, L, M, and N, tangent to circle B-G.

11d.1 - Semi-Regular Grid #1

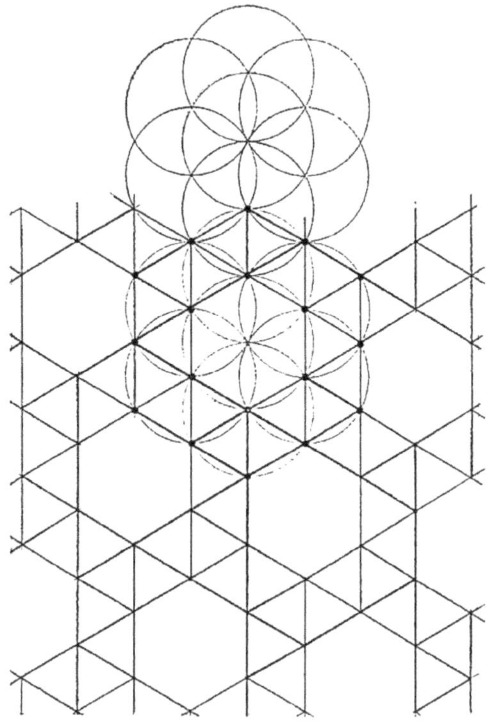

11d.2 - Semi-Regular Grid #2

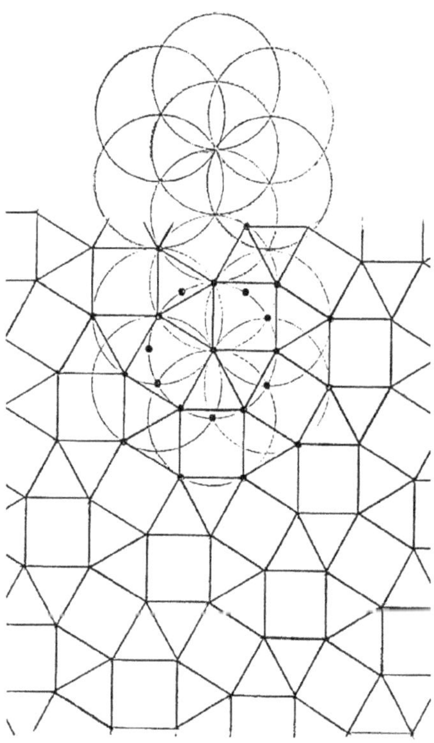

11d.3 - Semi-Regular Grid #3

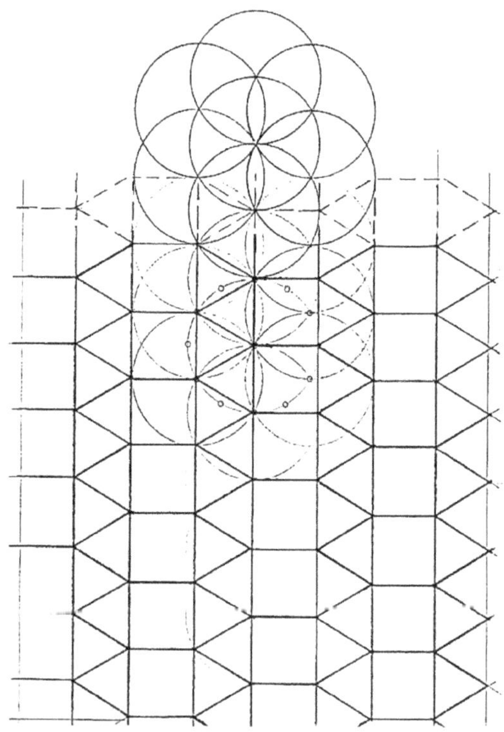

11d.4 - Semi-Regular Grid #4

FIGURE 11d.1–4
The Semi-Regular Grids

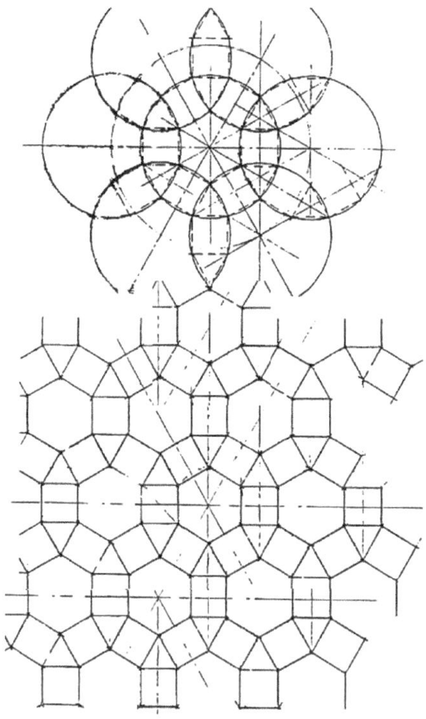

11d.5 - Semi-Regular Grid #5

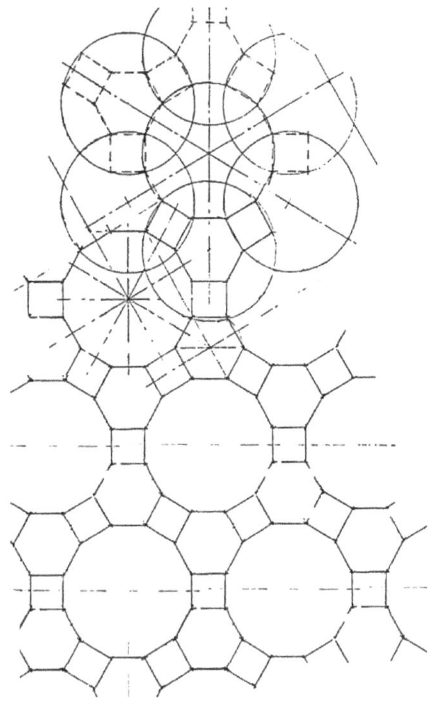

11d.6 - Semi-Regular Grid #6

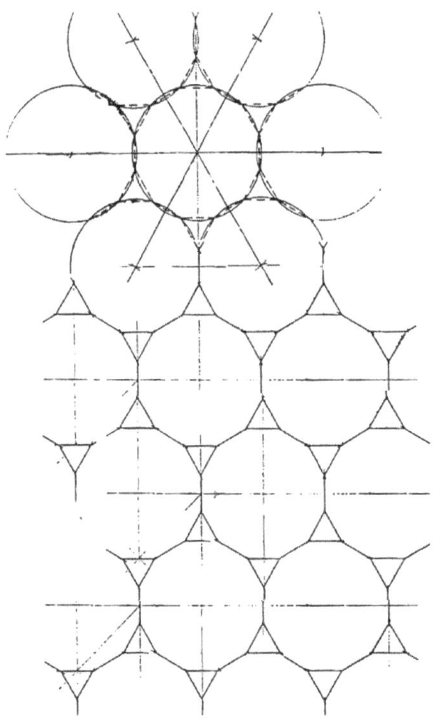

11d.7 - Semi-Regular Grid #7

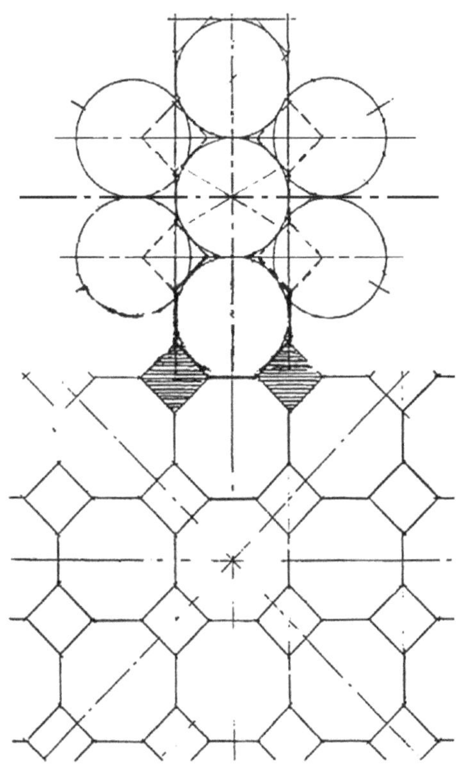

11d.8 - Semi-Regular GRid #8

FIGURE 11d.5–8

The Semi-Regular Grids

The intimacy between the triangular and hexagonal grids is indicated by the property of "dualing," **figure 11b.1-3**. If the centers of the triangles are connected, a hexagonal grid is produced; if the centers of the hexagons are joined, a triangular grid is produced. The square grid duals itself.

Only the triangle, square and hexagon, the 3-, the 4-, and the 6-fold geometries fill 2-dimensional space uniformly and completely. These are known as the regular grids because they use only one figure with equal sides, and all vertices of the grid are identical regardless of the number of figures forming the vertex. No other regular polygons have this property. But there are eight possible combinations of the 3-, 4-, 6-, 8-, and 12-sided polygons that are known as the semi-regular grids. "Semi" because different figures are used in the grid but each vertex is still identical.

To create these grids, return to the original monadic circle, **figure 11a,** and postulate a "simultaneous" differentiation in the six directions, **figure 11c.**[24] Stopping the movement at the vesica piscis position produces the 3, 4 and 6 fold regular grids. Continue the contraction inward, until the centers of the reflected circles fall on the circumference of the primary circle creating six simultaneous vesicas, an instant flower of life. In this instance, it is the generator of semi-regular grids #1 through #4, **figures 11d.1-4.**

Grids #1 and #2 are combinations of triangles and hexagons. #1 has four figures around each vertex, #2 has five figures at each vertex. Grids #3 and #4 are combinations of squares and triangles with five figures around each vertex.

Grid #5, **11d.5-8,** is composed of the three polygons that form the regular grids, the triangle, square, and hexagon. It is generated by continuing the sixfold expansion of the circles until one-quarter of their circumferences are in contact, dividing the primary circle into a peripheral division of twelve and an inner division of six. Grid #6, composed of the square, hexagon and dodecagon, is generated on the same circular expansion but the "interior" hexagon is not used, allowing the dodecagon, which is present in grid #5, to be expressed.

Grid #7, comprised of the triangle and the dodecagon, is generated by continuing the expansion of the six outer circles until only one-twelfth of their circumferences are in contact with the primary circle. The last of the semi-regulars, #8, comprised of the octagon and square, is generated from the fully expanded group of seven circles, as was the square grid. In the illustration the six outer circles are rotated one-twelfth, or 30° from their positions in figure 11b.3, to form the octagon. The interstitial spaces are squares.

The three regular grids are each made up of one type of polygon and one type of vertex. In the semi-regular grids, two or three types of polygons occur but there is still only one type of vertex. Grids in which there are more than one type of vertex are known as demi-regular. There are fourteen of these.[25] The beginning of pattern design with the grids involves further subdivision. A basic pattern, known as the "Inhalation and Exhalation," **figure 12a,** begins on the regular square grid, as in **figure 11a.7**. Within the primary circle two squares are placed in octagonal relationship. If the outline of the "star" octagon is emphasized the pattern is created.

A second level pattern, **figure 12b,** begins with the star octagon. Inscribe a circle within the octagon. From each vertex of the octagon project a line to the center. Where each line crosses the circumference of the circle mark points 1-8. Draw parallel diagonals 1-6 and 2-5; repeat three more times, from each pair of points to its opposite, to create a "barred star." To complete the pattern connect points A-C, and B-D. These give the outline of the intermediate octagons and asymmetric five-pointed stars. Originating in 3- and 6-fold geometries, unfolding in 4-fold geometry and reaching its fulfillment in the emergent 5-fold geometry indicates the intimate yet occult relationship of these informing powers.

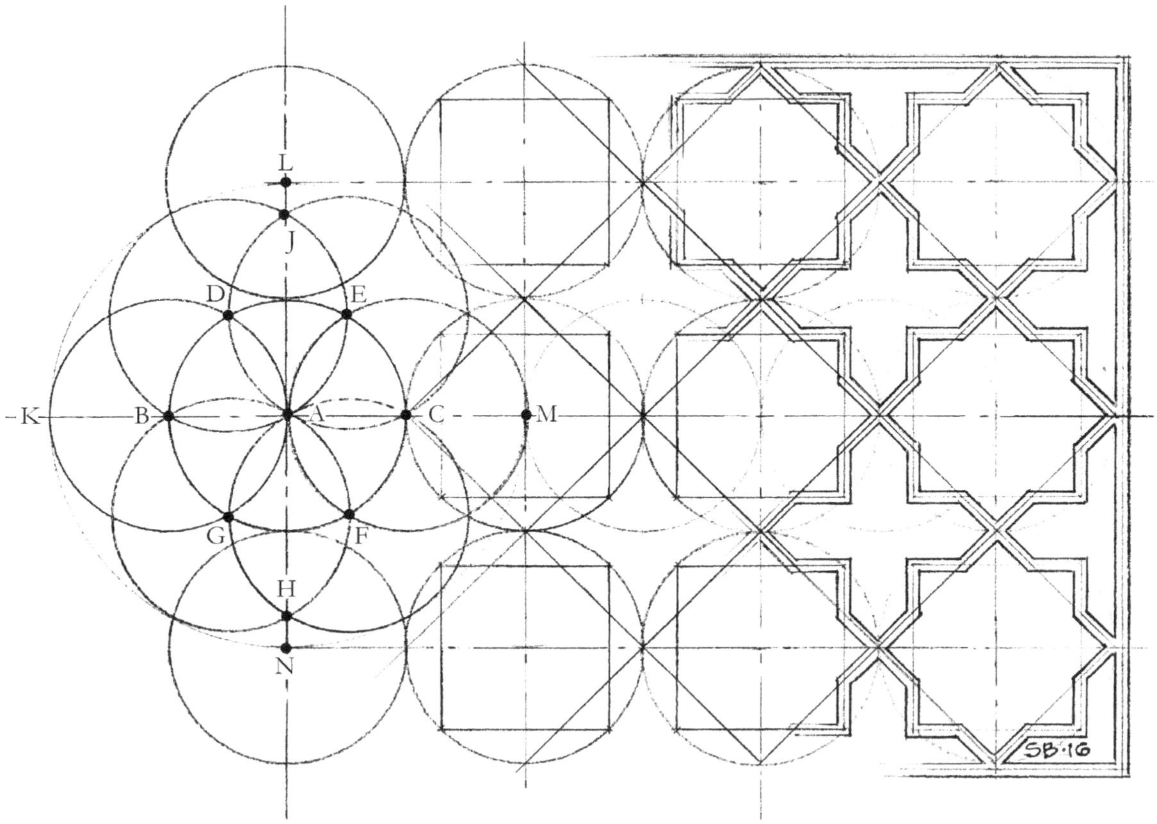

FIGURE 12a

The Inhalation and Exhalation

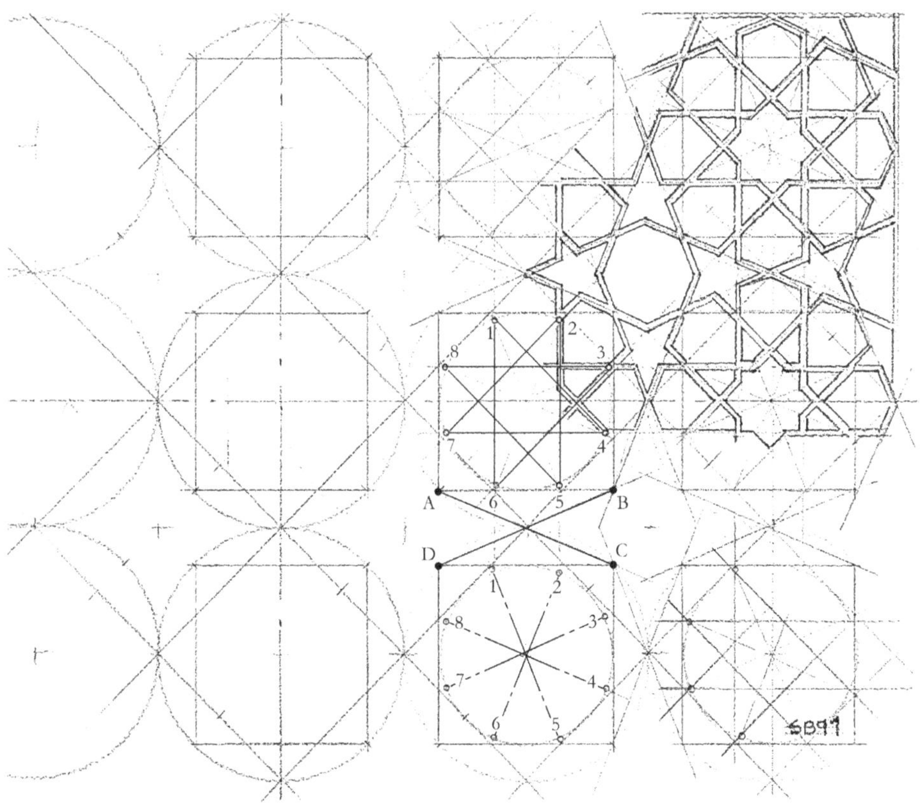

FIGURE 12b

Star Octagon Pattern

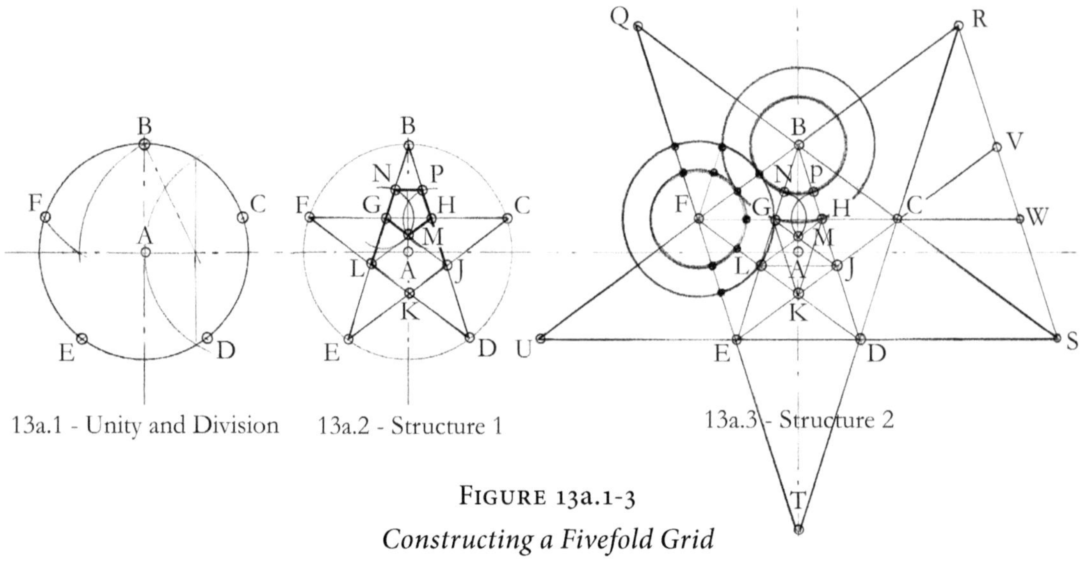

FIGURE 13a.1-3
Constructing a Fivefold Grid

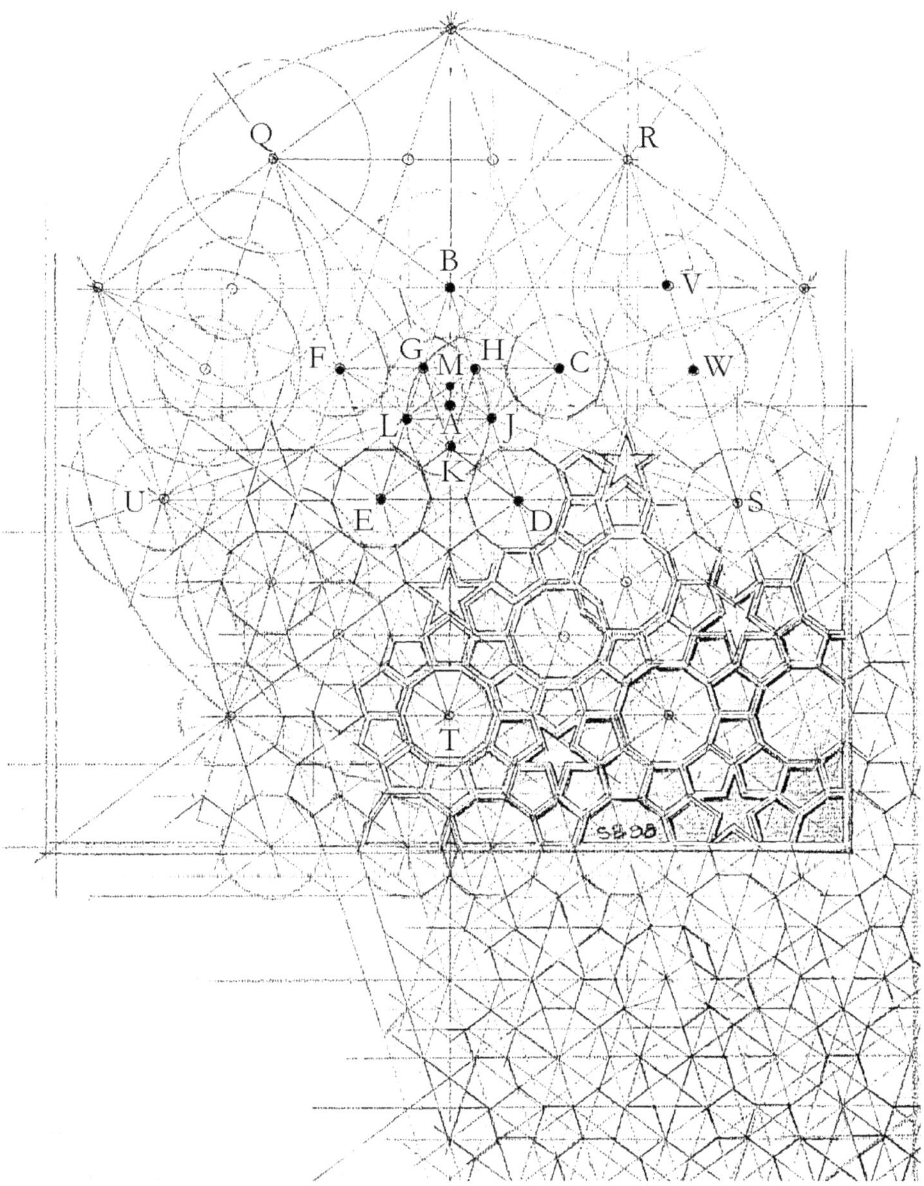

FIGURE 13b
A Fivefold Pattern

The pentagon cannot create a regular or semi-regular grid but may be used for pattern design. With center A draw circle AB, **figure 13a.1**, and find pentagonal points B-F.[26] Draw diagonals to give inner pentagon G-L, **13a.2**. Draw the diagonals of this pentagon to find point M. With center at G and radius GM find point N. Repeat to find point P. NPHMG is a pentagon. Draw circles with center at B, radius BN and BG, **13a.3**. Intervals NP and GH will divide the circumference of the two circles centered on B into ten parts. Repeat this at points C, D, E and F. Extend the sides of pentagon B-F to find points Q-U. Extend FC to find W and EC to find V. At each of these points draw the concentric circles with radii BN and BG. The pattern is then extended along its fivefold axes, **figure 13b**.

What has been described above is barely the threshold of the doorway to the vestibule of the subject. So many variants are possible that their numbers are effectively indefinite. Yet each pattern is a story in itself and can become a focus of meditation and teaching.

Chartres and the Gothic

A dramatic change in monumental Christian architecture began about the year 1200 in the Île-de-France region, focused on the town of Chartres. By that time several "streams" of traditional wisdom had mingled there. The site was a Druidic ritual center by about 1000 BC. It was dedicated to what might be called the feminine principle, the great mother, goddess of the agricultural cycle, of the dark earth, of nature. The Druids instituted the icon of the Black Madonna. On the surface the site was a sun altar but a grotto was discovered below the site and a well dug within it. Its water was considered to have healing properties. The icon was housed in the grotto.

The icon was a life-sized wood statue of a seated female figure holding an infant in her lap. While some say that the statue was blackened by fire or smoke, black is the color of the earth element; the earthly womb being a dark chamber from which new life emerges into light, whether that life be physical or spiritual. The icon was the center of an annual set of ritual cyclic movements. During the winter months she was kept in the grotto, later incorporated into the crypt of several successive churches, the focus of torchlight veneration. In the spring, as the power of the sun increased, she was brought out in hopeful celebration of new birth. During summer she remained above ground and devotions were made in the daylight. At the completion of the harvest in the fall, as the power of the sun waned, she was returned to the grotto.[27]

This is reminiscent of the myth of Demeter and Persephone celebrated in the Eleusinian Mysteries. It also sounds similar to the Egyptian ritual involving the exposing of the statue of Amon-Ra[28] and circulatory rituals with other such divinities. The icon of the mother and child is similar to ancient representations of Isis and Horus. In the first century BC the Greco-Roman Mystery stream arrived at Chartres with the Roman takeover. The Eleusinian Mysteries were quite consistent with the neolithic agricultural mythos. The site probably housed a Roman shrine incorporating the grotto and well.

About a hundred years later Joseph of Arimathea, uncle of Jesus and brother of Mary, left Palestine with her and other members of their family. Mary is said to have remained at Ephesus while John and others went on eventually arriving at Glastonbury, England, bringing with them the Grail, the cup with which John gathered the blood of Jesus at the crucifixion. John, moved by the ritual of the Black Madonna, dedicated the site to Mary. Chartres became associated with both esoteric Christianity and a Christianized feminine principle.

The stage was set for the school of Chartres in the ninth century by John Scotus Eriugena.[29] Eriugena was a Platonist scholar in the service of Charles the Bald. His cosmology included the Platonic doctrine of reincarnation, a concept declared heretical in 870 by the Council of Constantinople, but this did not seem to disrupt his career. At Eriugena's suggestion, in 876, Charles offered the "veil of Mary," said to have been worn by the Virgin Mary at the birth of Jesus, as the relic of foundation for a church at Chartres.[30]

The cathedral school as a Neoplatonic entity begins with Gerbert, 950–1003. Born in France, Gerbert studied in Spain, one of the leading centers of civilization of the day. Through Islamic culture Spain had direct access to Platonism and the liberal arts. Jewish, Christian and Muslim scholars studied together in the universities of Islamic Toledo and Cordova. They very likely also met outside of school and identified the mutual Platonic roots of the three traditions. After completing his studies in this milieu Gerbert returns to teach in Reims. After a time he is brought to Rome and introduced into high circles, eventually achieving the Papacy as Sylvester II in 999.

Gerbert's protégé is Fulbert, 960–1028, who accompanies him from Reims to Rome. In 990 Fulbert is appointed Chancellor of the school at Chartres. In 1006 he is elected Bishop of Chartres. It is Fulbert who transforms Chartres into a Neoplatonic school; and it is Fulbert's vision that is embodied in the cathedral today although he did not live to see it.

The teachings of the school sought to meld the Celtic and Greco-Roman streams with Christianity. But this was a Christianity *"based not on belief, but on the possibility of man's direct experience of Christ, ... attained through a meditative life translated into images."*[31] Explicit here is that the Mystery tradition is an aspect of religion of experience rather than religion of belief.

The schools most famous masters were Fulbert, Bernardus Silvestris, John of Salisbury and Alanus ab Insulis. The death of Alanus in 1203 marked the decline of the school. In the next generation the Cistercians, with their emphasis on self-sufficiency, manual labor, and direct experience lose influence while the urban, intellectual Dominicans become prominent. The new leading personalities, Albertus Magnus and his student Thomas Aquinas take an Aristotelian approach. The venue shifts from Chartres to Paris. Logic had overtaken Mystery.[32]

The course of study at Chartres was the liberal arts as formulated by Martianus Capella, c.415 AD.[33] In this vision the liberal arts were personified as seven female spiritual beings. Above the right door of the west portal, the main entrance to Chartres, were carved representations of the seven arts. Below each is a figure of that art's representative historical teacher. At the center of the tympanum is the mother and child, symbolizing perhaps the new birth from within, surrounded by the sevenfold pattern of guardian–teachers, or intellectual midwives. The Christian and pre-Christian Mysteries of Mary were linked to the Platonic educational structure.

The liberal arts at Chartres were not just a form of intellectual study but were a path to inner clarification. The study of an art was an approach to a spiritual being, a kind of bodhisattva. This was seen as a process of rebirth from within; of a coming forth from the darkness into light. The study would give birth, virgin-like, to a new, more refined soul; indeed even to the consciousness of the true self. In a parallel metaphor the sevenfold aspect of the liberal arts was related to the seven planetary spheres. The students work their way up, like ascending a ladder.[34]

Another formative source of the Gothic was Abbot Suger, 1081–1155, of St. Denis, traditionally the church patronized by French kings. Suger advocated what he called "the upward leading method," which he related to the writings of Dionysius the Areopagite [aka the Pseudo-Dionysius].

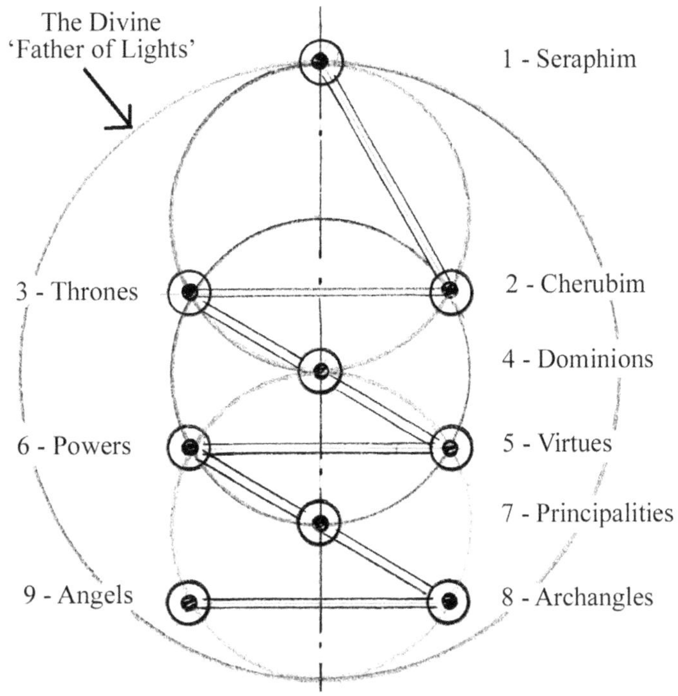

FIGURE 14
The Celestial Hierarchies

Denis is the French translation of Dionysius and the two were merged in French national myth. In his books Dionysius presents a Christianized Neoplatonic cosmology influenced by Plotinus and Proclus. His *Celestial Hierarchy* unfolds in nine emanative centers or stages,[35] perhaps in a similar image to our "circle diagrams,"[36] the same geometry that informs the Kabbalistic Tree, **figure 14**. The medium of spiritual transmission was light.[37]

Suger undertook to reconstruct St. Denis about 1130. Though he did not take a direct part in the design, his concept of self-elevation through movement into light and its relation to architecture is expressed in his dedication of one of the doors at St. Denis:

> The noble work is bright, but, being so
> Should brighten the mind, allowing travel
> Through the lights to the true light …
> The dull mind rises to the truth through material things,
> And is resurrected from its former submersion
> When the light is seen.

Suger's work at St. Denis, though experimental and transitional, was approximately contemporary with the work at Chartres. It would seem that shortly after the work began a new architectural spirit appeared in the Île-de-France. That area and neighboring Champagne comprise a core region of the French nation and are the genesis area for the earliest cathedrals in the pointed-arch style, the first and only indigenous Christian architecture.

In the shadows, behind the formation of Gothic architecture were the Knight Templars, a military-religious initiatic order consisting of soldier-priests, created in 1118 in Jerusalem.

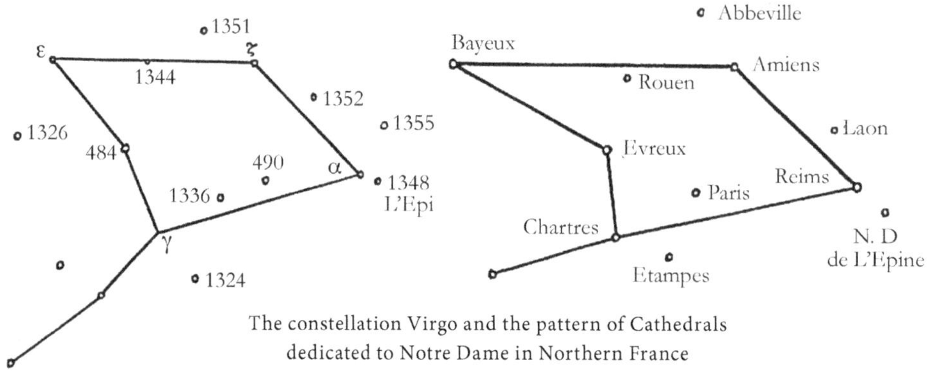

The constellation Virgo and the pattern of Cathedrals dedicated to Notre Dame in Northern France

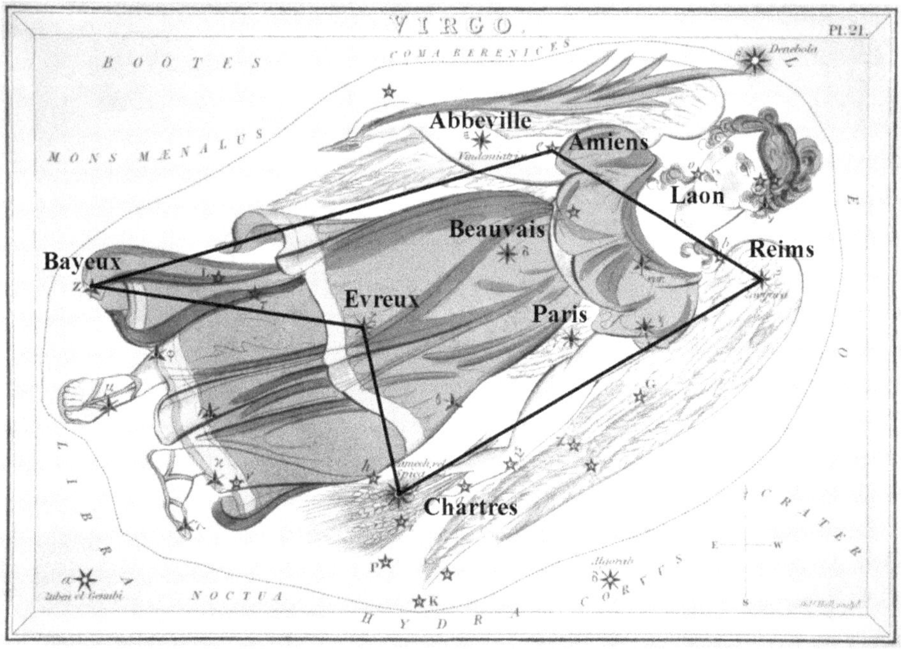

FIGURE 15

Virgo and France

The founders[38] all seem to have direct contact with Bernard of Clairvaux, characterized as "a supremely eloquent, strong-willed mystic,"[39] head of the recently founded Cistercian Order. The key to the Cistercians was the reintroduction of manual labor combined with ritual and a kind of intellectual meditation,[40] leading to ascension through direct experience. Whoever the founding Templars were, they seem to have gone right to the center of power. The Order quickly became immensely wealthy, with vast properties throughout Western Europe, a state unto itself.

The Order was called "Templar" because their headquarters occupied a building on the Temple Mount in Jerusalem, known today as the Al-Aqsa Mosque. The official business of the Order was the "protection" of the city and the Christian pilgrims. Charpentier speculates that their business, on an "occult" or hidden level, was to recover the Ark of the Covenant, said to have survived the destruction of the Temple through burial. He further speculates that the Ark, which was said to contain "the tables of the law," was mathematical in nature; the tables being "means," corresponding to the Greek concept of "logos."[41]

The founding members of the Order remained in Jerusalem for eight years and reportedly excavated the vaults below the temple platform. What the Templars actually found is not known but a "school of knowledge" rather than physical artifacts may have been involved. It might have

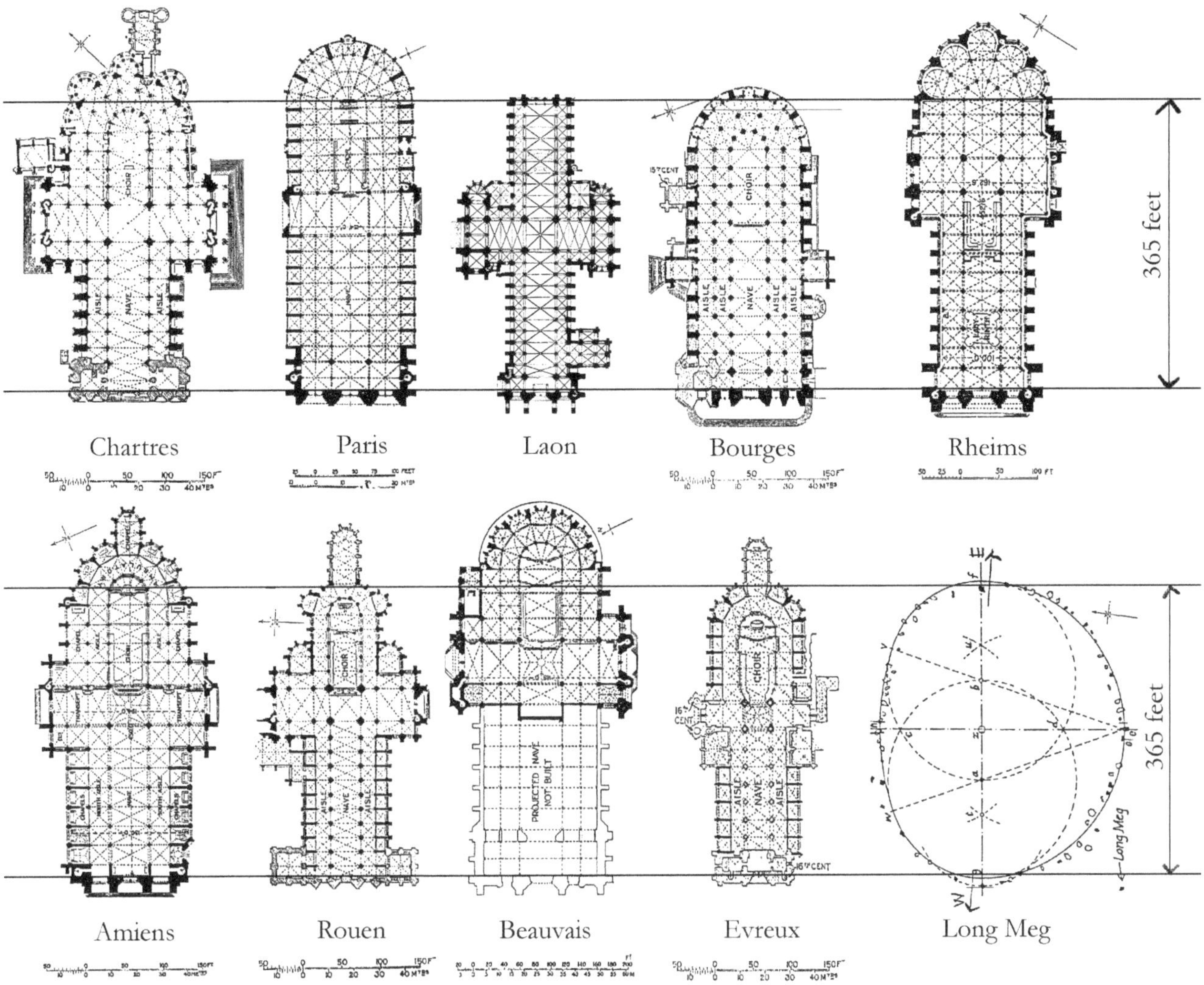

FIGURE 16

The "Virgo Cluster" and 365 feet

had an architectural aspect, as pointed arches had recently been introduced in Islam. The convergence in time and space of the secret revelation of the Templars and the Platonic School of Chartres, like spirit activating intellect, generated Gothic architecture

The Templars, along with the schools in Spain, may be considered lines of transmission of philosophical, mathematical and other material that had been lost in Europe; and new material developed in the Middle East and India in the centuries after the fall of the West. A sculpture on the north portal of Chartres depicts the Templars transporting the Ark to Chartres.

The scale and even audacity of the Gothic project is suggested in the remarkable illustration of Querido, **figure 15**. It indicates that the earliest group of cathedrals dedicated to the Virgin Mary, in the region of the Île-de-France, are set out in a geographic pattern that duplicates the pattern of stars in the constellation Virgo.

All these buildings were designed and, except for a few fragments, built during the heyday of the Templars. There was very likely a core of skilled master stone masons who worked on some or all of them. The set of buildings are all constructed with ad triangulum and all of them respond in a significant way to the dimension of 365 feet, **figure 16**. Included is the neolithic stone circle called Long Meg, in England, also 365 feet in width and constructed on the vesica piscis.

The cathedrals of the "Virgo Cluster" embody a kind of inspired energy that is lacking in the more than two hundred years the style lasted prior to the Renaissance. The pointed-arch style continued until the fifteenth or sixteenth centuries in France, England and Germany, but its initial energetic formative period was long over.

Chartres is sited on a granitic promontory that rises through a limestone plane. This geological condition attracted the Druids' attention. The two stones have a dyadic relationship. Limestone, or chalk, heavy with absorbed water, has a downward contractive tendency, dark and earthy, while granite, containing silicone, has an upward expansive tendency, seeking light. These contractive and expansive forces if considered "etheric" form a gateway allowing noetic forces to descend and earthly forces to ascend.[42]

The orientation of the cathedral is to the north-east as opposed to the traditional eastward orientation of Christian churches. Its direction points to the summer solstice sunrise, June 22. On this day the rising sun casts its rays onto the altar parallel to the axis of the building. Conversely, the setting sun on the winter solstice, December 22, would cast its ray parallel to the axis from the direction of the entry. Thus John the Baptist, whose day is June 24, diminishes but through his efforts the solar spirit enters Jesus whose day is December 25. It is this process of rebirth to a higher level, perhaps through the integration of such opposites, which the school sought to achieve on an inner level. The church's Marian imagery is related to birth from the winter darkness and by its orientation to cosmic elevation through sacrifice initiated by summer's growth. The space and light of the building itself reenacted this mystery annually and it was toward this mystery, reenacted within each individual, that the teaching of the school sought to lead.

Chartres Reconstruction

The reconstruction uses as a key the √3 rectangle of the crossing suggested by analyst John James,[43] beginning, **figure 17a.1,** on the ontological level of unity with a circle whose center is A, radius AB. Line BC is the primary ray, representing the initial act of division. It establishes the primary axis of the cathedral. The second ontological level, **17a.2,** sets the pattern of spatial division for the building. From point B draw a circle with radius AB to find points D and G. Repeat with center at C to find E and F, creating the sixfold pattern.

The third ontological level determines the placement of elements of physical structure, here divided into several steps. In **17a.3,** the centerline of the transept HJ runs at right angles to BC, the centerline of the nave and choir, establishing point A as the crossing. Points K and L lie on the circumference of circle BAC. With center at K and radius KL draw arc NLM. Repeat with center at L to draw MKN to create vesica piscis MKNL. Intervals KL and MN respectively mark the overall width and length of the cathedral's interior plan.

To define the triangular module, **17a.4**, construct hexagon PQKRSL within circle BAC. The side of the triangular module we seek will be one-fourth of radius AL. The module is found by drawing √3 rectangle PQRS, **17a.5**. Point U marks the half-point of radius AL. Repeating this procedure, **17a.6**, gives the module, equilateral triangle AF'A'. In the fully materialized building the central bay supporting the crossing is G'H'J'K'. It is a 2:√3 rectangle, or two √3 rectangles, or a 1:√3/2 rectangle, a ratio of 1:.867. A typical nave and choir bay K'J'XY is 2:√3/2, or half a √3 rectangle, a ratio of 1:.433. A typical transept bay M'G'K'L' is √3:1 or 1:.577. Side aisle bays such as N'VG'M' are 1:√3/2, similar to the crossing bay.

In the reconstruction, **figure 17b**, the north and south porches, and the plans of the towers are guided by one additional modular layer outside of points MKNL. The elevation is guided by the same grid. The key to the elevation is the placement of the rose window, which is superimposed on the labyrinth. Assuming a modular unit, A-F', is 28 feet, its altitude is 28 x √3/2 = 24-3". The distance from the front door to the turning point of the apse is 15 modules or about 365 feet. The north or solar tower is said to also be 365 feet high. Shown in the reconstruction is the south or Lunar tower, about 19 feet shorter, perhaps an allusion to the 19-year solar-lunar eclipse cycle.

The vesica piscis may be seen as representing the female birth organ, the yoni. In that context, circle BAC may be seen as the womb itself. Points P, Q, K, R, S, and L, while forming a hexagon may also be seen as six vertices of a cube, and point A as a seventh, **17a.4**. The cube symbolizes the earth element or the coming into manifestation. As the six faces of the cube may be "unfolded" to form the Latin cross this cube may symbolize the "Christic" possibility of return to unity through multiplicity. And this cubical form, in its 2-dimensional outline, becomes the module of the manifest church. Thus the icon of Christ in the vesica piscis is placed at the center of the cathedral's west portal.

The triangular and hexagonal geometry also has a purely symbolic reading. Our essential division, **17a.2,** recapitulated the six days of creation in drawing the circles centered on B, D, E, C, F, and G. The seventh passive center is at point A, the origin and center of the cathedral. While this point, a kind of "unmoved mover," can be identified with the Divinity, its manifestation in the Heptad, Sevenness, is identified with materialization of the divine (a kind of parthenogenous birth) through the feminine principle in figures such as Isis, Athena and Mary. In mythic astronomy the Pleiades are seven virgin sisters who form the core of Diana's girl gang. In medieval times the seven liberal arts are depicted as "maidens" presumably virgins.

Seven is "virginal" in the sense that it "neither multiplies nor is multiplied within the decade." Seven as a prime cannot be reached by multiplication of any whole numbers, and no number multiplied by seven is less than ten. By not engaging in "multiplication" the Heptad remains a "virgin." It may represent the spiritual birth from within, or "nature" as a whole that gives birth without an apparent external source. Sevenness is honored in the cathedral by the seven structural bays of the apse. Three methods of constructing the seven-sided regular polygon are shown in **figure 18**. The technique of the 13-interval knotted cord would have been available to the Druids.

Architectural Features of Chartres

Charpentier offers **figure 19**, applying musical intervals to the section through the nave of Chartres.[44] Charpentier uses the intervals of a tempered minor octave, but since this was not developed until the late fifteenth century, some 400 years after Chartres' construction, its use is unlikely.[45] He establishes a main aisle width of 40 units (the half-cubit, .369 meters = 1'-2.5" x 40 = 48.4'). Using this as a fundamental, and following Charpentier's octave intervals, the 3rd is 40 x 6/5 = 48, the spring point of the lower arches; 5th note interval = 40 x 3/2 = 60, marking the height of the gallery; the 7th note, 40 x 14/8 = 70, the height to the upper window sill; the octave interval is 40 x 2 = 80, giving the spring point of the vaults of the main aisle; and an octave and a 4th = 80 x 27/20 = 108, giving the crown of the main vault.[46] Charpentier's diagram is reminiscent of the Egyptian "royal apron."[47]

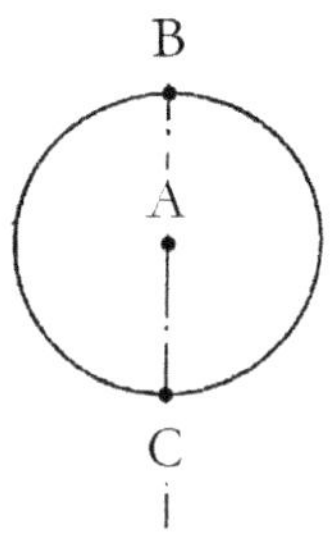

17a.1 - Unity
and the Ray

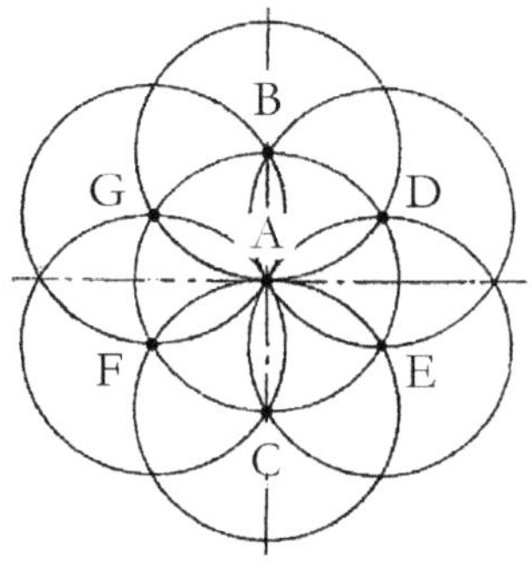

17a.2 - Division
The Six-Fold Pattern

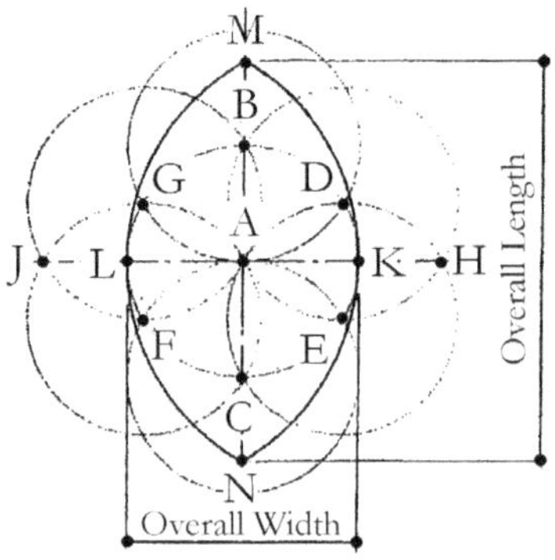

17a.3 - Structure 1
Vesica Piscis

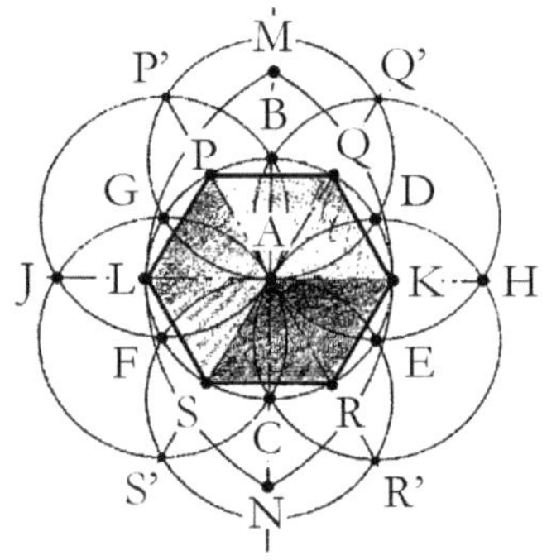

17a.4 - Structure 2
Hexagon and Cube

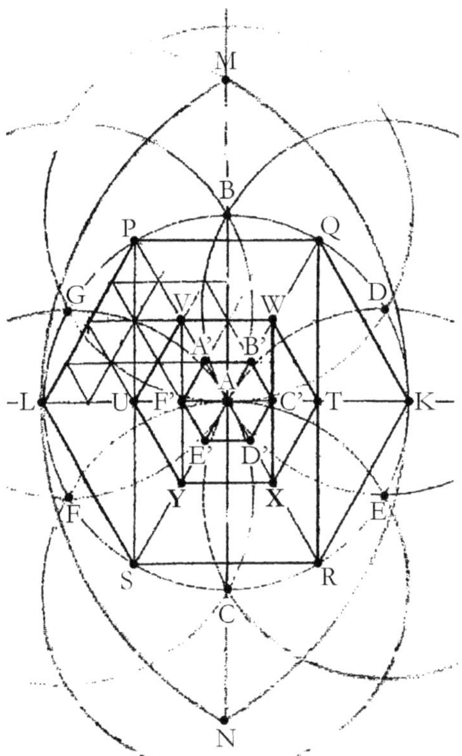

17a.5 - Structure 3
the Module

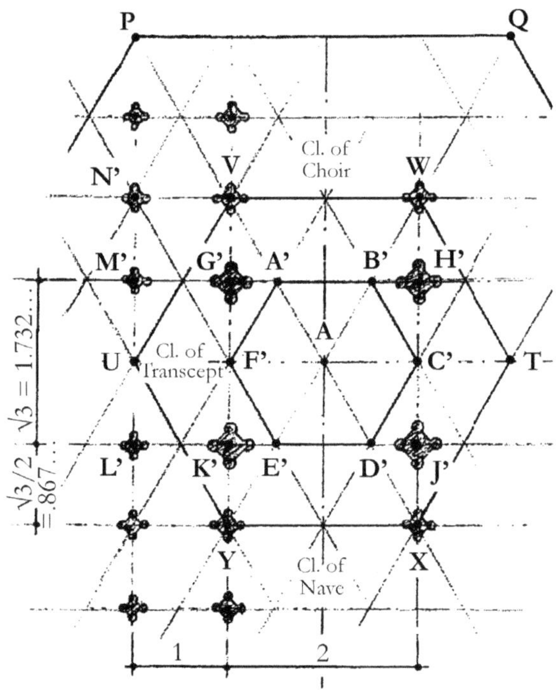

17a.6 - Materialization
Pillars of the Cathedral

FIGURE 17a
Chartres Reconstruction

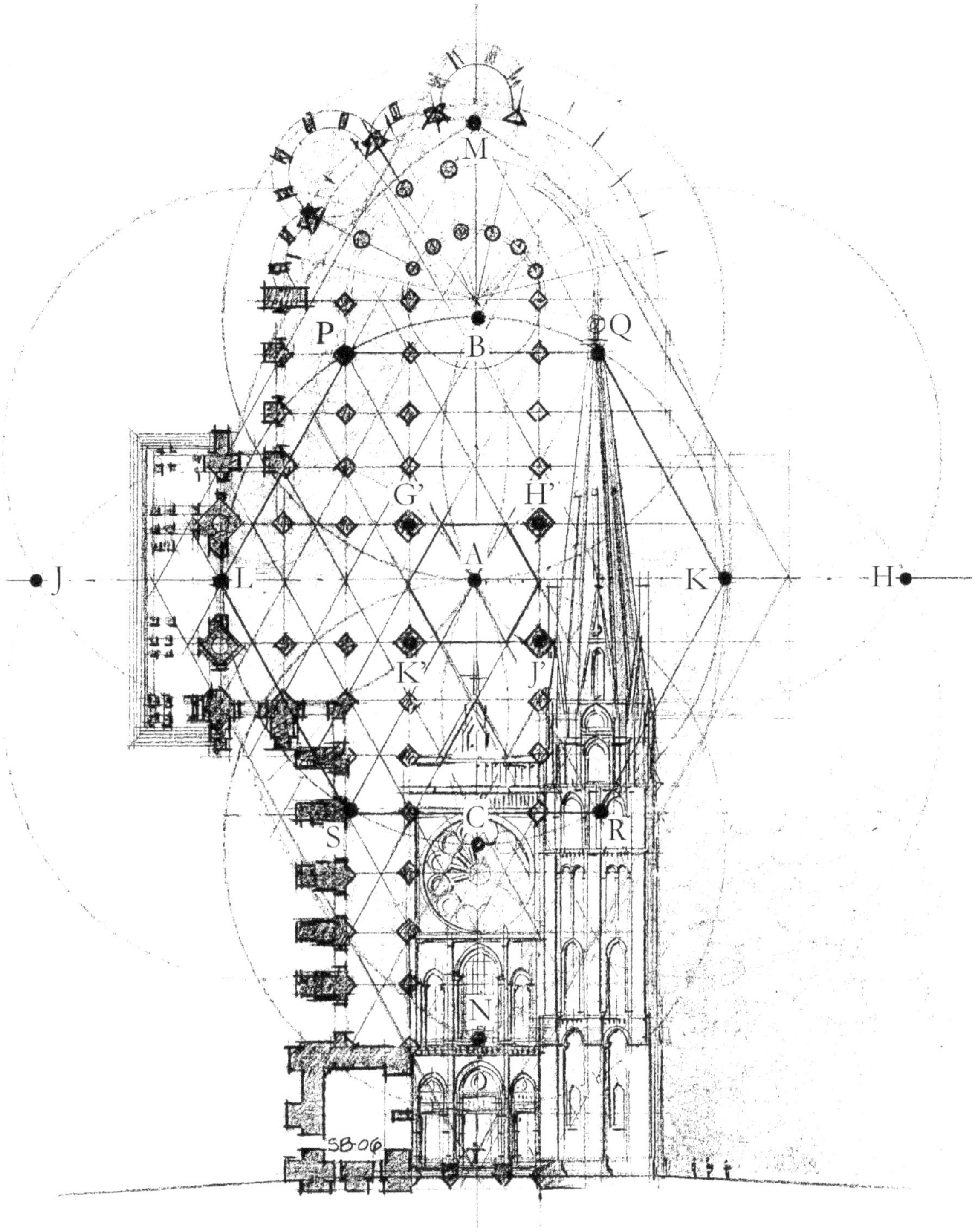

FIGURE 17b

Chartres Reconstruction

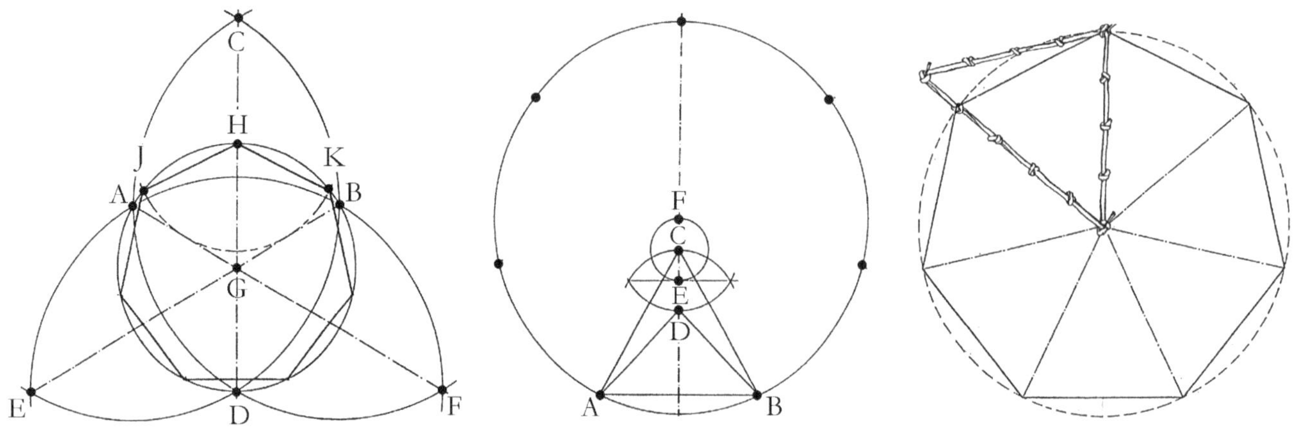

With centers at A and B draw Vesica ACBD. With center at D and radius AB draw arc EF. Draw AF and EB to find G. Draw circle ABD, center at G. With center at H draw arc JK. JH is a side of the heptagon.

ACB is an equilateral triangle, ADB is a half-square. Divide CD in half. Draw circle with radius CE. F is the center of the circumscribing circle of a heptagon.

Construction of a heptagon using a chord knotted in 13 intervals.

FIGURE 18

Construction of the Heptagon

FIGURE 19

Chartres Section and Musical Intervals

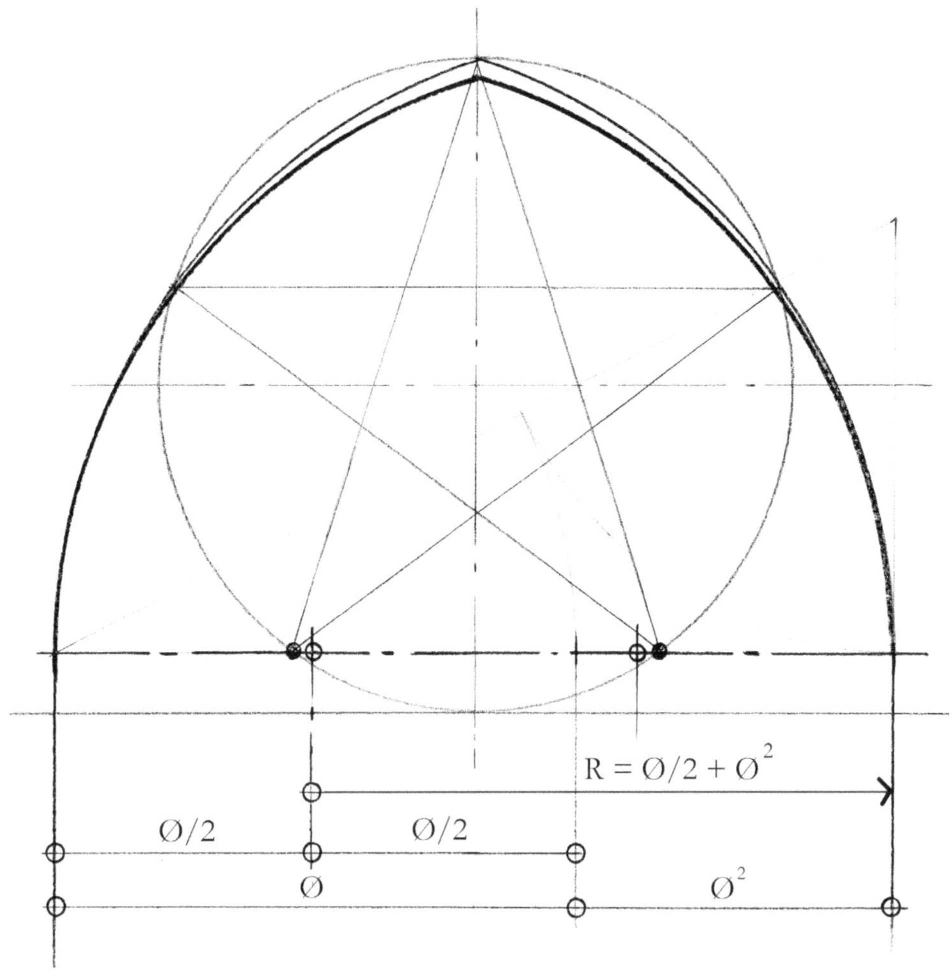

FIGURE 20
Chartres Arches

If a circle is drawn with a diameter equal to the height of the vault, **figure 20**, a pentagram inscribed within it gives the two centers of the vault.[48] These points can also be obtained by finding Ø of the span. Divide Ø in half and add $Ø/2 + Ø^2 = .309 + .382 = .691 = R$. As $\sqrt{2}/2 = .707$, the radii of the vault could have been obtained by a $\sqrt{2}$ method.[49]

But the presence of the pentagram and Ø, indirect and shadowy, peek out like Macavity the Mystery Cat. Its subtle presence here completes the Pythagorean 3-4-5 archetype: the threefold power in the plan; the three- and fourfold powers in the twelve-petalled rose windows; and the fivefold power in the arches.

One of the outstanding features of Chartres is the large circular "rose" or "rose of Mary" windows. Used in much smaller size in Romanesque architecture, they come into their own with the Gothic. Though called "rose" windows they are usually based on three- and fourfold geometries, whereas roses are fivefold. It may be that the term comes from the old French word "roué or "roe," from the Latin "Rota" meaning "wheel,"[50] as in the "wheel of fortune" or wheel of the zodiac.

At Chartres the west, north and south roses are based on twelvefold division. Critchlow offers an analytical diagram,[51] **figure 21a**, in which a circle's circumference is divided into twelve segments. In each of the segments a square is placed along its diagonal. Because of the orientation of the squares an equilateral triangular segment is left between them. The base of this triangle is the diagonal of the next incremental square, putting the successive squares in $\sqrt{2}$ progression and relating the radii of successive concentric circles in an approximate $\sqrt{3}/2$ relationship, **21b**.

Critchlow comments that this is a marriage of threeness, spirit, with fourness, matter, and advises us to contemplate the pattern "*as an expression of the twelveness of the heart, of the 'heart centre' of the Vedic Chakra system.*"[52] The geometry of the window as that of the sacred marriage reinforces the northeast orientation of the building. It is on the shortest day of the year that the setting sun's ray passes through this lens and along the axis of the building's interior space, like a fertilizing spirit penetrating matter, culminating the sacred marriage, signaling that a rebirth has taken place.

Figure 21c.1-3 reconstructs the west rose at Chartres. Begin with an enclosing circle, center at A, radius AB. Walk the radius along the circumference to find points B-G. Drawing circles with these centers creates the "flower" and a series of six vesica piscis each of which begins at A and ends at points 1-6. Connecting points 1-4, 2-5, and 3-6, find points H-N, dividing the circumference into twelve. Divide a typical interval, BH, in half to find point P, **21c.2**,. Draw a circle with center at P and radius PB, on its circumference mark point Q on centerline A7. Draw a circle with center at A, radius AQ. Find point R on its circumference on centerline AH. With center at R, radius RQ, draw a circle to find point S. Draw a circle with center at A, radius AS, to find point T. Draw another circle with center at T, radius ST. This process may be continued indefinitely in either direction. In **21c.3** the circles with center at R become the twelve outer rings, the twelve colonnettes "supporting" them have their top center at S. A further increment gives their height and the diameter of the center ring.

We could continue practically indefinitely here, as everywhere one looks at Chartres one encounters profound multilayered symbols. Not even mentioned here are the sculptural and stained-glass programs as these could easily command volumes in themselves. Not mentioned is the labyrinth, a map of the soul's journey, which dominates the floor of the nave and aligns with the rose window. Chartres cathedral is a great spiritual teaching machine whose tools are space, time and light, whose products are the clarification of consciousness and the elevation of the soul. It ranks as one of the most outstanding building projects in the experience of humanity.

Villard de Honnecourt

Villard de Honnecourt was a master builder in early thirteenth-century France. Though few names of medieval master builders have come down to us, Villard is known because parts of his professional notebooks found their way into the national library of France and are available to modern scholars. The "notebooks" date from about 1235, after Chartres, Paris and Laon had largely been completed, but during the period of construction of Bourges, Reims and Amiens. Villard was widely traveled and drawings of Chartres, Laon and other buildings appear in the notebooks.

The primary aspect of interest for us in the notebooks is the obvious domination of geometrical methods, for all scales of thinking, from overall planning to details such as window

21a - Rose Window Analysis
after Critchlow

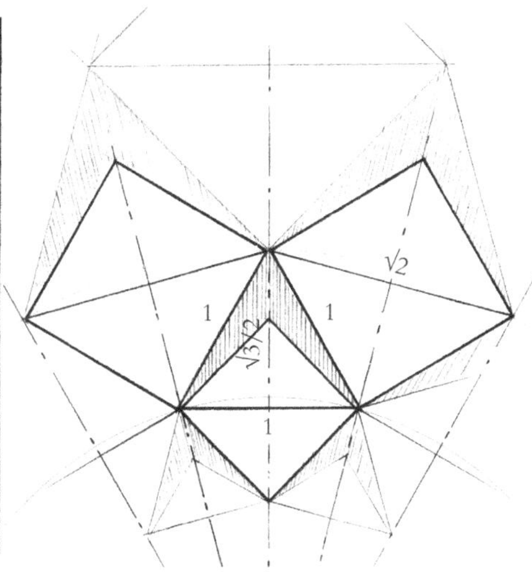

21b - Rose Window Geometrical Structure

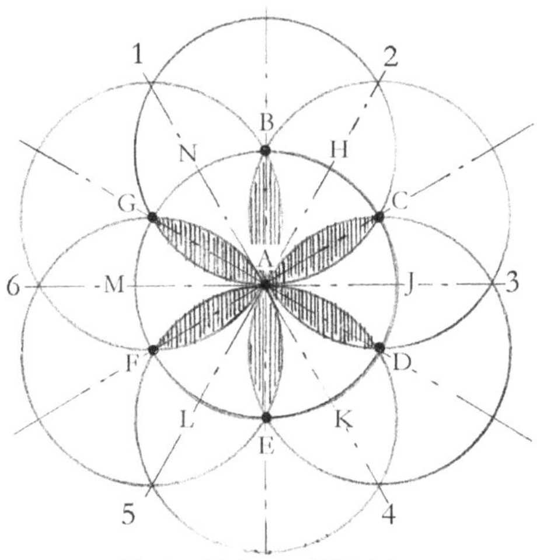

21c.1 - Unity and Division

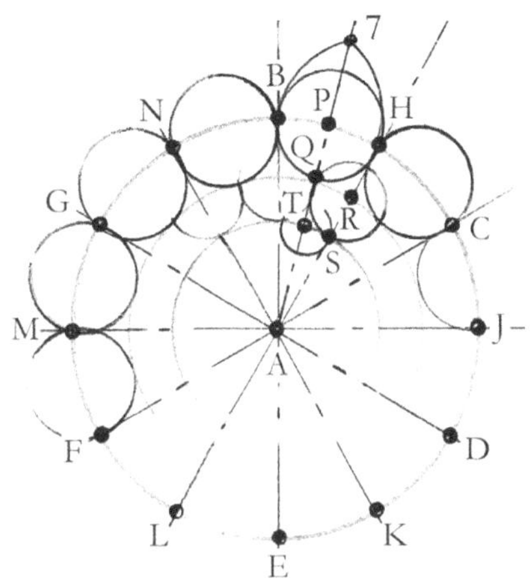

21c.2 - Structure

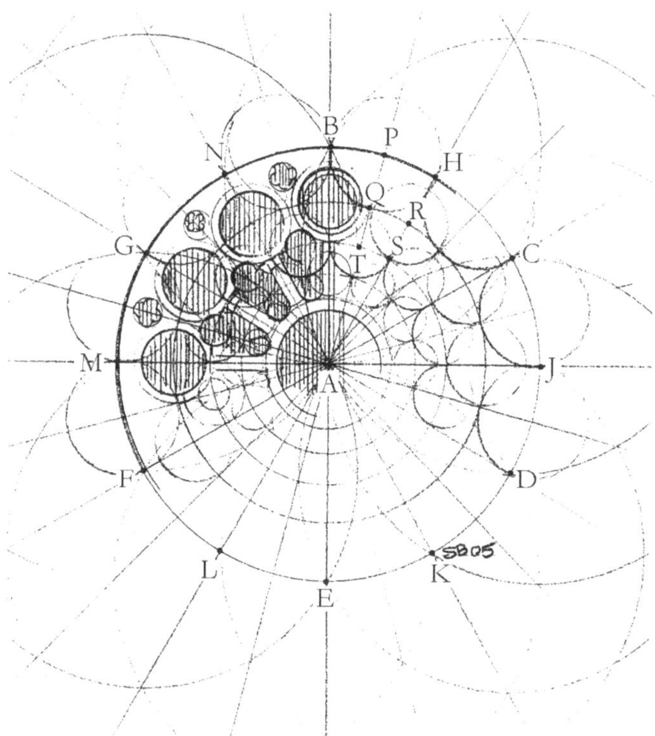

21c.3 - Manifestation

FIGURE 21a-c – *Rose Window Geometry and Reconstruction*

22a - Natural and Architectural Forms

22b - Vesica Geometry and Architectural Details

FIGURE 22

Villard de Honnecourt

fenestration, including natural and human representational ornaments. **Figure 22a** uses three-, four- and fivefold symmetries to construct a variety of architectural and natural elements. In **22b** Villard uses the vesica piscis to divide the diameter of a circle and set up a pier or window mullion. The notebooks provide a rare glimpse into premodern design methodology and establish that geometrical methods remained alive and well in the medieval era.

Early Renaissance

The Italian Renaissance

Although there have been many revivals of ancient knowledge in the history of the West the one that occurred in northern Italy in the fourteenth and fifteenth centuries, known simply as "the Renaissance," has had the most direct and lasting influence on us. Centered first in Tuscany, it soon spread to regions dominated by Rome and Venice.

Two major themes of this rebirth are rediscovery of ancient knowledge and emergence of the individual. In medieval society the individual's actions and options were considerably more circumscribed and subordinated to the community or group than they are today.[1] Builders of the early Gothic cathedrals, for example, did not leave us their names, only their collective work. This balance of sensibilities is shifted in the Renaissance, and the idea of the individual we recognize today begins to emerge.

Awareness of the ancients provided a model and measure for comparison. The Renaissance fascination with the ancient world stemmed from its serving as a route to individualism. This fascination is manifest in travel and collections.[2] For architects this meant measuring ruins; in the individual spirit you went to look with your own eyes. The Italians, of course, didn't need to go far to rediscover the ancient world. They were and still are living right on top of it.

The intellectual aspect of the shift from communal to individual identity is sometimes called humanism. One of its key metaphors is the phrase "Man is the measure of all things."[3] However, "Man" can be read two ways. Outwardly it is a reference to the physical or "rational" man but inwardly it refers to the spiritual man, to the human being as center and analog. Thus there was both an exoteric humanism and an esoteric humanism.

The visual manifestation of this shift of sensibilities is symbolized by "perspective." Medieval art was iconic and aspatial. The most important figure was largest; subsidiary figures or aspects were smaller and arranged around the principal element. There is a conceptual relation of the elements but not necessarily a spatial one. In Renaissance art a virtual, illusionary space is created and the subject of the work is placed within it.

At the same time the Italians were looking back to the ancients for new exemplars, the long twilight of the Byzantine Empire opened a window to antiquity. During more than a hundred-fifty years, as night slowly fell on the Eastern Empire, people began to move west to Italy, bringing with them books that had been quietly gathering dust in Greek libraries for generations.

Plethon

Most interesting in this context is the story of Plethon. Georgius Gemistus known as Plethon, meaning "student of Plato," was born in Constantinople c.1360. He was educated in the seven liberal arts[4] and for advanced study went to the Ottoman city of Adrianople.[5] There he was exposed to Platonism and Neoplatonism. He is said to have had a teacher who, while being ostensibly Jewish, was privately pagan. Whether this is true or not the story indicates that Plethon was absorbing ancient tradition, not just intellectually but in a spiritual sense as well.

About 1400, Plethon is appointed a judge in Mistra, on the Peloponnese near the site of ancient Sparta. He established a school there about 1410.[6] Among his students are the later prominent Cardinal Bessarion and Mark of Ephesus (Manuel Eugenikos), later a leader of the Eastern Church. In 1439, as Turks and Greeks prepared for the final struggle, a conference was held in Florence, known as the Council of Union, to discuss reuniting the Eastern and Western churches and obtaining Italian aid against the Turks.[7] Plethon was in the Byzantine delegation.

In parallel to the conference Plethon began to do what he probably enjoyed most: lecture on Platonic philosophy. In the audience were many of the leading personalities of the day including Paolo Toscanelli, Leon Battista Alberti, and most notably Cosimo de Medici.[8] Plethon found that although Aristotle was well known to Italian intellectuals Plato was not. His lectures and later writings explicate Platonic concepts, often in contrast to Aristotle. Plethon returned to Mistra and died there in 1452, almost a hundred years old.

In the story of Plethon a seed of the perennial tradition fell on fertile ground and took root in the "re-born" Italy. The rest of this chapter, in effect, describes the flowering of that seed. Plethon opened up Platonism to Italy by making it a respectable subject. His presentations stimulated Cosimo to follow the Alexandrine example and endow a study center, which was known as the Florentine Academy, and was headed by Marsilio Ficino. The academy's major project was to translate the dialogs of Plato, many later commentators on Plato, the so-called Neoplatonists, and the *Corpus Hermeticum*. It is likely that Plethon knew of the *CH* and mentioned it in his Italian lectures.[9] About 1460, a few years after Plethon's death, Cosimo[10] obtained a text of the *CH*, and had Ficino translate it. Because the *CH* was thought to predate Plato, and even Moses, its Platonic precepts could be used to counterbalance the influence of Aristotle.

Since the days of Aquinas teachers and theologians had relied on Aristotle for logical exposition of doctrines and the organization of knowledge. This was exoteric or outer-directed knowledge. Plato and, in particular, the Neoplatonists alluded to esoteric or inner-directed development. Since this work must take place within each individual it may be described as radically, personally empowering; that is to say, individualistic. Plethon's lectures kicked off more than two centuries of intellectual conflict between Aristotelians and Platonists.

In the later Middle Ages, after the fall of the School of Chartres, a Latinized Aristotleanism reigned supreme. Even the reading of Greek brought one under suspicion of heresy or paganism. Plethon's introduction of Plato, in a sense, gave the Italians a way out of the Middle Ages. They would not be afraid to look at ancient Greek philosophy (meaning Pythagorean and Platonic), religion, spirituality, or magic. The Plethon–Cosmo–Ficino connection in fifteenth-century Florence gave rise to the most influential flowering of esoteric philosophy since antiquity.

Plethon's circle of influence on the Renaissance closes with the remarkable story of his body's postmortem journey. During the Florence conference Plethon had come to the attention of the larger-than-life figure of Sigismondo Malatesta, ruler of Rimini. Sigismondo, quite impressed, invited Plethon to assume a position at his court, but he declined. In 1464 Sigismondo, in the employ of Venice, was campaigning against Turkish positions on the Peloponnese. His troops briefly occupied Mistra but could not hold it. As he withdrew he removed Plethon's body and brought it to Rimini. There he had it interred in his family church — the Tempio Malatestiano — designed by none other than Leon Battista Alberti.

Brunelleschi

Filippo Brunelleschi, 1377–1446, demonstrated a mathematical and mechanical aptitude from an early age, eventually being apprenticed to a goldsmith. Young Filippo excelled, quickly going on to engraving, sculpture in silver, then to clock-making, a craft skill in which mathematics, geometry and astronomy play key, closely related roles. The clock itself is a cosmological analog. During this time Brunelleschi becomes friends with the young sculptor Donatello and begins to investigate methods of architectural construction. In 1398 the 21-year-old Brunelleschi is admitted to the guild as a master goldsmith.

In 1401 a fateful competition is held in Florence to create a series of bronze relief panels for the doors of the Baptistery of San Giovanni, directly across the piazza from the unfinished cathedral. Brunelleschi and Donatello both enter, but the competition is won by the older and politically well-placed Lorenzo Ghiberti, setting the stage for future conflicts. Though Brunelleschi is offered a position under Ghiberti he refuses; he and Donatello "hit the road" for Rome. Brunelleschi spends much of the next twenty years in Rome surveying and recording ancient structures, particularly their vaulting.

The Dome

The completion of the dome of the Florence cathedral was the largest-scale achievement of Brunelleschi's career, **figure 1**. The cathedral in Florence was begun in 1294, enlarged and continued in 1357. In 1367 the span (about 120 feet), height (a 2:1 ratio) and curvature of the dome were established. The drum was built between 1410–13.[11] In 1418 a competition is held for design of the dome but the results are inconclusive. To force a decision by the hesitant city fathers Brunelleschi pulls the first of two major power plays he is to make during construction of the dome, "the incident of the egg."

The issue was this: a "conventional" dome, in which the stones of the vault are set on wood formwork during construction, which in turn would have to be supported from the ground, would have made the project logistically and financially impractical. Brunelleschi was the only builder who understood ancient vaulting techniques well enough to use both stone and metal in tension. Thus, the vault elements, as they leaned inward, actually cantilevered each other, and the scaffolding could be supported by the dome itself instead of the other way around. But Brunelleschi realized that once he explained his method any of his competitors, some of whom like Ghiberti were politically powerful, could build the dome.

At a 1420 meeting a heated argument ensues when Brunelleschi remains evasive. Finally, when pressed he suggests that whoever could make an egg stand on end should get the job. His competitors try but can't do it. When it's his turn Brunelleschi cracks off the bottom of the shell and the egg remains standing. When the others object that anyone could do that he tells them that the same is true of building the dome.[12]

Though he wins the argument he is not put in complete charge. He must still share authority and the money with his old rival Ghiberti. This sets the stage for the second and decisive power play: "the sick call." In 1426 the vaulting had reached about twenty-four feet, at which point a stone tension ring needed to be constructed and parts of the cantilevered scaffolding needed to be set. Only Brunelleschi knew how to perform these operations. Instead of appearing at the site to give directions Brunelleschi called in sick. The artisans went to Ghiberti but he, wisely, would

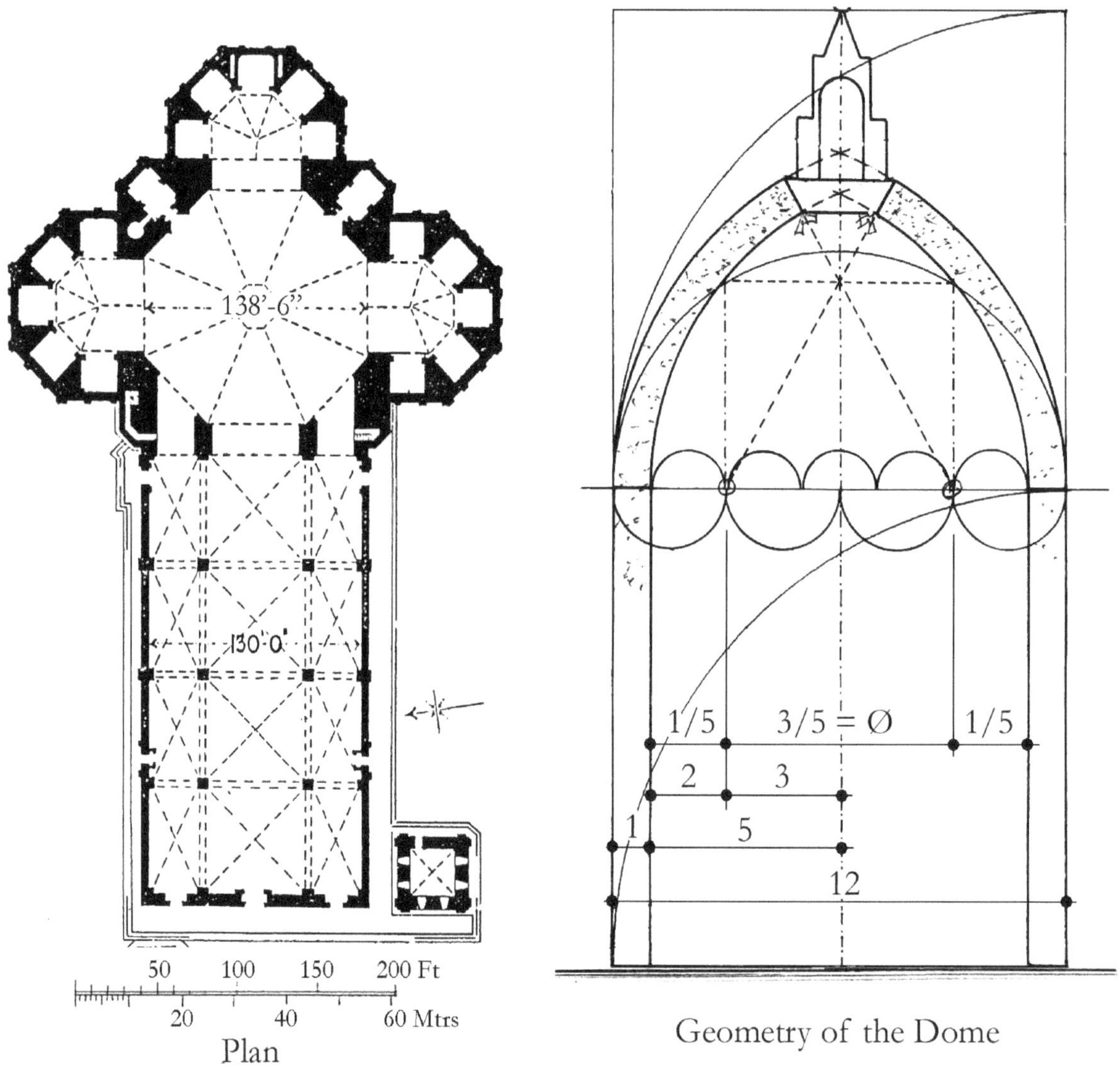

FIGURE 1
Brunelleschi's Dome

give them no directions. After a few days, seeing their livelihoods in jeopardy, they leaned on the administrators. Once again those in charge had to go to Brunelleschi. This time he forced Ghiberti to be "kicked upstairs," as we might say today, and was put in sole charge of the dome, a position he held for the rest of his life.

Brunelleschi's use of the module in design, based on his knowledge of the classical elements and proportions, allowed him to impose a uniform unit of measure on the project, the braccio, ± 2'-2" to 2'-3."[13] We take this for granted today but in medieval times each trade, such as masons, woodworkers, tile setters, etc., had its own metric units.

Brunelleschi imposed a new way of working based on his personal vision and knowledge rather than participation in a community of administrators, designers and builders.[14] Rather than contributing his concept to a larger goal as the medieval masons did Brunelleschi used his technical knowledge to leverage himself into sole charge of the project. The builders were relegated to the status of subordinate functionaries and the politicians to a passive audience. His refusal to work within the old collective tradition precipitated the authority struggle behind the power plays.[15]

Brunelleschi and Toscanelli

Parallel to this emergence of the individual visionary architect there develops a method of visually representing this psychological state called "perspective." The origins of modern perspective may be said to stem from the relationship of Brunelleschi and Toscanelli.

Paolo Toscanelli, 1397–1482, was born in Florence and studied medicine at Padua between 1418 and 1424.[16] His classmates included Nicholas of Cusa, he was a friend of Regiomontanus, and later a correspondent (through an intermediary) with Christopher Columbus. Toscanelli was one of Florence's leading intellectuals in the heyday of esoteric humanism, with a focus on geometry, in particular as applied to optics, geography and cartography. At this time medical diagnosis was done astrologically and at Padua mathematics was administered under the chair of astrology.[17] Observational and symbolic astronomy were still a single subject in this era. So, in effect Toscanelli was an astrologer.

Toscanelli was also apparently master of another art that came right down from the Neolithic: architectural sundialing. He and Brunelleschi designed a "meridiana" for the floor of Florence cathedral, though it was not built until 1475, almost thirty years after Brunelleschi's death.[18] A meridiana is essentially an opening in a roof or wall that allows a ray of the sun to hit the floor at a given time of day, usually noon. Over the course of a year a straight north–south line is traced out. The south end marks the summer solstice and the north end marks the winter solstice. The line is marked out on the floor in stone or metal and serves as a calendar.

Toscanelli and Brunelleschi studied geometry together, likely contributing to Brunelleschi's development of perspective.[19] Their studies were not restricted only to technical subjects but extended, for example, to Dante[20] and included reading Ptolemy's *Geographica.*

Optics

Foundational to the idea of perspective is the physics of light and vision, called optics. Its history[21] begins with the pre-Socratics such as Empedocles, whose explanation for sight was that objects radiate "eidola," "effluxes" or streaming substances that carried the visual image to the eye. How the image penetrated the eye and formed an image in the mind was not understood. The idea that a visual force came from outside the observer is called "intromission." The Pythagoreans however, perhaps with a different end in mind than the pre-Socratic atomists, took the opposite position, proposing that the visual force was projected out from within the person, called "extromission."

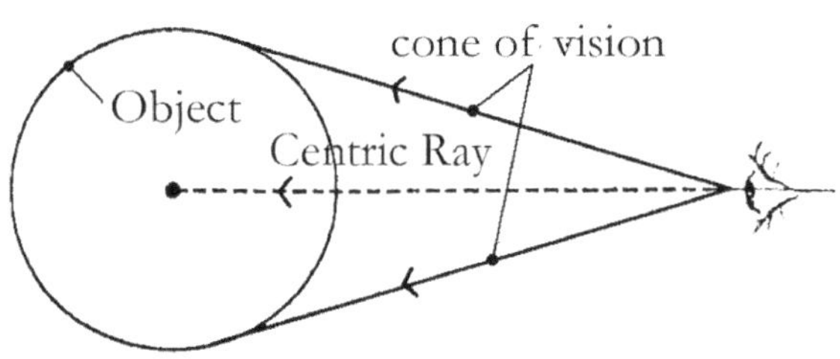

Figure 2 – *Visual Rays Create the Cone of Vision*

Euclid, c.300–250 BC provides the earliest geometrical model of vision. In his *Optics* he symbolizes the "effluxes," of visual force as straight lines, essentially inventing the "visual ray." Using the principle of extromission, perhaps revealing a Pythagorean root, he sets up a cone of vision with its apex at the eye, **figure 2**. The side view of a cone is a triangle, a figure subject to Euclidean analysis. The apparent size of an object is governed by the apex angle of the triangle, whose sides are visual rays. The same object close by will have a greater visual angle than if it is farther away. The greater the angle the more rays fall on the object and the more clearly we see it.

Ptolemy, 85–165 AD, contributed the idea of the "centric ray," the shortest one between the object and the eye, giving the clearest view. Though lenses were known in the craft traditions for many centuries, Ptolemy was the first to describe refraction, while Galen, c.130–200 AD, published the first anatomy of the eye, showing the pupil as a lens, and indicating that the seen rays were perpendicular to the curvature of the eye.

It is not possible through geometry to determine whether the rays of light enter the eye from outside or exit the eye from within; the geometry is the same. Theories of intromission and extromission continued to be debated until the Enlightenment era. Least one think that any "progress" has been made here, keep in mind that a definitive understanding of the phenomenon of light still does not exist, relativity, quantum mechanics, and string theory notwithstanding.

Cartography

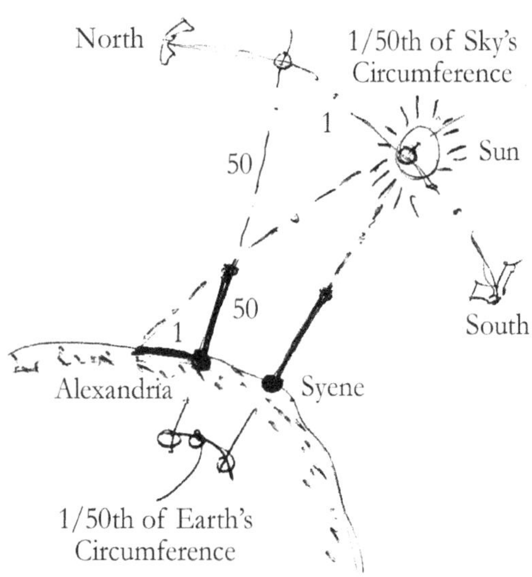

Figure 3

Eratosthenes' Measurement of the Earth

Contrary to popular belief, the ancients were well aware that the earth is a sphere. In fact, its circumference had already been measured rather accurately by Eratosthenes of Alexandria, c.200 BC, using the principle of similar triangles, **figure 3.** Eratosthenes estimate of 24,662 miles is rather close to the modern 24,883. Not bad for someone using a stick and a shadow. Ptolemy however in his *Geographica* uses a smaller incremental distance and so gets a circumference of about 18,000 miles.[22] This is the figure Toscanelli, via an intermediary, communicated to Columbus in 1474, leading that navigator to later incorrectly conclude he had reached East Asia.

In the *Geographica,* Ptolemy describes map-making techniques that utilize the optical theory of the visual rays. In one example he describes how to draw a map of the "oikumene," the known world.[23] His method is a mix of technical and practical procedures, which are abbreviated here.

Geometrically the task is to represent a spherical surface on a flat plane, **figure 4.** Ptolemy puts a grid on the sphere's surface, today called latitude and longitude; a concept inherited from Eratosthenes. Making use of Pythagorean extromission and Euclidean ray triangulation, he positions the observer over the center of the oikumene, **figure 4a,** point J, with the centric visual ray parallel to the circles of latitude. This center is between the equator and the tropic, thus these two circles will be seen as lines in an orthographic front view, but as ellipsoids in perspective. The curvature of these ellipsoids depend on the viewer's distance from them. To determine this, Ptolemy marks the north–south extent of the oikumene, points K and L, on the axis AB. Then, he locates the distance to the viewer's observation point by projecting a line from H to K and extended to intersect the line through J at point M. This procedure is a "rule of thumb," determined empirically.

To position the upper and lower points of the ellipses of the tropic and equator, **figure 4b,** turn the diagram 90° and treat it as a side view. Line AB is now treated as a picture plane. Points G, J and D which were in a straight line in front view are now on the circular edge of the sphere. Next, project lines from M through G to G' and through D to D'. These points will mark the nearest points of the two circles. To position the farthest points of the circles project lines from M to P and N. Where these lines cross AB find points N' and P'.

Now, turning again to a front view, we can draw the ellipses, **figure 4c**. Points G' and D' will mark the high points of the ellipses, N' and P' will mark the low points. The oikumene extends from K' to L'.

Perspective

Though Ptolemy does not mention it,[24] some ancient writers discuss "scenographia," a technical method of painting perspective-like theatrical backdrops. Little is known of this technique. Vitruvius gives this tantalizing hint:[25] *"Scenography is the shading of the front and retreating sides, and the correspondence of all the lines to the center of a circle ... if a fixed center is taken for the outward glance of the eyes and the projection of the radii, we must follow these lines in accordance with a natural law, such that ... images may give the appearance of buildings in the scenery of the stage and how what is figured upon the vertical and plane surfaces can seem to recede in one part and project in another."*

As usual with poor old Vitruvius, the text leaves a lot of room for ambiguity. By "a fixed center for the glance of the eye" does he mean a station point? Do the phrases "projection of the radii"" and "correspondence of all lines to the center of a circle" imply the use of a vanishing point? And what does Vitruvius mean by "lines in accordance with natural law"? Does he mean harmonic diminishment?

Toscanelli and Brunelleschi applied Ptolemy's cartographic method to illusionistic representation. As with the Vitruvian Man, no illustrations had survived and the breakthrough came in the re-geometricizing of the ancient written description. In **figure 4** Point M is the station point; J is the center of vision and the vanishing point. MJ is the centric ray and becomes the horizon line. Most importantly, line AB is understood to be both the one-dimensional axis but also to lie on the base of a cone, that is a two-dimensional plane; the picture plane. If this picture plane is moved toward the station point so that instead of lying along the center of the sphere it is in front of the sphere, the image on the picture plane is the same but smaller. All the necessary precursors to perspective are now present.

The geometrical technique they produced is at the center of the method still used today. In **figure 5a** a perspective is drawn of a grid on a floor. The picture plane is placed at the front of the grid, and it is represented as a square. The side view shows the relation of the picture plane to the grid and the station point. Though the station point can have any kind of relationship to the picture plane, in our example here the station point is placed at half the

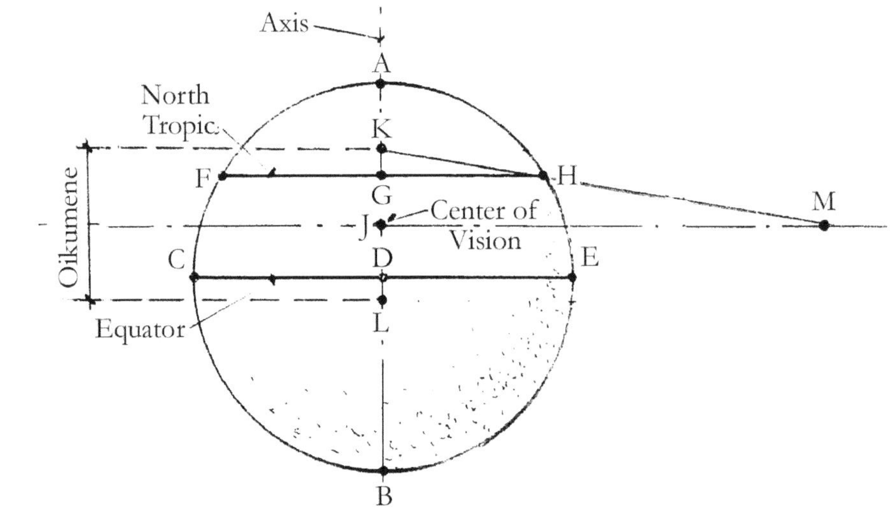

4a - Orthographic front view of the sphere of the earth

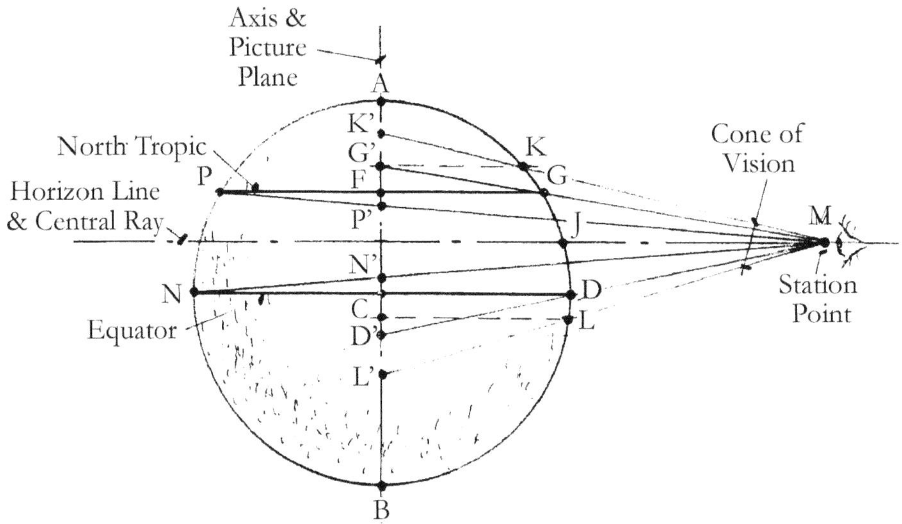

4b - Orthographic side view

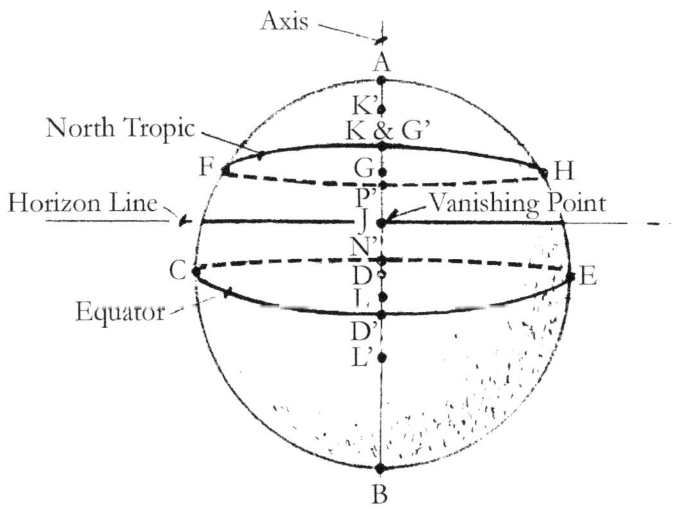

4c - Front view in perspective

FIGURE 4

Ptolemy's Perspective Method in the Geographica

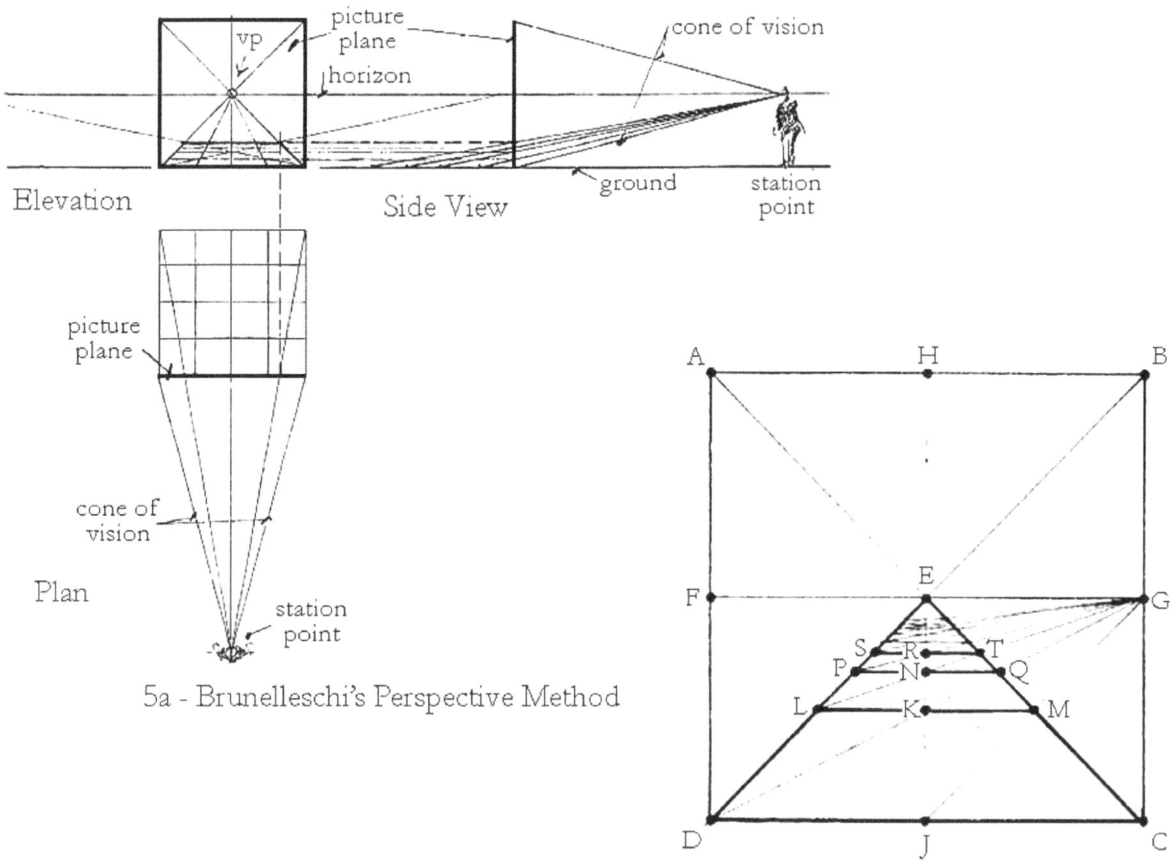

5a - Brunelleschi's Perspective Method

5b - Illusion of Depth by Subdivision of the Square

FIGURE 5 – *Perspective*

height of the grid and forms the horizon line. The station point's distance from the picture plane is determined here for convenience by drawing a line from the far edge of the grid through the picture plane at a height equal to 1 unit of the grid. Where this line crosses the horizon is the distance to the SP.

The front edge of the grid is touching the PP, thus it is seen as "true size" with no diminution. The sides of the grid in perspective are found by projecting rays from the front corners to the vanishing point, at the center of the square frame of the picture plane. The back corners of the grid may be found in both plan and side view by projecting a ray from those two points to the SP. Where they cross the PP mark the back corners of the grid. We can do this for the other points on the front and side to get the grid in perspective.

Because of the way we have set up our SP, object, and PP relationship, the illusion of perspective depth can be created, without plan or side view, by pure geometry alone. In **figure 5b** an elemental perspective is set up in a square divided by its diagonal AC and semi-diagonal GD, giving the 1/3rd point Q. This may be leading to something like the Vitruvian "accordance to natural law." It may be seen as alluding to the "pillar" of Egypt.[26] The square divided by its diagonals and semi-diagonals alone sets up a space illusion through harmonic division.

Brunelleschi's Demonstration

Brunelleschi was a consummate manipulative showman. Perspective as a theory was not enough for him. In 1425 he stages a public demonstration of the new vision on the steps of the very cathedral whose dome he was then building.[27] The first step, **figure 6**, was to paint a perspective picture of the Baptistery as seen from the cathedral steps on a wooden board with a small hole drilled in the board at the vanishing point. The observer would be placed at the station point, also the vanishing point, behind the wood panel, looking through the hole, toward the Baptistery, however, about a foot or so in front of the panel a mirror was placed. Keep in mind that a flat glass mirror, about one foot by one foot, was a high-tech novelty in fifteenth-century Florence.

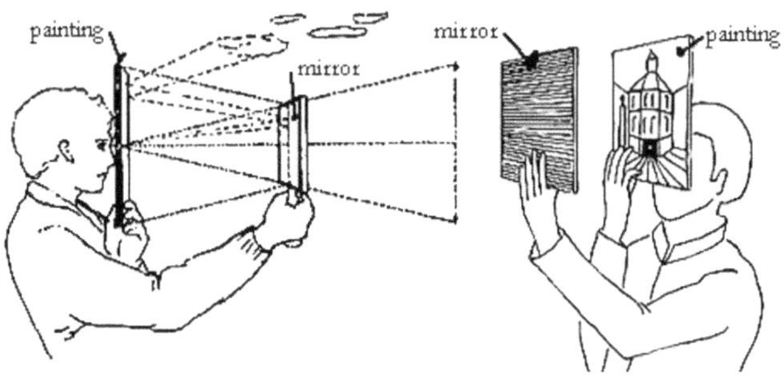

Figure 6
Brunelleschi's Demonstration

The observer would look through the opening in the panel and see the reflection of the painted perspective instead of the actual building. Around the edges of the mirror, the actual piazza would be visible, smoothly picking up where the painting left off. But Brunelleschi had one more trick up his sleeve. The sky above the building was painted in reflective silver, and the effect of this was to include the moving clouds in the actual sky through a double reflection.

It may be that Brunelleschi set up his demonstration on Sunday and caught the town's notables on their way out of church service, but whatever the day, observers were stunned; the event literally "went down in history." It was another public triumph for Brunelleschi; and perhaps all the sweeter as the subject of the painting, the Baptistery, was the scene of his loss to Ghiberti in the door competition. Brunelleschi must have taken heart from his success. It would be less than a year before his final power play on the dome would push Ghiberti aside for good.

The intimate relationship between painting and architecture established by perspective is illustrated in **figure 7**.

Perspective in Perspective

The method of perspective born in Brunelleschi's demonstration very quickly grew up to completely engulf the Western visual imagination. The timely coincidence of the beginnings of the use of movable type certainly played a role, but clearly a need was realized here. The desire for an individual viewpoint was tapped that was perfectly consistent with Brunelleschi's emergence

The Trinity, a fresco by Masaccio at Santa Maria Novella, Florence

Basilica of San Lorenzo, Florence by Brunelleschi

FIGURE 7

Masaccio and Brunelleschi: Space in Painting and Architecture

as an individual; as the first modern "starchitect." So powerful was the takeover of his perspective vision that today we take it for granted as an objective representation, but when seen in the context of the esoteric tradition it is anything but.

A perspective is a pattern on a flat surface that reminds us of what an object in space would look like if seen at a specific time and place. To create such a space illusion on a flat surface requires a single fixed, individuated station point.[28] Put in traditional terms, perspective is an illusion; it plays on what we think we know about the world, causing us to come to a "false" conclusion. It is a magical act; certainly not the only way to "see" the world.

How to read a perspective must be learned. Edgerton stresses that it is "*not natural to assume this attitude about a picture, either as viewer or artist. Young children, for instance, do not, nor did the ancient Chinese or the medieval Christians.*" [29] That perspective is learned and that it is not natural implies that the camera, which we take for granted as achieving an objective representation of "reality," is actually a machine for reproducing an illusion. The fact that perspective can be constructed on the same pattern as the musical octave indicates that harmonic division may be utilized in both sound and space perception as well as its illusionary reconstruction.

The point of this discussion is not to demean perspective or to "deconstruct" it (to render it meaningless) but to empower designers to use it as a tool of the imagination. Perspective is the vehicle of choice for representation of classical space in the visual arts. But whenever you draw one, remember that you are casting a spell over the observer; and try to avoid coming under it yourself.[30]

Architectural Work of Brunelleschi

The geometrical key to Brunelleschi's architecture, like Alberti's, is the cube[31] elegantly sliced up and reassembled. Brunelleschi's colonnades are usually 1:1 in plan. In elevation the columns may be 1 unit high with an arch 1/2 unit high, as in the Foundling Hospital; or the columns and arch may be 2 units high, as in Santo Spirito. Both the Old Sacristy at San Lorenzo and the Pazzi Chapel are shaped cubes in overall volume. Although Brunelleschi may seem preoccupied with modules his focus on unity is sufficiently maintained through adherence to the larger, informing cube.

Foundling Hospital, c.1420

The key architectural feature of this building is the nine-bay colonnade along the piazza. Using this as a starting point, **figure 8a**, a grid is set up with the colonnade plan bay as the unit. The 9 units of the colonnade are flanked by intervals of 3 units that Brunelleschi divides into 2 trabeated bays. Architectonically, these abutting masses contain and stabilize the vital rhythmic pulsation of the arcade. The overall building is then 15 units wide and the plan is placed in a 15 x 15 square. Its depth is 10 units. A 9 x 9 square informs the colonnade, entry hall, central courtyard sequence. The central courtyard plan is 3 x 3. The right side courtyard is 1 x 5 units and aligns with the grid layout.

A 15 x 15 grid can be created by arithmetic division, or approximated geometrically by $Ø^4/2$ = .073, 1/15th = .067. The ratio of the colonnade to the overall width, 9:15, is Ø. The central courtyard is 1/3rd of 9 and in the center of the 9 x 9 square. The overall enclosing rectangle is 10:15 or 2:3. The back row of rooms is centered at 9 or Ø.

The elevation is a bit more subtle. A geometric reconstruction starts from square, ABCD, **figure 8b**. Divide BC at Ø, point F. FC = $Ø^2$ = .382. Divide FC in half to find point J. JC = $Ø^2/2$ = .191. HJCD gives the outline of the facade. One might also start from the double square KLCD, **figure 8c**. Divide LC at Ø to find point J directly. Where semi-diagonals AE and BE intersect HJ find N and P, draw square NPQR. Draw squares SNRV and PTUQ. However the two end segments are not square as .191 x 3 = .573 leaving two intervals of .213. A square of sides .191 is placed within rectangle HSDV, **figure 8d**. This leaves space along SV to have a full free-standing column at the end of the arcade and along HD to smartly return the architrave. To space the arcade, **figure 8e**, divide RQ into thirds, points A' and B'. The top of the architrave is at the half point of PQ, point C'.

Looking at the elements, **figure 8f**, the center to center column interval A'B' is divided into 10 braccia. The spring point of the arch is at the top of the capital, about 8.75 braccia. Above this is an extra abacus or impost-like element at 9 braccia. The radius of the arch is 4.5 braccia and its apex is 13.25 braccia. The archivolt is about one column diameter wide; putting its apex at 14.25. The architrave above this is .75 braccia, putting its top at 15 braccia. The series of shapes above this are not an entablature but an uncut baluster or parapet on which the wall and windows of the second story sit, reading like an attic. Brunelleschi gets a lot out of this inventive element. Added to the architrave below, it reads as an entablature for the first story. It is 3 braccia deep

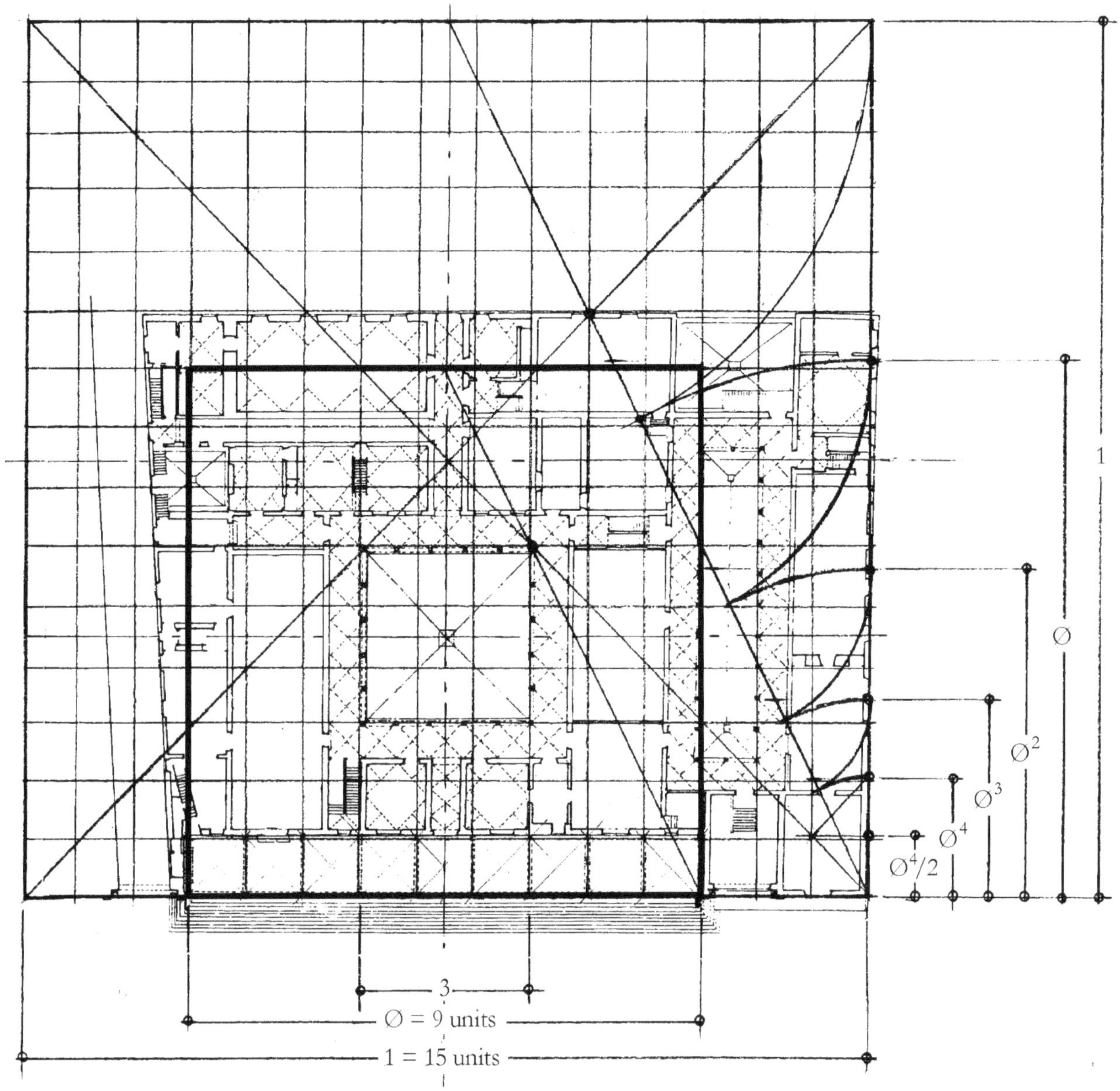

FIGURE 8a

Foundling Hospital Plan, Brunelleschi, 1421

giving an overall height of 18 braccia. The parapet's base reads as a cornice for the first-floor architrave; its flat middle fascia reading as a frieze; and its cymatium doubling as the window sill. An arithmetic method has been used in **figure 8f** but Ø of 30 braccia is 18.54. **Figure 8g** shows the overall elevation.

The lines we have drawn are not necessarily "object lines," outlines of actual members, but rather "linea occulti," hidden lines. They may be center-lines, outer or inner edges, or just lie somewhere within the object.

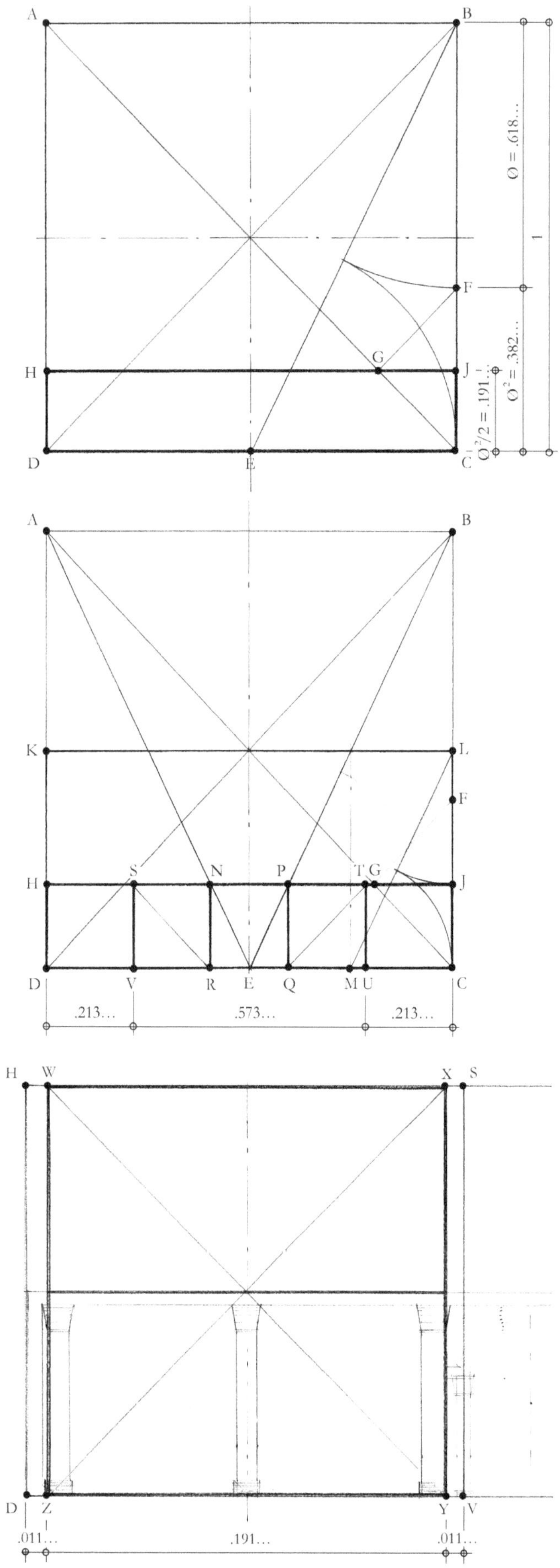

FIGURE 8b-d

Foundling Hospital Elevation

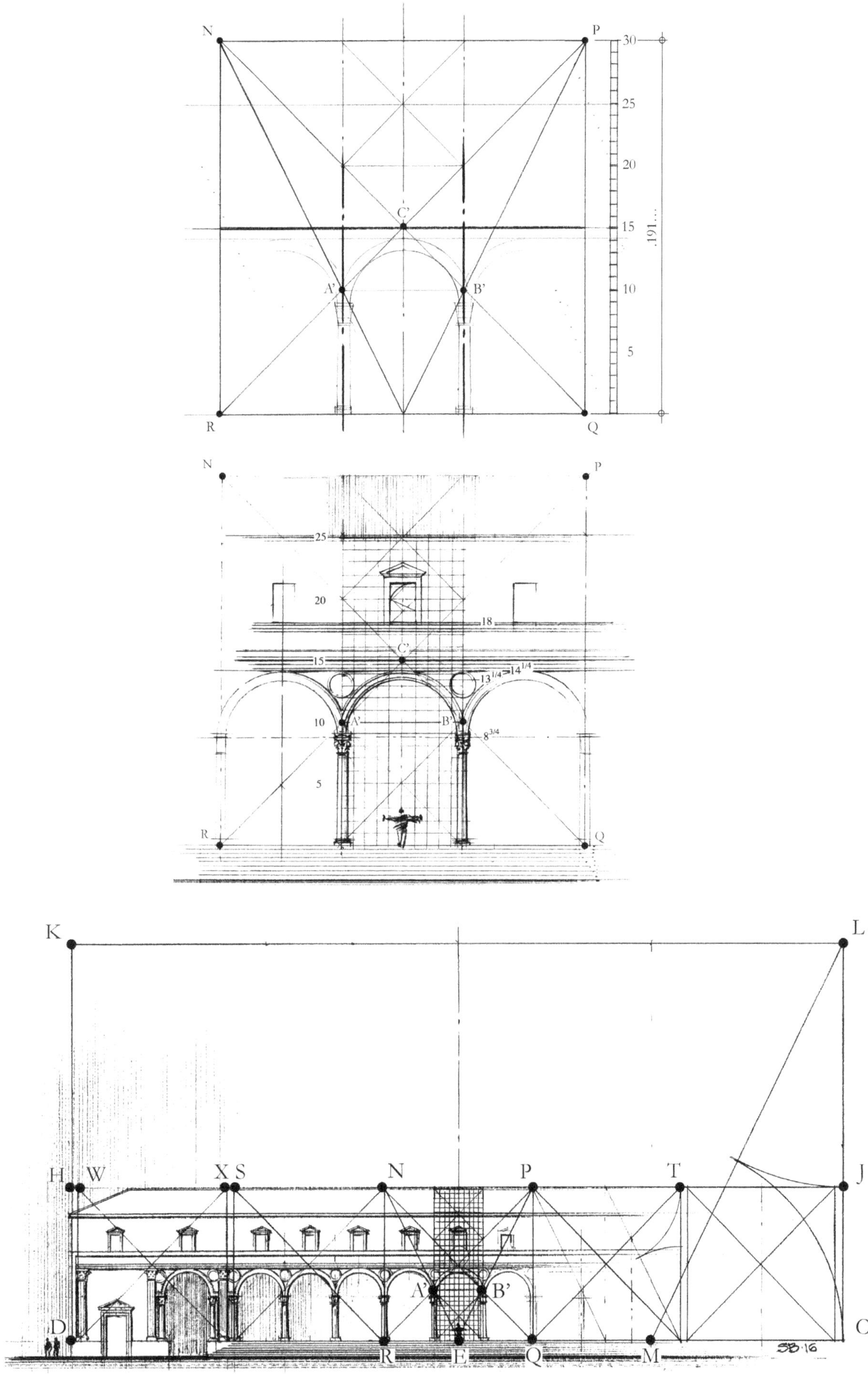

FIGURE 8e-g
Foundling Hospital Elevation

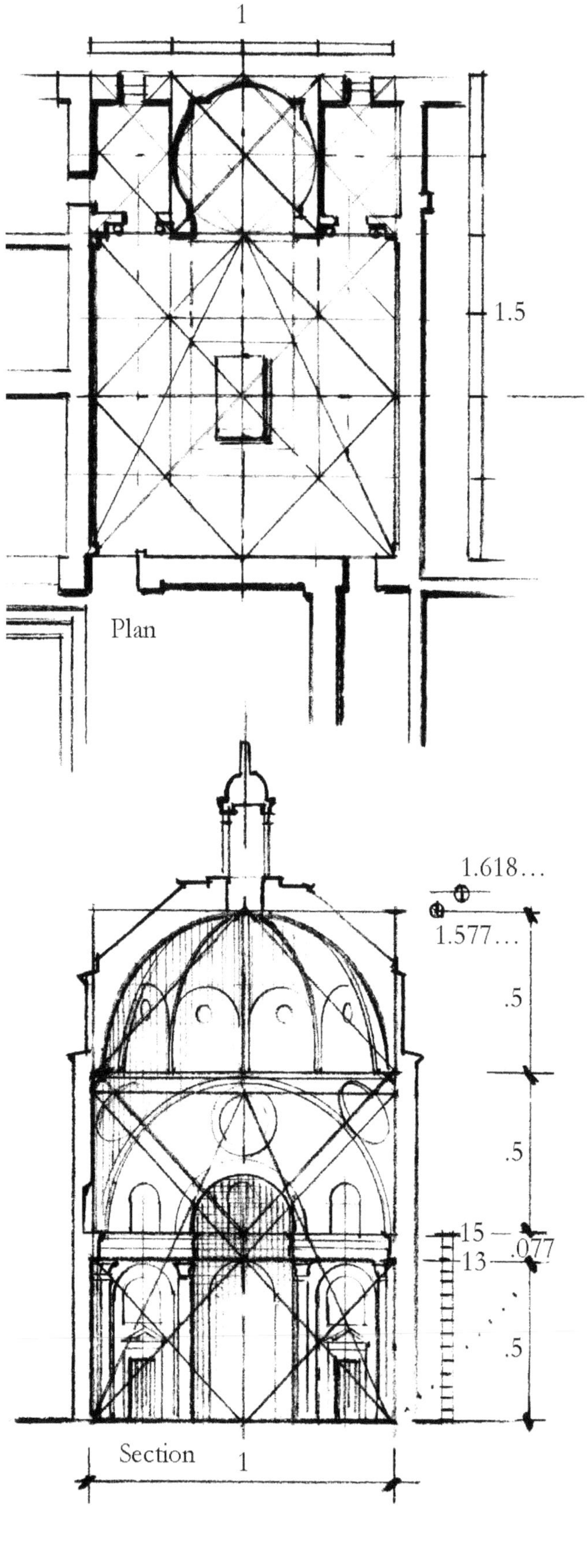

FIGURE 9

The Old Sacristy, San Lorenzo, Florence, 1422

The Old Sacristy

The Old Sacristy, **figure 9,** the Medici chapel at San Lorenzo, was designed by Brunelleschi in 1422, and completed in 1428. Its basic geometrical motif is a cube topped by a hemispherical dome, giving a 2 x 2 x 3 interior volume. The main cube is elevated by the depth of the entablature so the spring points of the pendentives are at the top of the entablature. The main cube is divided at its mid-height by the entablature, creating a three-tiered interior of 1x1 x1/2, or 2x2x1 volumes, the lower one completely cubical, the middle one partly cubical and partly spherical, and the third, completely spherical. If the cube is taken as representing matter and the sphere representing form or nous, the middle tier with the pendentives would represent mind or psyche, recapitulating the Platonic geometrical creation. The room is focused on the altar, located in a niche 1/3rd the width of the room. This makes the niche a 2x2x3 volume up to the entablature, with another cube on top of that containing its own dome on pendentives.

Santo Spirito

Santo Spirito designed some fifteen years after San Lorenzo is much tighter, much more clearly thought out than the earlier basilica. The plan is a "unified organism"[32] revealing Brunelleschi as an inventive visionary, integrating number, structural form and the classical elements to achieve a powerful sense of unity.

Planning began before Brunelleschi's time. He was brought in about 1428 two years after he had achieved complete mastery of the dome project and three years after the perspective demonstration. Brunelleschi lost a lengthy fight over the siting of the building, which delayed the start of construction until two years before his death.[33] Apparently there was a limit even to his remarkable manipulative powers. His vision, both on the urban site plan scale and the architectonic building scale proved too much for his successors. The great compromise of the interior was the loss of the vaulting Brunelleschi had planned for the nave, transept arms and presbytery. Had the vaults been built there would not have been a flat wall surface anywhere in the building's interior. Brunelleschi's successors also gave up on running chapels around the front, which in Brunelleschi's concept would have formed the entrance. They eliminated the aisle across the front, extended the nave by one bay, and put a traditional flat facade on the building. Though all the other chapels were built, sensibilities had fallen so far by the eighteenth century that it was felt necessary to further disfigure the building by putting a flat wall around the exterior of the chapels. Though much compromised the building is still an object lesson on number as a guide to design.

The building, **figure 10**, has three spatial layers,[34] 1) the nave, transept crossing and presbytery, 2) side aisles that run continuously around the first layer, and 3) the semi-circular chapels. The architectonic module, "M," may be taken as the square aisle bay of 11 braccia. Its height is two modules or 22 braccia making the spatial module a double cube 1 x 1 x 2. The inner layer is made of proportional volumetric units whose length intervals are twice that of the aisle sides. The crossing volume is 2 x 2 x 4 or 1x1x2, the same ratios as the aisle module. This is then repeated in the presbytery and transept arms. The nave is 2 x 4 x 8, or 1 x 2 x 4, that is four double cubes. In elevation both walls of the nave are 2:1, the short side being the reciprocal of the long side.[35] The half-round chapels are also 1-M wide, 2-M high but only 1/2-M deep, or 1x2x4, four double

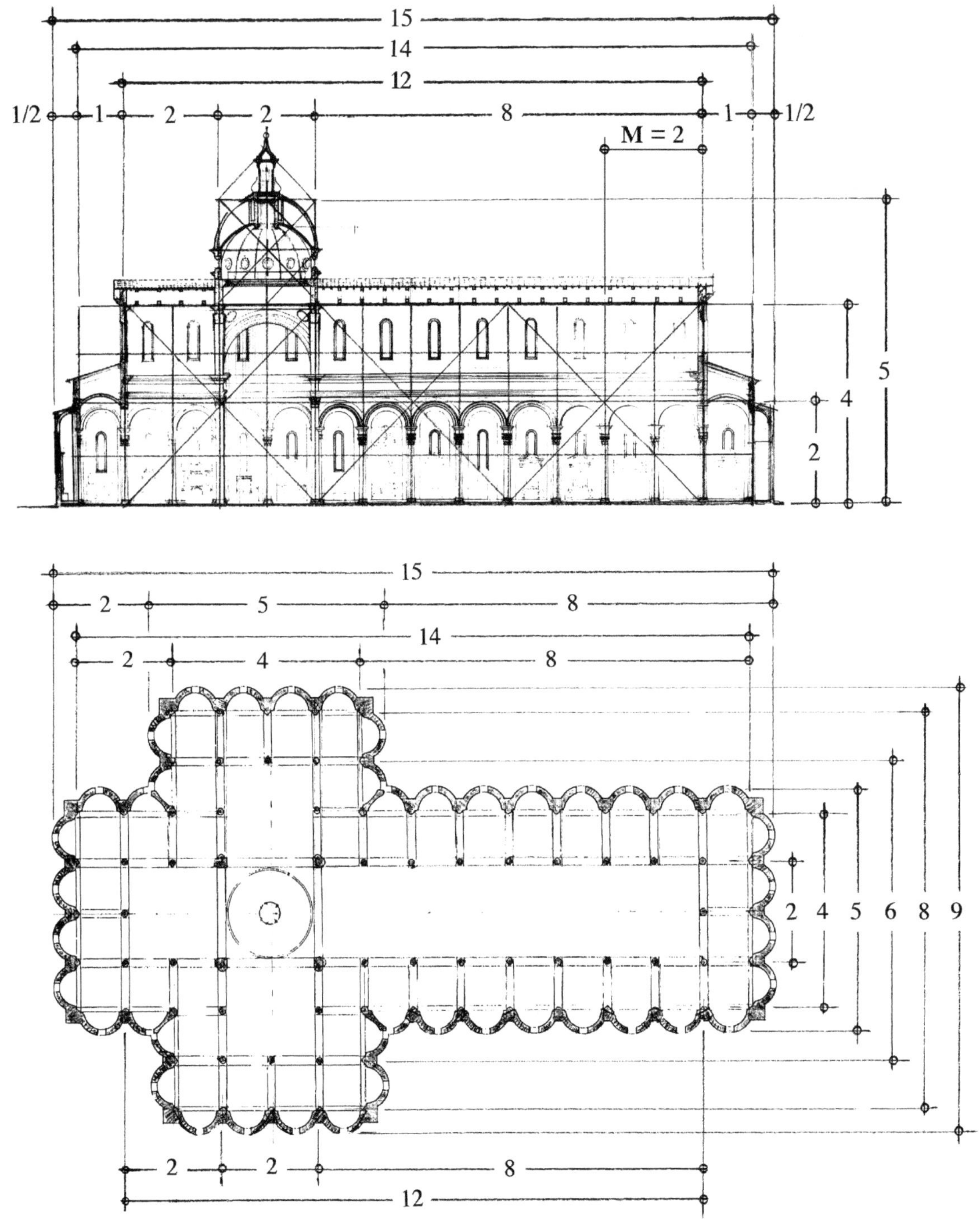

FIGURE 10
Santo Spirito, Brunelleschi, 1445

cubes. Each of the three spatial layers is made out of its own proportional volume, the aisle is primary, the nave is the same ratio but twice the length interval, four times the area and eight times the volume. The third layer, the chapels, is an aisle volume sliced in half.

Brunelleschi's use of the double cube indicates his desire to stay close to unity, as we may see the ontological progression, point, sphere, cube, double cube, half-double cube in the key volumes. In height the arcade spring point is 1.5 M, the apex of the arches is 2 M, the vault would have sprung from 3 M and had its apex at 4 M. The enclosing rectangle of the outermost layer is

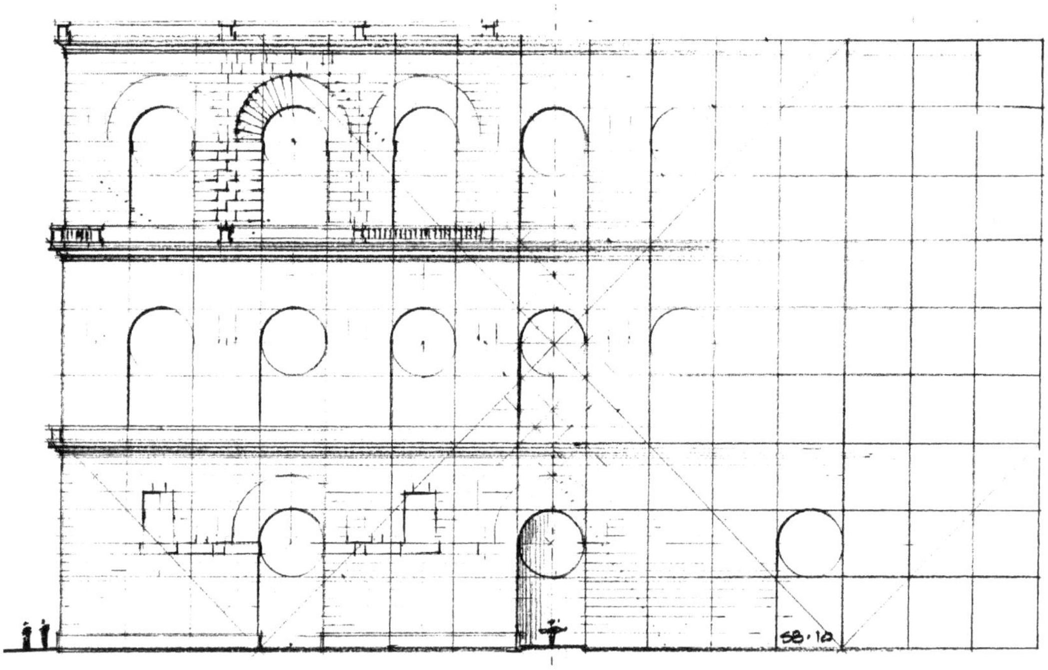

FIGURE 11
Palazzo Pitti, Brunelleschi, 1458

9 x 15 M, 3:5 or Ø. The second layer aisles are enclosed by an 8 x 14 rectangle, a 1:1.75 ratio, or 1:√3. The inner layer, is 6 x 12, 1:2. The nave, crossing and presbytery are 2 x 12 while the crossing and transept arms are 2 x 6. Though the primary theme seems to be doubling and halving, all three of the primary numerical powers are honored in the building's fabric.

The numbers generated in the analysis are .5, 1, 1.5, 2, 4, 5, 6, 8, 9, 12, 14, 15. Musically .5, 1, 2, 4, 8, are octaval notes; 1.5, 6, and 12 are fifths; 1:2:4:8 is a geometric progression of octaves, the even number side of the Platonic Lambda. 6:8:9:12 are the lowest whole numbers that can describe the four consonances of the octave. In an octave from 12 to 24 the 2nd note is 13.5 and the 3rd is 15.19. Although the concept of harmonic ratios in design was not yet fully articulated, its presence may be seen here. In fact, many of the seeds that were to inform Western architecture for the next four hundred years are already present here. Brunelleschi achieves a sense of unity by: use of harmonically related spatial blocks; use of the classical elements; continuity of structure and ornament; and complete continuity of the layering of the entire space, a vision of unity too scary even for his own followers.

The Palazzo Pitti

Designed in 1442, the original project had seven structural bays, **figure 11**. It was not constructed until after Brunelleschi's death, when his design was expanded dramatically into the building of today. Its powerful and direct conception set the tone for palazzo construction in Florence for the rest of the century. Several commentators agree[36] that the facade is designed using a square grid of 6.5 braccia. Although this is a correct analysis, none of them points out that the original seven bay project would have formed a 9 x 15 unit Ø rectangle.

Leon Battista Alberti

In fifteenth-century Italy some educated persons who obtained a harmony in their spiritual and material aspects to the most practically possible extent were called "many-sided men."[37] The "many-sided" personality mixed theoretical and practical knowledge. Rather than just reading Pliny, they also developed a natural history collection; they didn't just translate an ancient play, but also stage-managed the production; and beside all this, they conducted public service careers as judges, negotiators or recorders, not always to their own advantage. "*When this impulse to the highest individual development was combined with a powerful and varied nature, which had mastered all the elements of the culture of the age, then arose the 'all-sided man'— l'uomo universale.*" Such a person towered above the rest. Leon Battista Alberti was an exemplar of such a towering universal man. Thinking of him only as an architect is perhaps too limiting to gain a proper understanding of the emergence of classical architecture in the Renaissance.

There was athletics, especially horsemanship on one hand, rhetoric, music and fine art on the other. Alberti studied law as well as physics and math: "*he acquired every sort of accomplishment and dexterity, cross examining artists, scholars and artisans of all descriptions,... about the secrets of their craft.*" And on top of all this comes Alberti the literary figure. Most important are his books on fine art, which achieved authoritative status almost immediately; as well as prose and poetry, comparable in quality with writings of antiquity, including elegies, ecologs, humorous dinner speeches, even a funeral oration for his dog. While holding Latin in high esteem he encouraged people to write in the vernacular. Alberti had a "*close and mysterious communion with the world*"; to the extent that his friends said he had a gift of prophecy, foretelling a disaster in the d'Este family, the deaths of Popes and an ability "*to be able to read into the countenances and the hearts of men.*"

Battista Alberti, 1404–1472, was an out-of-wedlock son of one of the more important merchant families of Florence. Allied with the Medici, the Alberti came in for repression when the political climate in Florence shifted at the end of the fourteenth century.[38] The family was exiled and Battista was born in Genoa. At 14 he was sent to one of the leading prep schools of the day, the "gymnasium" of Barzizza in Padua, where a number of significant humanist thinkers, writers and teachers were educated, including Palladio's future patron Francesco Barbaro. From 1421–28 Battista attends the University of Bologna studying law, but things do not go as planned. During his first year of study his father dies, followed only months later by his guardian uncle. Worse yet, his father's relatives turn on him, cutting him out of the family estate by virtue of his out-of-wedlock status. Penniless and alienated from his primary supporters Battista suffers what today we would call a "breakdown."

His law studies disrupted for a time, he turns to literature and mathematics. By 1424 he publishes a play in Latin so skillfully written that he could pass it off as the work of an ancient author, Lepidus, also of his own invention. Though in later years Alberti took credit for the work, it was so well done that it was still causing confusion a hundred and fifty years later.[39] At this time Alberti already knew Toscanelli, the "mathematician-engineer-geographer-physician."[40] Alberti would dedicate his book *Intercenales* to him in 1439.[41] Alberti is said to be a good athlete, especially a good horseman. He is outgoing and has many friends, perhaps the most important of whom is his classmate Tommaso Parentucelli who later becomes the humanist Pope Nicholas V.[42]

Alberti graduates from Bologna in 1428 and, perhaps through Parentucelli, gets a spot in the retinue of Cardinal Albergati. In this same year Pope Martin V lifted the exile order on the Albertis[43]. Visiting Florence for the first time he is excited by the work of Donatello and Masaccio and comes under the influence of Brunelleschi, who was in his prime; the dome was almost enclosed, the Old Sacristy was complete, with San Lorenzo beginning, and the Foundling Hospital under way. Alberti's enthusiasm includes perspective and he becomes involved with Brunelleschi and Toscanelli in its continued development; Brunelleschi's demonstration having occurred only three years before.

In 1432 Alberti lands a position as a "Papal abbreviator," essentially a secretary, writing, editing, and translating diplomatic and legal documents; one of about a hundred such people working under the humanist Bishop Molin, right-hand man to Pope Eugenius IV. It is not clear if Alberti was ordained or not, but he was given the modest sinecure of Gangalandi, outside of Florence, thus acquiring an income.

One of the functions of the abbreviators was to translate Latin into vernacular. The Italian language was still developing at the time and Alberti's work with the abbreviators contributes to its development[44]. In Rome, between 1432–34, Alberti writes *On the Family*; experiments with the "camera obscura"[45]; and surveys Rome, creating a map, the "Descriptio Urbis Romae," using a kind of radiating polar projection.

In 1434 he is back in Florence and must have been involved again to some degree with Brunelleschi and Toscanelli. Though he "dabbled" in sculpture and painting[46] it was as a writer that he would make his major contributions. During this period he writes *Della Pittura* in Latin. In 1435, he translates it into Italian at Brunelleschi's request and dedicates the edition to him. Around 1437–38, Alberti writes *Della Statua*, in which he uses a module or "misura" of the foot to proportion the body.[47]

Architecture, Plato and the All-Seeing Eye

Alberti's involvement with architecture begins in 1438 when the pope sends him to the Council of Union, which begins in Ferrara, later moving to Florence, and is overseen by his former patron Cardinal Albergati. Ferrara was run by the d'Este family headed by Leonello with whom Alberti becomes friendly. What their friendship may have involved is indicated by the three books Alberti dedicates to Leonello: the public version of his faux Latin play, *Philodoxeos* (love of knowledge?); *De equo animanti,* on the nature, breeding, riding and racing of horses; and *Theogenius*, on governance. A few years later Alberti dedicates *Ludi matematici,* a collection of math problems and recreations, many involving geometry applied to surveying, to Leonello's brother Meliaduse.[48]

The subject of horses seems to have brought Alberti into contact with architecture. In 1442 Leonello sponsored a competition for an equestrian sculpture of his father, and asked Alberti to be one of the judges. Although there is no documentation extant, commentators assign the design of the sculpture's base to Alberti,[49] **figure 12**. The project uses the "arch upheld by columns" motif. Alberti would develop this motif over the remainder of his architectural career.

Put the base in half-square ABCD, BC = 1. Find points E, Ø of BC and G, Ø^2 of BC, rectangle JBCH, HC is the width of the base, including the "inside" half of the engaged column. EF marks

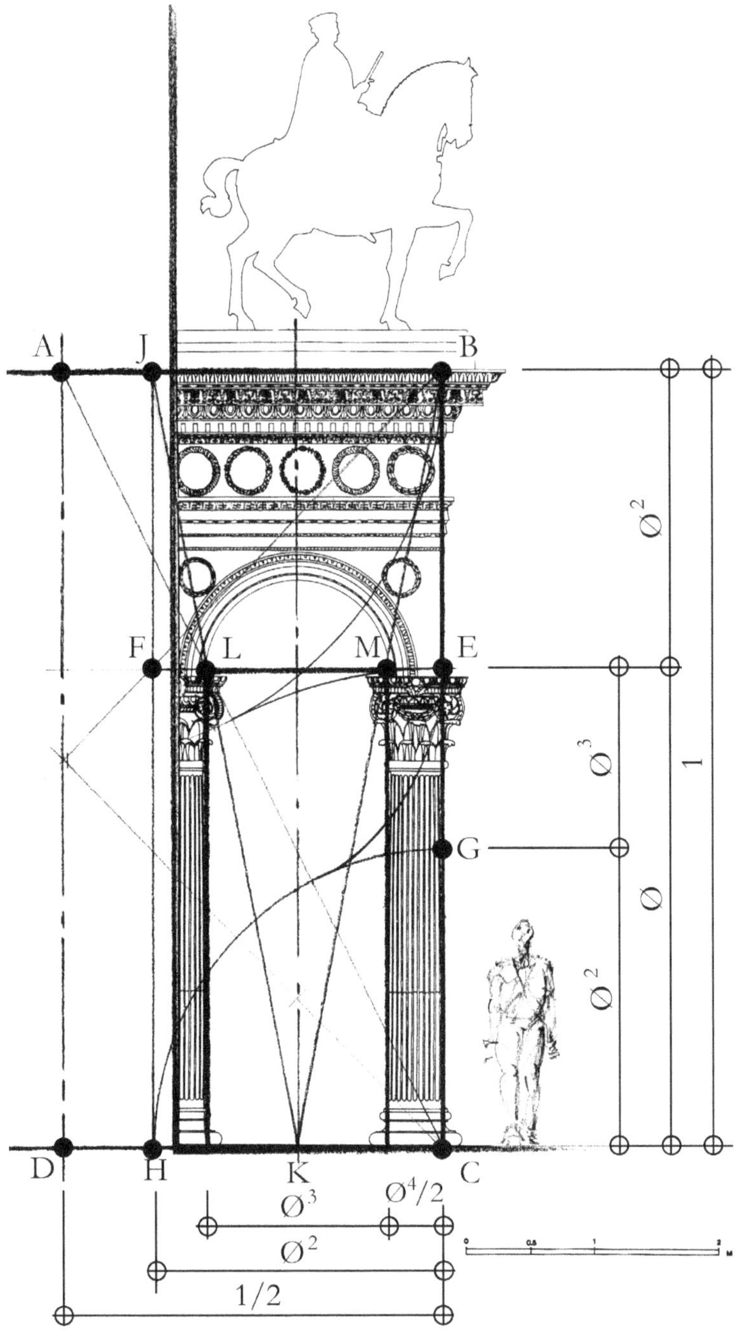

FIGURE 12

Arco del Cavallo, Ferrara, Alberti, 1442

the spring point of the arch. Draw triangle JBK. Where its sides cross EF find points L and M. Because EF is at Ø, LM = $Ø^3$, making EM the column D = $Ø^4/2$. H/D = .618/.073 = 8.47, by later standards a bit chubby for Corinthian.

These activities are going on parallel to the lectures of Plethon and it appears that Alberti encounters Plato and architecture in the same time frame. The book on horses was an outgrowth of his involvement with the sculpture project and the design of the base is approached the same way: it stimulates a literary investigation, planting the seed of *De re aedifactoria.* Alberti returns to Rome in 1443, where he writes *Momus,* a work involving descriptions of an ideal city, and begins work on *De re aedifactoria* while maintaining his position as papal abbreviator.

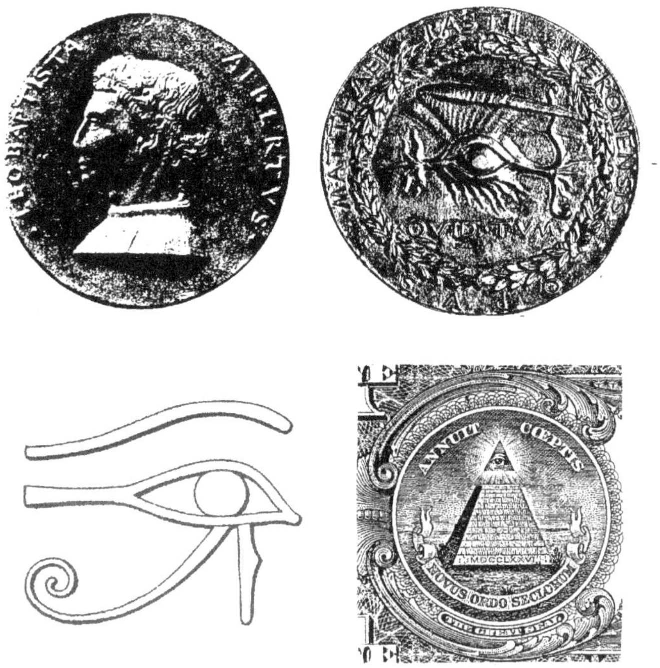

FIGURE 13
The Medal of Alberti

In 1447 Alberti's life takes a further architectural turn. His old school chum Parentucelli is elevated to the papacy as Nicholas V; a position he holds until his death in 1455. Alberti is now in effect an advisor to the pope. Though he is not advanced in formal rank, he is given another modest sinecure. At about the same time he adds the first name Leo, Leon or Leonis and has a personal medallion executed by Matteo de' Pasti of Rimini, **1446, figure 13.** The medal has Alberti's portrait in profile on the front and on the reverse, a very unusual symbol composed of a winged eye below which is the Ciceronean sound bite "Quid Tum," "What next?" These components are encircled by a laurel wreath.

Both the name and the medal might be outward effects of Alberti having joined an exclusive intellectual club, the Roman Academy, centered on the charismatic teacher and scholar Pomponio Leto.[50] The group went further than just academic studies, actively living out classical ideas, including what might be called pseudo-pagan rituals such as celebrating the birthday of Romulus. Each of the members of this club had to select an ancient name. Acquiring a new name is often part of initiatic rituals.

Rykwert[51] sees the winged eye as Alberti's answer to the challenge of human mortality, saying that the eye of the lion maintains its vitality after its death, linking the new name and the image. The winged eye had appeared in Alberti's work *Intercenales,*[52] representing divine omnipresence and omniscience. *Intercenales* was dedicated to Toscanelli and is not yet published in English.

For Wind[53], the symbol of the eye has both positive and negative connotations. It can be the positive all-seeing, life-giving, radiating sun, the organ of divine intelligence and omnipresence. Ficino is said by Wind to have cited the Orphic "infinite eye" as a symbol of divine intelligence.[54] It can also represent the negative "terriblita," a direct confrontation with the divine.

Wind notes that an earlier version of the medal had an eagle, the representative of Zeus, credited with the attributes of sharp vision and speed, similar to those given by Plutarch to the falcon of Horus. Alberti's winged eye is taken as a condensate of the eagle, highlighting its attributes while extending the symbolic range beyond the literal eagle to the ubiquity of the omniscient God. Here the motto Quid Tum takes on the terrible judgmental aspect. Cicero used the phrase to arouse the listener's expectations: If this, what next? The phrase is expanded here to include the threat of an angry God whose judgment can come in the twinkling of an eye.[55]

Gadol[56] cites a passage from a dialog of Alberti's called "Anuli," saying that the eye is *"more powerful than anything else, swifter, and more worthy. It is the first, chief, king; it is like a god of human parts"*; dismissing Wind's "angry God" concept. Gadol sees the winged eye as *"Alberti's symbol of this quasi-divine act of 'rational seeing'* [such as perspective theory], *a mode of imaginative vision which came to encompass all his aesthetic ideas in its gaze."*

י	10	10
יה	5 10	15
יהו	6 5 10	21
יהוה	5 6 5 10	26
		72

FIGURE 14
Gematria of the Tetragrammaton

March writes that Alberti's new name by gematria equals 72[57], the number of the tetragrammaton set up as a tetraktys, **figure 14,** and that Quid Tum equals the second perfect number, 28.

LEO		BAPTISTA		ALBERTUS		
2 5 5		2 1 6 1 9 9 1 1		1 2 2 5 8 1 2 9		
12	+	30	+	30	=	72

QUID		TUM		
7 2 9 4		1 2 3		
22	+	6	=	28

Gematria of Alberti's Name

However there are many possible gematria readings. March chooses here to use only single digits, making 10 and 100 equal to 1. Also note that 28 + 72 = 100, that is, the new monad 10 squared, signifying completion raised to a higher power; and that 28:72 = .388 ≈ $Ø^2$, .382.

The eye in Alberti's medal is referenced by Wind to the Egyptian eye of Horus, which represents both the intelligence and the instantaneous outreach of the divine. Light is assumed to project from the eye, human or divine, and in a sense is a medium of communication with the divine. The first act of the Divinity in Genesis is the projection of a ray of light, and such an eye of divine intelligence adorns every dollar bill in the United States, **figure 13**. Though the motto may be taken today as alluding to the terror of divine justice, a more traditional reading might be as a kind of call to travel the path set out by Diotima, after the inspiration of the initiatic moment, "What next?"

The eye is the organ of light and of its continuing mystery. Alberti's symbol may be seen in the context of the ray, the manifestation of divine intelligence. Its speed is instantaneous because the divine is omnipresent in the animate universe. The ray is instructive and constructive; Alberti built a visual world based on manipulation of its geometry. Thus the symbol may be taken to represent the calling or advancement to art and beauty, the challenge to engage the higher powers involved, the success of the endeavor indicated by the laurel wreath.

Later Life of Alberti

In the late 1440s Alberti becomes Nicolas' architectural and urban design consultant.[58] Two large-scale projects present themselves at this time. First is the conscious rebuilding of Rome as an imperial city in preparation for the jubilee year of 1450. The jubilee ritual symbolizes the renewal of life. Imhotep had overseen the jubilee of the pharaoh Zoser about four thousand years earlier. Second is the rebuilding of the Vatican, a massive undertaking that was to preoccupy the architectural world for the next hundred and fifty years. Another of Alberti's projects at this time was raising part of an ancient Roman boat from the bottom of Lake Nemi.[59]

Among the rebuilding work of the late 1440s is alteration of the San Stefano rotunda with its three Ø related rings and inner ring of 22 columns. Alberti's involvement in these, as in almost all of his architectural projects, is indirect, through "advice" to the actual builders/artisans. He is acting as a consultant in the contemporary sense, an expert who does not perform the work himself. In Alberti's case, however, he is not known to have taken fees for his architectural work. The series of renovation and repair projects are invaluable, enabling him to inspect, measure, and in some cases, de-construct and re-construct ancient and medieval buildings.

De re aedifactoria, begun in 1443 after his adventures in Ferrara, proved more difficult than expected to write (one thing, at least, that it has in common with this book). It was perhaps the interactions with Nicolas that helped to carry it to completion. By 1452 the book circulates widely in manuscript form, influencing a generation of designers, architects and patrons. The first published version with illustrations was by Bartoli in 1546.

Alberti was well known to Federico da Montefeltro, 1422–1482, one of the era's most successful condottieri, who governed Urbino 1444–1482. Federico was well educated and built up a library said to be second only to the Vatican. He was a special devotee of Vitruvius. Ironically, in 1469 he defeated Sigismondo, bringing an end to the construction of Alberti's Tempio Malatestiano in Rimini.

Alberti was a visitor at Federico's court from the late 1440s on. He is said to have advised Federico on the courtyard of the ducal palace, a project carried out later by Luciano Laurana and Francesco di Georgio Martini, assisted by the young Donato Bramante. Another member of the court was mathematician and painter Piero della Francesca. Borsi places them together at various locations in 1447, 1449 and 1451.[60] They would have had much to share, especially on the subject of perspective. Federico is succeeded by Guidobaldo da Montefeltro, who governs from 1482–1508. His court painter was Giovanni Sanzio, father of Raphael Sanzio, 1483–1520. Raphael grew up at court and absorbed the philosophical milieu of Urbino, much as the young Michelangelo grew up at the Medici court under the influence of Ficino's Platonic Academy.

In the 1460s Alberti is moving in the circle of Lorenzo de Medici in Florence. He attends lectures by Ficino[61] and writes for fellow abbreviator Leonardo Datti[62] *De componendis cifris,* a work on cryptography, a field long recognized as an aspect of the magical tradition. Here he uses the cipher wheel concept, later developed further by Giordano Bruno,[63] and the concept of number-letter substitution.

After the death of Nicolas, Alberti continues at the Vatican through two more papal administrations until 1466 when Paul II, 1464–71, liquidates the staff of abbreviators. Paul II was anything but an intellectual and an outspoken opponent of the humanists. A Venetian, rather than a Tuscan, he saw the humanist-heavy abbreviators as politically unreliable. Open dabbling with the classical gods was tolerated, perhaps even encouraged under Nicolas and his immediate successors, but the period of tolerance ends with Paul II. In 1466 Leto is charged with sodomy, but not convicted. In 1468, Paul II has the Academy leadership, not including Alberti, arrested for heresy and republican political conspiracy.[64] Though they are eventually pardoned, the Academy essentially ceases.

Alberti was not caught up in the scandals of the Academy, but he clearly was out of favor after 1466. Perhaps through the intercession of his patrons, he was still consulted by Paul II and is said to have influenced the design of his personal residence, the Palazzo Venezia in Rome. Though Alberti still travels a good deal, Rome remains his home base for the remaining eight years of his life.

It may said that Brunelleschi approached architecture from below: a master artisan with skills that brought him to the attention of the powerful. Alberti approached from above: the son of a governing family who, but for certain disadvantages, would himself have governed. Instead, he is forced by circumstances to trade on his intellectual skills and comes to advise those who actually govern, among whom he appears to have moved very smoothly. Where Brunelleschi would himself rig the winch to lift the stone, Alberti would issue instructions by letter from Rome. However, through Alberti many things flowed. If we see Renaissance architecture as a great tree growing upward, opening to the sun, Brunelleschi is certainly one of its roots; but Alberti is its trunk, from which many branches will emerge. The earth in which this great tree grows and draws its vitality is the ancient esoteric tradition.

Alberti on Beauty, Number and Proportion

Alberti is rather cautious on the subject of beauty. In fact he never tells us what it ultimately is. His famous definition that beauty is, "a state of harmony among the elements of a design or object such that nothing could be altered except to the detriment of that harmony,"[65] is essentially an exoteric definition, gauged by observation of an object. It tells us when an object achieves beauty but not what beauty is. What is clear in *De re Aedifactoria* is that beauty is essential to architecture. To Alberti the search for beauty is a "holy matter." It will take everything we've got to achieve it, and in any event its achievement is rare.

Paraphrasing Alberti's discussion: Everyone is attracted to beauty and is averse to the ugly or deformed. When we look at the works of the gods (plural) we admire the beauty of their work rather than its utility. Nature, he exclaims, basks in "a daily orgy of beauty."[66] People desire and protect beautiful buildings; while a building without beauty is just a pile of stones.[67] The ancients used beauty in architecture to substantiate the stature of the state.[68]

Beauty is an "inherent property" suffused all through the body of the beautiful object.[69] Beauty is achieved through art, and art requires a theory.[70] Beauty may be produced by three factors: 1) invention and intellect, 2) the hand of the artisan, or 3) imbued naturally. Intellect includes choice, distribution, and arrangement, giving the work dignity; craft includes laying, joining, trimming, polishing, etc., giving grace; nature includes weight, density, purity, durability, causing admiration.[71]

Alberti lists six "linements," that is, branches or components of architectural theory[72]: 1. locality (location, neighborhood or region), 2. area (site or room, footprint), 3. compartition (internal division, size and placement of elements), 4. wall (structure), 5. roof (enclosure), and 6. opening [penetration of enclosure]. These aspects of "theoria" are juxtaposed to a "materia" consisting of materials and construction techniques. However, these dyadically opposed aspects are united by the "hand and skills of the artisan." Four stages may be seen here; within the single subject of architecture there is a mental, noetic aspect and a material aspect. These dyadic opposites within unity are reunited by the triadic hand of the artificer, like nous and hule united by psyche. This results in the beautiful, complete, tetradic, material object.

Of most concern here is compartition. By compartition Alberti means what Vitruvius called "arrangement"; relating the elements so that they are harmonious to each other and to the whole, thus contributing to the sense of unity.[73] Alberti sees design, in effect, as drawing on a two-dimensional structural surface, the wall. The key design activity is creating a pattern of regular subdivisions, "close-fitting rectangles," or "compartments." These will give the size and placement of the elements. By "close fitting rectangles" Alberti is most likely referring to geometrical methods of design used to produce an "organic" effect, similar to Vitruvian symmetria and eurhythmy.

Surely we're on the trail of beauty here because Alberti tells us that compartition will take "all the inventive power, skill, and experience of the designer"[74]; and if it is not properly achieved the work will "lose all dignity."[75] If we are successful, the work will have an "organic" effect.[76] It is significant that in the earliest modern treatise on architecture this concept of the organic appears, indicating the age and substance of this essentially analogic idea.

To achieve proper compartition, Alberti invokes the image of a mystery, writing that we seek an entity that is the basic constituent of beauty and which "springs from every rule of beauty." Whatever that entity is, it is 1) drawn from the number and nature of each part, 2) imparted to each part by sure and constant method, and 3) handled so as to bond the elements into a single body by a consistent agreement and sympathy, achieving a sense of unity. To meet these criteria the entity must share some aspect ("force or juice") of each element, otherwise unity could not be achieved. Finding such an entity is neither obvious nor straightforward in any kind of work, but is "most ambiguous and involved" here because buildings are composed of many parts. Decisions about how to achieve beauty are not to be made on the basis of "mere fancy" of the designer but through the "workings of a reasoning faculty inborn of mind"; though he will not discuss how this works.[77]

As in Vitruvius,[78] the beautiful building is likened to an organic body. In this, art must imitate nature. Parts of the beautiful body have differences between them. In fact it is through their differences that we observe the entity that unites them. You may prefer one variant to another but they all have some attraction. What makes one person prefer one to the other, Alberti declines to inquire.[79]

Just as Vitruvius calls for symmetria (a pattern of proportion) to lead to eurhythmy (good movement), Alberti sees proper compartition as necessary to achieve what he calls "concinnitas." This is the entity sought earlier. Concinnitas composes the separate parts according to some "precise rule" so that they appear to correspond to each other or have "togetherness," the sense of unity. Concinnitas is based on number, outline and position.[80]

Concinnitas is recognized by the mind through the senses. We naturally desire the best, and experience it as pleasure.[81] Concinnitas is "the spouse of the soul and reason," running through human life and governance, it molds the whole of nature. Without concinnitas the "critical sympathy" of the parts would be lost. Alberti now offers another exoteric definition of beauty: it is a form of sympathy and consonance of the parts of a body, according to number, outline and position, governed by concinnitas. The achievement of concinnitas is the object of the art of building, the source of a building's dignity, charm, authority, and value.[82] The road to beauty is through concinnitas.

We have now been told out loud: the goal of the art of building is the attainment of beauty. The references to "dignity, charm and sympathy" throughout this discussion echo these terms as used in the Western magical tradition, and "consonance" in this context may be taken as a sympathetic or analogic concept.

By "outline" Alberti means the relation between the ratios of "areas," the floor and the walls, that is, between the length, width and height. The outline could be of walls or parts of walls.[83] The "precise rule" is expressed in number. By "number" Alberti does not mean quantitative or mathematical but qualitative number, number as symbol and as harmonic ratio.[84] Alberti now provides a brief summary of what is known as the "theology of arithmetic"; the symbolic references for the first ten numbers.[85]

The "precise rule" is rooted in music. It will be a mimesis of natural musical harmony. Alberti states his agreement with Pythagoras: nature is self-consistent, it can be modeled by number.[86] This profound Pythagorean idea, known as the "mathematica," is one of the fundamental concepts of the West; but remember, Alberti has just given us a lesson in qualitative rather than mathematical number. Now Alberti makes the musical analogy[87]: the same numbers that give rise to concinnitas in music also do so visually.[88]

Architects need to know three aspects of music: 1) harmonic string length ratios, 2) the three means, and 3) the trans-rational ratios. Alberti defines harmony as "the consonance of sounds pleasant to the ears." The ancients observed numerical ratios of string lengths that gave consonant sounds. Taking the fundamental, 1:1, as axiomatic, Alberti lists the following consonances:

Name	Fractional Ratio	Whole Number Ratio	Note
Diatesseron or sesquitertia	1&1/3:1	4:3	4th note
Diapente or sesquialtera	1&1/2:1	3:2	5th note
Diapason or double		2:1	octave
Diapason–diapente or triple		3:1	octave and fifth
Disdiapason or quadruple		4:1	two octaves
Tonus or sesquioctavus	1&1/8:1	9:8	whole tone

Alberti has used the numbers 1, 2, 3, and 4; but does not mention that $3/2 \div 4/3 = 9/8$.[89]

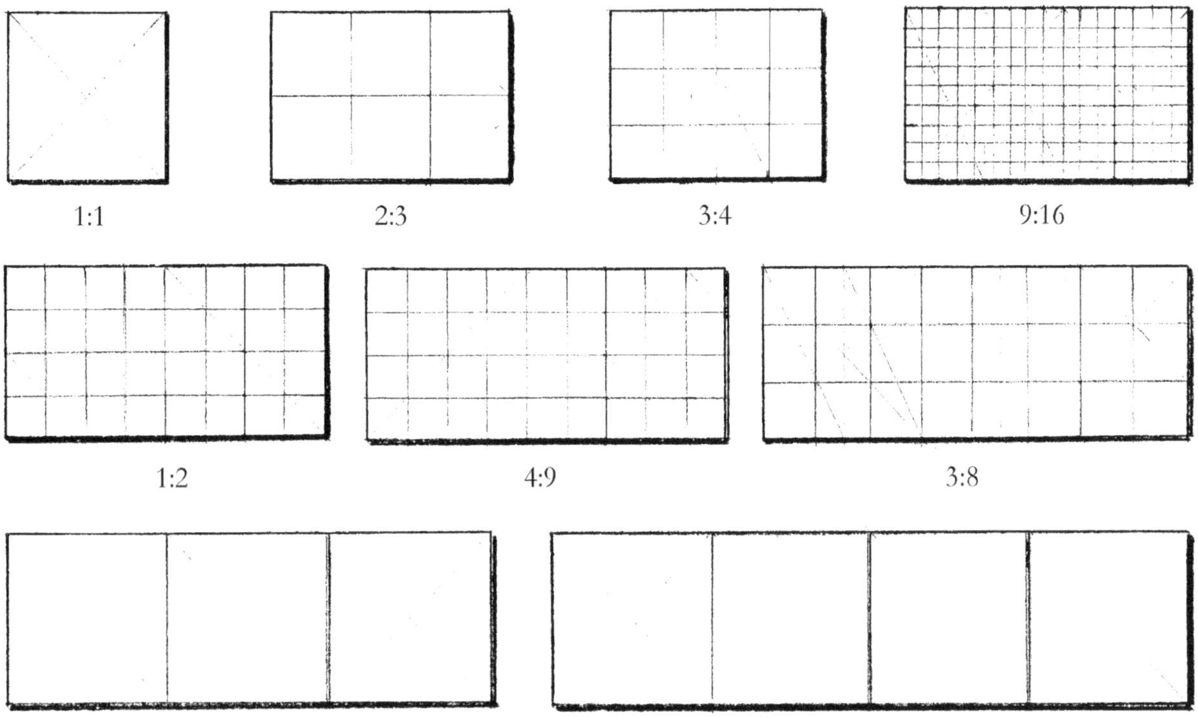

FIGURE 15 – *Alberti's Family of Plan Rectangles*

From these Alberti builds up a family of simple and compound rectangles classified as short, intermediate, and long, **figure 15.**[90] The last column in the table below refers to the combination of musical intervals that give the ratio in the second column; for example, 6/4 + 9/6 = 54/24 = 9/4.

Short			
First note	1:1	fundamental	
Sesquitertia	4:3	4th note	
Sesquialtera	3:2	5th note	
Intermediate			
Double sesquitertia	16:9	two 4ths	12:9 + 16:12
Double	2:1	octave, or 5th + 4th	3:2 + 4:3
Double sesquialtera	9:4	two 5ths	6:4 + 9:6
Long			
Double plus sesquitertia	8:3	octave + 4th	6:3 + 8:6
Double plus sesquialtera	3:1	octave + 5th	2:1 + 3:2
Double plus double	4:1	two octaves	2:1 + 4:2
		octave + 5th + 4th	2:1 + 3:2 + 4:3

Heights must be proportional to length and width. For any plan rectangle, but particularly the short ones, heights may be found by the three means — arithmetic, geometric and harmonic, which in Plato's *Timaeus* give rise to the octave itself.[91] If a room is 2:1, octaval, in plan it may have a range of "proportional" or "musical" ratios for its height. The 5th note gives H=1.5, the arithmetic mean; the 4th note gives 1.33, the harmonic mean. The geometric mean gives $\sqrt{3} = 1.732$.[92]

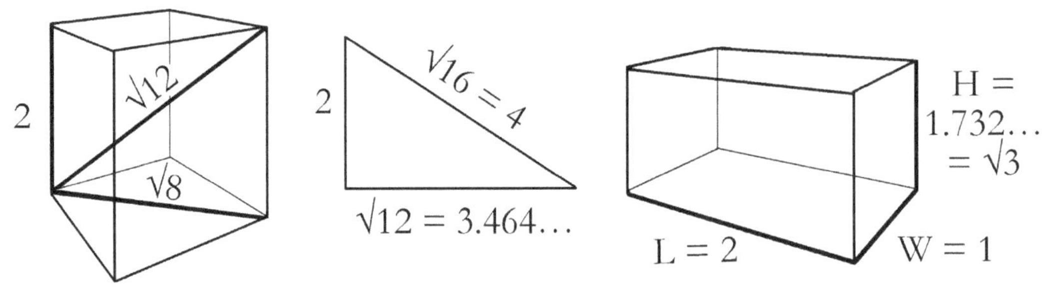

FIGURE 16
Trans-rational Heights for Rooms

Another method of elevating areas is the use of the trans-rational ratios. Alberti begins with the Pythagorean view that one is not a number but the wellspring of number. As $1^3 = 1$, the cube is consecrated to the Godhead; he cites the Vitruvian reference to cubic stability. Two is perhaps the first number. Alberti sets up a square whose side = 2. Its diagonal = $\sqrt{(2^2 + 2^2)} = \sqrt{8}$. The diagonal of a cube with side of 2 = $\sqrt{12}$, **figure 16.** Alberti now sets up a right triangle whose sides are 2 (the side of the cube) and $\sqrt{12}$ (the diagonal of the cube) giving a hypotenuse = $\sqrt{16}$ = 4. The longest and shortest intervals will give the plan and the intermediate interval the height. Thus, we have a 4:2 plan and a height of $\sqrt{12}$ = 3.46; or 2:1:1.732, the geometric mean in the above example. But, Alberti adds, these intervals may be modified to suit the design.[93]

FOOTPRINTS OF THE TEMPLE

Alberti's book has a large literary component; he has clearly read all of the most prominent Roman authors. In these references, when it comes to the "temple," he often speaks of the divinity in plural terms.[94] His frank and open discussion of the ancient pagan divinities gives some idea of the cultural and spiritual milieu of Renaissance Florence and Rome. Alberti writes[95] that Janus, Roman god of doorways, Ovid's celestial janitor, was the first to build a temple in Italy. As the god of doorways, Janus had two faces, one facing in and the other facing out. Wind associates Janus with the Mysteries, likening initiation to a door or gateway, citing the couplet:[96]

He that concealed things will find
Must look before him and behind.

Thus the first divinity cited by Alberti is intimately linked to initiatic process and esoteric vision.

Some say no temple buildings are needed; that the earth, sky, sun and sea are a kind of ultimate temple. But if one is to build, Alberti gives three kinds of geometrical plans: circular, rectangular, and polygonal, **figure 17.**[97] Both Leoni and Wittkower[98] use the word "square" but Rykwert uses the more ambiguous "quadrangle"; and Alberti does not recommend the square for use in plans, though he actually uses it in some of his church designs.

Wittkower cites nine geometrical plan types for the temple. The first form is, 1) the circle. It prompts Alberti to remark,[99] "*Nature delights primarily in the circle. Need I mention the earth, the*

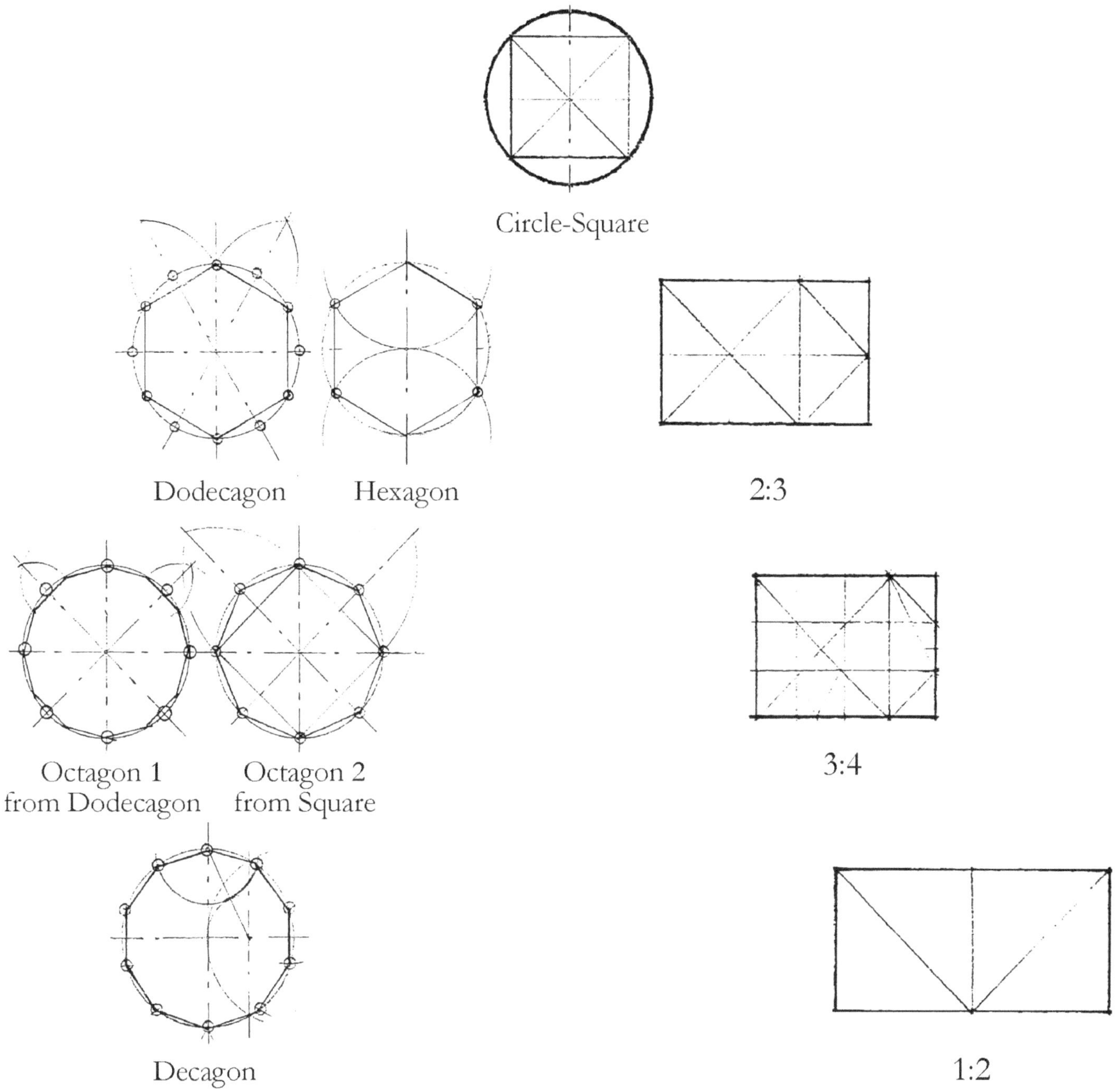

FIGURE 17
Alberti's Geometry of the Temple Plan

stars, the animals, and their nests, all of which she has made circular?" Next in line would normally be 2) the square, but this is only admitted provisionally. Next in order of dignification is 3) the hexagon, citing the beehive. Alberti now enumerates three rectangles, 4) 3:2, 5) 4:3, and 6) 2:1.

Lastly are three regular polygons, 7) the octagon with eight sides, 8) the decagon with ten sides, and 9) the dodecagon with twelve sides. For these three Alberti goes further, giving methods of construction. Beginning with the circle, strike off the radius on the circumference to create the hexagon. The dodecagon can be drawn by doubling the hexagon, or as Alberti puts it, finding the center of the side, drawing a line from the center through that point to the circumference. But interestingly he notes that from the dodecagon can be derived the octagon and the square. These polygons may be said to represent the threefold and fourfold powers and are transformationally related, that is to say, they transform into one another. The decagon introduces the fivefold powers. Alberti's construction of this polygon is a "golden section derivative" in that the side of the decagon is Ø of the radius of its circumscribed circle.[100]

March[101] sees a group of seven — 1) circle, 2) hexagon, 3) octagon, 4) decagon, 5) 4:3., 6) 3:2, 7) 2:1, suggesting a lambda arrangement:

circle
hexagon 4:3
octagon 3:2
decagon 2:1

Alberti gives the circle prime importance. After the circle, and subordinate to it, are the regular polygons. Among these is the square, which is the origin of the elongated rectangles. The four rectangles with side ratios of 1:1, 3:2, 4:3, and 2:1 comprise the positions of the Pythagorean tetrachord; the fundamental, fifth, fourth and octave. The polygons are a transformational family: triangle to hexagon to dodecagon, square to octagon, or dodecagon back to octagon to square; the triangle and square can also transform into the dodecagon.

The Centrally Planned Church vs. the Linear Church

Alberti's use of the regular polygons as the primary forms for the temple, and the linear or rectilinear plans as secondary, precipitates a lengthy debate in the Renaissance on the "best" planning principles for churches.[102] Renaissance artists operated on the assumption that the cosmos is a harmonically related structure that could be expressed mathematically. They were guided and supported by Plato, the later ancient Platonists, and early Christian theologians such as Augustine. The soul of the human being, to act as an intermediary mechanism between matter and spirit, must also be mathematically intelligible. Alberti maintains that we have an "inborn sense" of this harmony. We can perceive it with the senses because of its affinity with the soul. Thus if a church is built in accord with these harmonies we react intuitively, without, or prior to, rational analysis. Our inner sense tells us that the building partakes of those vital forces that form matter and bind the universe together. Rituals, Wittkower writes, are of little value if the sacred space does not have "correct proportions." It does not matter that the exact mathematical relationships are not manifest to the physical eye.

The circle, as the most perfect geometrical figure, was assigned special importance. Wittkower cites Nicolaus Cusanus (Nicholas of Cusa, 1401–1464) as having used a "pseudo-hermetic formula" to visualize the divine through the mathematical symbol of the circle and its center; the least tangible and at the same time the most perfect geometrical figure. Cusanus was a mathematician, Platonist, cardinal at the papal court of Pius II in 1458,[103] and certainly an acquaintance of Alberti. Cusanus was preoccupied with attempting to square the circle.[104]

Wittkower[105] maintains that Renaissance architects such as Alberti, di Georgio, Cesariano, and Palladio were well aware of such Platonic views, as they say in their writings. While they may not have been personally involved with esoteric philosophical speculation, they moved in a milieu saturated with such ideas "*which had spread quickly and irresistibly*" during the fifteenth century. This geometrical vision goes back to the Orphic poets, to Plato who utilized it in the *Timaeus*, to Plotinus; through him to Pseudo-Dionysius the Areopagite, and to the mystical authors of the medieval era, perhaps including the School of Chartres. Wittkower says that the centrally planned church took possession of the fifteenth-century architectural imagination because the artists developed a "new scientific approach" to the observation and modeling of nature: "*the mathematical interpretation of all matter.*" They regarded architecture as a mathematical science constructed of monadic modular units. They believed that they could reveal those harmonies through their reproduction in matter using geometric forms, including perspective.

The complex of ideas including the correspondence of microcosm and macrocosm; the harmonic structure of the cosmos; and the comprehension of the divine through the symbols of center, circle, and sphere, which were widespread in antiquity and the Middle Ages, were reborn or reintegrated in the Renaissance concept of the centrally planned church. The physical building was the materialization of intelligible mathematical symbols. The relationship was immediately and intuitively perceptible. This kind of architecture had strict geometry, *equipoise of its harmonic order,* formal serenity, and made use of the sphere, which mimed and revealed the perfection of the divine.

This aesthetic shift toward the centrally planned church indicates a shift in religious feeling more telling than an intellectual shift. The Renaissance continued to use ancient and medieval symbols, but with a change in emphasis, "*Christ as the essence of perfection and harmony superseded Him who had suffered on the Cross for humanity; The Pantocrator replaced the Man of Sorrows.*" Here is the triumph and tragedy of the era: the uniforming, homogenizing of space and the use of the pure geometrical form had "mathematized" space. While giving one a sense of control and having emerged from an esoteric viewpoint, this mathemetizing was also the opening wedge to devitalizing space, which was to take place in the Enlightenment era.

Alberti's Architectural Projects

Alberti's architectural work is always restrained, dignified and thoughtful. The works should be seen in the context of his literary studies. His intellectual influence was greater than that of his built work. His architectural work suffered from political and economic instabilities; he did not live to see the completion of any of his major projects. His early works are archetypal rather than specifically imitative. His middle-period designs are a search to integrate antique Vitruvian concepts with the actual building process of his day. His late work demonstrates a new integration of the ancient with the contemporary.

San Francesco, Rimini

Alberti's design for S. Francesco, aka the Tempio Malatestiano, c.1450, **figure 18,** applies a new classical layer to an existing Gothic building. The Tempio fronts on the same urban square as the first-century BC Arch of Augustus, and Alberti's design is related to it in the sense that it is a triumphful arch motif "grafted" onto a wall.

The facade is a composition guided by a series of √2-related squares, **figure 18a.**[106] Within the enclosing square, ABCD, the first story is two squares side by side, half the size of the enclosing square, HNGD and NFCG. The second story is a third square of the same size, PQRS. A fourth square, JKLM, is positioned halfway up the center bay. The imposts on both stories are related at the level of the half-square. The face-to-face distance of the interior columns equals their height, as Alberti suggests for the monumental arch.[107] The central opening is at the 5/8ths point, or Ø, making the opening 2/8ths wide and 3/8ths high. The pier is 1/8th wide and the side arch about 1/8th by 2/8ths. Alberti could have started with the geometrical figure of the astrological chart, perhaps learned from Toscanelli, and adjusted it as needed to fit over the existing building.

In the reconstruction, **figure 18b,** the enclosing square is divided into 8. The height of the lower floor is divided into 19. The pedestal including the sub-plinth is 4 units, the column is 12.5 and the entablature is 2.5. The outer columns are adjusted outward from the geometrical. Alberti may have done this to increase the width of the side arch, perhaps to 6/10ths from 5/10ths of the center arch. With the greatest respect this opportunity is taken to suggest a possible completion of the second story, based on the medal of Sigismundo Malatesta, made by Alberti's representative on the project, Matteo de' Pasti. A side scroll is suggested by Borsi,[108] and here is taken from Santa Maria Novella.

Santa Maria Novella, Florence

The body of the church dates from the thirteenth century. Alberti's work began in 1448 and continued to 1470, with the design dating from the late 1450s.[109] Alberti is associated only with the facade. He was limited by existing openings, particularly the side doors and central rose window, which had to be retained.[110] The facade is done in a Florentine medieval panel style, similar to San Miniato al Monte, which Alberti admired,[111] as well as the cathedral and baptistery. Alberti's use of this medieval system reveals two aspects of his architecture. First, Alberti was more flexible and synthetic than we might think today; second, that traditional practices were still vital and current in mid-fifteenth-century Florence.

The geometry, **figure 19**, is similar to S. Francesco, Rimini, an enclosing square ABCD divided into the √2 progression pattern, with the first story a double square, EFCD and the second story in a single same-size square placed in the center, GHJK. In this analysis the enclosing square ABCD is raised slightly off the ground to the level of the finish floor.

The top of the entablature of the first story is at $Ø^2$ of BC, point L; the top of the attic is at the half-point, line EF, making its height $Ø^3/2$ or .158. The column height is 1/3 of the enclosing square, point M. The entablature depth, LM, is .382 - .333 = .049, $Ø^5/2$ = .045, 1/24th = .042.

The top of the upper-story cornice is at the √2/2 point, N, of HJ. The centers of the inner columns of the tetrastyle are at the same point on both floors, point P, the √2/2 point of GH. The Ø point, Q, of AB comes very close to this; Ø being .618 and the √2/2 point of the upper square is .5 x .707 = .352 +.25 (interval HB) = .602. The curvilinear volutes reinforce the 45° lines pointing to the apex of the pediment while bonding the upper and lower floors. Alberti may have used a grid of 24 x 24 as .602 x 24 = 14.5, marking the center of the inner columns, points P and Q.

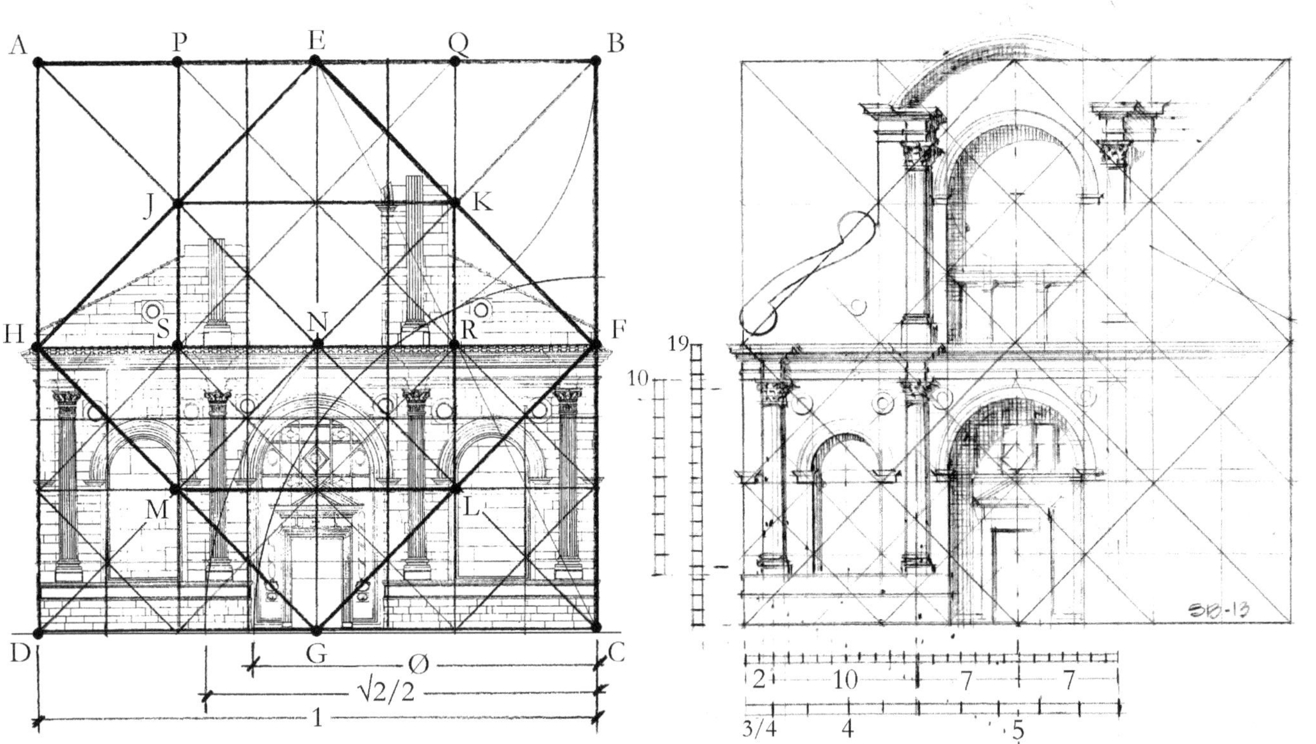

18a - San Francesco, Analysis

18b - San Francesco, Reconstruction

FIGURE 18a-b

San Francesco, Rimini, Alberti, c.1450

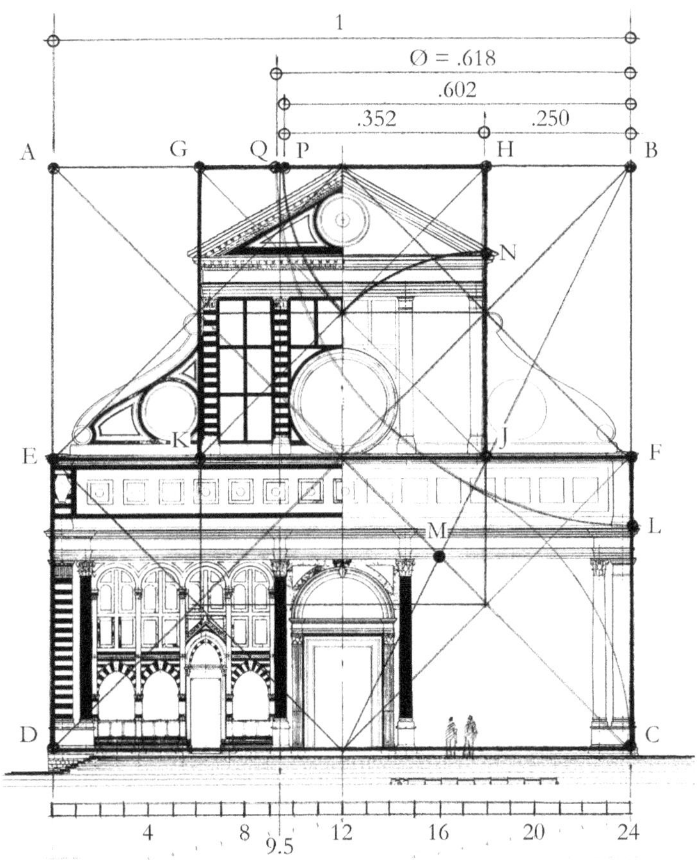

FIGURE 19

Santa Maria Novella, Alberti, c.1450

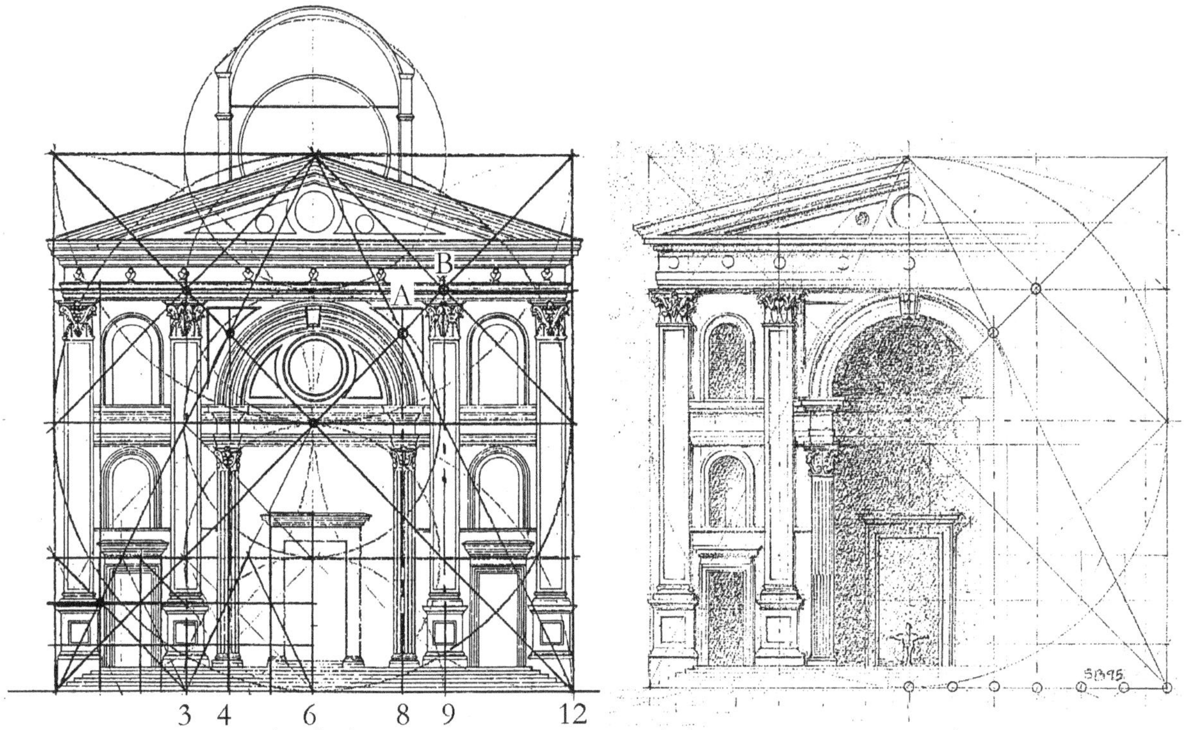

FIGURE 20
Sant'Andrea, Mantua, Alberti

SANT'ANDREA, MANTUA, 1470

Although the building was constructed entirely after Alberti's death, it is his most complete facade; designed in 1457, **figure 20**. Work was carried on by Luca Fancelli until 1485.[112] The interior was not completed until the eighteenth century and the decoration in the nineteenth. The nave was built to Alberti's plan, but the transept and apse were built after Fancelli's time.

Wittkower[113] sees in the facade an unclassical merger of the temple portico with the triumphal arch, built in the vocabulary of a wall architecture. In this last phase of his career Alberti *"used classical architecture as a storehouse which supplied him with material for free and subjective planning."* Gadol[114] characterizes Alberti's aesthetic outlook in Neoplatonic terms. Art is Aristotelian imitation of nature, "the greatest artist of all," and Alberti equates God with nature more than once in *De re aedefictoria.* But architecture is not the literal mimesis of the visible shapes of nature as in painting and sculpture but the imitation of the formative patterns of nature. Just as the divinity creates the natural world through the application of logos, the architect creates the building as microcosm by applying similar patterns. This ability to produce a microcosm recapitulates the role of Plato's demiurge, elevating the act of design.

The elevation may be enclosed in a square. Applying the same pattern as in previous facades and adding the semi-diagonals gives the 1/3rd and 1/4th points. This also suggests a 12 x12 grid. The 1/4 points position the inner pilasters and the 1/3 points position the central arch. In the reconstruction the tops of the columns are set exactly at the 3/4 point, but the analysis indicates that they are slightly below it. This lowers the pediment a bit, but it could have been made to penetrate the top of the square.

Looking at the compartition of the vertical centerlines we have the central arch 1/3 x 3/4 or 4:9. The central bay of the major order is 1/2 x 3/4 = 6:9 or 2:3. The side bays are 1/4 x 3/4 or 1:3. The four major horizontal divisions, the three stories, and the entablature and pediment are each 12 x 3 or 4:1. All these are among Alberti's recommended ratios. These are not literally rendered but form a kind of intellectual armature on which the "materia" of the building is developed.

Bramante

Donato Bramante, 1444–1514, was born in a small town near Urbino, Italy, and trained as a painter, although his major contribution was in architecture. Bramante's work has a sense of balance and stability, almost a serenity, that was achieved through a kind of intellectual clarity. His architecture raised the classical game a couple of notches beyond the level of Brunelleschi and Alberti. In his twenties he participated in the addition of a classical courtyard to the Ducal Palace built during the 1460s that was designed by the architect Luciano Laurana.[115]

Figure 21 – *Montefeltro Altarpiece, Piero della Francesca, 1472*

During his time in Urbino, Bramante was associated with Piero della Francesca, 1415–1492. Piero is a significant link in the transmission of geometrical wisdom in the arts from the Middle Ages into the Renaissance. Piero is a painter whose work is highly architectonic and utilizes dramatic perspective views to focus compositions. **Figure 21** is an altarpiece said to be commissioned by Federico da Montefeltro, Duke of Urbino, in 1472, to commemorate the birth of his son, Guidobaldo[116] Federico is seen kneeling in armor in the foreground. The Madonna is his wife Battista Sforza, and the Divine Child is their son Guidobaldo. The apse behind the Madonna is in a ratio slightly higher than 2:3. The vanishing point is the Madonna's third eye.

The apse of the niche is crowned by an exquisite shell from the apex of which is suspended an ostrich egg. The shell is an attribute of Venus. It may allude here to spiritual or symbolic birth without intercourse; as Aphrodite was not born in the usual way but rose from the foam of the sea and rode to land on a shell. A section through a shell is a geometrically determinable spiral. The egg is richly symbolic of origins and physical birth, at least as far back as the Orphics. The ostrich was a heraldic symbol of the Montefeltro family.[117]

Piero was a mathematician who published books on arithmetic, solid geometry and perspective. What effect Piero had on Bramante is not clear, but mastery of perspective geometry is a key to Bramante's later architecture.

Piero's best-known protégé was the mysterious mathematician Luca Pacioli, 1446–1517, known as Fra Pacioli.[118] In 1470, when Pacioli is 24, he is the houseguest of Alberti in Rome. He later publishes a mathematical compendium, *The Summa ...*, in 1494, including much that he learned from Piero. In 1498, Pacioli publishes a book on the Golden Section, called *The*

FIGURE 22
Fra Pacioli, attributed to Barbari, 1495

FIGURE 23
San Satiro, Milan, 1482, Trompe l'oeil Apse, Bramante

Divine Proportion, with illustrations by Leonardo da Vinci, written in Milan. One suspects that it is through Pacioli that Leonardo began to develop the insight to illustrate the Vitruvian Man.

In the *Divine Proportion,* Pacioli presents five ways that the Golden Section is like the Divinity[119]: 1) like God, it is unique; 2) as the Holy trinity is one substance in three persons, it is one single proportion in three terms; 3) as God cannot be defined in words, it cannot be expressed by any intelligible number or rational quantity but is always occult and secret and is called by the mathematicians "transcendental"; 4) like God, it is always similar to itself; 5)phi is the key to constructing the dodecahedron, the Platonic solid that contains the physical cosmos, putting it nearest to the Divinity. In a famous portrait, **figure 22** (above), Pacioli is depicted with numerous mathematical symbols and is accompanied by a young man who may be the very same Guidobaldo da Montefeltro of Piero's painting. Later as Duke of Urbino, Guidobaldo employed the father of Raphael as his court painter.

In 1474 at age thirty Bramante goes to Milan where he begins his independent architectural career with several small churches. This brings him to the attention of Duke Ludovico Sforza who gives him several large commissions in Milan, including rebuilding the choir of Santa Maria presso San Satiro for which Bramante creates a trompe l'oeil apse, 1482–1486, **figure 23,** which essentially recapitulates Piero's altarpiece. In 1499 the French occupy Milan, forcing out Bramante, Pacioli and da Vinci. Bramante relocates to Rome where he works with Cardinal della Rovere, soon to become Pope Julius II.

In 1502, Julius commissions Bramante's tour-de-force signature piece of Renaissance architecture, the Tempietto of San Pietro in Montorio, **figure 24a.** Geometrical analysis indicates a $\sqrt{2}$ construction. In plan the outer colonnade is within square ABCD. The cylinder is within JKLM, and the wall thickness is given by NPQR. The same geometrical net is applied to the elevation. Centerline HF is the center of the entablature. The spring line of the dome is point E.

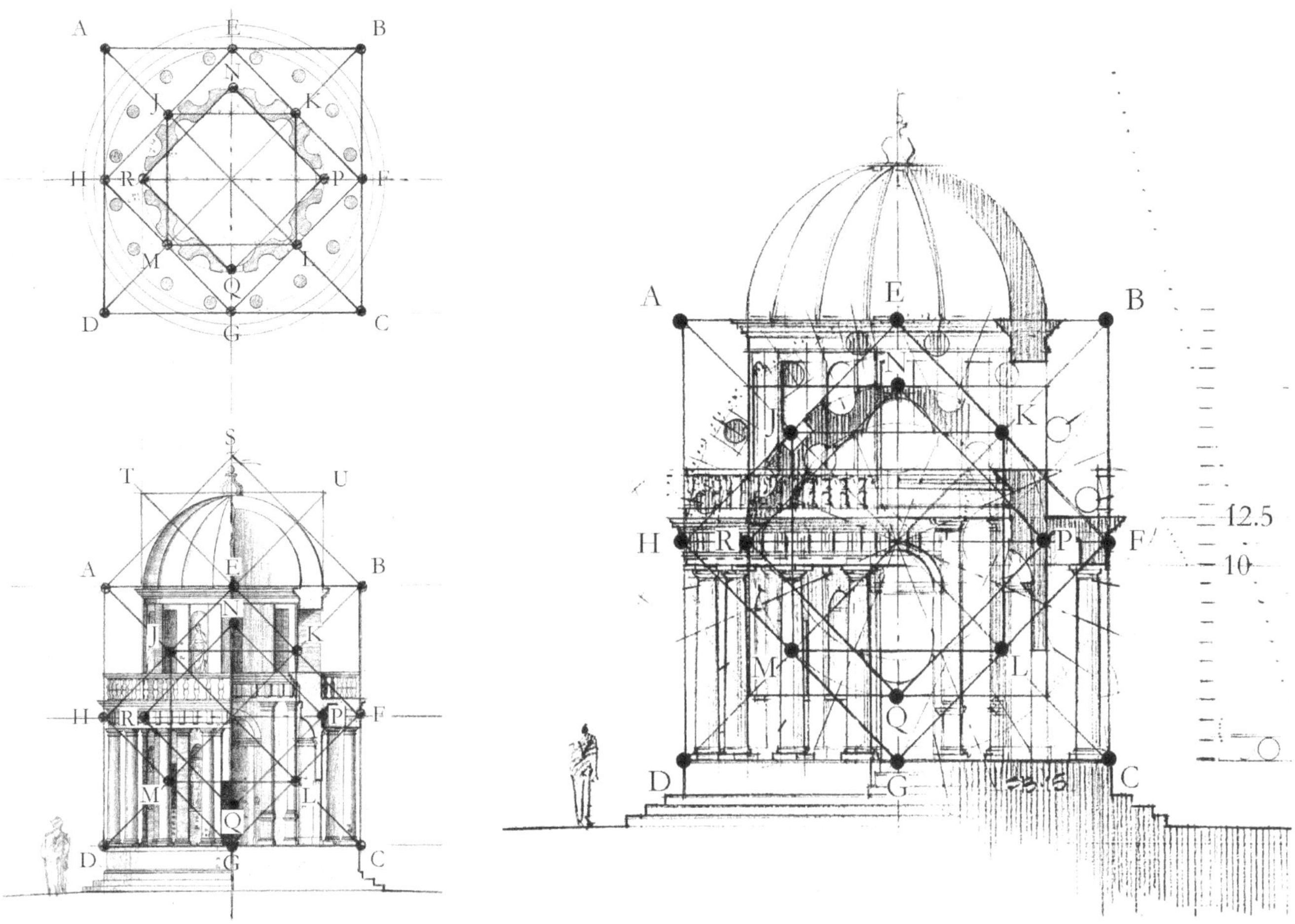

FIGURE 24a-b
Bramante's Tempietto, 1502. Analysis and Reconstruction

In the reconstruction, **figure 24b**, the plan, section and elevation are superimposed on the net, as they can be in such a completely integrated archetypal design.

This little building, less than fifteen feet in internal diameter, marks a coming of age of Renaissance architecture. All the lessons of ancient architecture had been integrated and the achievements of the ancient world would now be definitively challenged. Though one of the smallest buildings of the day, Bramante's Tempietto set the stage for the Baroque era to come. While being perfectly central in its circular plan, it is essentially a three-dimensional statement of cylinder and hemisphere; it is articulated by mass rather than line. *"Where earlier architects had drawn buildings, Bramante modeled them."*[120]

In 1503, Julius puts Bramante in charge of the most prestigious project of the age, the rebuilding of the Vatican. In a 1506 drawing he has significantly chosen a centralized plan for St. Peter's, also apparently based on a $\sqrt{2}$ progression, **figure 25**. In this sense it may be seen as related to the medieval Ad Quadratum system. The two major geometrical methods in the Middle ages were Ad Triangulum, the addition of triangles, and Ad Quadratum, the addition of rectangles. However just which triangles or rectangles remains in dispute.

Until his death at age 70 in 1514, Bramante is a central figure in Rome,[121] drawing around himself a circle of architects including Baldassare Peruzzi, Raphael, Gulio Romano, Pirro Ligorio and Guiliano da Sangallo; the faction that later comes into conflict with Michelangelo.

In spite of their personal conflict, Bramante's architecture laid the ground for Michelangelo's. Bramante utilized the method of Roman concrete, in which brick outer surfaces form a permanent mould for the poured cement.[122] The scale of St. Peter's is not conceivable without this material. Roman concrete also allows space to be treated dynamically rather than as the mere absence of mass. The relatively static geometry applied to flat wall surfaces by Brunelleschi and Alberti is superseded. Solids and voids now actively push and pull against one another.

Sebastian Serlio and the Five Books

Sebastian Serlio, 1475–1554, was born in Bologna into an artisan family and trained as a painter. His early work was in Pesaro, a small city about 120 miles south of Venice on the Adriatic coast. In 1514, he goes to Rome where he works with Peruzzi. After the sack of Rome in 1527 Serlio relocates to Venice where he moves in the circles of Titian and Sansovino. Among his architectural involvements during this period, Serlio works with Titian and Fortunio Spira in 1534 to implement alterations to the church of San Francesco della Vigna, which had been designed by Sansovino. These changes were spelled out in the "memo" of Francesco Giorgi, cited by Wittkower[123] as evidence for a living Platonic tradition in architecture in the early sixteenth century. Giorgi's numbers are based on the Platonic Lambda. Serlio is in Rome for several years in the mid-1530s to work with Sangallo under Pope Paul III.

Serlio's major legacy to us is his treatise on architecture. He began the project about 1520 and worked on it during the remainder of his life, some 34 years. It took the form of seven books, which were published in segments between 1537 and 1575. These have come down to us as Books I-V, with Books VI and VII published separately. In the late 1530s, Serlio is in Venice seeking grants to publish the Books. He appeals to Henry VIII of England and François I of France through their Venitian ambassadors. François not only funds a portion of the project but in 1541 invites Serlio to France where he is given an official position. Serlio conducted various civil and military projects until François' death in 1547. The new king, Henri II, replaced him with Philibert de l'Orme, another canonical author. Serlio retired to southern France and died at Fontainebleau in 1554, age 79. Although Henry VIII did not offer a grant, Serlio became known in Tudor court circles. In 1563, Robert Peake, painter to the Stuart court, published the first English translation of Serlio's first five books, which he dedicated to Prince of Wales Henry Stuart; although a 1560 Italian copy was already in the hands of the prince's young surveyor, Inigo Jones.[124]

Serlio's *Book I*, though published last, is "On Geometry," in which he illustrates the use of geometric methods to produce architectural and decorative objects. Serlio is the only one of the early Italian canonical authors to actually include the study of geometry in his treatise. While he may have done this as an introduction to *Book II*, "On Perspective,"[125] it is noteworthy that he begins at the beginning, so to speak, with the point. Later he emphasizes the square, which he sees as the origin, through transformation, of all plane figures. His presentation closely follows Euclid's first few axioms and constructions. In his introduction to *Book I,* Serlio writes that those who designed and built before learning geometry look back on their early work and, essentially, laugh. Having been through a similar education process, this author feels a strong sympathy for Serlio's approach, reinforced perhaps by the fact that we were both born on the same day of the year, though 472 years apart.

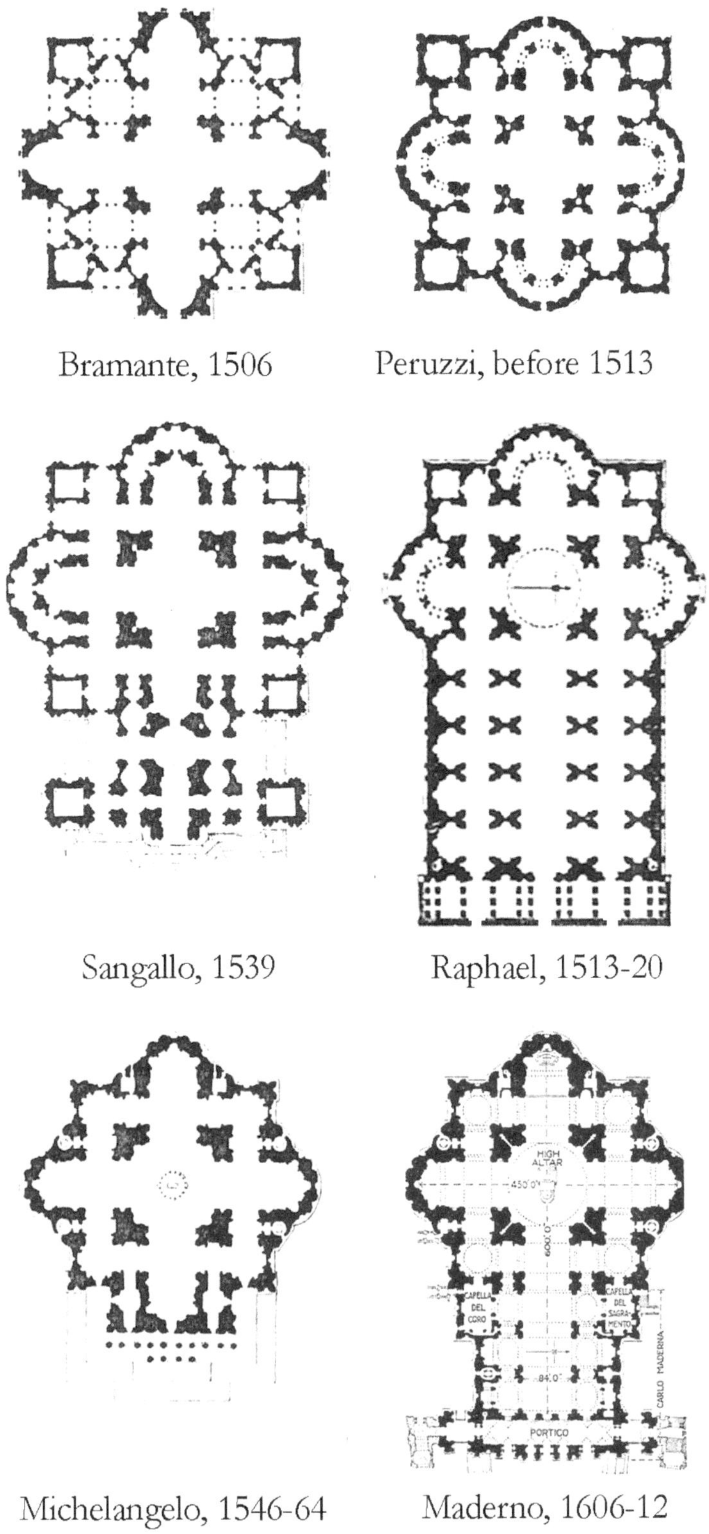

FIGURE 25

Plans for the Vatican, 1506–1612

Serlio's Vessel

After discussing several methods for drawing ellipses and ellipsoids, or eggs as he calls them, Serlio applies a geometrical method to designing decorative urns or vessels. In an echo of the old wisdom tradition in geometry Serlio writes,[126] *"It is an excellent thing to study or practice anything with the compass, whereby you may find out that which you never imagined; as this night it happened unto me, for in seeking to find an easier method to make the form of an egg, than Albrecht Dürer's, I found this way to make an antique vessel, placing the base at the foot of the egg, and the neck with the handles above upon the thickest part of the egg."*

In the spirit of Serlio, let's explore with compass and straightedge **figure 26**, utilizing a four-stage ontological design method:

1) Unity: Begin with a circle, center at A and radius AB. Draw horizontal and vertical axes which we have seen is the outcome of a geometrical creation story.[127]

2) Set the pattern of division of Unity: Divide the diameter into ten. This may be done with an arc centered at B with radius BC, which crosses AB at D. BC = AB x $\sqrt{2}/2$. This divides the radius AB into 2 parts plus 3 parts. Repeating this arc opposite hand creates a figure called a "square vesica" or "$\sqrt{2}$ vesica." This is not the vescia piscis, which is based on the $\sqrt{3}$. The square vesica is also "football" shaped but thinner.

3) Shape the elements: The upper surface of the vessel is a circle with center at A and radius AD tangent to the arcs of the vesica. Count down three units below A to point E. With center at E draw a circle tangent to the two arcs of the vesica. Lines from E to these two tangent points create a right angle. This arc forms the rounded bottom of the vessel. Serlio's description notes that this lower tangent point falls directly below the first point from the center F, which is half of AD.

4) & 5) Develop the details: The neck is guided by a vertical line through point F, AF = FD = 1 unit. The base is half of AF, point G. The starting point for the handle is placed at the 1/3rd point of the enclosing square. The neck, handles and base may now be individually ornamented.

Serlio's Doorway

Figure 27 is the brilliant, well-known image called Serlio's Doorway, which closes his book on geometry.[128] It uses the square, its diagonals and semi-diagonals to shape and position the door in the wall as well as its ornaments. Serlio's illustration eloquently speaks for itself with laconic restraint.

He writes, *"If you will make a door in a temple or church, which is to be proportioned according to the place then you must take the width within the church, or else the breath of the wall without. If the church has pilasters or pillars within it then you may take the width between them, and set the frame breath in a square* [inside of which], *the diagonal and* [semi-diagonal] *cross-cutting lines will not only show you the wideness of the door, but also the places and points of the ornaments."*

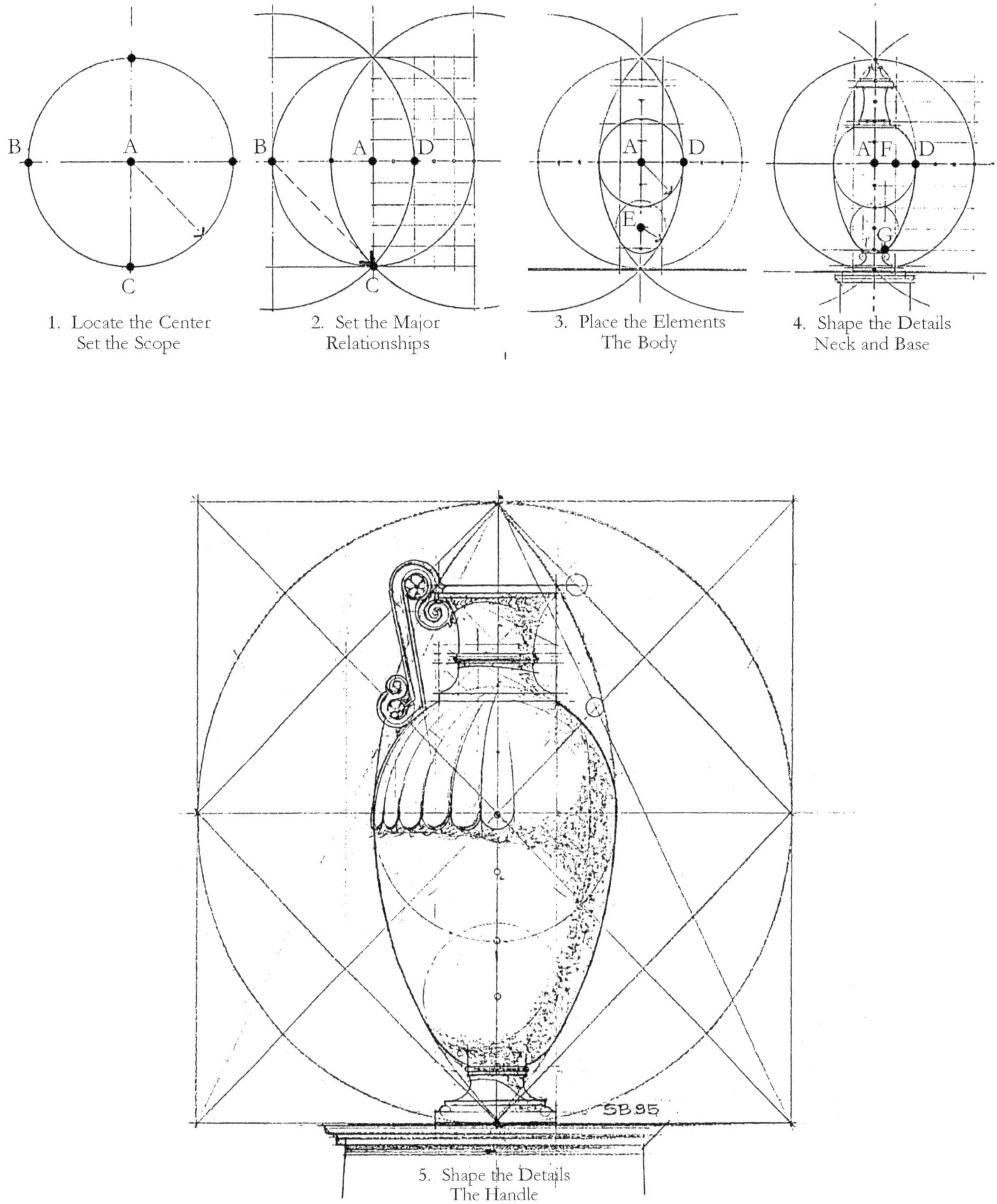

FIGURE 26
Serlio's Vessel

Serlio's reference to "cross-cutting" gives a hint of how to determine the ornaments. Subdivide the square of the upper half of the door by its diagonals and semi-diagonals, just as for the door itself, and find 1/3rd of the width of the door, which is the width of the framing. In the example the frame is divided in half, making the jamb or architrave 1/6th of the width of the opening; the ratio it assumes in later pattern books.

Serlio concludes, *"Although gentle Reader, the cross-cutting through or dividing is innumerable, yet for this time, lest I be too tedious, I here end my Geometry."* And just when the fun was beginning! Of course the "doorway" of geometry opens into all the other subjects necessary for architecture. Perhaps this door is an echo of the motto over the door of the Platonic Academy in ancient Athens, "Unless you know geometry, don't enter here."

FIGURE 27
Serlio's Doorway

Late Renaissance

Palladio

Venetian architect Andrea Palladio, 1508–1580, began his carrier as a stone mason and carver; a craft strongly associated with the aural, or spoken, tradition in geometry. The earliest known use of stone in construction (in chamber and passage monuments) is related to observing the geometry of sun, moon, and star movements. In practice, the necessity of moving large, massive objects and performing negative carving is greatly aided by geometric thinking. Palladio was a mason and sculptor for fourteen years and must have mastered all manner of practical techniques grounded in proportional ideas. Working with such methods, day in, day out, he would probably have formed proportional habits of thought.

At about age thirty, Palladio came to the attention of Count Trissino, a local nobleman in the Veneto region with a long history of study in the seven liberal arts. Wittkower calls him an *"all-round humanist."*[1] His areas of research and work included language structure, mythology, drama, literature, mathematics, music, astronomy, politics, architecture, and other subjects. Trissino applied these skills as the headmaster of an academy; a Neoplatonic school where the Quadrivium was studied with an orthodox program characterized by Wittkower as *"formal, esoteric and dogmatic, free from any popular tendencies."* The school was located *"in rural solitude,"* in his villa at Cricoli in the Venetian countryside. Activities went beyond the intellectual, *"students lived at Cricoli and their work was regulated from day-break to night-fall … strict moral conduct as well as physical cleanliness were peremptory demands."*[2] Wittkower points out the similarity to the medieval monastery, but certainly this concept of the "school" of higher knowledge goes back through Plato and Pythagoras to the temple schools of Egypt and Mesopotamia, and is probably even older. Study at such a school involved both thought and action.

Palladio began his involvement with the school during a work project. Trissino, acting on his study of classical knowledge, was reconstructing his villa based on Vitruvius. Palladio as a carver was asked to fabricate the classical building elements rendered by Trissino's scholarship. To facilitate this, Trissino began to acquaint Palladio with Vitruvius and other classical writers. But Trissino's academy was set up to deal with young aristocrats, not working men of thirty, so Palladio's education was skewed in favor of architecture. This represents a break with the ancient tradition of balance and in this way may be considered a precursor of modern professional education. Palladio is one of the early secular professional architects who was not first a priest or scholar.

In the manner of esoteric schools, this change of personal state was accompanied by a change of name. When he entered Trissino's academy our subject's name was Andrea di Pietro. It was Trissino who renamed him Palladio. Wittkower says that this was the name of a character who served as an architectural guide in a play written by Trissino.[3] Pallas, of course, is one of the appellations of Athena, the goddess who represented peace, wisdom and order. There may be more in the name than just a classical literary allusion. March claims that the name is "occultly" linked to Vitruvius through Latin gematria (number–letter substitution) and kabbalistic reduction, **figure 1.**

A	B	C	D	E	F	G	H	I
1	2	3	4	5	6	7	8	9
K	L	M	N	O	P	Q	R	S
10	20	30	40	50	60	70	80	90
T	V	X	Y	Z	(J	V	Hi	W)
100	200	300	400	500	600	700	800	900

This is the code given by the Renaissance magician known as Agrippa and is the one used by March. The ancient Latin alphabet had 23 letters, another 4, shown in parentheses were added later, bringing the total to 27, largest number of the Platonic Lambda. This code is not the same as "Roman numerals" used in arithmetic, C = 100, X = 10, etc.

V	I	T	R	V	V	I	V	S		
200	9	100	80	200	200	9	200	90 = 1088		
A	N	D	R	E	A	S				
1	40	4	80	5	1	90				
1	4	4	8	5	1	9			= 32	= 32
P	A	L	A	D	I	U	S			
60	1	20	1	4	9	200	90			
6	1	2	1	4	9	2	9 = 34			= 34
							32 x 34 = 1088			

In kabbalistic reduction the digits of a number are added until a single digit is reached. For example: 219 may be reduced to 2 + 1 + 9 = 12, then 1 + 2 = 3.

FIGURE 1 - *Gematria*

VITRVVIVS = 1088 and ANDREAS PALADIVS = 32 and 34; 32 x 34 = 1088.[4] Thus Palladio is a modern Vitruvius and through a kind of sympathetic magic accesses a "Vitruvian spirit."

Later in his career Palladio enters the circle of Venetian nobleman, scholar and diplomat Daniele Barbaro, 1514–1570. Palladio visited Rome with him in 1554,[5] and provided illustrations for Barbaro's translation and commentary on Vitruvius, 1556. Wittkower sees Barbaro as integrating Aristotelian and Platonic concepts, saying, "*The Aristotelian system is given a Platonic bias.*"[6] He notes that Palladio's work, influenced by Barbaro, represents "*a fusion of Aristotelian tenets with Plato's conception of ideas*"; or we may say, a fusion of categories and cosmological number; of external, sensory "mimesis" and internal, imaginal remembrance of formal archetypes.

Barbaro had been Venetian ambassador to the court of Queen Elizabeth, so British design circles may have known about Palladio. After Palladio's death, Inigo Jones, court designer for King James I, traveled to Italy and collected his drawings. When Jones returned to England they and the *Quattro Libri* (*QL*) became the basis for his royal architecture. Though this architecture went out of favor with the rise of Cromwell, it reemerged at the beginning of the eighteenth century in support of the Georgian kings. From this source it took root in the colonial United States.

As a continuation of intellectual study Palladio measured the ruins of ancient buildings. He made three trips to Rome in the 1540s with Trissino and others, one journey lasting two years.[7] Measuring, for an architect, has a special timeless magic in which idea becomes concrete and the concrete is returned to the idea state. It recalls the scene in Genesis[8] where Jehovah parades the animals before Adam and requires him to give each a name. Once Adam knows their names he has power over them. In the ancient mind, name and number were translated through gematria.

Palladio's designs achieved a new synthesis of the classical elements. His villas, palazzos, public buildings and churches did not have specific prototypical counterparts in the ancient world. He selected appropriate elements and composed them proportionally to make new statements. Taking the villas, for example, after a period of development, Palladio seems to have settled on variants of a three-part division both horizontally and vertically,[9] integrated by the use of harmonically related numbers, shown in diagrammatic form in **figure 2**. Looking at his life we see that Palladio worked at a trade in which he learned skills based on ancient traditions, studied at an academy that revived ancient knowledge, measured the physical remains of antiquity, and built new works based on ancient principles of harmony.

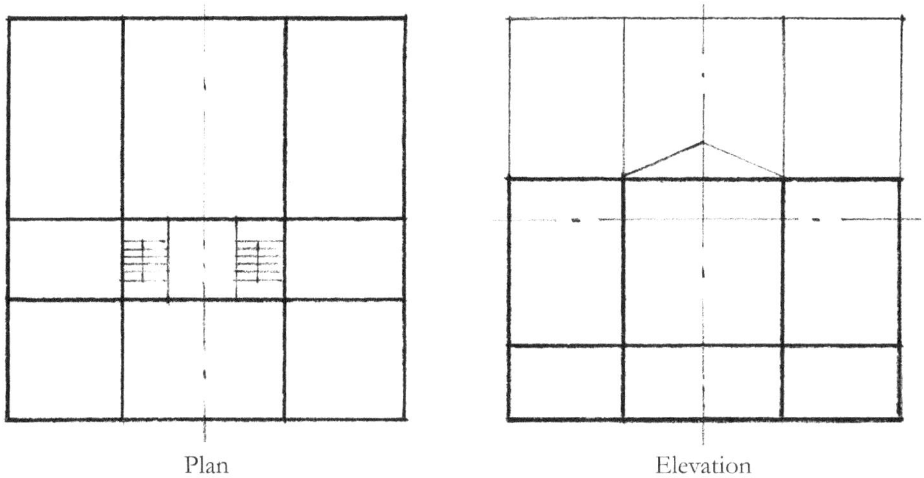

In these schematic diagrams the 3 x 3 pattern, vertically and horizontally, illustrates 'tripartite taxis' or three part structure in classical composition. Varying the division provides for a hierarchy of spaces

FIGURE 2 – *Palladio's Tripartite Taxis*

THE TEMPERED OCTAVE

To understand Palladio's use of number to create harmony in built form we might look, as Wittkower did, at music theory in the Quadrivium. In the system ascribed to Pythagoras, musical consonances are determined by ratios of small whole numbers 1, 2, 3, and 4.[10] These same numbers can be used to illustrate a story of creation.[11] In the *Timaeus*, Plato guides the creation of the world soul using the numbers 1, 2, 3, 4, 8, 9, and 27, **figure 3**. These are placed on an inverted "V" figure, called the lambda, the Greek letter L, with 1 at the apex, 2, 4, 8 on the left leg, and 3, 9, 27 on the right. The lambda may be seen as the "surface" of the tetraktys. The octaves are defined by the geometric sequence 1, 2, 4, 8 [$b = \sqrt{ac}$]. Then within each interval, between 1 and 2, for example where 1 is the position of the fundamental and 2 of the octave, are inserted the arithmetic mean [$b = (a+c)/2$] and harmonic mean, [$b = 2ac/(a+c)$], giving 3/2 and 4/3, which position the fifth and fourth notes respectively. The interval between these two notes, 9/8, is defined as the interval of the whole tone. Between the first and fourth notes are placed two whole tones and a fractional "leftover" called a "lemma," also known as a "half tone" or "semitone." Between the fifth and eighth notes are three whole tones and a lemma.

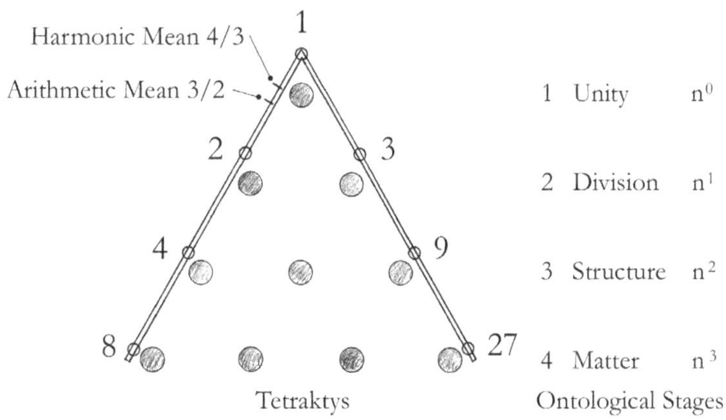

FIGURE 3 – *The Platonic Lambda*

Position		1		2		3		4		5		6		7		8
Note		C		D		E		F		G		A		B		C
Sound		DO		RE		MI		FA		SO		LA		TI		DO
Natural Octave	Name		Tone		Tone		Semi-Tone		Tone		Tone		Tone		Semi-Tone	
	Ratio		9/8		9/8		256/243		9/8		9/8		9/8		256/243	
	Length	1		9/8		81/64		4/3		3/2		27/16		243/128		2
Tempered Octave	Name		Major Tone		Minor Tone		Semi-Tone		Major Tone		Minor Tone		Major Tone		Semi-Tone	
	Ratio		9/8		10/9		6/15		9/8		10/9		9/8		6/15	
	Length	1		9/8		5/4		4/3		3/2		5/3		15/8		2

FIGURE 4
The Tempered Octave

This creates what may be called a "natural" octave, **figure 4**. The Greek musical system was based on the "tetrachord," consisting of the fundamental, the octave, the fifth note and the fourth note; or stated as ratios, 1:1, 2:1, 3:2 and 4:3. Also recognized were the octave and a fifth, 1:2:3; and the double octave, 1:2:4. In late fifteenth-century Italy the position of the third and sixth notes were moved, or "tempered," to create the system of major and minor scales, called "keys," which we use today.[12] The third note was moved from 81/64 to 5/4, a distance of 1/64 as 5/4 x 16 = 80/64, about 1.56% of the interval of the octave. The sixth note was moved from 27/16 to 5/3, a distance of 0.35/16, as 5/3 x 16 = 26.65/16, 2.08% of the octave interval. Thus in Palladio's time additional ratios used were, a third, 5:4, a sixth, 5:3, and a number of others. 5:3 of course is 1/Ø; 5:4 is a derivative of Ø. The natural octave is constructed using the three- and fourfold powers. Now the fivefold power is integrated into the harmonic pattern.

Villa Emo

The Villa Emo is an often cited example of harmonic number in action. In Palladio's *Quattro Libri* the plan of the main house, **figure 5a,** is noted with the numbers 12, 16, and 27.[13] 12:27 is an octave and a tone, 12:24 + 24:27 or 1:2 + 8:9. 12:16 is a fourth, 3:4. 16:27 is a fifth and a tone, as in 16:24:27, 2:3 + 8:9. The overalls are 59 wide x 55 deep, however these figures are not specified in the plan. The wings are noted with the numbers 12, 20, 24, and 48. 12:24:48 are octaves, 1:2:4. 12:20:24 is an octave composed of a sixth, 3:5 and a minor third, 5:6. The colonnade has the numbers 2, 3, 9, 12, and 15. 2:3, a fifth, is the pier. 3:9:12, the pier spacing, is two octaves 3:6 and 6:12, composed of an octave and a fifth plus a fourth. 12:15, a colonnade bay, is a third, 4:5.[14]

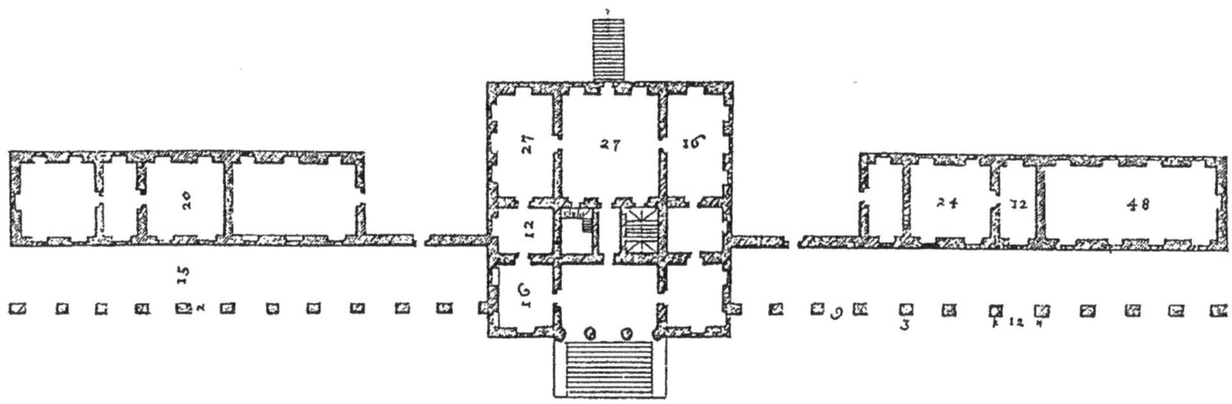

Plan

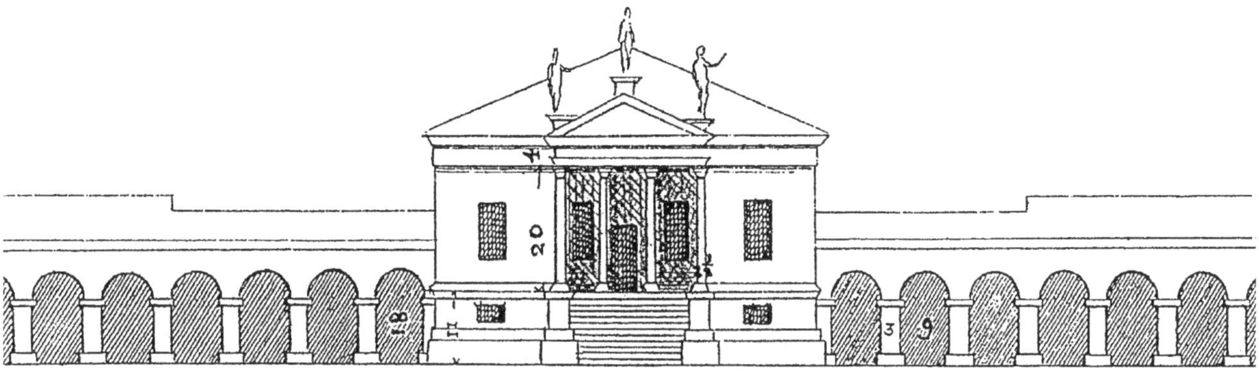

Elevation

FIGURE 5a
Villa Emo, Fanzolo, Palladio, 1559

Palladio is even more reticent with notation in elevation than in plan. The Emo's base is 11, column height 20, and cornice 4. 2.5, the width of the column, is 1/8th of the column height of 20. 4:20 is two octaves and a third. In the wings, the height of the colonnade arch is 18. This is twice 9, the open space between piers. The use of 11, as opposed to 10, 11.25 or 12, does not seem to have an exact musical explanation, and we must fall back on Timaeus' injunction not to search beyond the most "likely story."[15] The overall height is 35. 35/59 = .593. close to Ø.

Heights of interior rooms are determined by the three means.[16] In this villa we have 12x16 and 16x27. The arithmetic means are 14 and 21.5. The geometric means are 13.875 and 20.75. The harmonic means are 13.75 and 20.125. Square rooms are to be 1/3 higher than their plan dimension, 16x16 would get 21.25. This is compatible with a ceiling height in the principal rooms of either 20 or 21 feet, probably 20, as this is the height of the portico columns. The 27x27 room could not be 36 high. It could be a cube, but 27 is still too high. If it had a cornice at 20, its ceiling could be flat with vaulting up to 24. Palladio says that room heights may be adjusted to meet practical needs such as holding floor levels above.

The ensemble of numbers used by Palladio at the Villa Emo can be placed on a tempered octave scale, **figure 5b.**[17] 11 could be considered a whole number round-off of a pure harmonic, 11.25, a 2.35% discrepancy. 54 and 60 are within 1 foot of the length and width of the villa,

Notes								
Note #	1	2	3	4	5	6	7	8
Sound	DO	RE	MI	FA	SO	LA	TI	DO

Modules

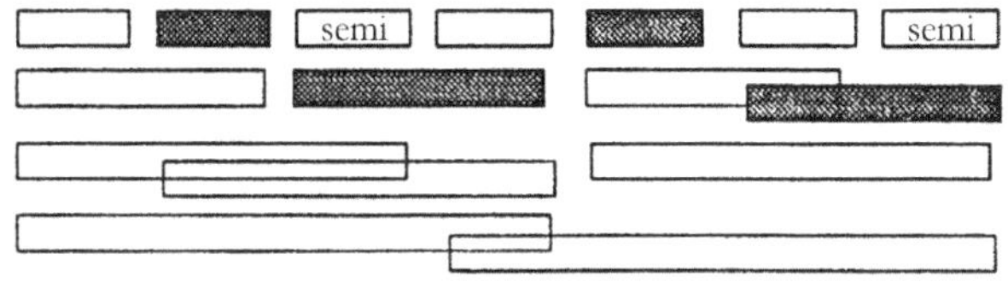

Intervals								
1st Octave	[1.5]			2		2.5		3
2nd	3			4				[6]
3rd	[6]				9	10	11.25	12
4th	12		15	16	18	20		24
5th	24	27						48
6th	48	54	60					[96]

Numbers in brackets [ ] are not used in the Emo. They are shown to indicate the octaves. Compositional modules of the octave are shown as rectangles. Minor scale modules are shaded.

FIGURE 5b
Villa Emo. Tempered Octave

about 2% off Palladio's dimensions.[18] In the octave progression 60:54 is the interval of a minor tone, 10/9.

Figure 5c is a geometrical analysis of the *QL* drawing applying √2. Taking the width of the building as unity, a square is set up in plan and elevation. It is immediately found that although the plan is drawn as a square, the noted numbers do not add up to a square, 16 + 27 + 16 = 59 and 16 + 12 + 27 = 55. Clearly then, the sixteenth-century engraving must be idealized either graphically or numerically. In elevation the height of the base seems to coincide with $Ø^2/2$ = .191; the tops of the columns are very slightly above the centerline of the square; the top of the cornice is positioned at 1/√3, .557; and the apex of the pediment is slightly below the √2/2 point.

LIMITS OF ANALYSIS

The inaccuracies of the *QL* drawings put limits on what we can know about Palladio's method and intentions.[19]

Just what were the numbers meant to signify?

Were the rooms placed within a given perimeter and inconstancies rounded off with "poché"?

Was a geometrical division made and the dimensions rounded off to the nearest harmonic?

Did Palladio start from the outside and work in or from the inside and build out?

Such questions remain unanswered.

It may be that the numbers on the plan and the elevation refer to different aspects. The elevation numbers appear to refer to actual object surfaces like column diameter, height,

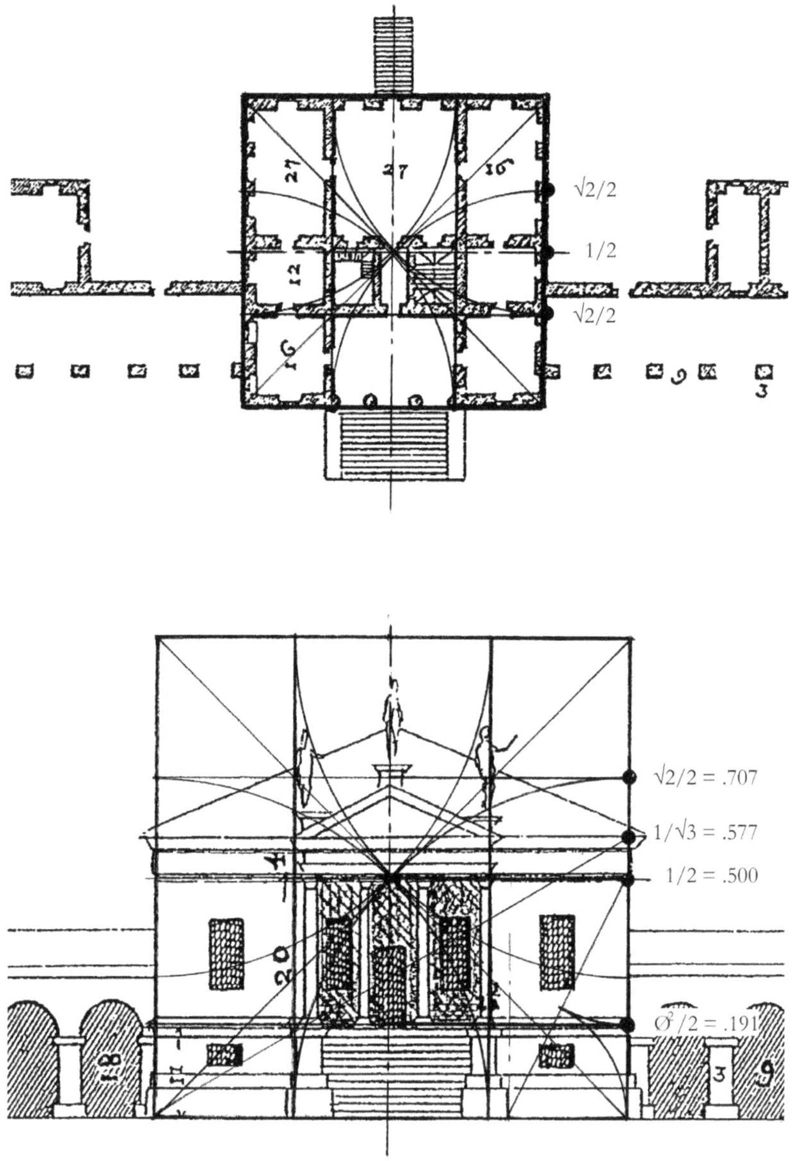

FIGURE 5C
Villa Emo. Analysis

intercolumniation; and they usually, though they do not always, have arrows indicating where they begin and end. The intent of the plan dimensions are probably surface to surface, but perhaps not, as no arrows are indicated on the plans and as-built dimensions are usually slightly smaller than the plan numbers. So geometrical lines could be centered on walls or fall on one side or the other.

As the purpose of the present exploration is to assist contemporary designers, rather than to insist on some definitive method, a variety of approaches are taken in reconstructing the villas.

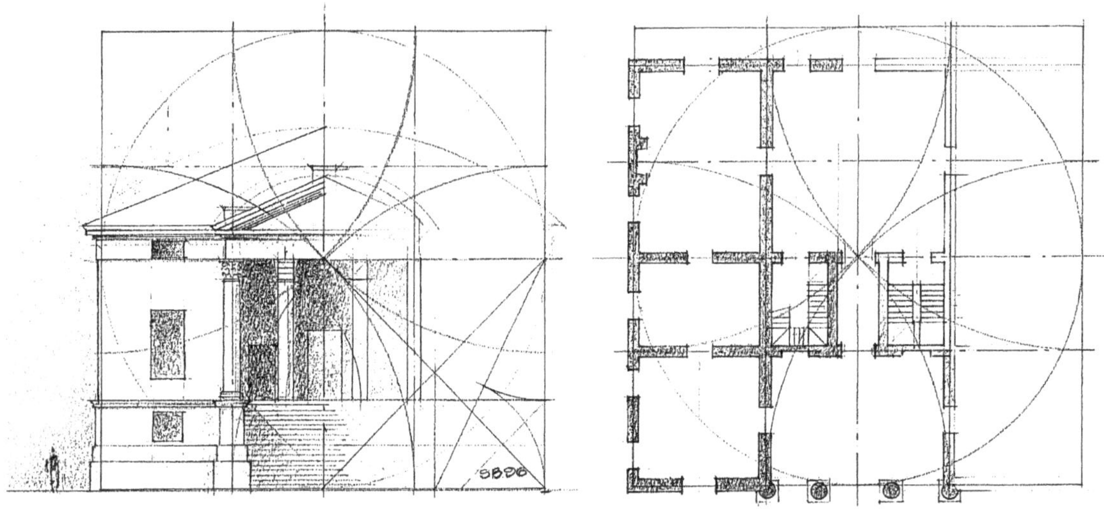

FIGURE 5d – *Villa Emo. Reconstruction Using √2*

EMO RECONSTRUCTIONS

An exploratory, "near approach" reconstruction based on the *QL* drawing, **figure 5d,** can be made featuring √2. Beginning with a square, mark off the √2/2 arcs from each corner. The front row of rooms is marked directly by the √2 cuts. The inner row is marked by the centerline of the square. The center of the back row of rooms is given by the back √2 cut. Taking the side of the square as 59 gives: 59 x .293 = 17.28'; x .414 = 24.42'; and x .207 = 12.21'. In elevation the basement height is set by $Ø^2/2$ of the square, 59 x .191 = 11.27. The center of the square is at the underside of the entablature. 59/2 = 29.5, minus 11.25 = 18.25'.

A closer geometrical reconstruction[20] begins with square ABCD, **figure 5e.1**. E is the center of AB. Draw semi-diagonal EC. With center at E and radius EB draw arc BF. Draw square FGHJ. Draw equal square GFMN, **5e.2**. Extend MN to PQ, marking the front of the villa. The front row of rooms is placed by square RSQM, **5e.3.** The elevation follows the same geometrical pattern, **5e.4**. Interval GF gives the centerlines of the outer columns of the portico. Take $Ø^2$ of half-square UT, point V. VU gives the height of the basement. The top of the cornice is placed by the apex of equilateral triangle WXY, or half-equilateral DZC. Dividing ZC into 6 gives the top of the columns and depth of the entablature, D is 1/10th of the column height, **5e.6**.

Taking the outside of the square as 61' gives the breakdown: GF = 61 x .447 = 27.24'; AH and JB = 61 x .276 = 16.83'; LQ = 27.24', SQ = 16.83. Factoring in wall thicknesses gives similar figures to actual measured dimensions.[21] The basement, VU, is 30.5 x .382 = 11.65'. The height of the order is the altitude of WXY, 27.25 x .867 = 23.63', giving a total height, ZC of 35.28'. 35.28/61 = .578, 1/√3 = .577.

Working with the archetype of the Emo, character alterations can be made by changing some of the factors. **Figure 5f** assumes a width of 60'. The portico is narrowed, its outside being at the √2 points, squared up and subdivided by the √2 and Ø.[22] It uses Palladio's dimensions integrated with a geometrical method.

While none of these reconstructions should be considered definitive, they do produce results within a rather close range to the actual Villa Emo. They begin to point to ways of working with arithmetic, geometry and musical ratios to "fabricate," as Palladio might have said, an aesthetic work with unified, cosmological roots.

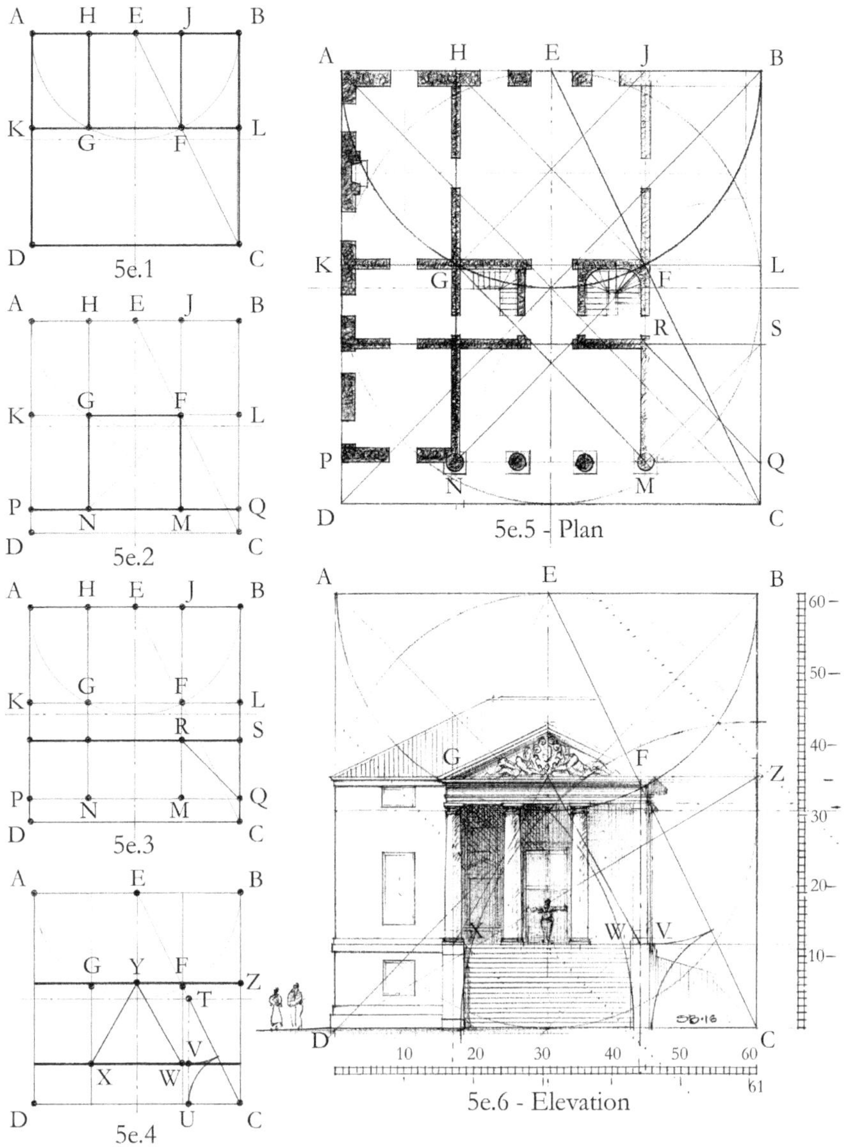

FIGURE 5e – *Villa Emo. Reconstruction Using √3 nd √5*

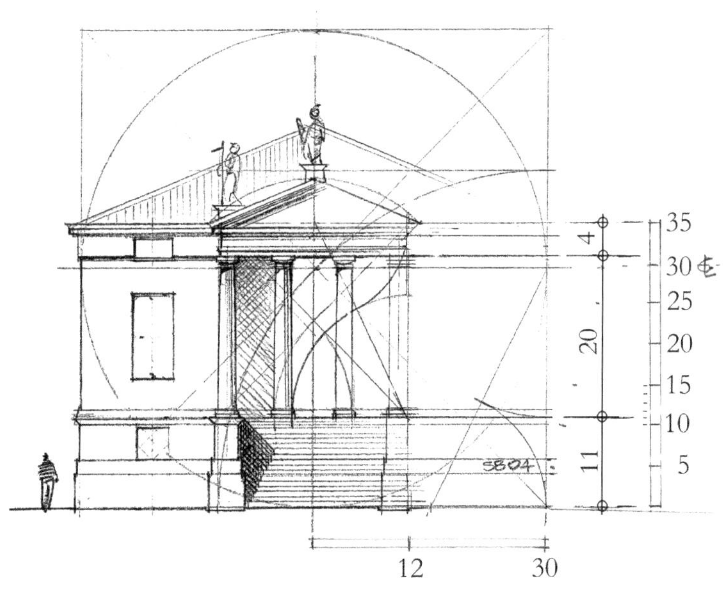

FIGURE *5f – Villa Emo. Reconstruction Using Geometry and Arithmetic*

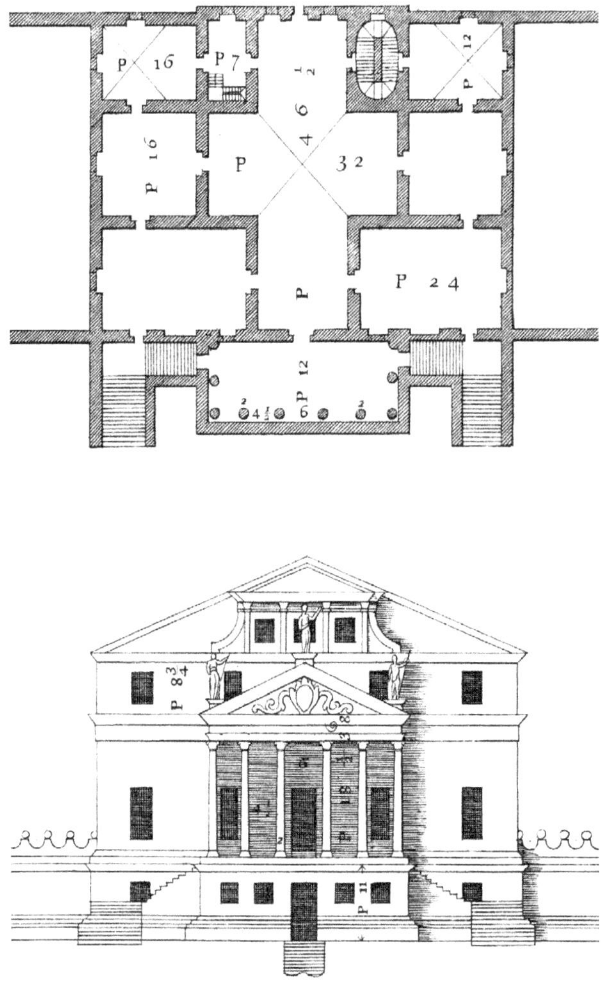

FIGURE 6a – *Villa Foscari, Palladio, 1549–1563*

Notes								
Note #	1	2	3	4	5	6	7	8
Sound	DO	RE	MI	FA	SO	LA	TI	DO

Modules

Tones
Thirds
Fourths
Fifths

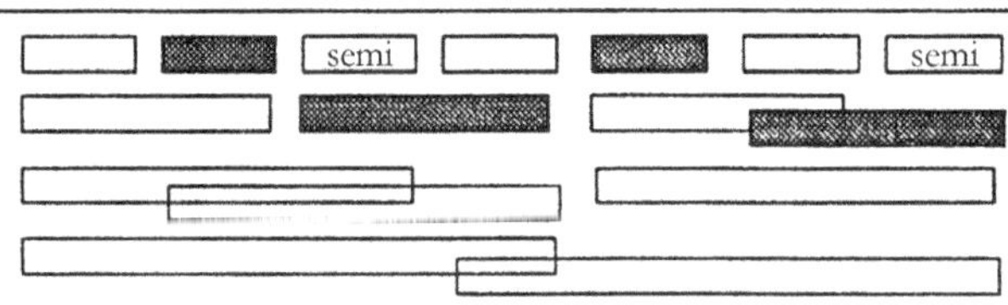

Intervals								
1st Octave	[1.5]			2				[3]
2nd	3		3.75	4	4.5			6
3rd	6	6.75	7.5	8	9		11.25	12
4th	12		15	16	18		22.5	24
5th	24	27		32	36			48
6th	48	54	60	64				[96]

FIGURE 6b – *Villa Foscari. Tempered Octave*

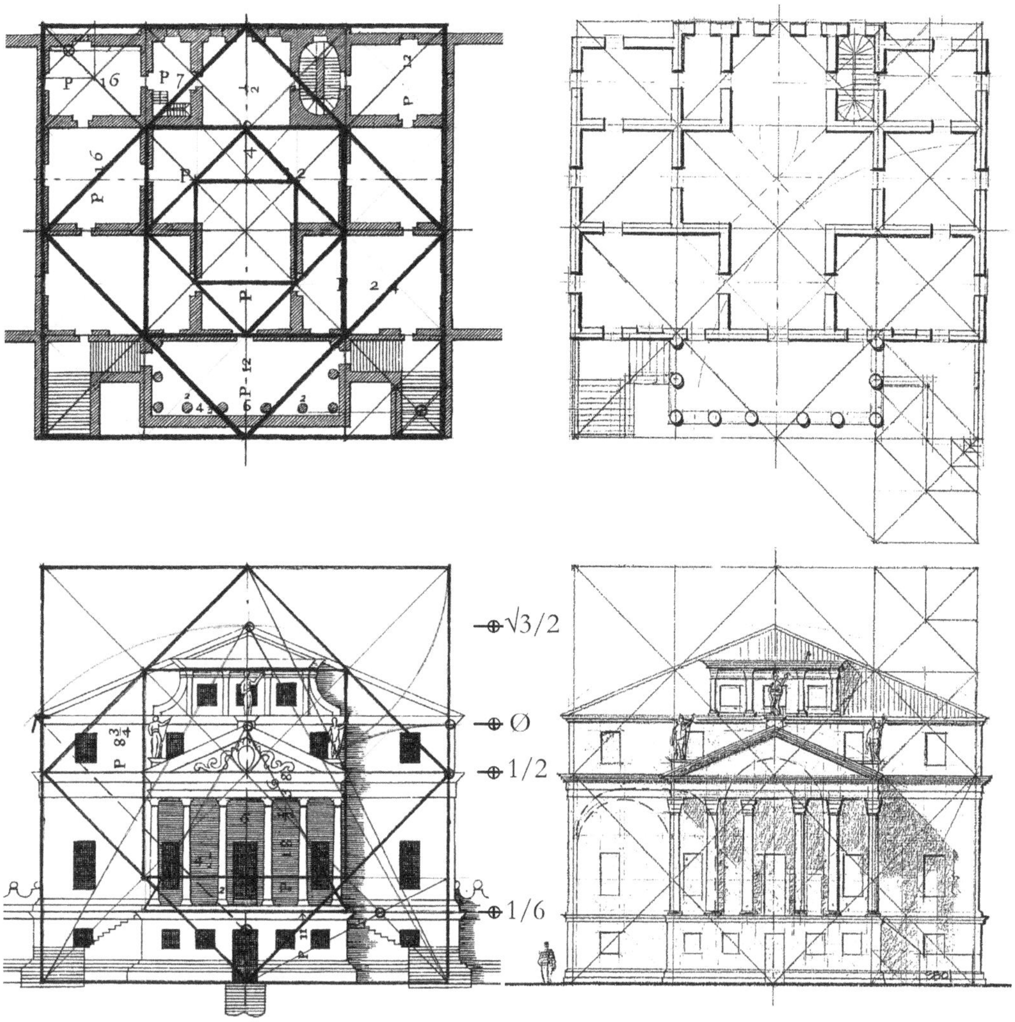

FIGURE 6c-d – *Villa Foscari. Analysis and Reconstruction*

VILLA FOCSARI

The Villa Foscari, **figure 6a,** is one of Palladio's most noble and dramatic villas. Set on a canal, with an elevated "piano nobile," the facade is centered by a six-column portico, reached by a symmetrical double stair. The architectural sequence culminates in a cruciform main hall with double height cross vaults.

Most of the numbers on the plan and elevation can be placed on the same tempered octave as those for the Emo, **figure 6b**. In plan, the rooms are 16 x 12 = 4:3, 16 x 16 = 1:1, and 24 x 16 = 3:2. The cruciform salon is 32 x 16 = 2:1 and 46.5 x 16 = 2.9:1 ≈ 3:1, overall it is 46.5 x 32 = 1.45:1 ≈ 3:2. The stair rooms are stated as 7 wide but their length is not given; it may have been intended to be 14 making them 1:2. 7 is not a harmonic in the scale of **figure 6b**, but 6.75 and 7.5 are. The portico is 36 x 12 = 3:1. The enclosed building is 64 x 48 = 4:3; including the portico gives 60:64, a semitone.

The basement is again the nonharmonic 11, the columns are 18.5, the entablature is 3.67 and the attic is 8.75. These are all nonharmonic in **6b** but have close equivalents: 11.25, 18, 3.75 and 9. The columns are 9.25 D high and the entablature is 1/5 of the column height = 3.7. The order is 22.17 high, its harmonic is 22.5.

Figure 6c is a geometrical analysis of the *QL* drawing starting with the plan as a whole in a square. Placing four smaller √2 related squares within it gives the key points of structure and modulation of spaces. This divides the plan square into 8 segments of 8' each, falling in the centers of walls. If the outermost segment is reduced by half, it gives the 12' interval for the back row of rooms and the front portico.

The elevation seems to respond to geometry as much as harmony. The portico is 36 wide x 22.17 high = 1:.63 ≈ Ø. The order plus the basement = 33.17. If the outside-to-outside dimension is taken as 66, the basement and order comprise a double square, the basement being 1/3rd of it. Adding the attic gives a total height of 41.92; 41.92/66 = .63 ≈ Ø. The height of both the overall roof and the portico's pediment are coincident with equilateral triangles. The rake angles are 22.5°

In the slightly idealized reconstruction, **figure 6d,** a 16' x 16' grid is used to mark the centers of walls in plan, except for the back wall of the salon, which is moved within the geometry. In elevation the same grid is used, and key heights are indicated by division into 2 and 3. The basement 11 is 1/3rd of 33. The top of the attic is positioned by the 5/8 point, .625 as opposed to Ø = .618. The apex of the roof is at .875 as opposed to .867. The portico is 34 wide as opposed to 36, however it could be extended without sacrificing the character of the facade.

Villa Ragona

An example of a two-story portico is the unbuilt Villa Ragona, **figure 7a**. In width the given numbers are 12 + 21.25 +12 = 45.25. The center row of rooms is 17 + 17, but the center stair hall width is not given. Subtracting 34 from 45.25 leaves 11.25. In depth 15 + 18 + 15 = 48. The portico and center back room are 1:√2; the corner rooms are 4:5; the stair hall is 11.25/18 = .625 ≈ Ø; the center side rooms are 18:17, which may be seen as a 1:1 approximate. If 5 is taken on either side of the stair hall for doorways, 12 + 5 = 17, however March notes that 18/17 is a "Boethian minor semitone,"[23] the overalls are 45.25/48 = 15/16. In elevation the basement is 12, the columns are 25, and the entablature 5. The numbers, or near equivalents, can be placed on the same tempered octave as the previous villas, **figure 7c**.

Figure 7a is a geometrical analysis of the *QL* drawing. It is immediately apparent that the plan is drawn as a square not in conformance to the numbers. Working with the plan as drawn, the inside width of the stair hall is placed by Ø, point A, which is very close to the 5/8ths point, B; the width of the central bay is set by √2/2 point, C, or the wall may fall between the √2/2 and the 3/4 point, D; the depth of the stair hall is set by the 1/3rd point, E. In elevation the portico begins very close to the 1/4 point, F; the top of the columns is at the 3/4 point, G. The outer columns of the portico seem to be centered slightly inboard from the √2/2 points, H and J.

Assuming a square of 48, the basement is 1/4 high. The top of columns is 1 unit above the 3/4 point, and the top of entablature is at the 7/8ths point.[24] The colonnade is a "squeezed" square, 23.5 wide and 25 high, D/H = 1/10. The entablature is 1/5th of the column, making the overall height 42, 42/48 = .875, very close to √3/2 x 48 = 41.6. The height of the second floor is at 16, approximately Ø of the column height. If the engaged corner columns are placed so that 3/5 of the column is inside the 21.25 portico, their outside dimension will be 23.5. As 24 x 30 = 4/5, this half Ø rectangle can become the frame for an elegant, uplifted portico. Adding one more 1/5th for the pediment gives a 2/3 frame.

Figure 7b is a geometricized reconstruction of the *QL* drawing. The front and back walls are placed outside the geometrical square and the side walls inside the square. While exact geometrical points of **7a** are held, the ratios of rooms and portico produced are close but not exactly Palladio's ratios. However, if the central bays are enlarged about 1/2 a wall thickness the

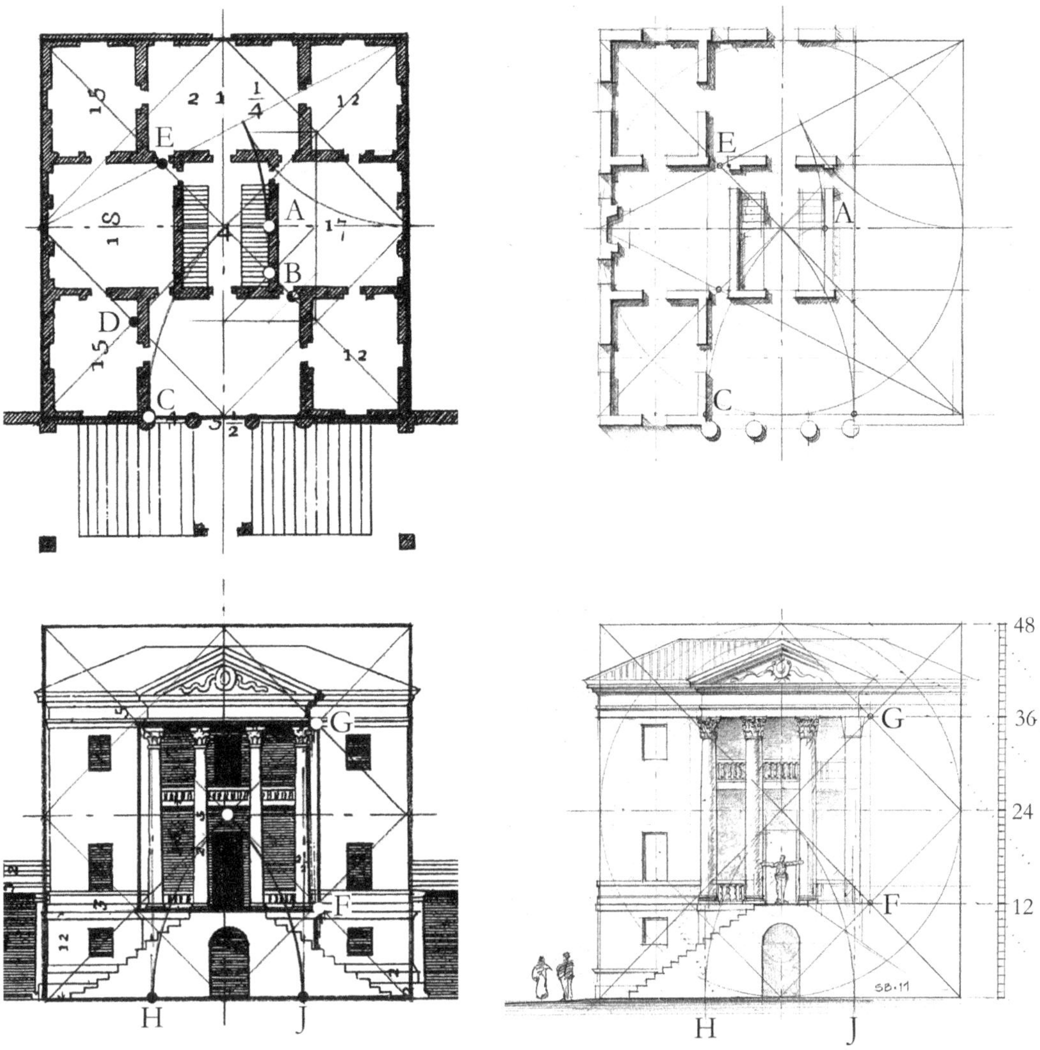

FIGURE 7a-b – *Villa Ragona, Palladio, Unbuilt, 1553. Analysis and Reconstruction*

Notes								
Note #	1	2	3	4	5	6	7	8
Sound	DO	RE	MI	FA	SO	LA	TI	DO

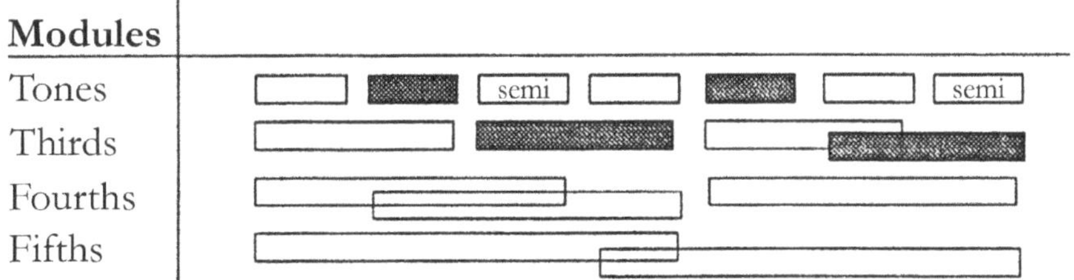

Intervals								
1st Octave	[1.5]					2.5		[3]
2nd	[3]			4		5	5.75	[6]
3rd	[6]							12
4th	12		15	16	18		22.5	24
5th	24		30	32	36	40	45	48
6th	48							[96]

FIGURE 7c – *Villa Ragona. Tempered Octave*

room ratios become closer to Palladio's.[25] The inner portico columns are placed by taking 1/Ø, 1.618 of the diameter, 2.5 x 1.618 = 4.04. The second-floor balcony is noticeably higher in the reconstruction. It is drawn at 16 units as stated in the *QL* drawing. As the portico is 1 unit lower in the reconstruction and a bit lower than 16 in the *QL* drawing the difference appears striking.

Villa Rotunda

Probably the most famous and iconic of Palladio's villas is the Rotunda, **figure 8**. The plan unfolds, flowerlike, from a square whose side is the diameter of the central circle. Its radius is 15 and this sets the grid in which the building develops in plan and elevation. Taking wall thicknesses into account the grid interval increases to 16 giving a width of 64. This leaves the two rectangular rooms as 15 x 15 and 15 x 30. But these are shaved to create the four passages. The front-back passage is 8 wide and the side passage is 6. The remaining spaces are 26 x 15 = √3:1[26] and taking wall thicknesses into account, 11:15, between 4:5 and 2:3. The porticos are 12 x 30 inside, 2/5 or $Ø^2$:1, adding 2 for the column and 1 more to the edge of the steps gives the modular 15.

In elevation the basement is given as 10, the order 21.75 and the attic 7, making the bulk of the building 38.75/64 = .605 ≈ Ø. Since it is not clear where the attic 7 ends, if 1.25 were added for the cornice the bulk would be 40/64, 5/8. The portico is 34 feet wide: six columns, D = 2, four side intercolumniations of 4 and 3D in the center, total = 12 + 16 + 6 = 34, 21.75/34 = .639, ≈ Ø, but is equally close to the 2/3rds point. The basement height 10 is 2/3 of 15, 1/4 of 40 or Ø of 16 = 9.89. In the center hall the crown of the dome is 55, 55/64 = .859 ≈ √3/2, .867, thus, as in the Pantheon,[27] the dome is contained, its thrust counteracted, through the equilateral triangle.

The Rotunda is decidedly cosmological. Its plan begins at the mysterious center, which inflates to form a sphere. The sphere "rises" to form the cylinder and dome of the center hall. It differentiates into a cube guided internally by √2 and √3, its exterior guided by Ø. Its mass rises like a sacred mountain, or the Benben stone atop its primal mound, awaiting the phoenix of eternal renewal. Just to "rub it in" it has recently come to light that the 12 statues crowning the four porticos are of the Olympian divinities arranged in order of the astrological signs they govern. Though these were carved and installed after Palladio's death, his design left the right number of pedestals for them. The statues represent the outermost aspect of full manifestation, number in space and time. The √2 geometry of the plan is that of an astrological chart.

Regarding the numbering of the villas, Palladio's intentions remain unclear. The plans are not drawn to scale; plans and numbers do not match. Maybe the drawings or numbers were not completely under Palladio's control.[28] Palladio's design method remains obscure. It may be that he began in geometry then adjusted the numbers to harmonic round-offs but the numbers are not necessarily harmonic. Perhaps Palladio was using different divisions of the octave to obtain the room dimensions.[29] The numbers could also have been adjusted for pragmatic reasons not apparent to us today.[30] Palladio may well have used a three-dimensional approach, starting with a harmonically related volume then dividing it harmonically and/or geometrically. Such spaces could be oriented and ornamented astronomically, encompassing all four subjects of the Quadrivium. Surely the science of harmony was involved but the integrated nature of the designs suggests the unifying presence of the geometrical powers.

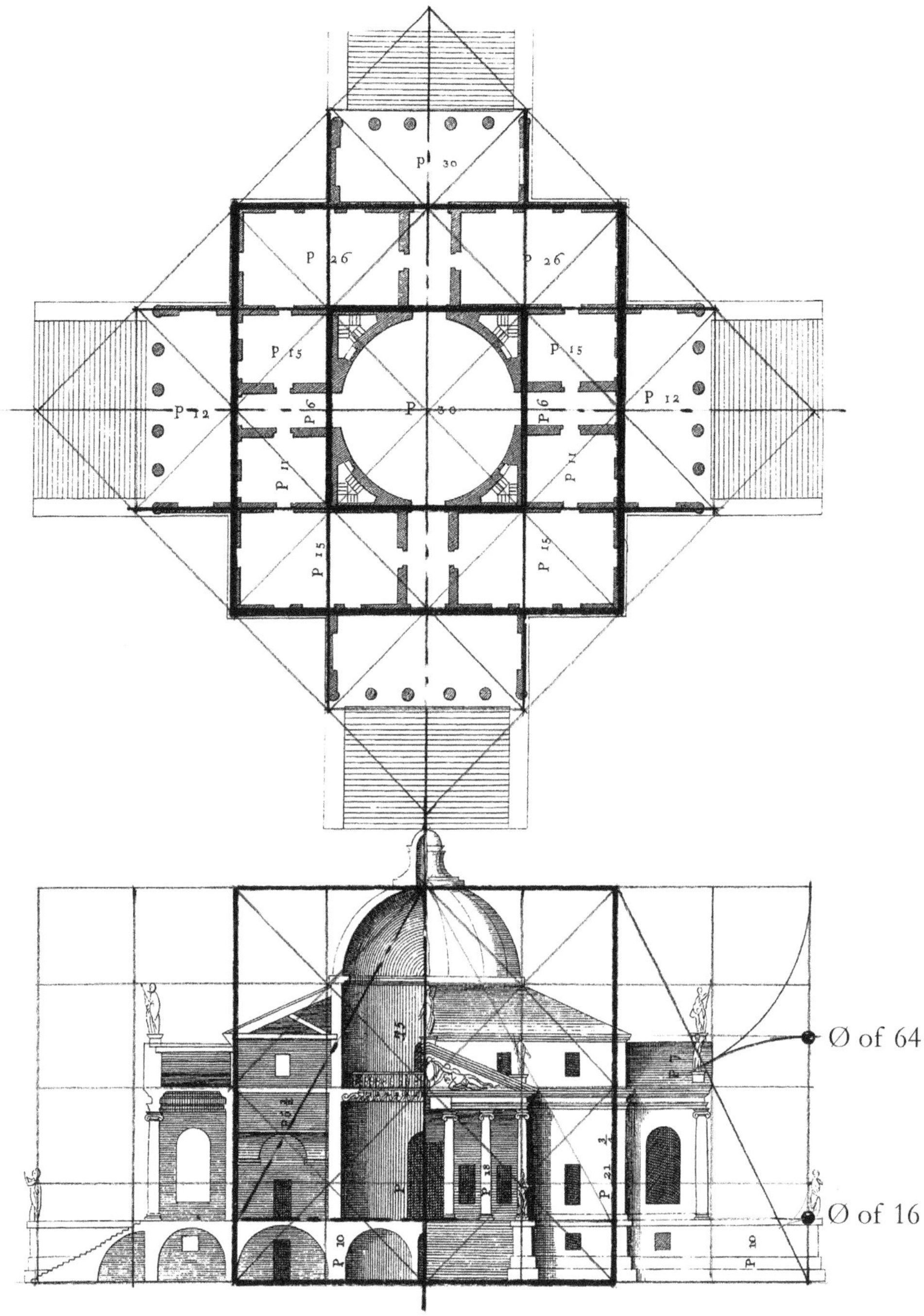

FIGURE 8
Villa Rotunda, Vicenza, Palladio, 1556. Analysis

FIGURE 9a – *Palazzo Porto, Vicenza, Palladio, 1571*

A Window Opening at the Palazzo Porto

Figure 9a shows the street facade of the Palazzo Porto.[31] The center-to-center distance of the columns on the side bays is (by inspection) 10' and the column height is stated as 18'. The window is given as 4' x 8'.

Figure 9b. The width of the opening is found by "squaring up" the distance between column centers, DC, and striking off the $\sqrt{2}/2$ points K and L. These divide the column bay into 10 units in the pattern of 3-4-3'.

Figure 9c. Set up rectangle MNLK; KL = 4, KM = 12. The upper 2:1 rectangle MNQP is the window and the square PQLK is the balustrade. In Bk. I Ch. XXV, Palladio tells us that the window frame, or architrave, is to be not less than 1/6th of the opening width KL and not more than 1/5th. In the reconstruction 1/6th is used, dividing KL/2 into 3 parts.[32]

Figure 9d. The balustrade, PQLK, has a base, a shaft or baluster, and a cap or rail. In his illustration Palladio shows four full balusters and two half balusters in the 4 unit opening. These may be placed by dividing into fifths either arithmetically or geometrically at point T. The base is 1/4 of the balustrade, 1 unit high, LV, making it equal to the column base. The rail is 1/5 of the balustrade, QU = QS/2. This procedure is similar to but not the same as the division of an archetypal order.[33]

Figure 9e. The frieze and cornice are added after Palladio's directions in Bk. I Ch. XXVI, using his first and simplest example. The architrave is divided into 4 parts. The frieze is 3 and the cornice is 5, totaling 12 parts in a recollection of the Pythagorean 3–4–5 archetype. The pediment, by inspection, has a rake angle of 28°. A test of the reconstruction is the placement of the human figures in the pediment in the same position as in Palladio's drawing.

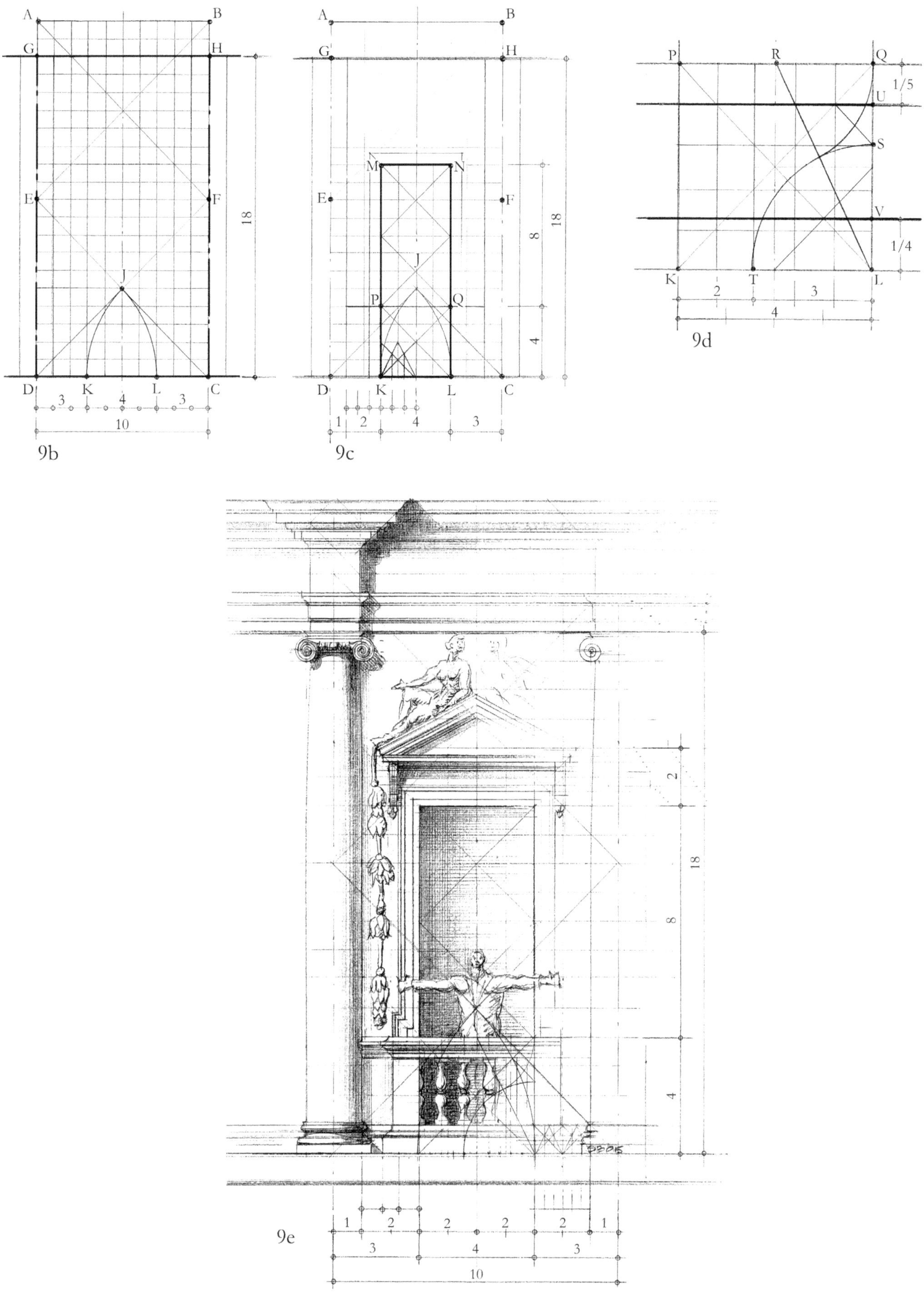

Figure 9b-e – *Palazzo Porto. Reconstruction*

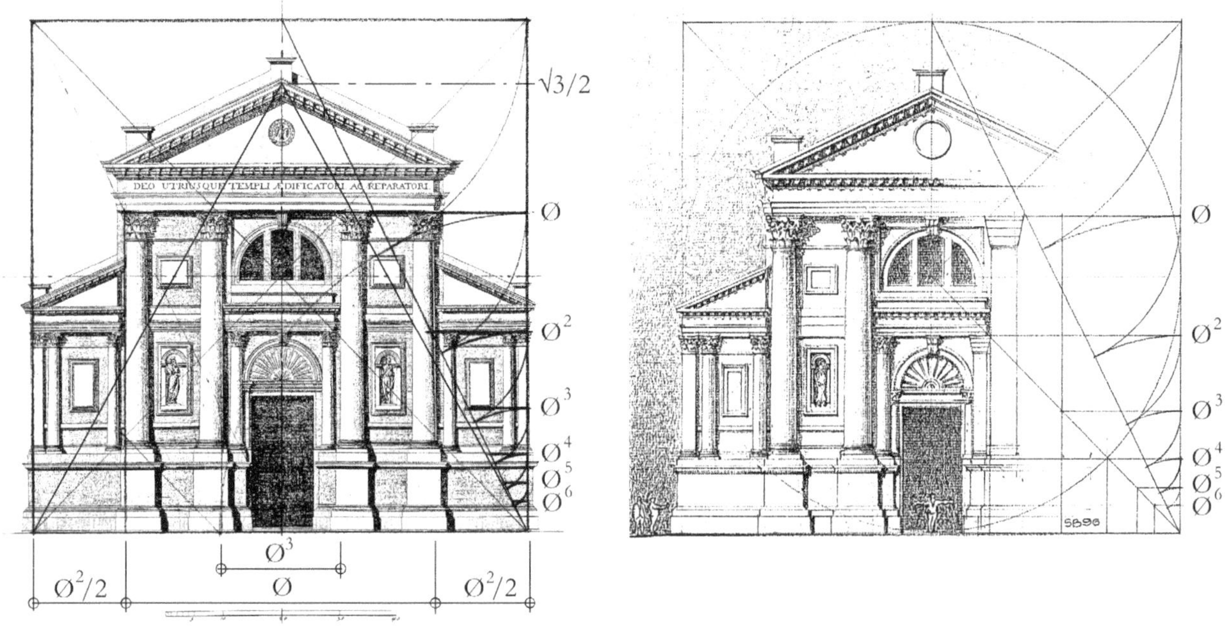

FIGURE 10a-b

San Francesco della Vigna, Venice, Palladio, 1564. Analysis and Reconstruction

SAN FRANCESCO DELLA VIGNA

The building was designed by Sansovino in 1534 and the facade by Palladio in 1564.[34] The planning of the church was the subject of the "memo of Zorzi" cited by Wittkower[35] as recapitulating the Platonic Lambda, using the numbers 1, 3. 9, and 27. Palladio's elevation is a masterpiece of integration of the classical elements, posing a brilliant solution to the problem of marrying the classical portico to the basilical church plan.

The elevation is analyzed using a Ø scale, **figure 10a**. The major columns and their pedestals are in a square of side Ø. The tops of the minor columns are at Ø^2, top of the pedestal at Ø^4 and the base is slightly lower than Ø^6. The entablature is slightly more than Ø^5, major column D is slightly less than Ø^6. The apex of the pediment is at the √3/2 point.

The facade reconstruction, **figure 10b**, also uses Ø as the key. The base is Ø^6, the pedestal is Ø^4, the tops of the minor columns are at Ø^2, the tops of the major columns are at Ø, and the entablature is Ø^5. The entry bay is Ø^3 wide, major column D is Ø^6, the inside of the outer major column is at Ø^4 from the side of the enclosing square. In this "pure" Ø reconstruction the major columns are Ø Ø^4 high, .618 - .146 = .472. H/D = .472/.056 = 8.43, a bit chunky for Corinthian capitals, and it increases the width of the portico at the expense of the end bays as shown by the inset panels. However Ø^5/2, .045 for D, would give an elegant H/D of 10.49. The entablature is 1/5.24 of the column.

THE PALLADIAN WINDOW

Figure 11a is an analysis of the "Palladian Window" or "Serliana" from the Basilica Palladiana at Vicenza guided by the division of the square into thirds and quarters.[36] The inner faces of the inner columns are at the 1/4 and 3/4 points. The height of the order is at the 2/3rds point. It is

11a

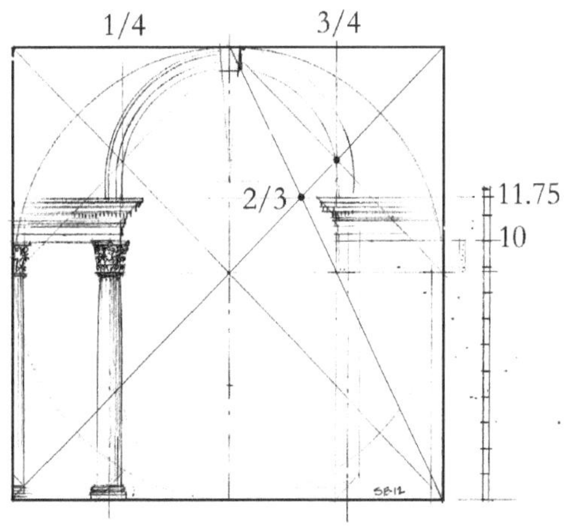

11b

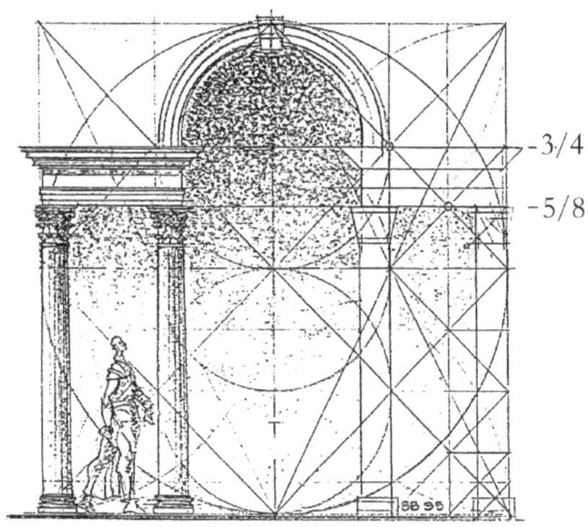

11c

FIGURE 11a-c

The Palladian Window. Basilica Palladiana, Vicenza, Palladio, 1546

divided by 8 for the column and 1 D for the abbreviated entablature, 1/2 D each for the architrave and cornice, totaling 9. The inside crown of the arch is below the enclosing square by 1/12th of the height of the square, making it a 12:23 rectangle. The arch can be made 1:2 by moving the columns inward by about 1/2 D each.

Figure 11b is a reconstruction guided by the same pattern but with slightly altered character. The Corinthian mode is used and the 2/3 height is divided into 11.75 D, 10 for the column, 3/4 for the architrave and 1 for the cornice.

The Palladian window is a "free" element, subject to a great deal of modification. In **figure 11c** the inner columns are placed with their outer face aligned with the quarter point. The relation of the arched center bay to the trabeated side bays can be varied widely, and the enclosing shape need not be a square. This flexibility has made the Palladian window an icon of classical design. It signals that the work it is part of is "classical," that no matter how humble the work its designer understood, or at least aspired to, the classical ideal.

Michelangelo: Early Life and Cultural Milieu

The high-water mark of visual art in the Renaissance was set by Michelangelo, 1474–1564. His extraordinary stature in painting, sculpture and architecture remains unsurpassed to this day. Michelangelo came from a middle-class professional family. As an infant he was nursed by the wife of a local stone cutter, leading him to remark later that, *"with my mother's milk I sucked down the hammer and chisels I use for my statues."*[37] He was sent to a grammar school but spends so much time drawing that, despite some family reservations as to the social status of artists, at the age of fourteen Michelangelo is apprenticed to the painter Domenico Ghirlandaio. Michelangelo shows precocious ability and soon comes to the attention of Florence's leading citizen, Lorenzo de Medici, when Ghirlandaio sends him to study with the sculptor Bertoldo di Giovanni whom Lorenzo had asked to form an art school utilizing the antique sculpture in the Medici collection.

In the garden of the Villa Medici the enthusiastic young Michelangelo makes a copy in marble of an antique sculpture of the head of a fawn, restoring parts of the mouth and teeth that had been damaged in the course of time. Lorenzo, impressed, makes a joke reminding Michelangelo that old people seldom have all their teeth, whereupon the young artist "distresses" the piece, knocking out some of the teeth. Lorenzo is further impressed, and Michelangelo is given the key to the garden where he works regularly. Within a year Lorenzo has him installed in a room in the Villa. *"Michelangelo always ate at Lorenzo's table with the sons of the family and other distinguished and noble persons who lived with that lord."*[38] He stayed for several years until Lorenzo's death in 1492.

By far the most "distinguished and noble" intellectual in the house in those years was Marcilio Ficino,1433–1499, installed in the household by Lorenzo's grandfather, Cosimo. Jacob Burckhardt writes, *"To Cosimo de Medici belongs the special glory of recognizing in the Platonic philosophy the fairest flower of the ancient world of thought, of inspiring his friends with the same belief, thus fostering within humanistic circles another, higher resuscitation of antiquity."* Cosimo was sufficiently involved that *"Ficino could style himself, as far as Platonism was concerned, the spiritual son of Cosimo."*[39] Having been inspired by the lectures of Plethon in Florence in 1439, Cosimo had resolved to found a new Academy in the Platonic mold. He is said to have immediately focused on Marsilio, the six-year-old son of his doctor.[40] After years of training in Greek, Latin and the seven liberal arts, Cosimo, in 1462, publicly sets up the twenty-nine-year-old Ficino and the new academy in his villa at Careggi.

Ficino's main task was to translate the entire body of Platonic writings and many of the later Neoplatonists such as Plotinus and Proclus from Greek to Latin, so they could be spread through the intelligentia. When the *Corpus Hermeticum* (*CH*) came to light in 1460, the now ailing Cosimo ordered Ficino to stop his ongoing work on Plato and translate the *Hermetica* so Cosimo could read it before he dies. Ficino succeeds. The *CH*, with its dramatic re-enactment of the Pythagorean–Platonic creation myth, its references to reincarnation, its frank presentations of alchemy, symbolic astronomy (that is, astrology), magical vitalization of matter, and especially its vision of life as an ongoing act of love between matter and spirit, electrified the Florentine Renaissance, powering it, one might say today, into a higher orbit, sending "gravitational" waves through Western culture, some of which ripple down to the present day.

Regarding Michelangelo's relation to all this, Panofsky writes[41] that he absorbed Platonism not just intellectually or as a fashion but as a *"metaphysical justification of his own self."* His life and work embody opposite aspects of Neoplatonism. On the one hand the idea of the *"presence of the*

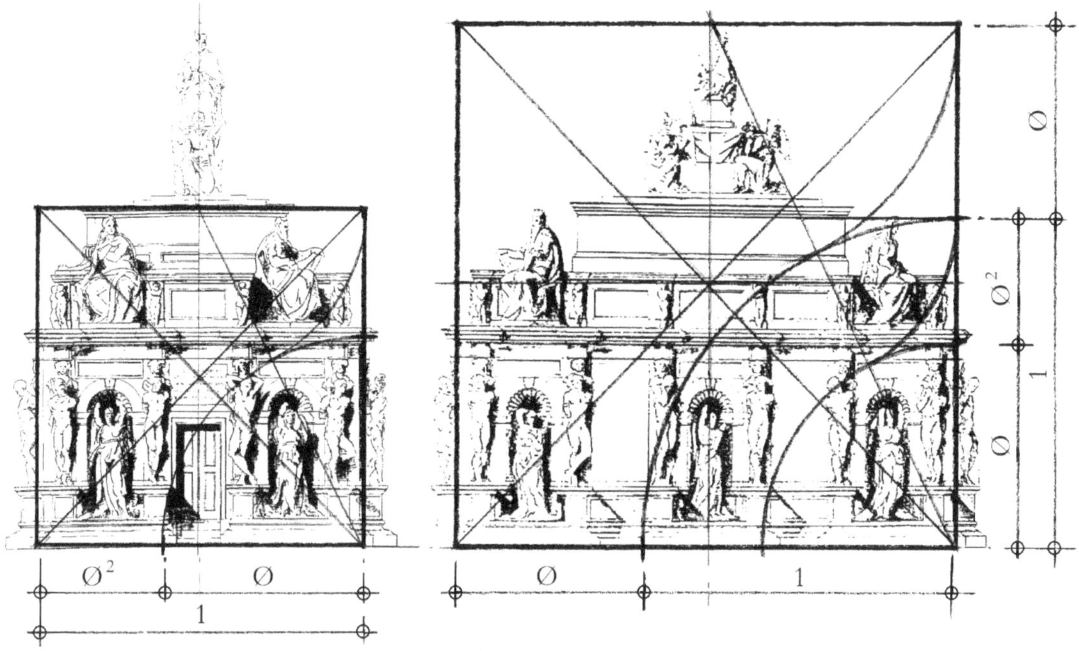

FIGURE 12
Tomb of Julius, Rome, Michelangelo, 1503

spiritual in the material," in other words, animism, stimulated his erotic pursuit of beauty. On the other hand the idea that the physical world was a kind of death, as in the motto "soma-sema," the body is a tomb, produced *"that unfathomable dissatisfaction with himself and the universe which is the very signature of Michelangelo's genius."*[42] Panofsky adds that in relationships like those with Tommaso dei Cavalieri and Vittoria Colonna, Michelangelo and his Florentine circle were living out the lecture of Diotima,[43] using attunement to physical beauty as a trigger for the elevation of consciousness.

Career of Michelangelo

With the death of Lorenzo in 1492, Michelangelo begins his independent career. In the following eleven years he executes the *Hercules,* the *Bacchus,* the *David,* the *Pietà* and others, establishing his brilliance as a sculptor. In 1503 he is summoned to Rome and begins work on the tomb of Julius II, pope from 1503–13, for which he carves the *Moses.*

The early version of the tomb, **figure 12,** is a block, 1 x 1 x 1+ Ø. The top of the lower section is at Ø. The top of the middle transitional section is at the half-point. The top of the upper section is at 1, completing the prismatic volume from which the mass of the tomb is carved. The top of the climactic sculpture is at the height of the enclosing square.

This project later falls prey to political and dynastic intrigues, and is not brought to fruition. Michelangelo is then maneuvered by Bramante's circle into painting the Sistine ceiling, which, for reasons of shape and construction technique, was considered a kind of artistic "mission impossible." But they had underestimated Michelangelo, whose stunning success capped his artistic reputation.

After this unprecedented twenty-five-year sculpture and painting career the forty-one-year-old Michelangelo begins his architectural life. Returning to Florence in 1515 at the order of the new Medici pope, Leo X, 1513–21, Michelangelo begins work on the San Lorenzo complex. The main body of the church had been built by Brunelleschi in 1420 but the facade had been left in rough masonry. The commission served the purpose of getting Michelangelo out of Rome, where

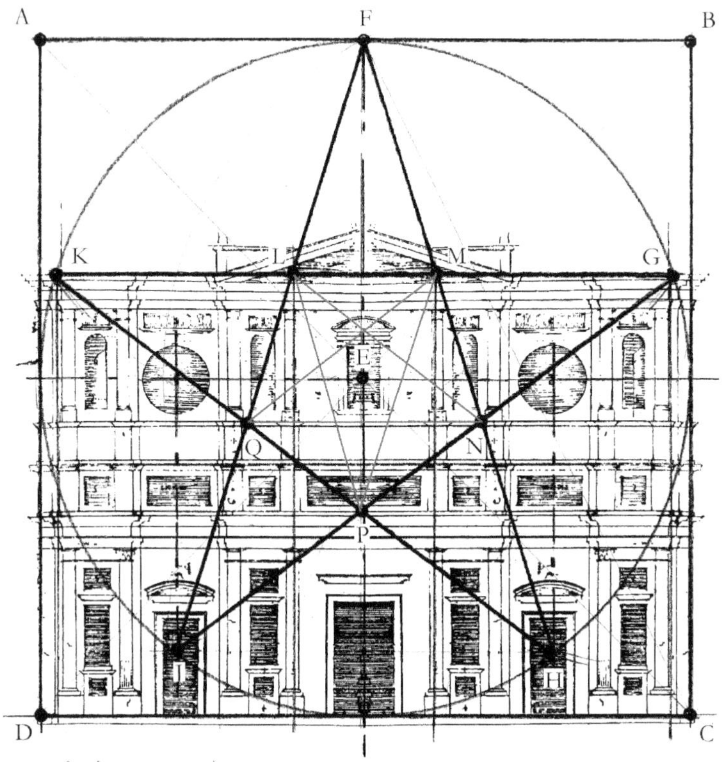

FIGURE 13
San Lorenzo, Facade, Florence, Michelangelo, 1515

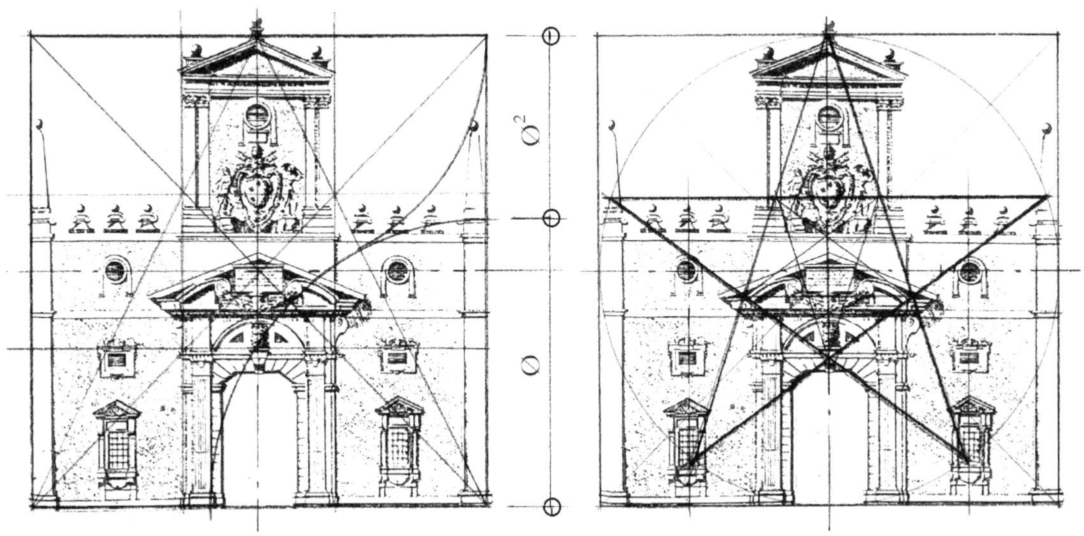

FIGURE 14
Porta Pia, Rome, Michelangelo, 1561

he was in conflict with the circle of Bramante and of preventing the completion of the tomb of Julius, who was from the della Rovere family, a dynastic line in competition with the Medici's.[44]

A drawing of the facade, likely made in connection with quarrying work,[45] is analyzed in **figure 13**. The drawing was taken from a large-scale wood model of the facade made under Michelangelo's direction. The overall width gives the side of square ABCD with center at E. Circle EF is inscribed within it and within that is drawn pentagram FGHJK, its diagonals forming pentagon LMNPQ. Diagonal KG gives the height of the cornice. Interval LM gives the width of the central bay. Points J and H mark the centers of the second and sixth bays. Along these center lines at height E are the centers of the circular panels. Points P and Q mark the heights of the two intermediate cornices. The middle cornice is not on the wood model.

Perhaps it seemed fitting to use the pentagram, the very symbol of the ancient Pythagorean brotherhood, which Michelangelo would likely have discussed with Ficino, on the facade of the church patronized by the family that supported them both. After several versions of the facade and several years spent in quarrying, the Medicis for dynastic reasons shift focus to the Medici chapel and tomb, known as the New Sacristy. The facade of the church remains unworked to this day.

After numerous projects including the Campidoglio and St. Peter's Basilica, and shortly before his death, Michelangelo designs the Porta Pia, 1562, **figure 14.** The elevation is informed by the square. The main body of the wall, its first story, attic and acroterion are approximately at the Ø point. The central feature is 1/3rd of the overall width. This design can also be analyzed using the pentagram. As at San Lorenzo the two circular panels in the side bays are positioned by the center of the square and the two lower points of the star. The width of the center bay, its enclosing aedicule, and the height of the opening are positioned by points on the inner pentagon.[46]

Michelangelo as Architect

In looking at the architecture of Michelangelo, geometrical arrangements, particularly pentagonal, have been used. But these are to be considered strictly analytical. They are unlikely to have been the method actually used by Michelangelo, who drew architecture as he would the human body, finding the right place for a division as if playing a fretless musical instrument.

Michelangelo maintained that he was a sculptor rather than an architect. This was not just modesty but rather a key to understanding his approach to architecture in which the building was *"conceived as if the masses were organic forms capable of expressing movement, of forming symphonies of light, shadow and texture, like a statue."* In a letter Michelangelo writes: *"architectural members derive from human members. Whoever is not a good master of the figure and most of all, of anatomy, cannot understand anything of it."*[47]

While analogies to the body go back at least through Vitruvius, fifteenth-century theorists thought of the body not as a pulsing breathing creature, but as a microcosmic carrier of the proportional forces of creation, in the same way as they thought of the musical octave or the periods of the planets as a kind of abstract, static perfection expressed through the analogies of ratio and geometry.[48] They illustrated the body in relation to a variety of ratios and polygons that were easily transferable to architecture. This had an abstracting effect on spatial concepts and may have assisted in the rise of the architect from medieval guild artisan to gentleman humanist.[49] From this context emerges the square or cubical module, a valid technique, but only approaching the beautiful when combined with a geometrical overview.[50] An overemphasis on the grid risks a loss of the critical sense of unity necessary to approach beauty. In the post-Alberti world, design came to be regarded as a weaving of harmonically proportioned planes into a static, balanced, three-dimensional structure.

Rather than making the analogy to the ideal harmonies that link the human to the cosmos, Michelangelo uses these numerical expressions to create an identification of our own physicality with the elements of the building, setting up a kind of sympathetic, even erotic bond. This method is based in understanding anatomy rather than geometry, but of course organic anatomy is also informed by harmonic proportion. The architectural elements are treated as though they were parts of an organism that swell or stretch in response to structural forces.[51] But these were not the actual structural forces. Those were handled by the mundane wall or mass on which the elements were placed. In Michelangelo's architecture the organic illusion always triumphed over "expression of structure."[52] The building acquires its vitality in a different way from the modular methods, the analogy is made on a visceral, emotional, erotic level. The building seems to live and breathe, establishing a link to the Egyptian magical tradition of vitalizing matter. This aesthetic approach is directly related to the work of Ficino, to his vision of a magical Hermetic cosmos, driven by eros and bound by love.[53]

These concepts informed Michelangelo's architectural drawing style.[54] He rarely used instruments, didn't indicate modules or include a scale. He worked in chalk or wash rather than ink line, emphasizing light-and-shade patterns rather than delineating parts in the manner of Alberti's outline method.[55] Michelangelo didn't think in perspective, equating architecture with sculpture; he did not design the building from a single fixed point, rather one was expected to move around or through the building as you would a statue.

Michelangelo's approach appears to be a "radical departure" from the main trends of the early Renaissance.[56] But here we choose to compare architectures in terms of their similarities rather than their differences; to look for manifestations of the "perennial" tradition of number and geometry as a guide to the remembrance of Unity through art. In this view, the architecture of Michelangelo is not a "radical departure," but rather represents, to continue the organic metaphor, a kind of ingestion or digestion of the system of Alberti and Brunelleschi, and an imaginative projection beyond them, yet rooted in them. After all, as noted, the same ratios govern the structure of the body and the conventional elements of architecture. But these ratios do not in themselves demand any particular manner of presentation.

The conflict with Bramante and his circle actually occurred; it is not imaginary. But in the view of this author, it can be largely explained by Michelangelo's failure, on all occasions, to be a "team player." He represents the ultimate development of "personality" or "artistic temperament." He knows his craft skill is superior to others and refuses to see the need for compromise, which, in any event, would destroy the complete integration of vision and skill that creates his very superiority.

Perhaps a more interesting conflict is that between the quasi-pagan, mystical humanists and orthodox Christian theologians. It continues the age-old push and pull between seeking knowledge to elevate consciousness and using knowledge to actually govern the material world. It manifests in the Renaissance in the debate over the merits of centrally planned churches as opposed to extended or "nave"-type churches; between "Greek" cross and "Latin" cross plans, or we might say, between circle or regular polygon and elongated rectangle. Advocates of the circle may be considered Pythagorean and may well be carriers of an "initiatic" tradition of some sort, theological, revived, or craft based. Governance of the civilized world, it seems, requires a hierarchy, a differentiation in which individual elements can find clearly distinct yet harmonically related linear positions. The Pythagorean is apt to take an "all in one" approach that mutes such distinctions in favor of some overall integration, relating it to the style of Michelangelo.

A major contribution of Michelangelo is the emphatic, dramatic restatement of the concept of anthropos, the analogy between the individual and the cosmos, but now seen from a viewpoint where the anamnesic effect is produced by the building as a whole taking on a vital animated quality, just as one would in making a statue of a living creature. Architectural elements, while still subject to the harmonious numbering systems of his predecessors, now breathe and flex at his command. They would be fragments without the whole, as would an eye or a nose. Here is the emergence of a theory of organic design in the modern world, one not unrelated to that of Sullivan and Wright.

Reaction to Michelangelo

Significant as the organic approach is, it always attracts criticism or worse because its inherently internal nature produces suspicion in those who govern the external world. In Renaissance Rome the response wasn't long in coming. Pirro Ligorio, 1514–1583, designer of the Villa d'Este, Tivoli, and the charming Villa Pia in Rome, savages Michelangelo in an unpublished manuscript.[57] Referring to the Porta Pia, he says *"If they make a city gate they put a mask in the center as if it were a temple of Bacchus ... and the more frightening they make it the more they consider it to be beautiful,* [instead of using orthodox ornamentation] *they put up certain nonsense, certain jolting discontinuities worthy of discord, and of the uncertainty of life, things truly dubious."* Ligorio is referring to such aspects as wall stepping and broken pediments. He sees Michelangelo's transformation of the elements as *"things proper only to the obsessed."* Speaking personally of Michelangelo, Ligorio says *"having got in his head the idea of being an architect, he has ruined as many orders and proportions as are found in the excellent ancient works, and makes poor Vitruvius' head spin."* Ligorio notes that the response from the partisans of Michelangelo was essentially that Vitruvius is trivialized by being taken literally, as an end rather than a beginning, and that strict imitation is mindless. Portoghesi says that for Ligorio, *"The only refuge from doubt is escape to the perfect classical order, and he who rejects this refuge is among the 'enemies of God, who has made every form of the world perfect,' and according to Ligorio he becomes the corruptor of youths."*[58]

The charge "corruptor of youth" echoes that of the trial of Socrates. It indicates, for this author, the continuing difficulty encountered by the initiatic–Orphic–Pythagorean–Platonic–Hermetic tradition, with its emphasis on direct experience of divinity, on the analog of the living individual and the cosmos, and on the human body, including its erotic aspect, as a vehicle for self-elevation.

The issue of doubt refers to the major political issue of the era, the Protestant Reformation and the response of the Roman Catholic Church, called the Counter-Reformation. It was this effort that provided the clientele for some of the greatest works of the period. The issue of disruption and discontinuity not only refers to the Reformation but also to the cosmological ideas it released. In 1609 Kepler published his *Astronomia nova* in which he perfected the heliocentric system of Copernicus and demonstrated that the planets move in elliptical orbits. Within a year the concept was dramatically confirmed by Galileo's telescopic observation: it could no longer be sidestepped, the earth now moved! Within thirty years the ellipse came to dominate Baroque architecture, prefigured by Michelangelo's elliptical dome for St. Peter's in the 1560s.

In the generation following his death *"behind the declared admiration for Michelangelo's genius, there lurked a censorious attitude towards the master for his dilettantism and above all for his tendency to attack the equilibrium of the classical language by critically interpreting its static and impassive quality, and forcing it to express a sense of human passion, imbuing it with doubt, with that disquieting sense of things still open to investigation."*[59]

The Baroque

In the last period of the Italian Renaissance the lessons of balance and stasis taught by ancient architecture had been absorbed, epitomized in Bramante's Tempietto. Michelangelo changed the rules of the game by introducing a dynamic aspect.[60] The era is known as the Baroque, a term derived from a Portuguese word referring to "an imperfectly shaped pearl." The setting is Rome, in the years ±1600 – 1700. This entire phase stands in the shadow of Michelangelo, who died in 1562. Vatican insiders such as Fontana, Ligorio, and della Porta take a negative attitude toward Michelangelo's organic, erotic, emotional approach. A generation later, in the 1590s, Carlo Maderno takes another look. His two principal associates are Bernini and Borromini. Bernini accepts some of the concept, but it is Borromini who enthusiastically embraces the Organic idea to accomplish a unique and dramatic personal vision that culminates the era.

Borromini, 1599–1667, is a younger relative of Maderno, 1556–1629, who, in turn, is a relative of Domenico Fontana, 1543–1607. All three are from the Lake Lugano area of Lombardy. This "Lombard clan in Rome"[61] begins with della Porta, 1533–1602. He works with the elderly Michelangelo on St. Peter's. Fontana comes to Rome in 1563, and working under della Porta they complete Michelangelo's dome, 1585–1590. Portoghesi refers to Fontana as *"the pope's engineer,"*[62] who implements the new street layout imposed on Rome by Pope Sixtus V, 1585–1590, including positioning of the obelisks. The influence of "the clan" is long-lived. Around 1700, Carlo Fontana, Domenico's grandson, is the teacher of the influential British architect James Gibbs. Perhaps because of the Lombard connection, but certainly under the impetus of the Counter-Reformation, the Baroque moved north into southern Germany where it continued to produce extraordinary work well into the eighteenth century.

Major themes of Baroque architecture are: the plastic use of mass to shape and effect space; an inventive license with the canonical elements; the use of hidden, indirect light sources; and merging actual and virtual or "trompe l'oeil" space through sophisticated perspective.[63] These themes are accomplished by creating a *"hierarchic-organic unity of the work"* through a dialectic between wall and column, structure and ornament, and careful use of shadows on modulated registers giving an *"atmospheric life of the wall."*[64]

Space is no longer just a static void to be counterpointed by a static solid. In the Baroque space it takes on a vital, active quality; it can be shaped and directed by the shaping and placing of solids. In particular the dynamically shaped facade modulates a push and pull relationship between the building's interior space and the urban space it fronts on, establishing an organic connection. The Baroque facade maintains its anthropomorphic analogies of the elements inherited from Michelangelo while at the same time actively shaping space on an urban scale.

Baroque space was both the passive container of mass and *"something corporeal and having density, something that can be modeled by acting on its surrounding shell with the flexible instrument of geometry."* This "corporeality" gives an anthropomorphic presence, *"a sense of pulsating vitality."* As the interior of the building shapes the facade, the facade shapes the external space around it, which is the interior space of the city. They are both *"filled with this vitality, their connection by means of facades and openings becomes the crucial nodal point of architecture."*[65]

Bernini writes that, *"the most beautiful moment that can be selected for* [representing] *the mouth is either when one has just finished speaking or when one is about to begin."*[66] The focus is on the moment of transformation of the potential to the actual as the vitalizing factor. The direct analogy is not ignored either: "*The projection at the center of the facade of the Filippini is explained by Borromini in the 'Opus Architectonicum' as the protrusion of the chest, while the articulated wings of the facade represent the arms with their joints. The necessity to connect the spatial configuration of the architecture to a vital, living rhythm also found expression in Bernini's device of the lateral dilation of the view, which had driven him to change the line of penetration of the ellipse to the short axis, as he does in Sant'Andrea al Quirinale,*"[67] **figure 17**. The vital quality is expressed differently in architecture than in sculpture through controlled curvature, perspective and proportion. Curvature in particular is used to create an *"organic connection between exterior and interior."*[68]

Mystery light, whose source is hidden or disguised, creates the illusion of a space having a light of its own, as though it were another world with its own sun.[69] This gives a transcendental quality to the experience of the image or space. These lighting and spatial effects are facilitated by the refined use of brick vaulting, in which Borromini was a specialist. Particular structural techniques are a factor always present in any genuine architecture, though they need not be expressed. Maderno and Borromini cut their structural teeth on the vaulting of the nave of St. Peter's.

These themes are a Baroque restatement of the principle of anthropos in architecture. The idea is descended from the work of Michelangelo and associated with the revival of the Hermetic, that is to say, Platonic philosophy. Portoghesi correctly labels this attitude toward space as "organic," that is to say, having a vital, living quality. In the ancient Mystery religions the experience of this vital quality of the entire cosmos was part of the candidate's apotheosis, the merging with divinity, in the initiatic moment. In Baroque architecture the anthropic principle is manifest in the stepping, curving and inflecting surfaces, and may be taken as a reference to a kind of Hermetic animism. It is an intentionally analogic architecture working on two scales, that of the building and that of the city.

In the architecture of the Counter-Reformation, illusionism was recruited consciously as a tool for propagating the Church's cause. Mystery light, organic curvilinear forms and virtual perspective space, all backed by structural virtuosity combine in the service of this cause. Exact adherence to geometry should not be expected here as these buildings are conceived as living cells that pulse and breathe. If the concept of treating the building as a single vital organism was brought to life in Renaissance architectural culture by Michelangelo, the Baroque architects, in effect, taught it to sing and dance.

Santa Susanna

Maderno's works include: 1) the church of Santa Susanna, Rome, 1585–1603, **figure 15**; 2) adding the nave of St. Peter's to the centralized plan of Michelangelo; 3) the facade of St. Peter's; and 4) the Palazzo Barberini, 1628, **figure 16,** completed after his death by Bernini and Borromini.

The stepped facade of Santa Susanna *"was conceived by Maderno… in terms of the opportunity it offered to characterize the surrounding space,* [and] *to create one of those urban poles postulated by Sistine street planning."* He does this by stepping the facade forward to give it mass when viewed from along the street at a sharp angle, and by use of the one-story side wings with their large scroll brackets to link the large-scale facade to the surrounding facades. Maderno's use of the elements vitalizes the wall through a *"syntactic revision that releases them from their immutability, giving them new life."* Vertical and horizontal registers, created by positioning of the elements and stepping of the wall, are thought of as carriers of light and shadow.[70]

The width of the facade, **figure 15a**, may be divided into 12 units and the height into 15, a 4:5 ratio. The inner pair of columns seems to be centered on the 1/3rd points. The first story is within a 1:2 rectangle, the entablature is 1/5th of the height of the order and lower D of the columns is

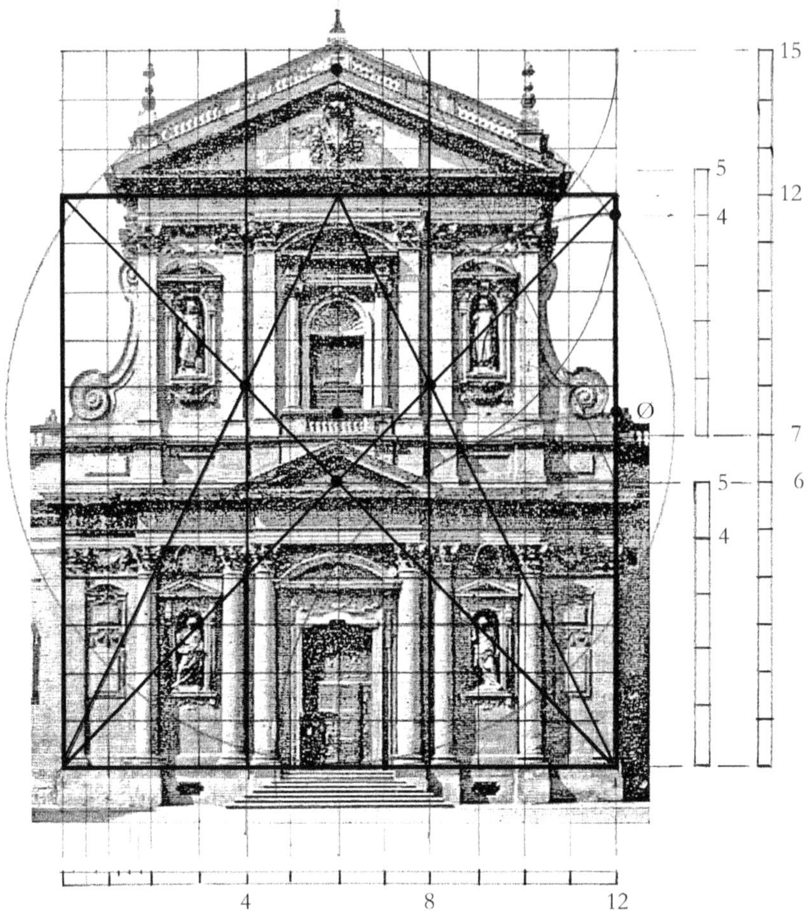

FIGURE 15a

Santa Susanna, Rome, Maderno, 1597

about 1/2 a unit or 1/24th of the width. The second story has a pedestal 1 unit high, the columns by inspection are about 4.5 units.

Reconstruction of Santa Susanna

15b.1. Begin with square ABCD. Divide width CD into thirds at J and K, and then into 12ths. The height CF will be 15 units, making EFCD a 4:5 rectangle. The first story of the facade will be within double square GHCD, 6 x 12 units.

15b.2. The entablature of the first story will be HL, 1/5th of HC. There are four full shafts on each side of the center, three engaged columns and a pilaster. The innermost two are paired at point J. Lower D of the columns is found by dividing each of the 12 units into 4 parts each, or overall width CD into 48 parts. D will be 2 parts, 1/24th of CD = .041. Setting CD = 1, the column height, CL ≈ .400, $Ø^2$, giving an H/D of 9.60. Since the Corinthian mode is used the pair of columns have a clear space of 1/2 D between them. The outermost pilaster is placed at the edge of the square, at D. The last column is placed 2 D from the outer column and 2.75 D from the inner pair, point Q. Points N and P which give the center bay are at a $Ø^3$ interval, ≈ 5.5 D.[71]

15b.3. The second story is within a square, RSTU, 9 x 9 units. Strike off 1 unit as a pedestal, WT. The top of the columns are at V which is Ø of ST making column height VW ≈ 4.5 units, .375 of BC. D of the second story columns = 5/6th of lower column D = .034; giving a slender H/D of 11.03.

15b.4. The principal doorway is Ø of the central bay NP and is a 1:2 rectangle. The second story opening is found by the √2 cut, taken between the pilasters. It is a 2:3 rectangle with a semi-circular

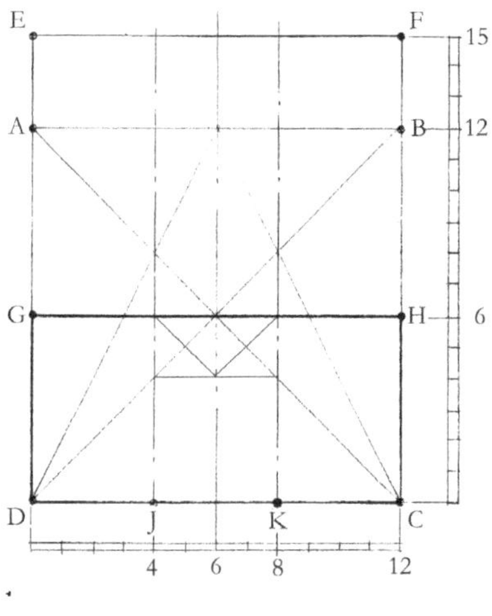

15b.1

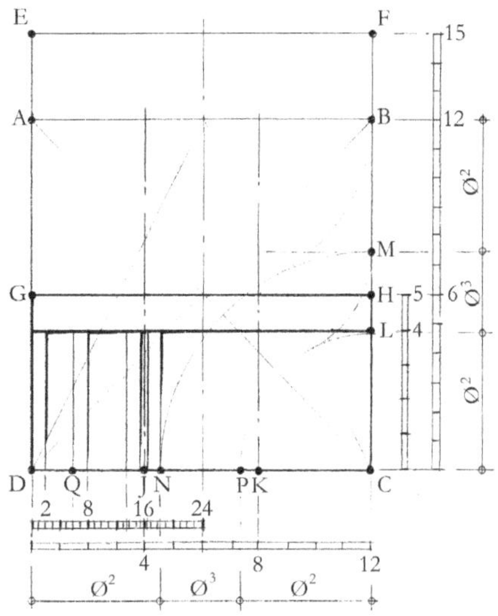

15b.2

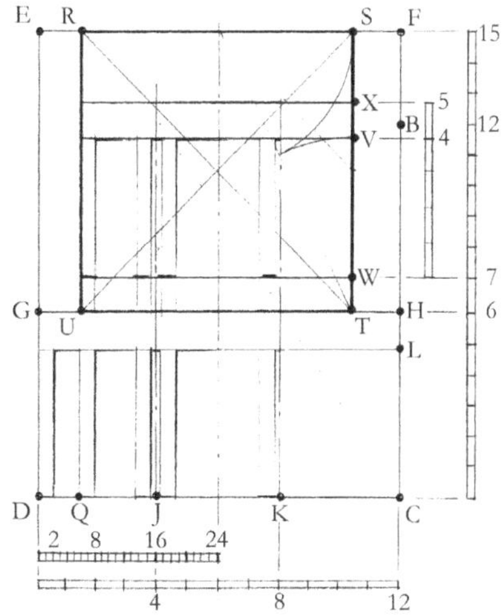

15b.3

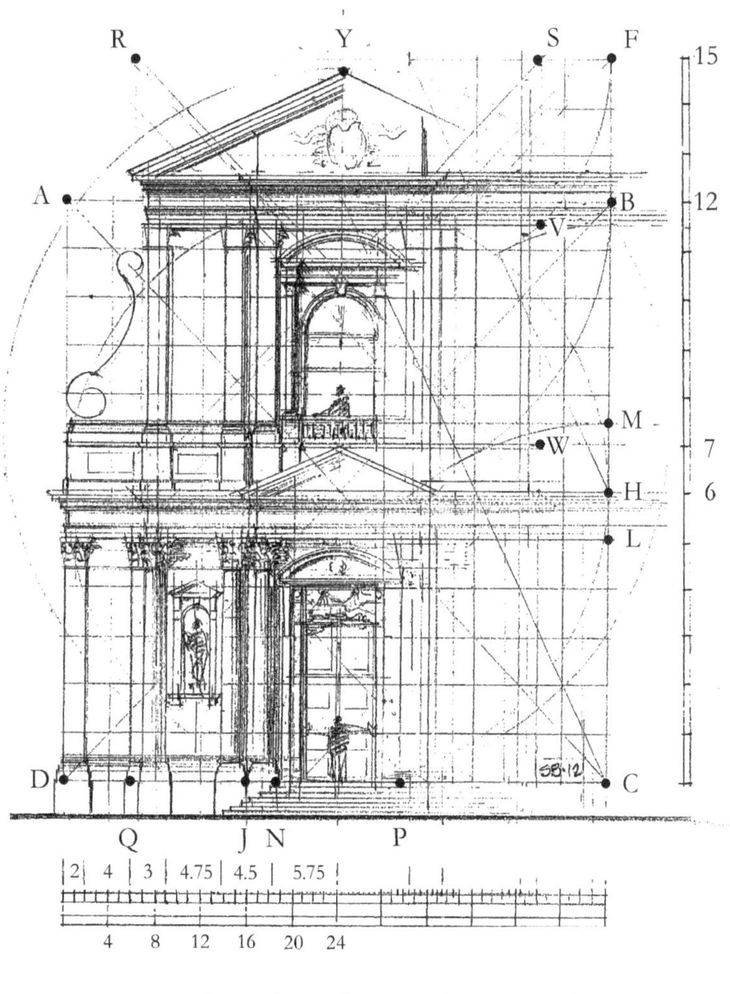

FIGURE 15b.4 – *Santa Susanna Reconstruction*

arch over it, making it 2:1. In the final step the outer column is moved 1/48th, about 2.1% inboard from Q to allow for placement of a half-pier. The niches in the intermediate bays are found either by the √2 cut or are 3/4 of their bay wide and about 2:5 in ratio. The ornamentation of these openings is found using similar procedures used in the reconstruction of an opening in Palladio's Palazzo

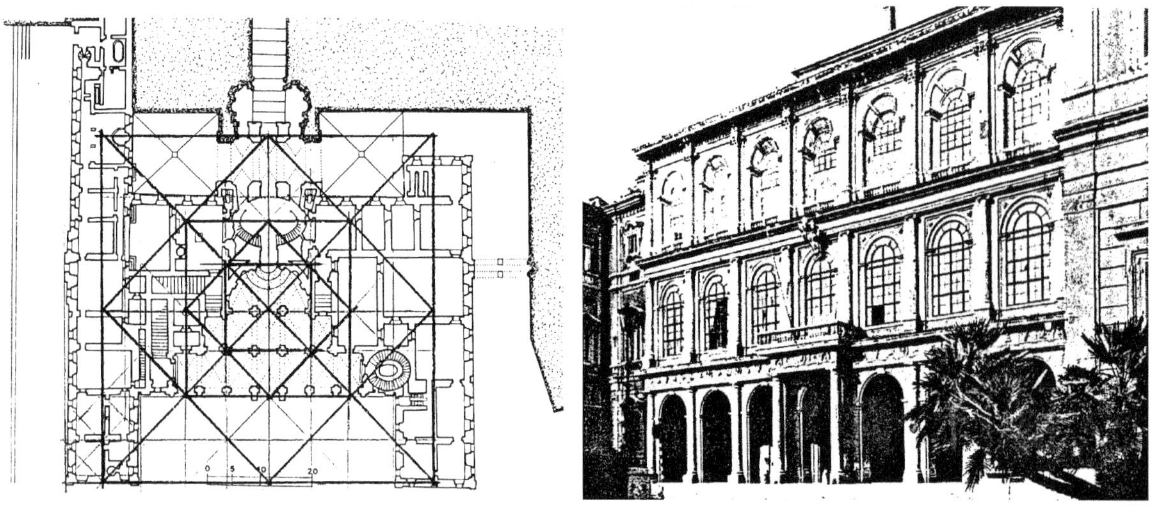

FIGURE 16
Palazzo Barberini, Rome, Maderno, 1628. Assisted by Bernini and Borromini

Porto, **figure 9.** The apex of the cyma, point Y, may be set at the height of line RS, giving a rake angle of about 28°. This point may also be created through the "squaring of the circle" procedure.[72]

Although we cannot be certain of the methods used by Baroque architects, our reconstruction has come very close using methods that can explicate the architecture of the previous two thousand years. Even the most elaborate Baroque "wedding cakes" of Vignola, Cortona or Rainaldi can be analyzed using similar methods. The presence of the "squared circle," in particular, indicates that the Baroque apples have not fallen far from the Vitruvian tree.

Bernini and Borromini

Though Borromini and Bernini worked together under Maderno on St. Peter's and the Palazzo Barberini, **figure 16,** they differed markedly in personality. Bernini was charming, chatty and outgoing. Borromini was introverted, depressive and distant. Bernini was the acknowledged leader in the arts of the day. His stunning success in painting, sculpture and architecture gave him a stature close to that of Michelangelo. At the same time Borromini labored in relative obscurity.

Bernini, 1598–1680, was the son of a successful sculptor of Florentine descent.[73] His father, Pietro, moved the family to Rome when his son was seven. Pietro participated in major commissions and moved in the patronage circle of Pope Paul V Borghese, 1605–1621, and his family. Bernini at age 19 began to work independently for the Borgheses. Within a few years he was a celebrity. By the time he was thirty he was running a studio with extensive painting, sculpture and monument commissions. His architectural works began in the mid 1620s when he designed the Baldacchino and culminated in the late 1660s with the colonnade at St. Peter's.

In the early seventeenth century it was determined by Kepler that the planets moved in elliptical orbits about the sun. Within a few years the ellipse became a major architectural motif in Rome. At S'Andrea al Quirinale, Rome, 1658–70, **figure 17,** Bernini uses the elliptical motif based on a dyadic pair of circles. The long axis gives the altitude for a pair of equilateral triangles, the bases of which give the long radii of the ellipse. A smaller pair of equilateral triangles position and size the altar and entrance. The vaulting of the dome uses a hexagonal pattern.

Borromini joined Maderno in Rome about 1620 as an ornamental carver. Maderno soon had him working at St. Peter's, where he specialized in brick vaulting. When Maderno died in 1629, Bernini was put in charge of St. Peter's and the Barberini. Borromini was in effect demoted from a colleague of Bernini to his employee. While by all reports Bernini was reasonable about the situation, apparently giving Borromini a fairly free hand on the completion of the Barberini palace,[74] Borromini smoldered, his resentment lasting lifelong.

He seized the chance for independence in 1634 with the design for the small church complex of San Carlo alle Quattro Fontane, Rome. The interior was built between 1638–41, the facade much later, 1665–70. Borromini also uses an elliptical motif in plan but to very different effect. Happily, Borromini has left a drawing of San Carlo, **figure 18,** showing the geometrical basis for the positioning of the interior columns and their ever-flowing entablature.

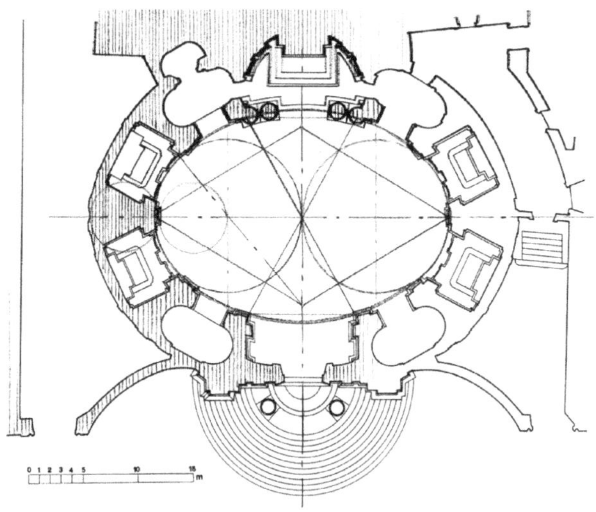

FIGURE 17

Sant'Andrea al Quirinale, Rome, Bernini, 1658

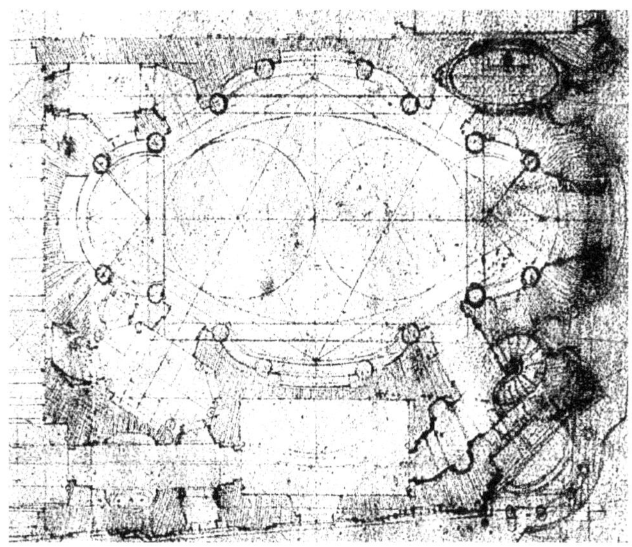

FIGURE 18

San Carlo alle Quattro Fontane, Rome, 1638

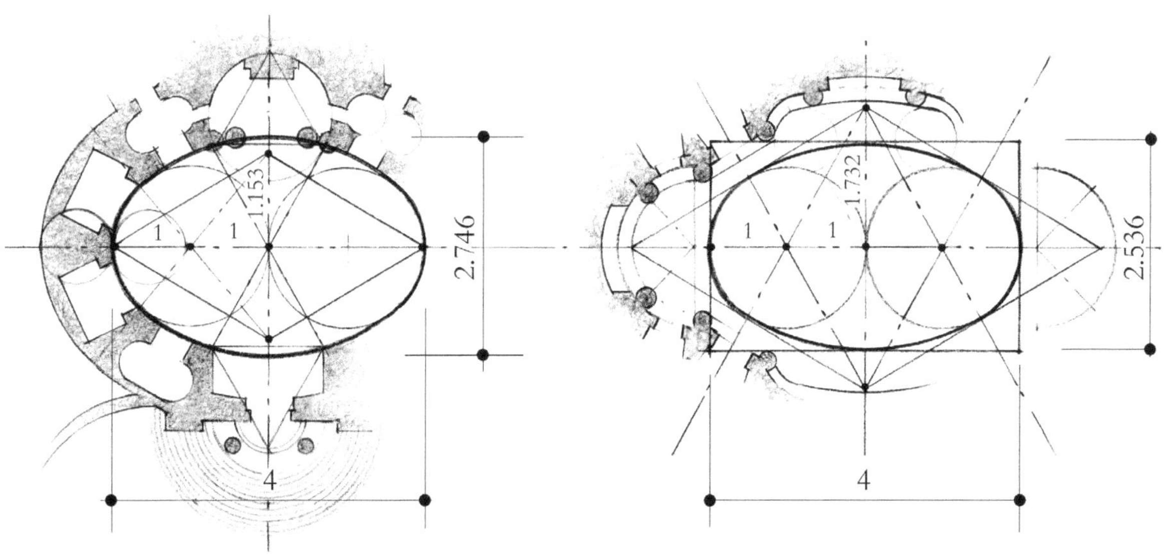

FIGURE 19

Geometry of Sant'Andrea and San Carlo

Their respective geometries are compared in **figure 19.** Both start with dyadic circles but Bernini inscribes an equilateral lozenge within them while Borromini circumscribes the lozenge. Bernini's ellipse is in the ratio of $4/2.746 = 1{:}1.456 \approx \sqrt{2}$. Borromini's ellipse is in the ratio of $4/2.536 \approx 8{:}5$, or Ø, and significantly he surrounds the ellipse with a Ø rectangle used to position the inner eight columns. This construction of the ellipse was published by Serlio almost a century earlier.[75] But of course this pattern is a continuation of the medieval tradition of ad triangulum. Both designers began with the same underlying division of unity, into the dyad, but ended with designs of markedly different character, in keeping with their personalities.

FIGURE 20 – *Palazzo Falconieri, Rome, Borromini, 1646*

Borromini brought a kind of popular or working class touch to design, perhaps in continuation of medieval traditional practices. His identification with popular tradition is illustrated by an ability to *"transfigure motifs of humble craft origin."*[76] This attitude can perhaps be seen in Borromini's work on the Palazzo Falconieri, **figure 20,** which has a distinct Gothic feeling in its proportions and its ornamental motifs, harking back to a more communal sense. *"Practical solutions are offered that make the work a communicative and didactic text even at the strictly technical level, these solutions being of interest not to the critics and the sophisticated, but rather to the artisans and workers."* Thus, in the last days of Italian supremacy in the arts, Borromini reverses the movement of Brunelleschi two hundred years earlier, of the architect as a controlling personality. This reversal, however, would help to suffuse the Baroque aesthetic through all levels of Roman culture, where sparks of it still smolder in the works of that era.

Borromini appears to achieve vitality and a sense of unity through the appearance of motion guided by geometry. Like a living creature, the elements at San Carlo seem to be caught at the still moment of the turning point of a breath. In the end, Borromini's work took the classical system of architecture down the "organic" pathway further than it had gone before and to a place seldom visited since. But the journey, in this case, proved too much for the traveler, and Borromini, consumed by despair, committed suicide at age 68.

The Enlightenment

After the Renaissance

Proportion is at the heart of the classical idea. Proportion sets the limits for a classical design, shapes the mass of the building, sizes and places the elements, and helps develop a building's character. The efficacy of proportion is traditionally linked with both the philosophical and magical systems. Both imply that there is a chain of being, emanating from a divine, or at least, mysterious center, guiding the appearance of the physical world. Links in the chain represent levels of informing principle, from general to specific, from Idea into Matter. While the philosopher works with the ideas in an internal process of self-elevation, the magician works with these subtle, nonphysical informing powers to effect the appearance of change in the outer world.

Links in the chain transmit their power through a kind of sympathetic, harmonic resonance or vibration. As the principles of harmony can be described by number, so number becomes symbolic of the informing powers. This gives rise to logos, a story of coming into being, illustrated by number and geometry. In a traditional unified cosmology, the same numerical principles guide visual art.

The fifteenth- to sixteenth-century Florentine Renaissance restated the magical theory in Christian form, couched in Neoplatonic terms. This magical atmosphere continued in the Italian arts through the Baroque era while the official church waxed hot and cold on this issue.[1] By the seventeenth century, proportion had been at the center of design theory and process for some forty-two hundred years, the entire span of civilization since the days of Imhotep. Beginning about 1650, however, the proportional heart of the classical idea was systematically cut out, leaving only its superficial appearance. To be intelligible such an unprecedented action needs to be seen in a larger context.

The shift of political and economic power from the Mediterranean to the Atlantic at the end of the sixteenth century marks the beginning of the era known as the "Enlightenment," or "Age of Reason," which runs into the early nineteenth century. The era's chief characteristic is the aggrandizement of the human rational faculty. For the first time in history a civilization rejected not only magical governance but the concept of magic itself. It rejected the idea that the cosmos is alive, intelligent and has a single center. The psychic and noetic realms were considered not to exist, or if they did, to be at an indefinite distance from the material realm, unable to exert any influence. Anyone claiming to utilize such non-material aspects was in danger of being ostracized, diagnosed, criminalized, even executed. This condition had dramatic effects. For example, in Platonism the Real is that which does not undergo change—the Forms or Ideas—while Matter, which is constantly changing, is referred to as the Actual. In the Enlightenment, the Real shifts from the Ideal to the Material, while the nonphysical Ideal is simply pushed off the table of acceptable discussion.

Magic, Math, and the Nation State

Several significant factors combined to set the stage for this dramatic transformation of consciousness and culture. First was the Protestant Reformation begun in 1517. In the Reformation the necessity of the intervention of the priest as a magical agent was attacked. One was to obtain access to higher states and ultimate salvation through ones own work and study. The scriptures were translated into the vernacular so they could be read by any literate person. The Reformation specifically rejected not only magical ritual but repudiated magical governance in general. Acts of governance would henceforth be based in "reason." They would be logical and substantiated by empirical observation, excluding anything metaphysical. This attitude extended to the direct investigation of nature rather than reliance on philosophical or religious orthodoxy.

A second factor in the fall of proportion was the change in mathematics when advanced algebra developed during the sixteenth century and calculus in the seventeenth. These forms are abstract and strictly logical. Calculus in particular involves the "infinitesimal" division, creating ontological difficulties.[2] Number reduced to arithmetic became a form of abstract logic completely divorced from number as a living symbol. The goal of this new math is to achieve power in the material world, not in the psychic or spiritual development of the person.

Another shock to traditional culture was the development of the telescope c.1600. This allowed Galileo and others to establish the "imperfections" of the astronomical heavens, whose perfection had long been a given in Aristotelian science. The official Ptolemaic theory was that the planets moved in exact circles, their irregular movements accounted for by "epicycles" or circles on circles. By Galileo's time-improved mathematical analysis indicated that the planets move in elliptical paths around the sun. The cosmological analogy of "as above so below" began to collapse as symbolic space was replaced by actual space.[3]

The late sixteenth-century writings of Francis Bacon, 1561–1626, outlined an approach to science as power over nature. Such a science goes further than just the organized study of nature. It presumes that matter is not alive and that "objects" can be separated from the rest of the universe to be studied in isolation. These two factors created "reductionism," the basis of modern science as distinct from ancient science. The mathematics of power became the model of Enlightened rationality, the primary tool of the new science, as in the mathematical determination of ballistic trajectory. Science had been reduced from natural philosophy to the study of materiality. It fragmented into numerous specialties from which reductionist ideology excluded any vision of unity or even any relation of the subject of study to anything else.

Rational governance and the mathematics of power came together in support of the development of the nation state, which took off after the Thirty Years' War, 1618-48. The seventeenth century marked the era of struggle between the kings and churches over who would collect the taxes necessary for a centralized administration and a standing army. Aside from not having their own military forces, religious institutions were inevitably wed to metaphysics, while secular forces were not. As governing decisions in the new state were to be based in reductionist rationality, the secular forces won the ideological, as well as the financial and military struggles.

This period saw the rise of the middle class, who administered the nation state, and still do today; whose wealth and power is based on trade and industry. In the preceding medieval system there were three classes, each symbolic of one of the stages of the ancient cosmogenic cycle. The aristocracy represented the proceeding; serfs and burghers, the maintaining; and clergy, the returning. With the rise of the middle class, the preoccupation with matter and its acquisition is raised to a principle of state.

While rational governance is a wonderful, optimistic idea, it is suggested here that it is not actually possible to put into practice. People just don't work that way. As Plato advises,[4] the challenge of governing a civilization is to harmonize the efforts and assumptions of non-sanguinely related groups. Plato suggests that governors use the "noble lie," that is, a myth of unified origin, often linked to astronomical symbols. Rational data-based argument is not without merit, but simply cannot trump myth as a motivator or coordinator of peoples' assumptions about life.

In the seventeenth century, Protestant and Catholic institutions, as well as the secular elite, rejected magic as a governing principle in public life. Yet, myth remains today essential to human governance. The resolution of this dilemma was that governance would now be exerted on two levels: a public rational level and a private magico-mythic level; the modern state underwent a personality split.

The Post-Magical State

The first response to this schizophrenic condition came in the early seventeenth century with the phenomenon of Rosicrucianism, a spiritually inspired vision of a revitalization of knowledge, and a new civilization that would be the outcome of its application. It drew on a combination of the work of Francis Bacon, calling for a new form of open knowledge, and John Dee, Queen Elizabeth's court astrologer and magician, whose methods utilized symbolic number. The Rosicrucian vision is centered around healing, using the system of the German doctor Paracelsus,[5] 1493–1541, firmly grounded in the Neoplatonic tradition of Ficino, including the use of astrology in diagnosis, and alchemy and talismans in treatment. Rosicrucianism arose in southern Germany in the circle of the Elector Palatinate, Frederick V, later known as the "winter king" of Bavaria. Frederick's wife was Elizabeth Stuart, daughter of England's James I. Frederick and James were part of an alliance of Protestant aristocrats opposed to the Catholic Hapsburgs.

Rosicrucianism surfaced as a pair of printed documents, the *Fama* and the *Confessio* published in 1614-15 in Cassel, a town near the Palatinate, shortly after the arrival of the royal couple. The *Fama*[6] tells the story of an inspired mystical teacher, Christian Rosenkreuz (CRC), who was born in Germany in the fourteenth century, traveled extensively in the "East" where he engaged in spiritual study, and returned home to practice as a healer and teacher. He began working with assistants and soon formed a private "Brotherhood." Over time, this Brotherhood grew and spread to various parts of the continent.

CRC eventually passed away at the age of 106, and the location of his tomb had been lost. Now, it was found again. The door was opened, symbolizing the opening of a new age, like dawn preceding the day. The time had come for the Brotherhood to reveal itself. Like-minded individuals were encouraged to come forward, respond to the *Fama,* and join the now public Brotherhood. Knowledge that had before been concealed would now be diffused to foster a return to an Edenic state: a unity of human and natural life. Combining influences from Bacon, Dee and Paracelsus, the universe was still magical, but open knowledge of matter would now be used publicly for human benefit.

CRC's tomb was a seven-sided room, with each wall facet a 5 x 8 unit panel. The ceiling vault was seven triangles, each with ten "figures," with writing. The floor was also divided into triangles, having zodiacal and astronomical markings. The sun did not penetrate the tomb; it was lit by a center light, an "inner" sun.[7] In the center was a round altar with an inscription stating that the tomb is a "compendium of the universe." Each wall panel contained a storage area for books and technical equipment, most likely alchemical, essentially containing all of the knowledge of the Brotherhood.

The image of the tomb with its "inner" light containing the knowledge of physical world, a shadow of the ideal world, is reminiscent of Plato's cave.[8] The seven sides may be taken to represent the seven liberal arts, a complete, concentrated microcosm of human knowledge.

Construction of the heptagon is related to the 5:8 pillar of the Egyptians.[9] Each of the wall panels is in phi ratio. Even CRC's age, 106, is the combination of 10 and 6, or Ø.

Rosecrucianism extends the Reformation to natural science and the structure of governance. It suggests a shared, nonsectarian, mystical Christianity[10] and a philosophy of nature explicated in a science subordinated to the search for unity in the cosmos. The means of the search is harmony expressed in symbolic number. The goal was to begin a new age in which human suffering would be alleviated through the sharing of material knowledge.

From 1613 to 1620, Frederick and Elizabeth governed the Palatinate. In 1620 Frederick maneuvered himself to become king of Bavaria but, before the winter was out, was defeated in battle by the Catholic Hapsburgs after James I withdrew his support.[11] This episode marks the end of public esoteric influence on governance in Europe. The optimistic Rosicrucian magical cosmos was obliterated by the witchcraft terror of the 1620s following Frederick's defeat.[12] Magic was in effect criminalized; its hold on the Western imagination permanently shattered. The advocacy of a magically linked harmonic universe combined with claims to secret knowledge exposed the Rosicrucian vision to accusations of dark magic and witchcraft, leading many, like Descartes, Newton, and others living in the new terror atmosphere to deny any connection to them.

Inigo Jones

Inigo Jones, 1573–1652, the son of a successful London businessman, began his career as a painter. He quickly came to aristocratic attention and was introduced into court circles.[13] Beginning in 1605 he became a theater and party producer for James I, and later for Charles I. Among his productions were two masques for the marriage of Frederick and Elizabeth in 1613.[14] His interest in architecture began after 1610, when he was appointed surveyor to the Prince of Wales. By 1612 he had acquired Palladio's *Four Books* and a number of his original drawings. He went to Germany with the royal newlyweds and then on to Italy in 1613–14. Thirty years after Palladio's death, Jones visited many of his projects. Jones' architectural influence, however, was limited to court circles and did not penetrate to the building trades or provincial gentry,[15] who continued to build in a slightly Gothicized Baroque style associated with the Tudors.

Jones was a contemporary of Shakespeare, John Dee, Robert Fludd, and Francis Bacon. He developed as an artist in the wake of the famous Hermetic magician Giordano Bruno's 1583 visit to England.[16] Jones was an intimate at the Stuart court, near the center of the Rosicrucian movement and within the gestation zone of Freemasonry.

Using Jones' preliminary drawing of the Banqueting House, **figure 1,** the building is put in square ABCD with center E. Applying the $\sqrt{2}/2$ find points F and G. The central three bays are marked by $\sqrt{2}$ cuts F and F'. The bay interval is then extended on either side. The height of the upper cornice is at Ø of BC, point H. The upper two floors are in double square LHJK. If BC = 1, CH = .618…, HJ = .5 and the basement, JC = .118 = $Ø^3/2$ = HM. This interval can be drawn directly by creating equilateral triangle ABN. Subtracting the altitude $\sqrt{3}/2$, .867 gives interval JC as .133, a difference of 1.5% of BC. Point G gives the height of the roof ridge and apex of the pediment. HJ is divided into 9 parts, 4 give the height of the lower floor columns. Both entablatures are 1/5 of their column's height. Though Jones' design method is not known, the geometrical analysis, showing the presence of the essential creative powers $\sqrt{2}$, $\sqrt{3}$ and $\sqrt{5}$, indicates that he has absorbed the lessons of Vitruvius and Palladio.

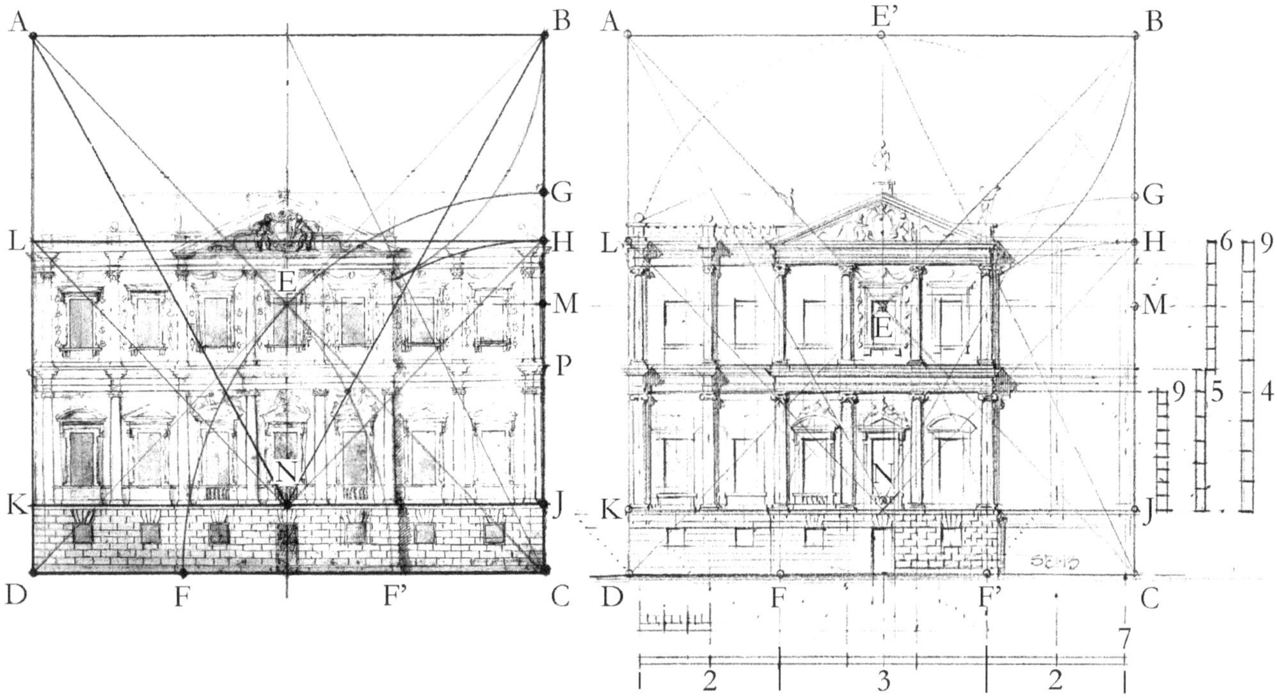

FIGURE 1
Banqueting House, London, Inigo Jones, 1619

FREEMASONRY

The second key post-magical ideological system was Freemasonry. In its mythic origin, modern Freemasonry arose from the remnants of the Knight Templars who took shelter in Scotland after their mid-fourteenth-century fall. If the relation of the Templars to the pointed arch style of architecture is considered, there would probably have been some geometrical aspects to their privately held knowledge. The surviving knights, unable to publicly enact their own rituals, began to integrate their activities with existing, legitimate, initiatic building craft guilds. As gentlemen non-artisans were "accepted" into these "operative" guilds "Speculative Masonry" arose.

The operative lodges dated from the Middle Ages, possibly earlier. Beyond practical services such as builder's insurance and credentials they were initiatic organizations, functional inheritors of the great ancient mysteries. It is presumed that some of their private teachings were geometrical, spiritualized in the initiatic context.

Speculative lodges emerged in England in the early seventeenth century with the Scottish Stuart king James I.[17] These lodges shared with the Rosicrucians the avoidance of sectarianism, an international scale outlook, and utilization of numerical and geometrical symbols. Rituals were private, but knowledge was transmitted through the brothers to the larger community.

The major figure in the Masonic myth is Hiram, the designer-builder of Solomon's temple. He organizes the workforce into three grades: apprentices, journeymen, and masters. Each grade has its own words and signs of recognition by which they are paid. As the temple nears completion Hiram is murdered by three overly ambitious artisans because he refuses to reveal the Master's means of recognition, the Masons "word," outside of the proper ritual setting. In the Masonic initiation the candidate plays the part of Hiram. He is duly "murdered," given certain information, and then "raised" by the Master. The ritual follows classic form in that the candidate enters living, then dies; is instructed and returned to life.

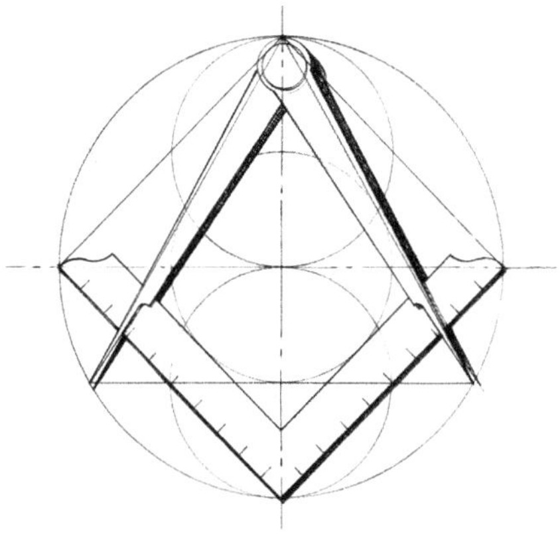

FIGURE 2
Masonic "Square and Compass" Archetypal Arrangement

In the imagery of Freemasonry, stages and incidents in the birth, life, death and rebirth of Solomon's Temple are metaphoric of the path of spiritual development of the individual. The Divinity is described as the "Great Architect of the Universe." The five classical Orders are used as references to the five senses. Archetypal lodge rooms are 2:1 in plan. They are symbolically oriented to the cardinal points with the Master stationed in the east, opposite the entry. One symbolically enters from the west and journeys toward the light in the east. Above the Master's chair in the east is a sunburst emblem with the letter G at its center, standing for God, Geometry, or some say Gnosis. The Masonic lodge room bears an uncanny resemblance to the temples of Mithra, the ancient initiatic organization to which Vitruvius might have belonged. The public logo of the Masons is the "square and compass." These are tools of construction and design, but also of instruction. While there is a spectrum of arrangements, the essential image responds to the cosmological circle diagram used earlier, Section II, **figure 2.**

The symbolic, cosmological and initiatory character of Freemasonry link it not just with Rosicrucianism but with the larger esoteric stream in Western civilization that has flowed from the Paleolithic. The close relation of Freemasonry to science and government in both their public rational form and non-public "speculative" form in the Georgian era was not an accident, a fatuous fad, or superstitious hangover. Freemasonry provided an essential venue for discussion of those values and studies that are not governed by metrics, where the universe is still continuous and not reduced. It was an essential training ground for the exercise of magical governance, now to be expressed publicly in strictly rationalistic terms. Freemasonry's architectural and construction symbolism indicate the close relationship within civilization of cosmology, spiritual development, governance, and architecture.

Palladianism

During the seventeenth century two political factions took shape in England: the Whigs, representing middle-class business interests, parliamentarianism and religious accommodation; and the Tories, representing old landed nobility, the monarchy and the established church. In 1714, after the death of Queen Anne, last of the Stuarts, the Whigs invited George I of the German House of Hanover to be king; and the period from 1714 to 1830 became known as the Georgian era.

Freemasonry attains quasi-official status in 1717 with the formation of the Grand Lodge. Its institutional mission was to purge Freemasonry of Catholic Jacobin elements and align it with the new Protestant–Hanoverian–Whig axis.[18] George I was a descendant of James I through Frederick V and Elizabeth, the Rosicrucian "winter king and queen." An aesthetic connection is made through the Palladian style of Inigo Jones, James I's court designer. This is now resurrected as the aesthetic symbol for support of the Whig Hanoverians. Palladianism was the semi-official style of the Whig governing faction, who also demanded a "purified" Freemasonry. A close relationship existed between these movements. The political climate after 1714 needed a style to convey continuity but be "purer" than the Baroque; to be connected with both antiquity and with current Georgian imperial ambitions. Jones' Palladianism suited these needs.[19] Baroque was associated with the Tories, absolutism, France, and Catholicism.

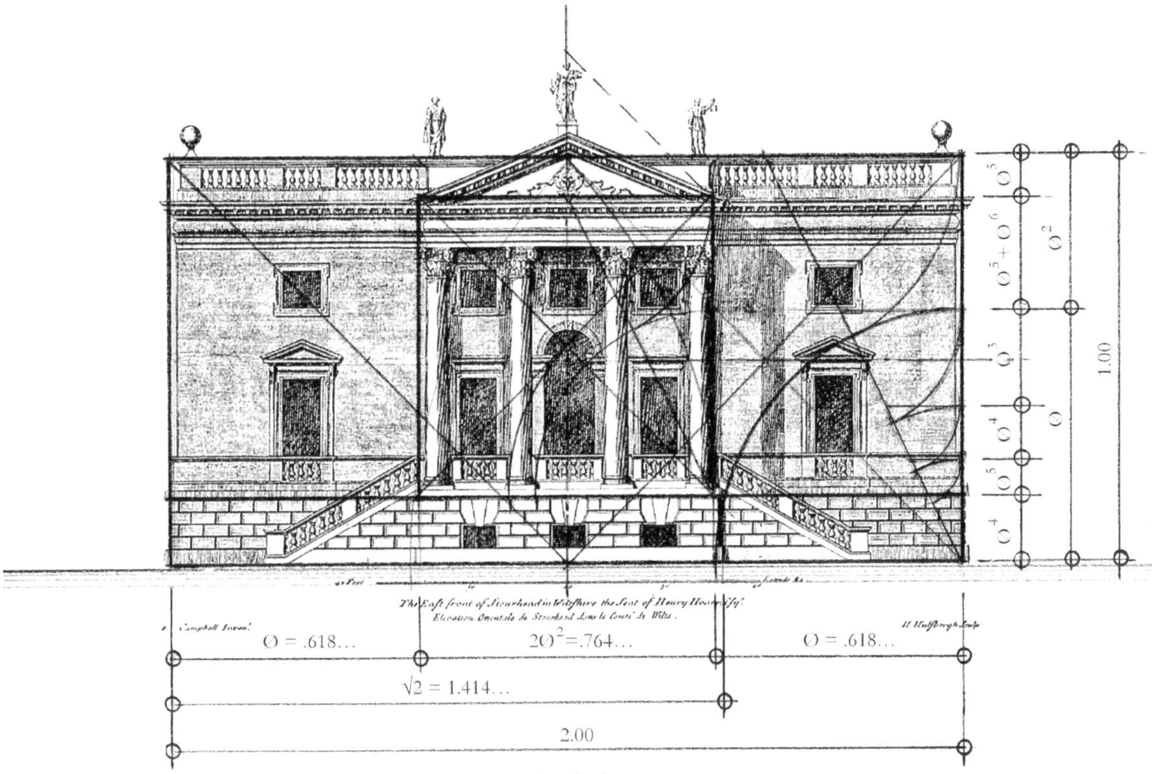

Analysis

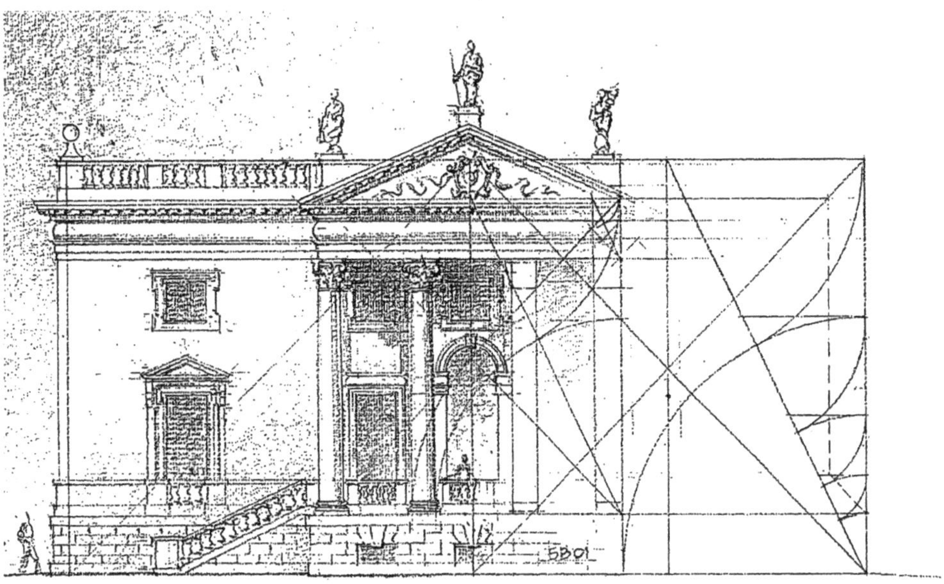

Reconstruction

FIGURE 3 – *Stourhead, Wiltshire, Campbell, 1719*

The Neo-Palladian movement was led by Lord Burlington, 1694–1753. In 1715 he and architect Colen Campbell, 1676–1729, published *Vitruvius Britannicus* a quasi-official manual of style. Burlington saw the fusion of old and new perfectly enshrined in Palladio. He had measured ancient buildings, his designs used ancient prototypes, his work achieved a high level of clarity of expression and harmony of proportions. His *Four Books,* published in 1570, contained theory, reconstructions of ancient buildings and examples of his own work.

The elevation of the house at Stourhead, Wiltshire, 1719,[20] **figure 3,** is based on the double square. If the overall width is taken as 2 and the height 1, the basement is $Ø^4$, .146, the central tetrastyle is in a square of $2Ø^2$ and each side wing is Ø, thus giving .618 + .764 + .618 = 2.0;

a doubling of the 3-4-3 $\sqrt{2}$ cut. Notice that .764 + .618 = 1.382 and $\sqrt{2}$ = 1.414; about a 2.3% difference, thus either geometrical key could be used to obtain the same pattern.[21] The parapet is $Ø^5$ = .090. The midpoint of the overall height sets the spring point of the entry arch.

Magic Obscured

During the course of the seventeenth century, the magical worldview was systematically marginalized in favor of reductionism and materialism. Being publicly associated with harmonic or magical views was dangerous. The West had thrown out the spiritual baby with the Medieval bathwater. As Goethe would later observe, the apprentices took over the sorcerer's workshop. But magical ideas had not been discarded, only turned away from in public.

A leading personality of the period who embodied this situation was Isaac Newton, 1643–1727. Newton's mathematical and optical works have been treated as foundational Enlightenment documents. He was an early member of the Royal Society, which played a key role in the development of experimental science, a Rosicrucian invisible college made visible. Recent revelations, though, indicate that Newton spent the overwhelming amount of his time studying a spectrum of occult and esoteric subjects like alchemy, astrology and symbolic arithmetic.

Newton was working on a Rosicrucian background. His researches, both published and unpublished, were undertaken in a search for Unity. Far from seeing God as a disinterested clockmaker, Newton sought unity utilizing rational science as part of a larger spiritual science in the traditional Rosicrucian manner. It is only in retrospect that he became a reductionist saint by exclusively focusing on his rationalistic achievements and obscuring, to the greatest extent possible, their esoteric background. Newton used new forms of knowledge in the service of traditional esoteric goals.

The Whigs, the Royal Society, and the Freemasons had significant overlapping membership. In such a context we are faced with the image that in the Georgian edifice of state, after the Royal Society has met in the high ceilinged, well-lit rooms of the piano noble, the gentlemen descended to the vaulted, dimly lit, crypt-like lodge room of the Freemasons. Or perhaps it was the other way around.

The Assault on Beauty

Problems for the idea of beauty begin in Europe after the fall of Frederick in 1620. Aesthetics underwent a "reduction" to the sensible. This reduced view of beauty is picked up in England by Henry Wotton, 1568–1639. He is James I's ambassador to Venice, another Hapsburg opponent, from 1604–24. He gives Inigo Jones the core of his Palladio drawing collection in 1612.[22]

Wotton translates beauty as "delight" in his 1624 edition-commentary on Vitruvius, using the elegant formulation "firmness, commodity and delight." Beauty we may say includes the feeling of "delight" meaning "a great joy or pleasure." Beauty may stimulate or be a source of joy and pleasure, but is not joy or pleasure itself. To translate "venustatis," pertaining to Venus, goddess of manifest beauty, as "delight" is to confuse cause with effect. It indicates an aversion to the idea of beauty. Since Wotton had to know about Rosicrucianism, it appears that the public-private split personality had already begun to set in.

The watershed event in the overthrow of beauty is produced by Claude Perrault, 1613–1688. He came from an upper middle class family of state officials. Perrault was a medical doctor and anatomist,[23] echoing the close relationship of the architect and the doctor that began with

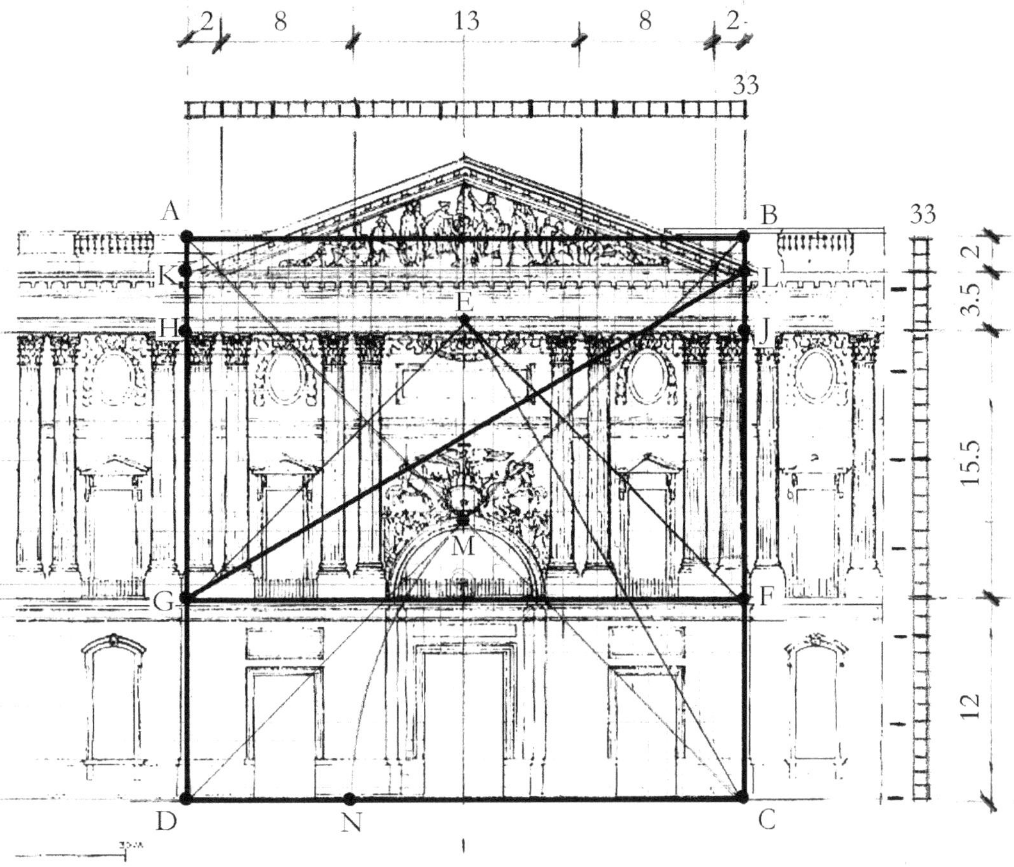

FIGURE 4

Louvre, East Wing Centerpiece, Paris. Perrault, 1665

Imhotep. In their traditional roles both use the macro-forces of the cosmos to maintain the micro-world of the body or the embodied community. Perrault wrote on physics, in particular musical acoustics, and on natural history. In 1666 he became an early member of the French Academy of Sciences. In the "querelle" between the Ancients and Moderns he and his brothers took the side of the Moderns,[24] who argued that the Ancients had been equaled or exceeded.

Claude's brother Charles was a literary figure, noted for recording the initial written versions of "folk tales" including "Cinderella," "Little Red Riding Hood," and "Sleeping Beauty." These were republished later by the Brothers Grimm and in our time became the basis of the classic Disney cartoons. They represent a kind of reduction and enclosure of the Western imagination. What had once been indigenous myths, alluding to the human spiritual potential, became rural tall tales, weirdly cute but meaningless, requiring a moral lesson to be added to make them acceptable as entertainment.

Charles worked for Colbert, leading minister of Louis XIV. After Louis and Colbert rejected Bernini's Baroque scheme for the east facade of the Louvre, Charles brought his brother into the project.[25] The east wing was built 1665–80. Perrault published a French translation of Vitruvius in 1673. The strict Vitruvianism of the east wing may be taken a sign of emerging historicism, academicism and literalness.

The centerpiece of the east wing, **figure 4**, may be put in square ABCD, which is divided into 33 units, the number of modillion intervals. By inspection the basement is 12 units high, FC, the column 15.5, FJ and the entablature 3.5, JL, total = 31, BC. In width the centers of the column pairs are at 2, 8, 13 in the center, 8, 2 = 33. The apex of the entry arch is at the center of ABCD, point M.

While Perrault may well have used a grid, the facade can be approximately reconstructed geometrically, in the spirit of Vitruvius. In height, $Ø^2$ x 33 = 12.6, the base; 33/2 = 16.5, point E, the colonnade; and 16.5/5 = 3.3, the entablature, coming out at 32.4 units high. Or considering that the top of the columns scale at 27.5 units, CJ, and $\sqrt{3}/2$ x 33 = 28.6 units, + 3.3, the entablature = 31.9 units high. Another approach notes that the colonnade and entablature are 19 units and $1/\sqrt{3}$, .557 x 33 = 19, making angle LGF 30^0. 12.6 + 19 = 31.6. In width, the center of the inner column pair is at 23 units, point N, while 33 x $\sqrt{2}/2$ = 23.3.

Perrault begins the public assault on beauty in his *Ordonnance* of 1683 with three main lines of attack. First and most critically he proposes that there are two kinds of beauty: natural, objective vs cultural, subjective. Objective or "positive" beauty is based on convincing, self-evident reasons, for example, musical harmony. Subjective or "customary" beauty is associated with fashion, not any inherent quality. It is beautiful by comparison, association, context or prejudice. While Diotima[26] had distinguished between levels of embodiment of the beautiful, these were not opposed to one another but were steps on a ladder of self-development.

The second point in Perrault's argument is that the eye and ear work differently. Here the magical-harmonic idea expressed by the musical analogy is directly trashed.[27] Ratios in music, Perrault says, must be exact but ratios in architecture are not subject to the same standards. All musicians agree on the ratio of the chord, but each architectural canon gives different ratios for the same elements.[28] Their inexactness indicates that their beauty is not inherent. The musical chord has an inherent natural mathematical beauty, but architectural designs have cultural subjective customary beauty, unintelligible without knowing history. This recalls the comments of Ligorio that Michelangelo's architecture inspired doubt.[29]

Perrault's third point is that, since objects or buildings are not seen orthographically but only in perspective, the eye never sees exact linear ratios. Thus proportion cannot play a role in beauty because we never see a building in orthographic view, but only at some perspective angle. For example, Perrault writes that a face with given proportions can be both ugly and beautiful: as when it laughs or cries; and two different faces with different proportions can be equally beautiful. Contrast this with Plotinus,[30] whose example of the face leads us away from a discussion of matter and turns us toward a deeper understanding of beauty. Use of the same ancient example with opposite conclusions is a hallmark of modern discourse.

Positive beauty's convincing self-evident reasons include[31]: 1) size and magnificence of the project, 2) richness of materials, 3) excellence of artisanship, and 4) symmetry. In other words, being beautiful is being big, rich and fancy. Perrault defines symmetry as the kind of proportion that produces a striking and unmistakable effect. There are two kinds: First is the traditional relation of parts to parts and to the whole. This he says is difficult to discern as we can't actually see a seventh or fifteenth part, etc. The second kind is bilateral, butterfly symmetry that is very apparent and exact, making it more important than relations between parts of the building that the eye cannot actually discern.

Here we see the reduction of the term "symmetry" and simultaneous loss of the ancient harmonic sensibility replaced by a total preoccupation with the physical world. The proportions associated with the ancient wisdom tradition, with achievement of higher states of consciousness, are simply dismissed, sent to their rooms like children after having been told a fairy tale of beauty. The tables have been turned; the Real, the Form of Beauty, has become the shadow, and the ever-changing "hule" has become the Real. The faculty of the imagination that once gave us access to the archetypal can now only take us to a private fantasy.

Custom alone, not imitation of nature, reason or good sense, makes the usual architectural proportions appear correct.[32] Custom causes us to accept some things, such as columns that lean inward, that might otherwise look misshapen to a rationalistic objective observer. These things should displease us because they don't make sense but, as customary, are declared correct by tastemakers. One must guard against arbitrary beauty being mistaken for positive beauty. Good taste uses both kinds, but depends more on the arbitrary.

Furthermore, Perrault tells us, the ancients had no rule, only "fancy" to guide them in establishing proportions. Thus the orders are arbitrary and since we know more than they did we are not bound by their rules; we can do better. There is no discussion anywhere in the *Ordonnance* of emotional, poetic or psychic content of the elements, nothing beyond the physical.

There is also a political connection.[33] Architectural proportions are correct by custom, which reason alone cannot determine, *"just as in civil law there are rules dependent on the will of legislators and on the consent of nations that a natural understanding of fairness will never reveal."* The analogy between architectural rules and political rules, neither of which makes sense on the surface but requiring knowledge of history to understand or property appreciate, is fascinating and revealing. Comparing the proportional system to arbitrary laws of the state indicates how far we have fallen.

Finally, we get a story of the origin of modernism.[34] Architects religiously venerate ancient works, especially admiring the mystery of proportions. They contemplate these with profound respect, not daring to question any decision of the ancients, though the reasons for these choices were unknown even to the ancients themselves. This exaggerated respect for antiquity originated in genuine respect for the sacred but medieval barbarism snuffed out all branches of knowledge except theology. Surviving culture took refuge in monasteries where reasoning and mental training were still practiced. The theologians, however, used these skills only to support scripture and doctrine. They lost the ability to think freely, without preconceptions. Renaissance secular scholars continued this outlook, taking greater pride in the linguistic aspects of text than in determining if the text was empirically correct. It was these "men of letters" who lost the distinction between positive and customary beauty and confused the whole thing with religion. Architecture suffered particularly from this problem. But we need not accept any mystery. After proper training and experience architects must be able to say that if a material reason cannot be found for a particular relationship of elements then there probably isn't any, freeing them to judge for themselves.

In his own day Perrault is answered by François Blondel, 1618-1686,[35] who argued that despite its being invisible, number was a basic source of beauty, while acknowledging that the power of number could not be either proved or disproved. Blondel devotes a chapter in his *Cours d'Architecture* to "scientifically" establishing proportion as a cause of beauty as found in nature. He uses examples from mechanics and optics to cite invisible mathematical causes that produce sensible results, such as refraction. In both the sciences "induction and experience" generated invariable principles. Through such "experience" there are proportions found in beautiful buildings that are not found in "ugly" ones. Blondel felt that architecture is a branch of mathematics and should be based on invariable principles. Number as the carrier of invariable principles is symbolic number.

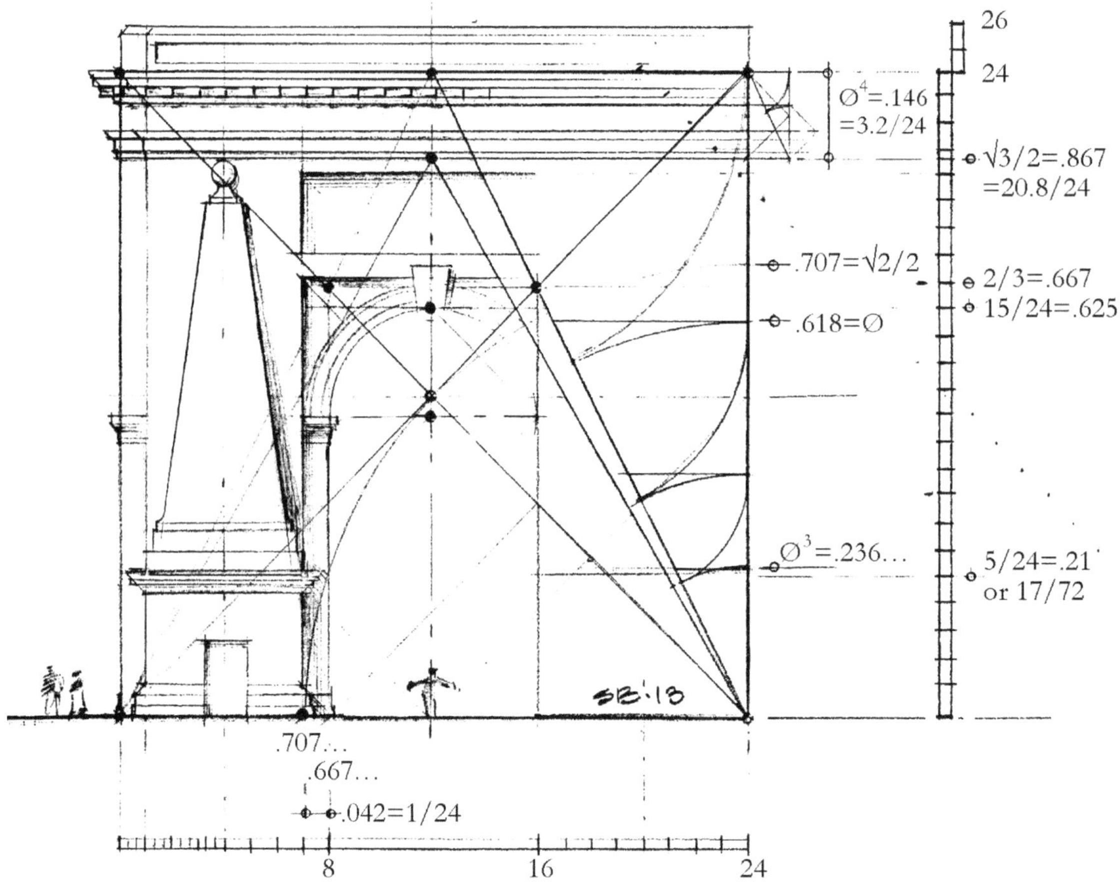

FIGURE 5

Porte Saint-Denis, Paris. Blondel, 1672

Blondel's traditional view allowed architectural meaning in terms of traditional philosophy; just what Perrault hoped to break by substituting a scientific logos for a mythic one. Prophetically, Blondel felt that cutting the link to archetypal principles would gravely affect the human intellect, that people would lose the sense of unity and lead restless anguished lives.[36]

His defense is weak at best and did not hold. Aesthetics were reduced and quantified. The classical elements became a cultural leftover in the ensuing frenzy to engineer the art of building. Once the rational-materialist view took over, beauty and its proportional trigger were declared subjective, marginalized, put "in the eye of the beholder" and not discussible by "reasonable" people.

Blondel's Porte Saint-Denis, **figure 5**, may be put in a square. The apex of an equilateral triangle gives the bottom of the entablature. The opening is 1/3 of the width. Its crown is slightly lowered from the 2/3 point in height, very close to Ø, at 5/8. The side piers are set by the √2/2 point. The relative purity of the geometry backs up Blondel's proportional ideas but the design can also be placed on a grid of 24, giving most of the key points; if multiplied by 3 to 72 it would give more points. If multiplied by 4 it gives 96, the number of parts the body is divided into by Vitruvius.

By the eighteenth century pure geometry pretty much drops out of use in design, and the grid takes over. The state of affairs is reflected in the contrasting approaches of two of the major canonical authors of the Georgian period: James Gibbs and William Chambers, who use the harmonic ratio method and arithmetic parts and minutes respectively.

Gibbs

James Gibbs, 1682–1754, absorbed the Baroque tradition while studying architecture in Rome with Carlo Fontana, 1638–1714. Fontana was the grandson of Domenico Fontana, who had surveyed and installed some of the major streets of Baroque Rome for Sixtus V, particularly those at whose foci obelisks were placed. Carlo had been a student and assistant to Bernini, Cortona, and Rainaldi.

Gibbs returned to England in 1708 and began architectural practice.[37] In 1710 he began work on the church of St. Mary le Strand.[38] The facade has two tiers of orders and a semi-circular portico. Above the center is a single arcuated tower with a base, four stages and a finial; translating a Gothic form into Classical terms. Its single spire design would have a significant effect on early American architecture. The design drew on English and Italian sources.[39] In spite of Whig suspicions of his being a Scot, a Catholic, and a Jacobite sympathizer, St. Mary's was so well received that Gibbs' career was made.[40]

The facade of St. Mary's, **figure 6,** is square, ABCD, with the top of the first-floor cornice at the half-point, E. The central tetrastyle feature spans both floors. Its width seems to be guided by the quarter points, F and G. The length of the main block of the building is twice its width, giving the main mass ratios of 1:1:2.

Overall height, including the tower, is approximately 3 to the width of 1. The modulation of the parts of the tower can be achieved by constructing isosceles triangle HJK. Where the sides intersect the top of the square find points L and M. Join points L and J. Draw MN parallel to LJ, repeat with PQ. This creates a series of similar trapezoids.

Although this may be close to an operative method of shaping the tower, it must be considered speculative. Gibbs was clearly not taking its network literally, as NP marks the top of its segment's entablature while QR marks the bottom of its entablature. The altitude of HJK is about 1:2.8; though it is a double square plus a 4:5 rectangle, this is not a compelling choice and, in fact, there are two possible apexes for HJK, the sphere and the weather vane. Further, the base of triangle HJK is on the ground rather than the first floor. But that such a technique can be applied at all recalls the pillar and plan-net of ancient Egypt.

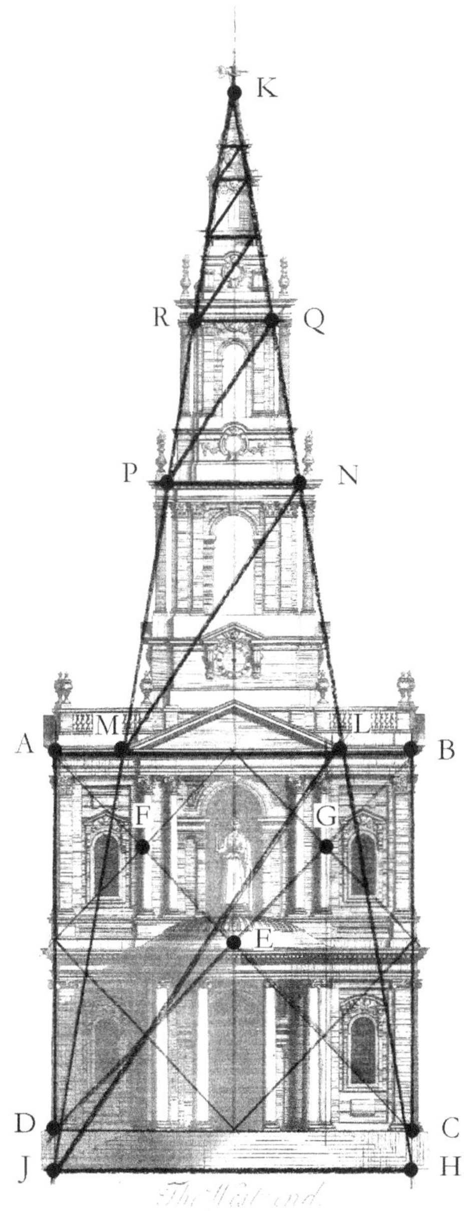

Figure 6
St. Mary le Strand, London, 1720

Gibbs' second major work is the church of St. Martin-in-the-Fields,[41] designed and built 1721-26. It set a precedent for Anglican churches for the next century, and its design was exported to the colonies through its publication in Gibbs' *Book of Architecture*. In elevation a

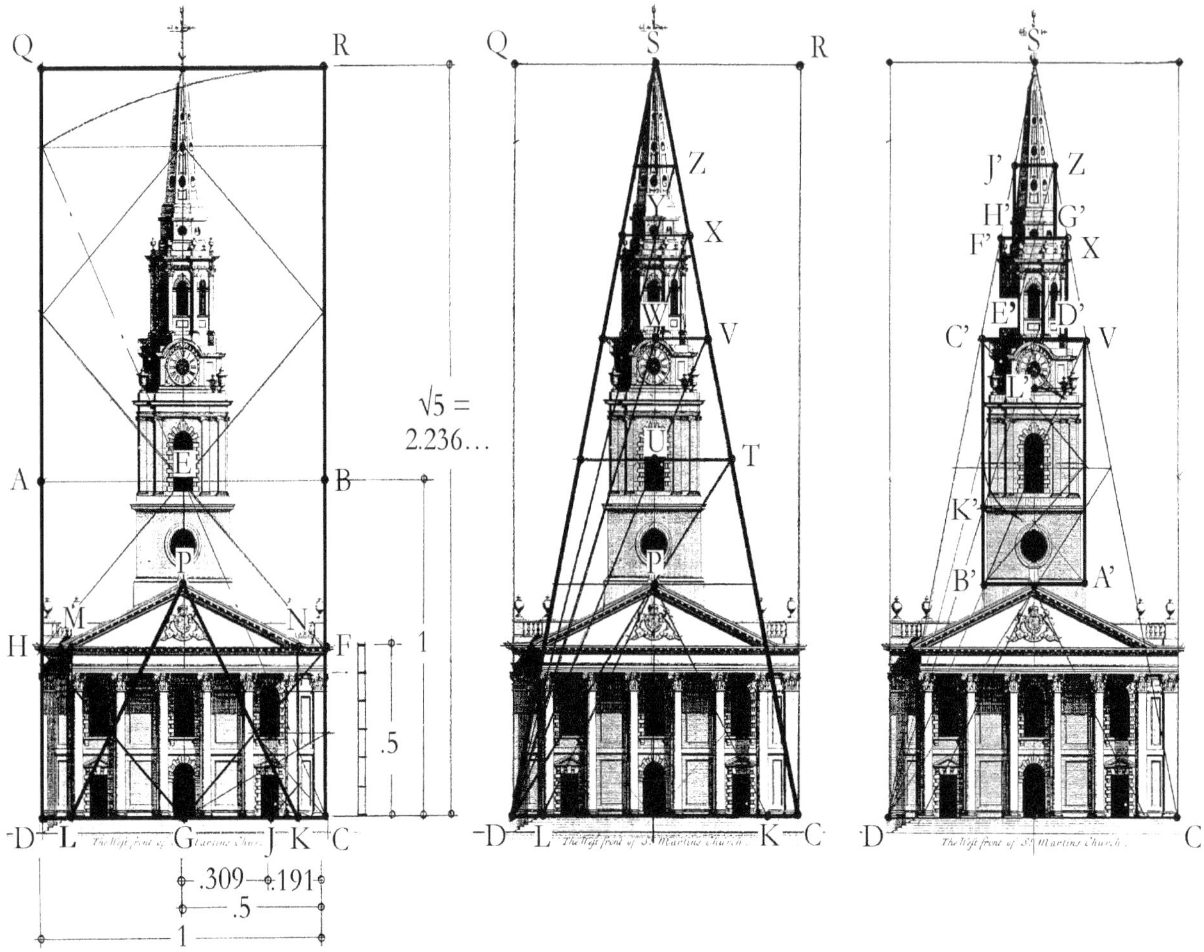

FIGURE 7a-c – *St. Martin, London, Gibbs, 1721. Analysis of West Facade*

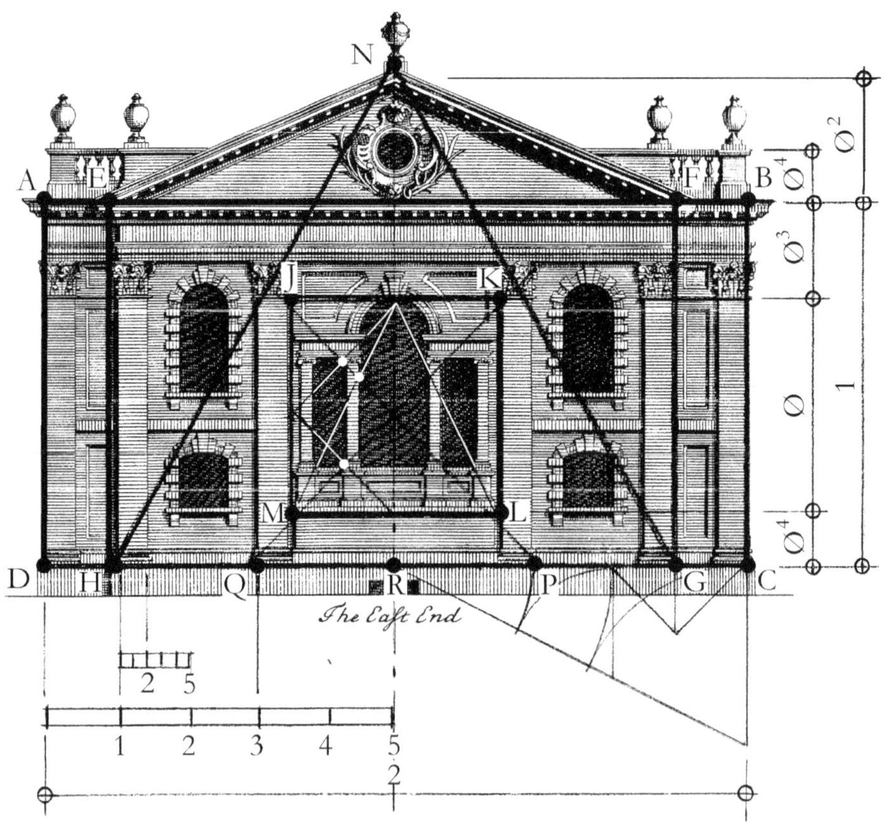

FIGURE 7d - *St. Martin Analysis of East Facade*

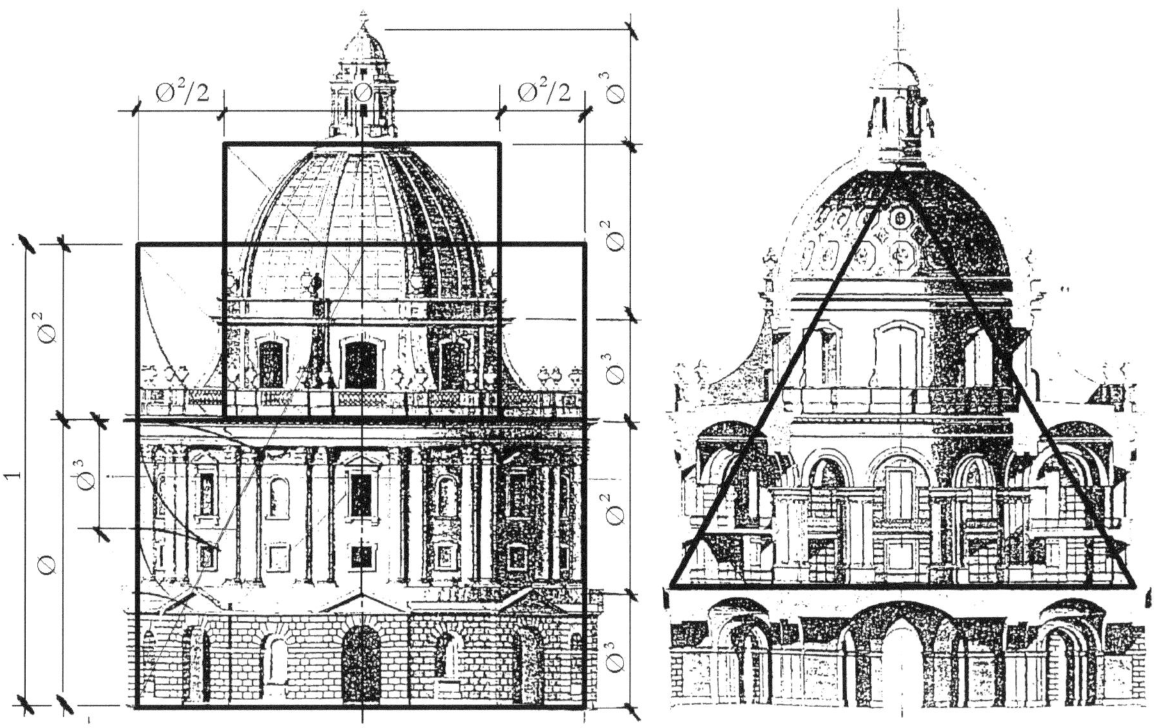

FIGURE 8
Radcliffe Camera, Oxford, Gibbs, 1737

monumental hexastyle Corinthian portico with two side bays is attached to a simple rectangular church body, the sides of which are pierced by two-story arcuated openings. The overall plan is a 2:1 rectangle. Behind and centered above the portico is a tower with a base and three stages, transiting from square to octagonal, and terminating in a spire.

Set the overall width of the west facade within square ABCD, **figure 7a.** Draw diagonal square EFGH. 2:1 rectangle HFCD will give the bulk of the elevation. The portico will be enclosed in Ø rectangle KLMN. This may be placed by finding Ø of GC, point J, then finding half of JC, point K. Repeat this on the other side to get point L.[42] Draw an equilateral triangle with base KL and apex P marking the apex of the pediment. To obtain the height of the tower draw √5 rectangle QRCD.

S is the center of QR, **figure 7b.** Draw triangle DSC. To define the tower draw a line from D through P and continue to point T. Draw horizontal line TU. Draw line DU and continue to V, draw horizontal to find W. Draw DW to find X. Draw DY to find Z.

The lower part of the tower is defined by rectangle VA'B'C', **figure 7c.** The second octagonal tier is defined by rectangle XD'E'F'. The upper section of the tower begins with rectangle ZG'H'J' and line G'S gives the slope of the obelisk form at the top of the tower. The lower section of the tower, double square VA'B'C', is further divided at the Ø points of the two squares, points K' and L' to give the three cubical parts of this lower section.

The east elevation, **figure 7d,** follows the pattern of a Ø rectangle, EFGH, placed within a double square, ABCD. On the west front, the Ø rectangle becomes a hexastyle; on the back it becomes a tetrastyle. The central bay of the tetrastyle is set by square JKLM, KL = Ø of FG. JKLM is divided by its diagonals and semi-diagonals to place the elements of the Serliana. The pediment is set at the apex of equilateral triangle HNG. Its altitude, NR, is 1.618 x .867 = 1.401, while 1 + $Ø^2$ = 1.382 and √2 = 1.414.

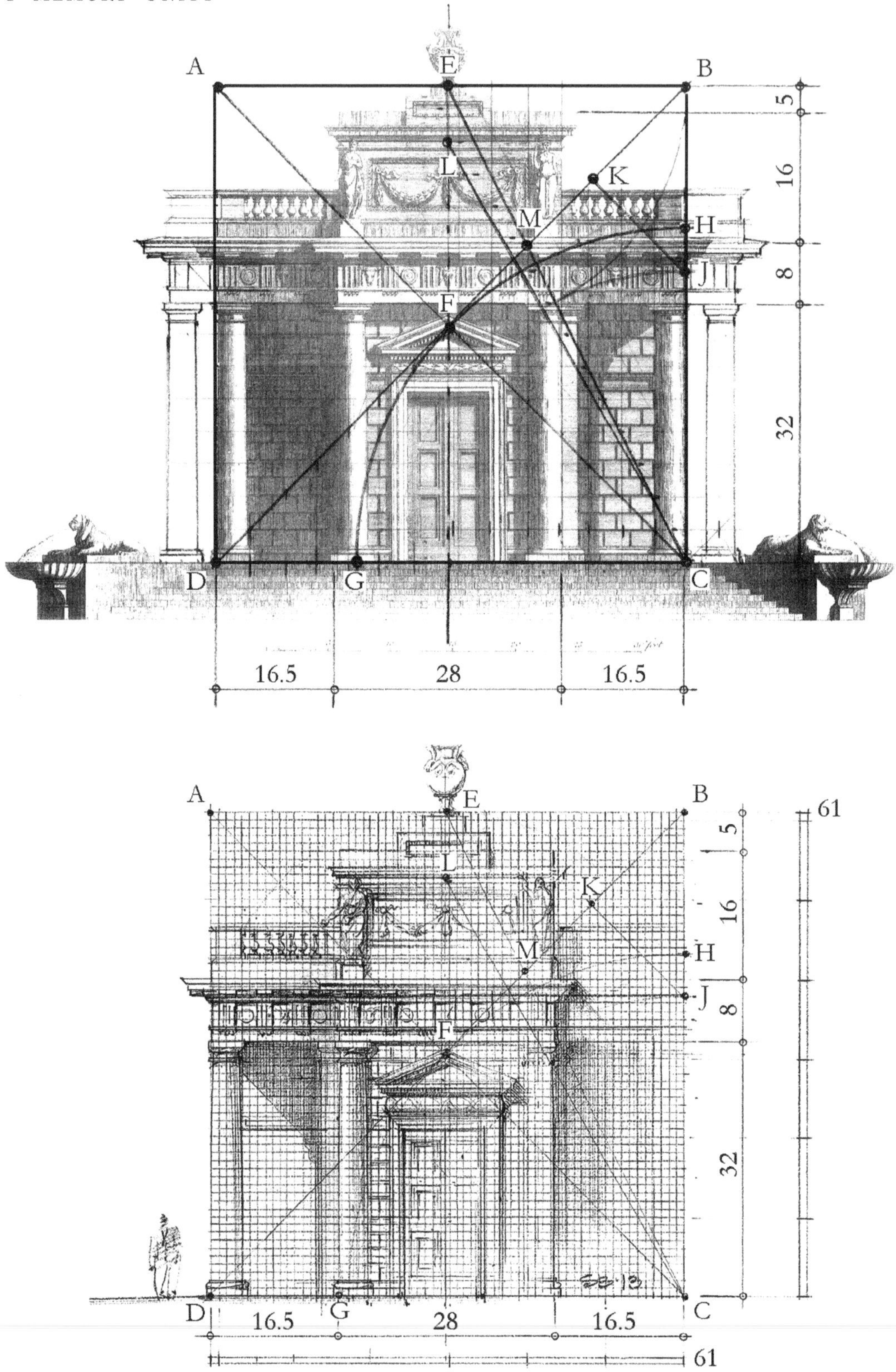

FIGURE 9a

The Casino at Marino, Dublin, Chambers, 1775

The tetrastyle within EFGH, however, is not exactly a Ø rectangle; it is squeezed just a bit from the geometrical $Ø^2/2$, .191 to 1/5 or .2, perhaps indicating that Gibbs used a harmonic division approach, dividing ABCD into 10 x 5. Further dividing each unit into 5 makes ABCD 25 x 50. The pilaster width is 2 units, entablature depth, 1/6 of 25 about 4 units and the pilaster W/H=2/21=1/10.5. By harmonic ratios NR would be 7 units high.

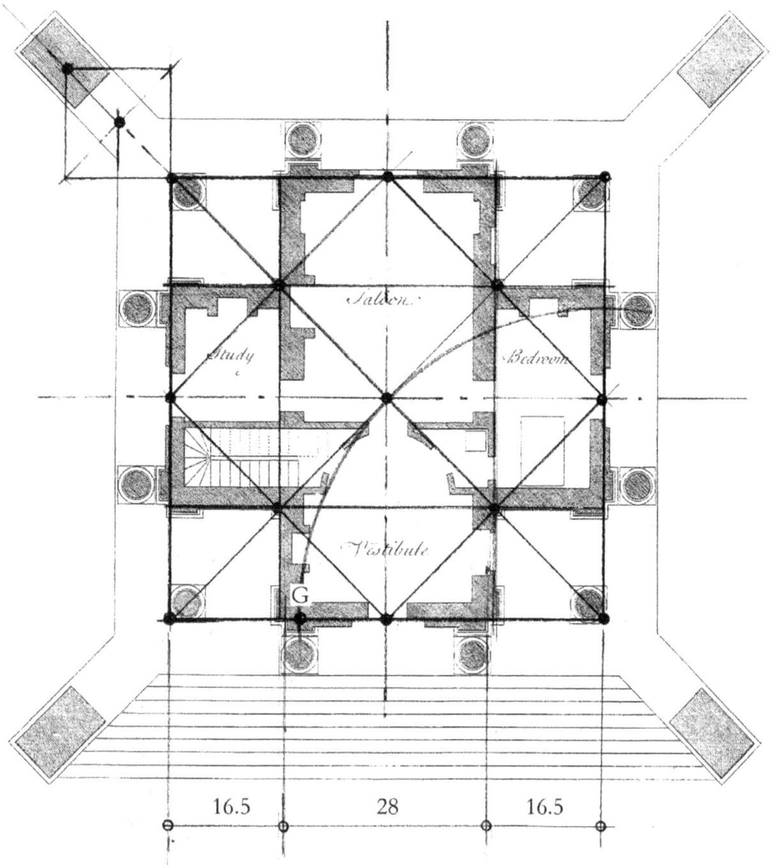

FIGURE 9b
The Casino, Chambers. Plan

The Radcliffe Camera at Oxford, 1737-48, is possibly Gibbs' best work. **Figure 8** shows some probable geometrical relationships of the massing. Setting the diameter as 1, the main cornice is at Ø and the diameter of the dome and drum is Ø. The exterior seems to have a vertical modulation of alternating $Ø^2$ and $Ø^3$ intervals. In section, the building seems to be guided by the equilateral triangle. This is not unique to Gibbs and was possibly a structural device to safely counter the thrust of the dome.

CHAMBERS

Sir William Chambers, 1723-1796, the son of a successful Scottish merchant, grew up in London. Between the ages of 17 and 26 he made three voyages to China with the Swedish East India Company. In 1750 he studied architecture with Blondel in Paris, then spent several years in Italy. Returning to London in 1755 he became architectural tutor to George III. He practiced for more than 15 years and in the 1760s began to accumulate official positions.

The "Casino," 1773, is a small stand-alone pavilion on an estate in Marino, near Dublin. In elevation, **figure 9a,** the center bay is five triglyph intervals. Taking these as 5/4 D gives 25 1/4 D units plus 1.5 at either end = 28 units. The end bays are 3 intervals at 5/4 D plus 1.5 units at the outer end = 16.5 units, making the overall width = 61 units. The Doric column is 8 D high, the entablature is 2 D; the attic centerpiece is 4 D and the base of the crowning vase is 1.2 D. The vertical count is column 32, entablature 8, attic 16, and crown base 5 = 61.

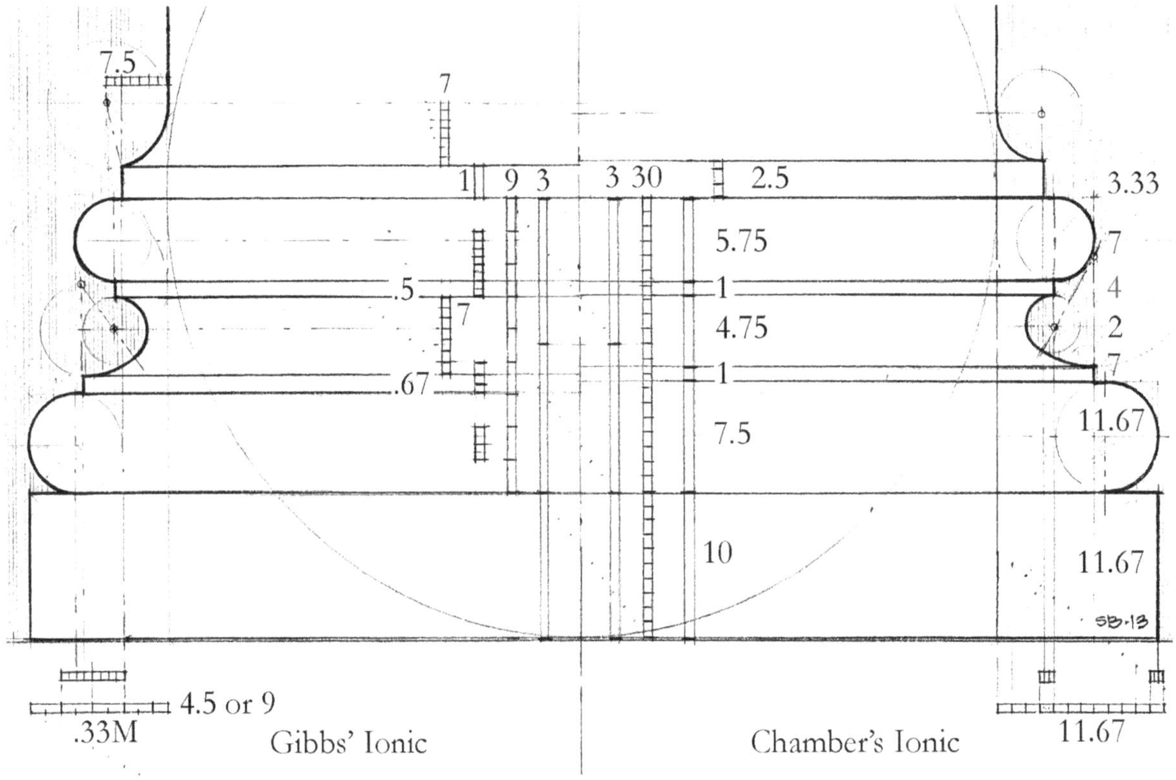

FIGURE 10

Attic Bases of Gibbs and Chambers

Geometrically the elevation may be put in square ABCD. The center F is at the apex of the entry door pediment. The top of the entablature, point M, falls at 40/61 = .656, the 2/3 point = .667, almost exactly between the √2/2 and Ø points. The top of the balustrade is almost at the $Ø^2/2$ point, K. The apex of equilateral triangle DLC, point L, falls just below the crown of the attic. In plan, **figure 9b,** the √2/2 point G falls at the center of the inner column as 61 x .707 = 43.1; by arithmetic it is 27 + 16.5 = 43.5.

While such relationships are not to be presumed entirely accidental or coincidental, there is no reason to assume that Chambers used anything but an arithmetical method. The power of the massing may be said to result from its being a cube that is carved into both above and below the entablature, and then augmented with the four aediculae. Though Chambers was clearly not a "mysterian," one can't help notice that the building scales at 38' in width, the double of 19.

PUBLICATIONS

In 1732 Gibbs published his canon, the *Rules for Drawing ...,* which makes use of "small whole number division," closer in method to Vignola than to Palladio. The small whole number method is linked to the musical-geometrical analogies of the Pythagoreans and Platonists. In both Gibbs and Vignola the columns of the three principle orders have height to diameter ratios of 8:1 for Doric, 9:1 for Ionic and 10:1 for Corinthian. These are multiples of the Pythagorean "usual suspects" 3, 4, and 5. They represent primary creative powers expressed as the three phases of the cosmological cycle: the Proceeding, symbolized by the dyad and tetrad; the Maintaining, by the triad; and the Returning, by the pentad. The Doric, Ionic and Corinthian orders are given these characters respectively by their association with multiples of these numbers. Chambers, like Palladio, uses the arithmetical method of describing the elements by parts, minutes and seconds.

It is most likely that Gibbs learned the "small whole number" method in the studio of Fontana; a method likely handed down within the craft tradition since medieval if not ancient times. The method may be seen to occupy a middle position between a purely geometrical construction and a completely arithmetical one. The small whole numbers involved are usually related to intervals of the musical octave, or are rationalizations of trans-rationals. The purely geometrical may, in practical situations, be cumbersome or restrictive, while the completely arithmetical does not maintain any natural link to unity.

Chambers begins his description of the orders in *Civil Architecture*, 1759, with harmonic number division.[43] The entablature is 1/4th of the column height. The entablatures of each of the orders except the Doric is divided into 10 parts, the Doric into 8. The architrave is 3, freeze 3 and cornice 4; the Doric is 2, 3 and 3. Since both 6:10 and 5:8 are Ø approximates[44] we're still on pretty traditional grounds here, but once we get to the lesser parts arithmetic takes over. Lower D is divided in half to be the module, M, which is divided into 30 parts. These will be the units of measurement for the elements. Where Gibbs takes a series of intervals and divided them by small whole numbers Chambers measures the intervals in uniform parts.

The Ionic or Attic base, **figure 10**, given by both Gibbs and Chambers,[45] is 1/2 D, 1 M or 30 P high. Chambers gives us a count of plinth, 10, lower torus, 7.5, scotia, including its fillets at 1P each, 6.75, and the upper torus, 5.75 = 30. In both canons the plinth is 1/3 of the height of the base. In Chambers, the remaining 2/3 is divided into 20 parts and the count is given in intervals of these. In Gibbs, the upper 2/3 is divided into 9, or 18. 1/3rd of this is the lower torus, 1/3 is scotia and its lower fillet, and 1/3 is the top fillet of the scotia and the upper torus. The scotia's lower fillet is 2/3 of 1/9 and the upper fillet is 1/2 of 1/9.

The entire difference between the two is that difference of 2 units, 20 vs. 18. Each of Chambers units is 1/60 of D, each of Gibbs units is 1/54th of D. The significant difference is not in the substance of the element but in the numerical method used to create it. Gibbs takes an interval, a unity, and divides it into a comprehendible number of parts. Chambers gives a string of seemingly unrelated numbers.

Chambers actually tells us that it is easier to remember the sequence 10, 7.5, 1, 4.75, 1, 5.75 than to divide a series of intervals by 3.[46] It's the psychology of these descriptions that is the issue. Methods are not neutral; by putting the relations abstractly, Chambers, knowingly or not, diverts our attention from the basic ratios that remind us of unity and focuses us on disconnected quantity.

As industrialism ramped up in the eighteenth century, the rate of construction rose and architectural design was guided by "pattern books." The pattern books institutionalized and spread Palladianism in Britain and the US.[47] One of the ultimate statements of this trend is in W. Halfpenny,[48] where design of the orders and elements is reduced to a series of charts, **figure 11.** Though expressed in linear measure, all the relationships in the chart recapitulate canonical proportions.

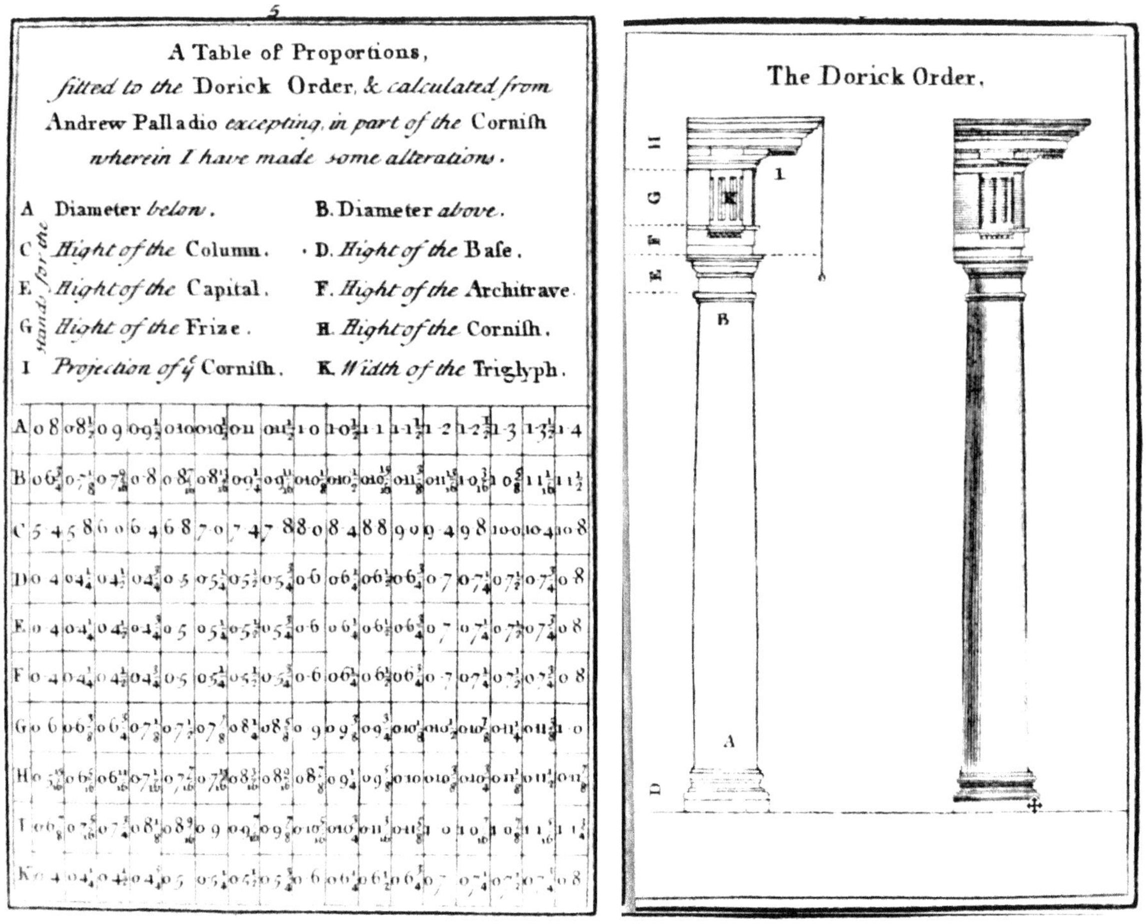

FIGURE 11
Halfpenny's Doric

Robert Morris

Robert Morris, 1703-1754, came from a successful London building family. He learned architecture from his older relative Roger Morris, 1695-1749. Robert Morris openly reiterates the musical analogy,[49] writing that as there are seven notes in the octave he will offer seven sets of ratios for rooms:

	Volume	H W L	Ratio of L:W	Ratio of H:W:L
1.	1 cube	1 : 1 : 1	fundamental	fundamental
2.	1.5 cube	1 : 1 : 1.5 or 2 : 2 : 3	fifth	fundamental & fifth
3.	2 cubes	1 : 1 : 2	octave	fundamental & octave
4.	6 cubes	1 : 2 : 3	fifth	octave & fifth
5.	24 cubes	2 : 3 : 4	fourth	fifth & fourth
6.	60 cubes	3 : 4 : 5	tempered third	fourth & third
7.	72 cubes	3 : 4 : 6	fifth	fourth & fifth

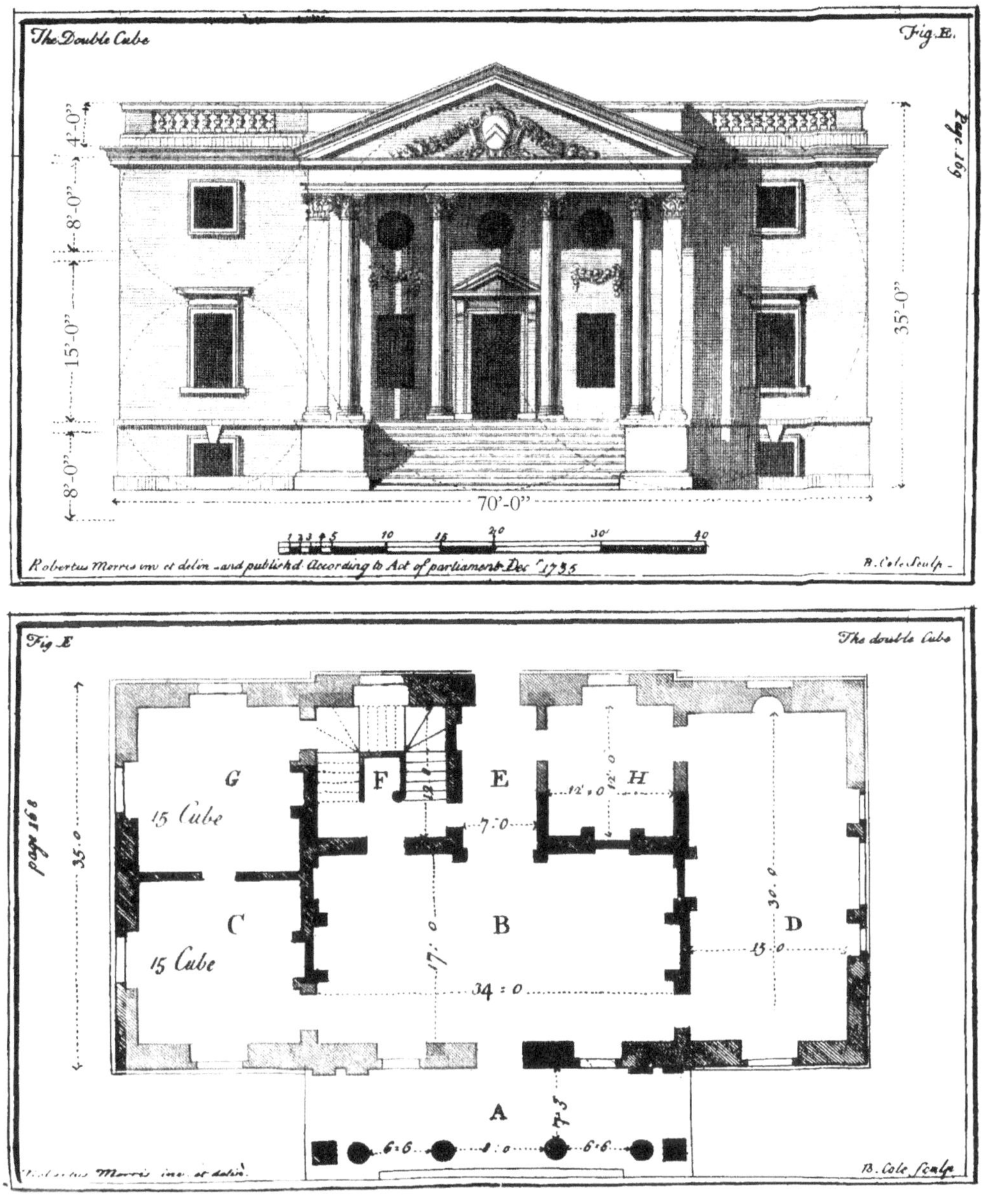

FIGURE 12

Double Cube House, Morris, 1734

Where Palladio had taken the height of the room as the mean between its length and width, Morris proposes a series of three-term progressions, or chords which give its length, width, and height. In Palladian rooms the long walls are horizontally oriented and the short walls are vertically oriented. While such rooms are experientially powerful, they are difficult to heat in the colder British climate. Morris' proposal is that the lowest number in the progression be the height of the room. Though this helps functional performance, while still keeping all the visible ratios harmonically related, all the walls will be oriented horizontally, somewhat diminishing the Palladian power.

An example is Morris' "Double Cube" house,[50] **figure 12.** The overall building volume is 1:1:2. The facade is a double square, 2:1. The side elevation is 1:1. All the room volumes are either a cube, double cube, or half cube. Space B is 17' by 34'; it has a 17' ceiling, raising the floor level above. Spaces C, D, and G have 15' ceilings. Spaces F and H are 12' cubes. Space E is 7' wide but is drawn as 14' long, and may be taken as 7' x 14' with a 14' ceiling, or 1/2 a cube.

Morris offers an algebraic method for determining the size of windows.[51] The minimum window area, A, is equal to the square root of the length x width x height of the room: $A = \sqrt{LWH}$. For example, a room of 24' x 18' x 12' has a window area of $\sqrt{5{,}184} = 72$ sf. If there are to be three windows each will have 24 sq.ft. Holding a 2:1 ratio each window would be a minimum of 3.5'x7'.

Although Morris shows himself to be a master of the Palladian volumetric method guided by harmonic number; a new spirit is present here. While Morris is unashamed in his presentation of the musical analogy, he also introduces abstract mathematics to govern lesser aspects. Though an echo of Rosicrucianism remains, design is being reduced to a set of soulless algebraic expressions.

Burke

One of the final body blows to beauty came in 1756 with the essay "A Philosophical Enquiry Into the Origins of Our Ideas of the Sublime and Beautiful" by British lawyer and Whig politician Edmund Burke, 1729–1797. The switch from the beautiful to the sublime as the goal of art marks a key step towards the emergence of the Romantic and the Modern. The essay was highly influential in its day and casts a shadow right down to the present.

Burke refers to "passions" as "organs of the mind," the strongest of which is self-preservation.[52] This passion is stimulated by pain and danger. When these forces actually affect us they are painful and dangerous, but when experienced in a setting where they cannot actually affect us they are "delightful." This is the experience Burke calls the "sublime." The experience of the sublime causes "astonishment," a state in which the psyche is so completely focused and preoccupied with its object that, in effect, it cannot do anything else; its other functions, including rationality, suspended. Other effects of the sublime are "admiration, reverence and respect."[53]

Some aspects of the sublime that excite delight when we are safe from their causes, are: fear and terror, obscurity and darkness, the experience of power, privations such as vacuity, solitude and silence, vastness and the appearance of infinity, indefinite succession and uniformity of parts, large magnitude, magnificence (*"a great profusion of things splendid or valuable"*), among others. You experience the sublime when you are outscaled, when the senses are on overload, when you encounter the appearance of the infinite; something to which the rational faculties cannot relate and so they surrender, freeze or collapse, and only the gut level emotional fear of annihilation remains.

Beauty, for Burke is quite different. Beauty is a quality of bodies that stimulates love or a similar passion.[54] There are two kinds of Love.[55] The first is mixed with lust, its object is a particular person. The second is not mixed with sexual desire and is directed generally to humankind and other creatures; its stimulus is beauty. However, these definitions are confined to "sensible qualities" of things to "preserve the utmost simplicity" in a distracting subject.

Comparing the sublime and the beautiful:[56] the sublime object is vast in size, rugged and textured; the beautiful object relatively small and smoothly polished. Sublime objects are edged by straight lines that vary sharply; beautiful ones are subtly and smoothly curved. The sublime is dark and gloomy, solid and massive; the beautiful is light and bright, airy and delicate. The sublime is "founded on pain," beauty on pleasure. Though these attributes may vary in intensity the polarity is always maintained. The sublime as the cause of admiration is focused on huge, terrible objects.[57] The beautiful dwells on small, delicate objects. Burke adds that we submit to what we admire but love what submits to us.

Wow! We're pretty far from Plotinus here, where beauty was the memory of unity and love was the attractive power that held the elements of the cosmos together. The difference is that Burke restricts discussion to the physical. In this "Enlightened" formulation we admire what can screw us, but love what we can screw.

Burke maintains that beauty has nothing to do with proportion.[58] Proportion, and other ideas of order, are matters of convenience, created by the mind, not a cause acting on mind. We know the beautiful when we experience it without intellectual analysis, whether we will it or not. The experience of beauty causes the experience of love in us as ice or fire causes the sense of cold or hot.

Proportion is a measure of relation between quantities.[59] Quantity can be divided into parts, and these parts must always have some ratio to each other. They are mathematical objects and essentially all alike to mind. If beauty were related to measure or quantity, to calculation or geometry, there would be some "certain measures" whose beauty could be demonstrated and could be found in natural objects. But there are no such certain measures. Various canons of human proportion do not agree with one another. The parts of the body that are compared often are far apart on the body and cannot be seen together. Similar relations of one part to another do not confer beauty; they are found in good- and not-good-looking people. Regardless of which canon is used, a painting may not be beautiful, but one that diverges from the canon can be.[60]

Perhaps surprisingly, I agree with much of the above, and so would Plotinus. The power is not in the numbers. Burke finds that proportion is unrelated to beauty because he is considering number only as quantitative or mathematical, and beauty only as the physical, to keep the discussion "simple." In fact many of these same points about proportion had been made by Perrault in 1683. For Perrault beauty has many of the qualities of Burke's sublime. Beauty must be obvious, consisting of richness of material, size and magnificence, precision of the work and bilateral symmetry.

Now Burke comes to a touchstone that may be used to position a commentator with regard to their attitude toward the relation of number to art: the Vitruvian Man. Burke considers the Vitruvian Man a "forced analogy," a "strange figure"; and the idea that proportions in buildings are related to those of the body as an urban legend, since the body is never seen in the "strained postures" of the Vitruvian Man. Any such analogy is "unaccountably whimsical," as a person looks nothing like a building.[61] Burke and Perrault agree that numerical analog ideas were an afterthought; that, in effect, people built what they needed to and rationalized it later by comparing their work to nature.[62] Perrault agrees that the ancients had no rules but their own "fancies."

Well, so much for about four thousand years of symbolic tradition; let's just chuck it in the rubbish bin and move on. In missing the point of the image completely, Burke sets the tone for much current-day writing on the subject, seeing the Vitruvian Man as a tortured prisoner of geometry.[63] Burke leaves no doubt what subjects he is discussing and who his audience is, *"The great chain of causes, which links one to another, even to the throne of God can never be unraveled by any industry of ours. When we go but one step beyond the immediate sensible qualities of things, we go out of our depth.… when I speak of a cause, … I only mean certain affections of the mind that cause certain changes in the body; or certain powers and properties in bodies that work a change in the mind."*[64] If he were to explain the motion of a falling body, Burke would say it is caused by gravity. He might be able to describe the action of this force mathematically, the "how," without having to make reference to the "why." He adds, *"a consideration of the rationale of our passions seems to me very necessary for all who would affect them upon solid and sure principles."*[65] The distinction between the sublime and the beautiful is *"never to be forgotten by any whose business it is to effect the passions."*[66]

This gives the game away. Burke's audience are those whose "business it is to effect the passions," or we might say, "manipulate phantasms." The passions, "organs of the mind," are not physical things but are composed of "pneuma,"[67] though he isn't going to say that. Mention of the great chain and what he calls "sympathy"[68] in the arts also evoke terminology associated with the magical tradition. Burke's project is the manipulation of the passions, certainly not clarification of the orbits of the soul, as we are advised in the *Republic,* or the use the passions to escape the passions, as we are advised by Diotima in the *Symposium.*

Some sixty years after Burke's essay comes Mary Shelley's archetypal romantic novel, *Frankenstein,* 1818. The creature is huge, misshapen, super-strong and incommunicable, in short, sublime. Its creator, Dr. Frankenstein, assumes the task of endowing inert matter with life, something we are told in the *Timaeus* is not ontologically possible for human beings.[69] If there ever was a sorcerer's apprentice it's Dr. Frankenstein, who creates the monster but can't control it. The first movie version, 1931 (and dozens of subsequent remakes and offshoots), intensifies this "horrific" vision, delighting mass audiences throughout the twentieth century. The modern horror show stock script is outlined in Burke. His "sublime" has an eerie similarity to the modernist architectural aesthetic.

As Freemasons Burke and most of his political associates would have been holders of the "Sublime Degree of Master Mason." The connection of the sublime to the manipulation of the passions could not have been lost on his law-making lodge brothers. Beneath all the rationalism is manipulation of the passions, aka the magical projection of pneumatic phantasms. Burke's project is not to destroy magical manipulation but rather to put it on a sure, engineered footing.

The old magical processes are being transformed, or more properly renamed, relocated socially, and given a rational exterior; very much in the way that *Vitruvius Britannicus* did for design (or that the work of Edward Bernays would later do for public relations). This supports the idea that the Masonic lodges were at least one principal venue for the transformation of the ancient magical system into what might be called the modern magical system. Or perhaps the modern world is like an Oreo cookie: dark, crispy and sublime on the rational outside; light, sweet and beautiful on the secret magical inside.

Romance

By the end of the seventeenth century there had been a Darwinian extinction of the magical viewpoint in public life.[70] It was physically unsafe to hold these views. In an age of uncertainty and doubt, dealing with spirits carried the death penalty, though often the motive of the denouncers was political, financial or personal. The arts reacted to this triumph of Reason, to the jettisoning of beauty and the brutality of the early industrial system, with the emergence of the "Romantic." The Romantic seeks beauty but utilizes the sublime. Its principal references are to an idealized nature and to the emotions, the "passions."

A trailblazer of the Romantic movement is Goethe, 1749–1832. In his treatment of *Faust,* 1805, the selling of one's soul to the Devil for power over matter, which then produces negative results, is a metaphor for the Enlightenment destruction of the vitality of the West. Goethe's *Sorcerer's Apprentice* is another metaphor of the present state of consciousness: wisdom, a sense of limits, is absent. Thus the powers can be turned on but not off.

Goethe is the last spokesperson for a non-reductionist science in which the experiment is a "mediator between subject and object."[71] It is a kind of science that uses "intuition," what might be called a "poetic science."[72] It is logical but not reductionist, allowing for objects to be connected.

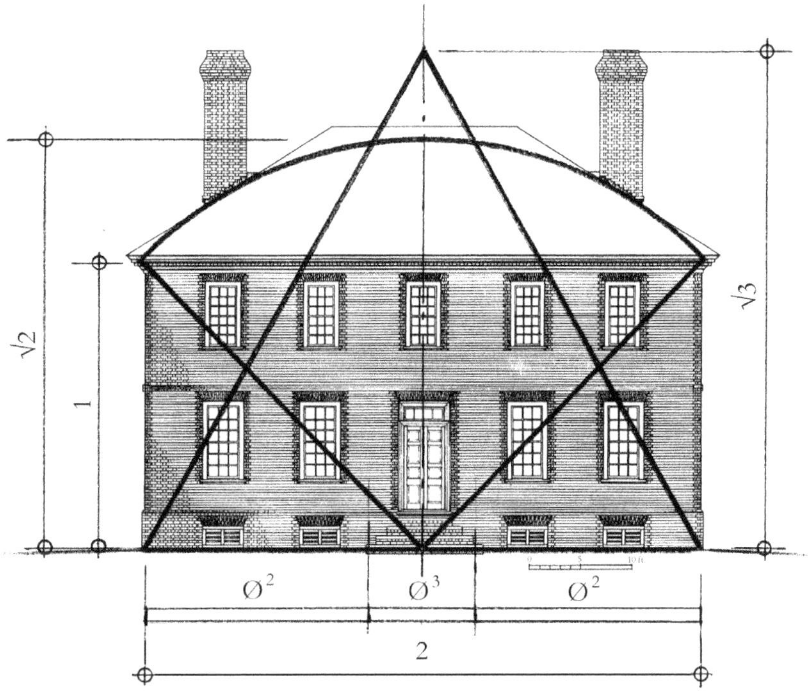

FIGURE 13
The Wythe House, Williamsburg, 1750

Under Romantic influence the intuition of Goethe becomes "feelings," emotions associated with the sublime. Though his method is repudiated by mainstream science in favor of strict reductionism, his work widely influenced thinkers in the nineteenth and twentieth centuries, including Emerson, who selects him as one of six "representative men," and Rudolf Steiner, who builds on his scientific method.

William Blake, 1757–1827, a poet and artist, not a scientist, did not attempt to mix the old with the new, but lamented its passing, using naturalistic images, as in:

The Sick Rose

O Rose, thou art sick:
The invisible worm,
That flies in the night
In the howling storm,
Has found out thy bed
Of crimson joy;
And his dark secret love
Does thy life destroy.

The relation of the worm to the rose is that of the supremacy of the rational to the beautiful. By dissecting nature its vitality is destroyed. In the image of the Blake's rose one cannot help recalling the sad fate of the Rosy-Cross (Rosicrucian) movement.

JEFFERSON

Thomas Jefferson, 1743–1826, was born in Albemarle County, Virginia. His father was a successful, self-made farmer and land surveyor. His mother was a member of the aristocratic, prominent Randolph family. From this he received a combination of nobility, high-mindedness

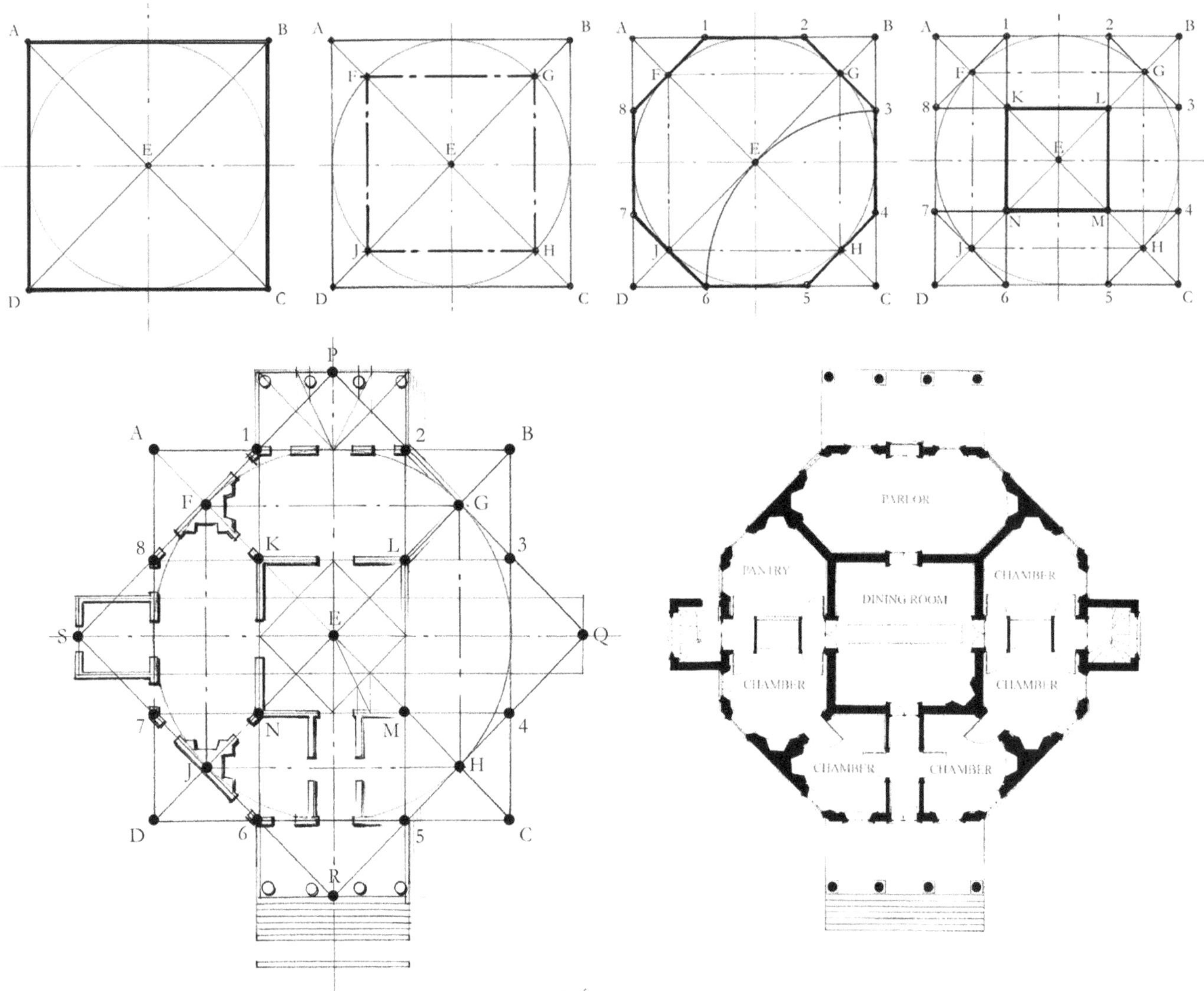

FIGURE 14a
Poplar Forest, Jefferson, 1806. Plan

and practical ingenuity. At 17 he goes to Williamsburg to attend the College of William and Mary where he studies law under the influence of George Wythe, followed by five years of legal apprenticeship. During this period he also lives in Wythe's house.

The Wythe House, **figure 13**, built about 1750, utilizes a powerfully direct geometrical method. In elevation the bulk of the house is a double square. The ridge line is set by the $\sqrt{2}/2$ of the width of the house.[73] The height of the chimneys is set by the altitude of an equilateral triangle, $\sqrt{3}/2$, whose base is the width of the house. The pattern leaves no doubt that we are looking at the Masonic square and compass. Yet the fivefold power is also honored in the five-bay modulation.

In 1806, during his presidency, Jefferson begins work on Poplar Forest, a personal retreat. At first glance the small house seems like a "poor man's" Villa Rotunda. Like the Rotunda it is clearly cosmological, though on a much smaller scale. Its plan, based on a similar $\sqrt{2}$ geometry, is octagonal rather than square, with a cubical center rather than a cylinder and dome. A version of Jefferson's plan appears in Morris' *Select Architecture*.[74]

In plan, it is a regular octagon strictly oriented to the cardinal points. It may be reconstructed geometrically, **figure 14a.** Draw a circle with center at E. Circumscribe it in a square, ABCD. Where diagonals AC and BD intersect the circle find points F, G, H, and J. Construct an octagon

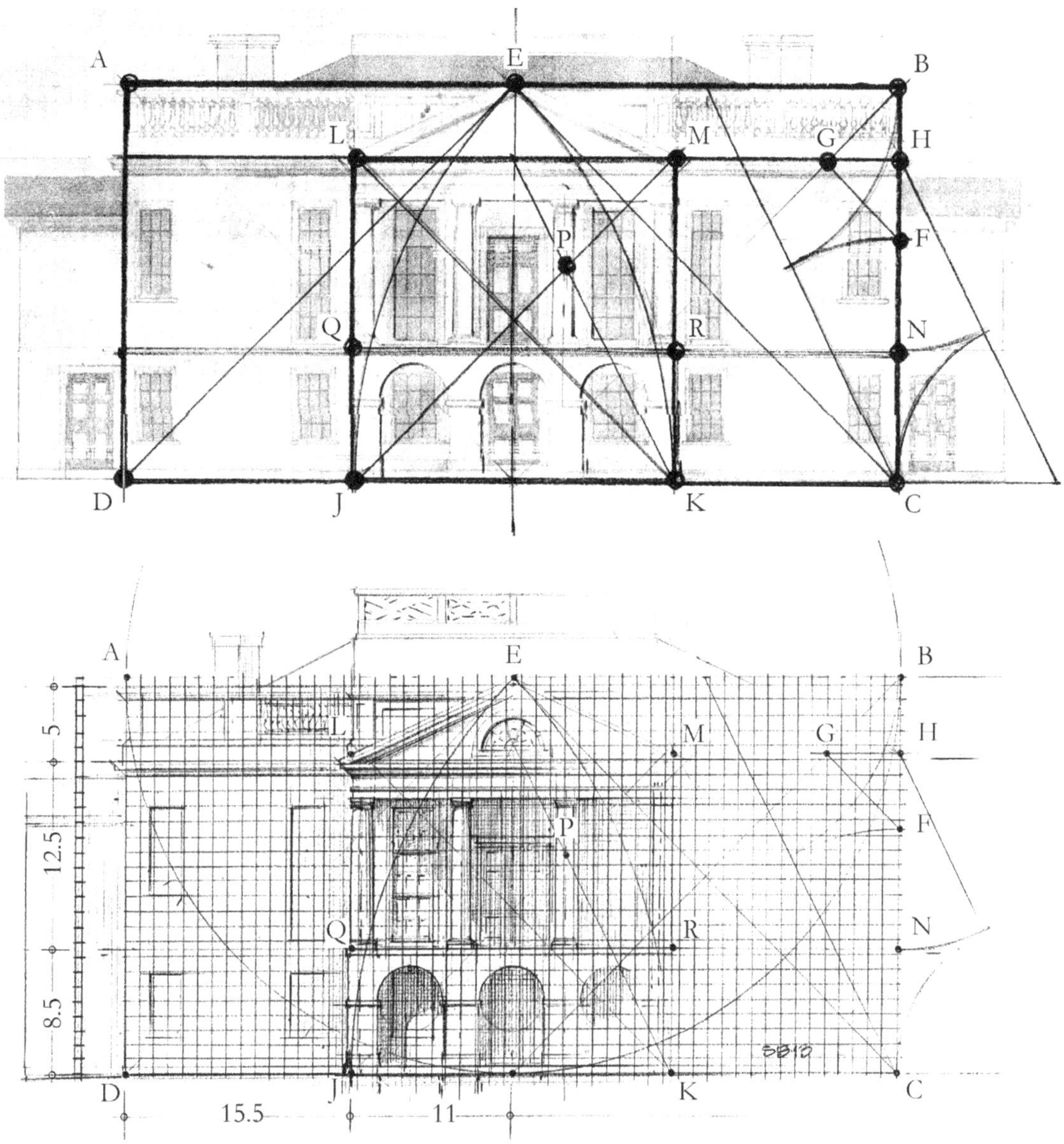

FIGURE 14b-c

Poplar Forest. Elevation. Analysis and Reconstruction

by drawing arc 3-6, with center at C and radius CE; repeat at A, B and D to find points 1 through 8. Draw the central square by connecting diagonals 1-6, 2-5, 3-8 and 4-7 to find points K, L, M, and N. Connecting points F and K, G and L, etc. gives the lozenge-shaped outer rooms. The north and south porticos are double squares marked by extending the sides of the octagon to points P, Q, R and S. The stair towers are square, half the length of exterior side 3-4.

In elevation, **figure 14b**, the bulk of the house fits within double square ABCD. Find Ø of overall height BC, point F. FC = Ø, FB = $Ø^2$. Divide FB in half to find point G. If BC = 1, BH = .191. This interval gives the unusually deep balustrade. To find the center surface, facing us orthographically, strike an arc with center at C and radius CE to find point J and from D to find K. Construct square LMKJ. If CD = 2, JK = MK = .828, while HC = .809; either construction could inform LMKJ. The height of the basement is found by taking Ø of HC, point N. The inner columns are centered on P, the 1/3rd point of JK.

This procedure has given all the key points needed to create the facade, but we can also use a harmonic ratio method. If we divide the height BC into 10 and length CD into 20 then BH = 2,

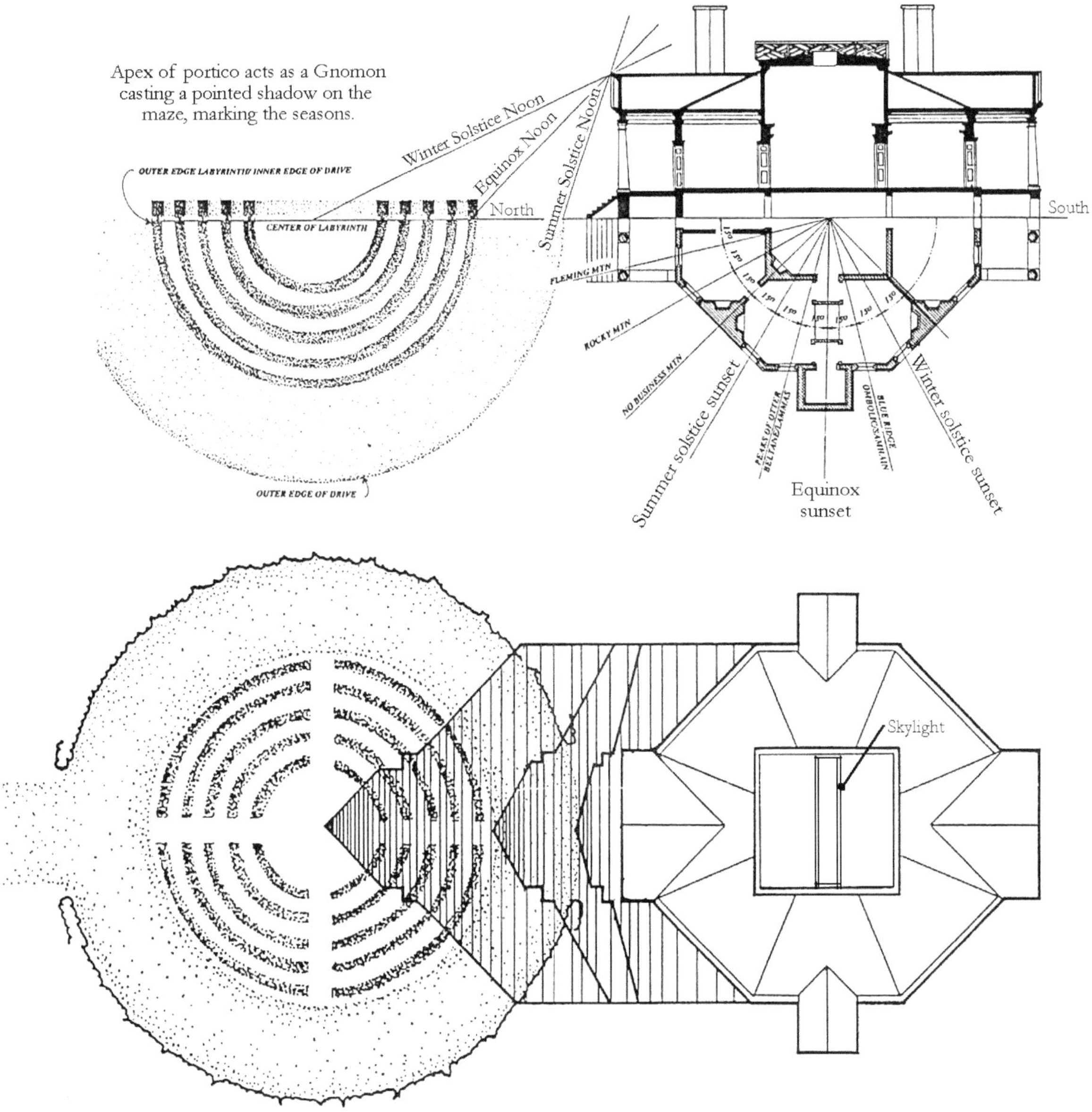

Plan showing the maze with the shadows of the pediment at noon on the summer solstice, equinox and winter solstice.

FIGURE 14d
Poplar Forest. Site Plan

HC = 8, HN = 5 and CN = 3. JK = MN = 8. The overall centerpiece is 8:10 or 4:5. The portico, LMRQ is a 5:8 rectangle; the basement QRKJ is 3:8; the attic is 1:4. Taking the entablature as 1/4th of the column = 1/5th of MR=1. The column rectangle is 4:8 or 1:2. We may see a skilful interweaving of the Fibonacci series here in the numbers 1, 2, 3, 5, 8 and some of their multiples.

That drawings of Jefferson and his circle are done on graph paper is a significant indicator that an arithmetic method was used. The facade is reconstructed in **figure 14c** using a drawing by John Neilson, a master carpenter who worked with Jefferson.[75] JK is 22 units and DJ=KC at 15.5 units making an overall width DC of 53. CN is 8.5, HN is 12.5, and BH is 5.5, making BC 26.5.

Comparing the arithmetic with the geometric finds that .707 x 53 = 37.47 units. 53 - 37.47 = 15.5, which equals DJ and KC, making JK = 22 units. Subdividing the height BC we get 26.5 x

.809 = 21.44 = CH, leaving BH = 26.5 - 21.44 = 5.06 units. Taking Ø of HC, 21.44 x .618 = 13.25 = HN leaving CN = 21.44 - 13.25 = 8.19. Now CH is either 21 arithmetically or 21.44 geometrically; BH is either 5.5 or 5.06. Thus the "adjustment" between arithmetic and geometry of height MK is 1 unit or less, about 3.6%.

The house and the site layout have several remarkable features. The first is the existence of two small earth mounds on the east-west axis about a hundred feet from either side of the house. These were intentional constructions by Jefferson. The rising and setting points of the sun on the equinoxes would be directly over the mounds when viewed from the house. The sunlight would enter the house through two half-circle windows in the stairwells. Inside the house the solar rays are terminated on the surfaces of the two sleeping structures he constructed.

A second site feature is a circular hedge maze on the north side, at the end of the driveway, centered on the main entry way, **figure 14d.** The circle is sized and positioned so that the shadow of the apex of the pediment marks the solstices and equinoxes. Two window openings in the west room are oriented to the winter and summer solstice sunsets and the other two mark the "cross quarter" days. East room windows mark the sunrise on these days. The cubical center room had a linear skylight along the east-west axis which would have thrown a strip of light onto the floor and north wall. The summer solstice, when the noon sun is at its highest, the strip would fall on the floor at the foot of the entry door. At the winter solstice, the strip would be on the wall about halfway between the door head and the ceiling. On the equinoxes, the strip would fall at the height of the door head. Thus when Jefferson got out of bed in the morning, or when he greeted visitors in the center hall, he would be reminded of the time of year by the structure of the house. The house would be less a "machine for living in" than a tuning devise, facilitating the observance of the very natural law that Jefferson refers to in the Declaration of Independence.[76]

It is not clear if Jefferson was actually a Freemason as no records exist of him having been a member of any specific lodge. However Jefferson moved in a Masonic milieu and shared many of their ideological views. For one thing he was a deist. This refers to the "clockwork" universe in which the Divinity "sets up" the cosmos but then allows it to proceed on the basis of "natural laws."[77] Thus the rational faculty, often mathematically expressed, becomes a path to contact the divine without miracles or revelations.

Jefferson is known to have attended meetings of the influential Lodge of the Nine Muses in Paris[78] which would have been closed to the general public. Voltaire and Ben Franklin were members, and Franklin was Master in 1779–81. Several of Jefferson's relatives were Masons as were his Virginia legislative associates Patrick Henry and George Washington. In 1801, Jefferson Lodge No. 65 was chartered in Virginia, an honor seldom bestowed on non-members. He is also known to have attended the Masonic cornerstone ritual and public parade at the site of the UV library in 1817. After his death there were several Masonic tributes to him.[79]

In 1809 Jefferson retires but continues to rework both Monticello and Poplar Forest until his death in 1826. During this time he becomes involved in the creation of the University of Virginia. The three achievements cited in his own epitaph, author of the Declaration of Independence, sponsor of the Statute of Virginia for religious freedom, and father of the University of Virginia, all relate to the esoteric sphere.[80]

In the Declaration, he is the author of the memorable words "*We hold these truths to be self-evident, that all men are created equal, that they are endowed by their Creator with certain unalienable Rights, that among these are Life, Liberty and the pursuit of Happiness—That to secure*

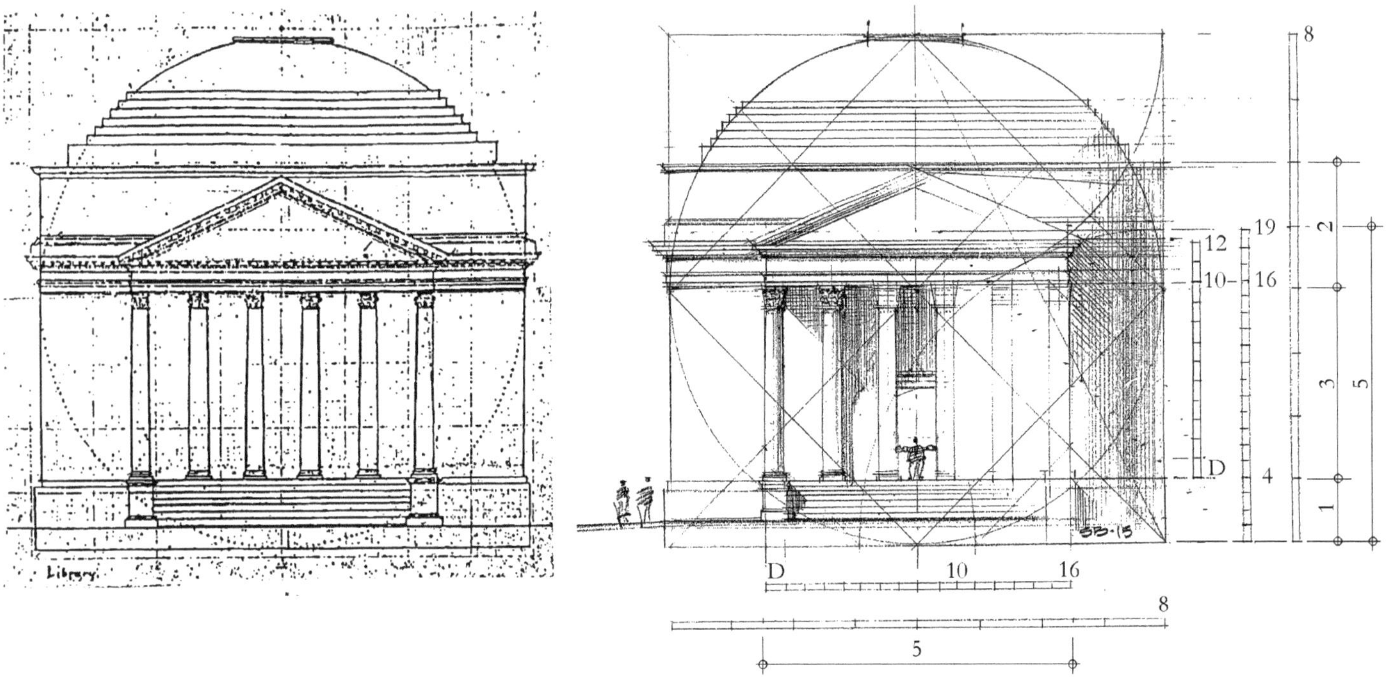

FIGURE 15

The Rotunda, University of Virginia, Charlottesville, Jefferson, 1825

these rights, Governments are instituted among Men, deriving their just powers from the consent of the governed."

"Created equal" refers to the individual's participation in the monad, a key to the macro-micro cosmological analogy. This participation manifests as "natural" laws, the state acknowledges this in the "rights" of the citizen as monad. Natural individual rights include "life, liberty and the pursuit of happiness" because the cosmos, as we are told by Timaeus,[81] is alive, intelligent and ultimately good. The individual having the power to choose based on intelligence, particularly the use of the rational faculty, will result in the achievement of happiness, the perpetual possession of the good.[82] In a very direct way this is the rational for democracy.

To facilitate movement toward the good, the church is separated from government, Jefferson's second achievement, so that individuals can choose. For choice to be meaningful, alternatives must exist, thus toleration is required. This deistic, nonsectarianism accomplished a major goal of the Rosicrucian vision and was an ideological mainstay of Freemasonry.

Jefferson's third achievement, the creation of UV, was the building of a community based on the sharing of knowledge, an elite whose members are openly selected by meritocracy. In a Rosicrucian context, UV is an invisible college made visible. In Jefferson's expression of this the living and learning spaces comprise a single focused layout surrounding a 3:1 rectangle, known as the Lawn. On the long north and south sides are a series of functional pavilions connected by a peristyle and focused on a single spherical building on the east side, representing both the origin and destination of the community's learning activity. The sun will rise behind it on the equinoxes, and it is the master's station in the Masonic lodge room. The west end was left open and would remain so for almost a hundred years, until the closing of the American frontier.

Counting the squares on Jefferson's elevation of the library, **figure 15,** the width and overall height are divided into 8 parts.[83] The portico is 5 parts wide. The base is 1 part high, the column is 3 parts, the entablature, pediment and attic are 2 parts, with the remaining 2 given to the dome. Behind the grid is the Fibonacci series, 1, 2, 3, 5, 8. Applying a scale of 19 to the 5-unit height of the portico gives the order. The base is $4/19 \approx 1/5$. Divide 12/19 into 10 to get D, 2/10 gives the entablature in the reconstruction. Jefferson's entablature is 1/6 of the column height, about 1.7/10.

In his life and career Jefferson embodies the Enlightenment. Without sacrificing noble bearing he looks at nature for himself, creating new practical devices. In politics Jefferson may be said to be an architect of our government, determining the relation and character of its structural elements. There is no clear separation of his activities as designer of the nation and his architectural works. In this relationship he joins a long line of statesmen-architects going back through Hadrian to Imhotep.

Jefferson's canonical references include: Palladio's *Four Books*; both of Gibbs' books; Morris' *Select Architecture*; and de Chambray's *Parallel of Ancient and Modern Architecture*.[84] His architectural work presents the classical idea on a national scale, drawn from European sources but revitalized in an American incarnation. His architectural palette includes red brick wall structure, sometimes arcuated, with white wood trim and details. Columns were usually brick with white painted stucco surfacing. The only carved ornaments are Ionic and Corinthian capitals; mouldings are uncut. The look is at the same time elegant but forceful; noble in its references while modest and restrained in expression.

These qualities of Jefferson's architecture are revealed in the building by McKim, Mead & White that later closed the west end of the Lawn. Though restrained by MMW standards it seems wildly overdressed in the presence of Jefferson's work. In the early nineteenth century, after the disappearance of the Founding Fathers, American history seems to take a distinct turn, the focus of vision shifting from contemplating the Golden Section to "going for the gold."

Beauty Bereft

The "Enlightenment" was an age of profound forgetting of innumerable centuries of wisdom expressed in the esoteric and magical traditions. Conceptually, the top half of our three-circle diagram was ripped off and thrown away. The theory of proportion did not survive this massive trauma. Imaged geometrically, rationalism has no center, being more analogous to a uniform grid than a centered circle. Instead of a center and a harmony we are left with emptiness and anxiety.

The Italian Baroque of the late seventeenth century was the last completely integrated and vital architectural vision, synthesized from the elements of tradition but living entirely on its own terms. Palladianism was the first of the historical revivals. The discarding of beauty as a goal objectified and materialized the elements of architecture, setting the stage for historicism and eclecticism. Once the proportional heart had been cut out, the soul denied and the sorcerer exiled, beauty, which had once provided entrée to the Real, became a fantasy, a ghost, and architectural design became a series of academic references rather than a living integration.

For these reasons this review of history will end here. Since we have already looked at the architectures of Egypt, Greece, Rome, the Medieval era and the Renaissance we have seen the indigenous forms of the revived architectures. Although there have been many worthy architectural works in the last two hundred years we need not examine them in detail here to substantiate the role of proportion in architecture.

IV

THE PRESENT MOMENT

AT THE OUTSET OF THIS WORK the reader was asked to participate in a journey. Now that the journey is coming to an end, let's look back at where we have been. Our origin point was a vision — a way of looking at the world as though it was a single unified entity. Our goal was the experience of the beautiful, defined as the memory of unity and guided by a "sense of unity" inherent in us. Our journey was energized by Eros, the desire to be one with the beautiful object. Our vehicle was the symbolic number and geometry of the Pythagoreans and Platonists. The journey proceeded through geometric, arithmetic and harmonic ratio methods of dividing unity while maintaining some relation to it, allowing for the possibility of the beautiful. Then we saw these methods developed through analysis and reconstruction of historic architectural structures. Parallel to this we followed the idea of symbolic number in the philosophy and spirituality of several phases of Western history.

Now we've arrived at the present moment and, in keeping with the ancient story, must begin our own work of return. This work begins when we reorient ourselves to be able to perceive the physical cosmos as a harmony, to see the continuities rather than the separations, to see wholes rather than collections of unconnected parts. Such work does not require a repudiation of the physical world but an absorption of it into a larger process. Our work will be in the physical realm, where it must, but it needs to be guided by higher ideas. What we're seeking, what's needed in design, is a new integration, a vital integration, a reconstruction of some of the elements combined with a transformation of others that results in a living entity; that allows us to experience the beautiful, to remember unity. We might recall the work of Plato's demiurge, who fuses the same and the different to create the living psyche.

The last such vitally integrated architecture, in the view of this author, was the Roman Baroque of the seventeenth century. Designers of the period, particularly Bernini and Borromini, building on the work of Bramante and others, looked at a variety of antique prototypes such as Hadrian's Villa, absorbed their lessons, and developed a new architecture. Much of the traditional architecture since that era, though worthy of study in its own terms, is largely "historic revival," that is to say, it is based on an academic reading of a defined past cultural era. But a vital integration gives birth to new life rather than reanimating the dead.

The Georgian architecture with which we concluded our historical review was among the first of these revivals, being based on a circumscribed reading of the architecture of Palladio. Early American architecture was dominated by Georgian influence. The nineteenth century saw a series of overt "revivals" such as Greek, Gothic and Romanesque. In the mid-nineteenth century, R. M. Hunt introduced a French Beaux-Arts influence in the United States. In the early twentieth century the first-rate artistic community that grew around the office of McKim, Mead & White fused Italian and French influences. Even the creditable style known as "Deco" was only a partial integration: it followed the theory of "progressive reduction," reducing the number of parts and editing and flattening the elements, while maintaining a core of classical sensibility.

Though retaining a vital spark, it represents a kind of "last gasp" of the traditional system rather than a new birth. Historicist architecture is by definition a version of something else, it does not go back to first principles and cannot form a vital integration of its own. This doesn't mean it can't be tasteful architecture, just not the kind of integration that will assist the elevation of consciousness, the work of return.

The aesthetics of modernism was an attempt at creating a new vision but it was based on negation, its principles an inversion of the classical. At present, the state of aesthetics is almost entirely negative. Any attempt at balance, harmony, or a sense of unity is considered an anathema. By seeing the "limit" as a restriction, modernism denies itself any relation to unity. In this atmosphere the search for beauty is a cynical joke suited, as modernists might say, only for "pathetic cultural retards"– such as this author and a few of his classicist buddies. The use of symbols to create meaning is prohibited. Choice in design must be strictly based on functionalism, which roots us in materialism. To grasp the classical, one must transcend functionalism. An archetypal form or massing is selected by the designer for its symbolic or characterological value. It is then adjusted, usually in a minor way, to accept the functional requirements. Mechanical functions are subordinated to symbolic ones. Further, in modernist ideology the building must "honestly" express its structure entirely through the actual display of its materials and parts. Any attempt at "fictive structure" in the service of character is considered unethical, a form of fraud or lying; "false teeth" as Le Corbusier is said to have called it.

Worse yet, the whole thing has been politicized. Modernist aesthetics was developed parallel to class struggle in Europe. Such ideas as "ornament is crime" come from this politicized milieu. Associating aesthetics with warring social classes or infamous dictators does not lead to productive discussion or any kind of new integration. We must not engage in a new "war of the styles" such as preoccupied architecture in the early twentieth century parallel to society's class struggles. Though this author is not a pacifist it must be noted that wars cannot be undertaken against ideas, only against people who, rightly or wrongly, are thought to hold these ideas. The new integration cannot be obtained by hurting people.

Nor is the search for unity a game. Games are sterile. Games ultimately are meaningless in themselves. They are setups; a reduced set of rules, strictly enforced. Seeing classicism this way is part of our modern problem. The attempt here is to seek an aesthetic that allows for meaning, an essential quality for establishing a living connection. No mathematized formula will be enough. Neither historicism, minimalism, functionalism or mathematizing is the path to a new vital integration.

Let's get our priorities straight. Work in the classical is done in the pursuit of beauty. Although rational means are employed the goal is trans-rational: to achieve the memory of unity. In the Platonic system, Unity is symbolically represented as the triadic cycle of the Good, the True and the Beautiful. Beauty is thus co-defined as the Good and the True. The manifest world proceeds from unity because of the Good, as Plato tells us in the *Timaeus;*[1] it is maintained in the True, the law, the way, maat or dharma; and it returns to unity in the Beautiful. Thus by attempting to create the beautiful, the artist is doing something good. The search itself elevates the artist and the finished product elevates the observer. The artist should remember that individuals can perceive beauty only to the extent of their own psychic clarity or refinement. Classical artists need to help in that refinement process; they should approach the public with compassion rather than contempt.

To find the way, designers might begin by simply choosing to look up. Socrates in the *Republic* tells us to imitate the heavenly pattern; to look up to the ideal cosmic patterns, then down to the material work at hand. Spiritual development, the work of return, begins in this world of sense perception and aesthetics, as we have been advised by Diotima. Traditionally the artist looks at nature, more properly at the patterns, the logoi of nature, its numerical and geometrical character. When these are reproduced or mimed in the artist's work, they stimulate the sense of unity, as we know intuitively that nature, that which comes to birth, is a unified living entity. Mimesis however must be in the service of anamnesis; that is, copying from nature must contribute to the remembrance of Unity. Mimesis as an end in itself will not achieve the vital quality we seek.

A theory is not a fact. It is a viewpoint backed by data, a pattern created by a connecting of the factual dots. The present work attempts to illuminate such a viewpoint, then to provide data through analysis and synthesis of archetypal and historical examples. As there may be many ways to organize such data, the proportional theory or viewpoint offered here should be evaluated on the basis of performance, asking "what do we get for it?" For your present author, what we get is the power to compel attention, to say something coherent and meaningful. Above all we get the power to generate desire. Any such power should be used for the good: for the achievement of unity. It is incumbent on anyone to use such a power for the good, not because you're a nice guy but because power is subject to the law of karma: what you put out is what you get back, only more-so. If one achieves such a power they must act for the good with restraint and forethought.

Classical artists place themselves in the position of the Platonic demiurge.[2] This is the being who gives the pattern, the logos, who enunciates the "word." Physical creation flows from this pattern. As the cosmos has a logos, every created work done in the service of return may also have its own logos, its own guiding pattern. As the demiurge of your cosmos you determine its composition, but you must also create or produce each element. As the logos is the source of life, vitality, the artist's work can remind the viewer of that which lives. This touches on the idea of the vitalization of matter. As the cosmos is alive and intelligent, the artist can implant some aspect of these qualities into the work. As these qualities are represented in the human intellect by symbolic number, proportion can be the tool of this achievement. In the Platonic tradition the ability to vitalize matter is a divine provenance. But human beings can endow matter with life-like qualities, a kind of ensoulment.

In the process of design, "ideal" or archetypal elements, when brought into the world of action, will always need to be particularized. In traditional design this is called "invention," perhaps a misnomer, as "transformation" might be a better term. In order to perform invention designers must have an intimacy with an element; it must be part of themselves. The act of drawing it should be like reciting a poem. At that point one can begin the work of transformation or particularization needed to give a design "character," a unified sense of being. Character in architecture is related to historia in painting and sculpture. It is a kind of rhetoric, explaining what the work is about.

To create the appearance of an orderly cosmos in a work of art is a form of illusionism. However, the craft skills necessary to create such illusions require lengthy discipline. The earlier in life one starts the better, but it's never too late. Proportional theory is not a substitution for artistic judgment. The designer must always remember: the numbers work for you; you don't work for the numbers. As my teacher in such matters, Keith Critchlow, told me, "If your work looks like geometry, keep working." Nor are the proportional methods suggested here a substitute for personal craft skill. This means manual skill. An important point here is that the less technology used, the older and simpler the tool, the more is required from the artist.

The computer or any digital media may have long-term value, but it is a "promised land" this author does not expect to enter. Such systems will undoubtedly become more sophisticated over time. New generations will be more familiar with them than mine, but the contemporary computer will probably not last very long. In traditional terms, unless a skill is part of you, of your mind and body, it isn't actually yours. If the skill isn't yours, any tool will represent a limitation.

Used properly, that is, in the search for beauty, classical disciplines are not a restraint but a form of liberation. For the Pythagoreans, the limit was good and the unlimited was not good. Classical methods develop the imagination by focusing on ideal form. Such methods allow us to elevate our consciousness, though to achieve illusionistic effects requires physical discipline. We have to remember that beauty is an ideal. In the world of action where we live we will always seek it but never ultimately possess it. The artist shouldn't be frustrated like poor Hephaestus: married to the ideal of beauty but unable to accept that it belongs to all and has a life of its own. In our work we can only allow for the possibility of it. We must accept the aesthetic equivalent of Plato's "most likely story."[3]

As we have seen, this search for the beautiful is not a simplistic or reduced process, nor is it a dualistic one. The forces of the universe are not fundamentally in dualistic conflict but triadic harmony. The structural forces of the cosmos have complex interactions. Working with them may be likened to driving the proverbial multi-horse chariot; if the parts are harmonically related the poiesis, the product, will allow for the beautiful and exert an erotic power.

This power would once have been called a magical one, presupposed in a cosmos where elements are related through harmonic resonance. The magician works with these subtle resonant forces. By magic we mean working with the subtle powers; in our present context it means creating visual images. The search for beauty in art may be considered a branch of the ancient magical tradition; certainly of the associated mythic tradition and later philosophic tradition. Working with such subtle energies is not a matter of belief but of experience. It need not be feared and pushed into some dark corner but could be embraced, like accepting Thoth's embrace in the transference of the ka; and like the ka, it has to do with the animation of matter.

Magic, of course, has been considered suspicious throughout Western history. Organized religions always frown on the use of magic by anyone other than their own representatives. Religions are after all organs of state that express outward aspects of the spiritual that validate the state's relationship with the cosmos. What we have here called spiritual development is an internal individual process. It is occult, not visible. Those who govern the state are naturally suspicious of that which they cannot see. By spirit is usually meant a flowing subtle energy, right on the border of the physical and noetic, that has a vitalizing effect. It is analogous to ka, chi, prana or pneuma. Within the soul the impressment of form into matter is carried out by this energy. It is also the carrier of external sense perceptions. Within psyche external perceptions are matched against noetic entities to extract meaning.

Working with these subtle, hard-to-find energies is also known as the "esoteric" system, its effects are "occult," or hidden, they are internal. The organized religions of the Book, Judaism, Christianity, and Islam, each have esoteric traditions: Kabbalah, Gnosticism, and Sufism, respectively. All are highly controversial within those traditions. Beyond the orthodox systems an independent "stream" continued from the pagan tradition, where it had been equally controversial. This consisted mainly of alchemy, astrology, and a kind of sympathetic magic known as theurgy.

A late author on the Western magical tradition was Henry Cornelius Agrippa. In his encyclopedic *De Occulta Philosophia,* Agrippa writes that the practice of magic, working with these subtle forces, requires knowledge in three areas of philosophy: natural, mathematical and celestial. By natural, he means what we now call science and technology, the manipulation of matter, which in his day was alchemy and sympathetic magic. By mathematical, he means the Quadrivium: arithmetic, geometry, harmony and astronomy (for Agrippa, principally astrology), what we have called symbolic number. By celestial, Agrippa means what we now call psychology and theology, the use of rituals and symbols (or manipulations of matter guided by symbols that could be geometrical or more literal). These are all methods of attunement that allow for a kind of ascension of the spirit. Such a tuning may be thought of as a "sympatheia," literally, getting on the same wavelength as the cosmic harmony. Since the artist works with images perceived through the agency of subtle energies, art and design could be considered a branch of the ancient magical tradition.

We could also look to the "white magic" of Ficino; after all, having Michelangelo as your student gives you serious bragging rights. Ficino's magic is aimed high, to planetary or angelic spirits, general governors rather than the lower more specialized spirits closer to physicality called daemons. The geometrical constructions of previous sections are also aimed at this higher impersonal type of power. For our purposes as designers, however, the techniques are neutral; it is one's intentions that determine the quality of the outcome. Faust, for example, opts consciously for power. Using his knowledge for the general good or his own good was not enough, thus insuring his downfall. The work of the artist inevitably causes an affectation, that is, it casts a spell over the observer. The only question is, "which way are you turning the observer?" But if such magical roads are problematic others are available.

In the search for a vital integration perhaps the science of Goethe could provide some signposts. He proposed a logical but nonreductionist science. Rather than extracting knowledge from nature Goethe saw the scientific process as mediating between the scientist and the object of study. His method aims at understanding the relationship of the object to the investigator rather than dissecting the object in isolation. For example, Newton considered color a property of light itself, a function of wavelength, without reference to anything else, and revealed, but not caused, by its interaction with objects. It was demonstrable through refraction but not caused by refraction. Goethe formulates the topic of color in a different way. Newton viewed color as a physical problem, involving light striking objects and entering our eyes. Goethe realized that the sensations of color we experience are also shaped by the mechanics of visual perception and by the way our minds process information.

Thus for Goethe, what we see of an object depends upon the object, the light and our perception. He sought to derive laws of color harmony, ways of characterizing how color affects us. He studied afterimages and colored shadows, and developed the idea of complementary colors, which is still one basis of our understanding of color vision today. Goethe appreciates that the sensation of complementary colors does not originate physically from the nature of light but perceptually from the actions of our visual system. Thus color is an experience rather than a physical property.

In *Metamorphosis of Plants,* 1790, he sees the plant as an organism in transformation, structured by harmonic analogy expressed through proportion; an idea later called "homolog," being similar in pattern. This view is "holistic" in the modern sense in that objects are related in "complex" ways, where nothing is isolated and everything affects everything else.[4] We may consider Holism–Reductionism on a spectrum of how data is obtained and interpreted. Where we place ourselves on that spectrum effects the nature of the questions asked. To utilize Goethe's method in classical design we would have to develop an "intuition" of the elements, to establish a relationship of intimacy, to have an examined inner experience of them. This kind of method might be seen to have informed the architecture of Rudolf Steiner.

The search for beauty in design could even be considered in a shamanic context: a journey of consciousness into an idealized realm in which the designer searches for an image to solve a problem. Just as a shaman might have spirit helpers in a noetic realm who take human, animal or plant forms, the designer may encounter geometrical patterns, specific elements or archetypal compositions. Designers might even meet and converse with their professional ancestors. These entities present themselves in response to the journeyer's expression of need. The shaman converses with the helper spirits to determine their appropriateness, perhaps in the way contemporary architect Louis Kahn conversed with a brick, which told him it wanted to be an arch.[5] The shaman returns to the "ordinary" world to apply the power of the spirit helper to a practical situation.

Before we dismiss such a method too quickly we should remember that for more than a hundred thousand years shamanism was the basic human spiritual form. Paganism and modern monotheism developed in the last seven or eight thousand years. These journeys of consciousness contributed to our survival for all that time, more than ninety percent of our existence. They can certainly be adopted for contemporary use.[6]

With, for many, magic demonized, Goethe marginalized, and shamanism considered barbaric, we may well need to develop a new vision all our own. But whatever the new integration will be, it will have to merge spiritual, artistic and material aspects. It will have to bridge art and science, which may require changes in our definition of both of these activities. Science may have to admit a Goethean aspect, and the artist will have to live within a framework of discipline. But the spiritual aspect is critical for the achievement of vitality.

The civilized world has always been governed through magical techniques. They are used to create a sense of unity among people who are not otherwise related. Magical methods continue to be used to govern society today, though their names have been changed to Psychology, Public Relations, Intelligence, etc. Although some say violence is at the bottom of society, violence by itself is not a governing technique. In fact it represents a failure of governance. Visual magic, symbols in the form of images, have played a key role in human governance since our beginning, not just of civilization but likely of our species. The use of proportional methods by artists today may thus provide a "psychic" connection to the whole of human ancestry.

Our present society seems to be run by sorcerers' apprentices who know how to turn the powers on but don't know how to shut them off. The levels of power continue to increase to the point where the inability to shut them off endangers us all. Perhaps the only way out of our present morass is to have, in some way, the sorcerer return. This would be a symbolic return. It would require us to re-enchant the world. This book is essentially a call for such re-enchantment, for the sorcerer's return. It is the artist, the poet of space-time, who is uniquely positioned to play the role.

Notes

Section I
The Search for the Beautiful

[1] Vit I.III.2
[2] Pevsner 1958, p 23
[3] *Timaeus* 30
[4] *Timaeus* 36
[5] *Timaeus* 33
[6] *Timaeus* 35
[7] Critchlow *SSA*, p 27
[8] *Timaeus* 42
[9] *Republic* 614-21
[10] *Meno* 84-85
[11] Plotinus I.6, 1.21
[12] Plotinus I.6, 1.43
[13] Plotinus I.6, 2.08
[14] Critchlow, in conversation
[15] Plotinus I.6, 3.34
[16] Plotinus I.6, 5.49
[17] Plotinus I.6, 6.01
[18] Plotinus I.6, 6.12
[19] Plotinus I.6, 6.23
[20] Plotinus I.6, 7.01
[21] Plotinus I.6, 7.29
[22] Plotinus I.6, 8.26
[23] Plotinus I.6, 9.07
[24] Plotinus V.8
[25] *Symposium* 205e
[26] *Symposium* 209e
[27] Genesis 1-2
[28] *Timaeus* 29-31
[29] Genesis 3-5
[30] *Timaeus* 28
[31] Graves 1955, 2a-b, p 30
[32] Genesis 6-8
[33] *Timaeus* 35
[34] Genesis 9-10
[35] *Timaeus* 31-32
[36] Taylor 1983, p 182
[37] Genesis 11-13
[38] Lawlor 1982, p 58
[39] *Timaeus* 55c
[40] Lawlor 1982, p 46
[41] Lawlor 1982, p 46
[42] Lawlor 1982, p 28
[43] Lawlor 1982, p 34
[44] Lawlor 1982, p 37
[45] Iamblichus 1988, Critchlow's intro, p 9
[46] Iamblichus 1988, Critchlow's intro, p 9
[47] Iamblichus 1988, Critchlow's intro, p 10
[48] *Timaeus* 35
[49] Theon 1963, p 63
[50] Iamblichus 1988, Critchlow's intro, p 13
[51] Iamblichus 1988, Critchlow's intro, p 20
[52] Theon 1963, p 49
[53] Taylor 1983, p 97
[54] Lawlor 1982, p 81
[55] Theon 1963, p 48
[56] Bateson 1985, pp 448-66
[57] Burchardt 1986, p 24
[58] Critchlow 1980, p 18
[59] *Republic* 500-01

Section II
Number – Harmony – Design

[1] Serlio 1996, book 1
[2] Ware 1977, preface, p 3
[3] Fideler 1993a, p 307, see Appendix I, pp 291-308 for an in-depth analysis of this Christian archytype.
[4] *Republic*, 618-21
[5] *Meno* 40-43
[6] Plotinus 1.6, and see Section I
[7] *Republic* 501
[8] *Poetics*, 1447
[9] Vitruvius III.I
[10] Vitruvius III.III.7
[11] Iverson 1975, plate 4; Fideler 1993b, p 95; Schwaller 1981 p 117, fig 45; West 1987, pp 187-88
[12] Ware 1977, p 32, figure 97
[13] Vitruvius, III.V.5; who echos Schwaller, 1981 ch VIII, p 115 on the use of the canon of 19.
[14] See Ware 1977, pp 29-31 for significant geometrical layout methods for the various entablatures.
[15] Serlio 1996, book IV, plate XXIIIv, p 294
[16] Normand 1936, Tiranti, London, "figure D" after the index of plates (there is no page number).
[17] Palladio 1965, bk I, ch XXI
[18] Palladio 1965, bk I ch XXIII
[19] Morris, 1734, lecture V, pp 74-77 and lecture VI, pp 94-95
[20] Badaway 1965, pp 25-32
[21] Lawlor 1980, pp 111-115
[22] Hambidge 1967, pp 105-117
[23] Bouleau 1963, pp 42-47

Section III
Proportion in Practice

Introduction

1 Ware 1977, p 3
2 Semes 2004, p 23

Egypt

1 As a scale comparison Americans might note that our country has been independent for 240 years. Even if one includes a 200-year colonial period, we are only about 1/7th as old as ancient Egypt.
2 Badaway 1965, pp 20-26
3 Rundle Clark 1991, p 235. After his murder by his evil twin brother Set, Osiris was nailed in a coffin and floated down the Nile. The coffin washed ashore in Lebanon and became incorporated into the trunk of a tree that was later used as a pillar supporting the local king's palace. Isis eventually finds the coffin and returns it to Egypt. This is symbolized by the "djed" column, a profound symbol of anthropic architecture.
4 See Section II, **figure 29**
5 Badaway 1965, pp 26-38
6 Badaway 1965, p 3:
- ▷ simple square (great pyramid, valley portal of Chephren, pl 2, p 70);
- ▷ square flanked by one 8:5 triangle (mastaba superstructure of Sekhemka, pl 5, p 5; rock cut tomb no. 100 in Thebes West, pl 39, p 46);
- ▷ double square (inner enclosure at Karnak, festival hall of Thutmosis III, pl 27, p 120; 18th dynasty temple at Medinet Habu, pl 28, p 122);
- ▷ square flanked by two 8:5 triangles (mastaba superstructure of Kanofer pl 5, p 76);
- ▷ square flanked by two 8:5 triangles on either side (temple at Qasr el Sagha, pl 11a, p 88).

7 Badaway 1965, p 28, pl 5
8 Rossi 2007, pp 32-56, offers a critique of Badaway, making the following points:

1. He uses small scale drawings and uses plans reconstructed from sometimes scanty remains; this is the "fat pencil" criticism discussed at Sect III.1. The example Rossi cites is Badaway's analysis of the great temple at Luxor, saying that the lines may be off by "a couple of meters." But this is about six feet in a building about 375 feet long, 1.6% of the overall. That the drawings have been reconstructed from fragmentary remains is significant, but usually the major points in the building are available.
2. His method is analytical, post-construction. Since the Egyptians did not use scale drawings, the triangles could not have been used in the planning process, but could they have been used in the field? Yes, Badaway's method is analytical, perhaps overly analytical, using huge numbers of lines. It is not a "workmanlike" method, and the adaptations of it in this book are much simpler. Although we do not have Egyptian construction documents, this is not proof that none ever existed. The triangle method could have been used in the field in some instances. Large-size layouts could have used convenient size templates to determine the angles. The "plan net" might be thought of as a kind of "cat's cradle," a two dimensional weaving rather than just a cord, a cross between a fishing net and a spider web that was literally unrolled.
3. If triangles were not used how were length and width of spaces justified?
4. The geometrical lines do not describe the building in detail leaving many decisions to be made; taking these two together – the position taken in this book is that proportional geometries are guides not laws, that designers must know what they want and that proportion serves design not the other way around. Thus many details are not specified by overall harmonic relations. Proportions help the designer to make appropriate choices. Hopefully designers would use compatible geometries for the whole and the parts, but this is not absolutely necessary to achieve some "sense of unity". As your present author was told by Keith Critchlow, "if your work looks like geometry, keep working."
5. The various triangles are geometrically unrelated, the 3-4-5 is unrelated to the 5:8; the position taken in this book is that they are not unrelated from a qualitative, symbolic point of view.

All these points are significant only if taken from a mathematical viewpoint; they are not design issues. As in all academic analysis there is a subtext of de-bunking here. The Egyptians couldn't have known about the Golden Section because they didn't write about it, they just "lurched uncontrollably" into it in building after building. Anyone maintaining that they knew of it is indulging in romantic anachronism. Rossi's thesis is the reasonable idea that we should only use what we know of Egyptian math to analyze their work. But do we presently or will we ever know all they knew? Not likely. In the end, Rossi admits that despite her critique "Badaway's schemes seem to work." She adds that no other such method has been able to be applied to over fifty Egyptian buildings and that his method has been followed by other scholars.

[9] Schwaller 1981, p 116; Iverson 1975, pp 28-29, pl 4; Fideler 1993b, p 97
[10] Schwaller 1981, pp 115-18
[11] Section II, **figure 17a**
[12] Fideler 1993b, p 95
[13] Fideler 1993b, p 108
[14] Badaway 1965, p 5-6
[15] Badaway 1965, p 5-6
[16] Badaway 1965, pp 58-59, fig 16
[17] Badaway 1965, p 60
[18] Badaway 1965, p 61 fig 17
[19] Wilkinson 1994, p 174, and fig 135, p 186
[20] Badaway 1965, p 9
[21] Hurry 1987, pp 3 & 98
[22] Giedion 1964, p 270
[23] Hurry 1987, p 95
[24] West 1987, p 112
[25] Hurry 1987, p 12
[26] Hurry 1987, p 16
[27] B-Fletcher 1963, p 29
[28] Hurry 1987, p 10, and B-Fletcher 1963, p 29, gives 410 feet x 358 feet
[29] Hurry 1987, p 10, and B-Fletcher 1963, p 29, gives 200 feet
[30] Giedion 1964, p 294
[31] Giedion 1964, p 283
[32] Rundle Clark, p 232, and Wilkinson 1994, p 140, fig 89
[33] Rundle Clark, p 234
[34] Hurry 1987, p 64
[35] Giedion 1964, p 275
[36] Hurry 1987, p 10
[37] West 1987, p 83
[38] Doczi 1981, p 41
[39] Breasted 1964, pp 220-35
[40] Giedion 1964, p 426
[41] Breasted 1964, p 226
[42] See Section III, Greece, **figure 1**
[43] Lawlor 1982, p 51
[44] Badaway 1965, p 102, pl 18
[45] De Cenival 1964, p 85, and Giedion 1964, p 47
[46] De Cenival 1964, p 150
[47] De Cenival 1964, p 150
[48] Hurry 1987, p 11 and Breasted 1984, pp 49 & 95
[49] Lloyd/Muller 1980, p 165 and West 1987, p 116, pp 175-80

Greece

[1] Gordon-Smith 2003, calls them "architectures" throughout the book, never using the term "orders." He also comments on the Morgan translation's confusion of "stylus," column, with "style."
[2] Coulton 1988, pp 32-33
[3] Semes 2015, p 32, Professor Economakis' recent article on the Doric in *Classicist* #12 takes this view.
[4] Wilson-Jones 2014, chapter 3, pp 63-86
[5] Hersey 1988, p 31
[6] The motif of three lines close together with a longer space between them was used as a border. See Section III, Egypt, figure 3, and Wilson-Jones 2014, chapter 3, pp 63-86.
[7] See Section II, **figures 3, 8, 10 and 11**
[8] The in-antis form has two projecting side walls, while the prostyle has four freestanding columns. See Section III, Rome I – Vitruvius, **figure 4**.
[9] Coulton 1988, p 88, gives 510-490 BC, or Lewis, p 161, gives 490-85 BC.
[10] Coulton 1988, pp 88-90
[11] Coulton 1988, pp 88-90
[12] Recent archeology has assigned this temple to Theseus, however it is traditionally assigned to Hephaestus.
[13] Graves 1982, 12.c
[14] Graves 1982, 12.c
[15] Graves 1982, 23.a
[16] Graves 1982, 23.b
[17] Graves 1982, 23.a
[18] Graves 1982, 23.1-2
[19] Graves 1982, 23.1-2
[20] The story is told by Graves. Graves 1982, 18a-c, p 67.
[21] A reconstruction drawing by L J André, 1853, *PRA* 1986, p 195, figure 2
[22] B-Fletcher 1963, p 160 and Normand, pl 6
[23] B-Fletcher 1963, gives the entablature's height as 4.2 M, making a total height 15.2 M. Normand 1998 gives 4.33 M for the entablature = 15.33 overall, a difference of .13 M or 4.5 parts.
[24] Note that the cap of the triglyph is included in the frieze, but continues over the square metope.
[25] As per Fideler 1993b, pp 108-09
[26] *PRA* 1986, p 165, elevation by Paccard 1845; p 231, plan drawing by Loviot, 1874
[27] Dimensions from B-Fletcher 1963, p 122
[28] 101.24/3.08 = 32.87 M 36/32.87=1.095, the ratio of lower M = 1.095 of FM. 1.096 x 30 parts = 32.85 = CM. The ratio of column M to frieze M is: 30/27 = 1.11 x 30 P = 33.33 P for CM.

[29] Normand 1998, plate 7

[30] Points G and H are very slightly offset from **figures 10b.1 to 10b.2**. In **10b.1,** if AD is set as 1, HG is at 1 from AD, or .126 from the building center. In **10b.2,** HG is Ø/4 from the center, .154, a difference of .028 of AD. The nomenclature is kept as a convenience.

[31] See Section III, Egypt, **figure 10**, for construction of the pentagonal pillar.

[32] The pentagonal pillar of the plan is not a similar triangle to the 2:1 pillar of the elevation. The translation is $1/Ø^2$ in plan = 1 in elevation, and 1 in plan = $Ø^2$ in elevation.

[33] Plotinus 1991, V.8.1

[34] Hambidge 1924, pp 95-96

[35] Angus 1925, chapters II and III, pp 39-144

ROME I — VITRUVIUS

[1] Bk III, I.1-4

[2] Bk I, II.1-4

[3] Bk III, I.2

[4] Bk III, I.3

[5] Bk III, I.1

[6] As per Theon 1979, p 47, sect XVIII

[7] There is also the Indian example called the Vatsu Purusha Mandala in which the cosmic man Purusha lies down within a square, see Michell 1988, p 72, fig 28.

[8] Bk III, I.5-7

[9] See Section II, **figure 6** and Granger, 1965, p 163, note 2.

[10] Bk III, I.7-8

[11] Bk III, II.6

[12] Bk III, III.8

[13] Bk III, III.8

[14] Bk IV, III.1

[15] Bk VII, pref.,12

[16] Bk III, III.8

[17] Bk III, III.9

[18] See Chaumont 1975, for a discussion of the close relation of Pythagorean, Orphic and Mithraic symbolism. Mithraism was gaining popularity with the army in Vitruvius' time and, although there is no positive evidence, it's far from impossible that he was a participant. During the civil war he spent time in Athens, which raises the possibility of participation in the Eleusinian system.

[19] Bk III, II.1-8

[20] Bk III, IV.3

[21] Bk IV, IV.1

[22] Bk III, IV.4

[23] Bk III, III.1-6

[24] Bk III, III.10

[25] Bk III, V.5-8

[26] See Section II, **figure 19**

[27] See Section II, **figure 19**

[28] Lawlor 1982, p 51

[29] Brennan 1983, pp 194-95, the double spiral is a possible representation of the movement of the sun during the course of the year, upward or outward in the winter-spring and downward or inward in the fall-winter.

[30] Bk III, V.8

[31] Bk III, V.8

[32] Vitruvius specifies at III, V.13 that all vertical surfaces of the entablature be leaned outward by 1/12th of their height to correct for what he claims is the perspective distortion of elements appearing to taper inward while getting smaller the higher they are. In **figure 9** this is done for the architrave, frieze and corona.

[33] Bk III, V.11

[34] An interval of 1 M is added for the width of the corona — this is a "working" approximation.

[35] Add the altitude of the tympanum plus the top of the corona plus the height of the cornice above the tympanum. Cornice =12.5 A parts = .65D, thus 11.4 + 1.4 + .63 = 13.45 D, the apex of the pediment.

[36] Bk IV, III.1-10 where the Doric canon is given.

[37] This strict centering also prevents column pairing, as the triglyphs are 1 D on center but the capitals and bases extend beyond 1D, causing them to "merge" in a detailing nightmare.

[38] This depends on how you count the cymatium; "as in the Ionic" could make the cymatium about 1/3 of the architrave, 4.5/14, or about 1/4 D, or 1/2 of Doric M. The Doric architrave is 1M making the cymatium 1/6D = 1/3M. Here 1/3M is used + the corona of 1/2M gives an overhang of 5/6M for each side x 2 = 10/6 = 1&2/3 M for the cornice.

[39] A half module is subtracted here as the tympanum sits on the corona, not on the cornice.

[40] See Section II, **figure 27.6** for an "occult" relationship of Ø and √2.

[41] Bk. VI, III.3

[42] *Timaeus* 55

[43] *Phaedo* 110

[44] Euclid's treatment of Ø is a deep and complex topic deserving far more detailed treatment than can be given here. Euclid's first pass at Ø is at II.11, the goal is to transform a square into a rectangle of equivalent area. Specifically to find a point in that transformation at which the extension beyond the square equals the area

taken from the original square, and the shape of that extension is also a square. What Euclid doesn't say is that the sides of the required squares are in Ø ratio. At IV.10 and 11, Euclid constructs a Ø triangle and then a pentagon without mentioning Ø, specifing the triangle by its angular relationships rather than its side lengths. At VI.30, Euclid directly proposes "to cut a given finite straight line in extreme and mean ratio." He begins by restating II.11 as a given and then proceeds directly to the proof, without referencing II.11. Euclid returns to Ø at the beginning of Book XIII.1-5, but does not reference VI.30 or II.11. Notice that at II.11 and IV.11, where Ø is defined as a construction, it is not mentioned by name. At VI.30, and later in Book XIII, where Ø is named, its construction is not specified or referenced. Such obscurity is unusual in a work of towering lucidity like Euclid's.

[45] Fideler 1993b, p 95
[46] Fideler 1993b, p 97
[47] Critchlow 1995, p 157
[48] Also discussed at Section III, intro to history.
[49] This account is taken from Book IV.I.3-10
[50] Graves 1982, 43.b
[51] As at Section II, **figure 20.1-5**
[52] Graves 1982, 96.b
[53] Graves 1982, 96.b
[54] Graves 1982, 96.b
[55] Graves 1982, 96.2 the Thesmophoria Festival was a prelude to the Eleusinian Mysteries.
[56] Graves 1982, 96.4

Rome II

[1] Jones 2000, p 182, though Boatwright 1987 disagrees, p 44.
[2] Jones 2000, p 182
[3] MacDonald 1976, p 12; Boatwright 1987, p 43
[4] Boatwright 1987, chap II, pp 33-73
[5] MacDonald 1976, p 12
[6] Boatwright 1987, p 205
[7] Jones 2000, p 192
[8] Here we combine two constructions: Section II, **figure 1** and Section III, Egypt, **figure 10a**.
[9] by B-Fletcher 1963, p 199
[10] Jones 2000, pp 199-206
[11] Jones 2000, Chapter 10, p 199
[12] Jones 2000, p 209
[13] Jones 2000, p 204
[14] Jones 2000, p 206
[15] Jones 2000, p 204
[16] Jones 2000, tells us this, p 203
[17] Jones 2000, p 209
[18] Jones 2000, p 208
[19] Jones 2000, p 211
[20] Jones 2000, p 211, but the Temple of Bacchus at Baalbek, illustrated at fig. 7.34, p 157, has unfluted 50-foot composite shafts.
[21] Jones 2000, p 210
[22] Jones 2000, p 212
[23] Jones 2000, p 202
[24] Jones 2000, p 212
[25] MacDonald 1976, p 83
[26] Giedeon 1964, p 515
[27] c.200 BC, B-Fletcher 1963, p 221
[28] MacDonald 1982, Vol. II, p 80
[29] B-Fletcher 1963, p 223
[30] B-Fletcher 1963, p 224
[31] The openings are 9'-8" + 9'-8" + 22'-2" = 41'-6". 76'-4"- 41'-6" = 34'-10", 34.83', divided by 4 = 8.71'.
[32] Interestingly, this interval, 1/64th , is the same interval the third and sixth notes of the natural octave were moved to create the tempered octave in the Renaissance.

Medieval

[1] I Kings, 6
[2] Halevi 1977, p 15, fig 6
[3] The Hennads are from Proclus 1987, Bk IV, 1049, p 408, and the extended tree from Halevi 1977, figure 19, p 120.
[4] Critchlow, K3
[5] Michell 1991, p 165
[6] Michell 1991, p 166
[7] Michell 1991, p 171
[8] See Section III, Medieval, **figure 11d.8,** semi-regular grid #8.
[9] Pajares-Ayuelo 2001, p 31
[10] See Section III, Medieval, **figures 11-15**
[11] Pajares-Ayuelo 2001, figure 4-34
[12] Pajares-Ayuelo 2001, p 167, figures 4-43 to 45, and figure 5-3 p 198
[13] Section II, **figure 27.6**
[14] Pajares-Ayuelo 2001, p 217
[15] Burckhardt 1976, pp 9-14
[16] Burckhardt 1976, p 14
[17] Burckhardt 1976, p 13
[18] Section I and Section II, **figure 1**
[19] Burckhardt 1976, p 12
[20] Azzam 1997, general
[21] Section II, **figure 1**
[22] *Timaeus* 35a
[23] See Section III, Medieval, **figure 17**, Chartres Cathedral reconstruction
[24] Critchlow 1976, p 20
[25] Critchlow 1969, p 62

[26] Section II, **figure 6c**
[27] Querido 1987, p 24
[28] Breasted 1964, pp 220-21
[29] "Born of Ireland," 815-877, http://plato.stanford.edu /entries/ scottus-eriugena
[30] Querido 1987, p 34
[31] Querido 1987, p 14
[32] Querido 1987, p 135
[33] Querido 1987, p 72
[34] Querido 1987, p 75
[35] Dionysis 1935, p 5 and Yates, 1979, p 118
[36] Section II **figure 1**
[37] Dionysis 1935, p 9
[38] Charpentier 1972, p 97
[39] wiki Hollister, p 210 – Hollister, C. Warren 1966, *The Making of England, 55 BC to 1399,* Vol I "A History of England," ed. by L. B. Smith, sixth ed., 1992, Lexington MA.
[40] Heald 2000, p 22
[41] Charpentier 1972, pp 47-60
[42] Querido 1987, p 21
[43] James 1990, p 52
[44] Charpentier 1972, pp 128-136
[45] Charpentier 1972, p 135, suggests the use of the Gregorian mode.
[46] Charpentier 1972. His source for all this is questionable. There are many ways to calculate octave intervals – it is not known which musical scales were used at Chartres. This is one of many deep and profound mysteries surrounding Chartres Cathedral and the early Gothic in general.
[47] Section II **figure 29a**
[48] Charpentier 1972, p 39
[49] Section II **figure 27.5**
[50] Cowen 2005, p 19
[51] Critchlow, K4
[52] Critchlow, K

Early Renaissance

[1] Burckhardt 1958, p 143
[2] Godwin 2005, chapter 6
[3] from Protagoras, c.485-421 BC
[4] Woodhouse 2000, p 17
[5] Woodhouse 2000, p 23
[6] Woodhouse 2000, p 30
[7] wikipedia.org/wiki/Council_of_Florence
[8] Woodhouse 2000, p 152
[9] Woodhouse 2000, p 60
[10] according to Mead 1978, p 8
[11] Fanelli 1980, p 1
[12] Vasari 1965, p 146
[13] http://dictionary.reference.com/browse/braccio, and http://www.convertunits.com/from/braccio+[Italy]/to/feet
[14] Fanelli 1980, p 17
[15] Fanelli 1980, p 11
[16] absoluteastronomy.com/topics/Paolo_dal_Pozzo_Toscanelli
[17] Edgerton 1975, p 61
[18] Heilbron 1999, pp 70-71 and Edgerton 1975, p 61, 121
[19] Vasari 1965, p 136 and Edgerton 1975, p 61, 121
[20] Vasari 1965, p 136
[21] Edgerton 1975, pp 67-68
[22] Eratosthenese knew that at noon on the summer solstice a stick or gnomon put in the ground at the town of Syene cast no shadow. He measured the shadow of a gnomon at Alexandria on the same day finding that the shadow was 1/50th of the height of the gnomon. He thus knew that the distance between the towns was 1/50th of the earth's circumference. The miscalculation was made by Poseidonius, c.100 BC. www.encyclopedia.com/doc/1G2-3437800489.html
[23] Edgerton 1975, pp 106-10
[24] Edgerton 1975, p 70
[25] Vitruvius Bk VII, Intro.11
[26] Section II, **figure 29**
[27] Edgerton 1975, p 124
[28] Edgerton 1975, pp 163-5 quotes optical physiologist M. H. Pirenne, *Vision and the Eye,* London 1948, p 15.ß
[29] Edgerton 1975, p 163. Another example may be cited from Colin Turnbull's *The Forest People,* an anthropological description of the Imbuti people of central Africa. Living in dense forest, they do not have the experience of long distance views. When Turnbull takes an Imbuti man to an open hilltop the man complains of "flies" that seem to be in front of his face, which Turnbull eventually realizes are cattle in the valley below.
[30] Perspective in Renaissance painting from the 16th century on are not "pure" but subtly adjust the geometry of the perspective until it becomes unnoticeable. This differs from 15th-century painting such as that of Piero della Francesca, where the perspective is rather too obvious, actually reducing the power of the illusion.
[31] Hersey 1976, p 64
[32] Fanelli 1980, p 74
[33] Furnari 1995, p 69
[34] Furnari 1995, p 90
[35] Section II **figure 5e**

[36] Furnari 1995, p 124; Fanelli 1980, p 76; Bartoli 1977, p 175
[37] Following Burckhardt 1958, V1, p 147
[38] Alberti 1988, p xi
[39] Alberti 1988, p xii
[40] Alberti 1988, p xii
[41] March 1998, p 85
[42] Alberti 1988, p xii
[43] Borsi 185, p 9; Gadol 1969, p 5, Alberti 1988, p xiii
[44] Alberti 1988, p xiii
[45] Gadol 1969, p 6, though exactly what he did is not clear.
[46] Burckhardt 1958, V1, p 147
[47] Gadol 1969, p 76
[48] Gadol 1969, p 8
[49] Borsi 1985, p 20, Gadol 1969, p 8, Alberti 1988, p xiv
[50] Alberti 1988, p xvi, Borsi 1978, p 96
[51] Alberti 1988, p xvi
[52] Alberti 1988, p xvi
[53] Wind 1968, p 231
[54] Proclus, *Platonic Theology*, IIx
[55] The reference is to Corinthians xv, 52
[56] Gadol 1969, p 69
[57] March 1998, p 194. Also note that 72 is 1/5 of a circle, setting up the pentagram and revealing the Golden Section.
[58] Gadol 1969, p 94
[59] Gadol 1969, p 94
[60] Borsi 1985, p 139
[61] Gadol 1969, pp 10-11
[62] Gadol 1969, p 10
[63] Yates 1979, chapter XI, for the discussion of "De Umbris Idearum" and the memory wheel.
[64] http://en.wikipedia.org/wiki/ Pope_Paul_II
[65] Alberti 1988, 6.2
[66] Alberti 1988, 6.2.2
[67] Alberti 1988, 6.2.3-4
[68] Alberti 1988, 6.2.2
[69] Alberti 1988, 6.2.5
[70] Alberti 1988, 6.2.6
[71] Alberti 1988, 6.4.1
[72] Alberti 1988, 1.1.1
[73] Alberti 1988, 1.9.1
[74] Alberti 1988, 1.9.1
[75] Alberti 1988, 6.5.1
[76] Alberti 1988, 1.9.1-2
[77] Paragraph, Alberti 1988, 9.5.1&3
[78] Vitruvius Bk III.1-5
[79] Paragraph, Alberti 1988, 9.5.2
[80] Paragraph, Alberti 1988, 9.5.4
[81] Alberti 1988, p 302, note 73, Rykwert denies that this is Neoplatonic, citing Aquinas.
[82] Alberti 1988, 9.5.6
[83] Paragraph, Alberti 1988, 9.5.13
[84] Alberti 1988, p 164, note 67. *"Concinnitas is a combination of numerus, finitio, and collocatio. The meaning of number is explained further in book 9 where certain 'perfect' numbers are described. Number is both a quantity ... and a quality, as defined by Pythagorean–Platonic number theory and later Christian biblical commentators."* Alberti is here referring to number ordered by natural laws of symmetry (proper correspondence).
[85] Paragraph, Alberti 1988, 9.5.10-11. The monad, in keeping with Pythagorean tradition, is not a number but the source of number. The dyad is "perhaps" the first number. The first unequivocal number is three. Of the odd numbers – Nature is composed of threes. Fiveness, the pentad, has so many occurrences that we may call it divine, and dedicated to the gods of the arts, Hermes in particular. Sevenness, the heptad, particularly delights God as there are seven planets and seven stages of human life. Nineness gives a key period in pregnancy and recovery from illness, 1/9th of a year being 40 days. Of the even numbers: Fourness is consecrated to divinity and oaths are taken upon it. Sixness is perfect because it is the sum of its factors. Eightness "exerts great influence on nature"; he cites pregnancy examples. Ten is considered the most perfect by Aristotle, some say because $10^2 = 1^3+2^3+3^3+4^3 = 100$. The ancients used an even number of solids and an odd number of voids in their porticos and rarely used more than nine voids and ten solids. See also Section I of this book, "A Pythagorean Creation Myth".
[86] Alberti 1988, 9.5.13-14
[87] Alberti 1988, 6.1
[88] Alberti 1988, 9.5.13
[89] Alberti 1988, 9.5.14
[90] Alberti 1988, 9.6.1-2
[91] Alberti 1988, 9.67, previously described at Section I, "ratio proportion logos," and *Timeaus* 36.
[92] Paragraph, Alberti 1988, 9.6.7-10
[93] Alberti 1988, 9.6.6
[94] Alberti 1988, 7.1-3
[95] Alberti 1988, 7.2
[96] Wind 1968, p 230
[97] Alberti 1988, 7.4.1-3
[98] Alberti 1986, p 138 and Wittkower 1971, p 3
[99] Wittkower 1971, p 3
[100] Alberti 1988, 7.4.1-4
[101] March 1998, p 185

[102] Summarizing Wittkower 1971 on the symbolism of the centrally planned church pp 27-30.
[103] March 1998, p 7
[104] March 1998, p 14
[105] Wittkower 1971, pp 27-32
[106] Gadol 1969, p 120
[107] Alberti 1988, 8.6.12
[108] Borsi 1978, p 100, figure 103
[109] Gadol 1969, p 112, and Furnari 1995, p 99
[110] Gadol 1969, p 120
[111] Borsi 1978, p 65; Wittkower 1971, p 43
[112] Borsi 1978, p 182
[113] Wittkower 1971, p 54
[114] Gadol 1969, p 149
[115] B-Fletcher 1963, p 606
[116] wikipedia.org/wiki/Montefeltro_Altarpiece and http://www.travelingintuscany.com/art/pierodellafrancesca/montefeltroltarpiece.htm
[117] As above, footnote 116
[118] Said to be the second from the right figure in the Montefeltro altarpiece, http://www.travelingintuscany.com/art/pierodellafrancesca/montefeltroltarpiece.htm
[119] Bouleau 1963, pp 75-76
[120] Ackerman 1961, p 27
[121] Lotz 1995, pp 1-23
[122] Ackerman 1961, p 28
[123] Wittkower 1971, p 102
[124] Serlio 1996, intro, p xxxiii
[125] Serlio 1996, p xxvii
[126] Transliteration from Serlio 1982, and Serlio 1996, p 24
[127] Section II, **figure 1a**
[128] Serlio 1996, pp 32-33

Late Renaissance

[1] Wittkower 1971, p 57
[2] Wittkower 1971, p 58
[3] Wittkower 1971, p 61, and Ackerman 1967, pp 20-21
[4] March 1998, pp 136 and 242-3, and Agrippa 1997, p 312. Gematria, number-letter substitution is a powerful tool to establish such occult correspondences, but its use, especially in Latin, is subject to many decisions that affect the outcome. In this case, March's argument is not entirely persuasive as he has used the value of U 200 for both the Us and Vs in Vitruvius, though V appears in Agrippa's code twice, once as 200 and later as 700. The letter U was often indicated by V in early printing, thus in the conflation of U and V, March could have used 700 for the Vs and/or the Us, but then the arithmetic would not work. Spelling is also an issue, though in this case March documents the unusual spelling of Palladio's name.
[5] Ackerman 1967, p 27
[6] Wittkower 1971, p 67
[7] Wittkower 1971, p 58
[8] Genesis 2, 19-20
[9] Wittkower 1971, p 73
[10] Section I, **figure 8**
[11] Section II, **figure 1**
[12] Wittkower 1971, p 133
[13] Palladio 1965, Bk II, ch XIV, pl XXXVIII. Dimensions in Bk II are given in Vicentine feet = 1'-1.75" or 1&1/7th English feet.
[14] Wittkower 1971, p 131 for the Emo, and see Part 4.5, pp 126-137 for a discussion of this method of musical proportional thinking.
[15] Wittkower 1971, p 131, analyzes only the plan dimensions; he simply ignores the elevations.
[16] Palladio 1965, Book I, chap. 23, and Section II, **figure 25**.
[17] The "modules" in **figure 6** are an attempt to represent the tempered octave diagram of Wittkower 1971, p 133, which he references to the sixteenth-century Venetian musicologist Zarlino. For example, the octave contains two 5ths, from notes 1 to 5 and from notes 4 to 8, the 5th being defined as three whole tones and a semitone.
[18] 11/11.25 = 97.8%, 54/55 = 98.2%, and 59/60 = 98.3%
[19] Scamozzi's presentation of Palladio's work is not much more help, coming over a generation later and taking various liberties with the built and unbuilt work. Interestingly, the Isaac Ware 1738 version on which the Dover 1965 edition is based uses much more refined line drawings in Books I, III and IV, and even in some parts of Book II.
[20] Based on Fletcher 2013, pp 184-91
[21] Ackerman 1967, p 169, figure 91. He gives: JB = 15.67', HJ 26.25', JF = 26.08', LS = 10.75' and SQ = 15.4'.
[22] As in Section II, **figure 10**
[23] March 1998, p 244
[24] The difference is between a 24' column with a 6' entablature, a ratio of 1:4, or 25 and 5, 1/5. Both comply with canonical values.
[25] Placing the walls between the $\sqrt{2}/2$ and 3/4 points.
[26] Also of note is that the relationship of the side of an equilateral triangle to the diameter of its circumscribing circle is $\sqrt{3}/2$:1, a circle of diameter 30 would circumscribe an equilateral triangle with side 26.
[27] The Pantheon's interior height, equal to its

interior width, is 142.5' and its outer width is about 180'. The side of an equilateral triangle of altitude 142.5' is 142.5' x 1.153' = 164.3', well within the building's circular retaining wall.

[28] Mitrovic 2004, p 35. Mitrovic notes that the *Quattro Libri* was long in development but "finished hastily." I know the feeling.

[29] As suggested by Mitrovic 2004, p 64, who cites March's translation of musical theorist and Palladio contemporary Silvio Belli – "On Ratio and Proportion", p 11, on the contra-harmonic mean; and Mitrovic 2004, p 87 and pp 91-93, where various ways of dividing the octave are discussed.

[30] Palladio 1965, Bk I, Ch XXIII. Heights of rooms may sometimes be adjusted to align floor heights above.

[31] Palladio 1965, Bk II, ch. III, pl V

[32] By the method of Section II, **figure 2**

[33] Section II, **figure 10**

[34] The illustration is from Scamozzi 2015, V 4, pl XVII. San Francesco della Vigna does not appear in Palladio 1965.

[35] Wittkower 1971, pp 102-07

[36] Palladio 1965, Bk III, plate XX

[37] Vasari 1965, p 325

[38] Vasari 1965, p 325

[39] Burckhardt 1958, p 227

[40] easyweb.easynet.co.uk/~orpheus/ficino.htm introduction to *The Letters of Marsilio Ficino*, Volume 1, © 1975 Fellowship of the School of Economic Science, London. *Opera Omnia*, p 1537.

[41] Panofsky 1972, p 180

[42] Panofsky 1972, p 180

[43] Symposium, 209e-212, and Section I

[44] Ackerman 1961, p 31

[45] Ackerman 1961, p 294

[46] As in Section II, **figure 8,** where the inner column is sized an positioned by the same points on the inner pentagon.

[47] Ackerman 1961, p 37

[48] Ackerman 1961, p 38

[49] Ackerman 1961, pp 43-44

[50] Fideler 1993b, p 108

[51] Ackerman 1961, p 44

[52] Ackerman 1961, p 45

[53] Symonds 1962, pp 405-08

[54] Ackerman 1961, p 45

[55] Alberti 1988, I.9, p 23

[56] Ackerman 1961, p 44

[57] Portoghesi 1970, pp 51-52

[58] Portoghesi 1970, pp 51-52

[59] Portoghesi 1970, p 51

[60] Portoghesi 1970, p 20

[61] Portoghesi 1970, p 52

[62] Portoghesi 1970, p 30 and p 50. The laying out of the obelisks is a topic that deserves further investigation. Time has run out, for now, for your present author.

[63] Portoghesi 1970, p 12

[64] Portoghesi 1970, p 58

[65] Portoghesi 1970, p 20

[66] Portoghesi 1970, p 13

[67] Portoghesi 1970, p 20

[68] Portoghesi 1970, p 13

[69] Portoghesi 1970, p 16

[70] Portoghesi 1970, p 56

[71] As in the octastyle portico, Section II, **figure 15-16**

[72] Section II, **figure 7**

[73] Wittkower 1973, p 143

[74] Wittkower 1973, p 198 – especially the wonderful elliptical spiral stairway. Note also the trompe-l'oeil perspective on the top floor arcade.

[75] Serlio 1996, p 27

[76] Portoghesi 1970, p 18

The Enlightenment

[1] As seen in the career of Alberti, Section III, Early Renaissance.

[2] Guénon 2004, passim, for a discussion of these complex issues, also see https://en.wikipedia.org/wiki/Integral.

[3] Perez-Gomez 1983, p 10

[4] *Republic* 415

[5] Yates 1978, p 107

[6] Yates 1978, pp 42-44

[7] Yates 1978, p 44

[8] *Republic* 514

[9] Section III, Egypt, **figure 6**

[10] Yates 1978, p 98

[11] Yates 1978, p 22. Like a good dynast, James I wanted another daughter to marry into the Hapsburgs in the hopes of creating a Catholic-Protestant ruling family, explaining his lack of support for his son-in-law.

[12] Yates 1978, p 103

[13] Harris & Higgott 1989, p 13

[14] Harris & Higgott 1989, pp 15, 33

[15] Curl 1993, p 23, and Harris & Higgott 1989, pp 298-303

[16] Yates 1979, chapters XII and XIII on Bruno in England and pp 392-93 on his influence on Jones

[17] Curl 1993, p 23

[18] Curl 1993, p 23

[19] Curl 1993, p 23

[20] Campbell 2009, vol III, pl 42
[21] As in Section II, **figure 27.6;** the tetrastyle is constructed as per Section II, **figure 10.5.**
[22] Harris & Higgott 1989, p 25
[23] Perrault 1993, p 5
[24] Perrault 1993, p 11
[25] Wikipedia, Charles Perrault
[26] See Section I, p 7
[27] Perrault 1993, p 49
[28] Perrault 1993, p 48
[29] Section III, Late Renaissance, p 281
[30] Section I, p 7, Plotinus I.6
[31] Perrault 1993, p 50
[32] Perrault 1993, pp 51-52
[33] Perrault 1993, p 54
[34] Perrault 1993, p 57
[35] Perrault 1993, intro p 35
[36] Perrault 1993, intro p 35
[37] Friedman 1984, p 7
[38] Curl 1993, p 115
[39] Friedman 1984, p 115
[40] Curl 1993, p 115; Friedman, p 13
[41] Curl 1993, p 115
[42] As in Section II, **figure 28**
[43] Chambers 2003, pp 36-7
[44] Section II, **figure 21**
[45] Chambers 2003, p 49 and Gibbs 1732, pl XXV
[46] Chambers 2003, p 38
[47] Curl 1993, p 41
[48] Halfpenny 1724, pl 1
[49] Morris 1734, lecture V, VI; and Section II, **figure 26**
[50] Morris 1734, lecture XI
[51] Morris 1734, lecture VII
[52] Burke 1757, I.XVIII
[53] Burke 1757, II.I
[54] Burke 1757, III.I
[55] Burke 1757, I.XVIII
[56] Burke 1757, III.XXVII
[57] Burke 1757, III.XIII
[58] Burke 1757, III.II
[59] Burke 1757, III.II
[60] Burke 1757, III.IV
[61] Burke 1757, III.IV
[62] Burke 1757, III.IV
[63] As does March 1998, ch XVIII. The modern view of the Vitruvian Man as imprisoned by geometry is the inverse of the ancient view of intellectual clarification through geometry as a source of liberation.
[64] Burke 1757, IV.I
[65] Burke 1757, I.XIX
[66] Burke 1757, III.XXVII
[67] Couliano 1987, pp 6-23, where pneumatic phantasms are discussed.
[68] Burke 1757, Pt III, IV.1 and Pt I, XII-XIV
[69] *Timaeus* 42 and *Hermetic* "Asclepius" pp 37-38
[70] Couliano 1987, p 183 for a Darwinian explanation of the rationalist take over.
[71] Wikipedia, Johann Wolfgang von Goethe 1792; Naydler 2000, ch 5, p 70; Seamon and Zajonic 1998, pp 1-14.
[72] https://en.wikipedia.org/wiki/Goethean_science.
[73] Whiffen 1990, in Whiffen's figure 16 the ridge is slightly higher, as Wiffen measures it from the first floor, but the discrepancy scales at only 1'-6", less than 3% of the 54'-6" width of the building.
[74] Lancaster 1951, p 4
[75] Howard 2003, p 129
[76] Holm 1995, p 3
[77] *Timaeus* 41. If we substitute "lesser divinities" for "natural laws" we in effect repeat what the demiurge tells the lesser creative powers.
[78] Creason 2011
[79] Creason 2011
[80] Needleman 2002, ch 4 pp 139-72
[81] *Timaeus* 39d
[82] *Symposium* 204d
[83] Jefferson's 8 x 8 enclosing square is larger than the square in the reconstruction. Jefferson includes the full width of the base, and the top of the square rises higher than the oculus.
[84] Nichols 2001, p 6

SECTION IV
THE PRESENT MOMENT

[1] *Timaeus* 29e
[2] *Timaeus* 40c
[3] *Timaeus* 29c-d
[4] https://en.wikipedia.org/wiki/Holism in science
[5] Your present author heard Kahn use this anecdote at a lecture in NYC in the early 1970s in reference to his work in Bangledesh. See also: www.archdaily.com/339111/video-louis-kahn-talks-to-a-brick/ and www.theguardian.com/artanddesign/2013/ feb/26/louis-kahn-brick-whisperer-architect
[6] See Harner 1986, in passim.

Figure Titles and Sources

All images are by the author unless otherwise noted. "Based on" means that the image has been modified sufficiently that it comprises a new illustration.

I - The Search for Beauty

II - Number Harmony Design

Figure 20	The Corinthian Capital. Using the Squared Circle and the Pentad	
Figure 21	Entablatures of the Three Principle Orders	
Figure 22	Pediments	
Figure 23	Superposition	
Figure 24	Arcades	
Figure 25	Palladio's Harmonic Ratios for Rooms	
Figure 26	Harmonic Volumes of Robert Morris	
Figure 27	An Expansion of the Tetrastyle. Using the Octave, √2 and Ø	
Figure 28	An Expansion of the Hexastyle. Using Ø and the Double Square	
Figure 29	The "Pillar" of Egypt	
Figure 29a	The King and Seshat Stretching the Cord	Wilkinson 1994, p 186, fig 135
Figure 30	Vertical Expansion. A Portico with a Steeple Using the Pillar	
Figure 31	Geometric Rectangles of Hambidge	
Figure 32	Division of the Frame	

III - Proportion in Practice

Egypt

Figure 1a	The Pillar	
Figure 1b	Constructional Diagrams	
Figure 2	The Temple at Amarna	based on Badaway 1965, p 28 , plate 5
Figure 3	The Canon of 19	based on Iverson 1975, pp 28-29, plate 4
Figure 4a	Seshat and Her Symbol	Badaway 1965, p 59, fig 16
Figure 4b	Phi and the Heptad	based on AEAD, p 61, fig 17
Figure 4c	Stretching the Cord	Wilkinson 1994, p 186, fig 135
Figure 5	Zoser's Complex, Saqqara, Imhotep, c.2700 BC	based on Lloyd/Muller 1980, p 83, fig 147 (after Lange-Hirmer, 1957)
Figure 6	The Ka Hieroglyph	Rossini 2007, p 42, no 60 (pd)
Figure 7.1-5	Zoser's Complex. Reconstruction	
Figure 7.6-7	Zoser's Complex. Plan Analysis	
Figure 7.8-9	Zoser's Complex and the Human Figure	
Figure 8	The Wadjet Eye	West 1987, p 83
Figure 9	The Great Pyramid	
Figure 10a.1-5	Pentagonal Phi Scale	
Figure 10b-c	The Pentagonal Pillar	
Figure 11a	Temple of Hatshepsut	based on De Cenival 1964, p 84
Figure 11b	Temple of Mentuhotep	based on Badaway 1965, p 103, plate 18
Figure 12a	Temple of Horus, Edfu. Plan	based on De Cenival 1964, p 143
Figure 12b	Temple of Horus. Pillar and Plan. Net reconstruction	based on De Cenival 1964, p 143
Figure 12c	Temple of Horus. Geometric Reconstruction	

Greece

Rome I – Vitruvius

Rome II

Figure 1a-b	Pantheon, Rome, 126 AD. Plan Reconstruction	based on *PRA* 1986, p 205, fig 10.12
Figure 1c-d	Pantheon. Plan Reconstruction	
Figure 2	Pantheon. Elevation Analysis	based on *PRA* 1986, p 205, fig 10.12
Figure 3	Pantheon. Elevation Reconstruction	
Figure 4	Pantheon. Reconstructed with Pedestals	
Figure 5a	Arch of Titus, Rome, 82 AD. Analysis	based on B-Fletcher 1963, p 223
Figure 5b	Arch of Titus. Reconstruction	
Figure 6a	Arch of Septimus Severus, Rome, 203 AD. Analysis	based on B-Fletcher 1963, p 224
Figure 6b	Arch of Septimus Severus. Reconstruction	

Medieval

Figure 1	Dimensions of Solomon's Temple	
Figure 2	The Tree of the Kabbalah	based on Halevi 1977, p 15, fig 6
Figure 3	The Tetraktys and the Tree	
Figure 4	Proclus, the Extended Tree and Chartres. Indicating Continuity of Ancient and Medieval Philosophy, Religion and Architecture	
Figure 5	Geometry of Jerusalem	based on Michell 1991, p 146, fig 74
Figure 6a	St. Front, Périgueux, 1120	based on B-Fletcher 1963, p 288
Figure 6b	St. Front. Reconstruction	
Figure 7a-b	Cosmatesque Ornament	7b based on Pajares-Ayuelo 2001, p 199, fig 5-3
Figure 7c	The Qunicunx Cosmos	
Figure 8	The Dome of the Rock	
Figure 9a	Pointed Arches. Directing Thrust Downward	
Figure 9b.1-9	Various Modulations of Pointed Arches	
Figure 10	Qaitbay Complex, Cairo. Reconstruction	
Figure 11a	Origin of the 3, 4 and 6-fold Grids	
Figure 11b	The Regular Grids and Their Duals	
Figure 11c	Simultaneous Development of the Flower	
Figure 11d	The Semi-regular Grids	
Figure 12a	The Inhalation and Exhalation	
Figure 12b	Star Octagon Pattern	
Figure 13a.1-3	Constructing a Fivefold Grid	
Figure 13d	A Fivefold Pattern	
Figure 14	The Celestial Hierarchies	
Figure 15	Virgo and France	Charpentier 1972, p 28
Figure 16	The "Virgo Cluster" and 365 Feet	based on B-Fletcher 1963, pp 531, 544, 560, 561. Long Meg from Critchlow 1979, p 43, fig 26
Figure 17a	Chartres. Reconstruction	
Figure 17b	Chartres. Reconstruction	
Figure 18	Construction of the Heptagon	1. & 2. Critchlow 1976, p 167, and 3. Critchlow 1979, p 101, fig 71

Early Renaissance

Late Renaissance

Figure 1	Gematria	March 1998, pp 136 and 242-43, and Agrippa 1997, p 312
Figure 2	Palladio's Tripartite Taxis	based on Wittkower 1971, p 73, fig 8
Figure 3	The Platonic Lambda	
Figure 4	The Tempered Octave	
Figure 5a	Villa Emo, Fanzolo, Palladio, 1559	Palladio 1965, Bk II, p 50, plate XXXVIII
Figure 5b	Villa Emo. Tempered Octave	
Figure 5c	Villa Emo. Analysis	
Figure 5d	Villa Emo. Reconstruction Using $\sqrt{2}$	
Figure 5e	Villa Emo. Reconstruction Using $\sqrt{3}$ nd $\sqrt{5}$	
Figure 5f	Villa Emo. Reconstruction Using Geometry and Arithmetic	
Figure 6a	Villa Foscari, Palladio, 1549-63	Palladio 1965, Bk II, p 49, plate XXXIII
Figure 6b	Villa Foscari. Tempered Octave	
Figure 6c-d	Villa Foscari. Analysis and Reconstruction	
Figure 7a-b	Villa Ragona, Palladio, unbuilt, 1553. Analysis and Reconstruction	based on Palladio 1965, Bk II, p 51, plate XL
Figure 7c	Villa Ragona. Tempered Octave	
Figure 8	Villa Rotunda, Vicenza, Palladio, 1556. Analysis	based on Palladio 1965, Bk II, p 41, plate XIII
Figure 9a	Palazzo Porto, Vicenza, Palladio, 1571	Palladio 1965, Bk II, p 40, plate V
Figure 9b-e	Palazzo Porto. Reconstruction	
Figure 10	San Francesco della Vigna, Venice, Palladio, 1564. Analysis and Reconstruction	based on Scamozzi 2015, bk 4, plate XVII
Figure 11a-c	The Palladian Window. Basilica at Vicenza, Palladio, 1546	based on Palladio 1965, Bk III, p 75, plate XX
Figure 12	Tomb of Julius, Rome, Michelangelo, 1503	based on Panofsky 1972, plate LXXI, figs 131 and 132
Figure 13	San Lorenzo, Facade, Florence, Michelangelo, 1515	based on Ackerman 1961, p 66, fig 15
Figure 14	Porta Pia, Rome, Michelangelo, 1561	based on Ackerman 1961, p 245, fig 124
Figure 15a-b	Santa Susanna, Rome, Maderno, 1597	15a based on B-Fletcher 1963, p 697b
Figure 16	Palazzo Barberini, Rome, Maderno, 1628, assisted by Bernini and Borromini	public domain
Figure 17	S. Andrea al Quirinale, Rome, Bernini, 1658	based on Norberg-Schultz, fig 86, p 75
Figure 18	San Carlo alle Quattro Fontane, Rome, 1638	public domain
Figure 19	Geometry of Sant'Andrea and San Carlo	
Figure 20	Palazzo Falconieri, Rome, Borromini, 1646	public domain

Enlightenment

Figure 1	Banqueting House, London, Inigo Jones, 1619	based on Harris & Higgott 1989, p 113, fig 3
Figure 2	The Masonic "Square and Compass." Archetypal Arrangement	
Figure 3	Stourhead, Wiltshire, Campbell, 1719	based on Campbell 2009, Vol III, plate 42
Figure 4	Louvre, East Wing Centerpiece, Paris, Perrault, 1665	based on Perrault 1993, p 6 fig 5

Figure 5	Porte Saint-Denis, Paris, Blondel, 1672	
Figure 6	St. Mary le Strand, London, Gibbs, 1720	based on Gibbs 2008, plate 17
Figure 7a-c	St Martin, London, Gibbs, 1721. Analysis of West Facade	based on Gibbs 2008, plate 3
Figure 7d	St. Martin. Analysis of East Facade	based on Gibbs 2008, plate 4
Figure 8	Radcliffe Camera, Oxford, Gibbs, 1737	source unknown
Figure 9a	The Casino at Marino, Dublin, Chambers, 1775	based on Chambers 2003, plate 1 end section
Figure 9b	The Casino, Chambers. Plan	based on Chambers 2003, plate 2 end section
Figure 10	Attic Bases of Gibbs and Chambers	
Figure 11	Halfpenny's Doric	public domain
Figure 12	The Double Cube House, Morris, 1734	Morris 1734, lecture XI, p 169
Figure 13	The Wythe House, Williamsburg, 1750	based on Whiffen 1990, p 72, fig 11
Figure 14a	Poplar Forest, Jefferson, 1806. Plan	Howard 2003, p 119
Figure 14b-c	Poplar Forest. Elevation. Analysis and Reconstruction	based on Nichols 2001, no. 30
Figure 14d	Poplar Forest. Site Plan	from Holm 1995
Figure 15	The Rotunda, University of Virginia, Charlottsville, Jefferson, 1825	Nichols 2001, no. 27

Bibliography

Alberti, L B, 1988 — *On the Art of Building in Ten Books,* trans by Rykwert, MIT Press

Alberti, L B, 1986 — *The Ten Books of Architecture,* trans by Leoni, Dover, original 1755

Angus, Samuel, 1966 — *Mystery Religions and Christianity,* Citadel, NY, written 1925

Aristotle, 1941 — *Basic Works of Aristotle,* trans by Richard McKeon, Random House, New York

Azzam and Critchlow, 1997 — *Geometry of the Arch in Islamic Architecture,* POW Inst. of Architecture, London

Badaway, Alexander, 1965 — *Ancient Egyptian Architectural Design,* U of Cal Press, Berkeley, CA

Bateson Gregory, 1985 — *Steps to an Ecology of Mind,* Ballantine, New York

Bartoli, Lando, 1977 — *La Rete Magica di Filippo Brunelleschi,* Nardini Editore, Firenze

Boatwright, Mary, 1987 — *Hadrian and the City of Rome,* Princeton U. Press

Borsi, Franco, 1978 — *Leon Battista Alberti,* complete works, Rizzoli, New York

Borsi, et al. 1985 — *Filippo Brunelleschi,* Ecole Nationale Superieure des Beaux-Arts, Paris

Bouleau, Charles, 1963 — *The Painter's Secret Geometry,* Thames & Hudson, London

Breasted, H, 1964 — *History of Egypt,* Bantam, New York, written 1905

Brennan, Martin, 1983 — *The Stars and the Stones,* Thames and Hudson, London

Burke, Edmund, 1757 — *A Philosophical Inquiry into the Ideas of the Origins of the Sublime and the Beautiful,* Kessinger reprint

Burckhardt, Jacob, 1958 — *Civilization of the Renaissance in Italy,* 2 vols., Harper, New York

Burckhardt, Titus, 1986 — *Sacred Art East and West, Perennial Books,* Bedfont, Middlesex, UK

Burckhardt, Titus, 1976 — *Art of Islam,* World of Islam Festival Publishing, Westerham, Kent, UK

Burr, David, — *Suger of St. Denis and Bernard of Clairvoux on Architecture,* http://www.history.vt.edu/Burr/S%26B.html

Campbell, Collen, 2009 — *Vitruvius Britannicus,* Dover, original 1715

Chambers, Sir William, 2003 — *Civil Architecture,* Dover, original 1759

Charpentier, L, 1972 — *The Mysteries of Chartres Cathedral,* RILKO/Thorsons, Wellingborough, UK

Couliano, Ian, 1987 — *Eros and Magic in the Renaissance,* U of Chicago

Coulton, J J, 1988 — *Ancient Greek Architects at Work,* Cornell U Press, Ithaca, NY

Cowen, Painton, 2005 — *The Rose Window,* Thames & Hudson, London

Creason, Todd, — toddecreason.blogspot.com/2011/10/thomas-jefferson-freemason-or-not.html

Critchlow, Keith, 1969 — *Order in Space,* Viking, New York

Critchlow, Keith, 1976 — *Islamic Patterns,* Schocken, New York

Critchlow, Keith, 1979 — *Time Stands Still,* Gordon Fraser, London

Critchlow, Keith, 1980 — *Soul as Sphere and Androgyne,* Golgonooza Press, London

Critchlow, Keith, 1995 — "Platonic Tradition on Proportion," in *Homage to Pythagoras,* ed by Bamford, Lindisfarne, Hudson, NY

Critchlow, Keith, K3 — *Dimensions and Proportions of Solomon's Temple,* Kairos Worksheet #3

Critchlow, Keith, K4 — *Proportioning of the Chartres Rose Windows,* Kairos Worksheet #4

Cumont, Franz, 1975 — *Mysteries of Mithra,* Dover, original 1903

Curl, James, 1993 — *Georgian Architecture,* David & Charles, Newton Abbot, Devon, UK

De Cenival, J L, 1964 — *Living Architecture: Egyptian,* Grosset & Dunlap, NY

Dionysius, Pseudo, 1935 — *The Celestial Hierarchies,* Shrine of Wisdom, London

Doczi, Gyorgy, 1981 — *The Power of Limits,* Shambhala, Boulder, CO

Edgerton, Samuel, 1975 — *The Renaissance Rediscovery of Linear Perspective,* Harper & Row

Fanelli, Giovanni, 1980 — *Brunelleschi,* Philip Wilson, Florence, Italy

Fideler, David, 1993a — *Jesus Christ Sun of God,* Quest, Wheaton, IL

Fideler, David, 1993b — "The Science and Art of Animating Statues," in *Alexandria 2,* Phanes, Grand Rapids, MI

Fletcher, Sir Banister, 1963 *A History of Architecture on the Comparative Method,* 17th ed, Scribners New York

Friedman, Terry, 1984 *James Gibbs,* Yale U. Press, New Haven, CT

Furnari, Michele, 1995 *Formal Design in Renaissance Architecture,* Rizzoli New York

Gibbs, James, 2008 *Book of Architecture,* Dover, original 1728

Gibbs, James, 1732 *Rules for Drawing the Several Parts of Architecture,* London

Giedion, Sigfried, 1964 *The Eternal Present,* Bollingen, New York

Gadol, Joan, 1969 *Leon Battista Alberti, Universal Man of the Early Renaissance,* U of Chicago Press

Godwin, Joscelyn, 2005 *Pagan Dream of the Renaissance,* Weiser, York Beach ME

Gordon-Smith, T, 2003 *Vitruvius on Architecture,* Monacelli, NY

Graves, Robert, 1982 *The Greek Myths,* 2 vols., Penguin, written 1955

Guénon, René, 2004 *The Metaphysical Principles of the Infinitesimal Calculus,* Sophia Perennis, Hillsdale, NY, original 1946

Guthrie, Kenneth, 1987 *The Pythagorean Sourcebook and Library,* Phanes, Grand Rapids MI

Halevi, Zev ben Simon, 1977 *A Kabalistic Universe,* Weiser, York Beach ME [aka Warren Kenton]

Halfpenny, William, 1724 *Practical Architecture: Or, A Sure Guide to the True Working According to the Rules of that Science,* originally published 1724

Hambidge, J, 1924 *The Parthenon,* Yale U Press, New Haven, CT

Harner, Michael, 1986 *The Way of the Shaman,* Bantam, New York

Harris & Higgott, 1989 *Inigo Jones Complete Architectural Drawings*, Drawing Center, New York

Heald, David, 2000 *Architecture of Silence,* Abrams, New York

Heilbron, J L, 1999 *The Sun in the Church,* Cambridge, Harvard U. Press

Hersey, G, 1988 *The Lost Meaning of Classical Architecture,* MIT Press, Cambridge, MA

Hersey, G L, 1976 *Pythagorean Palaces,* Cornell U. Press, Ithaca, NY.

Holm, Alvin, 1995 *Poplar Forest: Jefferson's Solar Calendar,* NEARA Journal, Vol. XXX, No. 1&2

Howard, Hugh, 2003 *Thomas Jefferson Architect,* Rizzoli, New York

Hurry J B, 1987 *Imhotep,* Ares, Chicago, IL, original 1926

Iamblichus (attributed), 1988 *Theology of Arithmetic,* trans by Waterfield, Phanes, Grand Rapids MI.

Iverson, Erik, 1975 *Canon and Proportion in Egyptian Art,* 2nd ed, Aris & Phillips, Warminster, UK

James, John, 1990 *Master Masons of Chartres,* West Grinstead Publishing, Leura, NSW, Australia

Jones, M W, 2014 *Origins of Classical Architecture,* Yale U Press, New Haven

Jones, M W, 2000 *Principles of Roman Architecture,* Yale U. Press, New Haven

Lancaster, Clay, 1951 *Jefferson's Architectural Indebtedness to Robert Morris*, JSAH, Vol. 10, No. 1, March

Lawlor, Robert, 1982 *Sacred Geometry,* Crossroad, NY

Lewis, Neville, 1987 *Delphi and the Sacred Way,* Michael Haag, London

Lloyd/Muller, 1986 *Ancient Architecture,* 1980, Electra/Rizzoli, New York

Lotz, Wolfgang, 1995 *Architecture in Italy,* 1500–1600, Yale U. Press, New Haven

MacDonald, William, 1976 *The Pantheon,* Harvard U. Press, Cambridge, MA

Macdonald, William, 1982 *Architecture of the Roman Empire,* 2 vols., Yale U Press

March, Lionel, 1998 *Architectonics of Humanism,* Academy Editions/Wiley, Chichester, West Sussex, UK

Mead, G R S, 1978 *Thrice-Greatest Hermes,* Hermes Press, Ferndale MI, original trans. 1906

Michell, George, 1988 *The Hindu Temple,* U of Chicago Press

Michell, John, 1991 *Twelve-Tribe Nations,* Thames & Hudson, London

Morris, Robert, 1734 *Lectures on Architecture,* London

Naydler, Jeremy, 2000 *Goethe on Science,* Floris, Edinburgh, UK

Nichols, F D, 2001 *Thomas Jefferson's Drawings,* Thomas Jefferson Memorial Foundation

Norberg-Schultz, C, 1979 *Baroque Architecture,* Rizzoli, New York

Normand, Charles, 1936 — *A Parallel of the Orders of Architecture,* Tiranti, London

Pajares-Ayuelo, P, 2001 — *Cosmetesque,* Norton, New York

Palladio, Andrea, 1965 — *The Four Books on Architecture,* Dover, USA

Panofsky, Erwin, 1972 — *Studies in Iconology,* Icon/Harper, original 1939

Perrault, Claude, 1993 — *Ordonnance for the Five Kinds of Columns,* trans. by McEwen, intro. by Perez- Gomez, Getty Center, Santa Monica, CA

Pevsner, Nikolaus, 1958 — *Outline of European Architecture,* Penguin, original 1945

Plato, — *Timaeus,* Loeb Classical, trans. by Bury, Harvard U Press, 1981; Penguin, trans. by D. Lee, NY, 1981, original 1965; trans. by Taylor, Wizards Bookshelf, Minneapolis MN, 1976, original 1793

Plato, 1991 — *Republic,* trans. by Jowett, Vintage, New York, original trans. 1892

Plato, 1981 — *Symposium,* trans. by Hamilton, Penguin

Plato, 1971 — *Meno,* trans. by Shrine of Wisdom, Letchworth, England

PRA no author, 1986 — *Paris Rome Athens,* École Nationale Supérieure des Beaux-Arts

Plotinus, 1991 — *Ennead,* 1.6, "On Beauty," Penguin, trans. by MacKenna, original trans. 1917

Proclus, 1987 — *Commentary on Parmenides,* trans. by Morrow, Princeton U Press

Querido, René, 1987 — *The Golden Age of Chartres,* Anthroposophic Press, Hudson NY

Rossi, C, 2007 — *Architecture and Mathematics in Ancient Egypt,* Cambridge U Press, NY

Rossini, S, 1989 — *Egyptian Hieroglyphics,* Dover, New York

Rundle Clark, R T, 1991 — *Myth and Symbol in Ancient Egypt,* Thames & Hudson, New York, original 1959

Scholfield, P H, 1958 — *Theory of Proportion in Architecture,* Cambridge U Press, NY

Schwaller, R A, 1981 — *The Temple in Man,* trans. by Lawlor, Inner Traditions, New York, original 1949

Scranton, R, 1965 — *Greek Architeture,* Braziller, New York

Seamon and Zajonc, 1998 — *Goethe's Way of Science,* SUNY Press, NY

Semes, Steven W, 2004 — *Architecture of the Classical Interior,* Norton, New York

Semes, Steven W, ed, 2015 — *Classicist #12,* Institute of Classical Architecture and Art, New York

Serlio, Sebastian, 1996 — *Sebastian Serlio on Architecture,* Vol. I, Books I-V, trans. by Hart and Hicks, Yale U. Press, New Haven, CT

Serlio, Sebastian, 1982 — *The Five Books of Architecture,* Dover, from the 1611 Peake edition.

Taylor, Thomas, 1983 — *Theoretic Arithmetic of the Pythagoreans,* Weiser, York Beach, ME

Theon of Smyrna, 1979 — *Math Useful for Understanding Plato,* trans. by R & D Lawlor, Wizards Bookshelf, San Diego

Vasari, Georgio, 1965 — *Lives of the Artists,* trans. by G. Bull, Penguin

Vitruvius, — *The Ten Books on Architecture,* trans. by M. H. Morgan, Dover, 1960, original 1914; and trans. by Granger, Lobe Classical, 1985, original, 1935

Ware, William R, 1977 — *The American Vignola,* Norton, New York, original 1905-6

West, John A, 1987 — *Serpent in the Sky,* Julian Press, New York

Whiffen, Marcus, 1990 — *The Eighteenth-Century Houses of Williamsburg,* Colonial Williamsburg Foundation/U Press of Virginia, Charlottesville, VA

Wilkinson, Richard H, 1994 — *Symbol & Magic in Egyptian Art,* Thames & Hudson, New York

Wind, Edgar, 1968 — *Pagan Mysteries in the Renaissance,* Norton, New York

Wittkower, Rudolf, 1971 — *Architectural Principles in the Age of Humanism,* Norton, New York

Woodhouse, C M, 2000 — *Gemistos Plethon: The Last of the Hellenes,* Oxford U. Press, New York

Wotton, Sir Henry, 1624 — *The Elements of Architecture,* written 1624

Yates, Frances A, 1979 — *Giordano Bruno and the Hermetic Tradition,* U of Chicago Press, Chicago, written 1964

Yates, Frances A, 1978 — *The Rosicrucian Enlightenment*, Shambhala, Boulder, CO

Index of Names